The Business Judgment Rule

Fiduciary Duties of Corporate Directors

Dennis J. Block

Nancy E. Barton

Stephen A. Radin

Fifth Edition

2001 Cumulative Supplement

Aspen Law & Business

Aspen Law & Business
1185 Avenue of the Americas
37th Floor
New York, NY 10036

Printed in the United States of America
ISBN 0-7355-1519-0

TABLE OF CONTENTS

VOLUME I

VOLUME II

ACKNOWLEDGMENT

We acknowledge with gratitude the assistance we received from Philip Barahona, Philip Bartlett, Anthony DeRose, Angela Chiarelli, Fran Fredrick, William Gordon, Julianna Mather, Samantha Masotti, Corbett Morris, Daniela Morrongello, Kenneth M. Murray and Simon C. Roosevelt in completing many of the tedious chores required to complete this project.

We owe particularly special thanks for the invaluable assistance we received from Theresa Kassim, who typed and revised countless drafts of this manuscript. Theresa's word processing and desktop publishing skills are second to none, and her diligence and good cheer is more than greatly appreciated.

Dennis J. Block
Nancy E. Barton
Stephen A. Radin

August 2001

ABOUT THE AUTHORS

Dennis J. Block, Nancy E. Barton and Stephen A. Radin are experienced counselors and litigators specializing in corporate governance, corporate, securities, class and derivative litigation, and mergers and acquisitions.

DENNIS J. BLOCK is a senior partner in the law firm Cadwalader, Wickersham & Taft in New York City. Mr. Block has been a member of the Council, and a Co-Chairman of the Committee on Corporate Counsel, of the Section of Litigation, and a member of the Committee on Corporate Laws of the Section of Business Law, of the American Bar Association. He is the co-editor of The Corporate Counsellor's Deskbook, co-author of a monthly column in the New York Law Journal, and a member of the editorial boards of several legal publications. Mr. Block is a frequent author and lecturer on corporate governance subjects, the business judgment rule, transactions involving corporate control, proxy contests, the federal securities laws, class and derivative litigation, special board and board committee investigations, indemnification and insurance of corporate officials, the attorney-client privilege, and professional responsibility. Prior to joining Cadwalader, Wickersham & Taft, Mr. Block was a senior partner of the law firm Weil, Gotshal & Manges LLP. Before entering private practice, Mr. Block was a Branch Chief of Enforcement at the New York Regional Office of the Securities and Exchange Commission. Mr. Block is a graduate of Brooklyn Law School.

Nancy E. Barton is Senior Vice President and General Counsel at General Electric Capital Corporation in Stamford, Connecticut. Prior to joining General Electric Capital Corporation in 1991, Ms. Barton was a member of the law firm Weil, Gotshal & Manges LLP. Ms. Barton is a frequent author and lecturer on corporate governance subjects, the business judgment rule, transactions involving corporate control, proxy contests, the federal securities laws, class and derivative litigation, special board and board committee investigations and the attorney-client privilege. Ms. Barton is a graduate of Boston University Law School.

Stephen A. Radin is a member of the law firm Weil, Gotshal & Manges LLP. He has written frequently and lectured on corporate governance subjects, the business judgment rule, transactions involving contests for corporate control, proxy contests, the federal securities laws, class and derivative litigation, special board and board committee investigations, and indemnification and insurance of corporate officials. Mr. Radin is a graduate of Columbia Law School, where he was named a Harlan Fiske Stone Scholar.

NOTE TO THE READER

This 2001 Supplement is intended to be used in conjunction with the fifth edition of *The Business Judgment Rule: Fiduciary Duties of Corporate Directors*, published in 1998. The 2000 Supplement should be discarded. Each entry in this Supplement is keyed in bold-faced italics to a particular paragraph or footnote of the main text, and, by reading this 2001 Supplement along with the 1998 text, the reader will be altered to noteworthy recent developments in the law as of December 31, 2000.

Throughout the text, federal court decisions are cited to the Federal Reporter, Federal Supplement or Federal Rules Decisions, and state court decisions are cited to regional reporters such as the Atlantic Reporter or Northeastern Reporter. California and New York state court decisions also are cited to the official and unofficial reporters in those jurisdictions. Decisions that cannot be cited to any of the above reporters are cited to the CCH Federal Securities Law Reporter service. Any decision that cannot be cited in any of the above forms is cited to LEXIS and/or WESTLAW if the decision is contained in one or both of these data bases, and otherwise is cited in slip opinion or transcript form.

The views expressed in *The Business Judgment Rule* and this Supplement are the views of the authors, and do not necessarily reflect the views of their clients.

CHAPTER I

Introduction

Add the following at the end of footnote 1 on page 1:

See also Skeen v. Jo-Ann Stores, Inc., 750 A.2d 1170, 1172 (Del. 2000); *Malone v. Brincat*, 722 A.2d 5, 10 (Del. 1998); *In re Gaylord Container Corp. S'holders Litig.*, 753 A.2d 462, 476 n.42 (Del. Ch. 2000) (quoting Veasey, *The Defining Tension in Corporate Governance in America*, 52 Bus. Law. 393, 397 (1997)); *Jackson Nat'l Life Ins. Co. v. Kennedy*, 741 A.2d 377, 386 (Del. Ch. 1999).

Replace the second sentence (immediately after footnote 8) in the paragraph beginning and concluding on page 2 with the following:

Section 8.30(a) of the Model Business Corporation Act, as it existed until it was amended in 1998, is typical of the language in these statutes and states as follows:

Replace the Model Act § 8.30 citation in footnote 9 on page 2 with the following:

Former Model Bus. Corp. Act § 8.30(a);

Replace the sentence between the two block quotes (immediately after footnote 9) in the paragraph beginning and concluding on page 2 with the following:

Section 8.30, as revised in 1998, reads as follows:

Replace the Model Act § 8.30 citation in footnote 10 on page 2 with the following:

2 Model Bus. Corp. Act Annotated §§ 8.30(a), (b) (3d ed. Supp. 1998/99).

Add the following at the end of footnote 11 on page 2:

See also Batchelder v. Kawamoto, 147 F.3d 915, 920 (9th Cir.), *cert. denied*, 525 U.S. 982 (1998).

Add the following at the end of footnote 12 on page 2:

See also Bradley v. First Interstate Corp., 748 A.2d 913 (unpublished opinion, text available at 2000 Del. LEXIS 113, at *1 and 2000 WL 383788, at *1) (Del. Mar. 21, 2000); *Wilson v. Tully*, 243 A.D.2d 229, 232, 676 N.Y.S.2d 531, 534 (N.Y. App. Div. 1st Dep't 1998).

Replace "1998" with "2001" in the Balotti citation in footnote 13 on page 3.

Add the following at the end of footnote 14 on page 3:

See also IBS Fin. Corp. v. Seidman & Assocs., L.L.C., 136 F.3d 940, 949-50 (3d Cir. 1998) ("[w]hen faced with novel issues of corporate law, New Jersey courts have often looked to Delaware's rich abundance of corporate law for guidance"); *In re Abbott Labs. Derivative S'holder Litig.*, 126 F. Supp. 2d 535, 536 (N.D. Ill. 2000) ("The parties . . . consider the requirements of . . . Illinois law . . . to be instructed by Delaware law, and they go directly to the Delaware cases. And so shall we.");

Strougo v. BEA Assocs., 2000 U.S. Dist. LEXIS 346, at *13, 2000 WL 45714, at *5 (S.D.N.Y. Jan. 19, 2000) ("the Court of Chancery has a well recognized expertise in the field of state corporation law"); *Flake v. Hoskins*, 55 F. Supp. 2d 1196, 1214 (D. Kan. 1999) ("Missouri looks to Delaware law in examining corporate actions"); *Lawson Mardon Wheaton, Inc. v. Smith*, 734 A.2d 738, 746 (N.J. 1999) ("[i]n analyzing corporate law issues, we find Delaware law to be helpful").

Replace the Model Act § 8.31 citation in footnote 15 on page 4 with the following:

Model Bus. Corp. Act § 8.31 Official Comment at 8-193;

Add the following at the end of footnote 15 on page 4:

See also Edge Partners, L.P. v. Dockser, 944 F. Supp. 438, 441 n.4 (D. Md. 1996).

Add the following at the end of footnote 16 on page 5:

See also Frater v. Tigerpack Capital, Ltd., 1999 U.S. Dist. LEXIS 6, at *12, 1999 WL 4892, at *4 (S.D.N.Y. Jan. 5, 1999) (quoting this text); *Univ. Clinical Assocs., Inc. v. Intracoastal Health Sys., Inc.*, 2000 WL 1466097, at *6 (Fla. Cir. Ct. Sept. 25, 2000) (business judgment rule does not apply in action seeking to enforce contract).

Add the following at the end of footnote 18 on page 5:

See also Flake v. Hoskins, 55 F. Supp. 2d 1196, 1213 (D. Kan. 1999) ("[w]hen a corporate director or officer's decision falls within the business judgment rule, the Court will not interfere with that decision").

Add the following at the end of the fourth sentence (immediately after footnote 18) of the paragraph beginning on page 4 and concluding on page 6:

"It is the essence of the business judgment rule that a court will not apply 20/20 hindsight to second guess a board's decision, except 'in rare cases [where] a transaction may be so egregious on its face that board approval cannot meet the test of business judgment.'" *In re Walt Disney Co. Derivative Litig.*, 731 A.2d 342, 362 (Del. Ch. 1998) (quoting *Aronson v. Lewis*, 473 A.2d 805, 815 (Del. 1984)), *aff'd with leave to replead on other grounds sub nom. Brehm v. Eisner*, 746 A.2d 244 (Del. 2000), *quoted in Greenwald v. Batterson*, 1999 Del. Ch. LEXIS 158, at *22, 1999 WL 596276, at *7 (Del. Ch. July 26, 1999). As stated by the Delaware Supreme Court in *Brehm v. Eisner*, 746 A.2d 244 (Del. 2000): "directors' decisions will be respected by courts unless the directors are interested or lack independence relative to the decision, do not act in good faith, act in a manner that cannot be attributed to a rational business purpose or reach their decision by a grossly negligent process that includes the failure to consider all material facts reasonably available." *Id.* at 264 n.66.

Replace the period at the end of footnote 19 on page 6 with the following:

, *quoted in Lamden v. La Jolla Shores Clubdominium Homeowners Ass'n*, 21 Cal. 4th 249, 257, 87 Cal. Rptr. 2d 237, 241 (1999).

Add the following at the end of the paragraph beginning on page 4 and concluding on page 6 (immediately after footnote 20):

The rule provides a defense; it "does not provide a theory of imposing liability upon officers and directors of the corporation who allegedly have not used independent judgment."

McIntyre v. Philadelphia Suburban Corp., 90 F. Supp. 2d 596, 600 n.4 (E.D. Pa. 2000).

Add the following at the end of the second sentence (immediately after footnote 27) in the paragraph beginning and concluding on page 7:

"[A]s long as directors of a corporation decide matters rationally, honestly, and without a disabling conflict of interest, the decision will not be reviewed by the courts." *Atkins v. Hibernia Corp.*, 182 F.3d 320, 324 (5th Cir. 1999); *see also White v. Panic*, 2000 Del. Ch. LEXIS 14, at *35 n.44, 2000 WL 85046, at *10 n.44 (Del. Ch. Jan. 19, 2000) ("[s]o long as the court determines that the process employed was either rational or employed in a *good faith* effort to advance corporate interests, a substantively wrong decision will not provide the basis for directorial liability") (quoting *In re Caremark Int'l Inc. Derivative Litig.*, 698 A.2d 959, 967-68 (Del. Ch. 1996)). The "wisdom or merit" of a "bad or shortsighted decision concerning how to deploy the company's cash" that will hinder the corporation's ability to pay dividends in the future is not "a proper subject for judicial review." *Weiss v. Samsonite Corp.*, 741 A.2d 366, 373 (Del. Ch. 1999), *aff'd*, 746 A.2d 277 (unpublished opinion, text available at 1999 Del. LEXIS 387 and 1999 WL 1254563) (Del. Nov. 12, 1999).

Add the following at the end of the paragraph beginning and concluding on page 7 (immediately after footnote 29):

"[M]ere allegations that directors made a poor decision . . . do not state a cause of action." *Ash v. McCall*, 2000 Del. Ch. LEXIS 144, at *33, 2000 WL 1370341, at *10 (Del. Ch. Sept. 15, 2000).

Add the following at the end of the paragraph beginning on page 7 and concluding on page 8 (immediately after footnote 33):

As stated in 1999 in *Odyssey Partners, L.P. v. Fleming Cos.*, 735 A.2d 386 (Del. Ch. 1999), "ordinary and traditional business decisions, such as what investments or ventures to pursue, . . . are generally within the business judgment of the board." *Id.* at 413.

Add the following at the end of the paragraph beginning and concluding on page 8 (between footnotes 34 and 35):

From January 1, 1998 through December 31, 2000, over 275 opinions containing the words "business judgment rule" have been published.

Section B

Add the following at the beginning of the first paragraph beginning and concluding on page 12 (immediately after footnote 51):

The business judgment rule is "a corollary common law precept" to "[o]ne of the fundamental principles" of corporate law: "that the business affairs of a corporation are managed by or under the direction of its board of directors." *McMullin v. Beran*, 765 A.2d 910, 916 (Del. 2000).

Add the following at the end of footnote 50 on page 12:

See also Wittman v. Crooke, 707 A.2d 422, 425 (Md. Ct. Spec. App. 1998) ("[d]irectors of a corporation . . . are not expected to be incapable of error") (quoting *Black v. Fox Hills N. Cmty. Ass'n, Inc.*, 599 A.2d 1228, 1231 (Md. Ct. Spec. App. 1992) and *Papalexiou v. Tower W. Condo.*, 401 A.2d 280, 286 (N.J. Super. Ct. Ch. Div. 1979)).

Add the following at the end of footnote 51 on page 12:

See also In re PSE&G S'holder Litig., 718 A.2d 254, 256 (N.J. Super. Ct. Ch. Div. 1998).

Add the following at the end of footnote 52 on page 12:

See also PSE&G, 718 A.2d at 256.

Add the following after the second block quote (immediately after footnote 56) in the paragraph beginning on page 12 and concluding on page 15:

The business judgment rule thus provides directors "broad discretion in making corporate decisions . . . without judicial second-guessing in hindsight." *Federal Deposit Ins. Corp. v. Castetter*, 184 F.3d 1040, 1044 (9th Cir. 1999).

Replace the semi-colon in footnote 57 on page 15 with the following:

, *quoted in Lamden v. La Jolla Shores Clubdominium Homeowners Ass'n*, 21 Cal. 4th 249, 259, 87 Cal. Rptr. 2d 237, 243 (1999).

Add the following at the end of footnote 58 on page 15:

See also Brehm v. Eisner, 746 A.2d 244, 263 (Del. 2000) ("[c]ourts are ill-fitted . . . to judge appropriate degrees of business risk") (quoting *Lewis v. Vogelstein*, 699 A.2d 327, 336 (Del. Ch. 1997)); *Einhorn v. Culea*, 612 N.W.2d 78, 84, 91 (Wis. 2000).

Add the following at the end of footnote 59 on page 15:

See also Drilling v. Berman, 589 N.W.2d 503, 507 (Minn. Ct. App. 1999), *review denied*, 1999 Minn. LEXIS 306 (Minn. May 18, 1999).

Replace the period at the end of footnote 66 on page 17 with the following:

, *quoted in Lamden*, 21 Cal. 4th at 259, 87 Cal. Rptr. 2d at 243.

Replace the period at the end of footnote 71 on page 18 with the following:

and In re Walt Disney Co. Derivative Litig., 731 A.2d 342, 366-67 n.58 (Del. Ch. 1998), *aff'd with leave to replead on other grounds sub nom. Brehm v. Eisner*, 746 A.2d 244 (Del. 2000).

Section C 1

Add the following at the end of footnote 77 on page 19:

See also Lippe v. Bairnco Corp., 230 B.R. 906, 917 n.6 (S.D.N.Y. 1999).

Add the following at the end of the first sentence (immediately after footnote 98) of the paragraph beginning on page 20 and concluding on page 21:

The Delaware Supreme Court also stated this presumption in 1999 in *Parnes v. Bally Entertainment Corp.*, 722 A.2d 1243 (Del. 1999), and *Emerald Partners v. Berlin*, 726 A.2d 1215 (Del. 1999), and in 2000 in *McMullin v. Beran*, 765 A.2d 910 (Del. 2000).

Add the following at the end of footnote 99 on page 21:

See also McMullin, 765 A.2d at 916; *Emerald Partners*, 726 A.2d at 1221; *Parnes*, 722 A.2d at 1246.

Add the following at the end of footnote 101 on page 21:

See also Brehm, 746 A.2d at 264 (quoting *Sinclair Oil Corp. v. Levien*, 280 A.2d 717, 720 (Del. 1971)).

Add the following at the end of the first sentence (immediately after footnote 102) of the paragraph beginning on page 21 and concluding on page 22:

As stated by the Delaware Supreme Court in *Brehm v. Eisner*, 746 A.2d 244 (Del. 2000), "[i]rrationality is the outer limit of the business judgment rule," and "directors' decisions will be respected by courts unless the directors are interested or lack independence relative to the decision, do not act in good faith, act in a manner that cannot be attributed to a rational business purpose or reach their decision by a grossly negligent process that includes the failure to consider all material facts reasonably available." *Id.* at 264 & n.66.

Add the following at the end of footnote 109 on page 22:

See also Barnes v. State Farm Mut. Auto. Ins. Co., 16 Cal. App. 4th 365, 378, 20 Cal. Rptr. 2d 87, 95 (1993).

Add the following at the end of footnote 112 on page 22:

See also In re Toy King Distribs., Inc., 256 B.R. 1, 168 (Bankr. M.D. Fla. 2000); *Univ. Clinical Assocs., Inc. v. Intracoastal Health Sys., Inc.*, 2000 WL 1466097, at *6 (Fla. Cir. Ct. Sep. 25, 2000).

Add the following at the end of footnote 113 on page 23:

See also Miller v. Thomas, 656 N.E.2d 89, 96 (Ill. App. Ct. 1995).

Add the following at the end of footnote 117 on page 23:

See also Lyon v. Campbell, 217 F.3d 839 (unpublished opinion, text available at 2000 U.S. App. LEXIS 17466, at *11-12 and 2000 WL 991650, at *4) (4th Cir. July 19, 2000); *Froelich v. Erickson*, 96 F. Supp. 2d 507, 520 (D. Md. 2000); *Edge Partners, L.P. v. Dockser*, 944 F. Supp. 438, 442 (D. Md. 1996); *Wittman v. Crooke*, 707 A.2d 422, 425 (Md. Ct. Spec. App. 1998).

Add the following at the end of footnote 119 on page 23:

See also Wigart v. Cervenka, 1999 Minn. App. LEXIS 426, at *9 n.1, 1999 WL 243231, at *3 n.1 (Minn. App. Apr. 27, 1999).

Add the following at the end of footnote 121 on page 23:

See also Matthews v. C.E.C. Indus. Corp., 202 F.3d 282 (unpublished opinion, text available at 1999 U.S. App. LEXIS 33396, at *18-19 and 1999 WL 1244491, at *6) (10th Cir. Dec. 21, 1999) (summarizing district court decision).

Add the following at the end of footnote 122 on page 23:

See also In re PSE&G S'holder Litig., 718 A.2d 254, 256 (N.J. Super. Ct. Ch. Div. 1998); *Maul v. Kirkman*, 637 A.2d 928, 937 (N.J. Super. Ct. App. Div. 1994).

Add the following at the end of footnote 123 on page 24:

See also Lippe v. Bairnco Corp., 230 B.R. 906, 916 (S.D.N.Y. 1999) (citing this text); *In re Dollar Time Group, Inc.*, 223 B.R. 237, 246 (Bankr. S.D. Fla. 1998); *In re Bakalis*, 220 B.R. 525, 536 (Bankr. E.D.N.Y. 1998); *Jones v. Surrey Coop. Apartments, Inc.*, 263 A.D.2d 33, 36, 700 N.Y.S.2d 118, 121 (N.Y. App. Div. 1st Dep't 1999).

Add the following at the end of footnote 124 on page 24:

See also Girard v. Krug Int'l Corp., 230 F.3d 1366 (unpublished opinion, text available at 2000 U.S. App. LEXIS 22149, at *7 and 1999 WL 1244491, at *2) (9th Cir. Aug. 24, 2000); *In re Ikon Office Solutions, Inc. Sec. Litig.*, 194 F.R.D. 166, 190 (E.D. Pa. 2000).

Add the following at the end of footnote 126 on page 24:

See also Haydinger v. Freedman, 2000 U.S. Dist. LEXIS 7924, at *29, 2000 WL 748055, at *8 (E.D. Pa. June 8, 2000); *McIntyre v. Philadelphia Suburban Corp.*, 90 F. Supp. 2d 596, 600 n.4 (E.D. Pa. 2000).

Add the following at the end of footnote 128 on page 24:

See also In re Performance Nutrition, Inc., 239 B.R. 93, 111 (Bankr. N.D. Tex. 1999).

Add the following at the end of the paragraph beginning on page 22 and concluding on page 24 (immediately after footnote 131):

The business judgment rule also has been stated as a presumption by courts applying, Kansas, Massachusetts and North Carolina law. *See In re Stoico Rest. Group, Inc.*, 2000 U.S. Dist. LEXIS 12523, at *6-7, 2000 WL 1146122, at *2 (D. Kan. July 20, 2000); *Harhen v. Brown*, 730 N.E.2d 859, 865 (Mass. 2000); *N.C. ex rel. Long v. ILA Corp.*, 513 S.E.2d 812, 821-22 (N.C. App. 1999).

Replace the Model Act § 8.31 citation in footnote 132 on page 25 with the following:

2 Model Bus. Corp. Act Annotated § 8.31 Official Comment at 8-197 (3d ed. Supp. 1998/99).

Section C 2

Add the following at the beginning of the paragraph beginning on page 25 and concluding on page 27 (immediately after footnote 133):

"The business judgment rule 'operates as both a procedural guide for litigants and a substantive rule of law.'" *McMullin v. Beran*, 765 A.2d 910, 916-17 (Del. 2000). (quoting *Citron v. Fairchild Camera & Instrument Corp.,* 569 A.2d 53, 64 (Del. 1989) and *Cinerama, Inc. v. Technicolor, Inc.,* 663 A.2d 1156, 1162 (Del. 1995)).

Replace the Parnes citation in footnote 135 on page 25 with the following:

Parnes v. Bally Entertainment Corp., 722 A.2d 1243, 1246 (Del. 1999);

Add the following at the end of footnote 135 on page 25:

See also In re Stoico Rest. Group, Inc., 2000 U.S. Dist. LEXIS 12523, at *6-8, 2000 WL 1146122 (D. Kan. July 20, 2000); *McLachlan v. Simon*, 31 F. Supp. 2d 731, 737-38 (N.D. Cal. 1998); *In re Toy King Distribs., Inc.*, 256 B.R. 1, 168 (Bankr. M.D. Fla. 2000); *Crescent/Mach I Partners, L.P. v. Turner*, 2000 Del. Ch. LEXIS 145, at *36, 2000 WL 1481002, at *10 (Del. Ch. Sept. 29, 2000); *Cooke v. Oolie*, 2000 Del. Ch. LEXIS 89, at *39, 2000 WL 710199, at *11 (Del. Ch. May 24, 2000); *Leung v. Schuler*, 2000 Del. Ch. LEXIS 41, at *39, 2000 WL 264328, at *11 (Del. Ch. Feb. 29, 2000) and 2000 Del. Ch. LEXIS 134, at *19, 2000 WL 1478538, at *6 (Del. Ch. Sept. 29, 2000); *State of Wis. Inv. Bd. v. Bartlett*, 2000 Del. Ch. LEXIS 42, at *11-12, 2000 WL 238026, at *4 (Del. Ch. Feb. 24, 2000); *Golaine v. Edwards*, 1999 Del. Ch. LEXIS 237, at *34-35, 1999 WL 1271882, at *10 (Del. Ch. Dec. 21, 1999); *Wittman v. Crooke*, 707 A.2d 422, 425 (Md. Ct. Spec. App. 1998); *Maul v. Kirkman*, 637 A.2d 928, 937 (N.J. Super.

Ct. App. Div. 1994); *Jones v. Surrey Coop. Apartments, Inc.*, 263 A.D.2d 33, 36-37, 700 N.Y.S.2d 118, 121 (N.Y. App. Div. 1st Dep't 1999).

Add the following at the end of the second sentence (immediately after footnote 136) of the paragraph beginning on page 25 and concluding on page 27:

"[T]he burden of pleading and proof is on the party challenging the decision to allege facts to rebut the presumption." *Solomon v. Armstrong*, 747 A.2d 1098, 1111-12, 1116 (Del. Ch. 1999), *aff'd,* 746 A.2d 277 (unpublished opinion, full text available at 2000 Del. LEXIS 30 and 2000 WL 140072) (Del. Jan. 26, 2000). "For example, where a shareholder proves that the board approved a transaction in which directors or the corporation's officers stood on both sides of the deal, thereby calling into doubt the satisfaction of the duty of loyalty, the presumption of the business judgment rule is rebutted." *In re Walt Disney Co. Derivative Litig.*, 731 A.2d 342, 367 (Del. Ch. 1998), *aff'd with leave to replead on other grounds sub nom. Brehm v. Eisner*, 746 A.2d 244 (Del. 2000).

Add the following at the end of footnote 137 on page 26:

See also Wis. Inv. Bd., 2000 Del. Ch. LEXIS 42, at *12, 2000 WL 238026, at *4.

Delete the Parnes and Potter citations in footnote 138 on page 27.

Add the following at the end of footnote 138 on page 27:

In *In re Gaylord Container Corp. Shareholders Litigation*, 753 A.2d 462 (Del. Ch. 2000), the Court of Chancery noted that while *Cede & Co. v. Technicolor, Inc.*, 634 A.2d 345 (Del. 1993), refers to a board's "triad of fiduciary duties – good faith, loyalty, due care" (quoting 634 A.2d at 361), the decision also "equates good faith with loyalty":

> In the following sentence from *Cede II*, the Supreme Court quotes its earlier opinion in *Barkan v. Amsted Industries, Inc.*, Del. Supr., 567 A.2d 1279, 1286 (1989), but adds bracketed text to clarify meaning. The sentence, with the bracketed text emphasized, reads as follows:
>
> > [A] board's actions must be evaluated in light of relevant circumstances to determine if they were undertaken with due diligence [*care*] and good faith [*loyalty*]. If no breach of duty is found, the board's actions are entitled to the protections of the business judgment rule.
>
> *Cede II*, 634 A.2d at 368 n.36 (*quoting Barkan*, 567 A.2d at 1286) (emphasis added) . . . . In *Barkan* itself, it is clear that the Supreme Court used the terms "due diligence" and "good faith" as a fresh way of referring to the "fundamental duties of care and loyalty" it discussed three sentences earlier in the same paragraph. *Barkan*, 567 A.2d at 1286. Moreover, *Cede II* contains two lengthy sections focusing on the duties of loyalty and care but has no comparable section on good faith, despite its putative equality in the triad. 634 A.2d at 361-66 (loyalty), 366-71 (due care); *see also id.* 359 (breaking down key issues on appeal into questions of loyalty and due care).

753 A.2d at 476 n.31.

Replace the Model Act § 8.31 citation in footnote 139 on page 27 with the following:

2 Model Bus. Corp. Act Annotated § 8.31 Official Comment at 8–197-98 (3d ed. Supp. 1998/99).

Add the following at the end of the paragraph beginning on page 25 and concluding on page 27 (immediately after footnote 139):

As stated most recently by the Delaware Supreme Court:

> Procedurally, the initial burden is on the shareholder plaintiff to rebut the presumption of the business judgment rule. To meet that burden, the shareholder plaintiff must effectively

> provide evidence that the defendant board of directors, in reaching its challenged decision, breached any *one* of its "triad of fiduciary duties, loyalty, good faith or due care." Substantively, "if the shareholder plaintiff fails to meet that evidentiary burden, the business judgment rule attaches" and operates to protect the individual director-defendants from personal liability for making the board decision at issue.

McMullin, 765 A.2d at 917.

Replace the Model Act § 8.31 citation in footnote 140 on page 27 with the following:

Id. at 8-193.

Replace the Parnes citation in footnote 141 on page 27 with the following:

Parnes, 722 A.2d at 1246 (quoting *In re Santa Fe Pac. Corp. S'holder Litig.*, 669 A.2d 59, 71 (Del. 1995));

Add the following at the end of footnote 141 on page 27:

See also Dean v. Dick, 1999 Del. Ch. LEXIS 121, at *10-17, 1999 WL 413400, at *3-5 (Del. Ch. June 10, 1999); *Solomon*, 747 A.2d at 1115.

Add the following at the end of the second sentence (immediately after footnote 141) of the paragraph beginning on page 27 and concluding on page 28:

On a motion to dismiss, Delaware courts thus "conduct a two-step analysis: first, to take the facts alleged as true and view all inferences from those facts in the light most favorable to the plaintiff; and, second, to determine whether with reasonable certainty, under any set of facts that could be proven, the plaintiff would succeed in rebutting the presumption of the business judgment rule." *McMullin*, 765 A.2d at 917. A motion to dismiss should be granted if a complaint "fail[s] to withstand that threshold level of judicial scrutiny" because "unless effectively pled factual allegations . . . successfully rebut the procedural presumption of the business judgment rule," directors are "protected by the substantive operation of the business judgment rule." *Id.* at 918.

Section C 3

Add the following at the end of footnote 144 on page 29:

See also Emerald Partners v. Berlin, 726 A.2d 1215, 1221-22 (Del. 1999) ("[A] breach of any one of the board of directors' triad of fiduciary duties, loyalty, good faith or due care, sufficiently rebuts the business judgment presumption and permits a challenge to the board's action under the entire fairness standard. . . . Emerald Partners has made a sufficient showing through factual allegations that entire fairness should be the standard by which the directors' actions are reviewed. Such a showing shifts to the director defendants the burden to establish that the challenged transaction was entirely fair."); *Solomon v. Armstrong*, 747 A.2d 1098, 1113 (Del. Ch. 1999), *aff'd*, 746 A.2d 277 (unpublished opinion, full text available at 2000 Del. LEXIS 30 and 2000 WL 140072) (Del. Jan. 26, 2000); *Apple Computer, Inc. v. Exponential Tech., Inc.*, 1999 Del. Ch. LEXIS 9, at *25, 1999 WL 39547, at *7 (Del. Ch. Jan. 21, 1999); *Maul v. Kirkman*, 637 A.2d 928, 937 (N.J. Super. Ct. App. Div. 1994).

Add the following at the end of the first sentence (immediately after footnote 144) of the paragraph beginning on page 28 and concluding on page 29:

Thus, "[i]f the shareholder plaintiff succeeds in rebutting the presumption of the business judgment rule, the burden shifts to the defendant directors to prove the 'entire fairness' of the transaction." *McMullin v. Beran*, 765 A.2d 910, 917 (Del. 2000).

Add the following at the end of the first sentence (immediately after footnote 144) of the paragraph beginning on page 28 and concluding on page 29:

In other words, "[i]f the presumption is rebutted, the board's decision is reviewed through the lens of entire fairness, pursuant to which the directors lose the presumption of good business judgment," and "the Court more closely focuses on the details of the transaction and decision-making process in an effort to assess the fairness of the transaction's substantive terms." *Solomon*, 747 A.2d at 1112.

Add the following between "is not rebutted," and "'the entire fairness . . .'" in the third sentence (immediately after footnote 145) of the paragraph beginning on page 28 and concluding on page 29:

courts do not decide whether directors' judgments are "reasonable" (*Brehm v. Eisner*, 746 A.2d 244, 264 (Del. 2000), and

Add the following at the end of footnote 147 on page 30:

See also In re Dairy Mart Convenience Stores, Inc. Derivative Litig., 1999 Del. Ch. LEXIS 94, at *63, 1999 WL 350473, at *17 (Del. Ch. May 24, 1999) (fairness review "is intended to ensure that the Company and the shareholders' best interests are served where the record indicates that the normal operation of the business judgment rule is inappropriate").

Add the following at the end of footnote 149 on page 30:

See also Emerald Partners, 726 A.2d at 1222.

Add the following at the end of the paragraph beginning on page 30 and concluding on page 31 (immediately after footnote 153):

"[E]ntire fairness requires the Court to strictly scrutinize all aspects of a transaction to ensure fairness." *Dairy Mart*, 1999 Del. Ch. LEXIS 94, at *65, 1999 WL 350473, at *18.

Add the following at the end of the paragraph beginning on page 31 and concluding on page 32 (immediately after footnote 156):

As discussed in Chapter II, the approval of an interested director transaction by disinterested directors or disinterested shareholders protects the transaction and makes a showing of fairness unnecessary. *See* Chapter II, Section B 2 a-c. As also discussed in Chapter II, the approval of a controlling shareholder transaction by disinterested directors who have real bargaining power or a majority of informed minority shareholders shifts the burden of proving fairness to the plaintiff challenging the transaction. *See* Chapter II, Sections B 3 h-k.

Section C 4

Replace "Imposition of the fairness test therefore" in the second sentence (immediately after footnote 157) of the paragraph beginning on page 32 and concluding on page 33 with the following:

"Burden shifting" therefore "does not create *per se* liability" (*McMullin v. Beran*, 765 A.2d 910, 917 (Del. 2000) (quoting *Cede & Co. v. Technicolor, Inc.*, 634 A.2d 345, 371 (Del. 1993) and *Cinerama, Inc. v. Technicolor, Inc.*, 663 A.2d 1156, 1162 (Del. 1995)), and imposition of the fairness test

Add the following at the end of the second sentence (immediately after footnote 158) in the paragraph beginning on page 32 and concluding on page 33:

Rather, this is the "procedure by which the Delaware judiciary determines the standard of review that is applicable to measure the board of directors' conduct." *McMullin*, 765 A.2d at 917.

Add the following at the end of the paragraph beginning on page 32 and concluding on page 33 (immediately after footnote 161):

As the Delaware Court of Chancery observed in 1999: "Delaware courts have always recognized the fact that the burden of proving entire fairness is often a daunting task, but some boards have been able successfully to carry that burden." *Solomon v. Armstrong*, 747 A.2d 1098, 1113 (Del. Ch. 1999), *aff'd*, 746 A.2d 277 (unpublished opinion, full text available at 2000 Del. LEXIS 30 and 2000 WL 140072) (Del. Jan. 26, 2000); *see also In re Walt Disney Co. Derivative Litig.*, 731 A.2d 342, 367 (Del. Ch. 1998) (the fairness standard of judicial review subjects challenged conduct to "exacting – but not outcome-determinative" scrutiny), *aff'd with leave to replead on other grounds sub nom. Brehm v. Eisner*, 746 A.2d 244 (Del. 2000).

Add the following at the end of the paragraph beginning and concluding on page 33 (immediately after footnote 162):

The trial court's powers thus "are very broad in fashioning equitable and monetary relief under the entire fairness standard as may be appropriate, including rescissory damages." *Int'l Telecharge, Inc. v. Bomarko*, 766 A.2d 437, 440 (Del. 2000). The question the court must decide is what "shares would have been worth" if there had been no breach of fiduciary duty. *Id.* at 441. Additionally, "the imposition of damages should eliminate the possibility of profit flowing to defendants from the breach of the fiduciary relationship." *Id.*

Add the following at the end of footnote 167 on page 34:

See also additional cases cited in Chapter II, Section A 1.

Add the following at the end of footnote 172 on page 35:

See also Apple Computer, Inc. v. Exponential Tech., Inc., 1999 Del. Ch. LEXIS 9, at *25, 1999 WL 39547, at *7 (Del. Ch. Jan. 21, 1999) (noting "the possibility of rescission or rescissory damages").

Add the following at the end of footnote 175 on page 37:

See also Wilson v. Tully, 243 A.D.2d 229, 238, 676 N.Y.S.2d 531, 538 (N.Y. App. Div. 1st Dep't 1998) ("[t]hat, in hindsight, such action or inaction may turn out to be controversial, unpopular or even wrong is insufficient").

Replace the Stuart Silver citation in footnote 177 on page 37 with the following:

Stuart Silver Assocs., Inc. v. Baco Dev. Corp., 245 A.D.2d 96, 100, 665 N.Y.S.2d 415, 418 (N.Y. App. Div. 1st Dep't 1997).

Add the following at the beginning of the paragraph beginning on page 37 and concluding on page 39 (immediately after footnote 187):

As stated by the Delaware Supreme Court in 2000 in *Brehm v. Eisner*, 746 A.2d 244 (Del. 2000), the court's inquiry "is not whether we would disdain the composition, behavior and decisions" of a board "if we were Disney stockholders. . . . That decision is for the stockholders to make in voting for directors, urging other stockholders to reform or oust the board, or in making individual buy-sell decisions involving Disney securities." *Id.* at 256.

Section D 1

Add the following at the end of footnote 188 on page 39:

See also In re Fruehauf Trailer Corp., 250 B.R. 168, 196 (D. Del. 2000) (citing earlier edition of this text for this proposition).

Add the following at the end of footnote 193 on page 40:

See also Harhen v. Brown, 710 N.E.2d 224, 232-33 (Mass. App. Ct.), *rev'd on other grounds*, 730 N.E.2d 859 (Mass. 2000) ("[T]he business judgment rule affords protection only to a 'business judgment.' This means that to be afforded protection a decision must have been consciously made and judgment must, in fact, have been exercised.") (quoting 1 Principles of Corporate Governance: Analysis and Recommendations § 4.01 comment c at 174 (1994)).

Section D 2

Replace the Model Act § 8.31 citation preceding the "('[i]f a director . . .')" parenthetical in footnote 198 on page 42 with the following:

2 Model Bus. Corp. Act Annotated § 8.31 Official Comment at 8-202 (3d ed. Supp. 1998/99)

Add the following at the end of footnote 199 on page 42:

See also Brehm v. Eisner, 746 A.2d 244, 255, 257 (Del. 2000); *In re Cooper Cos. S'holders Derivative Litig.*, 2000 Del. Ch. LEXIS 158, at *17, 20, 2000 WL 1664167, at *6, 7 (Del. Ch. Oct. 31, 2000); *McMillan v. Intercargo Corp.*, 768 A.2d 492, 503 (Del. Ch. 2000); *State of Wis. Inv. Bd. v. Bartlett*, 2000 Del. Ch. LEXIS 42, at *12, 2000 WL 238026, at *4 (Del. Ch. Feb. 24, 2000); *White v. Panic*, 2000 Del. Ch. LEXIS 14, at *28, 2000 WL 85046, at *8 (Del. Ch. Jan. 19, 2000); *Golaine v. Edwards*, 1999 Del. Ch. LEXIS 237, at *36, 1999 WL 1271882, at *10 (Del. Ch. Dec. 21, 1999); *In re Lukens Inc. S'holders Litig.*, 757 A.2d 720, 728-30 (Del. Ch. 1999); *Chaf-*

fin v. GNI Group, Inc., 1999 Del. Ch. LEXIS 182, at *16, 1999 WL 721569, at *5 (Del. Ch. Sept. 3, 1999); *Harhen v. Brown*, 730 N.E.2d 859, 845 (Mass. 2000).

Add the following at the end of footnote 200 on page 43:

See also In re Encore Computer Corp. S'holders Litig., 2000 Del. Ch. LEXIS 93, at *17, 2000 WL 823373, at *6 (Del. Ch. June 16, 2000) (business judgment rule governs decision made by two disinterested directors where the board included these two disinterested directors and two interested directors who recused themselves); *Cooke v. Oolie*, 2000 Del. Ch. LEXIS 89, at *46 & n.41, 2000 WL 710199, at *13 & n.41 (Del. Ch. May 24, 2000) (business judgment rule governs decision made by two disinterested and two interested directors, where the disinterested directors both approved the decision); *In re W. Nat'l Corp. S'holders Litig.,* 2000 Del. Ch. LEXIS 82, at *85-92, 2000 WL 710192, at *26-27 (Del. Ch. May 22, 2000) (business judgment rule governs decision made by three disinterested directors on a special committee where the board included these three directors and five additional directors that the court found lacked disinterestedness and independence, at least for the purpose of the motion for summary judgment before the court; discussed in Chapter II, Section B 3 k-1).

Section D 2 a

Add the following at the end of footnote 206 on page 44:

See also State of Wis. Inv. Bd. v. Bartlett, 2000 Del. Ch. LEXIS 42, at *12, 2000 WL 238026, at *4 (Del. Ch. Feb. 24, 2000).

Add the following at the end of footnote 207 on page 44:

See also Greenwald v. Batterson, 1999 Del. Ch. LEXIS 158, at *14, 21, 1999 WL 596276, at *5, 7 (Del. Ch. July 26, 1999).

Add the following at the end of footnote 209 on page 44:

See also Lewis v. Austen, 1999 Del. Ch. LEXIS 125, at *15, 1999 WL 378125, at *4 (Del. Ch. June 2, 1999) (business judgment rule presumption not overcome in action challenging adjustments to stock option plans made when Humana, Inc. spun off its Galen Health Care, Inc. subsidiary, where "the so-called option 'enhancements'" did not extend the options' expiration date, accelerate any vesting rights, or create any "new 'benefits'").

Add the following at the end of the paragraph beginning and concluding on page 44 (immediately after footnote 209):

A director who is a financial advisor who will receive compensation in connection with a transaction does not have a self-interest that precludes his ability to act independently where the director's and financial advisor's interests are "completely aligned with the interests of the stockholders in attempting to maximize the value of the interest of the corporation and the stockholders." *Crescent/Mach I Partners, L.P. v. Turner*, 2000 Del. Ch. LEXIS 145, at *39, 2000 WL 1481002, at *11 (Del. Ch. Sept. 29, 2000); *see also id.*, 2000 Del. Ch. LEXIS 145, at *39 n.42, 2000 WL 1481002 at *11 n.42 (summarizing *State of Wis. Inv. Bd. v. Bartlett*, 2000 Del. Ch. LEXIS 42, at *12-13, 2000 WL 238026, at *4 (Del. Ch. Feb. 24, 2000), as follows: "'[o]ne director's alleged interest, as here in a fee related to consummation of the merger, related to his work and tied to overall enhancement in the value of the merger transaction is simply not enough to mandate strict scrutiny of the Medco board's actions'" because the allegedly self-interested director had "every reason to attempt to negotiate the highest consideration possible for the stockholders").

Section D 2 b

Delete "and" in footnote 211 on page 45 and replace the period at the end of the footnote with the following:

and Brehm v. Eisner, 746 A.2d 244, 256 n.31 (Del. 2000).

Replace the Benerofe citation in footnote 216 on page 45 with the following:

Benerofe v. Cha, 1996 Del. Ch. LEXIS 115, at *20, 1996 WL 535405, at *7 (Del. Ch. Sept. 12, 1996), *subsequent proceedings*, 1998 Del. Ch. LEXIS 28, 1998 WL 83081 (Del. Ch. Feb. 20, 1998).

Add the following at the end of footnote 218 on page 46:

See also In re W. Nat'l Corp. S'holders Litig., 2000 Del. Ch. LEXIS 82, at *52-53, 2000 WL 710192, at *16 (Del. Ch. May 22, 2000); *In re Gaylord Container Corp. S'holders Litig.*, 753 A.2d 462, 465 n.3 (Del. Ch. 2000); *Odyssey Partners, L.P. v. Fleming Cos.*, 735 A.2d 386, 408 (Del. Ch. 1999).

Replace the period at the end of footnote 219 on page 46 with the following:

and Emerald Partners v. Berlin, 726 A.2d 1215, 1223 (Del. 1999).

Add the following at the end of footnote 221 on page 46:

See also Bansbach v. Zinn, 258 A.D.2d 710, 713, 685 N.Y.S.2d 332, 334 (N.Y. App. Div. 3d Dep't 1999) ("the mere allegation of personal friendships is insufficient to establish domination and control").

Add the following at the end of footnote 222 on page 46:

See also Crescent/Mach I Partners, L.P. v. Turner, 2000 Del. Ch. LEXIS 145, at *40, 2000 WL 1481002, at *11 (Del. Ch. Sept. 29, 2000) (an alleged "long-standing 15-year professional and personal relationship" does not "raise a reasonable doubt" of interestedness or lack of independence); *Fleming*, 735 A.2d at 409-10 (the fact that two directors were neighbors was of "no moment" because "conclusory allegations of 'personal affinity' are not sufficient to establish director interest"); *Apple Computer, Inc. v. Exponential Tech., Inc.*, 1999 Del. Ch. LEXIS 9, at *46-47, 1999 WL 39547, at *12 (Del. Ch. Jan. 21, 1999) (in a case where two of five directors of Exponential Technology, Inc. – Gordon Campbell and Donald Shriner – had a financial interest in challenged litigation support agreements, the court rejected a contention that a third director – George S. Taylor – lacked independence because "Campbell and Taylor founded Exponential together"; this conclusory allegation, the court held, "falls far short of raising a reasonable doubt . . . that a third Exponential director was incapable of exercising proper business judgment in approving the agreements").

Add the following at the end of the second paragraph beginning and concluding on page 46 (immediately after footnote 222):

Thus, by itself, "[e]vidence of personal and/or past business relationships does not raise an inference of self-interest." *State of Wis. Inv. Bd. v. Bartlett*, 2000 Del. Ch. LEXIS 42, at *20, 2000 WL 238026, at *6 (Del. Ch. Feb. 24, 2000), *quoted in Kohls v. Duthie*, 765 A.2d 1274, 1284 (Del. Ch. 2000); *see also Kohls*, 765 A.2d at 1284 (director's friendship with chief executive officer and the fact that the chief executive officer gave the director a summer job while the director was in business school does not establish lack of independence). Nor does a chief executive officer's or a large shareholder's "role in the nomination process" by itself "automatically foreclose a director's potential independence." *In re W. Nat'l Corp. S'holders Litig.*, 2000 Del. Ch. LEXIS 82, at *52-53, 2000 WL 710192, at *15 (Del. Ch. May 22, 2000), *quoted in Kohls*, 765 A.2d at 1284 n.20.

Family relationships such as a parent and his or her child, a grandparent and his or her grandchild, or brothers-in-law or sisters-in-law have been found sufficient in several cases to establish a lack of independence. *See, e.g., In re Cooper Cos. S'holders Derivative Litig.*, 2000 Del. Ch. LEXIS 158, at *18, 2000 WL 1664167, at *6 (Del. Ch. Oct. 31, 2000); *Grace Bros., Ltd. v. UniHolding Corp.*, 2000 Del. Ch. LEXIS 101, at *32 & n.23, 2000 WL 982401, at *10 & n.23 (Del. Ch. July 12, 2000); *Harbor Fin. Partners v. Huizenga*, 751 A.2d 879, 889 (Del. Ch. 1999); *Chaffin v. GNI Group, Inc.*, 1999 Del. Ch. LEXIS 182, at *17-18, 1999 WL 721569, at *5 (Del. Ch. Sept. 3, 1999); *Mizel v. Connelly*, 1999 Del. Ch. LEXIS 157, at *12 & n.3, 1999 WL 550369, at *4 & n.3 (Del. Ch. July 22, 1999); 2 Model Bus. Corp. Act Annotated § 8.60(3) (3d ed. Supp. 1998/99) (defining "related person" as "(i) the spouse (or a parent or sibling thereof) of the director, or a child, grandchild, sibling, parent (or spouse of any thereof) of the director, or an individual having the same home as the director, or a trust or estate of which an individual specified in this clause (i) is a substantial beneficiary; or (ii) a trust, estate, incompetent, conservatee, or minor of which the director is a fiduciary"). *But see Shapiro v. Greenfield*, 764 A.2d 270, 282 (Md. Ct. Spec. App. 2000) (rejecting "a per se rule based on a familial . . . relationship because a relationship between the parties does not necessarily destroy an individual's independent judgment").

Independence is measured with respect to the issue concerning which a decision is made and "does not require the individual director to have had no prior contact with the company in order to count as 'independent.'" *Nakahara v. NS 1991 Am. Trust*, 739 A.2d 770, 788 (Del. Ch. 1998). For example, "in a management buy-out independent outside directors are required to pass upon the entire fairness of the transaction" and "[i]nside directors are not allowed to vote on the entire fairness question, because they have an interest and are not independent." *Id.* "In such a situation, however, the 'independent' directors are not entirely independent of the corporation – they are, after all, directors of the corporation – they simply do not have a conflict of interest that would taint their fair judgment." *Id.*

Add the following at the end of footnote 223 on page 47:

In re Walt Disney Co. Derivative Litig., 731 A.2d 342, 357 (Del. Ch. 1998) (where one director, Stanley P. Gold, lacked independence from another director, Roy E. Disney, but Disney did not lack independence from a director alleged to have a financial interest in a challenged transaction, Michael D. Eisner, "the business judgment of Gold is similarly free from Eisner's alleged dominating influence"), *aff'd with leave to replead on other grounds sub nom. Brehm v. Eisner*, 746 A.2d 244 (Del. 2000).

Add the following at the end of the paragraph beginning on page 46 and concluding on page 47 (immediately after footnote 223):

The same is true with respect to directors who have a relationship with a controlling shareholder where there is no showing of interest on the part of the controlling shareholder. *Goodwin v. Live Entm't, Inc.*, 1999 Del. Ch. LEXIS 5, at *87, 1999 WL 64265, at *28 (Del. Ch. Jan. 22, 1999), *aff'd*, 741 A.2d 16 (unpublished opinion, text available at 1999 Del. LEXIS 238 and 1999 WL 624128) (Del. July 23, 1999).

Section D 2 c

Add the following at the end of the first paragraph beginning and concluding on page 47 (immediately after footnote 227):

As stated by the Delaware Court of Chancery in *Goodwin v. Live Entertainment, Inc.*, 1999 Del. Ch. LEXIS 5, 1999 WL 64265 (Del. Ch. Jan. 22, 1999), *aff'd*, 741 A.2d 16 (unpublished opinion, text available at 1999 Del. LEXIS 238 and 1999 WL 624128) (Del. July 23, 1999), a shareholder plaintiff's burden to rebut the presumption of the business judgment rule based upon an alleged interest on the part of board members requires that the shareholder plaintiff make two showings: "First, the plaintiff must proffer evidence showing that those members of the board had a material self-interest in the challenged transaction. . . . Second, the plaintiff must show that those materially self-interested members either: a) constituted a majority of the board; b) controlled and dominated the board as a whole; or c) i) failed to disclose their interests in the transaction to the board; ii) and a reasonable board member would have regarded the existence of their material interests as a significant fact in the evaluation of the proposed transaction." 1999 Del. Ch. LEXIS 5, at *77-78, 1999 WL 64265, at *25. "Absent such a showing, the mere presence of a conflicted director or an act of disloyalty by a director, does not deprive the board of the business judgment rule's presumption of loyalty." 1999 Del. Ch. LEXIS 5, at *78, 1999 WL 64265, at *25.

The Delaware Court of Chancery in *HMG/Courtland Properties, Inc. v. Gray*, 749 A.2d 94 (Del. Ch. 1999), held that the Supreme Court's decisions in *Cede & Co. v. Technicolor, Inc.*, 634 A.2d 345 (Del. 1993) and *Cinerama, Inc. v. Technicolor, Inc.*, 663 A.2d 1156 (Del. 1996), which require a showing of materiality in order to establish a disqualifying interest or lack of independence, do not apply in cases involving "classic self-dealing" where a director or directors "stand on both sides of a transaction." 749 A.2d at 113-15. To the contrary, the court in *HMG* stated, "self-dealing, in itself, is sufficient to rebut the presumption of the business judgment rule and invoke entire fairness review." *Id.* at 113. Thus, the court in *HMG* concluded, the *Technicolor* materiality analysis is inapplicable where a transaction involves a contract between the corporation and one or more of its directors and thus is governed by Section 144 of the Delaware General Corporation Law – Delaware's safe harbor statute that governs interested director transactions, which is discussed in Chapter II, Section B 2 a. *Id.* at 113-14; *see also Harbor Fin. Partners v. Huizenga*, 751 A.2d 879, 887 n.20 (Del. Ch. 1999) (stating that "[t]here is analytic force to the argument that § 144 should, like many statutes, be read as incorporating a 'materiality' element" in order to "ensure that a director who, for example, owns one share of stock worth $100 or even $1,000, in another entity with which the corporation of which he is a fiduciary is transacting business is not considered 'interested,'" but adding that "[t]he incorporation of a materiality element into § 144 as a matter of statutory interpretation should not, however, be confused with the 'materiality' test" articulated in the *Technicolor* decisions "to determine whether directors are 'interested' in a transaction in which § 144 does not apply").

Delete "the test somewhat differently, concluding that" in the first sentence (between footnotes 227 and 228) of the second paragraph beginning and concluding on page 47.

Replace the Model Act § 8.31 citation in footnote 228 on page 47 with the following:

2 Model Bus. Corp. Act Annotated § 8.31 Official Comment at 8-203 (3d ed. Supp. 1998/99).

Add "in Technicolor" between "the Supreme Court" and "rejected" in the first sentence (between footnotes 229 and 230) of the paragraph beginning on page 47 and concluding on page 48.

Add the following at the end of the paragraph beginning on page 51 and concluding on page 52 (immediately after footnote 249):

"Evidence of mere self-interest alone is not enough." *Live Entm't*, 1999 Del. Ch. LEXIS 5, at *77, 1999 WL 64265, at *25.

Add the following at the end of the paragraph beginning and concluding on page 52 (immediately after footnote 256):

The court in *In re Dairy Mart Convenience Stores, Inc. Derivative Litig*, 1999 Del. Ch. LEXIS 94, 1999 WL 350473 (Del. Ch. May 24, 1999), similarly rejected an allegation that outside directors were interested in a challenged transaction that included a grant of stock options to the directors "[b]ecause plaintiff has failed to plead the materiality of that potential self-interest." 1999 Del. Ch. LEXIS 94, at *66 n.57, 1999 WL 350473, at *8 n.57. The court in *Metropolitan Life Insurance Co. v. Aramark Corp.*, 1998 Del. Ch. LEXIS 70 (Del. Ch. Feb. 5, 1998), likewise found no disabling interest on the part of directors whose holdings were "not insignificant" but did not "constitute a material personal financial interest that would necessarily disable them from acting in what they in good faith perceive is the interest of the corporation as a whole." *Id.* at *4.

The same result was reached in *Dean v. Dick*, 1999 Del. Ch. LEXIS 121, 1999 WL 413400 (Del. Ch. June 10, 1999). The court dismissed a claim by Kenneth Becker, a limited partner in Mt. Airy-Regency Limited Partnership, challenging a decision by J. Simpson Dean, Jr., the sole owner of the general partner of Mr. Airy, to refinance a $100,000 note owed to Mt. Airy by Bard Investments Company, another limited partner in Mt. Airy, which was owned in part by Dean. 1999 Del. Ch. LEXIS 121, at *1-3, 1999 WL 413400, at *1. According to the plaintiff, "[b]y refinancing the Bard Note, Bard, which was owned in part by Dean, received an early distribution of its capital contribution." 1999 Del. Ch. LEXIS 121, at *3, 1999 WL 413400, at *1. The plaintiff also alleged that Dean had not sought to recover the amounts Mt. Airy had paid to service the notes from Bard but had attempted to recover these amounts from the plaintiff. 1999 Del. Ch. LEXIS 121, at *3-4, 1999 WL 413400, at *1. The court rejected plaintiff's contention that the refinancing of the Bard note "benefited Dean disproportionately, since he was a partner in Bard" because plaintiff "does not allege whether any benefit received by Dean in his role as a

Bard partner was even material to him." 1999 Del. Ch. LEXIS 121, at *12-13, 1999 WL 413400, at *4.

The court in *White v. Panic*, 2000 Del. Ch. LEXIS 14, 2000 WL 85046 (Del. Ch. Jan. 19, 2000), rejected an allegation that a director lacked independence because the plaintiff failed to allege facts indicating that a $33,440 consulting fee paid to the director's law firm was "so material as to taint" that director's judgment as a director. 2000 Del. Ch. LEXIS 14, at *26, 2000 WL 85046, at *8. The court reached the same conclusion with respect to a $12,000 consulting fee paid to another director, but did not reach $48,000, $50,000, and $75,000 consulting fees paid to other directors because even if those directors were assumed to lack independence "only a total of six out of fifteen ICN directors would be disqualified." 2000 Del. Ch. LEXIS 14, at *27-28 & n.36, 2000 WL 85046, at *8 & n.36.

The court in *In re Gaylord Container Corp. Shareholders Litigation*, 753 A.2d 462 (Del. Ch. 2000), held that the "mere fact" that a director is a managing director of an investment bank and had offered the investment bank's services but was not retained "does little to compromise his independence" because under these circumstances no "material financial relationship existed." *Id.* at 465 n.3. The court also held that a director who is "of counsel" to a law firm that "over the years" has "done some work" for the corporation does not lack independence in the absence of evidence that the law firm had "a material financial interest" in representing the corporation or that the director's "personal status as of counsel to that firm was material to him and somehow related to the continuation of the firm's relationship" with the corporation. *Id.* at 466 n.3.

The court in *In re Frederick's of Hollywood, Inc. Shareholders Litigation*, 2000 Del. Ch. LEXIS 19, 2000 WL 130630 (Del. Ch. Jan. 31, 2000), held that a director who was a senior vice president of the corporation's financial advisor, Janney Montgomery Scott, Inc. ("JMS"), was not interested in a merger despite plaintiffs' allegation that the terms of JMS's engagement letter with the corporation provided that JMS would receive approximately $2 million for its services once the merger was completed. "The difficulty with this claim," the court explained, "is that JMS would receive a fee for its services regardless of who the buyer was; moreover, the amount of the fee JMS was to receive would increase as the merger price increased." 2000 Del. Ch. LEXIS 19, at *23-24, 2000 WL 130630, at *7. As a result, the director's (and JMS's) interests "were completely aligned with the interests of the shareholders in obtaining the highest possible price" for the corporation's shares and there was no disabling self-interest. 2000 Del. Ch. LEXIS 19, at *24, 2000 WL 130630, at *7.

The court in *McMillan v. Intercargo Corp.*, 768 A.2d 492 (Del. Ch. 2000), characterized challenges to the disinterestedness and independence of three of eight directors on the board of Intercargo Corporation in connection with a merger of Intercargo Corporation and XL America, Inc. as "extremely weak" and "unaccompanied by allegations that any of these defendants dominated or controlled" the remaining five members – i.e., the majority – of Intercargo's board. *Id.* at 503, 504.

With respect to the first director, Stanley A. Galanski, plaintiffs alleged that Galanski was the president and chief executive officer of Intercargo and was "personally interested in the Merger because he is being hired by XL." *Id.* at 496. According to plaintiffs, the court stated, "Galanski was motivated to support a subpar deal with XL because XL promised him future employment, the terms of which the plaintiffs do not bother to specify." *Id.* at 503. The court stated that it was "skeptical" but did not need to decide whether a doubt is created concerning the disinterestedness of a chief executive officer who supported a "voluntary, uncoerced search for a buyer," "worked with his board to retain an investment banker to look for buyers," and "was asked by the ultimate buyer to stay on," where plaintiffs do not allege that he was hired by the buyer "on terms materially more favorable than his (apparently non-threatened) employment with Intercargo." *Id.* The court added that the reason for the lack of allegations concerning the terms of Galanski's employment agreement with XL was the fact – stated in the proxy statement used to obtain shareholder approval for the merger – that "he agreed to stay on with XL for . . . a rather modest increase of approximately 4%." *Id.* at 503 n.51.

With respect to the second director, Michael L. Sklar, plaintiffs alleged that Sklar was a partner of the law firm Rudnick & Wolfe, which served as Intercargo's primary outside counsel before the merger and that represented Intercargo in the merger. *Id.* at 496. The court stated that "[n]othing in the complaint indicates that Sklar or Rudnick & Wolfe stood to obtain legal work from XL after the merger." *Id.* Based upon the absence of an allegation that the law firm was promised work after the merger, the court reasoned as follows:

> If, as the plaintiffs allege, Intercargo had a long-term business plan that would make the company prosper, why would Sklar urge a change of control transaction at a less than optimum price? Would not this tend to be self-destructive in that it would subject Rudnick & Wolfe to the substantial risk of losing a client? Frankly, I don't get it, especially because the plaintiffs do not allege that Rudnick & Wolfe was promised a continued role as counsel for XL (on behalf, for example, of its new Intercargo operations).

Id. at 503.

With respect to the third director, Robert B. Sanborn, plaintiffs alleged that Sanborn served on Intercargo's board at the request of Orion Capital Corporation, which owned 26 percent of Intercargo's stock and had agreed to vote for the merger. *Id.* at 496. Plaintiffs pointed to two statements in Intercargo's proxy statement: one stating that "'as a designee of Orion, Mr. Sanborn's investment aims may differ from those of some stockholders,'" and another stating that "during at least one [Intercargo] board meeting at which XL's offer was discussed, 'Mr. Sanborn excused himself from the meeting upon the commencement of the discussion regarding the Company's strategic alternatives.'" *Id.* at 496-97. Plaintiffs alleged that "this unexplained recusal" demonstrated "'an undisclosed conflict between Orion and [Intercargo's] other stockholders.'" *Id.* at 497. According to plaintiffs, Orion had decided to sell its position in Intercargo and "was anxious to sell its position and was willing to sell at less than the best price." *Id.* at 504.

The court pointed to the "normal presumption" that "the owner of a substantial block who decides to sell is interested in obtaining the highest price" and held that plaintiffs alleged "no facts that reasonably support the inference that this presumption should not apply to Orion's investment in Intercargo." *Id.* Certainly, the court stated, "plaintiffs have not pled facts suggesting that Orion was anxious to engage in a fire sale," and "[h]ad Orion wished to sell out fast, it had options of its own and could have marketed its own quite valuable block." *Id.* With respect to plaintiffs' claim that Sanborn was conflicted because he recused himself from a board meeting due to his affiliation with Orion, the court noted defendants' response that "Sanborn stepped out of the meeting . . . because Orion was a potential rival bidder and Sanborn did not want to taint the process." *Id.* The court stated that if this was true, then Sanborn's "decision to recuse seems in keeping with high standards of directorial conduct." *Id.*

The same result was reached in *Hills Stores Co. v. Bozic*, 769 A.2d 88 (Del. Ch. 2000), a case involving a decision by the board of Hills Stores Company that a vote by shareholders in favor of a slate of directors proposed by Dickstein Partners Inc., an investment firm that promised either to buy all Hills shares for $22 in cash and $5 in payable-in-kind bonds or to sell Hills to the highest bidder in an auction, would constitute a change in control that would trigger employment agreement payments to three of the seven directors on the Hills board. Thomas Lee, a director who was not a beneficiary of an employment agreement, was alleged to be interested in the decision because Lee's firm received a $250,000 fee to act as a financial advisor to the corporation and because Lee was affiliated with entities that allegedly would have lost certain rights to purchase shares at a favorable price if a merger with Dickstein or other change in control occurred. *Id.* at 105.

On a motion for summary judgment, the court reasoned that "[t]he $250,000 that went to Lee's firm represents an infinitesimal proportion" of his more than $200 million annual income and that the plaintiffs had failed to produce evidence that the rights Lee's affiliates possessed would in fact have been extinguished by a merger or other change in control or that the rights Lee's affiliates possessed "overrode Lee's interest in maximizing his return" from the 800,000 Hills shares Lee and his affiliates owned, which "stood to receive over $20 million in proceeds if Dickstein's promised strategy panned out." *Id.* The court held that "[g]iven these facts and the plaintiffs' failure (through depositions and other discovery) to demonstrate that Lee was abnormally obsessed (apologies to Benjamin Franidin) with (what to Lee are) pennies rather than dollars, I conclude that there is no triable issue regarding Lee's disinterested status." *Id.* at 105-06.

The court in *Cooke v. Oolie*, 2000 Del. Ch. LEXIS 89, 2000 WL 710199 (Del. Ch. May 24, 2000), rejected a contention that the dual role of Sam Oolie and Morton Salkind, two of the four directors of The Nostalgia Network ("TNN"), a corporation operating under extreme financial distress, as directors and creditors of TNN at a time when TNN's board was seeking acquisition proposals gave rise to a potential conflict of interest. According to plaintiffs, "[t]he fiduciary duty of loyalty bound Oolie and Salkind, as directors, to seek out the best possible acquisition proposal for the shareholders of TNN," but "Oolie and Salkind also were creditors of TNN and knew that any acquisition of TNN might affect their financial interests as TNN creditors." 2000 Del. Ch. LEXIS 89, at *40, 2000 WL 710199, at *12. In plaintiffs' view, Oolie and Salkind's "fiduciary duties compelled them to seek the best deal possible for the shareholders, but their creditor status created the incentive to protect their personal loans despite the shareholders' interests." *Id.*

The court acknowledged "[t]he potential for a conflict of interest" but held that plaintiffs had failed to "show that an actual conflict existed" in the TNN board's vote in favor of the transaction favored by these directors. *Id.* The court reasoned as follows: "[Plaintiffs] must show that the actual terms of the USA deal created a basis for Salkind and Oolie to act disloyally. In other words, Oolie's and Salkind's vote to pursue the USA proposal signals potential disloyalty only if the USA proposal in fact offered superior terms for Oolie and Salkind and inferior terms for the plaintiff shareholders compared to the other proposals available to TNN." 2000 Del. Ch. LEXIS 89, at *40-41, 2000 WL 710199, at *12.

The court concluded that there was no "actual conflict of interest sufficient to rebut the business judgment rule" because the USA proposal, but not any of the competing proposals, capped TNN's debt, and it capped TNN's debt at $1,050,000 – an amount below the $1,514,000 owed by TNN to Oolie and Salkind. 2000 Del. Ch. LEXIS 89, at *41, 2000 WL 710199, at *12. "Oolie and Salkind, therefore, by electing to pursue the USA proposal, agreed to make a financial sacrifice on behalf of TNN. Clearly, the USA proposal did not benefit creditors." *Id.* The court also pointed to the fact that Oolie and Salkind owned a majority of TNN's stock and thus had no incentive "to pursue a transaction that benefited them as creditors if that transaction did not produce a total net gain to the defendants after considering their equity and debt positions." 2000 Del. Ch. LEXIS 89, at *41-42, 2000 WL 710199, at *12. According to the court, the evidence demonstrated that "Oolie and Salkind would receive less value under the terms of the USA proposal than any other proposals submitted to TNN." 2000 Del. Ch. LEXIS 89, at *42, 2000 WL 710199, at *12.

The same result also was reached in *Kohls v. Duthie*, 765 A.2d 1274 (Del. Ch. 2000), a case where plaintiffs alleged a lack of independence on the part of Gerald R. Morgan, Jr., a director of Kenetech Corporation, with respect to a transaction involving the corporation's chief executive officer, Mark D. Lerdal, based upon an investment by Kenetech in a fund of which Morgan was chief operating officer and chief financial officer. The court stated that "the fund at the time of the Kenetech commitment was valued at approximately $1.3 billion" and that since the time of Kenetech's investment the fund's value had reached $2 billion and the fund had been closed to new investors. *Id.* at 1285. Under these circumstances, the court held, "Kenetech's commitment of $5 million to be paid over 6 years is, thus, of immaterial concern." *Id.* The court added that even if Kenetech's investment in the fund "were somehow material to Morgan's employment (about which there is no evidence), the commitment is a contractual obligation of Kenetech, not subject to Lerdal's discretion." *Id.*

The court in *Harhen v. Brown*, 730 N.E.2d 859 (Mass. 2000), rejected an allegation that a director of Hancock Mutual Life Insurance Company lacked disinterestedness and independence in a decision involving a shareholder demand seeking corporate action against Hancock directors and employees who participated or acquiesced in illegal lobbying of members of the Massachusetts legislature. The director lacked disinterestedness and independence, plaintiff alleged, because he also was the chief executive officer of Polaroid and Hancock had purchased $18 million of long-term bonds issued by Polaroid. The court stated that Hancock's purchase of Polaroid bonds "constituted only a small fraction of Hancock's $107 billion portfolio, and the plaintiff's complaint does not set out the extent of Polaroid's assets or total indebtedness" and does not allege that the director alleged to lack disinterestedness and independence "had a material pecuniary interest in the transaction or indeed would benefit in any respect from a decision regarding the plaintiff's demand." *Id.* at 866.

The court in *In re General Motors Class H Shareholders Litigation*, 734 A.2d 611 (Del. Ch. 1999), a case involving two classes of GM common stock, GM $1 2/3 stock and GMH stock, stated that plaintiffs alleging that a director's independence was compromised by his or her ownership of greater amounts of GM $1 2/3 stock than GMH stock "must plead that the amount of such holdings and the predominance of such holdings over GMH holdings was of a sufficiently material importance, in the context of the director's economic circumstances, as to have made it improbable that the director could perform her fiduciary duties to the GMH shareholders without being influenced by her overriding personal interest in the performance of the GM $1 2/3 shares." *Id.* at 617. The court held that plaintiffs' complaint failed this test because the complaint was "devoid of any alleged facts supporting the materiality of the GM $1 2/3 holdings to the directors" or "an inference that the GM directors' holdings of GM $1 2/3 stock were so substantial as to have rendered it improbable that those directors could discharge their fiduciary obligations in an even-handed manner." *Id.* at 618.

The court in *Solomon v. Armstrong*, 747 A.2d 1098 (Del. Ch. 1999), *aff'd*, 746 A.2d 277 (unpublished opinion, full text available at 2000 Del. LEXIS 30 and 2000 WL 140072) (Del. Jan. 26, 2000), another case involving two classes of GM common stock, in this instance GM $1 2/3 stock and Class E stock, stated that "it is well established that when a party challenges a director's action based on a claim of the director's debilitating pecuniary self-interest, that party must allege that the director's interest is material to that director." *Id.* at 1118. Thus, "it is not enough for plaintiffs to plead that the outside directors held a disproportionate number of shares of GM $1 2/3 common stock. . . . [P]laintiffs must also plead that the . . . director defendants held shares in amounts that were *material* to them." *Id.* at 1117; *see also id.* at 1110 ("[a]lthough plaintiffs allege that the members of the Capital Stock Committee owned disparate holdings of Class E stock compared to the other classes, thereby implicating their personal interests, those breach of loyalty claims fail as a matter of law because plaintiffs do not allege the materiality of the holdings with reference to those particular directors").

The Delaware Court of Chancery's decision in In re *Walt Disney Co. Derivative Litigation*, 731 A.2d 342 (Del. Ch. 1998), *aff'd with leave to replead sub nom. Brehm v. Eisner*, 746 A.2d 244 (Del. 2000), contains an extensive discussion of director disinterestedness and independence in the context of a challenge to the Walt Disney Company board's 1995 approval of an employment agreement for Michael Ovitz and the board's 1996 decision to grant Ovitz a non-fault termination that resulted in a $140 million severance payment pursuant to the terms of the 1995 employment agreement. Among other things, the 1995 agreement included options to purchase 5 million shares of Disney stock: 1 million options would vest each year over a five year period, but 3 million options would vest immediately in the case of a non-fault termination. *Id.* at 350, 352.

The court explained that in order to allege disinterestedness or independence, a plaintiff must allege facts that, if true, would "demonstrate that a director 'will receive a personal financial benefit from a transaction that is not equally shared by the stockholders' or, conversely, that 'a corporate decision will have a materially detrimental impact on a director, but not on the corporation and the stockholders.'" *Id.* at 354 (quoting *Rales v. Blasband*, 634 A.2d 927, 936 (Del. 1993)). In those situations, the court stated, "a director cannot be expected to act 'without being influenced by the . . . personal consequences' flowing from the decision." *Id.* In other words, "a board member is considered to be disinterested when he or she neither stands to benefit financially nor suffer materially." *Id.* To disqualify the board as a whole, a disqualifying interest or lack of independence must be alleged with respect to a majority of the corporation's directors. *Id.*

Plaintiffs alleged that Michael D. Eisner, the chairman of the board and chief executive officer of Disney, was interested in the decision to enter into the challenged employment agreement and the decision to approve the non-fault termination. Plaintiffs also alleged that Eisner dominated a majority of the other directors on Disney's board at the time of each of these decisions.

Disney's board at the time the board approved Ovitz's employment agreement included 15 directors: Eisner and Stephen F. Bollenbach, Reveta F. Bowers, Roy E. Disney, Stanley P. Gold, Sanford M. Litvack, Ignacio E. Lozano Jr., George J. Mitchell, Richard A. Nunis, Sidney Poitier, Irwin E.

Russell, Robert A.M. Stern, E. Cardon Walker, Raymond L. Watson and Gary L. Wilson. Id. at 351 n.3. Disney's board at the time the board determined to grant Ovitz a non-fault termination included 17 directors: Eisner, Ovitz (who did not participate in the vote concerning the termination of his contract), Bowers, Disney, Gold, Litvack, Lozano, Mitchell, Nunis, Poitier, Russell, Stern, Walker, Watson, Wilson (i.e., all of Disney's directors at the time the employment agreement was entered into other than Bollenbach) plus two new directors: Leo J. O'Donovan and Thomas S. Murphy. *Id.*

The court held that Eisner had no disqualifying interest in the approval of the employment agreement or the determination to grant Ovitz a non-fault termination. The court rejected plaintiffs' contention that a long-time personal relationship between Eisner and Ovitz created an interest on the part of Eisner in Ovitz's employment agreement. *Id.* at 355. The court stated that this contention found "no support under Delaware law" because "[t]he fact that Eisner has long-standing personal and business ties to Ovitz cannot overcome the presumption of independence that all directors, including Eisner, are afforded." *Id.*

The court also rejected plaintiffs' contention that Eisner's interest in maximizing his own income from Disney created an interest on the part of Eisner in maximizing payments by Disney to Ovitz (according to plaintiffs, this would set a high baseline from which Eisner could negotiate upward for himself) and minimizing the controversy surrounding Ovitz's severance pay (according to plaintiffs, a public dispute with Ovitz would conflict with Eisner's desire to limit criticism of his compensation). *Id.* The court also pointed to Eisner's ownership of several million options to purchase Disney stock and stated that "it would not be in Eisner's economic interest to cause the Company to issue millions of additional options unnecessarily and at considerable cost" because this "would dilute the value of Eisner's own very substantial holdings." *Id.* at 355-56. Additionally, the court stated, "[e]ven if the impact on Eisner's option value were relatively small, such a large compensation package would, and did, draw largely negative attention to Eisner's own performance and compensation." *Id.* at 356. The Supreme Court affirmed this holding, stating that plaintiffs' theory "is not supported by well-pleaded facts, only conclusory allegations," and "we agree with the Court of Chancery." 746 A.2d at 257-58.

The court next held that even if Eisner were interested in Ovitz's employment agreement and/or the determination to grant Ovitz a non-fault termination, plaintiffs had failed to allege facts with respect to the independence of more than four directors: Litvack, Nunis, Russell and Stern. Accordingly, plaintiffs "still come up short; ten of the fifteen directors who approved the Agreement and eleven of the sixteen who voted to honor the Agreement were independent in deciding the issues of Ovitz's compensation and free of domination from Eisner." 731 A.2d at 361. In support of this conclusion, "the Court of Chancery proceeded meticulously to analyze each director's ties to Eisner to see if they could have exercised business judgment independent of Eisner." 746 A.2d at 258. Because the Supreme Court held that Eisner was disinterested, the Supreme Court determined that it "need not reach or comment on the analysis of the Court of Chancery on the independence of the other directors." *Id.*

With respect to the ten directors who approved the employment agreement who were found to be disinterested and independent, the Court of Chancery stated that there were no allegations of interestedness or lack of independence with respect to Bollenbach, Lozano and Watson, and the court rejected lack of independence allegations with respect to Bowers, Disney, Gold, Mitchell, Poitier, Walker and Wilson. With respect to the eleven directors who voted to approve the non-fault termination, the Court of Chancery stated that there were no allegations of interestedness or independence with respect to Lozano and Watson, and the court rejected lack of independence allegations with respect to Bowers, Disney, Gold, Mitchell, Murphy, O'Donovan, Poitier, Walker and Wilson.

Litvack and Nunis. Sanford M. Litvack and Richard A. Nunis were executive employees of Disney who "reported to" and were "accountable to" Eisner and were paid salaries set by Eisner and Disney's board. *Id.* at 356. Under these circumstances, the court held, there was "at least a reasonable doubt" concerning the ability of Litvack and Nunis "to vote independently of Eisner." *Id.* at 356-57.

Russell. Irwin E. Russell served as Eisner's personal counsel in "a small firm for which the fees derived from Eisner likely represent a large portion of the total amount of fees received by the firm." *Id.* at 360. Russell and Eisner also had "a long history of personal and business ties," including Eisner's use of Russell's law office as the mailing address for Eisner's personal residence, Russell's service as the registered agent for several entities in which Eisner is involved, and Russell's representation of Eisner in connection with the negotiation of Eisner's most recent compensation agreement with Disney. *Id.*

Stern. Robert A.M. Stern, an architect, had been commissioned to design several buildings for Disney and one for Eisner, "for which his firm had collected millions of dollars in fees from Disney and Eisner." *Id.* at 357. The court acknowledged that "the fees that Stern's architectural firm have received are in decline, and that Eisner has gone on record stating that 'Stern is unlikely to get new Disney contracts while on the Board.'" *Id.* at 358. The court nevertheless found a reasonable doubt concerning Stern's independence because "fees have continued to flow from Disney to Stern's firm, and the fees received in the past, from both Disney and Eisner, have been quite substantial." *Id.*

Disney and Gold. Roy E. Disney, like Litvack and Nunis, was a Disney executive who earned a "substantial salary" and received "numerous, valuable options on Disney stock." *Id.* at 356. Unlike Litvack and Nunis, however, Disney did not lack independence from Eisner because "[a]s a top executive" Disney's compensation is "set by the Board, not solely by Eisner," and "Disney, along with his family, owns approximately 8.4 million shares of Disney stock" worth over $2 billion. *Id.* The court stated that "[t]he only reasonable inference that I can draw about Mr. Disney is that he is an economically rational individual whose priority is to protect the value of his Disney shares, not someone who would intentionally risk his own and his family's interests in order to placate Eisner." *Id.*

Stanley P. Gold, the court held, lacked independence from Roy Disney because he was Disney's personal attorney and the president and chief executive officer of a company controlled by Disney's family. Because Disney's ability to exercise independent business judgment was not impaired by Disney's connection with Eisner, the court held, however, "the business judgment of Gold is similarly free from Eisner's alleged dominating influence." *Id.* at 357.

Walker and Wilson. Cardon Walker, a retired Disney executive who had been a senior executive of Disney for 25 years and who had served as Disney's president from 1971 to 1977 and as the chairman of Disney's board and Disney's chief executive officer from 1980 to 1983, was found not to lack independence from Eisner. *Id.* at 358. Gary L. Wilson, a retired Disney executive who had been an executive vice president and Disney's chief financial officer from 1985 through 1989, also was found not to lack independence from Eisner. *Id.*

With respect to Walker, plaintiffs alleged that "after Eisner became chairman of Disney, Walker consulted for Disney and has, in recent years, received substantial sums for his investments in certain Disney films." *Id.* The court stated that plaintiffs do not allege that Walker had any financial dealings with Eisner, and "[a]s for the substantial sums Plaintiffs allege Walker has received and continues to receive from Disney, these stem from contractual rights with the Company that are at least nineteen years old and that predate Eisner's reign with Disney." *Id.*

With respect to Wilson, plaintiffs alleged that Wilson was "beholden to Eisner because Eisner, by virtue of his authority as chairman, rewarded Wilson handsomely when the latter retired from Disney" and because Wilson receives "substantial compensation from Disney over which . . . Eisner had considerable influence." *Id.* The court rejected this allegation on the ground that "[w]hatever rights Wilson had when he left Disney have already been paid to him," and "[n]othing indicates that Wilson expects to receive additional financial benefits from Disney for acceding to Eisner's wishes." *Id.* The court also rejected plaintiffs' reliance upon a 1995 payment by Disney of $121,122 to a design firm owned by Wilson's wife for services performed by the firm. The court described this payment as "immaterial to Wilson, a man who received a bonus and stock options that, by Plaintiffs' own estimations, have resulted in over $70 million in income realized so far." *Id.*

O'Donovan. Father Leo J. O'Donovan, a Jesuit priest forbidden by his faith from collecting any director's fee and the president of Georgetown University, the recipient of over $1 million of donations from Eisner since 1989 and the alma mater of one of Eisner's sons, also was found not to lack independence. The court held that "Eisner's philanthropic largess to Georgetown" was not a disqualifying interest because there was no allegation that O'Donovan received "a direct, personal financial benefit" from any affiliation with Eisner. *Id.* at 359.

Bowers. Reveta F. Bowers, a principal of the elementary school that Eisner's children once attended, also was found not to lack independence. According to plaintiffs, Bowers lacked independence from Eisner because her salary as an elementary school principal was "low" compared to her director's fee and stock options she received from Disney. *Id.* at 359. The court stated that allegations that a director receives director's fees, "without more, do not establish any financial interest." *Id.* at 360. Any other rule, the court added, would "discourage the membership on corporate boards of people of less-than extraordinary means" because "[s]uch 'regular folks' would face allegations of being dominated by other board members, merely because of the relatively substantial compensation provided by the board membership compared to their outside salaries." *Id.* The court described itself as "especially unwilling to facilitate such a result." *Id.*

Mitchell. Senator George J. Mitchell, "a nationally known legal and political figure" who was "special counsel" to a law firm that had been engaged by Disney on various matters and that was paid $122,764 for the firm's services in 1996, and who on an individual basis had been retained by Disney to provide consulting services for which he was paid $50,000 in 1996, also was found not to lack independence. With respect to Mitchell's service as "special counsel" to his law firm, the court stated that "Plaintiffs have not indicated that Mitchell, as 'special counsel' (and not 'partner') shared in the legal fees paid to his firm." *Id.* With respect to Mitchell's service as a consultant on an individual basis, the court stated that plaintiffs had not alleged that the $50,000 Mitchell received in consulting fees was a material sum of money to Mitchell. *Id.*

Poitier. Sidney Poitier, a director who has earned millions of dollars through his relationship with Creative Artists – a talent agency Ovitz founded and had served as chairman of until Ovitz moved to Disney in 1995 – was held not to lack independence from Ovitz. The court acknowledged that Poitier had enjoyed a successful relationship with Ovitz and Creative Artists but concluded that Poitier's ability to render independent business judgment with respect to Ovitz's compensation was not "impermissibly conflicted" because Ovitz no longer was the head of Creative Artists and because Poitier did not continue to receive material benefits from Creative Artists. *Id.* at 360-61.

The court in *Goodwin v. Live Entertainment, Inc.*, 1999 Del. Ch. LEXIS 5, 1999 WL 64265 (Del. Ch. Jan. 22, 1999), *aff'd*, 741 A.2d 16 (unpublished opinion, text available at 1999 Del. LEXIS 238 and 1999 WL 624128) (Del. July 23, 1999), considered the disinterestedness and independence of directors of Live Entertainment, Inc. in the context of a challenge to a merger of Live Entertainment and Bain Capital, Inc. The court held that "a subjective expectancy" on the part of two directors of Live Entertainment, Roger Burlage and Ronald Cushey, that "they would continue as high-ranking managers" after the merger and that they "would be retained on an enhanced economic basis." 1999 Del. Ch. LEXIS 5, at *79, 1999 WL 64265, at *25. The court stated that "I am doubtful" that this subjective "expectancy" would be found to constitute a material interest following a full evidentiary hearing, but held that plaintiff had "produced sufficient evidence to generate a triable issue of fact regarding whether Burlage's and Cushey's expectations constituted a material interest in the merger not shared by the stockholders." 1999 Del. Ch. LEXIS 5, at *79-80, 1999 WL 64265, at *25.

The court, however, refused to find a triable issue of fact with respect to Melvin Pearl, a director of Live Entertainment who had discussed a possible consulting agreement with Bain Capital. The court stated that "more" was required than a possible consulting agreement in order to create a triable issue of fact with respect to whether Pearl had a material self-interest in the merger. "The 'more' that would be relevant," the court explained, "would be a showing that the potential sums Pearl would have received from the consulting arrangement would have, in the context of his annual income and net worth, been of such value to have made it difficult for him to examine the merger on the basis of its merits to Live's stockholders alone." 1999 Del. Ch. LEXIS 5, at *81-82, 1999 WL 64265, at *26. The court stated that Pearl was "a senior partner in a California law firm and has served on the boards of other companies" and plaintiff "has produced no evidence from which I could infer that the mere possibility or even probability of a consulting arrangement with Bain was of material importance to Pearl." *Id.*

The court also rejected allegations of interest on the part of five directors who were affiliated with Pioneer Electronics Corporation, the largest holder of Live Entertainment's common stock. Through its ownership of common stock and all shares of Live Entertainment's Series C preferred stock, Pioneer, while having the right to nominate only five of Live

Entertainment's thirteen directors, had effective voting control over the corporation and thus veto power over any transaction requiring shareholder approval. 1999 Del. Ch. LEXIS 5, at *6, 1999 WL 624128, at *2. The court stated that Pioneer did not stand on both sides of the merger between Bain and Live Entertainment because Pioneer had no ownership interest in Bain. 1999 Del. Ch. LEXIS 5, at *83, 1999 WL 624128, at *27.

The court rejected plaintiff's attempt "to show that Pioneer had some other material self-interest in the merger" based upon discussions between Pioneer and Live Entertainment concerning "making certain contractual arrangements conditions precedent to the merger," which plaintiff suggested "somehow constituted illicit 'side consideration.'" 1999 Del. Ch. LEXIS 5, at *83, 1999 WL 64265, at *27. The court explained that plaintiff had not "presented evidence regarding the value of these possible arrangements from which I could make an inference that Pioneer had a strong desire to consummate those arrangements and that a subjective belief on its part that Bain would agree to do so after the merger might have led it to support a merger at a price that was not desirable to it and the other common stockholders." 1999 Del. Ch. LEXIS 5, at *83-84, 1999 WL 64265, at *27.

The court stated that a shareholder challenging the independence of directors "based solely upon their election by and relationship to a controlling stockholder in a situation like this" has "an obligation to produce record evidence demonstrating that the controlling stockholder's commercial interests were of such a substantial nature as to possibly compromise its natural desire to obtain the best price for its shares." 1999 Del. Ch. LEXIS 5, at *84, 1999 WL 64265, at *27. Here, the court held, "the record is empty of evidence, rather than rhetoric, regarding the monetary or strategic significance of these matters to Pioneer." *Id.* The court concluded that "[t]he record lacks any evidence that Pioneer sought for itself better terms for its common stock than the other stockholders or that its elected representatives (who constituted only five of the thirteen board members) dominated the Board and used that domination to obtain an exorbitant price for its Series C shares at the expense of the common stockholders." 1999 Del. Ch. LEXIS 5, at *85, 1999 WL 64265, at *27.

The court added that there was no evidence concerning the relationship between Pioneer and its designees on Live Entertainment's board with respect to whether these directors were beholden to Pioneer other than the fact that each is or in the past has been employed by Pioneer. No facts were alleged, the court stated, suggesting that these directors received "significant remuneration" from Pioneer. 1999 Del. Ch. LEXIS 5, at *87, 1999 WL 64265, at *28.

In re Western National Corp. Shareholders Litigation, 2000 Del. Ch. LEXIS 82, 2000 WL 710192 (Del. Ch. May 22, 2000), provides another illustrative decision, in this case in the context of a merger between Western National Corporation and its 46 percent shareholder, American General Corporation, both of which were large, diversified insurance and financial service companies. Western National's chairman and chief executive officer was Michael J. Poulos, who had been a senior officer of American General until 1993, when Western National became a public company. Ten months later, American General acquired 40 percent (and a short time later an additional 6 percent) of Western National's shares and entered into a standstill agreement with Western National. The standstill agreement prohibited American General from doing any of the following before January 1, 1999 unless American General first obtained the approval of Western National's board: (1) acquiring more than 20 percent of Western National's shares in any 12 month period, (2) owning a total of more than 79 percent of Western National's shares, (3) engaging in an extraordinary transaction with Western National, or (4) nominating more than two directors to Western National's board. 2000 Del. Ch. LEXIS 82, at *7-8 & n.1, 2000 WL 710192, at *2 & n.1.

Western National soon needed additional capital, but American General's 46 percent interest made it difficult to raise equity from third parties and American General was unwilling to commit additional capital unless it could acquire absolute control of Western National. 2000 Del. Ch. LEXIS 82, at *8-12, 2000 WL 710192, at *3. Western National's board formed a special committee consisting of three outside directors, Donald G. Baker, Robert M. Hermance and Alan Richards, to explore strategic alternatives. 2000 Del. Ch. LEXIS 82, at *13, 2000 WL 710192, at *3. As discussed more detail in Chapter II, Section B 3 k-1, the committee ultimately negotiated a merger transaction with American General.

The court held that American General was not a controlling shareholder – a holding discussed in Chapter II, Section B 3 a – but also held that "a significant stockholder that does not, as a general matter, exercise actual control over the investee's business and affairs or over the investee's board of directors but does, in fact, exercise actual control over the board of directors during the course of a particular transaction, can assume fiduciary duties for purposes of that transaction." 2000 Del. Ch. LEXIS 82, at *70, 2000 WL 710192, at *20.

The court then focused upon each of Western National's eight directors – Donald Baker, Alan R. Buckwater, John A. Graf, Robert Hermance, Sidney Keeble, Michael J. Poulos, Alan Richards and Richard W. Scott – and held for the purpose of a motion for summary judgment by defendants that plaintiffs "raised (if barely so) triable issues of fact with respect to the independence of three of eight directors" (Buckwater, Keeble and Poulos) and "established that two other board members (otherwise totally unconnected to American General) might be burdened by potential conflicts of interest exclusively with respect to the merger transaction in question" due to employment contracts they entered into with American General at the time the merger was negotiated (Graf and Scott). 2000 Del. Ch. LEXIS 82, at *69, 2000 WL 710192, at *20. The court held that there was no showing of any lack of disinterestedness or independence with respect to the three directors on the special committee, Baker, Hermance and Richards.

Poulos. The court held that Western National's merger with American General posed no economic conflict of interest to Western National's chairman and chief executive officer, Michael J. Poulos, who planned to retire upon the completion of the merger and receive a $4.5 million severance payment and an accelerated vesting of options. The court explained that these payments were contractual benefits arising out of a 1994 employment agreement "negotiated *before* American General became a shareholder" of Western National. 2000 Del. Ch. LEXIS 82, at *39-40, 2000 WL 710192, at *12. More important, the court continued, at the time of the merger Poulos owned equity in both Western National and American General but "his interest in Western National significantly outweighed his interest in American General." 2000 Del. Ch. LEXIS 82, at *40, 2000 WL 710192, at *12. These facts, the court stated, "cannot possibly indicate (i.e., under any interpretation) that Poulos's *personal* economic and professional incentives were other than aligned with the public shareholders of Western National." 2000 Del. Ch. LEXIS 82, at *40-41, 2000 WL 710192, at *12. In the court's words:

> Poulos's significant equity interest in the Company aligned him economically with the public shareholders; his willingness to step aside from the Company's helm demonstrates, in my view, the absence of improper motivations such as a desire to maintain the perquisites and prestige attendant to the role of executive chairman. Finally, a $4.5 million cash severance payment coupled with accelerated vesting of certain options to an executive chairman of a large corporation does not strike me as so far beyond the pale that it would give rise to an improper motive to accomplish a merger.

2000 Del. Ch. LEXIS 82, at *41, 2000 WL 710192, at *12.

The court also rejected plaintiffs' reliance upon Poulos's 23 year career at American General prior to joining Western National in 1993 to demonstrate a disabling lack of disinterestedness or independence. The court acknowledged that "[i]t may indeed be true that Poulos enjoys fond recollections of his twenty-three year career at American General (prior to joining Western National) and it is undoubtedly true that he maintained close social and professional ties with his colleagues there." 2000 Del. Ch. LEXIS 82, at *41-42, 2000 WL 710192, at *12. Nevertheless, the court held, "such facts do not warrant the inference that Poulos favored the fortunes of American General over those of a company in which he holds substantial equity and has served as executive chairman for its entire existence as a publicly-held entity." 2000 Del. Ch. LEXIS 82, at *42, 2000 WL 710192, at *12. The court stated that "a liability theory predicated on an executive chairman preferring his friends' and colleagues' professional and economic interests over his own similar interests" has "inherent frailty." 2000 Del. Ch. LEXIS 82, at *42, 2000 WL 710192, at *12.

The court nevertheless pointed to "two facts with respect to Poulos's relationship with American General that give me some pause, particularly at summary judgment stage." 2000 Del. Ch. LEXIS 82, at *43, 2000 WL 710192, at *12.

First, the court described "the circumstances of American General's initial 40 percent acquisition of Western National stock" from Conseco Investment Company in 1994 as "unorthodox": Poulos knew that Conseco was anxious to sell its Western National shares, and Poulos, who at the time had just left American General to become the chief executive officer at Western National, solicited his former colleagues at American General and negotiated the transaction on behalf of both parties without the parties ever meeting, with no investment or legal advisors involved, and without Conseco being informed that American General was the buyer. *Id.* The court identified two potential inferences:

(1) plaintiffs' "sinister, though thinly supported hypothesis that Conseco's sale to American General evidenced a special relationship or some type of impermissible 'understanding' between Poulos and American General," and

(2) defendants' claim that Conseco, "a sophisticated market participant, would not casually leave itself exposed to double-dealing and opportunism from Poulos in a significant, multi-million dollar transaction such as the sale of a 40 percent equity stake in a sizable company" and that Conseco had "complete trust and confidence" in Poulos and was "completely satisfied with the consideration the undisclosed American General paid."

2000 Del. Ch. LEXIS 82, at *44-45, 2000 WL 710192, at *13. The court stated that defendants' claim was a "far more compelling" inference but acknowledged that plaintiffs had raised a factual issue worthy of "*some* credence" for the purpose of a motion for summary judgment. 2000 Del. Ch. LEXIS 82, at *45, 2000 WL 710192, at *13.

Second, the court pointed to a clause in the standstill agreement entered into by American General and Western National in 1994 providing for an end to the restrictions upon further purchases by American General of Western National shares if Poulos ceased to be Western National's chairman. 2000 Del. Ch. LEXIS 82, at *45, 2000 WL 710192, at *14. Again, the court identified "two plausible interpretations" for the provision:

(1) plaintiffs' interpretation, that "American General executives believed Poulos was, so to speak, their man at Western National," and that "Poulos was American General's *de facto* agent at Western National, impermissibly looking after its interest to the exclusion of all other shareholders (including himself)," and

(2) defendants' interpretation, that American General "had tremendous confidence in Poulos's management skills and wanted to reevaluate their investment should Poulos leave the Company."

2000 Del. Ch. LEXIS 82, at *45-47, 2000 WL 710192, at *14. The court stated that "[b]ecause I am considering a summary judgment motion, and the record is not fully developed with respect to this issue, I will give consideration to plaintiffs' more alarmist view." 2000 Del. Ch. LEXIS 82, at *47, 2000 WL 710192, at *14.

The court concluded that "[i]n light of the peculiar circumstances surrounding American General's initial investment in Western National and the not totally implausible inferences plaintiffs ask me to draw with respect to the so-called Poulos Provision, I cannot (at this stage) conclude that Poulos was entirely independent of American General" because "plaintiffs have adduced some evidence, although fairly tame, that Poulos *might* have considered this transaction not entirely as an advocate of Western National and its shareholders." *Id.*

Graf and Scott. John A. Graf, Western National's chief marketing officer, and Richard W. Scott, Western National's general counsel and chief investment officer, each were alleged to lack disinterestedness because they had entered into employment contracts pursuant to which they would serve American General following the merger. 2000 Del. Ch. LEXIS 82, at *48-50, 2000 WL 710192, at *14-15. The court accepted this allegation for the purpose of the summary judgment motion but noted the absence of "any other credible evidence to impugn their independence and impartiality" and "the dearth of evidence sullying these inside directors' independence from American General." 2000 Del. Ch. LEXIS 82, at *49, 2000 WL 710192, at *15. The court stated that "I suppose" that Graf's and Scott's retention of their jobs "technically placed them on both sides of the transaction" but added that "as conflicts of interest go, this one does not seem particularly egregious." 2000 Del. Ch. LEXIS 82, at *51, 2000 WL 710192, at *15.

The court noted that it did not read *In re Tri-Star Pictures, Inc., Litigation*, 634 A.2d 319 (Del. 1993), "to stand for the proposition that a subsidiary inside director who continues to participate in the combined company is automatically interested in the transaction, particularly at the summary judgment stage after plaintiffs have had an opportunity to engage in substantial discovery." 2000 Del. Ch. LEXIS 82, at *49, 2000 WL 710192, at *15. *Tri-Star*, the court in *Western National* stated, "involved a *de jure* parent-subsidiary merger where the parent corporation, Coca-Cola, held a 56 percent interest in Tri-Star (measured by direct holdings and voting agreements) and Coca-Cola executives filled four of Tri-Star's ten director slots." 2000 Del. Ch. LEXIS 82, at *48-49, 2000 WL 710192, at *14. According to the court in *Western National*, "[i]n the context of an appeal from a Rule 12(b)(6) dismissal," the court in *Tri-Star* stated only that "two Tri-Star executive directors, with ties to Coca-Cola affiliates, who would participate in the management of the combined entity (i.e., Coca-Cola's augmented entertainment unit) *appeared* interested." 2000 Del. Ch. LEXIS 82, at *49, 2000 WL 710192, at *14.

Buckwater. The court accepted plaintiffs' allegation that Alan R. Buckwater lacked independence from American General for the purpose of defendants' motion for summary judgment because Buckwater was the president of one of American General's lenders, Chase Texas Bank. The court noted defendants' contention that "the burden is on plaintiffs to show that the relationship between the director's employer and the merger partner affected the director's decision making process" and defendants' contention that "simply because a director is an employee of a company that has a commercial relationship with the other party in a merger does not mean that the director lacks independence." 2000 Del. Ch. LEXIS 82, at *62-63, 2000 WL 710192, at *18. The court agreed that "plaintiffs have not proffered any additional evidence that the banking relationship between Chase Texas and American General sterilized Buckwater's discretion or subverted his good faith evaluation of the merger's underlying corporate merits," and stated that the grounds for Buckwater's "lack of independence – an employment relationship with one of the parent company's lenders" – like "[t]he grounds for Graf's and Scott's conflict of interest – continued employment in the combined entity" – are "the sort of fiduciary problems that typically require additional evidence before the court will consider such directors interested in the transaction or beholden to the parent company." 2000 Del. Ch. LEXIS 82, at *63, 65-66, 2000 WL 710192, at *18, 19.

The court thus concluded that plaintiffs' "failure to impeach these three directors' disinterest and independence, coupled with their failure to establish" (as discussed below) that Baker, Hermance and Richards "labored under conflicts of interest or were in fact beholden to American General, would comfortably result in finding a disinterested and independent majority on the Western National board of directors." 2000 Del. Ch. LEXIS 82, at *67, 2000 WL 710192, at *19. The court nevertheless determined to "give some weight to the evidence casting doubt on Graf's and Scott's disinterest – their continued employment in the combined entity – and Buckwater's lack of independence – his employment relationship with Chase Texas – and not consider them wholly disinterested and independent, solely for purposes of this summary judgment motion." 2000 Del. Ch. LEXIS 82, at *67-68, 2000 WL 710192, at *19.

Keeble. The court held that there was "sufficient doubt" for the purpose of a motion for summary judgment concerning the independence of Sidney Keeble, a retired senior vice president of an American General subsidiary who had "large" and "troublesome" holdings in American General stock constituting approximately 40 percent of his total wealth at the time of the merger. 2000 Del. Ch. LEXIS 82, at *63-64, 66 n.60, 2000 WL 710192, at *18, 19 n.60. The court reached this conclusion "for purposes of this motion" despite (1) Keeble's submission of an affidavit swearing to a net worth of approximately $20 million outside of his holdings of American General stock and stating that "any speculative effect the merger might have had on the value of his American General stock played no role in his decision," and (2) plaintiffs' failure to make any "effort to establish that Keeble was improperly motivated as a result of his American General holdings." 2000 Del. Ch. LEXIS 82, at *63-65, 68, 2000 WL 710192, at *18, 19.

Baker and Buckwater. The court rejected plaintiffs' allegation that Donald Baker and Buckwater lacked independence because they were appointed to Western National's board by American General. The court rejected this allegation as unsupported by the record and wrong as a matter of law.

With respect to the record, the court stated that the relevant testimony "[a]t most" indicated that Poulos, Western National's chairman, conferred with Harold Hook, American General's chairman, before Western National's board nominated Baker and Buckwater as directors and that Baker and Buckwater "were 'known and trusted' by the Company's executive chairman and by the executive chairman of a large shareholder." 2000 Del. Ch. LEXIS 82, at *54-56, 2000 WL 710192, at *16. This fact, the court stated, "does not support a conclusion that these two directors were beholden to Hook and Poulos or were incapable of making independent judgments and exercising the discretion of a fiduciary with respect to the merger." 2000 Del. Ch. LEXIS 82, at *56, 2000 WL 710192, at *16.

With respect to the law, the court stated that "even if American General nominated some of the outside directors or if Poulos and Hook jointly nominated them, such nomination, without more, does not mandate a finding that these directors were beholden to American General, Poulos, or Hook, and incapable of exercising their independent business judgment." 2000 Del. Ch. LEXIS 82, at *52, 2000 WL 710192, at *15. The court explained that "[d]irectors must be nominated and elected to the board in one fashion or another," and "[t]he fact that a company's executive chairman or a large shareholder played some role in the nomination process should not, without additional evidence, automatically foreclose a director's potential independence." 2000 Del. Ch. LEXIS 82, at *52-53, 2000 WL 710192, at *15. The court acknowledged that "independent nominating committees may indeed have a salutary effect on board efficacy and independence, and are surely a 'best practice' which the corporate governance community endorses," but "they are not a *sine qua non* for director independence under Delaware law." 2000 Del. Ch. LEXIS 82, at *53, 2000 WL 710192, at *15.

Baker, Hermance and Richards. The court rejected challenges to the independence of Baker, Robert Hermance and Alan Richards, the three members of Western National's special committee, based upon consulting work these directors had performed for American General: Baker as a partner at Arthur Andersen who "supervised a single project for an American General subsidiary that lasted a year or two during the late 1970s and early 80s" (over 15 years before the merger) and who retired from Arthur Andersen in 1990 (seven years before the merger); Hermance, as a partner at Ernst & Young who supervised Ernst & Young's audit of American General until 1985 (12 years before the merger) and who retired from Ernst & Young in 1994 (three years before the merger); and Richards, who performed "a single, three-week consulting job for American General in the spring of 1987" (ten years before the merger). 2000 Del. Ch. LEXIS 82, at *58-61, 2000 WL 710192, at *17. The court stated that "a director's past employment with the company on whose board he sits does not alone establish that director's lack of independence" and that "for a court to conclude that a director lacks independence based on a past consulting relationship is an even more dubious proposition." 2000 Del. Ch. LEXIS 82, at *58, 2000 WL 710182, at *17.

The court also rejected a challenge to Richards' independence based upon "periodic consulting work" Richards performed for Western National "from October 1993 until June 1996 and a single, two-day assignment thereafter." 2000 Del. Ch. LEXIS 82, at *59-60, 2000 WL 710192, at *17. The court stated that this allegation "lacks logical support" and that Richards' consulting relationship with Western National "should have no bearing" on Richards' views of the merger. 2000 Del. Ch. LEXIS 82, at *60, 2000 WL 710192, at *17. Indeed, the court concluded, "if Richards harbored any self-interested motivation as a result of past consulting work for Western National (of which there is no indication), he would, if anything, likely resist American General's overtures to merge, as a combination with the much larger entity would terminate his relationship with the Company" because "[o]nce no longer in the corporate inner sanctum, the prospects for influencing future consulting arrangements are obviously diminished." *Id.*

The court then stated that the five potentially conflicted directors (Buckwater, Graf, Keeble, Poulos and Scott) "were not particularly involved in the merger process": there was "no evidence" that Buckwater, Graf or Keeble "played *any* role whatsoever (besides considering and approving the Special Committee's recommendation)" in the negotiation of the merger and that Poulos's and Scott's involvement in the merger process "was *de minimis*." 2000 Del. Ch. LEXIS 82, at *69-70, 2000 WL 710192, at *20. Instead, "the Special Committee – whose disinterest and independence is above reproach – and its advisors performed the bulk of the heavy lifting during the course of the merger negotiations." 2000 Del. Ch. LEXIS 82, at *70, 2000 WL 710192, at *20. The court then held that the business judgment rule governed the decision made by the special committee despite the court's conclusion for the purpose of the motion for summary judgment before the court that a majority of the board lacked disinterestedness and independence. *See* Chapter II, Section B 3 k-1.

The Delaware Court of Chancery's decision in *Odyssey Partners, L.P. v. Fleming Cos.*, 735 A.2d 386 (Del. Ch. 1999), contains another extensive discussion of director disinterestedness and independence, in the context of another corporation having a shareholder that owned approximately 46 percent of the corporation's stock. The *Fleming* decision is discussed in Chapter II, Section B 3 a.

Add the following at the end of footnote 258 on page 53:

See also Crescent/Mach I Partners, L.P. v. Turner, 2000 Del. Ch. LEXIS 145, at *40, 2000 WL 1481002, at *11 (Del. Ch. Sept. 29, 2000) ("[t]he allegations of Hunt's material interest in the Merger are wholly conclusory and even under the most strained of inferences would not survive a motion to dismiss").

Section D 2 d

Add "and chief executive officer" between "the corporation's president" and ", and had been placed" and delete "both of" in the fifth sentence (two lines following footnote 272) of the paragraph beginning on page 56 and concluding on page 57.

Add the following at the end of the paragraph beginning on page 56 and concluding on page 57 (immediately after footnote 274):

In a later decision in the case, however, the court held that an amended complaint sufficiently pleaded that this individual, Chang Kim, a director and the president and chief executive officer of the corporation, lacked independence from the controlling shareholder with which the corporation had entered into the challenged transaction. The court again noted the inadequacy by itself of an allegation that Kim was a designee of the controlling shareholder on the corporation's board, but stated that plaintiffs' amended complaint, unlike plaintiffs' prior complaint, alleged that Kim provided the corporation "day to day full-time management" and had "bought a house in suburban Philadelphia, near ICI's offices, and moved his principal residence there so he could live near his place of work," and that the amount of Kim's compensation for his services for the corporation was not public information but "has been and is his principal source of financial support." *Benerofe v. Cha*, 1998 Del. Ch. LEXIS 28, at *5-6, 10, 1998 WL 83081, at *2, 3 (Del. Ch. Feb. 20, 1998). The court stated that the court in *Rales v. Blasband*, 634 A.2d 927 (Del. 1993), "concluded that majority shareholders in the positions of Chairman of the Board and Chairman of the Executive Committee were 'in a position to exert considerable influence over' a fellow director who, like Kim, was also the President and CEO, even through the President's 'continued employment and substantial remuneration may not hinge solely on his relationship with' the majority shareholders." 1998 Del. Ch. LEXIS 28, at *11, 1998 WL 83081, at *4 (quoting 634 A.2d at 937). The court stated that it was "unable to conclude" that these allegations "should be viewed as presenting a situation any different than presented by *Rales*." 1998 Del. Ch. LEXIS 28, at *11-12, 1998 WL 83081, at *4.

Add the following at the end of the paragraph beginning on page 58 and concluding on page 61 (immediately after footnote 297):

- *Sonet v. Plum Creek Timber Co.*, 1999 Del. Ch. LEXIS 49, at *34-35, 1999 WL 160174, at *8 (Del. Ch. Mar. 18, 1999) (finding lack of independence with respect to a three member committee appointed by the general partner of a limited partnership to negotiate on behalf of unitholders where one member of the committee owned a brokerage firm that did business with the general partner and wished to continue that business relationship and a second member of the committee received compensation for serving as the chairman of the board of the general partner "plus $24,000 annually for the maintenance of a car supplied for his personal benefit"; the court rejected a claim that the third member of the committee was conflicted by the "possibility" that the general partner "might make a contribution" to a university of which the committee member was president);
- *Mizel v. Connelly*, 1999 Del. Ch. LEXIS 157, at *1-4, 6-14, 1999 WL 550369, at *1-2, 3-4 (Del. Ch. July 22, 1999) (finding lack of disinterestedness or independence for the purpose of a motion to dismiss in an action challenging a transaction entered into

by President Casinos, Inc. and a corporation owned by John E. Connelly, the chairman, chief executive officer and 32.7 percent shareholder of President Casinos, where the corporation's five member board included (1) Connelly, (2) John S. Aylsworth, the president and chief operating officer of President Casinos, who received more than $620,000 in annual compensation from the corporation, and (3) Terrence L. Wirginis, the vice president and vice chairman of the board of President Casinos, who received more than $239,000 in annual compensation from the corporation, and who also was Connelly's grandson; the court reasoned that (1) Connelly "as their boss . . . exerts 'considerable influence' over Aylsworth and Wirginis" because "Aylsworth and Wirginis each derive their principal income from their employment at President Casinos," (2) Connelly's ownership of 32.7 percent of President Casino's stock and the fact that he was the corporation's largest shareholder "undoubtedly . . . may not be sufficient to constitute control for certain corporation law purposes" but "great weight" should be attached "to be practical power wielded by a stockholder controlling such a block and to the impression of such power likely to be harbored by the stockholder's fellow directors," and (3) the fact that Wirginis is Connelly's grandson is "of great consequence" because "[t]he existence of a very close family relationship between directors should, without more, generally go a long (if not the whole) way toward creating a reasonable doubt" concerning independence);

- *Chaffin v. GNI Group, Inc.*, 1999 Del. Ch. LEXIS 182, at *16-18, 1999 WL 721569, at *5 (Del. Ch. Sept. 3, 1999) (finding lack of disinterestedness or independence where four directors voted in favor of a merger and one director voted against the merger but "only two disinterested directors approved the Merger, which was one vote short of the required disinterested majority"; one director who voted in favor of the merger, Carl V. Rush, lacked disinterestedness due to financial benefits he would receive from the merger, and another director who voted in favor of the merger, Titus H. Harris, Jr., lacked independence because his son, Titus H. Harris, III, was a senior officer of the corporation who would receive financial benefits as a result of the merger; the court stated that "[i]nherent in the parental relationship is the parent's natural desire to help his or her child succeed" and "most parents would find it highly difficult, if not impossible, to maintain a completely neutral, disinterested position on an issue, where his or her child would benefit substantially if the parent decides the issue a certain way");

- *Harbor Finance Partners v. Huizenga*, 751 A.2d 879, 882, 886-89 (Del. Ch. 1999) (finding lack of disinterestedness or independence for the purpose of a motion to dismiss in a case challenging an acquisition by Republic Industries, Inc. of AutoNation, Incorporated allegedly entered into for the benefit of Republic directors who owned a substantial block of AutoNation shares and on terms that allegedly were unfair to Republic, where three of Republic's seven directors, Wayne Huizenga, George D. Johnson, Jr. and John J. Melk, were conceded to have held enough AutoNation shares before the merger to render them interested in the transaction – Huizenga received Republic shares worth $235 million in exchange for over 29,375,000 AutoNation shares, Johnson received Republic shares worth over $20 million in exchange for 2.5 million AutoNation shares, and Melk received Republic shares worth over $6.6 million in exchange for 825,000 AutoNation shares – and a fourth director, Harris W.

Hudson, received Republic shares worth $825,000 in exchange for 100,000 AutoNation shares in the merger; the court stated that "at this pleading stage, it would be difficult for me to infer other than that Hudson desired to receive the highest possible price for his AutoNation shares" but acknowledged that "economic evidence might ultimately persuade me that it would have been irrational for Hudson to seek unfair economic advantage in the Merger for Auto-Nation stockholders at the expense of Republic because any such advantage would cause more than offsetting harm to him" due to his ownership of 10.1 percent of Republic's shares; the court also relied upon a "long-standing pattern of mutually advantageous business relations" between Hudson and Huizenga, Republic's chairman and chief executive officer, and the fact that Hudson and Huizenga were brothers-in-law);

- *In re Cooper Cos. Shareholders Derivative Litigation*, 2000 Del. Ch. LEXIS 158, at *17-21, 2000 WL 1664167, at *6-7 (Del. Ch. Oct. 31, 2000) (finding lack of disinterestedness or independence for the purpose of a motion to dismiss where a ten member board included (1) three directors, Gary, Steven and Brad Singer, who lacked disinterestedness because they were alleged to have profited from a wrongful scheme, (2) one director, Joseph C. Feghali, who lacked independence because he was Steven Singer's father-in-law, a family relationship "sufficient to create a reason to doubt" Feghali's ability to consider a demand, and (3) two directors, Robert S. Weiss, the corporation's chief financial officer and treasurer, and Robert S. Holcombe, the corporation's vice president and general counsel. With respect to Weiss and Holcombe, the court held that "it is reasonable to infer from the fact that Gary Singer was Messrs. Weiss's and Holcombe's corporate superior, that he (Gary) was in a position to exercise 'considerable influence' over them," and that "[t]hat inference, coupled with the allegation that Messrs. Weiss and Holcombe were among the directors who (along with the Singers) absented themselves" from – and thus ensured the lack of a quorum and therefore no corporate action at – an emergency board meeting called by two independent directors to consider how the corporation should respond to guilty pleas by two individuals who identified Gary Singer as a participant in criminal conduct, was sufficient to create a doubt concerning the disinterestedness or independence of Weiss and Holcombe);

- *Professional Management Associates, Inc. v. Coss*, 574 N.W.2d 107, 110-11 (Minn. Ct. App. 1998), *review denied*, 1998 Minn. LEXIS 196 (Minn. Apr. 14, 1998) (finding lack of disinterestedness or independence under Delaware law in an action challenging a compensation agreement entered into by a corporation and its chief executive officer and board chairman, Lawrence M. Coss, where the corporation's board consisted of five directors, one of whom was Coss and two of whom, Richard G. Evans and Robert D. Potts, were corporate officers who lacked independence from Coss because "[t]he bonus component of the officers' compensation is determined by the compensation committee on the basis of Coss's recommendation" and "the record demonstrates that even though Evans's and Pott's employment and compensation do not hinge solely on their relationship with Coss, Coss as chief executive officer and chairman of the board is in a position to exert considerable influence over Evans and Potts"); and

- *Bansbach v. Zinn*, 258 A.D.2d 710, 712-13, 685 N.Y.S.2d 332, 334 (N.Y. App. Div. 3d Dep't 1999) (finding lack of disinterestedness or independence

> where plaintiffs alleged that Michael Zinn, the president and chairman of the board of Besicorp Group Inc., harmed the corporation by violating federal campaign finance laws and that the following business relationships existed between Zinn and the three other members of Besicorp's board, George A. Habib, Harold Harris and Richard E. Rosen: "[P]laintiff alleges that [Zinn] and a third party had once formed a corporation with Harris and that such corporation, in turn, did business with Besicorp. When such corporation failed to meet its obligations with Besicorp, plaintiff alleges, Besicorp 'wrote off' a note payable to it in the amount of $127,500 and [Zinn] reimbursed Harris for a $14,000 payment made to finance the failed project. As to Habib and Rosen, plaintiff alleges that each had sought to do business with Besicorp and that Habib had submitted a written marketing and business consulting services proposal to Besicorp").

One court has concluded that an interest is not immaterial simply because the interest arises "after negotiations on terms are concluded but before the transactions close and receive board approval." *HMG/Courtland Props., Inc. v. Gray*, 749 A.2d 94, 113 n.23 (Del. Ch. 1999). The court stated that "[s]uch an exception would invite abuse" and "makes no public policy sense." *Id.*

Section D 2 e

Delete the citation to the Parnes case in footnote 301 on page 62.

Add the following at the end of footnote 301 on page 62:

See also Strougo v. Bassini, 1 F. Supp. 2d 268, 273 (S.D.N.Y. 1998); *Solomon v. Armstrong*, 747 A.2d 1098, 1126 (Del. Ch.

1999) ("[i]n most circumstances Delaware law routinely rejects the notion that a director's interest in maintaining his office, by itself, is a debilitating factor"), *aff'd*, 746 A.2d 277 (unpublished opinion, full text available at 2000 Del. LEXIS 30 and 2000 WL 140072) (Del. Jan. 26, 2000); *In re Walt Disney Co. Derivative Litig.*, 731 A.2d 342, 355 n.18, 360 (Del. Ch. 1998), *aff'd with leave to replead on other grounds sub nom. Brehm v. Eisner*, 746 A.2d 244 (Del. 2000); *Ciullo v. Orange & Rockland Utils., Inc.*, No. 601136/98, slip op. at 13 (N.Y. Sup. Ct. N.Y. Co. Jan. 8, 1999), *aff'd*, 271 A.D.2d 369, 706 N.Y.S.2d 428 (N.Y. App. Div. 1st Dep't), *leave to appeal denied*, 95 N.Y.2d 760, 737 N.E.2d 952, 714 N.Y.S.2d 710 (N.Y. 2000).

Add the following at the end of the second sentence (immediately after footnote 301) of the paragraph beginning on page 61 and concluding on page 62:

One court has held that the fact that a director also is a former employee who receives pension benefits does not create a disqualifying interest. *See Parnes v. Bally Entm't Corp.*, 1997 Del. Ch. LEXIS 70, at *6, 1997 WL 257435, at *2 (Del. Ch. May 12, 1997), *rev'd on other grounds and declining to reach this issue*, 722 A.2d 1243, 1246 n.12 (Del. 1999).

Add the following at the end of the paragraph beginning on page 61 and concluding on page 62 (immediately after footnote 302):

The same result has been reached in *Strougo v. Bassini*, 1 F. Supp. 2d 268, 273-74 (S.D.N.Y. 1998) and *Strougo v. BEA Associates*, 2000 U.S. Dist. LEXIS 346, 2000 WL 45714 (S.D.N.Y. Jan. 19, 2000); *cf. Krantz v. Fid. Mgmt. & Research Co.*, 98 F. Supp. 2d 150, 155-57 (S.D.N.Y. 2000) (declining to follow *Strougo v. Scudder, Stevens & Clark, Inc.*, 964 F. Supp. 783 (S.D.N.Y. 1997), and stating that "[e]ven the *Strougo* line of cases," which takes "a more jaundiced view of lucrative multiple directorships," "declines to rely solely on multiple board membership, but emphasizes the allegations of business decisions which so substantially prejudiced the shareholders to the benefit of the investment adviser that the court could reasonably draw an inference of control, rather than of poor business judgment or mere oversight"); *Marquit v. Dobson*, 1999 U.S. Dist. LEXIS 19964, at *6-7, 2000 WL 4155, at *2 (S.D.N.Y. Dec. 29, 1999) (distinguishing *Strougo v. Scudder* on the ground that under Maryland law "a shareholder demand would not be futile if the fund had at least two disinterested directors" and in the case of the three funds before the court, unlike the case of the fund before the court in *Strougo*, two of the three funds had more than two directors having no association with any other fund managed by the funds' advisor, and the third fund had "no director who does not serve on the board of at least one other fund" managed by the funds' advisor but "more than two of these serve only on one other board and there is no allegation that their compensation is so substantial that it would have an impact on their independence"; the court added its view that "[i]t is doubtful that the mere fact that a director serves on the board of two funds would be sufficient to compel the conclusion that he was not disinterested"), *aff'd on other grounds*, 229 F.3d 1135 (unpublished opinion, text available at 2000 U.S. App. LEXIS 25695 and 2000 WL 1529918) (2d Cir. Oct. 13, 2000).

Each of these cases (other than *Krantz*) construes Maryland law in the context of investment companies. A Maryland statute effective October 1, 1998 that governs cases filed on or after January 30, 1998 seeks to overrule the *Strougo* line of cases by providing that "[a] director of a corporation who with respect to the corporation is not an interested person, as defined by the Investment Company Act of 1940, shall be deemed to be independent and disinterested when making any determination or taking any action as a director." Md. Gen. Corp. Law § 2-405.3. *Strougo v. BEA Associates*, however, concluded that "the Maryland statute does not require a decision contrary to the one reached in *Bassini*." 2000 U.S. Dist. LEXIS 346, at *16, 2000 WL 45714, at *6.

The court in *BEA Associates* explained that the Investment Company Act defines an "interested person" as "any affiliated person," defines an "affiliated person" as "any person directly or indirectly . . . controlled by . . . such other person," and defines "control" as "the power to exercise a controlling influence over the management or policies of a company." 2000 U.S. Dist. LEXIS 346, at *14-15, 2000 WL 45714, at *5 (quoting 15 U.S.C. §§ 80a-2(a)(19)(A)(i), (a)(3)(C), (a)(9)). The court stated that the question of control was decided in *Strougo v. Bassini*, where the court had held that "well compensated service on multiple boards of funds managed by a single fund adviser can, in some circumstances, be indistinguishable in all relevant respects from employment by the fund manager, which admittedly renders a director interested." 2000 U.S. Dist. LEXIS 346, at *15, 2000 WL 45714, at *5 (quoting 1 F. Supp. 2d at 273). The court acknowledged that "the ICA definition of 'control' presumes that a natural person is not a control person" but stated that "[t]he next sentence of the definition . . . states that 'any such presumption may be rebutted by evidence'" and that on "a motion to dismiss on the pleadings" – the context in which the court was ruling – "the task is not to weigh the evidence." 2000 U.S. Dist. LEXIS 346, at *15-16, 2000 WL 45714, at *6. The court added that the ICA also defines an "affiliated person" as any employee (15 U.S.C. § 80a-2(a)(3)(D)) and that non-employee directors cannot be distinguished from employees for the purpose of determining whether they are affiliated persons. 2000 U.S. Dist. LEXIS 346, at *16, 2000 WL 45714, at *6.

The court in *In re Encore Computer Corp. Shareholders Litigation*, 2000 Del. Ch. LEXIS 93, 2000 WL 823373 (Del. Ch. June 16, 2000), held that two directors who received $566,525 and $398,750, respectively, under retention agreements entered into by the corporation with 49 key corporate employees upon the recommendation of an independent consultant in order to ensure their continued service through the closing of a transaction did not have a disabling financial interest in the transaction. The court stated that the retention agreements did not contractually obligate the directors to vote as directors in any particular way and were "independently recommended, shared by others, and made for legitimate business reasons." 2000 Del. Ch. LEXIS 93, at *18-19, 2000 WL 823373, at *6. The court reached the same conclusion with respect to a $50,000 incentive bonus paid to one of these directors four months after the transaction was approved. "[A]ny connection between these events," the court stated, "is far too remote to support the inference" that the incentive bonus disabled the director from impartially determining whether the transaction served the best interests of the corporation. 2000 Del. Ch. LEXIS 93, at *19, 2000 WL 823373, at *6.

Add the following at the end of the paragraph beginning on page 62 and concluding on page 63 (immediately after footnote 304):

Interestedness also is not established by terms in a merger agreement providing for the continuation of pre-existing indemnification and insurance obligations and protecting directors from personal liability to the full extent permitted by law. *In re Talley Indus., Inc. S'holders Litig.*, 1998 Del. Ch. LEXIS 53, at *12 & n.1, 38, 1998 WL 191939, at *4 & n.1, 12 (Del. Ch. Apr. 13, 1998). Provisions of this type "are typical of those commonly found" in merger agreements. 1998 Del. Ch. LEXIS 53 at *12 n.1, 1998 WL 191939, at *4 n.1. Nor is interestedness established by the fact that several directors would retain seats on the board of a merged entity. *Krim v. ProNet, Inc.*, 744 A.2d 523, 525, 528 & n.16 (Del. Ch. 1999).

Interestedness also is not shown by allegations that directors chose one bidder over another because the first bidder had agreed to honor stock options and compensation packages previously granted by the directors to themselves and the second bidder threatened litigation over these payments. *Golden Cycle, LLC v. Allan*, 1998 Del. Ch. LEXIS 237, at *36-37, 1998 WL 892631, at *12 (Del. Ch. Dec. 10, 1998). Neither is interestedness shown by allegations that all directors "are, functionally, officers" and a favored bidder "has a policy of retaining key management" but there is "no showing of an offer of employment, written or otherwise, or even discussions regarding post-transaction employment" of management directors. 1998 Del. Ch. LEXIS 237, at *37-38, 1998 WL 892631, at *12. The same conclusion has been reached with respect to allegations of "personal affront" on the part of directors "at having been the target of an unsolicited tender offer and a consent solicitation to remove them from office." 1998 Del. Ch. LEXIS 237, at *38, 1998 WL 892631, at *13. The court in that case described these allegations of interestedness as "unsupported" and "generalized" and stated that "I have been presented with no evidence that the Board harbors any untoward hostility" toward a bidder whose offer had been rejected or that the board discriminated against that bidder "as a result of this alleged 'animus' toward it." 1999 Del. Ch. LEXIS 237, at *38-39, 1998 WL 892631, at *13.

A similar result was reached in *Wittman v. Crooke*, 707 A.2d 422 (Md. Ct. Spec. App. 1998), a case holding that under Maryland law the directors of Baltimore Gas and Electric Company were not interested in a merger transaction with Potomac Electric Power Company simply because "at the time of the board meeting to vote upon the transaction, each director ha[d] a possibility of receiving a substantial benefit from supporting the transaction": "the possibility of 'entrenching' himself or herself on the board of the new corporation." *Id.* at 424. The court stated that "[t]he fact that many of the appellees were likely to become directors of the new corporation did not justify judicial intervention" and that this circumstance did not overcome the presumption of the business judgment rule. *Id.* at 425.

Interestedness also is not established by allegations that a merger agreement has been entered into by a board allegedly motivated by shareholder dissatisfaction resulting from poor performance and the possibility of a proxy contest at the corporation's next annual meeting and the directors' desire to avoid having to account for their mismanagement. *In re Lukens*

Inc. S'holders Litig., 757 A.2d 720, 729 (Del. Ch. 1999). The court in this case stated that "there is no logical force to the suggestion that otherwise independent, disinterested directors of a corporation would act disloyally or in bad faith and agree to a sale of their company 'on the cheap' merely because they perceived some dissatisfaction with their performance among the stockholders or because of the possibility that a third of their members might face opposition for reelection at the next annual stockholders meeting." *Id.*

Section D 2 f

Add the following at the end of the paragraph beginning on page 64 and concluding on page 66 (immediately after footnote 322):

- *Goodwin v. Live Entertainment, Inc.*, 1999 Del. Ch. LEXIS 5, at *71-72, 1999 WL 64265, at * 23 (Del. Ch. Jan. 22, 1999), *aff'd,* 741 A.2d 16 (unpublished opinion, text available at 1999 Del. LEXIS 238 and 1999 WL 624128) (Del. July 23, 1999) (describing the fact that Pioneer Electronics Corporation, a large shareholder, "accepted the same per share consideration for its common stock as the other stockholders and the fact that it – rather than the common stockholders – took the hit when Bain reduced its offer" as "strong evidence of the reasonableness of the Board's decision" and stating that plaintiff "failed to produce record evidence suggesting that Pioneer received (or was promised) side consideration that dampened its natural desire to obtain good value for its common shares" and that this failure was "fatal" to plaintiff's claim);
- *Krim v. ProNet, Inc.*, 744 A.2d 523, 528 & n.16 (Del. Ch. 1999) (in a case challenging a stock for stock merger entered into by the directors of ProNet,

Inc. with Metrocall Inc. that plaintiff alleged provided too low an exchange rate for ProNet shares, the court rejected a claim that the vesting of stock options held by certain ProNet directors upon the completion of a merger created a conflict of interest because "a high exchange ratio for ProNet shares benefits the option-holding directors as much as, if not more than, the regular stockholders");

- *In re IXC Communications, Inc. Shareholders Litigation*, 1999 Del. Ch. LEXIS 210, at *18-19, 1999 WL 1009174, at *6-7 (Del. Ch. Oct. 27, 1999) (rejecting claim that "a board of directors, consisting, in part, of three of the largest individual shareholders in the corporation and the largest single institutional investor . . . would completely ignore the best economic interests of the shareholders" and thus "ignore their own economic self-interests"; the court stated that "[p]laintiff has not demonstrated how the rational economic self-interest of these large shareholders differs from all IXC shareholders");
- *In re Gaylord Container Corp. Shareholders Litigation*, 753 A.2d 462, 484 (Del. Ch. 2000) ("[i]n the absence of countervailing evidence . . . stockholder-directors 'are presumed to act in their own best economic interest when they vote . . . .'") (quoting *Unitrin, Inc. v. Am. Gen. Corp.*, 651 A.2d 1361, 1380-81 (Del. 1995));
- *McMillan v. Intercargo Corp.*, 768 A.2d 492, 504 (Del. Ch. Apr. 20, 2000) ("[t]he normal presumption is that the owner of a substantial block who decides to sell is interested in obtaining the highest price");
- *In re Western National Corp. Shareholders Litigation*, 2000 Del. Ch. LEXIS 82, at *41, 2000 WL 710192, at *12 (Del. Ch. May 22, 2000) ("Poulos's

significant equity interest in the Company aligned him economically with the public shareholders");

- *In re Encore Computer Corp. Shareholders Litigation*, 2000 Del. Ch. LEXIS 93, at *19, 2000 WL 823373, at *6 (Del. Ch. June 16, 2000) ("Mr. Fisher owned 4 million shares of Encore, and had a significant self-interest in maximizing the value of that investment. If any inference is to be drawn, it is that Fisher's and the shareholders' financial interest were aligned"); and
- *Camden v. Kaufman*, 613 N.W.2d 335, 341 n.2 (Mich. Ct. App. 2000) ("[p]laintiff has failed to demonstrate that a director position in AJK would warrant accepting a lesser cash out value for their own stock in order to accept a position with AJK. While plaintiff has raised insinuations about the benefit to defendant directors, plaintiff has failed to present evidence that accepting a lesser cash out value for their own stock shares served a benefit to defendant directors").

Section D 2 g

Add the following at the end of the paragraph beginning on page 67 and concluding on page 68 (between footnotes 331 and 332):

To the contrary, "[o]n several occasions . . . courts have held that directors did not lack independence simply because they were required to balance the interests of different stockholder classes whose interests were at odds as to a particular transaction." *Gotham Partners, L.P. v. Hallwood Realty Partners, L.P.*, 2000 Del. Ch. LEXIS 146, at *72, 2000 WL 1476663, at *21 (Del. Ch. Sept. 27, 2000).

Add the following at the end of footnote 343 on page 69:

See also Jackson Nat'l Life Ins. Co. v. Kennedy, 741 A.2d 377, 391 (Del. Ch. 1999) (describing *In re FLS Holdings, Inc. S'holder Litig.*, 19 Del. J. Corp. L. 270 (Del. Ch. Apr. 2, 1993), *aff'd sub nom. Sullivan Money Mgmt., Inc. v. FLS Holdings, Inc.*, 628 A.2d 84 (unpublished opinion, text available at 1993 Del. LEXIS 251 and 1993 WL 245341) (Del. June 18, 1993), as a decision rejecting a proposed settlement after finding that "the absence of an independent agent negotiating on behalf of the preferred stockholders and the presence of only the 'relatively weak' procedural protection of an investment banker's *ex post* opinion that the allocation was fair . . . created a substantial issue that was fairly litigable"); *In re Gen. Motors Class H S'holders Litig.*, 734 A.2d 611, 619 n.6 (Del. Ch. 1999) (describing *FLS* as a case holding that "a board which: (i) negotiated the allocation of merger consideration between common and preferred stockholders; (ii) was 'exclusively' comprised of directors who owned 'large amounts of common stock' *or* were affiliates of the company's controlling common stockholder, and (iii) which utilized no other fairness mechanisms such as a vote of the preferred or a special committee bore the burden to show that the merger was fair to the preferred").

Add the following at the end of the paragraph beginning and concluding on page 69 (immediately after footnote 343):

The court in *In re General Motors Class H Shareholders Litigation*, 734 A.2d 611 (Del. Ch. 1999), likewise held that the fact that two shareholder groups have divergent interests does not permit a plaintiff to state a duty of loyalty claim "merely by alleging that the Board treated one group unfairly – even if it was for reasons unrelated to director self-interest." *Id.* at 618. "Rather, the plaintiffs must plead facts from which one could infer disloyalty or bad faith . . . in the sense that the directors acted for reasons inimical to their fiduciary responsibilities. An allegation that properly motivated directors, for no improper personal reason, advantaged one class of stockholders over the other in apportioning transactional consideration does not state a claim for breach of the duty of loyalty." *Id.*

As stated by the court in *Solomon v. Armstrong*, 747 A.2d 1098 (Del. Ch. Mar. 25, 1999), *aff'd*, 746 A.2d 277 (unpublished opinion, full text available at 2000 Del. LEXIS 30 and 2000 WL 140072) (Del. Jan. 26, 2000), "[d]irectors must often resolve conflicts among classes of stock, and the fact that a majority of the directors own more of one class than another does not necessarily implicate the directors' good faith or loyalty." *Id.* at 1118; *see also id.* at 1124 ("Delaware courts recognize that boards of directors routinely and properly have to make decisions that benefit one class of stock at the expense of another"). The court in *Solomon* described the following reasoning in *Freedman v. Restaurant Associates Industries, Inc.*, [1987-1988 Transfer Binder] Fed. Sec. L. Rep. (CCH) ¶ 93,502 (Del. Ch. Oct. 16, 1987), as "instructive" on this subject:

> It is easy to say that a director's duty runs to the corporation and all of its shareholders, but such a statement gives faint guidance to a director when conflicts among shareholder constituencies arise, as they do. For example, when merger considerations must be apportioned between Class A and Class B stock directors are inevitably faced with a conflict among classes of stock and, in most such instances, such directors will themselves own more of one class than another. Does such fact alone deprive such directors of the presumptions ordinarily accorded to their good faith decisions and require them to establish the intrinsic fairness of the apportionment? And, if so, do different directors have different burdens depending upon which class of stock they happen to own more of? It is not my impression that this is the law.

Id. at 97,221, *quoted in Solomon*, 747 A.2d at 1118 n.63.

The court in *Solomon*, however, also stated that "the ability of the board to act in all of the shareholders' best interests is seriously complicated" where "in a given transaction different shareholder classes have mutually exclusive interests." *Id.* at 1124. The court stated the "legally relevant" question to be the following: "[W]as the process for allocating value reasonably aimed at providing a fair result to all shareholders taken together and each and every class of shareholders taken separately?" *Id.* at 1124-25. The court's resolution of this question in the *Solomon* case, which involved a split-off of a wholly-owned subsidiary and a tracking stock linked to the performance of the subsidiary being split-off, is discussed in Chapter II, Section E 4 a below.

The court in *Harbor Finance Partners v. Huizenga*, 751 A.2d 879 (Del. Ch. 1999), similarly stated that in situations where a transaction "has different effects on two classes of the corporation's own stock . . . directors often own both classes of stock because corporations want to align the directors' interests with all the company's stockholders," and "[o]ur case law has long recognized that necessity requires directorial action in these circumstances and that such ownership interests do not necessarily strip directors of their disinterestedness status." *Id.* at 888 n.28. The court stated that "[i]n evaluating whether to accord business judgment rule protection to a decision" involving a transaction that has different effects on two classes of a corporation's stock and directors own shares of each class, it is "beneficial to shareholders" to weigh whether directors owned "so much more of one class . . . than the other as to render it improbable that they would evaluate the transaction impartially" (and not simply "assume that the necessity of decision-making in such circumstances renders it proper for the court to blind itself totally to the directors' economic motivations"). *Id.* This weighing process is beneficial to shareholders, the court explained, because it recognizes that "a board's personal economic circumstances might make it impossible for them to act as impartial broker between classes of the corporation's stockholders in a zero-sum transaction." *Id.* The court noted that "[u]se of the weighing analysis in such cases encourages directors to avoid acting unilaterally in situations where their disinterestedness might be reasonably questioned and to employ procedural protections such as class-specific votes or special committees to ensure fairness." *Id.*

Section D 2 h

Add the following at the end of footnote 345 on page 71:

See also Harhen v. Brown, 730 N.E.2d 859, 864-65 & n.5 (Mass. 2000) (adopting definition of the term "interested" in 1 Principles of Corporate Governance: Analysis and Recommendations § 1.23 (1994)).

Section D 3

Add the following at the end of the paragraph beginning on page 74 and concluding on page 75 (immediately after footnote 351):

Where a plaintiff fails to demonstrate the lack of a reasonable investigation by directors, allegations concerning "the soundness of the directors' actions based on the information" obtained by the directors – such as "the directors did not comprehend, or act appropriately upon, the information they received" – do not state a claim. *Fed. Deposit Ins. Corp. v. Castetter*, 184 F.3d 1040, 1045 (9th Cir. 1999).

Replace the Model Act § 8.31 citation in footnote 353 on page 75 with the following:

2 Model Bus. Corp. Act Annotated § 8.31 Official Comment at 8-207 (3d ed. Supp. 1998/99).

Add the following at the end of the first sentence (immediately after footnote 355) of the paragraph beginning on page 75 and concluding on page 77:

"[I]n making business decisions, directors must consider all material information reasonably available," and "the directors' process is actionable only if grossly negligent." *Brehm v. Eisner*, 746 A.2d 244, 259 (Del. 2000); *see also McMullin v.*

Beran, 765 A.2d 910, 921 (Del. 2000) (re-affirming gross negligence standard).

Replace the first semi-colon in footnote 357 on page 76 with the following:

and Wilson v. Tully, 243 A.D.2d 229, 235, 676 N.Y.S.2d 531, 536 (N.Y. App. Div. 1st Dep't 1998);

Add the following at the end of the third sentence (immediately after footnote 357) of the paragraph beginning on page 75 and concluding on page 77:

This gross negligence standard is "onerous," and "[s]econd-guessing about whether a board's strategy was 'reasonable' or 'appropriate' . . . does little to assist a plaintiff in meeting its obligation to set forth facts from which one could infer that the defendants' lack of care was so egregious" that it constitutes gross negligence. *McMillan v. Intercargo Corp.*, 768 A.2d 492, 505 n.56 (Del. Ch. 2000).

Add the following at the beginning of the paragraph beginning on page 77 and concluding on page 78 (immediately after footnote 367):

"[T]he standard for judging the informational component of the directors' decisionmaking does not mean that the Board must be informed of *every* fact. The Board is responsible for considering only *material* facts that are *reasonably available*, not those that are immaterial or out of the Board's reasonable reach." *Brehm*, 746 A.2d at 259.

Replace the Model Act § 8.30 citation in footnote 372 on page 80 with the following:

Model Bus. Corp. Act § 8.30 Official Comment at 8-169.

Add the following at the end of the paragraph beginning and concluding on page 80 (immediately after footnote 374):

"Due care in the decisionmaking context is *process* due care only." *Brehm*, 746 A.2d at 264. "Substantive due care" is a concept that "is foreign to the business judgment rule. Courts do not measure, weigh or quantify directors' judgments. We do not even decide if they are reasonable in this context." *Id.; see also Ash v. McCall*, 2000 Del. Ch. LEXIS 144, at *26, 2000 WL 1370341, at *8 (Del. Ch. Sept. 15, 2000) ("substantive due care" is "a concept that is foreign to the business judgment rule").

Section D 4

Change the period at the end of the first sentence (immediately before footnote 375) of the paragraph beginning on page 80 and concluding on page 81 to a comma and add the following immediately after footnote 375:

and thus good faith "is a key ingredient of the business judgment rule." *Brehm v. Eisner*, 746 A.2d 244, 264 (Del. 2000).

Replace footnote 375 on page 80 with the following:

2 Model Bus. Corp. Act Annotated § 8.31 Official Comment at 8-200 (3d ed. Supp. 1998/99).

Replace the period at the end of footnote 377 on page 80 with the following:

and Quadrangle Offshore (Cayman) LLC v. Kenetech Corp., 1999 Del. Ch. LEXIS 213, at *36 n.29, 1999 WL 893575, at *10 n.29 (Del. Ch. Oct. 13, 1999), *aff'd*, 751 A.2d 878 (unpublished opinion, text available at 2000 Del. LEXIS 147 and 2000 WL 431608) (Del. Apr. 4, 2000).

Add the following at the end of footnote 379 on page 81:

See also Leung v. Schuler, 2000 Del. Ch. LEXIS 41, at *39, 2000 WL 264328, at *11 (Del. Ch. Feb. 29, 2000) and 2000 Del. Ch. LEXIS 134, at *19, 2000 WL 1478538, at *6 (Del. Ch. Sept. 29, 2000) ("[u]nder the business judgment rule a board's good faith in making a decision is presumed" and "[t]hat presumption is heightened where, as here, the majority of the directors making the decision are independent or outside directors").

Add the following at the end of the first sentence (immediately after footnote 386) of the paragraph beginning on page 82 and concluding on page 83:

Accordingly, "[t]he presumptive validity of a business judgment is rebutted in those rare cases where the decision under attack is 'so far beyond the bounds of reasonable judgment that it seems essentially inexplicable on any ground other than bad faith.'" *Parnes v. Bally Entm't Corp.*, 722 A.2d 1243, 1246 (Del. 1999) (quoting *In re J. P. Stevens & Co. S'holders Litig.*, 542 A.2d 770, 780-81 (Del. Ch. 1988), *appeal refused*, 540 A.2d 1088 (unpublished opinion, text available at 1988 Del. LEXIS 102 and 1988 WL 35145) (Del. Apr. 12, 1988)); *see also Safety-Kleen Corp. v. Laidlaw Envtl. Servs., Inc.*, 1999 WL 601039, at *19 (N.D. Ill. Feb. 4, 1998) (courts may review a business judgment "for the limited purpose of assessing whether that decision is so far beyond the bounds of reasonable judgment that it seems essentially inexplicable on any ground other than bad faith") (quoting *J.P. Stevens*). "Irrationality . . . may tend to show that the decision is not made in good faith." *Brehm*, 746 A.2d at 264.

Replace the Model Act § 8.31 citation in footnote 388 on page 83 with the following:

Model Bus. Corp. Act § 8.31 Official Comment at 8-201.

Add the following at the end of the paragraph beginning on page 82 and concluding on page 83 (immediately after footnote 388):

The court in *Parnes v. Bally Entertainment Corp.*, 722 A.2d 1243 (Del. 1999), denied a motion to dismiss on this ground in a case challenging a stock-for-stock merger by Bally Entertainment Corporation with and into Hilton Hotels Corporation. The plaintiff in the case alleged that Arthur M. Goldberg, the chairman and chief executive officer of Bally Entertainment, controlled the negotiations that led to the merger and allegedly (1) "demanded that any potential acquiror pay Goldberg for his approval of the merger" and (2) received "several substantial cash payments and asset transfers that allegedly lacked any consideration and were conditioned upon the completion of the merger." *Id.* at 1246. The court stated that "[t]he presumptive validity of a business judgment is rebutted in those rare cases where the decision under attack is 'so far beyond the bounds of reasonable judgment that it seems essentially inexplicable on any ground other than bad faith.'" *Id.* (quoting *J.P. Stevens*, 542 A.2d at 780-81). Here, the court concluded, "the facts alleged . . . meet this test . . . . If . . . Goldberg tainted the entire process of finding an interested merger partner and negotiating the transaction by demanding a bribe, then it is inexplicable that independent directors, acting in good faith, could approve the deal." *Id.* at 1246-47. The court acknowledged that "[t]he facts that are developed during the course of the litigation may cast a very different light on the merger and the Bally directors' decisions," but stated that "[a]t the pleading stage . . . we must accept all . . . factual allegations as true and . . . all inferences that may be drawn from those facts." *Id.* at 1247.

The same result was reached in *Crescent/Mach I Partners, L.P. v. Turner*, 2000 Del. Ch. LEXIS 145, 2000 WL 1481002, at *10 (Del. Ch. Sept. 29, 2000). Plaintiff alleged that the directors of Dr. Pepper Bottling Holdings, Inc. ("Holdings") breached their fiduciary duties by approving a merger of a wholly-owned subsidiary of Dr. Pepper/Seven-Up Bottling

Group, Inc. with and into Holdings. Holdings' board included three directors: (1) Jim L. Turner, the corporation's controlling shareholder, chairman of the board and chief executive officer, (2) J. Kent Sweezey, a managing director of Donaldson Lufkin & Jenrette Securities Corporation ("DLJ"), an investment banking firm retained by Holdings, and (3) William O. Hunt. 2000 Del. Ch. LEXIS 145, at *2, 4, 2000 WL 1481002, at *1. Plaintiffs alleged that Turner negotiated a merger agreement that provided substantial benefits to him in "side-deals" not available to Holdings' minority stockholders, including obtaining equity in the surviving corporation without obtaining a proportionate opportunity for minority shareholders to obtain equity, diverting cash consideration to Turner-affiliated entities that could have been part of the merger consideration, negotiating employment contracts for himself that diverted consideration that could have been part of the merger consideration, securing a right to sell his own shares that was not offered on proportionate terms to other shareholders, and obtaining tax advantages in the merger that were unavailable to other shareholders. 2000 Del. Ch. LEXIS 145, at *7-10, 45 n.48, 2000 WL 1481002, at *3-4, 12 n.48.

The court held that the minority of Holdings' board – Sweezey and Hunt – were disinterested and independent but – quoting *Parnes* – also held that "the presumptive validity of the business judgment rule can be rebutted 'where the decision under attack is so far beyond the bounds of reasonable judgment that it seems essentially inexplicable on any ground other than bad faith.'" 2000 Del. Ch. LEXIS 145, at *42, 2000 WL 1481002, at *12 (quoting 722 A.2d at 1246). The court stated that "the presumption has been sufficiently rebutted by pleaded facts evidencing the remaining directors' 'indifference to their duty to protect the interests of the corporation and its minority stockholders.'" 2000 Del. Ch. LEXIS 145, at *42, 2000 WL 1481002, at *12 (quoting *Strassburger v. Earley,* 752 A.2d 557, 581 (Del. Ch. 2000)). The court explained that plaintiffs' allegations were similar to the allegations in *Parnes*:

> Turner, like Goldberg, has negotiated a merger agreement that conferred substantial benefits to him that will not be available to Holdings' minority stockholders. The allegations as framed in the Complaint suggest that Turner may have breached his fiduciary duty of loyalty. It may be inferred from plaintiffs' allegations in the Complaint that Sweezey and Hunt may have breached their fiduciary duty of loyalty "by acquiescing in [Turner's] self-interested negotiations and by approving the merger at an unfair price." In other words, it does not matter here that the Complaint fails to establish that Sweezey and Hunt were either interested directors or that they lacked the ability to form an independent judgment. Their approval of Turner's alleged self-interested "side-deals" allegedly taint the entire merger process and strips the board of the protection of the business judgment rule. Even though the remaining directors failed to benefit personally from the merger, their judgments were aligned with that of Turner and not that of Holdings or its minority stockholders.

2000 Del. Ch. LEXIS 145, at *45, 2000 WL 1481002, at *12 (footnotes omitted). In other words, "the remaining directors 'acted intentionally and in bad faith to enable [the majority shareholder] wrongfully to benefit at the corporation's expense'" (quoting *Strassburger,* 752 A.2d at 581). The court accordingly held that "[t]he Complaint adequately pleads a claim that Sweezey and Hunt failed to exercise, in good faith, their fiduciary duty of loyalty to Holdings and the minority stockholders." 2000 Del. Ch. LEXIS 145, at *46, 2000 WL 1481002, at *12. The court thus denied a motion to dismiss plaintiffs' duty of loyalty claims because "plaintiffs' Complaint has sufficiently pled non-conclusory allegations challenging the fairness of the price received in the merger and the process which led to the directors' approval." 2000 Del. Ch. LEXIS 145, at *48-49, 2000 WL 1481002, at *13.

Section D 5

Add the following between "815" and "; see also" in footnote 392 on page 84:

, *quoted in In re Walt Disney Co. Derivative Litig.*, 731 A.2d 342, 362 (Del. Ch. 1998), *aff'd with leave to replead on other grounds sub nom. Brehm v. Eisner*, 746 A.2d 244 (Del. 2000).

Replace the Model Act § 8.30 citation preceding the "('a director . . .')" parenthetical in footnote 394 on page 84 with the following:

2 Model Bus. Corp. Act Annotated § 8.30(a) Official Comment at 8-165 (3d ed. Supp. 1998/99)

Add the following at the end of footnote 394 on page 84:

Federal Deposit Ins. Corp. v. Castetter, 184 F.3d 1040, 1044 (9th Cir. 1999) ("[t]he general purpose of the business judgment rule is to afford directors broad discretion in making corporate decisions").

Replace the period at the end of footnote 405 on page 87 with the following:

, *quoted in part in Wilson v. Tully*, 243 A.D.2d 229, 238, 676 N.Y.S.2d 531, 538 (N.Y. App. Div. 1st Dep't 1998).

Add the following at the end of the paragraph beginning on page 87 and concluding on page 88 (immediately after footnote 406):

The Delaware Supreme Court's decision in *Parnes v. Bally Entertainment Corp.*, 722 A.2d 1243 (Del. 1999), states that "[t]he presumptive validity of a business judgment is rebutted in those rare cases where the decision under attack is 'so far beyond the bounds of reasonable judgment that it seems essentially inexplicable on any ground other than bad faith.'" *Id.* at 1246 (quoting *In re J.P. Stevens & Co. S'holders Litig.*, 542 A.2d 770, 780-81 (Del. Ch. 1988), *appeal refused*, 540 A.2d 1088 (unpublished opinion, text available at 1988 Del. LEXIS 102 and 1988 WL 35145) (Del. Apr. 12, 1988)). The

Parnes decision, however, does not address the question whether there are any such "rare cases" where an absence of good faith cannot be inferred.

Add the following at the end of footnote 422 on page 90:

See also Dean v. Dick, 1999 Del. Ch. LEXIS 121, at *12, 1999 WL 413400, at *4 (Del. Ch. June 10, 1999) ("that decision was well within Dean's business judgment as general partner, and I do not find it so egregious as to warrant second-guessing his judgment in contravention of the business judgment rule").

Section E

Add the following at the end of footnote 423 on page 91:

See also Great Rivers Coop. v. Farmland Indus., Inc., 198 F.3d 685, 704 (8th Cir. 1999) (fraud); *Harhen v. Brown*, 730 N.E.2d 859, 866 n.7 (Mass. 2000) (illegality).

Add the following at the end of the first sentence (immediately after footnote 423) of the paragraph beginning on page 90 and concluding on page 91:

These acts are void *ab initio*. *See Solomon v. Armstrong*, 747 A.2d 1098, 1114 (Del. Ch. 1999), *aff'd*, 746 A.2d 277 (unpublished decision, full text available at 2000 Del. LEXIS 30 and 2000 WL 140072) (Del. Jan. 26, 2000); *see also id.* at 1114 n.45 (adding that ultra vires acts that are void include "acts specifically prohibited by the corporation's charter, for which no implicit authority may be rationally surmised, or those acts contrary to basic principles of fiduciary law"); *State of Wis. Inv. Bd. v. Peerless Sys. Corp.*, 2000 Del. Ch. LEXIS 170, at *47-48, 2000 WL 1805376, at *14 (Del. Ch. Dec. 4, 2000) ("Delaware law divides improper acts by the board into two separate categories, void acts and voidable acts. Void acts include those that are *ultra vires*, fraudulent, gifts or waste, and are legal nullities incapable of cure. Voidable acts are performed in the interest of the company, but beyond the authority of management, and are also cause for relief. If the shareholders ratify the voidable act after the fact, as opposed to the void act, the ratification cures the defect and relates back to moot all claims provided that the ratification was 'fairly accomplished'") (footnotes omitted); *Harbor Fin. Partners v. Huizenga*, 751 A.2d 879, 896 n.61 (Del. Ch. 1999):

> A contract of a corporation, which is ultra vires, in the proper sense, that is to say, outside the object of its creation as defined in the law of its organization, and therefore beyond the powers conferred upon it by the legislature, is not voidable only, but wholly void, and of no legal effect. The objection to the contract is, not merely that the corporation ought not to have made it, but that it could not make it. The contract cannot be ratified by either party, because it could not have been authorized by either. No performance on either side can give the unlawful contract any validity, or be the foundation of any right of action upon it.

(quoting *Central Transp. Co. v. Pullman's Palace Car Co.*, 139 U.S. 24, 59-60 (1891)); *Apple Computer, Inc. v. Exponential Tech., Inc.*, 1999 Del. Ch. LEXIS 9, at *22, 1999 WL 39547, at *6 (Del. Ch. Jan. 21, 1999) ("Our law divides improper acts by the board into two categories: void and voidable. Void acts, acts that are ultra vires, fraudulent, gifts, or waste, are legal nullities incapable of cure. Voidable acts, acts performed in the interest of the company, but beyond the authority of management, are also (if challenged by a shareholder or other person with standing) cause for legal relief. The difference is that if the shareholders ratify the voidable act after the fact, the ratification cures the defect and relates back to moot all claims.").

Add the following at the end of the paragraph beginning and concluding on page 92 (immediately after footnote 432):

Harhen v. Brown, 710 N.E.2d 224 (Mass. App. Ct.), *rev'd on other grounds*, 730 N.E.2d 859 (Mass. 2000), involved a case where "the nub of the complaint" was illegal lobbying activities by F. William Sawyer, the senior registered lobbyist of John Hancock Mutual Life Insurance Company. *Id.* at 236. An "important issue" in the case was whether the involvement by the corporation's directors and officers with Sawyer, if any, "was so purposeful and knowing" that they "could not rationally have believed that that involvement, and Sawyer's illegal activities, were in the best interests of Hancock." *Id.* An intermediate appellate court in Massachusetts held that the business judgment rule "does not inexorably provide protection to the defendants individually if the allegations of the complaint are established." *Id.* The court explained that the Massachusetts business judgment rule "is rooted in the idea that 'action [by directors] taken in good faith, even though wanting in sound judgment, does not involve them in personal liability,'" but good faith is not limited to "the absence of subjective 'bad motives.'" *Id.* (quoting *Sagalyn v. Meekins, Packard & Wheat Inc.*, 195 N.E. 769, 771 (Mass. 1935) and 1 Principles of Corporate Governance: Analysis and Recommendations § 4.01(c) comment f at 181 (1994)).

Add the following at the end of the paragraph beginning on page 92 and concluding on page 93 (immediately after footnote 437):

The business judgment rule is inapplicable not just in cases involving fraud upon the corporation, but also in cases involving fraud on the board. *See, e.g., Cede & Co. v. Technicolor, Inc.*, 634 A.2d 345, 363 (Del. 1993); *Bomarko, Inc. v. Int'l Telecharge, Inc.*, 1999 Del. Ch. LEXIS 211, at *41, 1999 WL 1022083, at *14 (Del. Ch. Nov. 4, 1999), *aff'd*, 766 A.2d 437 (Del. 2000). "[T]he Court's 'reluctance to assess the merits of a business decision ends in the face of illicit manipulation of a board's deliberative processes by self-interested corporate fiduciaries.'" *Bomarko*, 1999 Del. Ch. LEXIS 211, at *41, 1999 WL 1022083, at *14 (quoting *Mills Acquisition Co. v. Macmillan, Inc.*, 559 A.2d 1261, 1279 (Del. 1989)); *see also HMG/Courtland Props., Inc. v. Gray*, 749 A.2d 94, 115 (Del. Ch. 1999) (stating that *Macmillan* holds that "where disinterested majority was manipulated by a deceptive CEO, entire fairness was appropriate standard of review").

Section F

Add the following at the end of footnote 438 on page 93:

See also Harbor Fin. Partners v. Huizenga, 751 A.2d 879, 890 (Del. Ch. 1999) ("so long as [a] claimant alleges facts in his description of a series of events from which a gift or waste may reasonably be inferred and makes a specific claim for the relief he hopes to obtain, he need not announce with any greater particularity the precise legal theory he is using") (quoting *Michelson v. Duncan*, 407 A.2d 211, 217 (Del. 1979)).

Replace the citation to the Parnes case in footnote 440 on page 94 with the following:

Parnes v. Bally Entm't Corp., 1997 Del. Ch. LEXIS 70, at *8, 1997 WL 257435, at *2 (Del. Ch. May 12, 1997), *rev'd on other grounds*, 722 A.2d 1243 (Del. 1999).

Replace the Benerofe citation in footnote 440 on page 94 with the following:

See also Benerofe v. Cha, 1996 Del. Ch. LEXIS 115, at *23, 1996 WL 535405, at *8 (Del. Ch. Sept. 12, 1996), *subsequent proceedings*, 1998 Del. Ch. LEXIS 28, at *12-13, 1999 WL 83081, at *4 (Del. Ch. Feb. 20, 1998);

Add the following at the end of footnote 440 on page 94:

See also Harbor Fin., 751 A.2d at 892, 893; *Sanders v. Wang*, 1999 Del. Ch. LEXIS 203, at *31, 1999 WL 1044880, at *10 (Del. Ch. Nov. 8, 1999); *Lewis v. Austen*, 1999 Del. Ch. LEXIS 125, at *24, 1999 WL 378125, at *6 (Del. Ch. June 2, 1999); *Apple Computer, Inc. v. Exponential Tech., Inc.*, 1999

Del. Ch. LEXIS 9, at *41-42, 1999 WL 39547, at *11 (Del. Ch. Jan. 21, 1999).

Add the following at the end of the second sentence (immediately after footnote 440) of the paragraph beginning on page 93 and concluding on page 95:

Directors thus "are only liable for waste when they 'authorize an exchange that is so one sided that no business person of ordinary, sound judgment could conclude that the corporation has received adequate consideration.'" *In re Walt Disney Co. Derivative Litig.*, 731 A.2d 342, 362 (Del. Ch. 1998), *aff'd with leave to replead on other grounds sub nom. Brehm v. Eisner*, 746 A.2d 244, 263 (Del. 2000) (quoting *Glazer v. Zapata Corp.*, 658 A.2d 176, 183 (Del. Ch. 1993)), *quoted in Leung v. Schuler*, 2000 Del. Ch. LEXIS 41, at *35 n.36, 2000 WL 264328, at *10 n.36 (Del. Ch. Feb. 29, 2000) and 2000 Del. Ch. LEXIS 134, at *11, 2000 WL 1478538, at *4 (Del. Ch. Sept. 29, 2000).

Add the following at the end of footnote 440 on page 94:

See also Ash v. McCall, 2000 Del. Ch. LEXIS 144, at *23, 2000 WL 1370341, at *7 (Del. Ch. Sept. 15, 2000); *Criden v. Steinberg*, 2000 Del. Ch. LEXIS 50, at *11 & n.13, 2000 WL 354390, at *3 & n.13 (Del. Ch. Mar. 23, 2000); *Hills Stores Co. v. Bozic*, 769 A.2d 88, 110 n.74 Del. Ch. 2000); *Wagner v. Selinger*, 2000 Del. Ch. LEXIS 1, at *10 n.12, 2000 WL 85318, at *3 n.12 (Del. Ch. Jan. 18, 2000); *Golaine v. Edwards*, 1999 Del. Ch. LEXIS 237, at *37 n.38, 1999 WL 1271882, at *10 n.38 (Del. Ch. Dec. 21, 1999).

Replace the period at the end of footnote 442 on page 95 with the following:

, *quoted in part in Golaine*, 1999 Del. Ch. LEXIS 237, at *37 n.38, 1999 WL 1271882, at *10 n.38.

Replace the period at the end of footnote 445 on page 96 with the following:

, *quoted in Austen*, 1999 Del. Ch. LEXIS 125, at *25, 1999 WL 378125, at *6 *and Harbor Fin.*, 751 A.2d at 892.

Replace the period at the end of footnote 447 on page 96 with the following:

, *quoted in Austen*, 1999 Del. Ch. LEXIS 125, at *24, 1999 WL 378125, at *6, *In re 3COM Corp. S'holders Litig.*, 1999 Del. Ch. LEXIS 215, at *12, 1999 WL 1009210, at *4 (Del. Ch. Oct. 25, 1999), *Wagner*, 2000 Del. Ch. LEXIS 1, at *9, 2000 WL 85318, at *3, *and Criden*, 2000 Del. Ch. LEXIS 50, at *9, 2000 WL 354390, at *3.

Add the following at the end of footnote 448 on page 96:

See also Leung, 2000 Del. Ch. LEXIS 134, at *11, 2000 WL 1478538, at *4 ("[t]he standard for pleading waste is stringent"); *Hills*, 769 A.2d at 110 n.74 ("the onerous test for waste"); *Sanders*, 1999 Del. Ch. LEXIS 203, at *31, 1999 WL 1044880, at *10 ("[t]he standard is stringent").

Replace the period at the end of footnote 449 on page 96 with the following:

and Brehm v. Eisner, 746 A.2d 244, 263 (Del. 2000), *3COM*, 1999 Del. Ch. LEXIS 215, at *12, 1999 WL 1009210, at *4, *and Wagner*, 2000 Del. Ch. LEXIS 1, at *9, 2000 WL 85318, at *3.

Replace the block quote and footnote 451 after the second series of ellipses (immediately after footnote 450) in the paragraph beginning on page 96 and concluding on page 97 with the following:

> The judicial standard for determination of corporate waste is well developed. Roughly, a waste entails an exchange of cor-

> porate assets for consideration so disproportionately small as to lie beyond the range at which any reasonable person might be willing to trade. Most often the claim is associated with a transfer of corporate assets that serves no corporate purpose; or for which no consideration at all is received. Such a transfer is in effect a gift. If, however, there is *any substantial* consideration received by the corporation, and if there is a *good faith judgment* that in the circumstances the transaction is worthwhile, there should be no finding of waste, even if the fact finder would conclude *ex post* that the transaction was unreasonably risky. Any other rule would deter corporate boards from the optimal rational acceptance of risk, for reasons explained elsewhere. Courts are ill-fitted to attempt to weigh the "adequacy" of the consideration under the waste standard or, *ex post*, to judge appropriate degrees of business risk.
>
> * * *
>
> [T]o find the plaintiff's claim sufficient I must be satisfied that the alleged facts establish a complete failure of consideration, and not merely the insufficiency of the consideration received. A complete failure of consideration is difficult to show since the acts alleged have to be so blatant that no ordinary business person would ever consider the transaction to be fair to the corporation. The company would literally have to get nothing whatsoever for what it gave. Under this standard I am not to examine the allegations to see whether consideration, once received, was excessive or lopsided, was proportional or not, or even whether it was a 'bad deal' from a business standpoint. If I were to do so I would not be deferring to the board's business judgment, as I am required to do here.
>
> * * *
>
> This strict standard requires the Court to apply a reasonable person standard and deny a claim of waste wherever a reasonable person might deem the consideration received adequate. When this difficult standard is applied in the liberal context of a motion to dismiss, in order for the complaint to survive the motion, the Court must find that in any of the possible sets of circumstances inferable from the facts alleged under the complaint, no reasonable person could deem the received consideration adequate.

Brehm, 746 A.2d at 263 (quoting *Lewis v. Vogelstein*, 699 A.2d 327, 336 (Del. Ch. 1997) (citations omitted)), *quoted in Leung*, 2000 Del. Ch. LEXIS 41, at *36, 2000 WL 264328, at *10 and 2000 Del. Ch. LEXIS 134, at *13-14, 2000 WL

1478538, at *4; *3COM*, 1999 Del. Ch. LEXIS 215, at *13, 1999 WL 1009210, at *4 (footnotes omitted); *Apple Computer*, 1999 Del. Ch. LEXIS 9, at *41-42, 1999 WL 39547, at *11; *see also Ash*, 2000 Del. Ch. LEXIS 144, at *23, 2000 WL 1370341, at *7 (to show waste, a plaintiff must show that the challenged transaction "either served no corporate purpose or was so completely bereft of consideration that it effectively constituted a gift"); *Criden*, 2000 Del. Ch. LEXIS 50, at *10-11, 2000 WL 354390, at *3 ("Insufficient or inadequate compensation is difficult to demonstrate since the alleged acts 'have to be so blatant that *no* ordinary business person would ever consider the transaction to be fair to the corporation.' In other words, the company would have to receive virtually nothing for what it gave.") (quoting *3COM*).

Add the following at the end of the paragraph beginning on page 96 and concluding on page 97 (immediately after footnote 452):

"To be sure, there are outer limits, but they are confined to unconscionable cases where directors irrationally squander or give away corporate assets." *Brehm*, 746 A.2d at 263, *quoted in Leung*, 2000 Del. Ch. LEXIS 41, at *36 n.37, 2000 WL 264328, at *10 n.37.

A waste claim cannot be established by "examining a corporate transaction with perfect 20/20 hindsight and declaring that it turned out . . . so horribly that it must be a waste of corporate assets." *Ash*, 2000 Del. Ch. LEXIS 144, at *26, 2000 WL 1370341, at *8. To the contrary, "the relevant time to measure" whether a board has committed waste is the time the board approves the transaction. *Id.* Accordingly,

> [i]f Company A exchanges $100 for an asset from Company B that Company A believes is worth $100, it is not "waste" if it later turns out that Company B's asset was worth only $10. Company B may have perpetrated a fraud on Company A or, perhaps, Company A's directors breached their duty of care, but Company A or its directors did not commit "waste."

Id.; see also Leung, 2000 Del. Ch. LEXIS 41, at *37, 2000 WL 264328, at *10 ("even if the complaint alleges facts that if true would show that in hindsight the consideration was inadequate, that alone will not satisfy the waste standard").

Section G

Add the following at the end of footnote 456 on page 98:

See also Flake v. Hoskins, 55 F. Supp. 2d 1196, 1213 (D. Kan. 1999) (Missouri law).

Replace "1997" with "2000" in the Fletcher citation in footnote 472 on page 100.

Add the following at the end of footnote 472 on page 100:

See also Hansen, *The Business Judgment Rule: Is There Any Doubt It Applies To Officers?*, LXX Corporation No. 17 (Aspen Law & Bus. Sept. 1, 1999) ("[b]oth as a matter of precedent, and as a matter of sound policy, it seems clear that officers do and should have the protection of the rule").

Replace the second sentence of the second paragraph beginning and concluding on page 100 (including footnote 473) with the following:

The Model Business Corporation Act states that "the business judgment rule will normally apply to decisions within an officer's discretionary authority." 2 Model Bus. Corp. Act Annotated § 8.42 Official Comment at 8-265 (3d ed. Supp. 1998/99).

Section H 1

Replace the first paragraph beginning and concluding on page 101 (including footnotes 474 through 477) with the following:

The Committee on Corporate Laws of the Section of Business Law of the American Bar Association is the drafter and custodian of the Model Business Corporation Act, a document designed to be "a clear, precise and state-of-the-art model for state legislatures to consider in revising state enabling acts." Veasey, *New Insights into Judicial Deference to Directors' Business Decisions: Should We Trust the Courts?*, 39 Bus. Law. 1461, 1462 (1984). The Committee undertook a complete revision of the Model Act during the first half of the 1980s, and, according to one of its members, "[p]erhaps more time and effort [was] devoted to the business judgment doctrine than to any other aspect of the [project]." *Id.* at 1462; *see also* Balotti & Hinsey, *Director Care, Conduct, and Liability: The Model Business Corporation Act Solution,* 56 Bus. Law. 35, 42-48 (2000); Goldstein, *Revision of the Model Business Corporation Act*, 63 Tex. L. Rev. 1471 (1985); Hamilton, *Reflections of a Reporter*, 63 Tex. L. Rev. 1455 (1985).

Replace "8-167" with "8-163" and replace "1996" with "Supp. 1998/99" in the Model Act § 8.30 citation in footnote 478 on page 101.

Replace the period at the end of footnote 482 on page 102 with the following:

, adopted in Changes in the Model Business Corporation Act Pertaining to the Standards of Conduct and Standards of Liability for Directors – Final Adoption, 53 Bus. Law. 813 (1998).

Replace the Model Act § 8.31 citation in footnote 483 on page 102 with the following:

Model Bus. Corp. Act Annotated § 8.31 Official Comment at 8-197.

Replace the Model Act § 8.31 citation in footnote 484 on page 103 with the following:

Id. at 8–197-98.

Replace the first sentence of the paragraph beginning and concluding on page 103 (immediately after footnote 484) with the following:

The director's standard of conduct in Section 8.30 of the Model Act, as it existed both before and after it was amended in 1998, is quoted at the beginning of this Chapter.

Replace the Model Act § 8.30 and § 8.31 citations in footnotes 485 through 489 on pages 103 and 104 with the following:

485. Model Bus. Corp. Act Annotated § 8.30 Official Comment at 8-163.
486. Model Bus. Corp. Act Annotated § 8.31 Official Comment at 8-199.
487. *Id.* at 8–199-200.
488. *Id.* at 8-200.
489. Model Bus. Corp. Act Annotated § 8.31(a); *see also* Balotti & Hinsey, 56 Bus. Law. at 51-57 (discussing Model Act § 8.31).

Delete the paragraph beginning and concluding on page 104 (between footnotes 489 and 490).

CHAPTER II

Section A

Replace the Model Act § 8.31 citation in footnote 10 on page 109 with the following:

2 Model Bus. Corp. Act Annotated § 8.31 Official Comment at 8-192 (3d ed. Supp. 1998/99).

Add the following at the end of the paragraph beginning on page 109 and concluding on page 110 (immediately after footnote 12):

There thus is an important distinction between "good corporate governance practices" and "principles of corporation law":

> All good corporate governance practices include compliance with statutory law and case law establishing fiduciary duties. But the law of corporate fiduciary duties and remedies for violation of those duties are distinct from the aspirational goals of ideal corporate governance practices. Aspirational ideals of good corporate governance practices for boards of directors that go beyond the minimal legal requirements of the corporation law are highly desirable, often tend to benefit stockholders, sometimes reduce litigation and can usually help directors avoid liability. But they are not required by the corporation law and do not define standards of liability.

Brehm v. Eisner, 746 A.2d 244, 256 (Del. 2000). Thus allegations in a complaint critical of a board's functioning because "directors own little stock," do not "hold a regular retreat," "don't meet regularly in the absence of company executives," and do not give the corporation's chief executive officer "'a written assessment of his performance,' as do '89% of the nation's biggest industrial corporations,'" state "very desirable practices to be sure, but they are not required by the corporation law." *Id.* at 256 n.29. In other words, "a case about whether there should be personal liability of the directors of a Delaware corporation to the corporation for lack of due care in the decisionmaking process and for waste of corporate assets" does not turn upon whether the directors failed "to establish and carry out ideal corporate governance practices." *Id.* at 255; *see also In re W. Nat'l Corp. S'holders Litig.*, 2000 Del. Ch. LEXIS 82, at *53 & n.47, 2000 WL 710192, at *15 & n.47 (Del. Ch. May 22, 2000) (noting "distinction between corporate governance 'best practices' and legal requirements" and stating that "[a]lthough independent nominating committees may indeed have a salutary effect on board efficacy and independence, and are surely a 'best practice' which the corporate governance community endorses, they are not a *sine qua non* for director independence under Delaware law"); *Cooke v. Oolie*, 2000 Del. Ch. LEXIS 89, at *58-59, 2000 WL 710199, at *17 (Del. Ch. May 24, 2000), *quoted in In re Digex, Inc. S'holder Litig.*, 2000 Del. Ch. LEXIS 171, at *49, 2000 WL 1847679, at *14 (Del. Ch. Dec. 13, 2000):

> Although we encourage directors to aspire to ideal corporate governance practices, directors' actions need not achieve perfection to avoid liability. Directors must adhere to the minimum legal requirements of the corporation law. Although the defendants failed to act as a model director might have acted . . . I conclude, as a matter of law, they did not breach a legal duty.

Section A 1

Replace the Model Act § 8.31 citation in footnote 20 on page 112 with the following:

2 Model Bus. Corp. Act Annotated § 8.31 Official Comment at 8-196 (3d ed. Supp. 1998/99).

Add the following at the end of footnote 21 on page 112:

See also In re Stoico Rest. Group, Inc., 2000 U.S. Dist. LEXIS 12523, at *8, 2000 WL 1146122, at *3 (D. Kan. July 20, 2000) (dismissing complaint where "plaintiff has not adequately pled the element of causation" because "conclusory assumptions, i.e. 'the breach of fiduciary duties by defendants directly resulted in monetary losses to SRG,' . . . do not inform defendants how they allegedly caused monetary losses to SRG" and do not "rule out the possibility" that plaintiff's losses were caused by other parties); *Ed Peters Jewelry Co. v. C & J Jewelry Co.*, 51 F. Supp. 2d 81, 99-100 (D.R.I. 1999), *aff'd*, 215 F.3d 182 (1st Cir. 2000) (stating that "[a] plaintiff may also recover tort damages 'for harm caused by the breach of a duty arising from the relation' according to normal tort rules that govern proof of claims, including the requirement of causation" and finding that "plaintiff presented no credible evidence at trial that it suffered damages") (citation omitted); *Koch v. Koch Indus., Inc.*, 37 F. Supp. 2d 1231, 1241-42 (D. Kan. 1998) *aff'd and rev'd on other grounds*, 203 F.3d 1202 (10th Cir.), *cert. denied*, 121 S. Ct. 302 (2000) (causation and damages are "essential elements" of a breach of fiduciary duty claim and "[l]ogically, the burden to prove causation and damages should lie with the party claiming both").

Add the following at the end of footnote 32 on page 115:

See also Strassburger v. Earley, 752 A.2d 557, 579 (Del. Ch. 2000) ("Rescissory damages is an exception to the normal out-of-pocket measure. They are exceptional, because such damages are measured as of a point in time *after* the transaction, whereas compensatory damages are determined at the time *of* the transaction. As a consequence, rescissory damages may be significantly higher than the conventional out-of-pocket damages, because rescissory damages could include post-transaction incremental value elements that would not be captured in an 'out-of-pocket' recovery."); *Bomarko, Inc. v. Int'l Telecharge, Inc.*, 1999 Del. Ch. LEXIS 211, at *57-78, 1999 WL 1022083, at *20-26 (Del. Ch. Nov. 4, 1999), *aff'd*, 766 A.2d 437 (Del. 2000) (granting equitable relief in the form of "a species of rescissory damages" in a case involving a challenged cash-out merger and debt restructuring of International Telecharge, Inc. ("ITI") in order to provide plaintiffs "at a minimum, what their shares would have been worth at the time of the Merger if Haan had not breached his fiduciary duties"; the court acknowledged that "before Haan acted disloyally there was uncertainty whether or not ITI could secure financing and restructure its debt and . . . the measure of damages I mean to allow removes these uncertainties and might overcompensate plaintiffs for that reason," but concluded that "the potentially harsh nature of this remedy is both appropriate, given the nature of Haan's misconduct, and necessary to avoid shortchanging plaintiffs"; the court rejected a claim for disgorgement of profits Haan earned from the corporation during the five years following the challenged merger and debt restructuring because "[o]n the record before me . . . there is no indication that Haan's receipt of monies after the Merger was on account of factors other than the Merger and the debt restructuring," "my valuation of ITI already takes into account the benefits of the debt restructuring and, as to these plaintiffs, deprives Haan of the value of the Merger," and thus "any order requiring disgorgement would constitute a double recovery for the plaintiffs"); *HMG/Courtland Props., Inc. v. Gray*, 749 A.2d 94, 122-24 (Del. Ch. 1999) (in a case where there was "no doubt" that "serious breaches of duty" had been committed and that "complete rescissory damages" would be a "permissible" remedy, the court instead "crafted a remedy tailored to the specific facts of this case" and stated that "[i]n doing so, I have done my best to 'craft from the 'panoply of equitable remedies' a damage award that approximates a price [and terms] the [HMG] board would have approved absent a breach of duty'"; the court stated that "this remedy makes HMG whole for the damages caused by the breaches of fiduciary duty and fraud committed by Gray and Fieber and holds Gray and Fieber properly accountable for their serious misconduct") (quoting *Ryan v. Tad's Enters., Inc.*, 709 A.2d 682, 699 (Del. Ch.), *reargument denied*, 709 A.2d 675, 677 (Del. Ch. 1996), *aff'd*, 693 A.2d 1082 (unpublished opinion, text available at 1997 Del. LEXIS 120 and 1997 WL 188351) (Del. Apr. 10, 1997)).

Add the following at the end of the first paragraph beginning and concluding on page 116 (immediately after footnote 36):

In *Strassburger v. Earley*, 752 A.2d 557 (Del. Ch. 2000), the Court of Chancery re-affirmed its ruling in *Cinerama, Inc. v. Technicolor, Inc.*, 663 A.2d 1134 (Del. Ch. 1994), *aff'd on other grounds*, 663 A.2d 1156 (Del. 1995). The court in *Strassburger* stated that "[i]n order to be equitably appropriate, rescissory damages must redress an adjudicated breach of the duty of loyalty, specifically, cases that involve self dealing or where the board puts its conflicting personal interests ahead of the interest of the shareholders." *Id.* at 581.

Applying this standard, the court held that three directors were liable for rescissory damages: one director who "personally obtained a unique benefit paid for entirely with corporate assets" and who thus "(a) was unjustly enriched, (b) engaged in self-dealing, and (c) placed his personal interests ahead of the interests of the minority shareholders"; and two directors who "were not unjustly enriched" and "did not otherwise obtain a personal benefit at the shareholders' expense" or act "intentionally and in bad faith" but who "did violate their fiduciary duty of loyalty" because "their primary loyalty was to the interest of their employer" and the "inevitable consequence" was that they "ignored their fiduciary obligation as Ridgewood directors to assure that *all* Ridgewood stockholders would be treated fairly." *Id.* In other words, "[t]heir sin was not one of venality, but, rather, of indifference to their duty to protect the interests of the corporation and its minority shareholders." *Id.* The court held that a fourth director was "differently situated from the rest" because this director "received no personal benefit . . . and had no conflicting interest that would motivate him to act in other than what he believed to be the corporation's best interests" and "at worst" acted without due care, which is not a legally sufficient ground for rescissory damages. *Id.* To the contrary, "a misguided decision" cannot subject a director "to even compensatory damages" because "[t]he business judgment rule shields directors from liability for good faith business decisions, even those that turn out to be mistaken." *Id.* at 581-82.

Section A 2

Replace the second sentence of the paragraph beginning on page 117 and concluding on page 118 (immediately after footnote 44) with the following:

This traditional formulation appeared in Section 8.30(a) of the Model Business Corporation Act until 1998 as follows:

Replace the Model Act § 8.30 citation in footnote 43 on page 117 with the following:

Former Model Bus. Corp. Act § 8.30(a).

Replace the Model Act § 8.30 citation in footnote 44 on page 118 with the following:

Former Model Bus. Corp. Act § 8.30 Official Comment;

Replace the first sentence (through the colon) between footnotes 46 and 47 of the paragraph beginning and concluding on page 119 with the following:

Section 8.30 was revised in 1998 to read as follows:

Replace the Model Act § 8.30 citation in footnote 47 on page 119 with the following:

2 Model Bus. Corp. Act Annotated §§ 8.30(a), (b) (3d ed. Supp. 1998/99).

Delete "proposed" in the first sentence (between footnotes 47 and 48) of the paragraph beginning and concluding on page 120.

Replace the Model Act § 8.30 citation in footnote 48 on page 120 with the following:

Model Bus. Corp. Act § 8.30 Official Comment at 8-163.

Replace "165" with "8-167" in the Model Act § 8.30 citation in footnote 49 on page 120.

Replace "163-64" with "8-165" in the Model Act § 8.30 citation in footnote 50 on page 121.

Replace "Id. at 166-67." in footnote 51 on page 123 with the following:

Id. at 8–168-70; *see also* Balotti & Hinsey, *Director Care, Conduct, and Liability: The Model Business Corporation Act Solution*, 56 Bus. Law. 35, 49-51 (2000) (discussing Model Act § 8.30); *Federal Deposit Ins. Corp. v. Castetter*, 184 F.3d 1040, 1046 (9th Cir. 1999) (the California Corporations Code "does not impose on directors a duty of possessing specialized knowledge").

Replace "proposed revision" with "revision in 1998" in the first sentence (between footnotes 51 and 52) of the paragraph beginning on page 123 and concluding on page 124.

Replace "proposed revision" with "revision in 1998" in the second sentence (between footnotes 53 and 54) of the paragraph beginning on page 123 and concluding on page 124.

Add the following at the end of footnote 52 on page 123:

See also Great Rivers Coop. v. Farmland Indus., Inc., 198 F.3d 685, 702 (8th Cir. 1999) ("[t]he standard of duty by which the conduct of a director of a corporation is to be judged should be that measure of attention, care, and ability which the ordinary director and officer of corporations of a similar kind would be reasonably and properly expected to bestow upon the affairs of the corporation") (Kansas law).

Add the following at the end of the first sentence (immediately after footnote 56) of the paragraph beginning on page 124 and concluding on page 126:

The statute thus "codifies the business judgment rule." *Byelick v. Vivadelli*, 79 F. Supp. 2d 610, 629 (E.D. Va. 1999).

Replace "proposed amendment" with "revision in 1998" in the second sentence (between footnotes 57 and 58) of the paragraph beginning on page 124 and concluding on page 126.

Section A 3

Replace the Model Act § 8.30 citation in footnote 65 on page 126 with the following:

2 Model Bus. Corp. Act Annotated § 8.30 Official Comment at 8-166 (3d ed. Supp. 1998/99).

Add the following at the end of the second sentence (immediately after footnote 67) of the paragraph beginning on page 126 and concluding on page 127):

"Although directors ultimately are responsible for a corporation's day-to-day management, most decisions do not require the board's attention." William B. Chandler III, *The Legal Framework for Analyzing Audit Committee Oversight*, The Corporate Governance Advisor, Jan./Feb. 2000, at 18. Directors thus "delegate management of day-to-day operations to corporate officers," but these delegations "must be monitored in order to ensure their quality and integrity." *Id.*

Add the following at the end of footnote 68 on page 127:

See also Chandler at 18 ("a director's duty to employ due care in performing his or her corporate functions includes a duty to oversee the subordinates to whom delegations have been made").

Replace "Dismissing this claim, the court stated that" in the third sentence (immediately after footnote 79) of the paragraph beginning on page 128 and concluding on page 129 with the following:

The court stated that "'directors are entitled to rely on the honesty and integrity of their subordinates until something occurs to put them on suspicion that something is wrong'" and dismissed the claim because

Replace the period at the end of footnote 80 on page 129 with the following:

(quoting *Graham v. Allis-Chalmers Mfg. Co.*, 188 A.2d 125, 130 (Del. 1963)); *see also In re Abbott Labs. Derivative*

S'holder Litig., 126 F. Supp. 2d 535, 538 (N.D. Ill. 2000) ("directors are entitled to rely upon the honesty and integrity of their subordinates until something occurs to alert suspicion").

Add the following at the end of footnote 90 on page 131:

See also Federal Deposit Ins. Corp. v. Castetter, 184 F.3d 1040, 1046 (9th Cir. 1999) (the business judgment rule does not protect "a director who has wholly abdicated his corporate responsibility, closing his or her eyes to corporate affairs"); *Benjamin v. Kim*, 1999 U.S. Dist. LEXIS 6089, at *46-47, 1999 WL 249706, at *14 (S.D.N.Y. Apr. 27, 1999) ("a director is not under a duty to 'install and operate a corporate system of espionage to ferret out wrongdoing which they have no reason to suspect exists,'" but "a director does have a duty to be reasonably informed about the company and make sure that appropriate information and reporting systems are in place so that the Board receives relevant and timely information necessary to satisfy its supervisory and monitoring role") (citation omitted).

Add the following at the end of the paragraph beginning on page 130 and concluding on page 131 (immediately after footnote 90):

The Delaware Court of Chancery in *White v. Panic*, 2000 Del. Ch. LEXIS 14, 2000 WL 85046 (Del. Ch. Jan. 19, 2000), stated that a contention by directors that they were "not 'on notice' of a need for corrective action" with respect to the presence of a company-wide sexual harassment problem and hostile work environment "concerns me because defendants appear to rely on an interpretation of *Graham v. Allis-Chalmers Mfg. Co.*, that was discredited in *Caremark*." 2000 Del. Ch. LEXIS 14, at *43, 2000 WL 85046, at *12 (citing *In re Caremark Int'l Inc. Derivative Litig.*, 698 A.2d 959 (Del. Ch. 1996)). The court dismissed the case "because the allegations of the complaint show that the board has *responded* to this perceived threat, not because the threat does not exist." *Id.*

The Court of Chancery's decision in *Ash v. McCall*, 2000 Del. Ch. LEXIS 144, 2000 WL 1370341 (Del. Ch. Sept. 15, 2000), points to "the problem of assessing claims, based on accounting irregularities, under the *Caremark* standard." 2000 Del. Ch. LEXIS 144, at *56 n.57, 2000 WL 1370341, at *15 n.57.

The case involved a merger of McKesson Corporation and HBOC & Co. into McKesson HBOC, Inc. Approximately 3-1/2 months after the acquisition became effective, Deloitte & Touche, the outside auditor for the combined company, informed the board of accounting irregularities at the combined company's HBOC subsidiary. McKesson HBOC's board, which included six former McKesson directors and six former HBOC directors, "responded to this information by initiating an internal investigation that culminated in a series of sweeping earnings restatements" and "sweeping managers changes, firing several senior managers and creating a new executive management structure." 2000 Del. Ch. LEXIS 144, at *53, 2000 WL 1370341, at *15.

The court stated that the alleged facts demonstrated that the McKesson directors "became aware of the accounting improprieties after the merger was consummated and immediately took decisive steps to disclose and cure them" – actions that "do not bespeak faithless or imprudent fiduciaries." *Id.* By contrast, the court continued, "[a] modicum of well-plead facts, sprinkled throughout the complaint, could lead to an inference that the HBOC directors might have had knowledge of suspect accounting practices and, therefore, *potential* accounting irregularities, in advance of the date of the Deloitte report." 2000 Del. Ch. LEXIS 144, at *53-54, 2000 WL 1370341, at *15. The court emphasized the word "potential" because plaintiffs did not assert "a single fact that might reasonably support such an allegation." 2000 Del. Ch. LEXIS 144, at *54 n.54, 2000 WL 1370341, at *15 n.54. To the contrary, the alleged facts "indicate[d] that HBOC, at some organizational level, knew of and responded to public criticism of its accounting practices" but not that "HBOC's directors had actual knowledge of these events and, therefore, possessed actual knowledge of potential accounting irregularities." 2000 Del. Ch. LEXIS 144, at *55, 2000 WL 1370341, at *15. The court granted leave to replead and stated that "[i]f plaintiffs can allege particularized facts that might enable this Court to infer that HBOC directors (or perhaps members of HBOC's audit committee) did possess knowledge of facts suggesting potential accounting improprieties . . . and took no action to respond to them until they were confronted (three months after the merger) with Deloitte's audit report, one could argue that the HBOC directors (or the audit committee members) failed to act in good faith." 2000 Del. Ch. LEXIS 144, at *55-56, 2000 WL 1370341, at *15.

The court noted that "the existence of an audit committee" at HBOC, "together with HBOC's retention of Arthur Andersen as its outside auditor to conduct annual audits of the company's financial reporting, is some evidence that a monitoring and compliance system was in place at HBOC premerger." 2000 Del. Ch. LEXIS 144, at *56 n.57, 2000 WL 1370341, at *15 n.57. The court stated that "the interesting question" if a properly framed complaint were filed "would be whether one could find directors liable on an oversight claim when those directors have retained a reputable independent, outside auditing firm and when the same directors have appointed an audit committee that is charged with overseeing the internal and external auditors." *Id.* The court added: "Would these facts support a finding that the directors had 'utterly failed to attempt to assure a reasonable reporting system exists' or exhibited a 'sustained and systematic failure to exercise reasonable oversight[?]'" *Id.* (quoting *Caremark*, 698 A.2d at 971). "Or," the court also asked, "do such facts indicate the malfunction or breakdown of the compliance system, rather than the absence of, or systematic failure to exercise, reasonable oversight?" *Id.* The court declined to decide these issues due to the absence of an adequately framed complaint. *Id.*

Add the following at the end of the third sentence of the paragraph (immediately after footnote 92) beginning on page 131 and concluding on page 132:

As stated by the Ninth Circuit in *Federal Deposit Insurance Corp. v. Castetter*, 184 F.3d 1040 (9th Cir. 1999), "California specifically eschewed a duty of inquiry 'such as the duty imposed by Section 11 of the United States Securities Act of 1933.' Cal. Corp. Code § 309 Legislative Committee Comment (1975). Rather, California allows non-officer directors to rely upon company employees and advisors without a duty of further inquiry absent special circumstances." 184 F.3d at 1045.

Section A 4

Replace "1998" with "2001" in the Balotti citation in footnote 95 on page 132.

Replace the Model Act § 8.31 citation in footnote 98 on page 133 with the following:

2 Model Bus. Corp. Act Annotated § 8.31 Official Comment at 8-192 (3d ed. Supp. 1998/99);

Section A 4 a

Add the following at the end of the third sentence (immediately after footnote 108) of the paragraph beginning on page 134 and concluding on page 135:

The court again reaffirmed the gross negligence standard in 2000 in *Brehm v. Eisner*, 746 A.2d 244, 259 (Del. 2000), and *McMullin v. Beran*, 765 A.2d 910, 921 (Del. 2000).

Add the following at the end of the paragraph beginning and concluding on page 135 (immediately after the parenthetical and period following footnote 117):

The Ninth Circuit, construing California law in *Federal Deposit Insurance Corp. v. Castetter*, 184 F.3d 1040 (9th Cir. 1999), held that directors are not liable for ordinary negligence such as a claim that "they negligently failed to investigate and inform themselves of the bank's financial condition." *Id.* at 1045.

Replace the Model Act § 8.31 citation in footnote 128 on page 137 with the following:

2 Model Bus. Corp. Act Annotated § 8.31(a)(2)(iv) (3d ed. Supp. 1998/99).

Add the following at the end of footnote 134 on page 139:

See also Stegemeier v. Magness, 728 A.2d 557, 562 (Del. 1999) (different standards of fiduciary duty govern corporate directors and trustees of a trust).

Replace "1998" with "2001" in the Balotti citation in footnote 137 on page 139.

Section A 4 b

Replace the Model Act § 8.31 citation in footnote 140 on page 140 with the following:

2 Model Bus. Corp. Act Annotated § 8.31 Official Comment at 8–204-06 (3d ed. Supp. 1998/99).

Replace "federal court" with "federal district court" in the first sentence (immediately after footnote 145) of the first paragraph beginning and concluding on page 141.

Add the following at the end of the first paragraph beginning and concluding on page 141 (immediately after footnote 149):

A federal appellate court construing Arizona law in *Federal Deposit Insurance Corp. v. Jackson*, 133 F.3d 694 (9th Cir. 1998), rejected the conclusion reached in *Resolution Trust Corp. v. Blasdell*, 930 F. Supp. 417 (D. Ariz. 1994), and held that "under Arizona law, where the business judgment rule applies to the conduct of a director, a showing of gross negligence is necessary to strip the director of the rule's protection," but "[w]here the threshold requirements of the rule are not met, however, a showing of simple negligence can be sufficient to impose liability on the director." *Id.* at 700. The court explained that "[l]ogically, two different standards must apply to acts within and without the business judgment rule; otherwise the rule has no meaning or purpose." *Id.* The court stated that "[i]f the business judgment rule insulates covered acts from charges of simple negligence, then it follows that a simple negligence standard must generally apply to acts outside the rule." *Id.*

Add the following at the end of footnote 153 on page 141:

See also Wilson v. Tully, 243 A.D.2d 229, 234, 676 N.Y.S.2d 531, 535 (N.Y. App. Div. 1st Dep't 1998) ("[i]t has been said that such a claim is possibly the most difficult theory in corporation law upon which a plaintiff might hope to win a judgment") (citing *In re Caremark Int'l Inc. Derivative Litig.*, 698 A.2d 959, 967 (Del. Ch. 1996)).

Add the following at the end of footnote 164 on page 143:

See also William B. Chandler III, *The Legal Framework for Analyzing Audit Committee Oversight*, The Corporate Governance Advisor, Jan./Feb. 2000, at 18, 20 ("*Caremark's* high standard for liability will also create a benefit. A high liability standard makes board service by qualified persons more likely because it puts risk-averse individuals at ease and, therefore, serves as an incentive for them to join boards and audit committees. A lower liability standard, as opposed to the *Caremark* standard, would expose directors to greater risk of personal liability and therefore be a disincentive for qualified, often risk-averse, individuals to serve on audit committees."); *In re Oxford Health Plans, Inc.*, 192 F.R.D. 111, 117 (S.D.N.Y. 2000) (stating that under *Caremark* "a violation of fiduciary duty exists if the directors 'either lack good faith in the exercise of their monitoring responsibilities or permitted a known violation of law by the corporation to occur" and that a lack of good faith "can be established by showing a sustained or systematic failure to exercise oversight and assure adequate record keeping"); *White v. Panic*, 2000 Del. Ch. LEXIS 14, at *42-43, 2000 WL 85046, at *12 (Del. Ch. Jan. 19, 2000) ("under the standard discussed in *Caremark*, the Director Defendants would face a substantial likelihood of liability only if plaintiff alleged facts showing a 'lack of good faith as evidenced by sustained or systematic failure . . . to exercise reasonable oversight'" and "this complaint, accepted as true, has not satisfied the high standard enunciated in *Caremark*"); *cf. Benjamin v. Kim*, 1999 U.S. Dist. LEXIS 6089, at *47, 1999 WL 249706, at *14 (S.D.N.Y. Apr. 27, 1999) (denying motion for summary judgment by defendants where "plaintiffs have submitted sufficient evidence that Silva was made aware of problems at GMR that should have prompted him to investigate, or that he was so negligent in his efforts to become informed about the affairs of GMR that his actions constituted a total failure to exercise reasonable oversight"; the court stated that "a claim of directorial liability 'predicated upon ignorance of liability creating activities within the corporation' will lie where the plaintiff shows a 'sustained or systematic failure of a director to exercise reasonable oversight'") (citation omitted).

Replace the Weinstock citation in footnote 175 on page 145 with the following:

N.Y.L.J., Mar. 28, 1996, at 29 (N.Y. Sup. Ct. N.Y. Co.), *subsequent proceedings*, No. 100151/95, Order (N.Y. Sup. Ct. N.Y. Co. Oct. 30, 1996), *aff'd sub nom. Teachers' Retirement Sys. v. Welch*, 244 A.D.2d 231, 664 N.Y.S.2d 38 (N.Y. App. Div. 1st Dep't 1997).

Replace the Teachers' Retirement citation in footnote 179 on page 145 with the following:

No. 113271/94 (N.Y. Sup. Ct. N.Y. Co. Apr. 16, 1996), *aff'd sub nom. Teachers' Retirement Sys. v. Welch*, 244 A.D.2d 231, 664 N.Y.S.2d 38 (N.Y. App. Div. 1st Dep't 1997).

Section A 4 c

Replace "1998" with "2001" in the Balotti citation in footnote 215 on page 151.

Replace "4–219-24" with "4–219-30.1" in the Balotti citation in footnote 217 on page 151.

Add the following at the end of the paragraph beginning and concluding on page 152 (immediately after footnote 224):

The Delaware Court of Chancery's decision in *Apple Computer, Inc. v. Exponential Technology, Inc.*, 1999 Del. Ch. LEXIS 9, 1999 WL 39547 (Del. Ch. Jan. 21, 1999), involved a motion to dismiss a duty of care claim asserted in a case where Apple Computer, Inc., the largest shareholder and biggest customer of Exponential Technology, Inc., challenged Exponential's sale of patents for $10 million to obtain funds to pay creditors and finance a $50 million lawsuit by Exponential against Apple Computer in California. The lawsuit in California alleged that Apple Computer had forced Exponential out of business by breach of contract, breach of fiduciary duty, and intentional and negligent interference with contractual relations and prospective economic advantage. 1999 Del. Ch. LEXIS 9, at *4-8, 1999 WL 39547, at *1-2. According to Apple Computer, the $10 million sale of the patents constituted the sale of "all or substantially all" of the corporation's assets because these patents were Exponential's most valuable asset and the sale precluded Exponential from continuing in the central processing unit ("CPU") design business. In Apple Computer's view, this was "a watershed event that fundamentally altered Exponential's business mission from designing CPUs to litigating the California Action." 1999 Del. Ch. LEXIS 9, at *20-21, 1999 WL 39547, at *5. The court concluded that these allegations, if proven at trial, would establish a sale of "all or substantially all" of Exponential's assets. Under Section 271 of the Delaware General Corporation Law, a sale of "all or substantially all" of a corporation's assets requires shareholder approval. 1999 Del. Ch. LEXIS 9, at *19-21, 1999 WL 39547, at *5.

The court held that Apple Computer alleged facts that, if true, would show that "Exponential completely failed to even attempt to comply with its statutory obligation to seek shareholder approval under § 271" and that "[i]f true, this allegation constitutes gross negligence." 1999 Del. Ch. LEXIS 9, at *25, 1999 WL 39547, at *7. The court noted that "[i]f a board's uninformed, hasty approval of a merger constitutes gross negligence in breach of its duty of care . . . , it follows that a failure to hold a shareholder vote under § 271 . . . would constitute gross negligence in violation of the board's duty of care under that statute." 1999 Del. Ch. LEXIS 9, at *26 n.30, 1999 WL 39547, at *7 n.30.

Section A 4 d

Add the following at the end of footnote 284 on page 163:

See also Bomarko, Inc. v. Int'l Telecharge, Inc., 1999 Del. Ch. LEXIS 211, at *54, 1999 WL 1022083, at *19 (Del. Ch. Nov. 4, 1999) (concluding that while "an overwhelming vote in favor of a transaction is evidence of fair dealing," there is "no logical force" to the contention that receipt of "only a bare majority of the stockholder vote is evidence of . . . unfairness"; the court added that "it is hard to see how compliance with a statutory mandate could ever be part of a showing of unfairness"), *aff'd on other grounds*, 766 A.2d 437 (Del. 2000).

Section A 4 e

Replace the Model Act § 8.31 citation in footnote 306 on page 168 with the following:

2 Model Bus. Corp. Act Annotated § 8.31 Official Comment at 8-204 (3d ed. Supp. 1998/99).

Add the following at the end of the first sentence in footnote 337 on page 172:

An additional case refusing to grant a motion to dismiss allegations of a lack of due care is *McMullin v. Beran*, 765 A.2d 910, 921-22 (Del. 2000); *cf. Apple Computer, Inc. v. Exponential Tech., Inc.*, 1999 Del. Ch. LEXIS 9, at *25, 30, 1999 WL 39547, at *7, 8 (Del. Ch. Jan. 21, 1999) (finding that allegations of a lack of due care were sufficiently pleaded, as discussed in Section A 4 c, but that the directors who had breached their duty of care were protected by a certificate of incorporation provision adopted pursuant to Section 102(b)(7) of the Delaware General Corporation Law, discussed in Chapter II, Section A 7).

Add the following at the end of the paragraph beginning on page 171 and concluding on page 172 (immediately after footnote 337):

Liability also was found in *Turner v. Bernstein*, 2000 Del. Ch. LEXIS 96, 2000 WL 776893 (Del. Ch. June 6, 2000), where the directors of GenDerm Corporation failed to provide GenDerm shareholders with material information needed to make an informed decision with respect to whether to approve a merger of GenDerm into a wholly-owned subsidiary of Medicis Pharmaceutical Corporation and thus whether to accept the merger consideration offered or to seek appraisal. On a motion for summary judgment by plaintiffs, the court stated that the directors "defaulted on this obligation and did not even attempt to put together a disclosure containing any cogent recitation of the material facts pertinent to the stockholders' choice." 2000 Del. Ch. LEXIS 96, at *33, 2000 WL 776893, at *10. The court concluded that "[g]iven the absence of evidence that the defendant directors made any attempt to comply with their disclosure obligations, it is clear that a due care violation has been demonstrated even under the exacting gross negligence standard." 2000 Del. Ch. LEXIS 96, at *33, 2000 WL 776893, at *10. The court added that "[b]ecause such a violation will suffice to establish liability, there is no need for the plaintiffs to produce evidence that the failure of disclosure was purposeful or otherwise indicative of disloyalty." 2000 Del. Ch. LEXIS 96, at *33-34, 2000 WL 776893, at *10.

The court in *Nagy v. Bistricer*, 770 A.2d 43 (Del. Ch. 2000), followed *Turner* and granted a motion for summary judgment in a case where David Bistricer and Nachum Stein, the directors of Riblet Products Corporation, distributed an information circular to Ernest J. Nagy, the sole minority shareholder of Riblet, in connection with a merger of Riblet with Coleman Cable Acquisition, Inc. Both corporations were controlled by Bistricer and Stein, and the merger provided for payment to Riblet shareholders of a tentatively set number of shares of Coleman stock (this tentative number was subject to an upward or downward adjustment by Coleman based upon the advice of Coleman's investment banker). *Id.* at 46-47. The court reasoned as follows:

> The Information Circular contains NO information from which Nagy would have an idea of the value of Coleman Acquisition or Riblet. The Information Circular contains NO information

> regarding the reasons Bistricer and Stein supported the Merger as directors of Riblet, or the process that they used in coming to their decision to support the Merger. The Information Circular contains NO information regarding Bistricer's and Stein's interest in Coleman Acquisition.
>
> Information of this kind is self-evidently material to Nagy's decision whether to accept the merger consideration or to seek appraisal. The failure of Bistricer and Stein to provide Nagy with ANY information in these categories was a breach of their fiduciary duties.

Id. at 60. "At the very least, the total lack of attention they paid to their disclosure duties merits a finding of gross negligence." *Id.*

Section A 4 f

Add the following at the end of the paragraph beginning and concluding on page 179 (immediately after footnote 369):

An additional case where there has been a finding of a lack of due care for the purpose of granting an injunction, *Chesapeake Corp. v. Shore*, 771 A.2d 293 (Del. Ch. 2000), is discussed in Chapter III, Section H 2 f-1. In another case discussed in Chapter III – *Phelps Dodge Corp. v. Cyprus Amax Minerals Co.*, 1999 Del. Ch. LEXIS 202, 1999 WL 1054255 (Del. Ch. Sept. 27, 1999) – the court found a reasonable probability of success on the merits of a lack of due care claim but denied a motion for a preliminary injunction due to the absence of irreparable harm. *See* Chapter III, Section D 7.

Section A 4 g

Add the following at the end of footnote 375 on page 180:

See also Crescent/Mach I Partners, L.P. v. Turner, 2000 Del. Ch. LEXIS 145, at *50-60, 2000 WL 1481002, at *13-16 (Del. Ch. Sept. 29, 2000); *Oliver v. Boston Univ.*, 2000 Del. Ch.

LEXIS 104, at *22, 2000 WL 1038197, at *7 (Del. Ch. July 18, 2000); *In re IXC Communications, Inc. S'holders Litig.*, 1999 Del. Ch. LEXIS 210, at *13-21, 1999 WL 1009174, at *5-7 (Del. Ch. Oct. 27, 1999); *In re 3COM Corp. S'holders Litig.*, 1999 Del. Ch. LEXIS 215, at *18-28, 1999 WL 1009210, at *5-8 (Del. Ch. Oct. 25, 1999); *Krim v. ProNet, Inc.*, 744 A.2d 523, 527-28 (Del. Ch. 1999); *Wittman v. Crooke*, 707 A.2d 422, 426 (Md. Ct. Spec. App. 1998).

Add the following at the end of footnote 377 on page 180:

See also State of Wis. Inv. Bd. v. Bartlett, 2000 Del. Ch. LEXIS 42, at *15-19, 2000 WL 238026, at *4-6 (Del. Ch. Feb. 24, 2000); *Am. Bus. Info., Inc. v. Faber*, No. 16265, Tr. at 123 (Del. Ch. Mar. 27, 1998), *interlocutory appeal refused*, 711 A.2d 1227 (unpublished opinion, text available at 1998 Del. LEXIS 137 and 1998 WL 188550) (Del. Apr. 2, 1998).

Add the following at the end of footnote 378 on page 180:

See also Federal Deposit Ins. Corp. v. Castetter, 184 F.3d 1040, 1043-46 (9th Cir. 1999); *Hills Stores Co. v. Bozic*, 769 A.2d 88, 109-10 (Del. Ch. 2000).

Add the following at the end of footnote 383 on page 184:

See also Castetter, 184 F.3d at 1045.

Add the following at the end of footnote 386 on page 185:

See also Crescent, 2000 Del. Ch. LEXIS 145, at *52-56, 2000 WL 1481002, at *14-15; *Wis. Inv. Bd.*, 2000 Del. Ch. LEXIS 42, at *16-17, 2000 WL 238026, at *5.

Add the following at the end of footnote 387 on page 186:

See also Castetter, 184 F.3d at 1045-46; *Chesapeake Corp. v. Shore*, 771 A.2d 293, 314, 334 (Del. Ch. 2000) (finding lack of due care where "impoverished deliberations were only once supplemented by expertise, and that consisted of less than five minutes of input").

Add the following at the end of footnote 390 on page 187:

See also *Chesapeake*, 771 A.2d at 314, 334 (finding lack of due care where no questions were asked).

Add the following at the end of footnote 395 on page 188:

See also Crescent, 2000 Del. Ch. LEXIS 145, at *53-54, 2000 WL 1481002, at *14 ("fairness opinions prepared by independent investments bankers are generally not essential, as a matter of law, to support an informed business judgment"); *Chesapeake*, 771 A.2d at 331 ("[t]here is no legal requirement that a board consult outside advisors, so long as the board has adequate information to make an informed judgment"); *In re Gaylord Container Corp. S'holders Litig.*, 753 A.2d 462, 479 n.57 (Del. Ch. 2000) ("I also reject as inadequate to generate a triable issue of fact the plaintiffs' assertion that the board needed to retain an investment bank in addition to [counsel]. . . . [T]he board felt that it was adequately positioned to make a judgment about the defensive measures based on the input of [counsel] and company management and using their own business acumen. . . . [T]he board was comprised of members with extensive managerial and board experience, as well as one member, Brown, who was an investment banker (and who testified that he discussed the measures during the two board meetings and during one or two conference calls with management), and another, Babb, who was a lawyer.").

Add the following at the end of footnote 398 on page 190:

See also Chesapeake, 771 A.2d at 305, 310 (finding lack of due care where board approved bylaw amendments without seeing the amendments).

Add the following at the end of footnote 402 on page 190:

See also Chesapeake, 771 A.2d at 305, 314 (finding lack of due care in case involving 30 and 45 minute meetings).

Add the following at the end of footnote 404 on page 190:

See also Chesapeake, 771 A.2d at 305, 314.

Add the following at the end of the paragraph beginning on page 189 and concluding on page 194 (immediately after footnote 411):

As the Delaware Supreme Court observed in *McMullin v. Beran*, 765 A.2d 910 (Del. 2000), "[t]he imposition of time constraints on a board's decision-making process may compromise the integrity of its deliberative process," and "[h]istory has demonstrated boards 'that have failed to exercise due care are frequently boards that have been rushed.'" *Id.* at 922 (quoting *Citron v. Fairchild Camera & Instrument Corp.*, 569 A.2d 53, 67 (Del. 1989)).

Replace "1998" with "2001" in the Balotti citation in footnote 412 on page 195.

Section A 5 a

Replace the first sentence (immediately after footnote 426, through the colon preceding the block quote) of the paragraph beginning on page 199 and concluding on page 200 with the following:

Sections 8.30(b) and (c) of the Model Business Corporation Act, as it existed until it was amended in 1998, are typical:

Replace the Model Act § 8.30 citation in footnote 427 on page 200 with the following:

Former Model Bus. Corp. Act §§ 8.30(b), (c).

Replace the first sentence (immediately after footnote 427, through the colon preceding the block quote) of the paragraph beginning on page 200 and concluding on page 201 with the following:

Section 8.30, as revised in 1998, reads as follows:

Replace the Model Act § 8.30 citation in footnote 428 on page 201 with the following:

2 Model Bus. Corp. Act Annotated §§ 8.30(d)-(f) (3d ed. Supp. 1998/99);

Add the following at the end of the paragraph beginning on page 201 and concluding on page 202 (immediately after footnote 434):

The Delaware Supreme Court in *Brehm v. Eisner*, 746 A.2d 244 (Del. 2000), stated that a board of directors "is entitled to the presumption that it exercised proper business judgment, including proper reliance on the expert." *Id.* at 261; *see also Ash v. McCall*, 2000 Del. Ch. LEXIS 144, at *31-32, 2000 WL 1370341, at *9 (Del. Ch. Sept. 15, 2000).

Replace the Model Act § 8.30 citation in footnote 437 on page 203 with the following:

Model Bus. Corp. Act § 8.30 Official Comment at 8-164.

Add the following at the end of footnote 438 on page 203:

See also Federal Deposit Ins. Corp. v. Castetter, 184 F.3d 1040, 1044-45 (9th Cir. 1999); *Koch v. Koch Indus., Inc.*, 37 F. Supp. 2d 1231, 1242 (D. Kan. 1998), *aff'd and rev'd on other grounds*, 203 F.3d 1202 (10th Cir.), *cert. denied*, 121 S. Ct. 302 (2000); *Brehm*, 746 A.2d at 261-62; *Crescent/Mach I*

Partners, L.P. v. Turner, 2000 Del. Ch. LEXIS 145, at *54-57, 2000 WL 1481002, at *15 (Del. Ch. Sept. 29, 2000); *In re W. Nat'l Corp. S'holders Litig.*, 2000 Del. Ch. LEXIS 82, at *77 & n.67, 2000 WL 710192, at *23 & n.67 (Del. Ch. May 22, 2000); *Hills Stores Co. v. Bozic*, 769 A.2d 88, 109 n.70 (Del. Ch. 2000); *In re Gaylord Container Corp. S'holders Litig.*, 753 A.2d 462, 479 (Del. Ch. 2000); *Camden v. Kaufman*, 613 N.W.2d 335, 341 (Mich. Ct. App. 2000).

Add the following at the end of footnote 439 on page 203:

See also Brehm, 746 A.2d at 261 n.51 (the right to rely "is not without limitation, as in a case of corporate waste").

Add the following at the end of footnote 475 on page 209:

See also Crescent/Mach I Partners, L.P. v. Turner, 2000 Del. Ch. LEXIS 145, at *52-54, 2000 WL 1481002, at *14 (Del. Ch. Sept. 29, 2000) (rejecting claim that reliance upon a nationally recognized investment banking firm, Donaldson, Lufkin & Jenrette Securities Corporation ("DLJ"), was grossly negligent conduct that deprived directors of the benefit of the business judgment rule because, plaintiffs alleged, "DLJ's opinion was influenced by its financial interest in the consummation of the merger" and the fact that a DLJ managing director, J. Kent Sweezey, served on the corporation's board; the court reasoned as follows: "[P]laintiffs provide nothing more than conclusory allegations that DLJ was motivated by personal interests. Rather, they suggest that the mere existence of Sweezey's affiliation with DLJ is enough to taint the process. This does not constitute a breach of the duty of care for the following reasons. First, DLJ was entitled to compensation for its efforts in consummating the merger transaction. There is nothing in the record to suggest that this compensation was excessive or extraordinary. Second, plaintiffs fail to plead any allegations that DLJ's or Sweezey's interest in the merger was not completely aligned with that of the stockholders in attempting to maximize the value of the interest of the corporation. Third, fairness opinions prepared by independent investment bankers are generally not essential, as a matter of law, to support an informed business judgment. Yet, the challenged directors obtained an evaluation of the $25 per share consideration offered by Cadbury and Carlyle from an investment banking firm and fully disclosed that fact in the proxy statement.") (footnote omitted); *In re Unocal Exploration Corp. S'holders Litig.*, 2000 Del. Ch. LEXIS 92, at *8 n.10, 2000 WL 823376, at *2 n.10 (Del. Ch. June 13, 2000) (rejecting claim that "PaineWebber's 'contingency fee' ($600,000 if it rendered an opinion or $150,000 if it did not) makes its work unreliable" because PaineWebber "would be paid the same $600,000 whether its opinion was favorable or not" and thus "[n]othing about the compensation arrangement compelled or gave PaineWebber a direct incentive to render a *favorable* opinion").

Add the following at the end of the paragraph beginning and concluding on page 209 (immediately after footnote 475):

The court in *Solomon v. Armstrong*, 747 A.2d 1098 (Del. Ch. 1999), *aff'd*, 746 A.2d 277 (unpublished opinion, full text available at 2000 Del. LEXIS 30 and 2000 WL 140072) (Del. Jan. 26, 2000), a case involving a negotiation between GM and its wholly-owned EDS subsidiary concerning the terms of a split-off by GM of EDS, granted a motion to dismiss in a case where plaintiffs challenged a fee structure providing for financial advisors chosen by GM to represent the EDS negotiating team to earn $6.5 million of a $7.5 million fee upon the completion of a transaction. The court held that this fee structure did not form a sufficient basis for an inference that these advisors "were willing to opine, or lean toward, better terms for GM during the negotiation of the transaction." *Id.* at 1119. The court reasoned that the GM board "independently decided that the split-off was in the best interest of the corporation – the advisors were simply employed to aid the directors (at least indirectly through the use of the negotiating teams) in obtaining all reasonably available information and to better estimate the value attributable to each of the GM operations." *Id.* The court pointed to the absence of allegations other than the fee structure that these financial advisors "erred in their underlying analyses or mislead the board or its agents." *Id.* The court stated that "[n]o basis exists for *assuming* wrongdoing on the banks' part (and by implication the board's part) without allegations of an actual manifestation of bias in favor of GM through the investment banks' manipulation of financial information." *Id.*

The court in *Wittman v. Crooke*, 707 A.2d 422 (Md. Ct. Spec. App. 1998), rejected a claim that directors breached their duty of care by relying upon advice from a financial advisor that plaintiff contended had a financial interest in a challenged merger because the advisor stood to earn $8.5 million more by recommending the merger than by advising against the merger. The court stated its agreement with the trial court's statement that "to say that they just [approved the merger] because they want to make 8 million dollars, well, there has to be more than that. That's a conclusion that is not supported by facts. And I don't think that is a fair inference to draw under these circumstances." *Id.* at 426.

Add the following at the end the paragraph beginning on page 210 and concluding on page 211 (immediately after footnote 485):

The court in *In re Gaylord Container Corp. Shareholders Litigation*, 753 A.2d 462 (Del. Ch. 2000), rejected a contention that a board consisting of a chief executive officer and ten disinterested and independent outside directors could not rely upon the corporation's long-standing outside law firm in the context of the adoption of defensive measures because, plaintiffs contended, counsel was "beholden" to the chief executive officer. The court stated that it has "no doubt" that counsel was "appropriately loyal" to the chief executive officer as a client but it was "not clear why I should infer" that counsel "would tilt its advice" to help the chief executive officer "if that meant alienating the other ten directors." *Id.* at 465, 479 n.57. The court stated that "it would be unusual to require a board dominated by independent directors to retain special counsel simply because company counsel of long-standing had a traditional lawyer-client relationship with the company's CEO." *Id.* at 479 n.57.

Add the following at the end of the paragraph beginning and concluding on page 211 (immediately after footnote 487):

Directors also may rely upon fairness opinions from financial advisors rendered as of the date a transaction such as a merger is approved by the directors without also obtaining a "full bring-down opinion" on the date the transaction is completed so long as "changes between the date of a fairness opinion and the date of merger completion" are not "so great as to render an earlier fairness opinion unreliable." *In re Unocal Exploration Corp. S'holders Litig.*, 2000 Del. Ch. LEXIS 92, at *58-59, 2000 WL 823376, at *15 (Del. Ch. June 13, 2000).

Add the following at the end of the paragraph beginning and concluding on page 214 (immediately after footnote 504):

Of course, "no board is obligated to heed the counsel of any of its advisors." *In re IXC Communications, Inc. S'holders Litig.*, 1999 Del. Ch. LEXIS 210, at *16, 1999 WL 1009174, at *6 (Del. Ch. Oct. 27, 1999). Otherwise, a court would "simply substitute[ ] advice from Morgan Stanley or Merrill Lynch for the business judgment of the board charged with ultimate responsibility for deciding the best interests of the shareholders." *Id.*

Section A 5 b

Add the following at the end of footnote 506 on page 215:

See also Schoonejongen v. Curtiss-Wright Corp., 143 F.3d 120, 127 (3d Cir. 1998) ("unless otherwise provided by the certificate of corporation and subject to the limitations set forth in 8 Del. Code Ann. § 141(c), the board may freely delegate the authority to manage the business and affairs of the corporation").

Add the following at the end of footnote 507 on page 215:

See also William B. Chandler III, *The Legal Framework for Analyzing Audit Committee Oversight*, The Corporate Governance Advisor, Jan./Feb. 2000, at 18 ("Although directors ultimately are responsible for a corporation's day-to-day management, most decisions do not require the board's attention. Thus, under Delaware's statutory regime, while Section 141(a) empowers a board to manage the corporation, it also authorizes directors to delegate management of day-to-day operations to corporate officers."); *Curtiss*-Wright, 143 F.3d at 127 ("the ability to delegate is the essence of corporate management, as the law does not expect the board to fully immerse itself in the daily complexities of corporate operation").

Replace the Model Act § 8.30 citation in footnote 508 on page 216 with the following:

2 Model Bus. Corp. Act Annotated § 8.30 Official Comment at 8-170 (3d ed. Supp. 1998/99).

Add the following at the end of the paragraph beginning on page 215 and concluding on page 216 (immediately after footnote 509):

"Directors of Delaware corporations quite properly *delegate* responsibility to qualified experts in a host of circumstances." *Ash v. McCall*, 2000 Del. Ch. LEXIS 144, at *30, 2000 WL 1370341, at *9 (Del. Ch. Sept. 15, 2000); *see also* 2000 Del. Ch. LEXIS 144, at *30-31, 2000 WL 1370341, at *9 (adding that "[o]ne circumstance is surely due diligence review of a target company's books and records").

Add the following at the end of the second sentence (immediately after footnote 520) of the paragraph beginning on page 217 and concluding on page 218:

Thus, "[t]he board may not either formally or effectively abdicate its statutory power and its fiduciary duty to manage or direct the management of the business and affairs of th[e] corporation." *Grimes v. Donald*, 1995 Del. Ch. LEXIS 3, at *27, 1995 WL 54441, at *9 (Del. Ch. Jan. 11, 1995), *aff'd*, 673 A.2d 1207 (Del. 1996), *quoted in Quickturn Design Sys., Inc. v. Shapiro*, 721 A.2d 1281, 1292 n.43 (Del. 1998). Accordingly, "[t]o the extent that a contract, or a provision thereof, purports to require a board to act *or not act* in such a fashion as to limit the exercise of fiduciary duties, it is invalid and unenforceable." *Quickturn*, 721 A.2d at 1292 (quoting *Paramount Communications, Inc. v. QVC Network, Inc.*, 637 A.2d 34, 51 (Del. 1994)) (emphasis added by court in *Quickturn*).

Add the following at the end of the third sentence (immediately after footnote 523) of the paragraph beginning and concluding on page 218:

The court stated that an action that "tends to limit in a substantial way the freedom of [newly elected] director decisions on matters of management policy . . . violates the duty of each [newly elected] director to exercise his own best judgment on matters coming before the board." *Abercrombie v. Davies*, 123 A.2d 893, 899 (Del. Ch. 1956), *rev'd on other grounds*, 130 A.2d 338 (Del. 1957), *quoted in Quickturn*, 721 A.2d at 1292.

Add the following at the end of the paragraph beginning and concluding on page 218 (immediately after footnote 525):

Nagy v. Bistricer, 770 A.2d 43 (Del. Ch. 2000), provides a third example. There, the two directors of Riblet Product

Corporation, who owned 85 percent of the corporation's stock, entered into a merger agreement with Coleman Cable Acquisition, Inc., which these two directors also controlled. The exchange rate was tentatively set, subject to an upward or downward adjustment by the Coleman board based upon the advice of investment bankers. *Id.* at 46. In the court's words: "Bistricer and Stein negotiated a Merger Agreement that enabled the board of the acquiring corporation to adjust the merger agreement upward or downward in its discretion. Although that discretion was loosely tethered to the advice of an investment bank, that bank itself was one that Coleman Acquisition could unilaterally select." *Id.* at 61. The court held that "Bistricer and Stein essentially abdicated their duty to determine a fair merger price to the Coleman Acquisition board" and that "[t]his abdication is inconsistent with the Riblet board's non-delegable duty to approve the Merger only if the Merger was in the best interests of Riblet and its stockholders." *Id.* at 62. The court asked the following question: "If a director cannot negotiate a merger agreement with a firm price without an adequate basis to believe it to be fair, how can a director support a merger agreement that gives the buyer with whom the director's corporation is supposedly negotiating at arm's length the right to set the final price?" *Id.* at 62 n.50.

Add the following at the end of the paragraph beginning on page 220 and concluding on page 221 (immediately after footnote 539):

The Delaware Supreme Court in *McMullin v. Beran*, 765 A.2d 910 (Del. 2000), held that an improper delegation claim was stated in a suit alleging that Atlantic Richfield Company ("ARCO"), the owner of 80 percent of the shares of ARCO Chemical Company ("Chemical"), "unilaterally initiated, structured and negotiated" an acquisition by Lyondell Petrochemical Company of Chemical's shares at a price of $57.75 per share by means of a tender offer for all shares and a second-step merger at the same price, with ARCO obligated to tender its shares. *Id.* at 914-15. Plaintiff alleged that Chemical's board "made no determination of Chemical's entire value as a going concern before making" an "expedited decision to recommend approval of ARCO's proposed third-party Transaction with Lyondell." *Id.* at 924-25. The court held that Chemical's board "could properly rely on the majority shareholder to conduct preliminary negotiations" but stated that the board had the "ultimate" duty "to make an informed and independent decision on whether to recommend approval of the third-party transaction with Lyondell to the minority shareholders" or to urge minority shareholders "to refrain from tendering their shares to Lyondell" and instead pursue "an appraisal action during the second step of the Transaction." *Id.* at 924. The court stated that "[o]ne can reasonably infer" from the alleged facts that "Chemical's minority shareholders might have received more than $57.75 cash in an appraisal proceeding, if the Chemical Directors had fulfilled their fiduciary duties to *ascertain* whether the proposed sale to Lyondell maximized value for all shareholders." *Id.* at 925.

Delete the comma immediately before footnote 540 and "by contrast," immediately after footnote 540 in the paragraph beginning on page 221 and concluding on page 222.

Add the following at the end of the first paragraph beginning and concluding on page 224 (immediately after footnote 557):

The court in *State of Wisconsin Investment Board v. Bartlett*, 2000 Del. Ch. LEXIS 42, 2000 WL 238026 (Del. Ch. Feb. 24, 2000), rejected an improper delegation claim in a case involving a merger between Medco Research Inc. and King Pharmaceuticals, Inc. Plaintiff alleged that Medco's directors abdicated their fiduciary duties by permitting Richard Williams, the chairman of Medco's board and who also held 30,000 options to purchase Medco shares, to negotiate the merger with limited participation from other directors after the board had agreed (at the start of the negotiations) that Williams would receive 0.75 percent of the aggregate value of the consideration to be paid to Medco in any strategic alliance involving Medco. 2000 Del. Ch. LEXIS 42, at *4-5 & n.1, 11 n.5, 13-14, 2000 WL 238026, at *1 & n.1, 4 n.5, 4. The court stated that Williams' interest was "aligned with that of the shareholders" because "[h]is stake rises with the value of the deal," and "[w]hile it may well be so that Williams would get nothing if no deal gets done he has every reason to attempt to negotiate the highest consideration possible for Medco's shareholders." 2000 Del. Ch. LEXIS 42, at *13, 2000 WL 238026, at *4. Under these circumstances, the court held that "the decision by the Medco board to delegate responsibility to Williams can only be regarded as a valid exercise of business judgment" because the record did not demonstrate "any self-interest or lack of independence on the part of the Medco board which caused them to delegate responsibility to Williams to negotiate the merger and to abandon any responsibility to review his work." 2000 Del. Ch. LEXIS 42, at *14, 2000 WL 238026, at *4. To the contrary, the court stated, "[w]hat the record actually shows is that: four of five directors had no economic interest in the outcome of the merger negotiations; they had no entrenchment motive," and there was "no evidence that Williams controlled any other directors through any power to affect their related or unrelated economic interests." *Id.*

The court in *Schoonejongen v. Curtiss-Wright Corp.*, 143 F.3d 120 (3d Cir. 1998), construing Delaware law, upheld a board decision to "delegate its authority to administer and amend" the corporation's retirement benefits plan. *Id.* at 127. The court explained that "[t]he business decision of appointing a corporate officer to manage retirement health benefits for the corporation does not have the effect of 'removing from directors in a very substantial way their duty to use their own best judgment on management matters.'" *Id.* (quoting *Abercrombie v. Davies*, 123 A.2d 893, 899 (Del. Ch. 1956), *rev'd on other grounds*, 130 A.2d 338 (Del. 1957)). The court added that "nothing in the record demonstrates that a delegation of authority in this context would 'formally preclude the ...

board from exercising its statutory powers and fulfilling its fiduciary duty.'" *Id.* (quoting *Grimes v. Donald*, 673 A.2d 1207, 1214 (Del. 1996)).

Section A 6

Add the following at the end of the paragraph beginning and concluding on page 225 (immediately after footnote 565):

As stated by the Court of Chancery in *Solomon v. Armstrong*, 747 A.2d 1098 (Del. Ch. 1999), *aff'd*, 746 A.2d 277 (unpublished opinion, full text available at 2000 Del. LEXIS 30 and 2000 WL 140072) (Del. Jan. 26, 2000), "breaches of the duty of care are voidable rather than void and can be entirely extinguished by informed shareholder ratification." *Id.* at 1114; *see also Harbor Fin. Partners v. Huizenga*, 751 A.2d 879, 890 & n.37 (Del. Ch. Nov. 1999) ("the effect of untainted stockholder approval of the Merger is to invoke the protection of the business judgment rule and to insulate the Merger from all attacks"); *Wittman v. Crooke*, 707 A.2d 422, 426 (Md. Ct. Spec. App. 1998) ("the stockholder vote ratified the transaction and therefore extinguished appellant's duty of care claim"). The court in *Solomon* also held that "when it comes to claiming the sufficiency of disclosure and the concomitant legal effect of shareholder ratification after full disclosure (e.g., claim extinguishment . . .) it is the defendant who bears the burden." 747 A.2d at 1128; *see also Harbor Fin.*, 751 A.2d at 890 n.36. The courts permit defendants to overcome this burden in the procedural context of a motion to dismiss due to "[t]he substantial difficulty of winning such a motion (the plaintiff is given the benefit of every doubt), the illogic of requiring the court and defendants to identify disclosure deficiencies not complained of by experienced plaintiffs' lawyers, and the interests of judicial economy." *Harbor Fin.*, 751 A.2d at 890 n.36.

Plaintiffs in *In re Santa Fe Pacific Corp. Shareholder Litigation*, [1995 Transfer Binder] Fed. Sec. L. Rep. (CCH)

¶ 98,845 (Del. Ch. May 31, 1995), *aff'd in part and rev'd in part*, 669 A.2d 59 (Del. 1995), did not appeal the Court of Chancery's dismissal of their duty of care claims, but in a decision on an appeal with respect to plaintiffs' duty of loyalty claims in the case, which the Court of Chancery had held were not extinguished by the shareholder vote (this aspect of the Court's decision is discussed in Chapter II, Section B 2 c), the Delaware Supreme Court held that the duty of loyalty claims had not been ratified by the shareholder vote. *In re Sante Fe Pac. Corp. S'holder Litig.*, 669 A.2d 59, 67-68 (Del. 1995). The Supreme Court relied upon two considerations that arguably apply to duty of care claims as well as duty of loyalty claims.

First, the court stated, the case involved claims challenging defensive measures, including the adoption of a poison pill shareholder rights plan and the use of no shop and break-up fee provisions in a merger agreement that allegedly favored the bidder with whom the merger agreement had been entered into over another bidder. Board action of this type, the court explained, is subject to "enhanced judicial scrutiny" under cases discussed in Chapter III, Sections A 2-4 such as *Unocal Corp. v. Mesa Petroleum Co.,* 493 A.2d 946 (Del. 1985), and *Revlon, Inc. v. MacAndrews & Forbes Holdings Inc.*, 506 A.2d 173 (Del. 1986). The court stated that "[p]ermitting the vote of a majority of stockholders on a merger to remove from judicial scrutiny unilateral Board action in a contest for corporate control would frustrate the purposes" underlying *Unocal* and *Revlon*. 669 A.2d at 68.

Second, the court stated, the shareholder vote was a vote in favor of a merger with a preferred bidder. The choice offered shareholders in the shareholder vote was a choice between approving that merger and doing nothing. Shareholders were not given an opportunity to vote specifically upon the defensive measures challenged in the litigation, including the adoption of a poison pill shareholder rights plan and the use of no shop and break-up fee provisions in a merger agreement that allegedly favored the bidder with whom the merger agreement had been entered into over another bidder, and that thus "allegedly already worked their effect before the stockholders had a chance to vote." *Id.* "Since the stockholders of Santa Fe merely voted in favor of the merger and not the defensive measures," the court concluded, "we decline to find ratification." *Id.*

The Court of Chancery in *In re Cencom Cable Income Partners, L.P. Litigation*, 2000 Del. Ch. LEXIS 90, 2000 WL 640676 (Del. Ch. May 5, 2000), followed *Santa Fe* on a motion for summary judgment in a case involving a vote by limited partners to approve a sales transaction that effectively terminated the limited partners' right to priority distributions, where the governing partnership agreement provision provided no authority for the partnership's general partners to terminate priority distributions before the termination of the partnership. The court rejected a claim by the general partner that the vote on the sales transaction constituted ratification of the general partner's authority to terminate priority distributions.

Under *Sante Fe*, the court in *Cencom* stated, "[r]atification can effectively occur only where the specific transaction is clearly delineated to the investor whose approval is sought and that approval has been put to a vote." 2000 Del. Ch. LEXIS 90, at *19, 2000 WL 640676, at *5. Here, the court explained, the general partner "never specifically proposed an amendment to the Partnership Agreement." 2000 Del. Ch. LEXIS 90, at *20, 2000 WL 640676, at *6. To the contrary, the general partner "simply structured a Sales Transaction that would suspend priority distributions on July 1, 1995 and sought the Limited Partners' approval of the terms of the Sales Transaction." *Id.* The court stated that "[l]ike the shareholders confronted by the defensive measures on which they had no vote in *Sante Fe*, the Limited Partners were not asked to approve the General Partner's unilateral decision to terminate priority distributions upon the effective date of sale; rather, they were only asked to approve the terms of the Sale Transaction as proposed in the Disclosure Statement." *Id.*

Accordingly, the court concluded, it was "unclear whether the reasonably prudent Limited Partner asked to approve the Sales Transaction would have understood that approval was tantamount to an amendment of the Partnership Agreement authorizing termination of priority distributions or ratification of the General Partner's actions in structuring a sales transaction that effectively terminated the Limited Partners' contractual right to priority distributions." 2000 Del. Ch. LEXIS 90, at *18, 2000 WL 640676, at *5. As a result, "I cannot now comfortably conclude that I know that the Limited Partners did 'consent' to the termination of their priority distributions as that term is defined in the Partnership Agreement." 2000 Del. Ch. LEXIS 90, at *20, 2000 WL 640676, at *6.

The Court of Chancery distinguished *Santa Fe* in *In re Lukens Inc. Shareholders Litigation*, 757 A.2d 720 (Del. Ch. 1999), a case involving a shareholder vote approving a merger agreement entered into by Lukens Inc. and Bethlehem Steel Corporation following a bidding contest for Lukens between Bethlehem and Allegheny Ludlum Corporation. Lukens and Bethlehem initially entered into a merger agreement providing that Bethlehem would pay Lukens shareholders a combination of cash and stock having a value of $25 per share. Allegheny then offered to pay Lukens shareholders $28 in cash per share. Bethlehem responded by raising its offer to cash and stock valued at $30 per share, and Lukens and Bethlehem entered into a revised merger agreement. *Id.* at 725-26.

Bethlehem and Allegheny then entered into "secret discussions" with each other and agreed that Bethlehem would acquire Lukens and sell Lukens' stainless steel operations to Allegheny. This agreement resulted in an end to the bidding for Lukens between Bethlehem and Allegheny. Plaintiffs alleged that Lukens' directors breached their fiduciary duties by allowing Bethlehem and Allegheny to "carve up" Lukens and by not refusing to go forward with any merger until they extracted "the complete value of Lukens from both Bethlehem and Allegheny." *Id.* at 726. According to plaintiffs, Lukens' shareholders received less than they would have received "had an open and fair sale process for Lukens taken place." *Id.* In other words, Lukens' directors "dropped the ball by failing to protect against the 'carve up.'" *Id.* at 738.

The court held that plaintiffs' allegations all were duty of care violations and that "[u]nlike the situation in *Santa Fe*, the proposition voted on by the Lukens stockholders fairly framed the question whether or not to ratify the job done by the Lukens directors in managing the bidding process." *Id.* at 737. The court stated that the Bethlehem-Allegheny carve up of Lukens "was well-known to the stockholders when they voted and was itself contingent on their approval of the Bethlehem merger proposal." *Id.* at 738. The court stated that "[i]n a very clear and real sense, the vote to approve the Bethlehem merger proposal represents a decision that it was better to approve that transaction (*notwithstanding* the known possibility that the 'carve up' deprived Lukens's stockholders of some incremental value) than to reject the $30 proposal and either 'do nothing' or remarket the Company in a way that prevented collusion among bidders." *Id.*

Unlike the situation in *Santa Fe*, the court held, "it would not 'frustrate the purposes underlying *Revlon* and *Unocal*' to '[p]ermit[ ] the vote of a majority of stockholders on a merger to remove from judicial scrutiny' this sort of duty of care based claim." *Id.* (quoting *Santa Fe*, 669 A.2d at 68). To the contrary, the court observed, "one is prompted to ask what purpose would be served by a rule that allowed the Lukens stockholders both to approve the $30 proposal (knowing of the 'carve up') and to maintain an action against their directors for failing to do better." *Id.* The court accordingly held that *Santa Fe* does not preclude a finding of ratification "where there was an active bidding process, no measures precluded any participant from bidding, and the merger agreement presented to stockholders represented the highest offer made by anyone." *Id.* at 737; *see also In re Gen. Motors Class H S'holders Litig.*, 734 A.2d 611, 617 (Del. Ch. 1999) (distinguishing *Santa Fe* on the ground that "this is not a case in which the defendants are attempting to use the stockholder vote to insulate themselves from responsibility for decisions not directly at issue in the vote").

Apple Computer, Inc. v. Exponential Technology, Inc., 1999 Del. Ch. LEXIS 9, 1999 WL 39547 (Del. Ch. Jan. 21, 1999), involved a motion to dismiss a duty of care claim asserted in a case where Apple Computer, Inc., the largest shareholder and biggest customer of Exponential Technology, Inc., challenged Exponential's sale of patents for $10 million to obtain funds to pay creditors and finance a $50 million lawsuit by Exponential against Apple Computer in California. The lawsuit in California alleged that Apple Computer had forced Exponential out of business by breach of contract, breach of fiduciary duty, and intentional and negligent interference with contractual relations and prospective economic advantage. 1999 Del. Ch. LEXIS 9, at *4-8, 1999 WL 39547, at *1-2. According to Apple Computer, the $10 million sale of the patents constituted the sale of "all or substantially all" of Exponential's assets because these patents were Exponential's most valuable asset, and the sale precluded Exponential from continuing in the central processing unit ("CPU") design business. In Apple Computer's view, this was "a watershed event that fundamentally altered Exponential's business mission from designing CPUs to litigating the California Action." 1999 Del. Ch. LEXIS 9, at *20-21, 1999 WL 39547, at *5.

Apple Computer alleged that Exponential's directors violated Section 271 of the Delaware General Corporation Law, which requires shareholder approval of a sale of "all or substantially all" of a corporation's assets, and breached their fiduciary duties by failing to comply with Section 271. The court held that a post-transaction ratification of the patent sale by Exponential's shareholders after the litigation had been commenced could moot Apple Computer's Section 271 and breach of fiduciary duty claims. The court explained that Apple Computer alleged a violation of the duty of care and no "selfish acts" that "implicated the duty of loyalty"; rather, "Exponential unintentionally, and in good faith, sold the patent portfolio without seeking shareholder approval." 1999 Del. Ch. LEXIS

9, at *24, 1999 WL 39547, at *6. The court stated that "Exponential's conduct, because it was not in bad faith, constitutes a voidable, not a void act." 1999 Del. Ch. LEXIS 9, at *25, 1999 WL 39547, at *7. Thus, the court held, subsequent ratification of the patent sales would invoke judicial review under the business judgment rule. 1999 Del. Ch. LEXIS 9, at *27, 1999 WL 39547, at *7.

The court described this conclusion as "particularly apt here because the harm alleged by Apple was precisely the *opportunity* to vote on the patent sale." 1999 Del. Ch. LEXIS 9, at *27, 1999 WL 39547, at *7. The court accordingly held that "[a]ssuming § 271 was triggered, but overlooked, the ratification vote itself goes a long way in remedying the harm incurred by the erstwhile disenfranchised shareholders. Thus, I conclude that Exponential's board has already taken the step most appropriate to cure the injury alleged by Apple." *Id.*

The court, however, did not dismiss the case on this basis due to a dispute concerning the ratification vote created by the fact that some of Exponential's shareholders failed to date their consents. Exponential contended that the undated consents should be treated as valid because the requirement that consents be dated in Section 228(c) of the Delaware General Corporation Law is intended to facilitate enforcement of the 60 day time limit provided for in Section 228(c) for returning consents, and here, according to Exponential, there was "no possibility that the sixty-day limit was not fulfilled." 1999 Del. Ch. LEXIS 9, at *28, 1999 WL 39547, at *7. The court deferred a decision concerning whether the undated consents should be treated as valid until a record was developed on this issue and briefing was completed concerning "the legal implications of § 228(c)'s date requirement within the context of *ex post* shareholder ratification." 1999 Del. Ch. LEXIS 9, at *29, 1999 WL 39547, at *7.

Add ",it has been said," between "because" and "'a transaction . . . '" in the first sentence of the paragraph beginning on page 225 and concluding on page 226.

Add the following at the end of footnote 566 on page 225:

See also Harbor Fin., 751 A.2d at 890 & n.37; *Solomon*, 747 A.2d at 1114 & n.46.

Delete ", it has been said," in the second sentence of the paragraph beginning on page 225 and concluding on page 226.

Add the following at the end of the paragraph beginning on page 225 and concluding on page 226 (immediately after footnote 567):

The Court of Chancery in *Harbor Finance Partners v. Huizenga*, 751 A.2d 879 (Del. Ch. 1999), questioned the rule requiring a unanimous shareholder vote (rather than a majority shareholder vote) to ratify waste on the ground that "its actual application has no apparent modern day utility . . . except as an opportunity for Delaware courts to second-guess stockholders." *Id.* at 897. The court rejected the view that "a transaction that satisfies the high standard of waste constitutes a *gift* of corporate property and no one should be forced against their will to make a gift of their property" as "inadequate" to justify the rule requiring unanimous shareholder approval in order to ratify waste because "property of the corporation is not typically thought of as personal property of the stockholders" and "it is common for corporations to undertake important value-affecting transactions over the objection of some of the voters or without a vote at all." *Id.* at 899-900.

The court pointed to several additional bases for questioning the rule requiring a unanimous shareholder vote to ratify waste.

First, the court stated, the origin of this rule is rooted in the distinction between voidable and void acts: "[v]oidable acts are traditionally held to be ratifiable because the corporation can lawfully accomplish them if it does so in the appropriate manner" and "[t]hus if directors who could not lawfully effect a transaction without stockholder approval did so anyway, and the requisite approval of the stockholders was later attained, the transaction is deemed fully ratified because the subsequent approval of the stockholders cured the defect"; "void acts are said to be non-ratifiable because the corporation cannot, in any case, lawfully accomplish them." *Id.* at 896. The court stated that "[s]uch void acts are often described in conclusory terms as '*ultra vires*' or 'fraudulent' or as 'gifts or waste of corporate assets.'" *Id.* The court explained that "it is unsurprising that it has been held that stockholders cannot validate such action by the directors, even on an informed basis" because "at first blush it seems it would be a shocking, if not theoretically impossible, thing for stockholders to be able to sanction the directors in committing illegal acts or acts beyond the authority of the corporation." *Id.* "[T]he types of 'void' acts susceptible to being styled as waste claims," the court continued, however, "have little of the flavor of patent illegality about them, nor are they categorically *ultra vires*" – a doctrine that rests "on notions about corporations which originated at a time when corporations were created by special act and largely for public purposes for the exercise of special franchises" and that "statutory and case law changes . . . have essentially whittled the doctrine down to nothing." *Id.* at 897 & n.62.

"Put another way," the court continued, "the oft-stated proposition that 'waste cannot be ratified' is a tautology that, upon close examination, has little substantive meaning." *Id.* at 897. The court asked "what rational person would ratify 'waste'?," and stated that "the answer is, of course, no one." *Id.* To the contrary, "real world stockholders are not asked to ratify obviously wasteful transactions"; rather, the transactions that have been attacked as waste in Delaware courts "are ones that are quite ordinary in the modern business world," including "stock option plans; the fee agreement between a mutual fund and its investment advisor; corporate mergers; the purchase of a business in the same industry as the acquiring corporation; and the repurchase of a corporate insider's shares in the company." *Id.* (footnotes citing cases omitted). The court described these as "all garden variety transactions that may be validly accomplished by a Delaware corporation if supported by sufficient consideration, and what is sufficient consideration is a question that fully informed stockholders seem as well positioned as courts to answer." *Id.* These transactions, the court stated, "are neither *per se ultra vires* or illegal; they only become 'void' upon a determination that the corporation received no fair consideration for entering upon them." *Id.*

Second, the court stated, the rule requiring unanimous shareholder approval in order to ratify conduct alleged to constitute waste "is not necessary to protect stockholders and it has no other apparent purpose." *Id.* The court acknowledged that "I would hesitate to permit stockholders to ratify a blatantly illegal act – such as a board's decision to indemnify itself against personal liability for intentionally violating applicable environmental laws or bribing government officials to benefit the corporation." *Id.* at 898. The court, however, stated that not permitting stockholders to ratify waste "has little to do with corporate integrity in the sense of the corporation's responsibility to society as a whole." *Id.* Accordingly, the justification for not allowing a majority of shareholders to ratify waste must be to protect stockholders but "where disinterested stockholders are given the information necessary to decide whether a transaction is beneficial to the corporation or wasteful to it, I see little reason to leave the door open for a judicial reconsideration of the matter." *Id.*

The court pointed to "[t]he fact that a plaintiff can challenge the adequacy of the disclosure" as "in itself a substantial safeguard against stockholder approval of waste" because "[i]f the corporate board failed to provide the voters with material information undermining the integrity or financial fairness of the transaction subject to the vote, no ratification effect will be accorded to the vote." *Id.* As a result, the court stated, "it is difficult to imagine how elimination of the waste vestige will permit the accomplishment of unconscionable corporate transactions, unless one presumes that stockholders are, as a class, irrational and that they will rubber stamp outrageous transactions contrary to their own economic interests." *Id.* at 899.

The court also pointed to the fact that "[t]he burden to prove that the vote was fair, uncoerced, and fully informed falls squarely on the board" and the fact that "Delaware law imposes no heightened pleading standards on plaintiffs alleging material nondisclosures or voting coercion" and "the pro-plaintiff bias inherent in Rule 12(b)(6)." *Id.* Accordingly, "it is difficult for a board to prove ratification at the pleading stage," and, "[i]f the board cannot prevail on a motion to dismiss," then the directors must "submit to discovery and possibly to a trial." *Id.* For all these reasons, the court stated, "Delaware law does not make it easy for a board of directors to obtain 'ratification effect' from a stockholder vote." *Id.*

The rule requiring unanimous shareholder approval in order to ratify conduct alleged to constitute waste, the court continued, also is not "necessary to protect minority stockholders from oppression by majority or controlling stockholders." *Id.* The court reasoned that "a corporation with a controlling or majority stockholder may, under current Delaware law, never escape the exacting entire fairness standard through a stockholder vote, even one expressly conditioned on approval by a 'majority of the minority,'" because "our law limits an otherwise fully informed, uncoerced vote in such circumstances to having the effect of making the plaintiffs prove that the transaction was unfair." *Id.* at 900-01. "[D]efendants appreciate this shift, but it still subjects them to a proceeding in which the substantive fairness of their actions comes under close scrutiny by the court – the type of scrutiny that is inappropriate when the business judgment rule's presumption attaches to a decision." *Id.* at 901; *see also* Chapter II, Section C 3 h-k (discussing this principle).

Third, the court stated, "I find it logically difficult to conceptualize how a plaintiff can ultimately prove a waste or gift claim in the face of a decision by fully informed, uncoerced, independent stockholders to ratify the transaction." 751 A.2d at 901. The court explained that "[t]he test for waste is whether any person of ordinary sound business judgment could view the transaction as fair" and "[i]f fully informed, uncoerced, independent stockholders have approved the transaction, they have, it seems to me, made the decision that the transaction is 'a fair exchange.'" *Id.* (quoting *Michelson v. Duncan*, 407 A.2d 211, 224 (Del. 1979)).

According to the court, "it is difficult to see the utility of allowing litigation to proceed in which the plaintiffs are permitted discovery and a possible trial, at great expense to the corporate defendants, in order to prove to the court that the transaction was so devoid of merit that each and every one of the voters comprising the majority must be disregarded as too hopelessly misguided to be considered a 'person of ordinary sound business judgment.'" *Id.* (quoting *Michelson*, 407 A.2d at 224). The court added that "[i]n this day and age in which investors also have access to an abundance of information about corporate transactions from sources other than boards of directors, it seems presumptuous and paternalistic to assume that the court knows better in a particular instance than a fully informed corporate electorate with real money riding on the corporation's performance." *Id.*

Fourth, the court stated, "it is unclear why it is in the best interests of disinterested stockholders to subject their corporation to the substantial costs of litigation in a situation where they have approved the transaction under attack." *Id.* The court stated that "[e]nabling a dissident who failed to get her way at the ballot box in a fair election to divert the corporation's resources to defending her claim on the battlefield of litigation seems, if anything, contrary to the economic well-being of the disinterested stockholders as a class." *Id.* The court asked "[w]hy should the law give the dissenters the right to command the corporate treasury over the contrary will of a majority of the disinterested stockholders?" *Id.*

"For all of these reasons," the court concluded, a "re-examination of the waste vestige would seem to be in order." *Id.* at 902. The court acknowledged that "there may be valid reasons for its continuation" but stated that "those reasons should be articulated and weighed against the costs the vestige imposes on stockholders and the judicial system." *Id.* "Otherwise, inertia alone may perpetuate an outdated rule fashioned in a very different time." *Id.*

Section A 7

Add the following at the end of footnote 571 on page 227:

See also McMullin v. Beran, 765 A.2d 910, 926 (Del. 2000) (Section 102(b)(7) provisions "cannot provide protection for directors who breach their duty of loyalty").

Add the following at the end of the second sentence (immediately after footnote 571) of the paragraph beginning on page 226 and concluding on page 227:

It has been said that "[m]ost of the statute's exceptions simply iterate particular examples of breaches of the duty of loyalty" because "conduct not in good faith, intentional misconduct, and knowing violations of law" are "quintessential examples of disloyal, i.e., faithless, conduct." *McMillan v. Intercargo Corp.*, 768 A.2d 492, 501 n.41 (Del. Ch. 2000); *see also Grace Bros., Ltd. v. UniHolding Corp.*, 2000 Del. Ch. LEXIS 101, at *35 n.27, 2000 WL 982401, at *11 n.27 (Del. Ch. July 12, 2000) ("The pertinent exceptions in § 102(b)(7) relating to unlawful actions and actions taken in bad faith are quite obvious examples of disloyal acts. Arguably, the improper personal benefits provision of § 102(b)(7)(iv) could be seen as preventing a director from benefiting from his own gross negligence in the context of a self-dealing transaction, but this, too, can properly be seen as raising loyalty concerns, given that it involves a fiduciary who has personally benefited from his own lack of care at the expense of the beneficiaries of his service.").

Add the following at the end of footnote 576 on page 228:

See also Goodwin v. Live Entm't, Inc., 1999 Del. Ch. LEXIS 5, at *76 n.17, 1999 WL 64265, at *24 n.17 (Del. Ch. Jan. 22, 1999), *aff'd*, 741 A.2d 16 (unpublished opinion, text available at 1999 Del. LEXIS 238 and 1999 WL 624128) (Del. July 23, 1999) ("[w]here a corporate electorate has adopted an exculpatory charter provision, it has presumably decided that it prefers a board more insulated from liability either because the board's insulation from negligence claims may lead it to undertake potentially profitable but riskier transactions that it might otherwise eschew or because the company will be able to attract better directors to serve on the board").

Add the following at the end of footnote 582 on page 229:

Cf. Harhen v. Brown, 710 N.E.2d 224, 238 (Mass. App. Ct. 1999), *rev'd on other grounds*, 730 N.E.2d 859 (Mass. 2000) (exculpatory provision adopted pursuant to Massachusetts law held inapplicable to the extent that claims against defendants who were both directors and officers "arise out of the alleged failure of their performance as officers and members of the management committee" because "[t]he fact that these defendants are also directors may be regarded as a mere happenstance").

Replace the paragraph beginning and concluding on page 229 and the paragraph beginning on page 229 and concluding on page 230 (including footnotes 584 through 589) with the following:

The protection provided by Section 102(b)(7) is limited to actions brought by "the corporation or its stockholders." Del.

Gen. Corp. Law § 102(b)(7). A federal bankruptcy court in Illinois construing Delaware law in *In re Ben Franklin Retail Stores, Inc.*, 225 B.R. 646 (Bankr. N.D. Ill. 1998), *aff'd on this ground and rev'd on other grounds*, 2000 U.S. Dist. LEXIS 276, 2000 WL 28266 (N.D. Ill. Jan. 12, 2000), has held that a Section 102(b)(7) charter provision does not shield directors from a breach of fiduciary duty claim by creditors because the protection provided by Section 102(b)(7) is limited to "the corporation or its stockholders" and makes no mention of creditors. *Id.* at 652. The court added the following:

> [S]hareholders' elect directors; creditors do not. Creditors should not be bound by limitations on the scope of the duties of fiduciaries they had no part in selecting because, unlike shareholders, they cannot protect themselves by being careful in their selection of managers.
>
> More broadly, shareholders' investments in corporations are subject to the rights and limitations of the certificate of [in]corporation. Creditors' "investments" are not; they are subject to specific contracts. The Defendants' duties to creditors arose, if at all, to protect the value of those contract claims from diminution by reason of improper conduct. Those duties cannot be reduced by a provision in a certificate that forms no part of the creditors' contracts or the inducement for their "investments."

Id. The district court affirmed this ruling because "the provision explicitly states that '[a] director of the Corporation shall not be personally liable to the Corporation or its stockholders for monetary damages'" and "[n]o mention is made of the potential liability to creditors that directors may incur." 2000 U.S. Dist. LEXIS 276, at *23-24, 2000 WL 28266, at *8. Accordingly, the court concluded, "[n]othing in the exculpatory provision prevents suits brought by the creditors or those acting on their behalf." 2000 U.S. Dist. LEXIS 276, at *24, 2000 WL 28266, at *8.

Where only money damages are sought and the directors are immune from personal liability for due care violations, allegations of a lack of due care cannot be examined even "solely for purposes of determining whether the presumption of the business judgment rule has been rebutted" and whether "the burden shifts to the defendants directors to prove that the transaction was entirely fair to the plaintiff shareholder." *Goodwin*, 1999 Del. Ch. LEXIS 5, at *76 & n.17, 1999 WL 64265, at *24 & n.17; *see also* Chapter I, Sections C 1-4 (discussing business judgment rule presumption, the shareholder plaintiff's need to rebut this presumption, and the fairness standard that governs when the presumption is rebutted). To examine alleged due care violations even for this limited purpose "would gut § 102(b)(7) . . . by restoring many of the inhibitions to director risk-taking which existed prior to its enactment" because "[a] board might rightly fear that the chances for exposure to liability and for a court to upset its decisions would materially be enhanced if a breach of the duty of care – although not justifying a damage recovery itself – could produce a possibly outcome determinative shift of the burden of proof to the directors to demonstrate the 'entire fairness' of transactions they approve." 1999 Del. Ch. LEXIS 5, at *76 & n.17, 1999 WL 64265, at *24 & n.17. The court added that "if upon such a burden shift the defendants fail to demonstrate entire fairness solely because their own breaches of the duty of care resulted in, for example, an unfair price," there would be no remedy "if the transaction has been consummated and money damages are all that are at issue." *Id.*

Courts have rejected claims that a "knowing violation of the law" requires only that a director "have an awareness of the facts constituting a breach of fiduciary duty" and "not necessarily a subjective understanding that the Court would characterize those facts as a breach of fiduciary duty." *Frank v. Arnelle*, 1998 Del. Ch. LEXIS 176, at *40, 1998 WL 668649, at *10 (Del. Ch. Sept. 16, 1998), *aff'd*, 725 A.2d 441 (unpublished opinion, text available at 1999 Del. LEXIS 25 and 1999 WL 89284) (Del. Jan. 22, 1999). Thus, an "intentional decision" by directors to disseminate a proxy statement does not lead "ineluctably to a finding that they deliberately violated their disclosure obligations." *Arnold v. Soc'y for Savs. Bancorp, Inc. ("Arnold I")*, 650 A.2d 1270, 1288 n.35 (Del. 1994). Instead, there must be "affirmative proof that the director defendants knowingly or deliberately failed to disclose facts that *they knew were material.*" *Frank*, 1998 Del. Ch. LEXIS 176, at *41, 1998 WL 668649, at *10.

A frequently litigated issue involves the applicability of Section 102(b)(7) provisions to disclosure claims – a subject discussed later in this Chapter. *See* Chapter II, Section C. Where the disclosure claim involves a claim based upon a good faith omission of a material fact rather than a knowing failure to disclose a material fact, dismissal is required. *See, e.g.*, *Zirn v. VLI Corp. ("VLI II")*, 681 A.2d 1050, 1062 (Del. 1996); *Arnold I*, 650 A.2d at 1288 & n.36 ("the single disclosure violation which we have found was consistent only with a good faith omission"); *see also Cinerama, Inc. v. Technicolor, Inc.*, 663 A.2d 1156, 1163 n.9 (Del. 1995) ("a violation of the duty of disclosure is not necessarily a breach of the duty of loyalty"); *Lewis v. Vogelstein*, 699 A.2d 327, 330 n.5 (Del. Ch. 1997) (distinguishing between "(1) innocently incomplete or defective (including negligent omission) disclosure" and "(2) knowing attempts to manipulate shareholders through deliberately false or misleading disclosures"); Veasey, *The Defining Tension in Corporate Governance in America*, 52 Bus. Law. 393, 398 (1997) (a failure to disclose material information "could be fraud or a good-faith omission").

Accordingly, disclosure claims "allegedly due solely to the directors' lack of care, and not in any way motivated by bad faith, disloyalty or misconduct . . . can . . . be dismissed because of the presence of the § 102(b)(7) Provision." *In re Lukens Inc. S'holders Litig.*, 757 A.2d 720, 735 n.47 (Del. Ch. 1999). Likewise, where a complaint challenges a self-tender offer pursuant to which shares are repurchased to benefit the corporation rather than the corporation's directors, "alleged disclosure violations simply cannot implicate the duty of loyalty. Rather, they involve the directors' duty of care, which fits squarely within the protection of the Company's § 102(b)(7) provision." *Frank*, 1998 Del. Ch. LEXIS 176, at *39, 1998 WL 668649, at *10.

The same result was reached in *McMillan v. Intercargo Corp.*, 768 A.2d 492 (Del. Ch. 2000), where a complaint included a "conclusory allegation that the defendants breached their duty of disclosure in a 'bad faith and knowing manner'" but, the court concluded, "no facts pled in the complaint buttress that accusation." *Id.* at 507. The court held that "even if the complaint states a claim that there were material omissions from the proxy statement, it does not allege facts from which one can reasonably infer that any such omission resulted from more than a mistake about what should have been disclosed," and, "[a]s a result, the plaintiffs' disclosure claims shall be dismissed." *Id.; see also VLI II*, 681 A.2d at 1062; *Arnold I*, 650 A.2d at 1288; *In re Dataproducts Corp. S'holders Litig.*, [1991 Transfer Binder] Fed. Sec. L. Rep. (CCH) ¶ 96,227, at 91,183 (Del. Ch. Aug. 22, 1991) (each dismissing disclosure claims); *cf. Emerald Partners v. Berlin*, 726 A.2d 1215, 1223 (Del. 1999) (reversing dismissal pursuant to Section 102(b)(7) certificate provision where disclosure claims were not properly categorized as due care claims); *Zirn v. VLI Corp. ("VLI I")*, 621 A.2d 773, 783 (Del. 1993) (holding that a Section 102(b)(7) provision did not apply to a disclosure claim based upon equitable fraud), *subsequent proceedings*, *VLI II*, 681 A.2d at 1052 n.7 (declining to follow *VLI I* on this issue because *VLI I* was decided "before the record here had been fully developed and before the developments in the law represented by *Arnold*"); *In re Wheelabrator Techs. Inc. S'holders Litig.*, 18 Del. J. Corp. L. 778, 802 n.18 (Del Ch. Sept. 1, 1992) (Section 102(b)(7) provision did not require dismissal where plaintiffs alleged that "the breach of the duty of disclosure was an intentional violation of the duty of loyalty").

Another frequently litigated issue is the extent to which a Section 102(b)(7) certificate provision may be raised as a defense in the context of a motion to dismiss. The Delaware Supreme Court's decision in *Emerald Partners v. Berlin*, 726 A.2d 1215 (Del. 1999), describes "the shield from liability provided by a certificate of incorporation provision adopted pursuant to 8 *Del. C.* § 102(b)(7)" as being "in the nature of an affirmative defense" and states that "[d]efendants seeking exculpation under such a provision will normally bear the burden of establishing each of its elements" – a burden the court in *Emerald Partners* stated may be "slight." *Id.* at 1223-24, *quoted in McMullin v. Beran*, 765 A.2d 910, 926 (Del. 2000). The Supreme Court then held that the Court of Chancery incorrectly had ruled that the plaintiff in the case "was required to establish *at trial* that the individual defendants acted in bad faith or in breach of their duty of loyalty." *Id.* at 1224.

Emerald Partners involved directors alleged to have "breached their fiduciary duties . . . of fair dealing and fair price" by approving a merger between corporations having the same chairman and chief executive officers – claims that the court stated were not properly categorized as due care claims. *Id.* at 1221-22. The concluding sentence of the paragraph of the decision describing a Section 102(b)(7) certificate provision as being "in the nature of an affirmative defense" and stating that directors seeking exculpation "normally bear the burden of establishing each of its elements" reads as follows: "Nonetheless, where the factual basis for a claim *solely* implicates a violation of the duty of care, this Court has indicated that the protections of such a charter provision may be properly invoked and applied." *Id.* at 1224.

Numerous decisions by the Court of Chancery – both before and after *Emerald Partners* – have held that motions to dismiss based upon certificate provisions adopted pursuant to Section 102(b)(7) may be granted notwithstanding the absence of any allegation in the complaint sought to be dismissed concerning these certificate provisions and notwithstanding the fact that a Section 102(b)(7) certificate provision is "in the nature of an affirmative defense" and the requirement that directors "normally bear the burden of establishing each of its elements." *Id.* at 1223-24. As illustrated by the cases discussed below, where there is no dispute that a director protection certificate provision has been adopted, the courts have taken judicial notice of the certificate provision on motions to dismiss and/or converted the motion to dismiss into a motion for summary judgment and decided the motion without discovery (or permitted discovery only concerning the adoption of the certificate provision). Directors protected by a Section 102(b)(7) certificate provision have not been required to endure discovery with respect to due care claims and await the summary judgment stage of the litigation or trial for a ruling concerning the applicability of the certificate provision. *Cf. Harhen v. Brown*, 710 N.E.2d 224, 238 (Mass. App. Ct. 1999), *rev'd on other grounds*, 730 N.E.2d 859 (Mass. 2000) (rejecting reliance on motion to dismiss based upon exculpatory provision adopted pursuant to Massachusetts law where "the record contains no secretary's certificate as to whether this exculpatory provision . . . was adopted as required").

Pre-Emerald Partners Decisions. The first decision to consider a motion to dismiss pursuant to a Section 102(b)(7) certificate provision, *In re Dataproducts Corp. Shareholders Litigation*, [1991 Transfer Binder] Fed. Sec. L. Rep. (CCH) ¶ 96,227 (Del. Ch. Aug. 22, 1991), involved a challenge by shareholders of Dataproducts Corporation to a merger that the corporation's directors had approved. *Id.* at 91,179-80. The directors moved to dismiss duty of care claims pursuant to a Section 102(b)(7) certificate provision, the parties stipulated that Dataproducts' certificate could be considered by the court on the motion to dismiss, and the court granted the motion. *Id.* at 91,180 n.1, 91,182-83.

Rothenberg v. Santa Fe Pacific Corp., 18 Del. J. Corp. L. 743 (Del. Ch. May 18, 1992), involved claims arising out of a decision by the directors of Santa Fe Pacific Corporation to lower the exchange value in an exchange offer for debentures even though some debenture holders already had tendered their debentures at the original, higher exchange value. *Id.* at 748-49, 752. Santa Fe's directors moved to dismiss duty of care claims pursuant to a Section 102(b)(7) certificate provision. Unlike the case in *Dataproducts*, the plaintiff in *Santa Fe* contended that Santa Fe's certificate of incorporation could not be considered on a motion to dismiss because the certificate provision was not referred to in the plaintiff's complaint. The court acknowledged that a Section 102(b)(7) provision is an affirmative defense but stated that in this case "no one disputes its substantive content." *Id.* at 752. Accordingly, even if the charter provision "could not be considered on the defendants' motion to dismiss under Rule 12(b)(6) (an issue that the Court need not decide), it may properly be considered on the defendants' separate dismissal motion grounded upon their affirmative defense(s)." *Id.* The court then reasoned as follows:

> Because Article TENTH is an affirmative defense, the defendants would normally shoulder the burden of establishing each of its elements, and the inapplicability of each of its four exceptions. . . . In this case, however, the Court determines that to the extent that the amended complaint states a claim for breach of the duty of care, Article TENTH is applicable, and its four exceptions are inapplicable, to that claim as a matter of law.
>
> Section 102(b)(7) permits a corporation, by so providing in its certificate of incorporation, "to protect its directors from monetary liability for duty of care violations, i.e., liability for gross negligence." Santa Fe has done that in Article TENTH, which (to repeat) is modeled on § 102(b)(7). Because the plaintiff undisputedly alleges in his complaint that Santa Fe's directors breached their duty of care, that claim is clearly covered by Article TENTH. . . . Because Article TENTH's exceptions track those set forth in § 102(b)(7), those exceptions are therefore inapplicable to the plaintiff's duty of care claim as a matter of law.

Id. at 752-53 (citations omitted).

Boeing Co. v. Shrontz, 18 Del. J. Corp. L. 225 (Del. Ch. Apr. 20, 1992), involved breach of fiduciary duty claims arising out of alleged oversight failures by the directors of Boeing Co., a defense contractor, in connection with illegal activity including the acquisition of classified documents and overcharging the government. *Id.* at 231-32. Boeing's directors moved to dismiss plaintiffs' duty of care claims pursuant to a Section 102(b)(7) certificate of incorporation provision. The court accepted plaintiff's contention that a Section 102(b)(7) certificate provision "constitutes an affirmative defense and is thus not properly before this Court on a motion to dismiss" and accordingly "defer[red] ruling" on the Section 102(b)(7) aspect of the motion to dismiss. *Id.* at 234. The court recognized, however, that plaintiff did not contest the legal effect of the certificate provision and stated that "a motion to dismiss may be converted into a motion for summary judgment" and allowed plaintiffs only "[v]ery limited discovery as to the steps taken to adopt" the certificate provision. *Id.*

In *In re Wheelabrator Technologies Inc. Shareholders Litigation*, 18 Del. J. Corp. L. 778 (Del Ch. Sept. 1, 1992), shareholders of Wheelabrator Technologies, Inc. challenged a merger between Wheelabrator and Waste Management, Inc. *Id.* at 784-86. Wheelabrator's directors sought to dismiss plaintiffs' duty of care claims based upon a Section 102(b)(7) provision in Wheelabrator's certificate of incorporation. Plaintiffs opposed the motion on the ground that the complaint did not plead or otherwise refer to the Section 102(b)(7) provision. The court held that the court could "judicially notice the contents of a certificate of incorporation of a Delaware corporation on a Rule 12(b)(6) dismissal motion." *Id.* at 800-01. The court relied upon Rule 201(b) of the Delaware Uniform Rules of Evidence, which states as follows:

> A judicially noticed fact must be one not subject to reasonable dispute in that it is either (1) generally known within the territorial jurisdiction of the trial court or (2) capable of accurate and ready determination by resort to sources whose accuracy cannot reasonably be questioned.

Id. at 801 (quoting Del. Unif. R. Evid. 201(b)).

The court held that "[t]he certificate of incorporation of a Delaware corporation falls within the ambit of that Rule" because "[b]y law it is filed with, and is obtainable by resort to, the office of the Secretary of State of Delaware. That office is located within the territorial jurisdiction of Delaware and is a source 'whose accuracy cannot reasonably be questioned.'" *Id.* at 801. The court stated that it was "not barred from taking judicial notice of a Delaware corporation's certificate of incorporation simply because the procedural setting is a motion to dismiss under Rule 12(b)(6)"; to the contrary, "[j]udicial notice may be taken at any stage of the proceeding." *Id.* The court then concluded as a matter of law that Wheelabrator's certificate provision "bars the plaintiffs' duty of care claim insofar as it seeks monetary damages against WTI's directors." *Id.* at 801-02.

Leslie v. Telephonics Office Technologies, Inc., 19 Del. J. Corp. L. 1237 (Del. Ch. Dec. 30, 1993), involved claims that the directors of Telephonics Office Technologies (1) "diverted income from the sale of corporate assets to their personal benefit, through a series of self-dealing transactions" that provided the directors "disproportionate personal consideration from the buyer of substantially all of the assets of Telephonics," and (2) did not "properly obtain shareholder concurrence in the sale as was allegedly required by the certificate of incorporation and by Section 271 of the General Corporation Law." *Id.* at 1240-41 The plaintiffs also alleged that "even assuming that the written consent of shareholders containing a majority of voting shares had been obtained . . . it was ineffective because [plaintiffs] were never informed of the transaction, pursuant to the requirements of Section 228." *Id.* at 1250.

Defendants moved to dismiss the duty of care allegations in the complaint based upon the corporation's Section 102(b)(7) certificate provision. The court rejected plaintiffs' contention that "since their complaint did not reference the provision, defendants cannot invoke it to support a motion to dismiss under Rule 12(b)(6)." *Id.* at 1254 n.16. The court explained that "[e]ven if this is so defendants' motion can be viewed as a summary judgment motion," and held that "any claim for compensatory damages stemming from a duty of care violation by the defendants would be barred by the 102(b)(7) provision." *Id.* at 1254 & n.16. The court, however, held that "the thrust of the complaint is that defendants embarked on an *intentional* scheme to siphon off the company's assets" and "to the extent plaintiffs seek equitable relief for any alleged breaches of the duty of care, or to the extent any claim for compensatory damages is connected to a duty of loyalty claim, this provision would not bar them." *Id.*

In re Baxter International, Inc. Shareholders Litigation, 654 A.2d 1268 (Del. Ch. 1995), involved breach of fiduciary duty claims arising out of alleged oversight failures by the directors of Baxter International, Inc., a seller of medical supplies, in connection with systematic overcharging of the Veterans Administration. *Id.* at 1268-69. In the context of a motion to dismiss based upon plaintiffs' failure to make a pre-litigation demand, the court took judicial notice of a Section 102(b)(7) certificate of incorporation provision and held that "[w]hen the certificate of incorporation exempts directors from liability, the risk of liability does not disable them from considering a demand fairly unless particularized pleading permits the court to conclude that there is a substantial likelihood that their conduct falls outside the exemption." *Id.* as 1270. Applying this standard, the court held that demand was required and dismissed the case. *Id.* at 1270-71.

Green v. Phillips, 22 Del. J. Corp. L. 360 (Del. Ch. June 19, 1996), involved a challenge to a consulting and non-competition agreement between Phillips-Van Heussen Corporation and its former chairman and chief executive officer, Lawrence Phillips. *Id.* at 363-64. The directors named as defendants in the case other than Phillips moved to dismiss the duty of care allegations in the case. The court stated that it could take judicial notice of a Section 102(b)(7) certificate provision in deciding a motion to dismiss and dismissed the case against all directors other than Phillips "because there are no well-pleaded allegations that (i) the defendants (other than Phillips) were financially interested, or that (ii) the other defendants acted in other than good faith." *Id.* at 372-73.

Apple Computer, Inc. v. Exponential Technology, Inc., 1999 Del. Ch. LEXIS 9, 1999 WL 39547 (Del. Ch. Jan. 21, 1999), involved claims by Apple Computer, Inc., the largest shareholder and biggest customer of Exponential Technology, Inc., arising out of Exponential's sale of patents for $10 million to obtain funds to pay off creditors and finance a $500 million lawsuit by Exponential against Apple in California alleging that Apple had forced Exponential out of business by breach of contract, breach of fiduciary duty, and intentional and negligent interference with contractual relations and prospective economic advantage. According to Apple, Exponential's sale of the patents constituted a breach by Exponential of Section 271 of the Delaware General Corporation Law, which prohibits the sale of all or substantially all of the corporation's assets without shareholder approval, and a breach of fiduciary duty by Exponential's directors. 1999 Del. Ch. LEXIS 9, at *1-8, 1999 WL 39547, at *1-2. The court dismissed the claims against Exponential's directors to the extent that those claims sought money damages because no facts were alleged that, if true, would "indicate that the Exponential board's failure to seek shareholder approval was anything more than a good faith error" and thus liability was precluded by a charter provision adopted pursuant to Section 102(b)(7). 1999 Del. Ch. LEXIS 9, at *30, 1999 WL 39547, at *8.

Post-Emerald Partners Decisions. Post-*Emerald Partners* Court of Chancery decisions reach the same conclusion.

In *In re General Motors Class H Shareholders Litigation*, 734 A.2d 611 (Del. Ch. 1999), the court stated that "I do not read *Emerald Partners* as precluding a Rule 12(b)(6) dismissal of claims that the directors breached their fiduciary duty of care on the *basis* of an exculpatory charter provision so long as dismissal on that *basis* does not *thereby* preclude plaintiffs from pressing well-pleaded allegations that the directors breached their fiduciary duties of loyalty and good faith." *Id.* at 619 n.7. The court declined to rely upon this ground, however, because plaintiffs' claims in the case were subject to dismissal on other grounds. *Id.*

In *Green v. Phillips*, No. 14436 (Del. Ch. May 5, 1999), the court denied a motion for reconsideration of the court's prior decision in that case, which is discussed above. According to the plaintiff in the case, *Emerald Partners* held that a director protection certificate provision never can be the basis for a motion to dismiss at the pleading stage regardless of the violation alleged. *Id.*, slip op. at 1-2. The court stated that "[i]n *Emerald Partners* the Supreme Court explicitly noted that its holding will not prevent the dismissal of breach of fiduciary duty claims where 'the factual basis for [the] claim *solely* implicates a violation of the duty of care . . . .'" *Id.* at 2. In the case before the court, the court stated that "the claim against the individual defendants other than Mr. Phillips was of that character, because the complaint contained no allegations that those defendants either were financially interested, or that in approving the challenged agreement they acted in other than good faith." *Id.* at 2-3.

The court in *In re Lukens Inc. Shareholders Litigation*, 757 A.2d 720 (Del. Ch. 1999), reached the same conclusion. The court distinguished the result in *Emerald Partners* on the ground that in *Emerald Partners* "[t]he Supreme Court concluded that, in the context of an entire fairness analysis, disclosure claims are not easily categorized as arising under only the duty of care, holding that '[s]ince we conclude that the disclosure claims here alleged are not so categorized, the analysis falls short.'" *Id.* at 733 (quoting 726 A.2d at 1224). The court stated that "the *Emerald Partners* court explicitly recognized that 'where the factual basis for a claim *solely* implicates a violation of the duty of care . . . the protections of such a charter provision may properly be invoked and applied.'" *Id.* (quoting 726 A.2d at 1224). According to the court in *Lukens*, this language, when read with the *Emerald Partners* court's description of a Section 102(b)(7) charter provision as being "*in the nature of* an affirmative defense" and the *Emerald Partners* court's statement that defendants "will normally bear the burden of establishing each of its elements," does not require that a 102(b)(7) provision be raised only as an affirmative defense and on the basis of a well developed factual record. To the contrary, the court in *Lukens* stated, *Emerald Partners* "strongly suggests" the applicability of a Section

102(b)(7) charter provision "in the context of a motion to dismiss where *only* duty of care claims are alleged." *Id.*

The court in *Lukens* thus "read *Emerald Partners*' treatment of 8 *Del. C.* § 102(b)(7) to mean that where a complaint adequately alleges an entire fairness claim (implicating, at least initially, elements of good faith, loyalty and care), the burden will be on a director defendant to show his or her entitlement to the immunizing effect of the charter provision." *Id.* at 733-34. Similarly, "if a complaint adequately alleges bad faith or disloyalty, or some other exceptional circumstance under 8 *Del. C.* § 102(b)(7), or if the nature of the alleged breach of duty is unclear, the complaint will not be dismissed on a motion made under Rule 12(b)(6) on the basis of an exculpatory charter provision." *Id.* at 734.

Applying these rules, the court in *Lukens* granted a motion to dismiss because the complaint in *Lukens* "alleges, if anything, only a breach of the duty of care." *Id.* at 734. The court pointed to the functions of Section 102(b)(7) provisions: "to render duty of care claims not cognizable and to preclude plaintiffs from pressing claims of breach of fiduciary duty, absent the most basic factual showing (or reasonable basis to infer) that the directors' conduct was the product of bad faith, disloyalty or one of the other exceptions listed in the statute." *Id.* The court concluded: "*Emerald Partners* supports the conclusion that the Director Defendants are entitled to this dismissal at this stage of the process, without having to engage in discovery or shoulder the burden of proving that they acted loyally and in good faith." *Id.*

The court in *Chaffin v. GNI Group, Inc.*, 1999 Del. Ch. LEXIS 182, 1999 WL 721569 (Del. Ch. Sept. 3, 1999), also granted a motion to dismiss a duty of care claim to the extent plaintiff sought money damages, noting that "[b]oth sides agree on the content and legal effect" of the corporation's Section 102(b)(7) provision. 1999 Del. Ch. LEXIS 182, at *19-21, 1999 WL 721569, at *6. The court did not, however, dismiss plaintiff's duty of care claim to the extent that plaintiff sought the equitable remedy of rescission. Defendants contended that this remedy was unavailable as a matter of law in light of the passage of time because the merger challenged in the case had been consummated and cash had been paid in the merger to 370 people who were not before the court. The court, however, held that "[o]n a motion to dismiss all that need be decided is whether a claim is stated upon which any relief could be granted" and "[i]f that question is answered in the affirmative, the nature of the relief is not relevant and need not be addressed." 1999 Del. Ch. LEXIS 182, at *22, 19999 WL 721569, at *7. The court stated that "[a]t this stage, to decide whether rescission relief is (or is not) feasible would not only go beyond the scope of a motion to dismiss, but also would be imprudent, because the issue is fact driven and cannot be decided in the absence of an evidentiary record." *Id.*

The court in *In re Frederick's of Hollywood, Inc. Shareholders Litigation*, 2000 Del. Ch. LEXIS 19, 2000 WL 130630 (Del. Ch. Jan. 31, 2000), also rejected a claim that *Emerald Partners* "precludes any consideration of this § 102(b)(7) defense on a motion to dismiss" because "*Emerald Partners* holds that a § 102(b)(7) charter provision is 'in the nature of an affirmative defense . . . [and that the Defendants] will normally bear the burden of establishing each of its elements.'" 2000 Del. Ch. LEXIS 19, at *19-20, 2000 WL 130630, at *6 (quoting *Emerald Partners*, 726 A.2d at 1224). Citing *GM Class H* and *Lukens*, the court reasoned as follows:

> The plaintiffs misread *Emerald Partners*. This Court has interpreted the above-quoted language as not precluding a Rule 12(b)(6) dismissal of claims that the directors breached their fiduciary duty of care on the basis of an exculpatory charter provision, so long as a dismissal on that ground does not prevent a plaintiff from pursuing well-pleaded claims that the directors breached their fiduciary duty of loyalty. Under this reading of *Emerald Partners*, where a complaint alleges actionable disloyalty the burden will shift to the defendants to show the immunizing effect of the charter provision, but where the complaint only alleges a breach of the duty of care, that claim may be dismissed at the pleading stage.

2000 Del. Ch. LEXIS 19, at *20-21, 2000 WL 130630, at *6 (footnote omitted).

The court in *McMillan v. Intercargo Corp.*, 768 A.2d 492 (Del. Ch. 2000), reached the same conclusion. The court took judicial notice of an exculpatory provision authorized by Section 102(b)(7) in Intercargo Corporation's certificate of incorporation and explained that "the defendants do not obtain a dismissal of the plaintiffs' loyalty claims as a result of the exculpatory charter provision; they obtain a dismissal *because* the complaint fails to plead a loyalty claim or another claim premised on behavior not immunized by the exculpatory charter provision." *Id.* at 501 & n.40. The court stated the governing rule as follows: "By showing that the certificate of incorporation bars duty of care claims *and* by further demonstrating that the well-pled allegations of the complaint fail to support a claim that the defendant directors engaged in non-immunized conduct, the defendant directors meet their affirmative duty to justify dismissal of the entire complaint under *Emerald Partners*." *Id.* at 501 n.43. The court added that "[t]he effect of the exculpatory charter provision is to guarantee that the defendant directors do not suffer discovery or a trial simply because the plaintiffs have stated a non-cognizable damages claim for a breach of the duty of care," and "[t]o give the exculpatory charter provision any less substantial effect would be to strip away a large measure of the protection the General Assembly has accorded directors through its enactment of 8 *Del. C.* § 102(b)(7)." 768 A.2d at 501-02.

The same result was reached in *Ash v. McCall*, 2000 Del. Ch. LEXIS 144, 2000 WL 1370341 (Del. Ch. Sept. 15, 2000), a case challenging a merger of McKesson Corporation and HBOC & Co. into McKesson HBOC, Inc. Within three months of the merger, McKesson HBOC's outside auditor informed the board of accounting irregularities within HBOC. The board responded "by initiating an internal investigation that culminated in a series of sweeping earnings restatements. 2000 Del Ch. LEXIS 144, at *53, 2000 WL 1370341, at *15. Plaintiffs alleged that the directors of HBOC and McKesson HBOC "failed to exercise proper oversight of the companies' financial reporting process so as to prevent accounting improprieties; that the McKesson directors breached their duty of care in the course of investigating HBOC's books and records before the merger; and, finally, that McKesson's acquisition of HBOC constituted an act of corporate waste." 2000 Del. Ch. LEXIS 144, at *3-4, 2000 WL 1370341, at *1. The court stated that "this aspect of plaintiffs' complaint, which sounds in negligence and seeks money damages as a remedy, must be dismissed" due to Section 102(b)(7) provisions in McKesson's and McKesson HBOC's certificates of incorporation. 2000 Del. Ch. LEXIS 144, at *35 n.31, 2000 WL 1370341, at *10 n.31. The court explained that the complaint "fails to allege adequately either pre-merger or post-merger bad faith or disloyalty by the McKesson or McKesson HBOC boards." *Id.*

The court in *O'Reilly v. Transworld Healthcare, Inc.*, 745 A.2d 902 (Del. Ch. 1999), denied a motion to dismiss claims arising out of a merger of Health Management, Inc. ("HMI") into Transworld Healthcare, Inc., where plaintiff alleged that HMI faced substantial financial problems and the possibility of a bankruptcy filing, that Transworld owned 49 percent of HMI's stock, an option to purchase an additional 2 percent of HMI's stock, and substantially all of HMI's debt, that two of HMI's four directors had financial interests in the merger, that "Transworld used its status as a large stockholder and creditor to coerce the HMI board into reducing the Merger price" from $1.50 per share to $0.30 per share, that Transworld prevented HMI from negotiating with Counsel Corporation, a competitor of HMI that had expressed an interest in acquiring a primary line of HMI's business, that Transworld sold HMI's assets to Counsel after the merger and thus "usurped, to its benefit, the opportunity to sell HMI's assets to Counsel Corp.," that the proxy statement distributed to HMI's shareholders contained "materially false and misleading statements . . . regarding Transworld's purpose for engaging in the Merger and the 'arm's length' nature of the Merger negotiations," and that the

$0.30 per share merger price was half of HMI's book value and unfair. *Id.* at 909-11, 913.

The court stated that "despite the looming spectre" of a Section 102(b)(7) certificate provision, "I cannot conclude at this stage of the proceedings that O'Reilly's allegations of bad faith, knowledge and intent are merely conclusory" given the allegations "of self-interest among two of HMI's four board members and the reasonable inference that the pleaded disclosure allegations were part of a plan to deceive HMI's stockholders in order to consummate the Merger and fulfill the two HMI directors' and Transworld's self-interests." *Id.* at 915. The allegations, the court held, were sufficient to trigger the first, second and fourth exceptions to the Section 102(b)(7) certificate provision: "any breach of the directors duty of loyalty," "acts or omissions not in good faith or which involve intentional misconduct or a knowing violation of law" and "any transaction from which the directors derived an improper personal benefit." *Id.* at 915-16.

The court noted that plaintiff's allegation that the merger price resulted from an unfair process included an allegation that HMI's directors breached their duty of care. *Id.* at 915. The court stated that it was "reasonable to infer from the two HMI directors' self-interest and Transworld's self-interest and alleged threats" that "these alleged violations of the duty of care were made to consummate the Merger and to fulfill their respective self-interests." *Id.* at 916. As a result, the court continued, plaintiff's duty of care allegations fell within the exculpation provision's exceptions for "acts or omissions not in good faith or which involve intentional misconduct or a knowing violation of law" and for "any transaction from which the directors derived an improper personal benefit." *Id.* Accordingly, the court held, "the Exculpation Provision cannot at this stage in the proceedings be a basis for dismissing that claim against HMI directors." *Id.*

The court in *Sanders v. Wang*, 1999 Del. Ch. LEXIS 203, 1999 WL 1044880 (Del. Ch. Nov. 8, 1999), also denied a motion to dismiss based upon a Section 102(b)(7) provision. The court stated that "[t]he Delaware Supreme Court's decision in *Emerald Partners v. Berlin* instructs this court that the use of exculpatory provisions to shield fiduciaries from personal liability presents an affirmative defense not amenable to pre-trial disposition," but "where the *only* alleged acts are breaches of the duty of care, then this Court may consider the defense for the purpose of pre-trial disposition." 1999 Del. Ch. LEXIS 203, at *35, 1999 WL 1044880, at *11. The court concluded that "the nature of the defendants' breach of fiduciary duty remains unclear at this time" and that "[a]t this stage of the proceedings, I cannot conclude as a matter of law that the Board acted in good faith and that their actions constituted no more than mere carelessness." *Id.*

The court in *Oliver v. Boston University*, 2000 Del. Ch. LEXIS 104, 2000 WL 1038197 (Del. Ch. July 18, 2000), similarly denied a motion to dismiss based upon a Section 102(b)(7) provision because "plaintiffs adequately plead that the alleged misrepresentations and omissions were the product of self-dealing, not good faith errors in judgment." 2000 Del. Ch. LEXIS 104, at *26 n.25, 2000 WL 1038197, at *8 n.25; *see also Rosser v. New Valley Corp.*, 2000 Del. Ch. LEXIS 115, at *26-27, 2000 WL 1206677, at *8 (Del. Ch. Aug. 15, 2000) (denying motion to dismiss where plaintiffs alleged that defendants proposed a recapitalization "in order to shift equity from the former Class B holders, thereby diluting the value of their investment and to funnel that equity to the former Class A holders" in a self-interested manner, and that "misleading partial disclosure and omissions in the Proxy Statement were intended to effectuate defendants' self-interested objections"; "[a]ccordingly," the court held, "New Valley's § 102(b)(7) charter provision will not protect defendants against plaintiffs' remaining disclosure claims if plaintiffs can continue to tie those allegations to a claim that defendants breached their duty of loyalty"); *Grace Bros., Ltd. v. UniHolding Corp.*, 2000 Del. Ch. LEXIS 101, at *34-49, 2000 WL 982401, at *11-15 (Del. Ch. July 12, 2000) (denying motion to dismiss based upon

Section 102(b)(7) charter provision where plaintiffs alleged that three directors, with "the active support of their fellow directors, effected a scheme" pursuant to which a controlling group "was able to gain the benefits of a squeeze-out merger without having to ensure that the merger was fair" to minority shareholders, and thus "rid themselves of the expense of being stockholders in a publicly listed and regulated corporation that provides its minority stockholders with important benefits such as regular financial disclosures, access to books and records, and a liquid market for their securities").

The court in *Brown v. Perrette*, 1999 Del. Ch. LEXIS 92, 1999 WL 342340 (Del. Ch. May 14, 1999), likewise denied a motion to dismiss. The *Brown* case involved allegations that directors knowingly participated in a flawed bidding process. The court explained that "I cannot resolve the issue of whether § 102(b)(7) applies until I have had the opportunity to examine the evidence pertaining to the allegedly flawed bidding process and the board's knowledge of it." 1999 Del. Ch. LEXIS 92, at *44, 1999 WL 342340, at *13; *see also In re Trump Hotels S'holder Derivative Litig.*, 2000 U.S. Dist. LEXIS 13550, at *52-53, 2000 WL 1371317, at *17-18 (S.D.N.Y. Sept. 21, 2000) (denying motion to dismiss where plaintiffs alleged breaches of the duties of due care, loyalty, good faith and candor; the court considered this issue on a motion to dismiss despite the fact that the certificate of incorporation was "clearly outside of the pleadings" because "both sides have briefed the issue, Plaintiffs were thus clearly on notice" and thus "this point is ripe for determination"); *Kahn v. Roberts*, [1993-1994 Transfer Binder] Fed. Sec. L. Rep. (CCH) ¶ 98,201, at 99,414 (Del. Ch. Feb. 28, 1994) (denying motion for judgment on the pleadings because "[w]hether or not the directors acted in bad faith in approving the repurchase is a question of fact not reached at this stage"), *subsequent proceedings*, 21 Del. J. Corp. L. 674 (Del. Ch. Dec. 6, 1995) (granting summary judgment on other grounds), *aff'd*, 679 A.2d 460 (Del. 1996); *Freedman v. Braddock*, N.Y.L.J., May 19, 1993, at 25 (N.Y. Sup. Ct. N.Y. Co.) (construing Delaware law and denying motion to dismiss where directors allegedly "clearly had knowledge" of government reports that "expressly notified" the directors that mortgage banking practices were 'unsound and unsafe'" and that made recommendations that the directors did not implement; this conduct, the court stated, "[a]t this juncture, prior to discovery, ... arguably fall[s] within the exception" set forth in Del. Gen. Corp. Law § 102(b)(7)), *aff'd mem.*, 202 A.D.2d 197, 609 N.Y.S.2d 777 (N.Y. App. Div. 1st Dep't 1994).

Decisions dismissing duty of care claims pursuant to Section 102(b)(7) certificate provisions on motions for summary judgment include *John Hancock Capital Growth Management, Inc. v. Aris Corp.*, [1990 Transfer Binder] Fed. Sec. L. Rep. (CCH) ¶ 95,461, at 97,380 (Del. Ch. Aug. 24, 1990), *Arnold v. Society for Savings Bancorp, Inc. ("Arnold I")*, 650 A.2d 1270, 1288 (Del. 1994), *Levy v. Stern*, 1996 Del. Ch. LEXIS 25, at *8-10, 1996 WL 118160, at *3-4 (Del. Ch. Mar. 12, 1996), *rev'd on other grounds*, 687 A.2d 573 (unpublished opinion, text available at 1996 Del. LEXIS 468 and 1996 WL 742818) (Del. Dec. 20, 1996), *Cooke v. Oolie*, 1997 Del. Ch. LEXIS 92, at *40 & nn. 86-87, 44 & n.95, 1997 WL 367034, at *10 & nn.86-87, 11 & n.95 (Del. Ch. June 23, 1997), *Frank v. Arnelle*, 1998 Del. Ch. LEXIS 176, at *37-41, 1998 WL 668649, at *10 (Del. Ch. Sept. 16, 1998), *aff'd*, 725 A.2d 441 (unpublished opinion, text available at 1999 Del. LEXIS 25 and 1999 WL 89284) (Del. Jan. 22, 1999), *Goodwin v. Live Entertainment, Inc.*, 1999 Del. Ch. LEXIS 5, at *14-15, 1999 WL 64265, at *5 (Del. Ch. Jan. 22, 1999), *aff'd*, 741 A.2d 16 (unpublished opinion, text available at 1999 Del. LEXIS 238 and 1999 WL 624128) (Del. July 23, 1999), *Hills Stores Co. v. Bozic*, 769 A.2d 88, 110 n.73 (Del. Ch. 2000), and *In re Healthco International, Inc.*, 208 B.R. 288, 308 (Bankr. D. Mass. 1997) (discussed in Chapter II, Section F 2 d).

The court in *Odyssey Partners, L.P. v. Fleming Cos.*, 735 A.2d 386 (Del. Ch. 1999), held in a post-trial decision that plaintiffs had no duty of care claim due to a Section 102(b)(7) provision in the corporation's certificate of incorporation. *Id.* at 388, 392, 406 & n.19, 415, 419 n.31. The court in *HMG/Courtland Properties, Inc. v. Gray*, 749 A.2d 94 (Del. Ch. 1999), held in another post-trial decision that a Section 102(b)(7) certificate provision did not protect a director, Norman Fieber, who disclosed his own interest in a transaction with the corporation but who concealed the interest in the transaction of another director, Lee Gray, who desired to participate in the transaction and who was invited to do so after Gray had negotiated the transaction on behalf of the corporation. *Id.* at 121. The court stated that "[t]his conduct was not the product of mere inadvertence, but a conscious decision by Fieber not to come clean with the Board." *Id.* The court added that "to the extent that Fieber had simply violated his duty of care . . . § 102(b)(7) seems to contemplate liability for a director who personally benefits from his own gross negligence" because Section 102(b)(7) does not reach "any transaction from which the director derived an improper personal benefit." *Id.* at 121 n.32.

Change "Two" to "Three" in the first sentence of the second paragraph beginning and concluding on page 231.

Replace the Teachers' Retirement citation in footnote 598 on page 232 with the following:

Teachers' Retirement Sys. v. Welch, 244 A.D.2d 231, 231-32, 664 N.Y.S.2d 38, 39 (N.Y. App. Div. 1st Dep't 1997).

Replace the Teachers' Retirement citation in footnote 599 on page 233 with the following:

Id. at 232, 664 N.Y.S.2d at 39.

Add the following at the end of the paragraph beginning on page 232 and concluding on page 233 (immediately after footnote 601):

The same result was reached in *Ciullo v. Orange & Rockland Utilities, Inc.*, No. 601136/98 (N.Y. Sup. Ct. N.Y. Co. Jan. 8, 1999), *aff'd on other grounds*, 271 A.D.2d 369, 369, 706 N.Y.S.2d 428, 429 (N.Y. App. Div. 1st Dep't), *leave to appeal denied*, 95 N.Y.2d 760, 737 N.E.2d 952, 714 N.Y.S.2d 710 (2000), an action alleging waste by shareholders against directors of Orange & Rockland Utilities who faced possible criminal prosecution due to conduct by a corporate officer who had pleaded guilty to coercing corporate vendors into making contributions to various political candidates and causes and had arranged for those contributions to be reimbursed through inflated invoices paid by the corporation. *Id.*, slip op. at 1-2. The directors who faced possible criminal prosecution allegedly took a series of actions motivated by personal goals rather than corporate interests in an "attempt to buy goodwill to repair any damage to their reputations." *Id.* at 2.

These actions allegedly included agreements with the District Attorney's office pursuant to which the corporation paid for an independent investigation, the creation of a special committee of directors to conduct the investigation and retain outside law firms, accounting firms and consultants outside of the corporation's standard spending approval process, an agreement that shareholders rather than ratepayers would bear all costs of the investigation, and the expenditure of $25 million pursuing a civil action seeking $5 million from an employee who was alleged to have improperly used $29,575 of corporate funds and who was indicted a short time after the corporation commenced its civil action. This employee was acquitted of all criminal charges, the trial judge criticized the District Attorney's office for pursuing the case and offered the employee a public apology, and the employee was awarded over $5 million in an arbitration proceeding against the company alleging wrongful termination. *Id.* at 2-4.

Plaintiffs alleged that the corporation lost additional money by not adequately defending the corporation's books in a regulatory proceeding, where the corporation allegedly failed to state that "its books and records were accurate in all but a small part," and as a result the New York State Public Service Commission found that the corporation's financial statements "were not sufficiently trustworthy to justify a rate increase." *Id.* at 5. The corporation also allegedly agreed to a $10 million rate refund notwithstanding the fact that the corporation had sought only $5 million of alleged damages for the wrongdoing for which money was refunded to ratepayers. *Id.* All of these payments by the corporation, plaintiffs alleged, were "more than the amounts they would have been if they were designed to protect shareholders." *Id.*

The court held that the directors were shielded from liability by a certificate of incorporation provision adopted pursuant to section 402(b). *Id.* at 13. The court acknowledged that section 402(b) "cannot be used to shield directors from liability for intentional misconduct, bad faith, knowing violation of the law or for obtaining some advantage, financial or otherwise," to which "he or she was not legally entitled," but held that "the allegations in the complaint fail to satisfy that exception." *Id.* at 13-14.

Replace "1996" with "Supp. 1998/99" in the Model Act § 2.02 citation in footnote 609 on page 234.

Replace "1998" with "2001" in the Balotti citation in footnote 616 on page 238.

Section A 8

Replace "1997" with "1999" in the Cary citation in footnote 642 on page 243.

Replace "1997" with "2000" in the Fletcher citation in footnote 643 on page 244.

Add the following at the end of the paragraph beginning and concluding on page 244:

A fourth court – *Federal Deposit Insurance Corp. v. Ornstein*, 73 F. Supp. 2d 277 (E.D.N.Y. 1999) – has reached the same conclusion.

Add the following at the end of the paragraph beginning on page 244 and concluding on page 245 (immediately after footnote 654):

The court in *Federal Deposit Insurance Corp. v. Ornstein*, 73 F. Supp. 2d 277 (E.D.N.Y. 1999), followed *Resolution Trust Corp. v. Gregor*, 872 F. Supp. 1140 (E.D.N.Y. 1994). The court in *Ornstein* stated that the *Gregor* decision "thoroughly examined this question and concluded that New York law holds directors of a 'banking institution' liable for simple negligence." 73 F. Supp. 2d at 280. The court stated that "[t]he defendants have not cited any subsequent authority that would undermine the analysis in *Gregor*, which I adopt." *Id.*

Add the following at the end of paragraph beginning and concluding on page 247 (immediately after footnote 670):

The Ninth Circuit in *Federal Deposit Insurance Corp. v. Castetter*, 184 F.3d 1040 (9th Cir. 1999), construing California law, rejected a contention by the Federal Deposit Insurance Corporation that directors of a bank have "a duty of possessing specialized knowledge." *Id.* at 1046. To the contrary, the court stated that "in the national banking context, directors may well be chosen not solely for their business acumen, but for their relationship to the borrowing community." *Id.* at 1046 n.4. The court pointed to the Community Reinvestment Act of 1977 (the "CRA"), which requires financial institutions to '"help meet the credit needs of the local communities in which they are chartered'" and stated that "[t]o that end, the CRA encourages lending to segments of the community that otherwise might not have easy credit access, such as 'low- and moderate income neighborhoods.'" *Id.* (quoting 12 U.S.C. §§ 2901(a)(3), 2903(a)(1)). "In furtherance of those goals," the court continued, "many banks include on their boards persons representative of their lending community, some of whom may lack an extensive knowledge of banking procedure, but whose contributions to the board are nonetheless valuable because of their knowledge of community needs." *Id.* at 1046 n.4. The court stated that "[a] requirement of encyclopedic bank knowledge as a pre-requisite to board service" or "imposing personal liability for lack of such specialized knowledge" would "thwart the purpose" of the Community Reinvestment Act. *Id.*

Add the following at the end of footnote 703 on page 252:

See also Federal Deposit Ins. Corp. v. Castetter, 184 F.3d 1040, 1043-44 (9th Cir. 1999):

> In this instance, the FDIC alleges that the directors were guilty of ordinary negligence. The directors assert the defense of statutory immunity under California's business judgment rule. Because the simple negligence standard is stricter than the gross negligence standard provided for in 12 U.S.C. § 1821(k) and because the immunity defense does not implicate the "floor" of gross negligence under the facts of this case, California law is the applicable standard for assessing liability in this instance under *Atherton*.

Section B

Add the following at the end of footnote 763 on page 263:

See also Cooke v. Oolie, 2000 Del. Ch. LEXIS 89, at *49, 2000 WL 710199, at *14 (Del. Ch. May 24, 2000) ("[i]f a fiduciary pursues interests other than those of the corporation and its shareholders, he may breach his duty of loyalty").

Section B 2 a

Replace "Today, however" in the first sentence of the paragraph beginning on page 266 and concluding on page 267 with the following:

"Over the last century there has been a gradual shift in how the law has conceived of transactions between the corporation and its officers and directors and the type of recourse that shareholders have been entitled to in those instances." *Solomon v. Armstrong*, 747 A.2d 1098, 1115 (Del. Ch. 1999), *aff'd*, 746 A.2d 277 (unpublished opinion, full text available at 2000 Del. LEXIS 30 and 2000 WL 140072) (Del. Jan. 26, 2000). While the common law still prohibits self-dealing by the trustee of a trust, "the standards of trust law and corporation law are different." *Stegemeier v. Magness*, 728 A.2d 557, 562 & n.22 (Del. 1999); *see also Oberly v. Kirby*, 592 A.2d 445, 466-67 (Del. 1991) (principles of corporate law are "far more flexible and adaptable" than principles of trust law); *Wittman v. Crooke*, 707 A.2d 422, 424 (Md. Ct. Spec. App. 1998) ("[t]he duty of loyalty owed by a trustee to his beneficiaries . . . ordinarily is more intense than . . . that owed by a corporate director to the corporation"). Under corporate law,

Replace "8-387" with "8-372" and replace "1996" with "Supp. 1998/99" in the Model Act §§ 8.60-8.63 citation in footnote 774 on page 266.

Add the following at the end of footnote 774 on page 266:

See also Shapiro v. Greenfield, 764 A.2d 270 (Md. Ct. Spec. App. 2000) (citing this text for this proposition).

Add the following at the end of footnote 776 on page 267:

See also Sobek v. Stonitsch, 995 F. Supp. 918, 921 (N.D. Ill. 1998) ("[i]n the real world, corporations often have dealings, fair to the corporation, with interested directors," and thus "[v]oiding the vote of interested directors would unnecessarily inhibit otherwise fair transactions without any common sense reason"; "[t]he real issue in this type of transaction is whether it was fair and who has to prove it was fair"); *In re Walt Disney Co. Derivative Litig.*, 731 A.2d 342, 367 (Del. Ch. 1998) ("[i]nstead of imposing *per se* liability for board members who approve a self-interested transaction, this Court and the Delaware statutes recognize that in certain circumstances the shareholders may well be served notwithstanding the fact that the deal might be characterized as an interested transaction"), *aff'd with leave to replead on other grounds sub nom. Brehm v. Eisner*, 746 A.2d 244 (Del. 2000).

Replace the period at the end of footnote 778 on page 267 with the following:

, *quoted in Shapiro*, 764 A.2d at 282.

Add the following at the end of footnote 780 on page 268:

See also Cooke v. Oolie, 2000 Del. Ch. LEXIS 89, at *44 n.39, 2000 WL 710199, at *13 n.39 (Del. Ch. May 24, 2000) (Del. Gen. Corp. Law § 144 does not apply simply by reason of the fact that directors considering a potential transaction with a third party face a potential conflict of interest as directors and creditors; in this case, the court held, Section 144 did not apply (1) because the directors "neither sit on both sides of the potential USA transaction nor do they have a financial interest in USA" and (2) because "§ 144 applies to a 'contract or transaction,' but, in this case, no transaction has occurred"; rather, "[t]he plaintiffs merely challenge defendants' decision to pursue a transaction which ultimately never took place").

Delete the period at the end of the first sentence (immediately after footnote 780) of the paragraph beginning on page 268

and concluding on page 269 and add the following immediately after footnote 781:

; put another way, "a self-dealing transaction that falls within the statute's reach is voidable unless, at minimum, one of the statutory categories that creates an exception to voidability is satisfied." *Nagy v. Bistricer*, 770 A.2d 43, 54 n.21 (Del. Ch. 2000).

Add the following at the end of footnote 782 on page 268:

See also HMG/Courtland Props., Inc. v. Gray, 749 A.2d 94, 114 (Del. Ch. 1999):

> Section 144 provides that a self-dealing transaction will not be "void or voidable solely for this reason" if the transaction is ratified by a majority of the disinterested directors or by a shareholder vote. 8 Del. C. § 144(a)(1), (2). Such ratification is valid, however, only if the "material facts as [to the director's] relationship or interest and as to the contract or transaction are disclosed or are known to the [relevant ratifying authority] . . . ." *Id.* Neither Fieber nor Gray disclosed Gray's "interest" in the Transactions" to the HMG Board. *Id.* In the absence of such disclosure, 8 Del. C. § 144(a)(1), the Transactions can only be rendered non-voidable if they were "fair as to [HMG] as of the time [they were] authorized."

Add the following at the end of footnote 783 on page 268:

See also Stegemeier, 728 A.2d at 562 (describing "safe harbor for the directors of a corporation if the transaction is approved by a majority of disinterested directors").

Add the following at the end of the third sentence (immediately after footnote 783) of the paragraph beginning on page 268 and concluding on page 269:

Self-dealing transactions thus are "not automatically voidable if they are not approved by disinterested directors or ratified by fully informed shareholders" because "[t]he interested parties to the transaction may still be able to demonstrate that the transaction was entirely fair to the corporation and therefore valid." *Solomon*, 747 A.2d at 1115 n.49.

Add the following at the end of footnote 784 on page 269:

See also Cooke, 2000 Del. Ch. LEXIS 89, at *46 n.41, 2000 WL 710199, at *13 n.41 ("Under § 144, plaintiffs bear the burden of demonstrating that the defendants have engaged in an interested transaction. . . . Once the plaintiffs demonstrate interest, the burden shifts to the defendants to show that one of § 144's safe harbor provisions protects them and the transaction. . . . Once the defendants demonstrate that a safe harbor protects the transaction, the plaintiffs can attempt to prove to the Court that the interested directors controlled or dominated the disinterested directors, which would destroy the disinterested ratification.").

Add the following at the end of the paragraph beginning on page 268 and concluding on page 269 (immediately after footnote 784):

Section 144 has been held to apply to all interested director transactions that involve contracts between the corporation and one or more of its directors and not just transactions where the interest is material. Transactions falling within the terms of Section 144 thus differ from transactions not falling within the terms of Section 144 because in the latter case the Delaware Supreme Court's decisions in *Cede & Co. v. Technicolor, Inc.*, 634 A.2d 345 (Del. 1993) and *Cinerama, Inc. v. Technicolor, Inc.*, 663 A.2d 1156 (Del. 1996), require a showing of materiality before an interest or lack of independence becomes disqualifying. *See Harbor Fin. Partners v. Huizenga*, 751 A.2d 879, 887 n.20 (Del. Ch. 1999) (stating that "[t]here is analytic force to the argument that § 144 should, like many statutes, be read as incorporating a 'materiality' element" in order to "ensure that a director who, for example, owns one share of stock worth $100 or even $1,000, in another entity with which the corporation of which he is a fiduciary is transacting business is not considered 'interested,'" but adding that "[t]he incorporation of a materiality element into § 144 as a matter of statutory interpretation should not, however, be confused with the 'materiality' test" articulated in the *Technicolor* decisions "to determine whether directors are 'interested' in a transaction to which § 144 does not apply"); *id.* at 888 & n.28 (to require a plaintiff in a case involving an interested director transaction governed by Section 144 "to demonstrate that a director's material holdings on the other side of the table from the corporation are not outweighed by his stockholdings in the corporation itself . . . would encourage directors to eschew procedural protections for the public stockholders in the hope that a court will later find that the directors' conflicting interests in other businesses were outweighed by the stockholdings in the company of which they were fiduciaries"); *HMG*, 749 A.2d at 112-14; *see also Beneville v. York*, 769 A.2d 80, 84 n.4 (Del. Ch. 2000) (noting distinction between *Cede/Technicolor* materiality analysis in context of interests that do and do not implicate § 144).

Add the following at the end of footnote 789 on page 269:

See also In re Digex, Inc. S'holders Litig., 2000 Del.. Ch. LEXIS 171, at *88, 2000 WL 1847679, at *24 (Del. Ch. Dec. 13, 2000); *Odyssey Partners, L.P. v. Fleming Cos.*, 735 A.2d 386, 414 (Del. Ch. 1999).

Replace the period at the end of footnote 790 on page 270 with the following:

, *quoted in Fleming*, 735 A.2d at 414 *and Digex*, 2000 Del. Ch. LEXIS 171, at *88, 2000 WL 1847679, at *24; *see also Digex*, 2000 Del. Ch. LEXIS 171, at *98, 2000 WL 1847679, at *27 ("*Weinberger*'s suggestion of either an 'independent negotiating structure' or 'total abstention' is not to be taken lightly").

Replace "1998" with "2001" in the Balotti citation in footnote 791 on page 270.

Add the following at the end of the paragraph beginning on page 269 and concluding on page 270 (immediately after footnote 792):

In re Digex, Inc. Shareholders Litigation, 2000 Del. Ch. LEXIS 171, 2000 WL 1847679 (Del. Ch. Dec. 13, 2000), illustrates this principle. *Digex* involved a proposed merger between WorldCom, Inc. and Intermedia Communications, Inc., the holder of 52 percent of the outstanding stock of Digex and 94 percent of the voting power of all of Digex's outstanding stock. 2000 Del. Ch. LEXIS 171, at *2, 6, 2000 WL 1847679, at *1, 2. Digex's board included eight directors. Five of these Digex directors also were directors or officers of Intermedia and "stood to personally profit tremendously upon a sale of Intermedia, but to profit very little, or not at all, upon a sale of Digex" because they owned large numbers of Intermedia shares and stock options and much smaller numbers of or no Digex stock and stock options. The remaining three Digex directors were not affiliated with Intermedia. 2000 Del. Ch. LEXIS 171, at *7 & n.5, 2000 WL 1847679, at *2 & n.5. At the time of the events underlying the decision, Intermedia faced severe financial problems, but Digex was "a rapidly growing company that was extremely attractive to potential suitors." 2000 Del. Ch. LEXIS 171, at *12, 2000 WL 1847679, at *3.

The court described the potential conflicts of interest that faced the individuals who served as directors of Intermedia and Digex "due to their dual directorships and their direct, personal financial interests in any potential transaction" involving the sale or all or part of Intermedia, Digex and/or Intermedia's ownership position in Digex as follows:

> If Intermedia sold itself (which, of course, would include its majority stake in Digex), Intermedia's shareholders stood in a position to reap a substantial premium on their shares, largely due to the acquiror's presumable desire to obtain control over

> Intermedia's "crown jewel," Digex. This was especially true with regard to Intermedia's officers and directors, who, as discussed above, stood to profit tremendously from a sale of Intermedia. In contrast, Digex's shareholders stood to gain comparatively little under this possibility, at least in the short term, other than a new controlling shareholder.
>
> If Intermedia sold part or all of its Digex holdings, Intermedia could expect a significant payoff to fund its own operations, but Intermedia's shareholders, and especially its officers and directors, would not personally benefit to the extent they would if Intermedia itself were sold. Under this possibility, Digex shareholders could expect to reap a significant premium if Intermedia sold its holdings to an acquiror who decided to then tender for all outstanding Digex shares.

2000 Del. Ch. LEXIS 171, at *12-13, 2000 WL 1847679, at *3-4.

Against this backdrop, the Digex board, by a vote of "four to three, with only the interested directors . . . voting in favor" (one director did not participate due to health problems), approved a request by Intermedia to Digex to waive the protections provided to Digex by Section 203 of the Delaware General Corporation Law in order to facilitate a sale of Intermedia to WorldCom. 2000 Del. Ch. LEXIS 171, at *26, 2000 WL 1847679, at *7. As discussed in Chapter III, Section B 3 i-1, the court concluded on a motion for a preliminary injunction that Intermedia and the four Digex directors who voted to waive Section 203's protections were "not reasonably likely to meet their burden as to the entire fairness of the Digex board's decision to waive Digex's § 203 protections and, therefore, that plaintiffs have demonstrated a reasonable probability of success on the merits of their § 203 claim." 2000 Del. Ch. LEXIS 171, at *113, 2000 WL 1847679, at *31.

Add the following at the end of footnote 793 on page 270:

See also Byelick v. Vivadelli, 79 F. Supp. 2d 610, 628 (E.D. Va. 1999) (stating that Virginia's safe harbor statute, Va. Stock Corp. Act § 13.1-691, "is a statute which regulates conflict of interest transactions" and "does not address the potential liability of a director who has a conflict of interest"; this statute thus governs claims seeking to void an interested director transaction but does not govern claims seeking to hold an interested director liable for the transaction).

Replace "1996" with "Supp. 1998/99" in the Model Act §§ 8.60-8.63 citation in footnote 794 on page 270.

Add the following at the end of footnote 794 on page 270:

Cf. Camden v. Kaufman, 613 N.W.2d 335, 339 (Mich. Ct. App. 2000) (dismissing breach of fiduciary duty claim because "once proper approval of an interested transaction is obtained, the type of challenges available are limited to waste, fraud, illegality, or the like").

Add the following at the end of the paragraph beginning and concluding on page 270 (immediately after footnote 794):

Thus, "while non-compliance with §§ 144(a)(1), (2)'s disclosure requirement by definition triggers fairness review rather than business judgment rule review, the satisfaction of §§ 144(a)(1) or (a)(2) alone does not always have the opposite effect of invoking business judgment rule review that one might presume would flow from a literal application of the statute's terms." *HMG*, 749 A.2d at 114 n.24. "Rather, satisfaction of §§ 144(a)(1) or (a)(2) simply protects against invalidation of the transaction 'solely' because it is an interested one. As such, § 144 is best seen as establishing a floor for board conduct but not a ceiling." *Id.* (citation omitted). Put another way, "in a case where § 144 is directly applicable, compliance with its terms should be a minimum requirement to retain the protection of the business judgment rule." *Id.* at 113.

Section B 2 b

Add the following at the end of the first sentence (immediately after footnote 795) of the paragraph beginning and concluding on page 271:

"The disinterested directors' ratification cleanses the taint of interest because the disinterested directors have no incentive to act disloyally and should be only concerned with advancing the interests of the corporation." *Cooke v. Oolie*, 2000 Del. Ch. LEXIS 89, at *44, 2000 WL 710199, at *13 (Del. Ch. May 24, 2000).

Add the following at the end of 796 on page 271:

See also Cooke, 2000 Del. Ch. LEXIS 89, at *44-45, 2000 WL 710199, at *13; *Cooke*, 2000 Del. Ch. LEXIS 89, at *44-45, 2000 WL 710199, at *13; *Stegemeier v. Magness*, 728 A.2d 557, 562 (Del. 1999); *Odyssey Partners, L.P. v. Fleming Cos.*, 735 A.2d 386, 406 (Del. Ch. 1999).

Add the following at the end of footnote 797 on page 271:

See also In re Encore Computer Corp. S'holders Litig., 2000 Del. Ch. LEXIS 93, at *17, 2000 WL 823373, at *6 (Del. Ch. June 16, 2000) (business judgment rule governs decision made by two disinterested directors where the board included these two disinterested directors and two interested directors who recused themselves); *Cooke v. Oolie*, 2000 Del. Ch. LEXIS 89, at *46 & n.41, 2000 WL 710199, at *13 & n.41 (Del. Ch. May 24, 2000) (business judgment rule governs decision made by two disinterested and two interested directors, where the disinterested directors both approved the decision); *In re W. Nat'l Corp. S'holders Litig.*, 2000 Del. Ch. LEXIS 82, at *85-92, 2000 WL 710192, at *26-27 (Del. Ch. May 22, 2000) (business judgment rule governs decision made by three disinterested directors on a special committee where the board included these three directors and five additional directors that the court found lacked disinterestedness and independence, at least for the purpose of the motion for summary judgment before the court; discussed in Chapter II, Section B 3 k-1).

Add the following at the end of footnote 800 on page 272:

See also McMullin v. Beran, 765 A.2d 910, 923 (Del. 2000) (denying motion to dismiss where plaintiff alleged that interested directors did not abstain from participation in the board's approval of the challenged transaction).

Replace the Model Act § 8.31 citation in footnote 801 on page 273 with the following:

2 Model Bus. Corp. Act Annotated § 8.31 Official Comment at 8-207 (3d ed. Supp. 1998/99).

Add the following at the end of footnote 801 on page 273:

See also McMillan v. Intercargo Corp., 768 A.2d 492, 504 (Del. Ch. 2000) (describing a "decision to recuse" as being "in keeping with high standards of directorial conduct").

Add the following at the end of the paragraph beginning on page 273 and concluding on page 274 (immediately after footnote 809):

The mere fact of seeking board approval, "[p]resumably . . . to avoid any argument that it was required for some reason," does not "subject[ ] the transaction (or . . . the board's approval of it) to an interested party analysis." *Fleming*, 735 A.2d at 412-13 & n.25. Where shareholders who have board representation do not oppose a board decision at the time the decision is made but later commence litigation challenging the decision, "[t]he absence of dissent by plaintiffs' own board representatives" at the time of the decision "substantially discredits their after-the-fact charges that their fellow directors acted with disloyalty or in bad faith." *Id.* at 406.

Section B 2 c

Add the following after the heading in the paragraph beginning on page 274 and concluding on page 275:

Courts recognize that "shareholders themselves are often in the best position to judge the merits of a deal even when it is tainted by board self-interest." *In re Walt Disney Co. Derivative Litig.*, 731 A.2d 342, 367-68 (Del. Ch. 1998), *aff'd with leave to replead on other grounds sub nom. Brehm v. Eisner*, 746 A.2d 244 (Del. 2000).

Add the following at the end of footnote 810 on page 274:

See also In re 3COM Corp. S'holders Litig., 1999 Del. Ch. LEXIS 215, at *10-11, 1999 WL 1009210, at *3 (Del. Ch. Oct. 25, 1999); *Solomon v. Armstrong*, 747 A.2d 1098, 1111, 1116 & n.51, 1117 & n.60, 1127, 1129 (Del. Ch. 1999), *aff'd*, 746 A.2d 277 (unpublished opinion, full text available at 2000 Del. LEXIS 30 and 2000 WL 140072) (Del. Jan. 26, 2000); *Disney*, 731 A.2d at 368-69.

Add the following at the end of footnote 811 on page 274:

See also Rosser v. New Valley Corp., 2000 Del. Ch. LEXIS 115, at *23, 2000 WL 1206677, at *7 (Del. Ch. Aug. 15, 2000); *Harbor Fin. Partners v. Huizenga*, 751 A.2d 879, 890 & n.37 (Del. Ch. 1999); *In re Gen. Motors Class H S'holders Litig.*, 734 A.2d 611, 616-17 (Del. Ch. 1999); *Lewis v. Austen*, 1999 Del. Ch. LEXIS 125, at *23 n.24, 1999 WL 378125, at *6 n.24 (Del. Ch. June 2, 1999). The courts permit defendants to overcome this burden in the procedural context of a motion to dismiss due to "[t]he substantial difficulty of winning such a motion (the plaintiff is given the benefit of every doubt), the illogic of requiring the court and defendants to identify disclosure deficiencies not complained of by experienced plaintiffs' lawyers, and the interests of judicial economy." 751 A.2d at 890 n.36.

Add the following at the end of the second sentence (immediately after footnote 811) of the paragraph beginning on page 274 and concluding on page 275:

Indeed, "the right to affirm or veto" a board decision "at the corporate ballot box" is "the ultimate procedural production." *GM Class H*, 734 A.2d at 616-17 n.2.

Add the following at the end of footnote 812 on page 275:

See also Rosser, 2000 Del. Ch. LEXIS 115, at *21, 23, 2000 WL 1206677, at *7 (quoting *Smith v. Van Gorkom*, 488 A.2d 858, 890 (Del. 1985), and adding that "while fully informed shareholder ratification may not be tantamount to the death penalty for breach of fiduciary duty claims, application of the business judgment rule will lead to the same end result in virtually every case").

Add the following at the end of the third sentence (immediately after footnote 812) of the paragraph beginning on page 274 and concluding on page 275:

This make sense: if shareholders are "fully informed," then the court should conclude that the shareholders "fully understood" the transaction, were "content" with the transaction "as it applied to them," and "never expected the Court to step in and save them from themselves." *Rosser*, 2000 Del. Ch. LEXIS 115, at *25, 2000 WL 1206677, at *7. Accordingly, "shareholder ratification can have a penetrating legal effect . . . where shareholder approval is sought (e.g., approval of a merger) and where there is *no* controlling shareholder, control group or dominating force that can compel a particular result. Absent any other allegations that might cast doubt on the board's disinterest vis-a-vis the merits of the transaction, an informed and uncoerced shareholder vote on the matter provides an independent reason to maintain business judgment protection for the board's acts." *Solomon*, 747 A.2d at 1117 (footnotes omitted); *see also id.* at 1127. As a result, "[f]ar from being seen as a mere additional burden, corporations may seize the power of fully informed shareholder approval as a sort of safe harbor." *Disney*, 731 A.2d at 369.

Add the following at the end of footnote 813 on page 275:

See also Solomon, 747 A.2d at 1127 ("plaintiffs may defeat the business judgment rule's presumptions . . . by alleging materially false or misleading statements in the disclosure statements on which the vote was predicated"); *Disney*, 731 A.2d at 368 & n.70 (under section 144 the validity of ratification is "expressly condition[ed]" upon "full disclosure of all material facts," and thus section 144 "codifies the board's duty of disclosure as a prerequisite to obtaining shareholder ratification of interested deals involving a director").

Add the following at the end of the fourth sentence (immediately after footnote 813) of the paragraph beginning on page 274 and concluding on page 275:

Thus, where the vote is "a foregone conclusion by reason of defendants' control . . . the business judgment rule could never apply," and "[a]n informed vote in that situation would only shift the burden to plaintiffs to show that the transaction was not entirely fair." *Rosser*, 2000 Del. Ch. LEXIS 115, at *24-25, 2000 WL 1206677, at *7.

Add the following at the end of footnote 814 on page 275:

See also Harbor Fin., 751 A.2d at 899 ("Delaware law does not make it easy for a board of directors to obtain 'ratification effect' from a stockholder vote. The burden to prove that the vote was fair, uncoerced, and fully informed falls squarely on the board."); *Solomon*, 747 A.2d at 1116 n.58 ("the party offering the defense of shareholder ratification bears the burden of proof of showing that the disclosure was legally sufficient"); *id.* at 1128 ("when it comes to claiming the sufficiency of disclosure and the concomitant legal effect of shareholder ratification after full disclosure (e.g., claim extinguishment, the retention of the business judgment rule presumptions, or the shift of the burden of proof of entire fairness from the defendant to the plaintiff) it is the defendant who bears the burden"); *Disney*, 731 A.2d at 369 ("[t]o obtain this Court's deference to shareholder ratification, directors "must show this Court that the shareholders possessed all information germane to the transaction at the time they voted to ratify it"); *id.* ("[w]here a board seeks shareholder action, it is charged with the obligation to provide shareholders with the requisite information"); *id.* at 369 ("the simple requirement that a board seeking shareholder ratification of a self-interested transaction provide shareholders all information material to the transaction" is "an essential component of the duty of loyalty in a situation where the board seeks to comply with its fiduciary obligations by obtaining shareholder approval for the board's otherwise potentially conflicted interests"); *id.* at 369 n.75 (quoting *Van Gorkom*, 488 A.2d at 893 (Del. 1985) ("The burden must fall on defendants who claim ratification based on shareholder vote to establish that the shareholder approval resulted from a fully informed electorate.")); *id.* at 369 n.76 (quoting *Cahall v. Lofland*, 114 A. 224, 234 (Del. Ch. 1921), *aff'd*, 118 A. 1 (Del. 1922) ("One cannot ratify that which he does not know. The burden is on him who relies on a ratification to show that it was made with a full knowledge of all material facts.")).

Add the following at the end of footnote 815 on page 275:

See also Harbor Fin., 751 A.2d at 900.

Add the following at the end of the second paragraph beginning and concluding on page 280 (immediately after footnote 843):

The Court of Chancery in *Lewis v. Austen*, 1999 Del. Ch. LEXIS 125, 1999 WL 378125 (Del. Ch. June 2, 1999), restated its view that ratification does not extinguish a duty of loyalty claim. 1999 Del. Ch. LEXIS 125, at *23 n.24, 1999 WL 378125, at *6 n.24.

Replace "On appeal, the Delaware Supreme Court in In re Sante Fe Pacific Corp. Shareholder Litigation" and footnote 844 in the first sentence of the third paragraph beginning and concluding on page 280 with the following:

On an appeal of the Court of Chancery's decision in *In re Sante Fe Pacific Corp. Shareholder Litigation*, [1995 Transfer Binder] Fed. Sec. L. Rep. (CCH) ¶ 98,845 (Del. Ch. May 31, 1995), *aff'd in part and rev'd in part*, 669 A.2d 59 (Del. 1995), the Delaware Supreme Court

Replace footnote 845 on page 280 with the following:

In re Sante Fe Pac. S'holder Litig., 669 A.2d 59, 67 (Del. 1995).

Add the following at the end of footnote 851 on page 281:

See Chapter II, Section A 6 (discussing decisions following and distinguishing result in *Santa Fe*).

Add the following new footnote 856.1 at the end of the paragraph beginning on page 281 and concluding on page 282:

See also Wittman v. Crooke, 707 A.2d 422, 425-26 (Md. Ct. Spec. App. 1998) (conduct alleged to constitute a violation of the duty of loyalty may be ratified).

Add the following at the end of the paragraph beginning on page 281 and concluding on page 282 (immediately after new footnote 856.1):

The Delaware Court of Chancery's decision in *Kohls v. Duthie*, 765 A.2d 1274 (Del. Ch. 2000), considered a contention that a tender offer conditioned upon the acceptance by a majority of shareholders other than the corporation's chief executive officer, who controlled 35 percent of the corporation's shares, "should be given the same effect as a ratifying vote." *Id.* at 1285. The court stated that "[t]he argument has considerable force although, before deciding the question, I would want to consider further whether the decision to tender or not is one that can be exercised without incurring the economic risk of being treated materially differently than other stockholders – a risk not associated with the right to vote." *Id.* at 1285-86. The court noted that "the plan" was to complete a second-step merger "immediately after the completion of the tender offer" but that "there is always some risk" with respect to the timing and completion of a second-step merger. *Id.* at 1286 n.24.

Section B 2 d

Add the following at the end of footnote 858 on page 282:

See also Byelick v. Vivadelli, 79 F. Supp. 2d 610, 629 (E.D. Va. 1999).

Add the following at the end of footnote 859 on page 283:

See also Cooke v. Oolie, 2000 Del. Ch. LEXIS 89, at *40, 2000 WL 710199, at *12 (Del. Ch. May 24, 2000) (acknowledging "potential for a conflict of interest" where directors of a corporation operating under extreme financial distress also are creditors but holding that plaintiffs had failed to show that an "actual conflict exists" and thus that plaintiffs had failed to rebut the presumption of the business judgment rule; case discussed in Chapter I, Section D 2 c).

Add the following at the end of the paragraph beginning on page 282 and concluding on page 283 (immediately after footnote 861):

"[A] plaintiff's mere allegation of 'unfair dealing,' without more, cannot survive a motion to dismiss." *Rabkin v. Philip A. Hunt Chem. Corp.*, 498 A.2d 1099, 1105 (Del. 1985), *quoted in In re Boston Celtics LP S'holders Litig.*, 1999 Del. Ch. LEXIS 166, at *13 n.16, 1999 WL 641902, at *4 n.16 (Del. Ch. Aug. 6, 1999); *see also Boston Celtics*, 1999 Del. Ch. LEXIS 166, at *12, 1999 WL 641902, at *4 ("[i]n the context of a challenge to the fairness of certain transactions, such as the cash-out merger of minority limited partners by a majority limited partner, it also is necessary for the plaintiff to allege specific items of misconduct that demonstrate unfairness, in order to survive a motion to dismiss").

Add the following at the end of footnote 862 on page 283:

See also Byelick, 79 F. Supp. 2d at 629 ("No inflexible rule has been established by which to test the 'fairness' of a transaction. It depends largely on the nature and circumstances of the business action, but, generally, a director must act in good faith, and the transaction must, 'as a whole, [be] open, fair and honest at the time it was consummated.' In sum, 'a transaction in which a director has a conflict of interests should bear 'the earmarks of an arm's length bargain' in order to be deemed 'fair to the corporation''") (citations omitted).

Add the following at the end of the paragraph beginning on page 283 and concluding on page 284 (immediately after footnote 865):

As stated by the Court of Chancery in *In re Digex, Inc. Shareholders Litigation*, 2000 Del. Ch. LEXIS 171, 2000 WL 1847679 (Del. Ch. Dec. 13, 2000):

> As often summarized in our caselaw, the concept of entire fairness has two basic components, fair dealing and fair price. Fair dealing concerns how the board action was initiated, structured, negotiated, and timed. Fair dealing asks whether all of the directors were kept fully informed not only at the moment in time of the vote, but also during the relevant events leading up to the vote while negotiations were presumably

> occurring. Fair dealing also asks how, and for what reasons, the approvals of the various directors themselves were obtained. Fair price relates to the economic and financial considerations of the proposed decision, including any relevant factors that affect the intrinsic or inherent value of a company's stock. "

2000 Del. Ch. LEXIS 171, at *90, 2000 WL 1847679, at *24 (footnotes omitted). "The entire fairness test is not simply a bifurcated analysis of these two components, fair dealing and fair price"; rather, "these two aspects" – fair dealing and fair price – "as well as any other relevant considerations" are part of the analysis of the entire fairness of any board action. *Id.*

Replace the second bullet (including footnotes 868 and 869) in the paragraph beginning on page 284 and concluding on page 288 with the following:

- *Boyer v. Wilmington Materials, Inc.*, 754 A.2d 881, 885, 886, 889-90 (Del. Ch. 1999) (holding, following a trial, that a sale of a substantially all of the assets of Wilmington Materials, Inc. ("WMI") to Delaware Aggregates, Inc. ("DAI") approved by WMI's board by vote of five to three was not fair, where three of the five WMI directors who voted to approve the transaction owned DAI and the other two WMI directors who voted to approve the transaction had entered into a contract providing them a right to become DAI shareholders, and where a principal purpose of the sale was to eliminate two shareholders from continued participation in the ownership and management of WMI's assets and business without compensating them for the value of their shares; the court stated that the impetus for the transaction was an agreement that would provide two of the WMI directors who voted for the transaction $1.5 million in the event WMI relocated its business, that WMI's board was not advised by independent legal or financial advisors, and that "[i]f corporate fiduciaries engage in self-dealing and fix the . . . price by procedures not calculated to yield a fair price, these facts should, and will, be considered in assessing the credibility of [their] valuation contentions").

Add the following at the end of the paragraph beginning on page 284 and concluding on page 288 (immediately after footnote 875):

- *HMG/Courtland Properties, Inc. v. Gray*, 749 A.2d 94, 115-18 (Del. Ch. 1999) (holding, following a trial, that real estate transactions entered into by HMG/Courtland Properties, Inc. as seller and two of HMG's directors, Norman Fieber and Lee Gray as buyers, were not fair where Fieber's self-interest in the transactions was disclosed but neither Fieber nor Gray "informed their fellow directors that Gray – who took the lead in negotiating the sales for HMG – had a buy-side interest"; with respect to the fair dealing component of fairness, the court stated that the process was "anything but fair" because "the HMG Board unwittingly ratified Transactions in which a conflicted negotiator was relied upon" by HMG "to negotiate already conflicted Transactions"; with respect to the fair price component of fairness, the court stated that "[t]he defendants have failed to persuade me that HMG would not have gotten a materially higher value . . . had Gray and Feiber come clean about Gray's interest" and "have not convinced me that their misconduct did not taint the price to HMG's disadvantage").

Section B 2 e

Replace "8-386" with "8–371-72" and replace "1996" with "Supp. 1998/99" in the Model Act §§ 8.60-8.63 citation in footnote 881 on page 289.

Replace "Id." with "Id. at 8-372" in the Model Act §§ 8.60-8.63 citation in footnote 882 on page 289.

Add the following at the end of footnote 883 on page 289:

See also Mizel v. Connelly, 1999 Del. Ch. LEXIS 157, at *12 & n.3, 1999 WL 550369, at *4 & n.3 (Del. Ch. July 22, 1999) (noting that Model Business Corporation Act § 8.60 does not include "grandparents" in its definition of "related person," "perhaps because the drafters did not foresee an occasion where a grandchild-director would be evaluating a transaction involving his or her grandparent," and concluding that "[l]ogically, it only makes sense to include grandparents . . . if grandchildren are included" and that "I hesitate to ascribe a one way view of grandparent-grandchild loyalty . . . even to the authors of the MBCA, who claim to have set forth an exclusive, 'bright line' definition").

Section B 2 f (i)

Add the following after heading in the paragraph beginning on page 294 and concluding on page 295:

"[D]efining what constitutes a corporate opportunity is often an elusive task." *United States v. Rodrigues*, 229 F.3d 842, 846 (9th Cir. 2000).

Add the following at the end of footnote 902 on page 294:

See also *In re Digex, Inc. S'holders Litig.*, 2000 Del. Ch. LEXIS 171, at *29, 2000 WL 1847679, at *8 (Del. Ch. Dec. 13, 2000).

Add the following at the end of the first sentence of the paragraph beginning and concluding on page 296:

Accordingly, there is no corporate opportunity where the corporation lacks the financial capacity to pursue the opportunity. *See Odyssey Partners, L.P. v. Fleming Cos.*, 735 A.2d 386, 412 n.24 (Del. Ch. 1999) (citing cases).

Add the following at the end of footnote 926 on page 300:

See also Delta Envtl. Prods., Inc. v. McGrew, 56 F. Supp. 2d 716, 717-19 (S.D. Miss. 1999) (under Mississippi law, the corporate opportunity doctrine does not apply to "an employee with neither executive nor administrative authority").

Add the following at the end of the paragraph beginning and concluding on page 299 (immediately after footnote 922):

The corporate opportunity doctrine does not reach an opportunity to sell a corporation to the highest bidder, such as, for example, a controlling shareholder allegedly steers a potential bidder for the corporation away from a bid for the corporation and towards a bid for the controlling shareholder. As the court in *In re Digex, Inc. Shareholders Litigation*, 2000 Del. Ch. LEXIS 171, 2000 WL 1847679 (Del. Ch. Dec. 13, 2000), explained, "the perceived corporate opportunity" under these circumstances "is not really a *corporate* opportunity at all" because there is no "interest or expectancy" of "the corporation qua corporation"; "[r]ather, the purported opportunity is that of the . . . *shareholders* to sell their . . . shares to the highest bidder." 2000 Del. Ch. LEXIS 171, at *35, 2000 WL 1847679, at *10. In other words, "where a majority shareholder of a corporation can block any unacceptable transaction, the corporation cannot take advantage of the opportunity to enter into an unsanctioned transaction and, thus, there is no opportunity that fairly belongs to the corporation." 2000 Del. Ch. LEXIS 171, at *36, 2000 WL 1847679, at *10. "[W]hile majority shareholders may breach their duty of loyalty on similar facts, the powers inherent in the majority status generally preclude a plaintiff from claiming that a corporate opportunity has been usurped where the majority shareholder could have blocked the transaction in any event." 2000 Del. Ch. LEXIS 171, at *39, 2000 WL 1847679, at *11. "This is so because no 'interest or expectation' fairly belonged to the corporation since the majority could block the transaction at any time." *Id.*

Section B 2 f (ii)

Replace "8-391" with "8-376" and replace "1996" with "Supp. 1998/99" in the Model Act §§ 8.60-8.63 citation in footnote 929 on page 301.

Add the following at the end of the first paragraph of footnote 946 on page 303:

See also Agranoff v. Miller, 1999 Del. Ch. LEXIS 78 at *61-68, 1999 WL 219650, at *18-21 (Del. Ch. Apr. 9, 1999), *aff'd*, 737 A.2d 530 (unpublished opinion, text available at 1999 Del. Ch. LEXIS 256 and 1999 WL 636634) (Del. July 28, 1999); *Benerofe v. Cha*, 1998 Del. Ch. LEXIS 28, at *13-15, 1998 WL 83081, at *4-5 (Del. Ch. Feb. 20, 1998); *N.E. Harbor Golf Club, Inc. v. Harris ("N.E. Harbor II")*, 725 A.2d 1018, 1021-23 (Me. 1999); *Demoulas v. Demoulas Super Markets, Inc.*, 677 N.E.2d 159, 179-87 (Mass. 1997); *Hanover Ins. Co. v. Sutton*, 705 N.E.2d 279, 290-92 (Mass. App. Ct. 1999) (each finding that business opportunity was a corporate opportunity that had been usurped).

Replace the Cooke citation in the second paragraph of footnote 946 on page 303 with the following:

Cooke v. Oolie, 1997 Del. Ch. LEXIS 92, at *45-46, 1997 WL 367034, at *12 (Del. Ch. June 23, 1997), *subsequent proceedings*, 2000 Del. Ch. LEXIS 89, 2000 WL 710199 (Del. Ch. May 24, 2000),

Add the following at the end of the second paragraph of footnote 946 on page 303:

See also In re Digex, Inc. S'holders Litig., 2000 Del. Ch. LEXIS 171, at *29-49, 2000 WL 1847679, at *8-14 (Del. Ch. Dec. 13, 2000); *Rypac Packaging Mach. Inc. v. Coakley*, 2000 Del. Ch. LEXIS 64, at *23-27, 2000 WL 567895, at *6 (Del. Ch. May 1, 2000); *Kahn v. Icahn*, 1998 Del. Ch. LEXIS 223, at *11-16, 1998 WL 832629, at *3-4 (Del. Ch. Nov. 12, 1998), *aff'd*, 746 A.2d 276 (unpublished opinion, text available at 2000 Del. Ch. LEXIS 22, 2000 WL 140018) (Del. Jan. 24, 2000) (each finding that business opportunity was not a corporate opportunity that had been usurped).

Add the following at the end of the third paragraph of footnote 946 on page 303:

See also Kohls v. Duthie, 2000 Del. Ch. LEXIS 103, at *27-37, 2000 WL 1041219, at *7-11 (Del. Ch. July 26, 2000) (denying motion to dismiss claim that director usurped corporate opportunity belonging to Kenetech Corporation "to repurchase a large block of its own stock for little or no consideration (thus providing nearly cost-free returns to its stockholders")), *subsequent proceedings*, 765 A.2d 1274, 1277, 1279-80, 1287-88 (Del. Ch. 2000) (subsequent decision denying a motion seeking to enjoin a management buy-out tranaaction sponsored by a third party venture capital firm that would cause plaintiffs to lose standing to pursue their corporate opportunity claim; the court stated that "the evidence now in the record strongly suggests that the likelihood of success on the merits" of the claim "is remote" due to testimony that the seller of the shares, the Hillman Company, "did not offer and would not have sold its shares to Kenetech due to Kenetech's distressed financial condition and Hillman's need for a certain and final sale to meet its tax planning objectives").

Replace footnote 947 on page 305 with the following:

Broz, 673 A.2d at 159.

Add the following at the end of the paragraph beginning and concluding on page 305 (immediately after footnote 949):

Section 122(17) of the Delaware General Corporation Law, adopted in 2000, permits a corporation to "[r]enounce, in its certificate or by action of its board of directors, any interest or expectancy of the corporation in, or in being offered an opportunity to participate in, specified business opportunities or specified classes or categories of business opportunities that are presented to the corporation or one or more of its officers, directors, or stockholders." Del. Gen. Corp. Law § 122(17). This statute "permits the corporation to determine in advance whether a specified business opportunity or class or category of business opportunities is a corporate opportunity rather than to address such opportunities as they arise." *Id.* L. '00 Synopsis of Section 122. This statute "does not change the level of judicial scrutiny that will apply to the renunciation of an interest or expectancy of the corporation in a business opportunity." *Id.*

Replace the Northeast Harbor citation in footnote 950 on page 305 with the following:

N.E. Harbor II, 725 A.2d at 1021-22 (quoting *N.E. Harbor Golf Club, Inc. v. Harris ("N.E. Harbor I")*, 661 A.2d 1146, 1151 (Me. 1995)).

Add the following at the end of the first sentence following the block quote (immediately after footnote 952) in the paragraph beginning on page 305 and concluding on page 306:

This rule is "designed to prevent individual directors and officers from substituting their own judgment for that of the corporation when determining whether it would be in the corporate interest, or whether the corporation is financially or otherwise able to take advantage of an opportunity." *N.E. Harbor II*, 725 A.2d at 1022. Under this rule, "[f]airness to the corporation is no defense . . . if the opportunity is taken without first offering it to the corporation." *Id.* at 1023 n.5. This rule has been said to protect directors and officers because "after disclosing the potential opportunity to the corporation, they can pursue their own business ventures free from the possibility of a lawsuit," and thus directors and officers "have a strong incentive to disclose any business opportunity even remotely related to the business of the corporation." *Id.* at 1022.

Replace the Northeast Harbor citation in footnote 952 on page 307 with the following:

N.E. Harbor I, 661 A.2d at 1151

Replace the Northeast Harbor citation in footnote 953 on page 307 with the following:

Northeast Harbor I, 661 A.2d at 1150-52, *subsequent proceedings, Northeast Harbor II*, 725 A.2d at 1021-23;

Add the following at the end of the paragraph beginning on page 305 and concluding on page 307 (immediately after footnote 953):

Courts in Massachusetts also have adopted this approach. *See Demoulas*, 677 N.E.2d at 180-82, 183; *Hanover*, 705 N.E.2d at 290-91.

Section B 2 g

Add the following at the end of footnote 961 on page 308:

See also Leonhardt, *Executive Pay Drops Off the Political Radar*, N.Y. Times, Apr. 16, 2000, § 4, at 5.

Replace the period at the end of footnote 964 on page 309 with the following:

, *quoted in Odyssey Partners, L.P. v. Fleming Cos.*, 735 A.2d 386, 410 (Del. 1999), *and quoted in part in In re 3COM Corp. S'holders Litig.*, 1999 Del. Ch. LEXIS 215, at *17 n.21, 1999 WL 1009210, at *5 n.21 (Del. Ch. Oct. 25, 1999) ("[t]here is, of course, no single template for how corporations should be governed and no single compensation scheme for corporate directors").

Add the following at the end of the paragraph beginning on page 308 and concluding on page 309 (immediately after footnote 964):

The Delaware Supreme Court observed in *Brehm v. Eisner*, 746 A.2d 244 (Del. 2000), that "the size of executive compensation for a large public company in the current environment often involves huge numbers" and that "[t]his is particularly true in the entertainment industry" – the industry involved in the *Brehm* decision – "where the enormous revenues from one 'hit' movie or enormous losses from a 'flop' place in perspective the compensation of executives whose genius or misjudgment, as the case may be, may have contributed substantially to the 'hit' or 'flop.'" *Id.* at 259 n.49.

Replace "1996" with "Supp. 1998/99" in the Model Act § 8.11 citation in footnote 965 on page 309.

Add the following at the end of footnote 967 on page 309:

See also Technicorp Int'l III, Inc. v. Johnston, 2000 Del. Ch. LEXIS 81, at *186-246, 2000 WL 713750, at *50-56 (Del. Ch. May 31, 2000).

Replace "1997" with "2000" in the Corpus Juris Secundum citation in footnote 970 on page 311.

Add the following at the end of footnote 971 on page 311:

See also Kahn v. Buttner, No. 600456/97, slip op. at 4 (N.Y. Sup. Ct. N.Y. Co. Sept. 28, 1999).

Add the following at the end of footnote 973 on page 312:

See also Brehm v. Eisner, 746 A.2d 244, 262 n.56 (Del. 2000); *Grimes v. Donald*, 673 A.2d 1207, 1215 (Del. 1996).

Add the following at the end of the paragraph beginning on page 311 and concluding on page 312 (immediately after footnote 973):

Directors thus "have the power, authority and wide discretion to make decisions on executive compensation," but "there is an outer limit to that discretion, at which point a decision of the directors on executive compensation is so disproportionately large as to be unconscionable and constitute waste." *Brehm*, 673 A.2d at 262 n.56.

Add the following at the end of the first sentence (immediately after footnote 975) of the paragraph beginning on page 313 and concluding on page 314:

The Delaware Court of Chancery in *In re Walt Disney Co. Derivative Litigation*, 731 A.2d 342 (Del. Ch. 1998), *aff'd with leave to replead sub nom. Brehm v. Eisner*, 746 A.2d 244 (Del. 2000), thus observed that "if a 'particular individual warrant[s] large amounts of money, whether in the form of current salary or severance provisions, the board has made a business judgment,'" and "this Court's deference to directors' business judgment is particularly broad in matters of executive compensation." *Id.* at 362 (quoting *Grimes v. Donald*, 673 A.2d 1207, 1215 (Del. 1996)), *quoted in White v. Panic*, 2000 Del. Ch.

LEXIS 14, at *36, 2000 WL 85046, at *10 (Del. Ch. Jan. 19, 2000). On appeal, the Delaware Supreme Court agreed that "the size and structure of executive compensation are inherently matters of judgment." *Brehm v. Eisner*, 746 A.2d 244, 263 (Del. 2000). As a result, "[c]ompensation to executives for their efforts on behalf of a corporation has consistently been approached . . . with caution by our courts," and "where, as here, there is no reasonable doubt as to the disinterest of . . . the Board, mere disagreement cannot serve as grounds for imposing liability based on alleged breaches of fiduciary duty and waste." *Disney*, 731 A.2d at 364, *quoted in State of Wis. Inv. Bd. v. Bartlett*, 2000 Del. Ch. LEXIS 42, at *31, 2000 WL 238026, at *9 (Del. Ch. Feb. 24, 2000). "To rule otherwise would invite courts to become super-directors, measuring matters of degree in business decisionmaking and executive compensation." *Brehm*, 746 A.2d at 266, *quoted in Wis. Inv. Bd.*, 2000 Del. Ch. LEXIS 42, at *32, 2000 WL 238026, at *9. Thus, "to effectively challenge a board's decision about executive compensation as waste, the plaintiff must demonstrate that the board acted 'unconscionably' by 'irrationally squandering or giving away assets.'" *Hills Stores Co. v. Bozic*, 769 A.2d 88, 110 n.74 (Del. Ch. 2000); *see also In re Abbott Labs. Derivative S'holder Litig.*, 126 F. Supp. 2d 535, 537 (N.D. Ill. 2000) ("executive compensation is a business judgment left to the board except in the most exceptional circumstances").

Add the following at the end of the paragraph beginning and concluding on page 314 (immediately after footnote 988):

The Delaware Supreme Court's decision in *Brehm v. Eisner*, 746 A.2d 244 (Del. 2000), illustrates these principles in the context of a $140 million severance package granted by The Walt Disney Company to Michael Ovitz in December 1996. The court stated that "it appears from the Complaint" that "the compensation and termination payout for Ovitz were exceedingly lucrative, if not luxurious, compared to Ovitz' value to the Company," that "the processes of the boards of directors in dealing with the approval and termination of the

Ovitz Employment Agreement were casual, if not sloppy and perfunctory," and that "the sheer size of the payout to Ovitz, as alleged, pushes the envelope of judicial respect for the business judgment of directors in making compensation decisions." *Id.* at 249. The court nevertheless dismissed the case due to plaintiffs' failure to plead the particularized facts required to excuse demand in a shareholder derivative action. *See* Chapter IV, Section B (discussing demand requirement).

The case involved a five year employment agreement entered into on October 1, 1995 by Disney and Ovitz, a Hollywood talent-broker and a long-time friend of Disney's chairman and chief executive officer, Michael D. Eisner. 746 A.2d at 249. The agreement provided for Ovitz to become president of Disney and receive an annual salary of $1 million, a discretionary bonus, and two sets of stock options ("A" options and "B" options) that collectively could enable Ovitz to purchase 5 million shares of Disney common stock. The "A" options would vest in three annual increments of 1 million shares each, in September of 1998, 1999 and 2000, but would vest immediately if Disney granted Ovitz a non-fault termination of the employment agreement. The "B" options would vest in two annual installments of 1 million shares each, in September of 2001 and 2002, but would be forfeited if Ovitz's employment ended in less than five years for any reason, including a non-fault termination, or if Ovitz and Disney did not agree to extend Ovitz's employment beyond the five year term of the employment agreement. *Id.* at 250.

Under the agreement, Ovitz's employment at Disney could end in one of three ways: (1) Ovitz could serve the five year term of the agreement and, if Disney determined not to offer Ovitz a new contract, Disney would owe Ovitz a $10 million severance payment; (2) Disney could terminate Ovitz for "good cause" before the end of the five year term of the agreement if Ovitz committed gross negligence or malfeasance or if Ovitz resigned voluntarily and owe Ovitz no additional compensation; or (3) Disney could terminate Ovitz without cause (a non-fault termination) before the end of the five year term of the agreement and owe Ovitz the present value of his remaining salary through September 30, 2000, a $10 million severance payment, an additional $7.5 million for each year remaining under the agreement, and the immediate vesting of his 3 million "A" options. *Id.* Ovitz's employment with Disney did not work out, and, in September 1996, Ovitz sent a letter to Eisner stating Ovitz's desire to leave Disney. In December 1996, Disney's board approved a non-fault termination. *Id.* at 251-52.

The court held that the Disney board's approvals of the employment agreement in 1995 and the non-fault termination in 1996 were protected by the business judgment rule because plaintiffs did not allege interestedness or a lack of independence on the part of a majority of Disney's directors – this portion of the court's decision is discussed in Chapter I, Section D 2 c – and, as discussed below, that plaintiffs did not allege facts overcoming the business judgment rule presumption that the board's decisions to approve the employment agreement in 1995 and the non-fault termination in 1996 were proper exercises of business judgment.

With respect to the approval of the employment agreement in 1995, plaintiffs alleged that Disney's board "failed properly to inform itself about the total costs and incentives" of Ovitz's employment agreement and "failed to realize that the contract gave Ovitz an incentive to find a way to exit the Company via a non-fault termination as soon as possible because doing so would permit him to earn more than he could by fulfilling his contract." 746 A.2d at 251. In support of this allegation, plaintiffs relied upon an admission, made after Ovitz's departure from Disney, by Graef Crystal, a compensation expert who advised Disney's board concerning the employment agreement that "'nobody' – not Crystal and not the directors" – had quantified the potential severance benefits to Ovitz for an early termination without cause, and, according to Crystal, "I wish we had." *Id.* at 251, 260-61.

The court rejected this allegation because the complaint "admits that the directors were advised by Crystal as an expert and that they relied on his expertise." *Id.* at 261. The question thus was "whether the directors are to be 'fully protected' (i.e., not held liable) on the basis that they relied in good faith on a qualified expert under Section 141(e) of the Delaware General Corporation Law." *Id.* The court stated that the board "is entitled to the presumption that it exercised proper business judgment, including proper reliance on the expert," and that "[p]laintiffs must rebut the presumption that the directors properly exercised their business judgment, including their good faith reliance on Crystal's expertise." *Id.* The court held that "[w]hat Crystal *now* believes *in hindsight* that he and the Board *should have done* in 1995 does not provide that rebuttal." *Id.*

The court also rejected plaintiffs' allegation that the board's approval of the employment agreement constituted waste – "an exchange that is so one sided that no business person of ordinary, sound judgment could conclude that the corporation has received adequate consideration." *Id.* at 263. The court explained that "a board's decision on executive compensation is entitled to great deference," and "[i]t is the essence of business judgment for a board to determine if "a 'particular individual warrant[s] larger amounts of money, whether in the form of current salary or severance provisions.'" *Id.* (quoting the Court of Chancery's decision in the case, *In re The Walt Disney Co. Derivative Litig.*, 731 A.2d 342, 362 (Del. Ch. 1998), *aff'd with leave to replead sub nom. Brehm v. Eisner*, 746 A.2d 244 (Del. 2000), and *Grimes v. Donald*, 673 A.2d at 1215 (Del. 1996)). Here, the court concluded, Disney's board determined "it had to offer an expensive compensation package to attract Ovitz" and that "he would be valuable to the Company." *Id.* The court also pointed to the fact that "the vesting schedule of the options actually was a disincentive for Ovitz to leave Disney" and "[w]hen he did leave . . . he left 2 million options . . . 'on the table.'" *Id.* at 263.

In sum, the court concluded, plaintiffs' case with respect to the Disney board's approval of Ovitz's employment agreement was "basically a quarrel" with the board's "judgment in evaluating Ovitz's worth *vis a vis* the lavish payout to him." *Id.* The court stated, however, that "the size and structure of executive compensation are inherently matters of judgment." *Id.*

With respect to the decision to grant a non-fault termination in 1996, the court reached the same conclusion. The court explained that "[t]he terms of the Employment Agreement limit 'good cause' for terminating Ovitz's employment to gross negligence or malfeasance, or a voluntary resignation without the consent of the Company." *Id.* at 265. The alleged fact that Ovitz "sought alternative employment while he was the president of Disney," the court stated, does not constitute gross negligence or malfeasance. *Id.* The alleged fact that Ovitz failed to follow Eisner's directive to meet with Disney's senior executive vice president and chief financial officer, the court stated, "may demonstrate that Ovitz failed to become familiar with Disney's finances or that he bucked authority at Disney," but "it does not demonstrate, without more, that Ovitz was grossly negligent or committed malfeasance." *Id.* at 265 (quoting 731 A.2d at 363-64). The alleged fact that Ovitz wrote a letter to Eisner "stating his dissatisfaction with his role and expressing his desire to leave the Company" and the alleged fact that Ovitz searched for another job, the court stated, "'provide strong evidence of Ovitz's lack of commitment to the Company" but "are not legally tantamount to a voluntary resignation.'" *Id.* at 252, 265 (quoting 731 A.2d at 364).

Construed most favorably to plaintiffs, the court concluded, the facts in plaintiffs' complaint "show that Ovitz's performance as president was disappointing at best, that Eisner admitted it had been a mistake to hire him, that Ovitz lacked commitment to the Company, that he performed services for his old company, and that he negotiated for other jobs (some very lucrative) while being required under the contract to dedicate his full time and energy to Disney." *Id.* at 265. "All this shows," the court stated, is that Disney's board "had *arguable* grounds to fire Ovitz for cause," but "what is alleged is only an *argument – perhaps* a good one – that Ovitz's conduct constituted gross negligence or malfeasance." *Id.* Disney still "would have had to persuade a trier of fact and law of this argument in any litigation dispute with Ovitz," and "that process of persuasion could involve expensive litigation, distraction of executive time and company resources, lost opportunity costs, more bad publicity and an outcome that was uncertain at best and, at worst, could have resulted in damages against the Company." *Id.*

In sum, plaintiffs contended that Disney's directors "committed waste by agreeing to the very lucrative payout to Ovitz under the non-fault termination provision because it had no obligation to him, thus taking the Board's decision outside the protection of the business judgment rule," and that the board's "available arguments of resignation and good cause" gave the board "the leverage to negotiate Ovitz down to a more reasonable payout than that guaranteed by his Employment Agreement." *Id.* at 265-66. These allegations, the court held, fail to meet the standard for a waste claim because these facts did not "show that no reasonable business person would have made the decision" that Disney's board made. *Id.* at 266. Rather, plaintiffs simply disagreed with the board's business decision to grant Ovitz a non-fault termination. "[M]ere disagreement," the court held, "cannot serve as grounds for imposing liability based on alleged breaches of fiduciary duty and waste." *Id.* (quoting 731 A.2d at 364). The court stated that "[t]o rule otherwise would invite courts to become super-directors, measuring matters of degree in business decisionmaking and executive compensation." *Id.* at 266. "Such a rule," the court concluded, "would run counter to the foundation of our jurisprudence." *Id.*

The same result was reached in *Wagner v. Selinger*, 2000 Del. Ch. LEXIS 1, 2000 WL 85318 (Del. Ch. Jan. 18, 2000), a case challenging a separation agreement involving Irwin Selinger, the chief executive officer and chairman of the board of Graham Field Health Products, Inc. ("GFI"), whose employment agreement expired on July 8, 2001 but who left GFI in mid-1998 due to disagreements between Selinger and GFI's board concerning the future direction of GFI. The agreement provided for GFI to continue paying Selinger his $550,000 base salary through July 31, 1999, to forgive $2.2 million in past loans by GFI to Selinger in return for a $500,000 unsecured note bearing no interest, to return to Selinger $3 million in GFI stock that had been pledged by Selinger as security for the $2.2 million in loans, to release Selinger from all potential claims held by GFI, and to pay Selinger's legal fees. 2000 Del. Ch. LEXIS 1, at *5, 2000 WL 85318, at *2. In return, Selinger agreed to extend the duration of non-competition and confidentiality provisions in his employment agreement from one year to five years, to provide limited consulting services if requested to do so by GFI, and to make himself available for pending litigation in which he and GFI were co-defendants. 2000 Del. Ch. LEXIS 1, at *11-12 & n.16, 2000 WL 85318, at *3 & n.16. The court stated that if the litigation provision "constituted the sum of the alleged consideration for the additional benefits conferred, I may have ruled differently on this motion," but held that based upon all of the alleged facts plaintiff did "not sufficiently state facts that if true would create reasonable doubt that, in approving the Separation Agreement, GFI's Board acted in a manner that no person of ordinary, sound business judgment would act" or that "the results of the Board's bargain show bad faith, a lack of honest belief that the terms were in the best interest of the company, or that the Board did not fully inform itself before reaching its conclusions." 2000 Del. Ch. LEXIS 1, at *12-13 & n.16, 2000 WL 85318, at *3 & n.16. Accordingly, the court concluded, "I am not permitted to second-guess the Board's decision-making process or to appraise whether, in my personal opinion, the exchange of consideration was fair." 2000 Del. Ch. LEXIS 1, at *13, 2000 WL 85318 at *4.

Replace "1997" with "2000" in the Fletcher citation in footnote 992 on page 315.

Add the following at the end of footnote 994 on page 315:

See also Seinfeld v. Coker, 2000 Del. Ch. LEXIS 172, at *5 & nn. 6-7, 2000 WL 1800214 at *2 & nn. 6-7 (Del. Ch. Dec. 4, 2000) (approving $2,500,000 settlement paid for by directors' and officers' insurance carrier of case challenging payment of $300,000 in cash and stock to each of 19 directors – a total of $5,700,000 – whose positions were eliminated following a merger of two banks, and stating the following with respect to the merits of the case: "First, defendants might characterize the payments as awards to former directors for prior service. Though older cases would not support such an argument [citing *Blish v. Thompson Automatic Arms Corp.*, 64 A.2d 581, 606-08 (Del. 1948)], more recent cases question the reasoning of these older decisions [citing *Zupnick v. Goizueta*, 698 A.2d 384 (Del. Ch. 1997)]. Second, defendants would likely insist that the 'consideration' BankAmerica received from the payments was the continued goodwill of influential businessmen who could direct future business to the bank. This issue would give rise to a debate regarding contract law that is plainly one on which each side would have substantial arguments. . . . '[N]either side could predict with confidence that its contentions would prevail.'") (footnotes omitted).

Add the following at the end of the footnote 1003 on page 317:

See also Ciullo v. Orange & Rockland Utils., Inc., No. 601136/98, slip op. at 13 (N.Y. Sup. Ct. N.Y. Co. Jan. 8, 1999), *aff'd*, 271 A.D.2d 369, 706 N.Y.S.2d 428 (N.Y. App. Div. 1st Dep't), *leave to appeal denied*, 95 N.Y.2d 760, 737 N.E.2d 952, 714 N.Y.S.2d 710 (2000) ("conclusory allegations do not state a cause of action in the absence of factually based allegations of wrongdoing or waste in determining directors' compensation") (citing *Marx v. Akers*, 88 N.Y.2d 189, 204, 666 N.E.2d 1034, 1043, 644 N.Y.S.2d 121, 130 (1996)).

Add the following at the end of the second paragraph beginning and concluding on page 317 (immediately after footnote 1005):

The court in *Sanders v. Wang*, 1999 Del. Ch. LEXIS 203, 1999 WL 1044880 (Del. Ch. Nov. 8, 1999), granted judgment on the pleadings in favor of shareholders of Computer Associates, Inc. ("CA") on a breach of fiduciary duty claim in a case involving a shareholder approved key employee stock ownership plan that permitted a board compensation committee to grant up to 6,000,000 shares of common stock to plan participants. The committee increased the 6,000,000 number to more than 20,000,000 in order to reflect stock splits, and granted more than 20,000,000 shares to plan participants. 1999 Del. Ch. LEXIS 203, at *5-7, 1999 WL 1044880, at *2. The court held that the 6,000,000 share ceiling in the plan was clear and unambiguous and that the award of more than 6,000,000 shares was a "clear violation" of the plan "without any legal justification." 1999 Del. Ch. LEXIS 203, at *17-31, 1999 WL 1044880, at *6-9.

Under these circumstances, the court stated, "as a matter of law . . . the Board exceeded its authority" and as a result "plaintiffs are entitled to judgment on the pleadings that the directors wrongfully authorized the award and that the director executives who received the award must disgorge the benefit received in order to avoid being unjustly enriched." 1999 Del. Ch. LEXIS 203, at *32-33, 1999 WL 1044880, at *10. The court accordingly ordered that the shares be returned to the corporation, that a constructive trust be imposed on the plan participants who received the shares, and that an accounting be rendered for any economic benefit derived from the shares. 1999 Del. Ch. LEXIS 203, at *40, 1999 WL 1044880, at *13.

The court left open for further proceedings a ruling with respect to "the nature of the breach of fiduciary duty giving rise to the imposition of a constructive trust in order to redress the unjust enrichment" – i.e., whether the wrongful acts "were breaches of the duty of care or duty of loyalty or whether they resulted from negligent or grossly negligent conduct." 1999 Del. Ch. LEXIS 203, at *33-34, 1999 WL 1044880, at *10. The court explained that a provision in the corporation's certificate of incorporation adopted pursuant to Section 102(b)(7) of the Delaware General Corporation Law shielded outside directors from liability for money damages for breaches of the duty of care but not for breaches of the duty of loyalty. Accordingly, the court concluded, "the management executives/directors who received the improper share grants . . . may face personal liability for monetary damages if they are necessary to make the shareholders whole," and "[t]he directors authorizing the share grants face damage claims, yet to be proved, for which they may be liable or from which, depending upon the proof of the nature of their conduct, they may be exculpated" by the corporation's Section 102(b)(7) charter provision. 1999 Del. Ch. LEXIS 203, at *34-35, 1999 WL 1044880, at *10-11.

The court noted that the three plan participants still would keep a total of almost $320 million. 1999 Del. Ch. LEXIS 203, at *24, 1999 WL 1044880, at *7. The court stated that "$320 million is no mere bagatelle," and "I find it remarkable that defendants would have me believe that CA's shareholders would consider that $320 million for three individuals failed to 'encourage, recognize, and reward sustained outstanding individual performance by certain key employees.'" *Id.* (quoting § 1.1 of the Key Employee Stock Ownership Plan). The court acknowledged that "[i]t is certainly the province of shareholders, by way of their franchise, to compensate their executives as lavishly as they deem necessary to ensure the growth and prosperity of their company," but concluded that "it is critical as a matter of governance policy that this Court ensure that these compensation plans when approved by shareholders are administered in strict accordance with the terms of the Plan and as the shareholders had the right to anticipate." 1999 Del. Ch. LEXIS 203, at *39, 1999 WL 1044880, at *12.

Replace "6-115" with "6-110" and replace "1996" with "Supp. 1998/99" in the Model Act § 6.24 citation in footnote 1006 on page 318.

Section B 2 h

Replace "1996" with "Supp. 1998/99" in the Model Act §§ 3.02 and 6.24 citation in footnote 1015 on page 321.

Add the following at the end of the fourth sentence (immediately after footnote 1027) of the paragraph beginning on page 322 and concluding on page 323:

Thus, "the pleaded facts must show 'an absolute lack of consideration, rather than inadequate consideration.'" *Lewis v. Austen*, 1999 Del. Ch. LEXIS 125, at *24, 1999 WL 378125, at *6 (Del. Ch. June 2, 1999).

Section B 2 h (i)

Replace "6-115" with "6-110" and replace "1996" with "Supp. 1998/99" in the Model Act § 6.24 citation in footnote 1031 on page 324.

Add the following at the end of the paragraph beginning and concluding on page 324 (immediately after footnote 1032):

The same rules governing materiality of director interestedness in any other context govern the materiality of director interestedness in this context. *See In re Dairy Mart Convenience Stores, Inc. Derivative Litig.*, 1999 Del. Ch. LEXIS 94, at *66 n.57, 1999 WL 350473, at *18 n.57 (Del. Ch. May 24, 1999) (rejecting an allegation that outside directors were interested in a challenged transaction that included a grant of stock options to the directors "[b]ecause plaintiff has failed to plead the materiality of that potential self-interest").

Add the following at the end of footnote 1050 on page 327:

See also Lewis v. Austen, 1999 Del. Ch. LEXIS 125, at *28, 1999 WL 378125, at *7 (Del. Ch. June 2, 1999).

Section B 2 h (ii)

Add the following at the end of the fifth sentence (immediately after footnote 1092) of the paragraph beginning on page 332 and concluding on page 333:

The court thus "found that the waste standard for options" granted under shareholder approved plans "has gradually evolved from a proportionality test, which required examining the sufficiency of the consideration, to a traditional waste standard, which requires showing an absence of consideration or an effective gift of corporate assets." *In re 3COM Corp. S'holders Litig.*, 1999 Del. Ch. LEXIS 215, at *14 n.16, 1999 WL 1009210, at *4 n.16.

Add the following at the end of the paragraph beginning on page 336 and concluding on page 337 (immediately after footnote 1123):

The Delaware Court of Chancery's decision in *In re 3COM Corp. Shareholders Litigation*, 1999 Del. Ch. LEXIS 215, 1999 WL 1009210 (Del. Ch. Oct. 25, 1999), using the waste standard stated in *Lewis v. Vogelstein*, 699 A.2d 327 (Del. Ch. 1997), dismissed a complaint challenging stock options approved by shareholders having "quite large (at least $650,000 per director)" dollar values. 1999 Del. Ch. LEXIS 215, at *14, 1999 WL 1009210, at *4. The court concluded that plaintiff's "legal allegations flowing from these facts, specifically that the compensation is 'grossly excessive' and that 'no reasonable person not acting under compulsion and in good faith would have done it,' are wholly conclusory." *Id.* The court explained that "[a]lthough 'the consideration typically involved in stock options, i.e., continued and greater efforts by employees, is ephemeral and not susceptible to identification and valuation in dollar terms,' the plaintiff must still allege some bare minimum facts showing that 3COM failed to receive *any* benefit from issuing those options" and that in this case "[p]laintiff simply has not done so." 1999 Del. Ch. LEXIS 215, at *14-15, 1999 WL 1009210, at *4.

The court rejected plaintiff's suggestion that "by comparing the alleged values of the 3COM options (at least $650,000 per director) to the values of the options the *Vogelstein* Court found wasteful ($180,000) one must infer that he has established the minimum factual support for his waste claim." 1999 Del. Ch. LEXIS 215, at *16, 1999 WL 1009210, at *4. The court acknowledged plaintiff's assertion that an allegation of waste is "inherently factual" but held that "I can only draw inferences in his favor from the facts he alleges in his Complaint, not from facts found in another case." 1999 Del. Ch. LEXIS 215, at *16, 1999 WL 1009210, at *5. The court stated that "the facts in *Vogelstein* only help me discern the legal standard to be applied and are not, as plaintiff argues, a benchmark for what specific dollar amounts may constitute excessive director compensation." 1999 Del. Ch. LEXIS 215, at *16-17, 1999 WL 1009210, at *5. That legal standard, the court continued, requires that a plaintiff allege "a complete *failure* of consideration" and not simply that the consideration is "inadequate," which was all plaintiff alleged that a comparison between plaintiff's alleged facts in this case and the alleged facts in *Vogelstein* would show. 1999 Del. Ch. LEXIS 215, at *17, 1999 WL 1009210, at *5.

In sum, the court concluded, "plaintiff alleges only that certain amounts of compensation were given to the director defendants and then concludes that these amounts are excessive," without alleging facts that "indicate why 3COM did not benefit from these grants, and that they, therefore, amounted to a gratuity and corporate waste." 1999 Del. Ch. LEXIS 215, at *17-18, 1999 WL 1009210, at *5. According to the court, "[b]are allegations that the alleged option values are excessive or even lavish, as pleaded here, are insufficient as a matter of law to meet the standard required for a claim of waste." 1999 Del. Ch. LEXIS 215, at *18, 1999 WL 1009210, at *5.

The Delaware Court of Chancery's decision in *Criden v. Steinberg*, 2000 Del. Ch. LEXIS 50, 2000 WL 354390 (Del. Ch. Mar. 23, 2000), reached the same result using the *Vogelstein* standard in a case challenging an allegation that the directors of Individual Investor Group, Inc. ("IIG") breached their duty of loyalty and wasted corporate assets by repricing stock options to employee directors (on November 19, 1998) and to non-employee directors (on December 23, 1998). The options had been issued under a shareholder approved plan that included a repricing provision. Plaintiff alleged that the repricing of the employee director and the non-employee director options "should be treated as a singular transaction because of their proximity in time and the circumstances surrounding their approval." 2000 Del. Ch. LEXIS 50, at *1-4, 2000 WL 354390, at *1-2.

The court concluded that plaintiff's allegation that the directors wasted corporate assets by authorizing the repricing was "unaccompanied by any facts demonstrating that the corporation received nothing in kind and is merely conclusory." 2000 Del. Ch. LEXIS 50, at *11, 2000 WL 354390, at *3. The court stated that "[t]he re-pricing objected to here was a part of an overall plan, approved by the shareholders, to incentivize performance or encourage retention of key employees and non-employee directors." 2000 Del. Ch. LEXIS 50, at *12, 2000 WL 354390, at *3. The court continued:

> [P]laintiff calls into question the defendant directors' "diversion of corporate assets for improper and unnecessary purposes" in the face of a shareholder plan authorizing a re-pricing that was carried out, concededly, according to its terms.

> Under these circumstances the complaint cannot raise a reasonable doubt that any business person of ordinary judgment could conclude that IIG received nothing in exchange for re-pricing the director defendants' options. Is not the only reasonable inference to be drawn from the shareholders' approval of the plan that the shareholders themselves believed the re-pricing to be an appropriate performance incentive for the corporation's managers and directors? Must I infer that the majority of shareholders who approved the plan were persons lacking "ordinary, sound business judgment?"
>
> * * *
>
> Plaintiff has failed to allege facts that either directly, or inferentially, indicate why the shareholders, who approved the plan allowing the re-pricing, were so ill informed about the plan they approved that neither they or any reasonable person could not believe that IIG would benefit from the re-priced options and that the re-priced options they authorized would amount to a gratuity and thus, corporate waste.

2000 Del. Ch. LEXIS 50, at *12-14, 2000 WL 354390, at *3-4 (footnote omitted).

The court thus held as follows:

> Plaintiff's allegations that IIG received no consideration for the director employee and non-employee benefit from the stock option re-pricing, are nothing more than conclusory and are insufficient, as a matter of law, to meet the standard required for a claim of waste. Carrying out a predetermined stock option plan, approved by shareholders, entirely consistently with the plan can hardly be characterized as an act of a "disloyal" fiduciary. Because the plaintiff has failed to make out a claim of waste, there can be no underlying breach of the fiduciary duty of loyalty.

2000 Del. Ch. LEXIS 50, at *15, 2000 WL 354390, at *4. "To rule otherwise," the court stated, "would invite courts to become super-directors, measuring matters of degree in business decision making and executive compensation." *Id.* (quoting *Brehm v. Eisner*, 746 A.2d 244, 266 (Del. 2000)).

Section B 3

Add the following at the end of footnote 1150 on page 342:

See also In re Walt Disney Co. Derivative Litig., 731 A.2d 342, 367 & n.64 (Del. Ch. 1998) (stating that "[i]nstead of imposing *per se* liability for board members who approve a self-interested transaction, this Court and the Delaware statutes recognize that in certain circumstances the shareholders may be well served notwithstanding the fact that the deal might be characterized as an interested transaction," and offering "a merger with a majority shareholder at a price well above the current market value for the company's shares" as an example), *aff'd with leave to replead on other grounds sub nom. Brehm v. Eisner*, 746 A.2d 244 (Del. 2000).

Add the following at the end of footnote 1151 on page 342:

See also Locati v. Johnson, 980 P.2d 173, 175 (Or. Ct. App. 1999).

Section B 3 a

Add the following at the end of the paragraph beginning and concluding on page 344 (immediately after footnote 1154):

"[A] shareholder who owns less than 50% of a corporation's outstanding stock, without some additional allegation of domination through actual control of corporation conduct, is not a 'controlling stockholder' for fiduciary duty purposes." *Emerald Partners v. Berlin*, 726 A.2d 1215, 1221 n.8 (Del. 1999). "A party alleging domination and control of the majority of a company's board of directors, and thus the company itself, bears the burden of proving such control by showing a lack of independence on the part of a majority of the directors." *Odyssey Partners, L.P. v. Fleming Cos.*, 735 A.2d 386, 407 (Del. Ch. 1999); *see also Solomon v. Armstrong*, 747 A.2d

1098, 1117 n.61 (Del. Ch. 1999) ("[i]n order for a plaintiff to successfully allege domination in the absence of controlling stock ownership, a plaintiff must allege literal control of corporate conduct"), *aff'd*, 746 A.2d 277 (unpublished opinion, full text available at 2000 Del. LEXIS 30 and 2000 WL 140072) (Del. Jan. 26, 2000).

Add the following at the end of the paragraph beginning on page 344 and concluding on page 345 (immediately after footnote 1157):

The Delaware Court of Chancery's decision in *Odyssey Partners, L.P. v. Fleming Cos.*, 735 A.2d 386 (Del. Ch. 1999), provides a noteworthy illustration of these principles in a case concluding that a 46.8 percent shareholder was not a controlling shareholder. The case involved ABCO Holdings, Inc., the owner of ABCO Markets, Inc., a chain of grocery stores based in Phoenix and Tuscon, Arizona. *Id.* at 388-89. ABCO financed an acquisition of 38 stores in 1988 by (1) the issuance of notes to investors, (2) a credit agreement with Manufacturers Hanover Trust Company (later Chemical Bank), which was secured by a first priority interest in substantially all of ABCO's assets, and (3) additional financing from Fleming Companies, Inc., a large food wholesaler headquartered in Oklahoma City, Oklahoma and that operated in the Phoenix market and that previously had entered into an agreement to supply grocery products to ABCO for sale in ABCO stores. *Id.* at 389, 391.

Financial problems led to a restructuring in 1992. Fleming provided new financing and became the owner of 46.8 percent of ABCO's shares and a warrant that Fleming could exercise under certain circumstances to acquire ownership of a total of 50.1 percent of ABCO's shares. *Id.* at 391-92. Fleming's supply agreement with ABCO was extended and amended to require ABCO to purchase at least 51 percent of its dry groceries, perishables and general merchandise from Fleming. *Id.* at 392. The restructuring also included a stockholders agreement providing that ABCO's board would include five directors, that noteholders would designate three of these directors (one of these three directors was required to be a member of senior management), and that Fleming would designate the remaining two directors. The agreement also provided that if Fleming exercised its warrant and acquired 50.1 percent of ABCO's shares, then Fleming would have the right to replace the member of senior management designated by the noteholders with a member of senior management designated by Fleming. *Id.* In sum, the restructuring resulted in Fleming became ABCO's largest shareholder, ABCO's largest supplier, and one of ABCO's two principal creditors (Chemical Bank was the other). *Id.*

Pursuant to the stockholders agreement, the noteholders appointed Edwin M. Banks, Edward C. Geiger, Jr. and Edward G. Hill, Jr. (Hill was ABCO's president and chief operating officer) to ABCO's board, and Fleming appointed R. Randolph Devening and Thomas W. Field, Jr. to ABCO's board. As discussed in more detail below, Devening resigned from his positions at Fleming in 1994 and Fleming appointed William M. Lawson to replace Devening as one of Fleming's two designees to ABCO's board. The board, however, determined to increase it size from five directors to six directors in order to retain Devening as a director "because his experience and advice were valued by the other directors." *Id.* at 393, 408. As a result, the stockholders agreement was amended to expand the board to six directors and allow the appointment of the sixth director by the other five members of the board. *Id.* at 393.

ABCO continued to experience financial problems and was unable to raise new capital. The court found that "ABCO's inability to raise new capital resulted from the failure of ABCO's various constituencies to agree on a plan to recompose or restructure the rights arising out of the 1992 Restructuring and held by them under the Stockholders Agreement, the Certificate of Incorporation and, in Fleming's case, the Supply Agreement and its loans to ABCO." *Id.* at 410-11. A recapitalization plan and rights offering failed because "the minority stockholders chose overwhelmingly: (i) not to participate in the offering through the investment of additional capital; and (ii) not to agree to the proposed changes in the Agreement and Certificate of Incorporation that were required before Fleming would proceed alone in providing needed financing without minority stockholder participation." *Id.* at 411. The court stated that "ABCO's search for more capital was stymied by the very structures in the Agreement and Certificate of Incorporation that were intended to protect the stockholders from overreaching by each other or by the board of directors. Fleming was eager to contribute more capital, but the others would not accept its terms. The others wanted the company sold, but Fleming's opposition to a sale and its refusal to surrender the value of the Supply Agreement made that option impracticable or impossible." *Id.* at 411-12. In the court's view, "the dire financial situation confronting ABCO . . . was no more the result of Fleming's control over the corporation than it was the result of the negative control exercised by the other stockholders." *Id.* at 411.

By 1995, Fleming determined to exercise its warrant and become the owner of 50.1 percent of ABCO's stock, to purchase the Chemical Bank loan (the senior loan and security interest in ABCO), and to foreclose on Fleming's junior security interest. *Id.* at 400. Fleming agreed to satisfy all of ABCO's secured and unsecured debt obligations, and on this basis ABCO's board approved Fleming's purchase of the Chemical Bank loan and determined not to authorize the filing of a Chapter 11 bankruptcy petition, which would protect ABCO against a foreclosure by Fleming. *Id.* at 400-04. At the foreclosure, Fleming bid $66 million, the exact amount of the indebtedness being foreclosed, for all of the collateral identified in the notice of sale. All secured and unsecured creditors were paid in full, and the owners of ABCO equity received nothing. *Id.* at 405. The foreclosure sale thus "resulted in ABCO's 50.1% stockholder (Fleming) owning 100% of its assets, while ABCO's other stockholders ended up holding shares worth nothing." *Id.* at 406.

The court held that Fleming did not control ABCO's board of directors prior to Fleming's exercise of its warrant in 1995. The court stated that the noteholders' designees – Banks and Geiger – "[i]ndisputably" were not controlled by Fleming, and that "[j]ust as clearly, Lawson was" controlled by Fleming. *Id.* at 407-08. The court then found that ABCO's remaining three directors – Devening, Field and Hill – were independent of Fleming. As a result, the court held, Fleming controlled one of five directors before 1994 and one of six directors beginning in 1994. The court reasoned as follows:

R. Randolph Devening. R. Randolph Devening became Fleming's executive vice president and chief financial officer in 1989 and was given the responsibility of overseeing Fleming's business interest in ABCO. Devening joined ABCO's board as a Fleming designee in 1992. *Id.* at 389. Devening was promoted to vice chairman and chief financial officer of Fleming in 1993, but in 1994 he left Fleming to become chairman, president and chief executive officer of Food Brands America, Inc., where he "earned a very high level of compensation." *Id.* at 389-90. Devening also entered into a two year consulting agreement with Fleming, the purpose of which was to fulfill the age and length of service requirements for an enhanced retirement package from Fleming. During the term of this consulting agreement, Devening was not asked to provide any services and received two annual payments of $1,000. *Id.* at 390. Devening was replaced by William M. Lawson, Jr. as Fleming's designee on ABCO's board, but at the same time "[h]is fellow directors asked him to continue serving as a director because his experience and advice were valued by the other directors." *Id.* at 408.

The court found that from 1992 through 1994, while Devening served as a senior officer of Fleming and a Fleming designee on ABCO's board, Devening "was in a position of conflicted loyalty and cannot be considered to have been independent of Fleming." *Id.* at 408. Once Devening stopped serving as a senior officer of Fleming, however, Devening's status as a former Fleming officer and a former Fleming designee to ABCO's board was "not, alone, a sufficient basis for a finding that he was controlled by Fleming." *Id.* The court reasoned that "[i]t is not enough to charge that a director was nominated by or elected at the behest of those controlling the outcome of the corporate election"; to the contrary, "[t]hat is the usual way a person becomes a corporate director." *Id.* (quoting *Aronson v. Lewis*, 473 A.2d 805, 816 (Del. 1984)). The court also held that Devening's consulting agreement with Fleming was not a basis for a finding that Devening was controlled by Fleming because "in the context of Devening's compensation from non-Fleming sources, it is meaningless as a financial issue." *Id.* at 408. The court also stated that "Geiger and Banks would not have agreed to Devening's appointment as the sixth director, or permitted his continued service without objection, if they regarded him as a Fleming loyalist." *Id.*

The court also held that Devening's participation in lobbying efforts with minority shareholders in connection with a recapitalization plan favored by Fleming but rejected by the minority shareholders did "not evidence any lack of independence." *Id.* at 409. The court pointed to Devening's testimony that he attended these meetings as a favor to Lawson, who indisputably was controlled by Fleming, in order to introduce Lawson to the minority shareholders with whom Devening previously had worked. *Id.* at 398. The court also pointed to the fact that the recapitalization plan had been approved by a unanimous vote of the directors for submission to the stockholders (although one director, Banks, testified that he had stated his opposition to the plan as a shareholder to the board but voted for the plan as a director because he thought – incorrectly, according to the court – that Fleming had conditioned its guarantee of a necessary lease on a unanimous vote of directors and because he knew he would be outvoted if he voted against the plan). *Id.* at 397 n.12, 409. The court stated that Devening's actions in support of a recapitalization plan that was approved by a unanimous vote of all directors for submission to shareholders and that the entire board believed was in the best interests of the company did "not evidence any lack of independence." *Id.* at 408-09.

Thomas W. Field, Jr. Thomas W. Field, Jr. was hired by Fleming as a consultant in 1991, and in 1992 Field was appointed to ABCO's board as a Fleming designee. A short time later, Field became chairman of ABCO's board, and in 1993 he became ABCO's chief executive officer. *Id.* at 390. Fleming paid Field a consulting fee until be became ABCO's chief executive officer, at which time ABCO began paying Field a $273,000 annual salary. Both before and after becoming chief executive officer of ABCO, Field received a $24,000 annual director fee from Fleming for his service as one of Fleming's two designees to the ABCO board. *Id.*

The court held that Fleming's annual payment of $24,000 to Field for his services as a Fleming board designee was "not so great as to give rise to an inference of impropriety" or subject him to Fleming's domination or control. *Id.* at 410. In the circumstances, the court stated, "it is unremarkable that Fleming assumed the responsibility to compensate its own board designee for his board service, or that it continued to do so after he became a member of ABCO's management." *Id.* The court held that the fact that Field and Devening were neighbors was of "no moment" because "conclusory allegations of 'personal affinity' are not sufficient to establish director interest." *Id.* at 409-10.

The court also held that Field's scheduling of ABCO's annual board meeting at Fleming's headquarters in Oklahoma City "as a favor to Fleming" did not establish a lack of independence on the part of Field. The court explained that "Field had sensible business reasons for planning an annual board meeting at Fleming's headquarters": "Fleming's financing and lease guarantees were instrumental to ABCO's continuing operations," and "ABCO's business plans were customarily presented at this meeting, so it was an opportunity to involve

Fleming executives in discussions regarding ABCO's long-term goals." *Id.* at 393, 409-10 & n.22. The court stated that "nothing in the record suggests that meeting once a year at Fleming's headquarters allowed Fleming to dominate or control the actions of the Company's board of directors." *Id.* at 410.

The court also rejected allegations that "Field consulted with Fleming regarding possible acquisition candidates for ABCO and stated that Fleming's acquisition of ABCO 'made perfectly logical sense to him'" as insufficient to establish a lack of independence on the part of Field. *Id.* at 409. The court explained that as chairman of ABCO's board and ABCO's chief executive officer Field had "legitimate business reasons . . . to consult with Fleming about acquisition possibilities because ABCO would have looked to Fleming as a principal source of financing for such transactions." *Id.* at 410. The court also explained that "the fact that Field stated that a Fleming/ABCO combination 'makes perfectly logical sense' does not evidence his control by Fleming" because "Fleming was ABCO's largest stockholder, largest supplier and (by the time of the foreclosure sale) its only secured creditor." *Id.* Under these circumstances, the court stated, "[i]t is hardly surprising that a knowledgeable observer would see the logic in the combination of Fleming and ABCO." *Id.*

Thus, the court concluded, Field's status as a Fleming designee, like Devening's status as a Fleming designee, "does not deprive him of his independence." *Id.* at 410 n.23.

Edward G. Hill, Jr. Edward G. Hill, Jr. served as president and chief operating officer of ABCO from ABCO's formation in 1984 until the 1996 foreclosure. *Id.* at 390. Hill also was a noteholder designee to ABCO's board. *Id.* at 393, 409. The court held with respect to Hill, as it had with respect to Devening, that participation in lobbying efforts with minority shareholders in connection with the recapitalization plan favored by Fleming but rejected by minority shareholders did not demonstrate control by Fleming. The court relied upon the same considerations with respect to Hill that the court had relied upon with respect to Devening, and also pointed to Hill's testimony that "due to his positions in management, he was the person the best suited to explain ABCO's precarious financial situation to the minority shareholders." *Id.* at 409. The court also held that a public statement by Hill to ABCO's customers, vendors and suppliers that Fleming's foreclosure would not result in negative financial or operational consequences for the company did not demonstrate a lack of independence because the statement was intended to reassure customers, venders and suppliers and was the type of statement that "would have been expected of him as President of ABCO." *Id.*

The court also held that Fleming did not control ABCO's board of directors even after the exercise of its warrant in 1995 to become a 50.1 percent shareholder of ABCO. The court acknowledged that "[w]hen Fleming became the majority stockholder, it could be argued to have obtained such control over ABCO to support an inference that Field and Hill, ABCO's senior executives, could no longer act independently of it." *Id.* at 408. The court nevertheless concluded that "[u]ltimately, however, the question of a director's loyalty is one of fact to be decided from the entirety of the record" and "[t]he record of this matter, as a whole, leads me to conclude that Field and Hill acted independently of Fleming and at all times acted in what they reasonably believed to be the best interests of ABCO." *Id.*

The Delaware Court of Chancery's decision in *In re Western National Corp. Shareholders Litigation*, 2000 Del. Ch. LEXIS 82, 2000 WL 710192 (Del. Ch. May 22, 2000), also illustrates these principles. *Western National* involved American General Corporation, a 46 percent shareholder of Western National Corporation. American General and Western National both were large, diversified insurance and financial service companies. Western National's chairman and chief executive officer was Michael J. Poulos, who had been a senior officer of American General until 1993, when Western National became a public company. Ten months later, American General acquired 40 percent (and a short time later an additional 6 percent) of Western National's shares and entered into a standstill agreement with Western National. The standstill agreement prohibited American General from doing any of the following before January 1, 1999 unless American General first obtained the approval of Western National's board: (1) acquiring more than 20 percent of Western National's shares in any 12 month period, (2) owning a total of more than 79 percent of Western National's shares, (3) engaging in an extraordinary transaction with Western National, or (4) nominating more than two directors to Western National's board. 2000 Del. Ch. LEXIS 82, at *7-8 & n.1, 2000 WL 710192, at *2 & n.1.

The court stated that a shareholder is a controlling shareholder and owes fiduciary duties to other shareholders only "if it owns a majority interest in or exercises control over the business and affairs of the corporation," and that "[i]n the absence of majority stock ownership, a plaintiff must demonstrate that the minority shareholder held a dominant position and actually controlled the corporation's conduct." 2000 Del. Ch. LEXIS 82, at *18, 2000 WL 710192, at *6. The court rejected plaintiffs' contention that the combination of American General's 46 percent equity position and its ability to purchase an additional 20 percent of Western National's stock during any twelve month period gave it "effective control." 2000 Del. Ch. LEXIS 82, at *21, 2000 WL 710192, at *6. The court explained that "substantial non-majority stock ownership, without more, does not indicate control" and that "the fact that American General *could* acquire a numerical majority stock interest in Western National in the open market is not sufficient to convert its status as a substantial minority shareholder to that of a fiduciary." 2000 Del. Ch. LEXIS 82, at *21, 2000 WL 710192, at *6. The court added that "the Standstill Provision further militates against a finding of domination or control, as it limited to two the number of directors that American General could nominate." 2000 Del. Ch. LEXIS 82, at *22, 2000 WL 710192, at *6.

The court also held that joint ventures entered into by Western National and American General pursuant to which Western National "borrowed" American General's ratings in order to offer insurance products that Western National's own ratings could not support did not demonstrate control by American General of Western National. The court explained that "[w]hen two entities join together as co-venturers in a common enterprise, each brings to the table particular assets that will, hopefully, make the enterprise successful," and "[m]anagement of the enterprise and division of its profits (if indeed successful) should, presumably, bear some, direct relation to the contributions of each party." 2000 Del. Ch. LEXIS 82, at *23-24, 2000 WL 710192, at *7. The court stated that there was no evidence that American General "forced" Western National into these joint ventures, "exercised disproportionate control over them, or extracted a disproportionate amount of the benefits flowing from them." 2000 Del. Ch. LEXIS 82, at *24, 2000 WL 710192, at *7.

The court also held that control was not established by American General's (1) "veto" of a potential business combination between Western National and U.S. Life Insurance Company in 1996 (by stating that it would not vote its 40 percent block in favor of the transaction) and (2) subsequent acquisition of U.S. Life itself. The court distinguished *Kahn v. Lynch Communication Systems, Inc.*, 638 A.2d 1110 (Del. 1994), where a 43 percent shareholder holding five of eleven board seats was found to have exercised control based upon its veto of a merger and threat to employ a tender offer if a "negotiated" agreement could not be reached, and where the 43 percent shareholder's directors "rather colorfully stated that the other directors must comport with their demands" because "[w]e are a forty-three percent owner" and "[y]ou have to do what we tell you" and "you are pushing us very much to take control of the company." 2000 Del. Ch. LEXIS 82, at *24-25, 2000 WL 710192, at *17. Unlike the case in *Lynch*, the court in *Western National* explained, there was "not a scintilla of evidence" in *Western National* that demonstrated that

"American General threatened Western National when the U.S. Life merger was under consideration or two years later when Western National and American General merged," "no American General managers, employees, agents, or even nominees sat on Western National's board of directors," and "under the terms of the Standstill Provision, American General could not plausibly (or at least easily) 'threaten' the Western National board as it was prohibited from appointing more than two directors and could not acquire more than 79% of the Company's shares through a tender offer or otherwise." 2000 Del. Ch. LEXIS 82, at *26-27, 2000 WL 710192, at *7-8.

The court stated that "[t]he mere fact that Western National management solicited the view of a 40 percent shareholder with respect to an extraordinary business transaction and ultimately agreed with the view expressed by that shareholder does not indicate a relationship of domination and control." 2000 Del. Ch. LEXIS 82, at *27, 2000 WL 710192, at *8. To the contrary, the court continued, the fact that a large but not majority shareholder "takes steps to 'veto' a business combination" between the corporation and a proposed merger partner is not even "particularly probative of whether the large shareholder exercises actual control over the business and affairs of the corporation." 2000 Del. Ch. LEXIS 82, at *28, 2000 WL 710192, at *8. The court explained:

> Section 141(a) of Delaware's corporation statute provides that the *business and affairs* of a Delaware corporation fall under the direction of its board of directors. Similarly, the standard for determining whether a large, though non-majority shareholder, exercises control over the corporation requires a judicial finding of actual control over the *business and affairs* of the corporation. Notwithstanding the explicit statutory grant of authority over the business and affairs of a Delaware corporation to its board of directors, certain events in the life of the corporation, such as a merger, require the affirmative participation of the corporation's shareholders. [*See* 8 *Del. C.* § 251(c).] The shareholders' right to voice their view as to the advisability of a proposed merger, however, does not indicate that they exercise actual control over the corporation's *business and affairs*.

2000 Del. Ch. LEXIS 82, at *28-29, 2000 WL 710192, at *8. "American General's exercise of its statutory rights as a stockholder to oppose a merger with U.S. Life," the court stated, thus was "of no legal consequence." 2000 Del. Ch. LEXIS 82, at *29, 2000 WL 710192, at *8.

In short, the court concluded, "American General did not exercise actual control over the Company's business and affairs." 2000 Del. Ch. LEXIS 82, at *68, 2000 WL 710192, at *20. Instead, "American General was generally a passive investor, only expressing its views with respect to extraordinary transactions such as the U.S. Life merger and appropriately engaged in the co-management of Western National-American General joint ventures." *Id.* The court added that there was "no evidence to suggest that American General directly or indirectly participated, or was in any way involved, in the functioning of the Western National board of directors before the merger." *Id.*

Add the following immediately after footnote 1159 in the first sentence of the paragraph beginning on page 345 and concluding on page 346:

shareholders who were married and together owned 10 percent of the corporation's stock, where one of these shareholders was an "affiliate" of the corporation and the chairman of a strategic partner of the corporation and the other was an "affiliate" of an entity that "invested heavily" in the corporation (*Oliver v. Boston Univ.*, 2000 Del. Ch. LEXIS 104, at *4-5, 20-21, 2000 WL 1038197, at *1-2, 7 (Del. Ch. July 18, 2000)),

Add the following at the end of footnote 1175 on page 347:

See also Korsinsky v. Granlund, No. 605635/99, slip op. at 14-15 (N.Y. Sup. Ct. N.Y. Co. Aug. 16, 2000) (a tender offeror who acquired 72.7 percent of the corporation's stock pursuant to a tender offer and an agreement with the corporation's controlling shareholders pursuant to which the tender offeror would acquire the controlling shareholders' shares after the completion of the tender offer was not a controlling shareholder and owed no fiduciary duty to shareholders prior to the expiration of the tender offer period and the completion of the tender offer).

Add the following at the beginning of the paragraph beginning and concluding on page 347 (immediately after footnote 1175):

Likewise, an entity that has entered into a merger agreement with a corporation owes no fiduciary duties to the corporation or its shareholders until the merger agreement is consummated. *In re Lukens Inc. S'holders Litig.*, 757 A.2d 720, 726 (Del. Ch. 1999).

Add the following at the end of the paragraph beginning on page 347 and concluding on page 348 (immediately after footnote 1183):

The court in *O'Reilly v. Transworld Healthcare, Inc.*, 745 A.2d 902 (Del. Ch. 1999), found for the purpose of a motion to dismiss a challenge to a merger of Health Management Inc. ("HMI") with a subsidiary of Transworld Healthcare, Inc. that Transworld was "a controlling stockholder with concomitant fiduciary status," where it was alleged that (1) Transworld held 49 percent of HMI's stock and an option to purchase another 2 percent of HMI's stock, (2) Transworld owned substantially all of HMI's debt, (3) "two of HMI's four directors had conflicts of interest because one of those directors would receive payments contingent on the Merger's consummation and both of those directors stood to benefit personally from the Merger's elimination of HMI's need to file for bankruptcy," (4) "in response to Transworld's 'threat' that it would not consummate the Merger unless the Merger price was reduced, HMI's board agreed to reduce the Merger price from $1.50 to $0.30," and (5) a third party, Counsel Corporation, expressed an interest in acquiring a HMI's primary line of business, but HMI's board "refrained from negotiating with Counsel Corp." in response to Transworld's statement that negotiations with Counsel Corp. "would place the Merger at risk." *Id.* at 913. The court stated that "[o]n the basis of these allegations, one may reasonably infer that Transworld used its position as a large stockholder and creditor to dictate the terms of the Merger to HMI's board, to prevent the HMI board from negotiating with Counsel Corp., and to force the HMI board to approve the Merger, and that HMI acceded to these demands because of Transworld's status and certain directors' interest in the Merger's consummation." *Id.; see also In re Dairy Mart Convenience Stores, Inc., Derivative Litig.*, 1999 Del. Ch. LEXIS 94, at *64 n.56, 1999 WL 350473, at *17 n.56 (Del. Ch. May 24, 1999) (declining to decide whether two individuals should be considered controlling shareholders "despite the fact that they did not control a mathematical majority of the voting stock" because, it was alleged, their "influence over corporate policy essentially amounted to de facto control"; the court stated that "[b]ecause I have already concluded that the transaction is subject to entire fairness review, and because that strict level of scrutiny will examine all parts of the transaction, at this point there is no reason to specifically reach this issue").

The court in *Emerald Partners v. Berlin*, 726 A.2d 1215 (Del. 1999), declined to decide whether a merger of May Petroleum, Inc. and thirteen sub-chapter S corporations was a controlling shareholder transaction. At the time the merger agreement was entered into, Craig Hall was the owner of 52.4 percent of May's common stock, the chairman and chief executive officer of May, and the sole owner and the chairman and chief executive officer of the thirteen sub-chapter S corporations merging with May, but, between the time the merger agreement was entered into and the record date for the vote by May's shareholders on the merger, Hall's 52.4 percent ownership of May was reduced to 25 percent ownership by a transfer of shares by Hall to independent irrevocable trusts created for the benefit of Hall's children. *Id.* at 1218, 1221 n.8. The court declined to decide whether the merger was a controlling shareholder transaction because "the circumstances attendant upon the events leading to the negotiation of the merger would appear to implicate the entire fairness standard" whether or not Hall was a controlling shareholder since "Hall, as Chairman and Chief Executive Officer of both May and the Hall corporations and sole owner of the Hall corporations, clearly stood on both sides of the transaction." *Id.* at 1221.

An Oregon court in *Locati v. Johnson*, 980 P.2d 173 (Or. Ct. App. 1999), held that each "member of a small group of shareholders who collectively own a majority of shares or otherwise have . . . domination or control" is a controlling shareholder who "has individual fiduciary duties toward the minority." *Id.* at 176-77. As a result, "one member of the group may breach those duties even if a different member did not." *Id.* at 177.

Section B 3 b

Add the following between "minority shareholders" and ", but also" in the first sentence (between footnotes 1184 and 1185) of the paragraph beginning on page 349 and concluding on page 350:

and "may not use corporate assets to advantage itself to the corporation's disadvantage" (*T. Rowe Price Recovery Fund, L.P. v. Rubin*, 770 A.2d 536, 555 (Del. Ch. 2000))

Add the following at the end of footnote 1185 on page 349:

See also In re Digex, Inc. S'holders Litig., 2000 Del. Ch. LEXIS 171, at *36, 2000 WL 1847679, at *10 (Del. Ch. Dec. 13, 2000).

Add the following at the end of footnote 1186 on page 349:

See also McMullin v. Beran, 765 A.2d 910, 919 (Del. 2000) ("the majority shareholder has the right to vote its shares");

Frankino v. Gleason, 1999 Del. Ch. LEXIS 219, at *11, 1999 WL 1032773, at *3 (Del. Ch. Nov. 5, 1999) (also quoting *Bershad), aff'd sub nom. McNamara v. Frankino*, 744 A.2d 988 (unpublished opinion, text available at 1999 Del. LEXIS 418 and 1999 WL 1319365) (Del. Dec. 9, 1999); *In re Frederick's of Hollywood, Inc. S'holders Litig.*, 1998 Del. Ch. LEXIS 111, at *20 n.19, 1998 WL 398244, at *6 n.19 (Del. Ch. July 9, 1998).

Replace the period at the end of footnote 1189 on page 350 with the following:

, *quoted in McMullen v. Beran*, 1999 Del. Ch. LEXIS 227, at *12 n.18, 1999 WL 1135146, at *4 n.18 (Del. Ch. Dec. 1, 1999), *rev'd on other grounds*, 765 A.2d 910 (Del. 2000).

Add the following at the end of the second paragraph beginning and concluding on page 356 (immediately after footnote 1220):

The Court of Chancery in *HMG/Courtland Properties, Inc. v. Gray*, 749 A.2d 94 (Del. Ch. 1999), noted that *CERBCO* "simply required defendant directors who pursued a corporate opportunity for themselves to reimburse the corporation for outside counsel fees the corporation incurred to obtain advice for a special committee of outside directors regarding the self-interested transaction the defendants proposed because such fees were 'made necessary by the course of events initiated by the [defendants'] breach.'" *Id.* at 124 n.35 (quoting *Thorpe v. CERBCO, Inc.*, 1996 Del. Ch. LEXIS 110, at *5, 1996 WL 560173, at *2 (Del. Ch. Sept. 13, 1996), *aff'd*, 703 A.2d 645 (unpublished opinion, text available at 1997 Del. LEXIS 438 and 1997 WL 776169) (Del. Dec. 3, 1997)). The court in *HMG* stated that *CERBCO* does not hold that "any investigative and litigation costs incurred by a corporation to prosecute a breach of loyalty case against its directors are automatically recoverable." *Id.* at 124 n.35.

The Court of Chancery in *In re Digex, Inc. Shareholders Litigation*, 2000 Del. Ch. LEXIS 171, 2000 WL 1847679 (Del. Ch. Dec. 13, 2000), summarized the *CERBCO* litigation as follows:

> In *CERBCO*, the third party approached the Eriksons, in their capacity as officers and directors, about the potential purchase of the subsidiary, East. The Eriksons, however, immediately steered the third-party towards purchasing their controlling block of CERBCO in order to gain control of East.
>
> The Eriksons never informed the other CERBCO board members of this interest in the subsidiary East, but did inform them of the proposed sale of the Erikson's stock. In fact, a member of the CERBCO board later specifically asked the Eriksons whether there had been any interest in a purchase of East. "The Eriksons denied that [the third-party] had ever made such an offer, and had [they] done so, the Eriksons indicated that they would likely vote their shares to reject it."
>
> Ultimately, it was this lack of candor that led both the Chancellor and the Supreme Court to find that the Eriksons had breached their duty of loyalty.

2000 Del. Ch. LEXIS 171, at *42-43, 2000 WL 1847679, at *12 (citing *Thorpe v. CERBCO, Inc.*, 676 A.2d 436, 438-39, 441 (Del. 1996)). The court in *Digex* then distinguished *CERBCO* on the ground that "Digex, through its officers and non-interested directors, was apprised of the status of the various proposed transactions at all times." 2000 Del. Ch. LEXIS 171, at *45-46, 2000 WL 1847679, at *13. The court stated that the controlling shareholder "only had to give fair notice of the opportunity to Digex" and had no "duty to see that a particular transaction involving Digex was consummated." 2000 Del. Ch. LEXIS 171, at *48-49, 2000 WL 1847679, at *14.

Add the following at the end of the paragraph beginning on page 357 and concluding on page 358 (immediately after footnote 1227):

The court in *Cooke v. Oolie*, 2000 Del. Ch. LEXIS 89, 2000 WL 710199 (Del. Ch. May 24, 2000), likewise held that the fact that a shareholder also is a director "does not disable the director-shareholder from negotiating the most favorable terms achievable for the sale of his stock" so long as the director-shareholder does not "misuse his corporate office to his own advantage and to the exclusion of the other shareholders." 2000 Del. Ch. LEXIS 89, at *56, 2000 WL 710199, at *16. Applying this rule, the court held that a sale by two directors of their controlling interests in The Nostalgic Network, Inc. ("TNN"), a corporation operating under extreme financial distress, for a premium above market value did not constitute a breach of the directors' duty of loyalty. The court reasoned as follows:

> The defendants, in this case, have not misused their corporate offices in any way. As I will discuss in later sections, the defendants neither sold their stock using confidential corporate information, nor sold their corporate offices outright. The defendants also did not sell their shares to a buyer who looted the company. Accordingly, the defendants, as majority shareholders, did not breach any fiduciary duty when they elected to sell their control block for a premium. Thus, the only question that remains is whether the defendants, purely as directors, have, in some way, breached their duty of loyalty to the company.
>
> I find as a matter of law that the defendants have not breached their duty of loyalty. The defendants vigorously pursued transactions in the shareholders' best interests, contacting 59 companies. The board considered five (5) proposals and elected to pursue the USA deal, which unfortunately collapsed. At that point defendants found themselves in a precarious position – the company faced financial disaster in a matter of weeks and had just lost the deal it had been negotiating. The defendants did not "jump ship" as the plaintiffs contend. It is undisputed that the defendants solicited TCI and Concept. They also contacted DLJ for assistance. Janas solicited Lifetime. In spite of these attempts, new options never materialized. The defendants wrote a letter to Gold asking it to launch a tender offer for all shares of all shareholders. Gold refused. The defendants suggested that Gold purchase company shares as opposed to defendants' personal shares. Gold refused. Ultimately, Gold only offered to buy defendants' shares. Even at that point, defendants did not completely abandon TNN. Instead, the defendants negotiated a contract provision with Gold which mandated that Gold fund TNN when necessary.

> These undisputed actions are not the actions of faithless directors acting in their own self-interest.
>
> The plaintiffs implore me to find a breach of loyalty because the defendants did not disclose their discussions with Gold to the board in a timely fashion and because the defendants did not contact AMC after USA terminated its proposal. Although I agree that, in a more perfect world, the defendants would have immediately and completely disclosed their discussions with Gold to the board and would have called AMC, I do not believe that plaintiffs can hold defendants captive in perpetuity to locate a buyer for TNN. Ultimately, I conclude, as a matter of law, that these facts do not rise to the level of a breach of loyalty. Although we encourage directors to aspire to ideal corporate governance practices, directors' actions need not achieve perfection to avoid liability. Directors must adhere to the minimum legal requirements of the corporation law. Although the defendants failed to act as a model director might have acted, for the above reasons and on the undisputed facts I conclude, as a matter of law, that they did not breach a legal duty.

2000 Del. Ch. LEXIS 89, at *56-59, 2000 WL 710199, at *16-17 (footnotes omitted).

Replace the citation to the Fleming case in footnote 1235 on page 358 with the following:

1996 Del. Ch. LEXIS 91, 1996 WL 422377 (Del. Ch. July 24, 1996), *subsequent proceedings*, 1998 Del. Ch. LEXIS 40, 1998 WL 155543 (Del. Ch. Mar. 26, 1998), *subsequent proceedings*, 735 A.2d 386 (Del. Ch. 1999).

Replace the citation to the Fleming case in footnote 1238 on page 359 with the following:

1996 Del. Ch. LEXIS 91, 1996 WL 422377 (Del. Ch. July 24, 1996), *subsequent proceedings*, 1998 Del. Ch. LEXIS 40, 1998 WL 155543 (Del. Ch. Mar. 26, 1998), *subsequent proceedings*, 735 A.2d 386 (Del. Ch. 1999).

Add the following at the end of the paragraph beginning on page 359 and concluding on page 360 (immediately after footnote 1241):

Following a trial, the court in *Odyssey Partners, L.P. v. Fleming Cos.*, 735 A.2d 386 (Del. Ch. 1999), reaffirmed the principles previously stated by the court: "[f]iduciary obligation does not require self-sacrifice," and "one who may be both a creditor and a fiduciary (e.g., a director or controlling shareholder) does not by reason of that status alone have special limitations imposed upon the exercise of his or her creditor rights." *Id.* at 415 (quoting *Odyssey Partners, L.P. v. Fleming Cos.*, 1996 Del. Ch. LEXIS 91, at *10-11, 1996 WL 422377, at *3 (Del. Ch. July 24, 1996)). The court quoted the following statement in *Thorpe v. CERBCO, Inc.*, 19 Del. J. Corp. L. 942 (Del. Ch. Oct. 29, 1993): "[C]ontrolling shareholders, while not allowed to use their control over corporate property or processes to exploit the minority, are not required to act altruistically towards them." 735 A.2d at 411 (quoting 19 Del. J. Corp. L. at 956).

The court accordingly held that Fleming's rejection, at a time when it was a 46.8 percent shareholder of ABCO, of a proposal requiring Fleming to give up "for nothing" a supply agreement pursuant to which ABCO, the owner of a chain of grocery stores, was required to purchase at least 51 percent of its dry groceries, perishables and general merchandise from Fleming, did not constitute a breach of fiduciary duty. *Id.* at 392, 410-411. Nor, the court held, did Fleming's rejection of another proposal requiring "significant and disproportionate self-sacrifice by Fleming," including "suffering material dilution of its equity interest," providing additional vendor credit, deferring principal payments, guaranteeing new store leases for ABCO and subordinating its debt, constitute a breach of fiduciary duty by Fleming. *Id.* at 411. The court explained that "Fleming was under no obligation to agree to any of these things, either as a stockholder, a supplier or a creditor." *Id.* To the contrary, "Fleming's refusal to waive its preemptive rights or to assume further financial obligations on behalf of ABCO without adequate compensation cannot seriously be thought to have been a breach of its fiduciary duties." *Id.*

The court also held that Fleming's "mere status as a fiduciary" after it obtained 50.1 percent ownership of ABCO "did not impose on it extra-statutory obligations in the conduct of the foreclosure sale." *Id.* at 415 (quoting *Odyssey Partners, L.P. v. Fleming Cos.*, 1998 Del. Ch. LEXIS 40, at *5, 1998 WL 155543, at *2 (Del. Ch. Mar. 26, 1998)). To the contrary, "Fleming was not acting in a fiduciary capacity when it bid at the foreclosure sale and, thus, its conduct thereat is not subject to a fiduciary duty analysis." *Id.* at 415. In short, "Fleming's rights to control the foreclosure sale were statutory rights derived from its status as a secured creditor," and "[s]ince these rights did not derive from any fiduciary relationship, the law will not impress upon them special limitations that pertain to the conduct of fiduciaries." *Id.*

The court acknowledged that "this rationale would not extend to actions taken by Fleming, as majority stockholder, to prevent the board of directors from acting to protect ABCO or its stockholders from the 'threat' posed by the notice of foreclosure." *Id.* As discussed above, the court previously had denied a motion to dismiss based upon allegations that Fleming used its majority shareholder status in an impermissible manner. 1996 Del. Ch. LEXIS 91, at *12-14, 1996 WL 422377, at *4-5. Following the trial of the action, however, the court held that the record "does not support a conclusion that any action or decision of the ABCO board of directors taken or not taken in response to Fleming's notice of foreclosure was the product of Fleming's domination or control." 735 A.2d at 415.

Replace the period at the end of the Marriott citation in footnote 1242 on page 360 with the following:

, *subsequent proceedings*, 2000 Del. Ch. LEXIS 17, at *23, 61-62, 2000 WL 128875, at *7, 18 (Del. Ch. Jan. 24, 2000).

Add the following at the end of the fifth sentence (immediately after footnote 1248) of the paragraph beginning on page 360 and concluding on page 362:

The court in *In re Life Technologies, Inc. Shareholders Litigation*, No. 16513 (Del. Ch. Nov. 24, 1998), reiterated this principle. The court held that a majority shareholder making a tender offer has no duty to offer minority shareholders a fair price. *Id.*, Tr. at 4. This rule, the court explained, "is premised on the understanding that tender offers are voluntary transactions; that is, that stockholders each have a free choice . . . to tender or not at a given price." *Id.* "[W]here one shareholder offers to purchase the shares of another, or even where a corporation offers to purchase its own shares from its stockholders, or a majority shareholder offers to purchase shares held by minority shareholders, no person or entity stands on both sides of the transaction." *Id.*

Add the following at the end of footnote 1249 on page 362:

See also In re Marriott Hotel Props. II LP Unitholders Litig. ("Marriott III"), 2000 Del. Ch. LEXIS 17, at *48-49, 56-61, 2000 WL 128875, at *14, 16-17 (Del. Ch. Jan. 24, 2000) (stating that "the law provides a framework that is well-suited to the individual and essentially voluntary nature" of a tender offer by a controlling shareholder or a general partner, that there is a "fundamental difference between a merger, in which . . . the board of directors . . . plays an integral role, and a tender offer, in which the offeror deals directly with the . . . stockholders," and that "the entire fairness test properly applies to protect minority stockholders from the tyranny of the controlling entity" but where a general partner stands on one side of a transaction and limited partners stand on the other side "[i]t would be exceedingly paternalistic and intrusive to hold that the entire fairness test is required to protect the limited partners from themselves"; and rejecting a claim that the combination of a tender offer and a consent solicitation seeking approval of amendments to a limited partnership agreement that would permit affiliates of the general partner to vote limited partnership units acquired in the tender offer and remove a prohibition against the transfer of more than 50 percent of the partnership units within a 12 month period "amounted to a reorganization akin to a merger": unlike a merger, the court stated, "no act of 'corporate governance'" – "except for allowing the Amendments to be voted upon" – such as board or general partner approval "is required to complete the transaction"); *Korsinsky v. Granlund* No. 605635/99, slip op. at 13-14 (N.Y. Sup. Ct. N.Y. Co. Aug. 16, 2000) ("[T]he 'entire fairness' doctrine only applies to 'freeze-out' or 'cash out' mergers or 'self-tender' offers, and not to a voluntary tender offer by a third party, as is the case here. In the 'freeze-out' transaction, the minority is simply forced out of the corporation by majority vote, regardless of whether any individual shareholder ever wishes to sell his or her shares, and the directors and the majority shareholders are duty-bound to ensure the 'entire fairness' of the transaction, including a fairly determined price. In the context of tender offers, however, where minority shareholders have a choice to hold or sell their holdings as they see fit, New York law does not impose this broad obligation of 'entire fairness,' and hence does not require fiduciaries to ensure a fair tender offer price.") (citations omitted).

Add the following at the end of the sixth sentence (immediately after footnote 1249) of the paragraph beginning on page 360 and concluding on page 362:

This rule – that in the absence of coercion or disclosure violations a tender offer need not be made at a fair price – applies equally to self-tender offers. *Frank v. Arnelle*, 725 A.2d 441 (unpublished opinion, text available at 1999 Del. Ch. LEXIS 25, at *6, 1999 WL 89284, at *2) (Del. Jan. 22, 1999), *aff'd*, 1998 Del. Ch. LEXIS 176, at *15, 1998 WL 668649, at *4 (Del. Ch. Sept. 16, 1998); *Cottle v. Standard Brands Paint Co.*, [1990 Transfer Binder] Fed. Sec. L. Rep. (CCH) ¶ 95,306, at 96,431 (Del. Ch. Mar. 22, 1990); *Lewis v. Fuqua Indus., Inc.*,

1982 Del. Ch. LEXIS 575, at *7, 1982 WL 8783, at *3 (Del. Ch. Feb. 16, 1982).

Add the following at the end of the third sentence (immediately after footnote 1254) of the paragraph beginning and concluding on page 362:

A court construing Virginia law reached the same conclusion in a case involving directors of a close corporation. *See Berman v. Physical Med. Assocs., Ltd.*, 225 F.3d 429, 433-34 (4th Cir. 2000).

Add "controlling shareholders of" between "cases involving" and "close corporations" in the fourth sentence (immediately after footnote 1254) of the paragraph beginning and concluding on page 362.

Section B 3 c

Add the following new footnote 1257.1 at the end of the fourth sentence of the paragraph beginning and concluding on page 363:

See Cheff v. Mathes, 199 A.2d 548, 555 (Del. 1964) ("it is elementary that a holder of a substantial number of shares would expect to receive the control premium as part of his selling price"), *quoted in Strassburger v. Earley*, 752 A.2d 557, 572 n.35 (Del. Ch. 2000).

Add the following at the end of footnote 1258 on page 363:

See also Cooke v. Oolie, 2000 Del. Ch. LEXIS 89, at *56, 2000 WL 710199, at *16 (Del. Ch. May 24, 2000); *Strassburger*, 752 A.2d at 572 n.35; *McMullen v. Beran*, 1999 Del. Ch. LEXIS 227, at *11 & n.17, 1999 WL 1135146, at *3 & n.17 (Del. Ch. Dec. 1, 1999), *rev'd on other grounds*, 765 A.2d 910 (Del. 2000).

Add the following at the end of footnote 1259 on page 363:

See also Korsinsky v. Granlund, No. 605635/99, slip op. at 13 (N.Y. Sup. Ct. N.Y. Co. Aug. 16, 2000).

Add the following at the end of footnote 1267 on page 365:

See also Cooke, 2000 Del. Ch. LEXIS 89, at *64, 2000 WL 710199, at *19 ("Courts have regularly upheld agreements for the sale of a majority of the outstanding shares of stock in a corporation, or of less than a majority but enough to ordinarily carry voting control, which contain a provision that the seller will arrange for a majority of the existing directors to resign and be replaced by the purchaser's designees. Courts have upheld these provisions because they have realized that such a contractual provision merely accelerates a change that would occur anyway at the next shareholders' meeting.") (footnote omitted).

Add the following at the end of the paragraph beginning and concluding on page 365 (immediately after footnote 1271):

As the court in *McMullen v. Beran*, 1999 Del. Ch. LEXIS 227, 1999 WL 1135146 (Del. Ch. Dec. 1, 1999), *rev'd on other grounds*, 765 A.2d 910 (Del. 2000), summarized the holding in *Thorpe v. CERBCO, Inc.*, 676 A.2d 436 (Del. 1996), a controlling shareholder is entitled to a control premium so long as the controlling shareholder does "not obtain that premium by using its control of the corporate board to divert opportunity for such premium from corporation to itself." 1999 Del. Ch. LEXIS 227, at *11 & n.17, 1999 WL 1135146, at *3 n.17.

Add the following at the end of the paragraph beginning on page 367 and concluding on page 368 (immediately after footnote 1287):

A third court in New York in *Korsinsky v. Granlund*, No. 605635/99 (N.Y. Sup. Ct. N.Y. Co. Aug. 16, 2000), thus summarized the law as follows: "'[A]bsent looting of corporate assets, conversion of a corporate opportunity, fraud or other acts of bad faith, a controlling shareholder' is permitted to obtain a 'premium' when selling his/her shares, in order to reflect the added value accompanying his/her control." *Id.*, slip op. at 13 (quoting *Zetlin v. Hanson Holdings, Inc.*, 48 N.Y.2d 684, 685, 397 N.E.2d 387, 388-89, 421 N.Y.S.2d 877, 878 (1979)).

Replace "1998" with "2001" in the Balotti citation in footnote 1290 on page 368.

Section B 3 d

Add the following at the end of footnote 1293 on page 369:

See also Strassburger v. Earley, 752 A.2d 557, 570 (Del. Ch. 2000).

Add the following at the end of the paragraph beginning on page 368 and concluding on page 369 (immediately after footnote 1294):

Fairness may be required even where a controlling shareholder receives the same consideration in amount and form per share as all other shareholders but gains a financial advantage by timing or structuring the transaction in a manner that favors the controlling shareholder at the expense of minority shareholders (for example, by insisting upon an immediate cash sale of the corporation at a time when the controlling shareholder needs cash and greater consideration would be available by accepting non-cash consideration such as stock or waiting to complete the sale of the corporation until a later time). *See McMullin v. Beran*, 765 A.2d 910, 921 (Del. 2000).

Where multiple transactions are part of "a single, unified package" that are "inextricably linked" (such as repurchases of a total of 83 percent of a corporation's outstanding shares from its two largest shareholders and the sale of the corporation's principal operating assets to finance the repurchases), each of the transactions must be fair. *Strassburger*, 752 A.2d at 570.

Add the following at the end of footnote 1296 on page 370:

See also T. Rowe Price Recovery Fund, L.P. v. Rubin, 770 A.2d 536, 552 (Del. Ch. 2000) ("the entire fairness standard of review applies . . . to interested transaction[s] involving controlling stockholders").

Replace "Shareholders involved in such" in the sentence following the block quote in the paragraph beginning on page 369 and concluding on page 370 (immediately after footnote 1296) with the following:

Goodwin v. Live Entertainment, Inc., 1999 Del. Ch. LEXIS 5, 1999 WL 64265 (Del. Ch. Jan. 22, 1999), *aff'd*, 741 A.2d 16 (unpublished opinion, text available at 1999 Del. LEXIS 238 and 1999 WL 624128) (Del. July 23, 1999), similarly held that Pioneer Electronics Corporation, which had effective voting control of Live Entertainment, Inc. – and thus veto authority over any transaction requiring shareholder approval – through its ownership of common stock and all shares of the corporation's Series C preferred stock did not stand on both sides of a merger of Live Entertainment with Bain Capital, Inc. 1999 Del. Ch. LEXIS 5, at *6, 83, 1999 WL 624128, at *2, 27. The court rejected plaintiff's attempt "to show that Pioneer had some other material self-interest in the merger" based upon discussions between Pioneer and Live Entertainment concerning "making certain contractual arrangements conditions precedent to the merger," which plaintiff suggested "somehow constituted illicit 'side consideration.'" 1999 Del. Ch. LEXIS 5, at *83, 1999 WL 64265, at *27. The court explained that plaintiff had not "presented evidence regarding the value of these possible arrangements from which I could make an inference that Pioneer had a strong desire to consummate those arrangements and that a subjective belief on its part that Bain would agree to do so after the merger might have led it to support a merger at a price that was not desirable to it and the other common stockholders." 1999 Del. Ch. LEXIS 5, at *83-84, 1999 WL 64265, at *27.

The court stated that a shareholder challenging the independence of directors "based solely upon their election by and relationship to a controlling stockholder in a situation like this . . . has an obligation to produce record evidence demonstrating that the controlling stockholder's commercial interests were of such a substantial nature as to possibly compromise its natural desire to obtain the best price for its shares." 1999 Del. Ch. LEXIS 5, at *84, 1999 WL 64265, at *27. Here, the court held, "the record is empty of evidence, rather than rhetoric, regarding the monetary or strategic significance of these matters to Pioneer." *Id.* The court concluded that "[t]he record lacks any evidence that Pioneer sought for itself better terms for its common stock than the other stockholders or that its elected representatives (who constituted only five of the thirteen board members) dominated the Board and used that domination to obtain an exorbitant price for its Series C shares at the expense of the common stockholders." 1999 Del. Ch. LEXIS 5, at *85, 1999 WL 64265, at *27. The court thus held that plaintiff failed to overcome the presumption of the business judgment rule. 1999 Del. Ch. LEXIS 5, *19 & n.4, 74-76, 1999 WL 64265, at *7 & n.4, 24.

Odyssey Partners, L.P. v. Fleming Cos., 735 A.2d 386 (Del. Ch. 1999), involved the purchase by Fleming Companies, which at the time owned 50.1 percent of the outstanding shares of ABCO Holding, Inc., of (1) a loan to ABCO by Chemical Bank and (2) all of the corporation's assets at a foreclosure sale. The court held that these transactions "*involved* ABCO" but were not transactions "*with* ABCO" and thus were not subject to review under a fairness standard. *Id.* at 412. The court explained that "[i]n theory, an entire fairness standard of review is appropriate where the controlling stockholder has actually used its power over the corporation 'to impair the normal and primary protection the law affords the corporation and its stockholders: the judgment of its independent board of directors'" (*id.* at 412, quoting what now appears at I Rodman Ward, Jr., Edward P. Welch & Andrew J. Turezyn, *Folk on the Delaware Corporation Law* § 151.6, at GCL-V-39 (4th ed. Supp. 2001-2)), but that in this case Fleming did not use its power over ABCO to impair ABCO's shareholders of the judgment of an independent board of directors.

With respect to Fleming's purchase of the Chemical Bank loan, the court held, there was no evidence that ABCO's board "had any occasion to become involved in negotiating the terms of Fleming's deal with Chemical Bank," and "[n]or is there evidence that Fleming used its position as ABCO's largest stockholder to secure terms from Chemical Bank that might not otherwise have been available." *Id.* at 412. The court stated that "[n]either the process by which Fleming negotiated its deal with Chemical Bank nor the terms of the agreement between Fleming and Chemical Bank were relevant to ABCO and its stockholders." *Id.* at 413. To the contrary, "[t]he only matter of interest to ABCO was that all of its defaulted, secured indebtedness would, as a consequence of the transaction, be held in the same hands," a result that "would marginally decrease ABCO's room to maneuver by eliminating the theoretical possibility of negotiating with Chemical Bank to restructure its debt" and "marginally increase Fleming's powers as a creditor to notice and supervise the foreclosure sale." *Id.* These considerations, the court stated, "are not the sort of considerations that have ever caused a Delaware court to invoke the entire fairness standard of review." *Id.*

With respect to Fleming's purchase of ABCO's assets at the foreclosure sale, the court held that this transaction, like Fleming's purchase of the Chemical Bank loan, "was not a negotiated transaction *between* Fleming and ABCO." *Id* at 414. The statutory process that governs a foreclosure sale, the court stated, "did not require ABCO directors' approval of either the notice of foreclosure or the terms of the winning bid at the foreclosure." *Id.* Accordingly, "Fleming did not owe a fiduciary duty to ABCO, or its minority shareholders to bid or pay a 'fair price' at the foreclosure sale." *Id.*

Shareholders involved in

Section B 3 e

Add the following at the end of footnote 1302 on page 371:

See also Stegemeier v. Magness, 728 A.2d 557, 564 (Del. 1999) (quoting *Sinclair Oil Corp. v. Levien*, 280 A.2d 717, 720 (Del. 1971); *Solomon v. Armstrong*, 747 A.2d 1098, 1113 & nn. 35 & 36 (Del. Ch. 1999), *aff'd*, 746 A.2d 277 (unpublished opinion, full text available at 2000 Del. LEXIS 30 and 2000 WL 140072) (Del. Jan. 26, 2000).

Add the following at the end of the paragraph beginning on page 370 and concluding on page 371 (immediately after footnote 1303):

In other words, "[s]elf-dealing attacks on the business judgment rule require that there be something more than a simple transaction between a parent and its subsidiary; there must be some cognizable allegation of wrongdoing." *Solomon*, 747 A.2d at 1113 n.36.

Add the following at the end of footnote 1341 on page 376:

See also In re Dairy Mart Convenience Stores, Inc. Derivative Litig., 1999 Del. Ch. LEXIS 94, at *36 n.28, 1999 WL 350473, at *10 n.28 (Del. Ch. May 24, 1999) (citing *Citron v. E.I. Du Pont de Nemours & Co.*, 584 A.2d 490, 500 n.13 (Del. Ch. 1990) as a "But cf." case "suggesting that the controlling stockholder relationship alone raises an inference of improper dealing, thus immediately subjecting the transaction to entire fairness review"); *Solomon*, 747 A.2d at 1113 n.35 (also citing *Citron* as a "But cf." case and describing *Citron* as "citing conflicting cases and suggesting that the parent-subsidiary or controlling stockholder relationship *alone* can raise an inference of improper dealing during a transaction").

Add the following at the end of the paragraph beginning on page 375 and concluding on page 376 (immediately after footnote 1342):

The Delaware Supreme Court's decision in *McMullin v. Beran*, 765 A.2d 910 (Del. 2000), reversed the denial of a motion to dismiss a claim that the directors of a controlled subsidiary breached their fiduciary duty to the subsidiary and its shareholders by approving a sale of the corporation to a third party in a transaction where all shareholders received the same consideration. The court based its ruling upon an allegation that the controlling shareholder insisted upon an immediate all-cash transaction when greater value could have been achieved by a differently timed or structured agreement involving cash and securities. The court held that plaintiff had alleged a duty of loyalty claim and overcome the presumption of the business judgment rule because a majority of the subsidiary's directors lacked disinterestedness or independence from the controlling shareholder. *Id.* at 923; *see also* Chapter III, Section A 4 g (discussing duty of care ruling in the *McMullin* decision). The court did not address the holdings in *Sinclair Oil Corp. v. Levien*, 280 A.2d 717 (Del. 1971), and its progeny.

Section B 3 f

Add the following at the end of footnote 1345 on page 376:

See also Shaev v. Wyly, 1998 Del. Ch. LEXIS 2, at *7, 1998 WL 13858, at *2 (Del. Ch. Jan. 6, 1998), *motion for reargument denied*, 1998 Del. Ch. LEXIS 33, 1998 WL 118200 (Del. Ch. Mar. 6, 1998), *aff'd*, 719 A.2d 490 (unpublished opinion, text available at 1998 Del. LEXIS 356 and 1998 WL 764168) (Del. Oct. 1, 1998).

Add the following at the end of footnote 1346 on page 376:

See also Richardson v. Reliance Nat'l Indem. Co., 2000 U.S. Dist. LEXIS 2838, at *32-34, 2000 WL 284211, at *12 (N.D. Cal. Mar. 9, 2000) (holding that officers of wholly-owned subsidiary owe fiduciary duties to shareholders of the parent corporation); *Grace Bros., Ltd. v. UniHolding Corp.*, 2000 Del. Ch. LEXIS 101, at *40-42, 2000 WL 982401, at *12-13 (Del. Ch. July 12, 2000) ("a wholly-owned subsidiary functions to benefit its parent" and "[t]o the extent that members of the parent board are on the subsidiary board or have knowledge of proposed action at the subsidiary level that is detrimental to the parent, they have a fiduciary duty, as part of their management responsibilities, to act in the best interests of the parent and its stockholders"; the court rejected a claim that there is a "safe harbor in our corporate law for fiduciaries who purposely permit a wholly-owned subsidiary to effect a transaction that is unfair to the parent company on whose board they serve" in order to benefit the controlling shareholders of the parent corporation); *Cochran v. Stifel Fin. Corp.*, 2000 Del. Ch. LEXIS 58, at *37, 2000 WL 286722, at *11 (Del. Ch. Mar. 8, 2000) ("a wholly-owned subsidiary is to be managed solely so as to benefit its corporate parent"); *Solomon v. Armstrong*, 747 A.2d 1098, 1123 (Del. Ch. 1999), *aff'd*, 746 A.2d 277 (unpublished opinion, full text available at 2000 Del. LEXIS 30 and 2000 WL 140072) (Del. Jan. 26, 2000); *Shaev*, 1998 Del. Ch. LEXIS 2, at *7, 1998 WL 13858, at *2.

Add the following at the end of the second sentence (immediately after footnote 1345) of the second paragraph beginning and concluding on page 376:

This principle, the court stated in *Solomon v. Armstrong*, 747 A.2d 1098 (Del. Ch. 1999), *aff'd*, 746 A.2d 277 (unpublished opinion, full text available at 2000 Del. LEXIS 30 and 2000 WL 140072) (Del. Jan. 26, 2000), "contemplates on its own terms that the best interest of *all* of the shareholders of the parent company will be considered by the Board." *Id.* at 1123.

The *Solomon* case involved the split-off of a wholly-owned subsidiary of a corporation where the performance of a tracking stock was linked to the performance of the subsidiary being split-off. The court stated that the "legally relevant" question was whether "the process for allocating value" was "reasonably aimed at providing a fair result to all shareholders taken together and each and every class of shareholders taken separately." *Id.* at 1123-24. This decision is discussed further in Chapter II, Section E 4 a.

Add the following at the end of the second paragraph beginning and concluding on page 376 (immediately after footnote 1344):

The court in *First American Corp. v. Al-Nahyan*, 17 F. Supp. 2d 10 (D.D.C. 1998), a case construing Virginia law, rejected a claim that directors of a wholly-owned subsidiary owe a fiduciary duty only to the subsidiary's parent corporation. The court stated that "[t]he duties of the directors of wholly owned subsidiaries have not been articulated in the law" and that "[c]ase law leaves subsidiary directors wondering whether their duty runs primarily to the parent corporation as shareholder, to the subsidiary corporation itself as an entity, or even to other constituencies such as creditors, regulators, employees, and communities." *Id.* at 26 (quoting Gouvin, *Resolving the Subsidiary Director's Dilemma*, 47 Hastings L.J. 287, 324 (1996)).

The court then stated that "the directors of a wholly-owned subsidiary owe the corporation fiduciary duties, just as they would any other corporation" and that "the subsidiary has standing to sue for breach of those duties." *Id.* at 26. The court stated that the "far more perplexing issue is to define the scope of those duties." *Id.* The court posed the following questions: "[A]ssuming the director's principal duty to the wholly-owned subsidiary corporation is to manage it in the best interests of its sole shareholder, the parent corporation, who is to determine what the best interests of the parent are?," and "May (or must) the subsidiary's Board make an independent business judgment about the parent's best interests or is the subsidiary's Board obliged to accept the edict of the parent's Board in all circumstances?" *Id.* These questions, the court stated, "will await future cases and further commentary for answers." *Id.* (footnote omitted). In the meantime, the court held that the directors in the case before the court had fiduciary duties to manage the wholly-owned subsidiary in a manner that avoided violations of law, and that sufficient evidence had been produced with respect to whether the directors did so to warrant denial of the directors' motion for summary judgment "[w]hatever the precise language required to articulate this duty." *Id.* at 26-27.

The court rejected the directors' contention that *Anadarko Petroleum Corp. v. Panhandle Eastern Corp.*, 545 A.2d 1171 (Del. 1988), holds that "a wholly-owned subsidiary's director's fiduciary duties flow only to the parent corporation." 17 F. Supp. 2d at 26. This contention, the court stated, "overstates the 'narrow confines' of the court's holding" in *Anadarko*. *Id.* The court in *First American* reasoned that *Anadarko* involved claims by purchasers of contingent equity interests in a planned spin-off of a wholly-owned subsidiary, who alleged that the board of the spun-off corporation breached its fiduciary duties by agreeing to modify contracts between the parent and the spun-off corporation in the interim period between the date when the interests were sold and the date the spun-off corporation became an independent entity. *Id.* According to the court in *First American*, the court in *Anadarko* held only that "during that liminal period, the spin-off's Board did not owe any fiduciary duties to the prospective owners." *Id.* The court in *First American* stated that "[e]ven assuming the Virginia courts would follow *Anadarko*, they would understand it to apply only to the question of who are the shareholders to whom the directors of a wholly-owned subsidiary owe duties when the corporation is being spun-off – the parent or the prospective purchasers," and "*Anadarko* teaches that the answer to that question lies in a careful examination of the nature of the prospective purchasers' interests in the spin-off." *Id.*

Change the word "director" to "directors" in the second sentence of the paragraph beginning and concluding on page 377 (between footnotes 1347 and 1348).

Section B 3 g

Add the following at the end of footnote 1350 on page 377:

See also Popp Telcom v. Am. Sharecom, Inc., 210 F.3d 928, 931 n.2 (8th Cir. 2000) ("[a] 'freeze-out' merger is one which forces the minority interest to give up its equity in the corporation in exchange for cash or senior securities while allowing the controlling interest to retain its equity") (quoting *Sifferle v. Micom Corp.*, 384 N.W.2d 503, 506 n.1 (Minn. Ct. App. 1986)); *Solomon v. Armstrong*, 747 A.2d 1098, 1120 (Del. Ch. 1999) ("in a classic freeze-out the minority shareholders have no choice"; "by virtue of its majority control, the parent corporation can force the transaction through without the consent of the minority"), *aff'd*, 746 A.2d 277 (unpublished opinion, full text available at 2000 Del. LEXIS 30 and 2000 WL 140072) (Del. Jan. 26, 2000).

Add the following at the end of footnote 1353 on page 378:

See also Solomon, 747 A.2d at 1120 ("our law imposes heightened fiduciary duties on the parent corporation" because "the parent corporation can force the transaction through without the consent of the minority").

Add the following at the end of the second sentence (immediately after footnote 1360) of the paragraph beginning and concluding on page 378:

As stated by the Delaware Court of Chancery in *In re Unocal Exploration Corp. Shareholders Litigation*, 2000 Del. Ch. LEXIS 92, 2000 WL 823376 (Del. Ch. June 13, 2000):

> Section 251(b) of the DGCL [Delaware General Corporation Law] provides that a 50.1% majority stockholder seeking to purchase the corporation's remaining shares through a merger *cannot complete the transaction* without obtaining the recommendation and approval of the corporation's directors. This procedural hurdle is critical because directors are obliged to make that recommendation in a manner consistent with their fiduciary duties. By exercising control over the corporation's board of directors, the 50.1% stockholder may, *in breach of its fiduciary duties to the minority stockholders*, cause the board, in breach of their respective fiduciary duties, to approve a merger that is not fair to the minority stockholders. Delaware law is therefore clear that if a controlling stockholder engages in a long-form merger to eliminate the minority, this court will review the transaction for entire fairness.

2000 Del. Ch. LEXIS 92, at *21, 2000 WL 823376, at *6 (footnotes omitted).

Add the following at the end of the paragraph beginning and concluding on page 379 (immediately after footnote 1362):

As stated in *International Telecharge, Inc. v. Bomarko*, 766 A.2d 437 (Del. 2000), "[t]he fair dealing prong of the entire fairness inquiry relates to how a transaction is structured and negotiated" and "[t]he fair price prong 'relates to the economic and financial considerations of the proposed merger.'" *Id.* at 440.

Add the following at the end of the second sentence (immediately after footnote 1364) of the paragraph beginning on page 379 and concluding on page 380:

"When making a determination of the transaction's entire fairness courts examine the transaction as a whole looking at both fair price and fair dealing, without focusing on one component over another." *Int'l Telecharge*, 766 A.2d at 440.

Add the following at the end of footnote 1366 on page 380:

See also Strassburger v. Earley, 752 A.2d at 557, 572 & n.35, 576-77 (Del. Ch. 2000) (finding unfair dealing in case where price was fair).

Add the following at the end of the fourth sentence (immediately after footnote 1366) of the paragraph beginning on page 379 and concluding on page 380:

Another Court of Chancery decision states that an unfairness claim "consists of two elements, unfair dealing and unfair price, also known as procedural fairness and substantive fairness, respectively," and that "[b]oth of these aspects of fairness have to be met for a board's decision to be found entirely fair to the minority shareholders." *Onti, Inc. v. Integra Bank*, 751 A.2d 904, 930 (Del. Ch. 1999).

Add the following at the end of the paragraph beginning on page 379 and concluding on page 380 (immediately after footnote 1369):

This fairness standard does not govern short-form mergers provided for by Section 253 of the Delaware General Corporation Law, which "allows a corporate parent holding 90 percent or more of each class of another corporation's stock unilaterally to file a certificate of merger eliminating the minority stock interest" without "any action by the board of directors or stockholders of the subsidiary to accomplish such a merger." *Unocal*, 2000 Del. Ch. LEXIS 92, at *1-2, 2000 WL 823376, at *1. "Each minority stockholder of the subsidiary, if dissatisfied with the terms of the merger," is permitted to exercise appraisal rights. 2000 Del. Ch. LEXIS 92, at *2, 2000 WL 823376, at *1. The court reasoned as follows:

> The function and purpose of § 253 is both inconsistent with and undermined by the application of a heightened judicial standard of review, and the concomitant heightened incentive for procedural safeguards, that applies to long-form mergers involving a controlling stockholder. Put simply, long-form and

> short-form mergers should be subject to a different set of rules because one form of transaction requires the subsidiary board's participation and assent while the other does not. The entire fairness standard of review governs long-form mergers with a controlling stockholder and consists of both "fair dealing" and "fair price." It cannot apply meaningfully to a pure short-form merger, in which no "dealing" is required. Plaintiffs' argument that the entire fairness standard applies, although finding some support in decided cases, contradicts the basic principle that, absent fraud, gross overreaching, or other such wrongful conduct, appraisal is the exclusive remedy to minority stockholders in a short-form merger.
>
> * * *
>
> To do otherwise would gut the short-form merger statute of its meaning. For better or worse, the legislature granted a 90% parent corporation the right to merge the subsidiary out of existence unilaterally and provided an appraisal remedy for the minority stockholders in each such instance. It is simply inconsistent with that grant of power to superimpose on its exercise, in every case, an analysis of the "procedure" employed in fixing the terms of the merger.

2000 Del. Ch. LEXIS 92, at *22-23, 50-51, 2000 WL 823376, at *6, 13. Even where the majority does negotiate with the minority – for example, by utilizing a special committee process "mimicking the mechanism often used in connection with transactions in which the entire fairness standard applies" – the fairness standard does not govern, at least where the process is "not a sham or one adopted to lull investors into abandoning their appraisal remedy." 2000 Del. Ch. LEXIS 92, at *25, 2000 WL 823376, at *7.

Add the following at the end of the paragraph beginning on page 393 and concluding on page 397 (immediately after footnote 1468):

- *Nebel v. Southwest Bancorp, Inc.*, 1999 Del. Ch. LEXIS 30, at *21, 23-24, 1999 WL 135259, at *6, 7 (Del. Ch. Mar. 9, 1999) (denying motion to dismiss and motion for summary judgment in an action challenging a short-form merger where no independent committee of directors represented the interests of minority shareholders and the "significant gap" between the $41 per share merger price and the $85 per share fair value of the shares adjudicated in an appraisal action, combined with allegations that defendants "made no genuine effort to determine MGB's 'fair value,' as opposed to the 'fair market value' of the plaintiffs' shares" and other substantive unfairness allegations, "create an inference that the Merger was the product of unfair dealing . . . sufficient to state a claim upon which relief may be granted"); and

- *O'Reilly v. Transworld Healthcare, Inc.*, 745 A.2d 902, 929-30 (Del. Ch. 1999) (denying motion to dismiss a challenge to a merger of Health Management Inc. ("HMI") into Transworld Healthcare, Inc., where plaintiff alleged that HMI faced substantial financial problems and the possibility of a bankruptcy filing, that Transworld owned 49 percent of HMI's stock and an option to purchase an additional 2 percent of HMI's stock, that Transworld owned substantially all of HMI's debt, that two of HMI's four directors had financial interests in the merger, that "Transworld used its status as a large stockholder and creditor to coerce the HMI board into reducing the Merger price" from $1.50 per share to $0.30 per share, that Transworld prevented HMI from negotiating with Counsel Corporation, a third party that had expressed an interest in acquiring a primary line of HMI's business, that Transworld sold HMI's assets to Counsel after the merger and thus "usurped, to its benefit, the opportunity to sell HMI's assets to Counsel Corp.," that the proxy statement distributed to HMI's shareholders contained "materially false and misleading statements . . . regarding Transworld's purpose for engaging in the Merger and the 'arm's length' nature of the Merger negotiations" and that the $0.30 per share merger price was half of HMI's book value and unfair; the court noted, however, that although plaintiff had pled a *prima facie* case of unfairness that survived the motion to dismiss, "it seems possible that the Defendants may be able to show that HMI acted under economic pressure, and after dealing with Transworld at arm's length, accepted the best deal available").

Add the following at the end of the paragraph beginning on page 398 and concluding on page 399 (immediately after footnote 1480):

- *Metropolitan Life Insurance Co. v. Aramark Corp.*, 1998 Del. Ch. LEXIS 70, at *5-7 (Del. Ch. Feb. 5, 1998) (granting motion for preliminary injunction enjoining a stock reclassification plan where the directors assessing the value of shares being cashed out pursuant to the plan improperly applied a private company discount; the court concluded that "if a private company discount, which was very substantial in this case, is illegal, the price wasn't fair, and if the price wasn't fair, it doesn't matter whether the process was fair");
- *In re Dairy Mart Convenience Stores, Inc. Derivative Litigation*, 1999 Del. Ch. LEXIS 94, at *60-61, 1999 WL 350473, at *17 (Del. Ch. May 24, 1999) (denying motion for summary judgment where two directors, one of whom also was an officer, allegedly "entered into a buyout transaction with the Company for their continuing controlling interests in the Company," "threatened to unseat the board if their demands were not met," "the Company met their demands with a transaction that ensured the re-election of the incumbent board at the upcoming annual meeting," and "that transaction was restructured placing two management directors with the

ability to secure near 41% of the voting power and effective voting control for the Company at no cost to those insiders");

- *Strassburger v. Earley*, 752 A.2d 557, 576-77 (Del. Ch. 2000) (finding fair price but unfair dealing following a trial in a case where Ridgewood Properties, Inc. repurchased a total of 83 percent of its outstanding shares from its two largest shareholders, Triton Group, Ltd. and Hesperus Limited Partners, to finance these repurchases Ridgewood sold its principal operating assets, and as a result of the repurchases N. Russell Walden's stock ownership interest increased from 6.9 percent to 55 percent; the court reasoned as follows: "[T]he board's decision to repurchase the Triton and Hesperus stock was triggered by Triton's announcement of its plan to exit its investment. The board's response to that announcement – the repurchases – was initiated by Walden, whose intense self interest in making that happen guided his conduct. To assure that the board would arrive at the specific outcome (structure) he desired, Walden subtly assumed control of the decision making process – a feat that was not difficult to carry off because the remaining directors trusted Walden and followed his lead. In that sense the three relevant fair dealing factors – initiation, structure and negotiation – converged. The board, at Walden's initiation and urging, approved a transaction structure that would benefit only Walden and the two largest shareholders whose holdings were to be repurchased. Walden then negotiated with those two shareholders to obtain favorable price and other terms. Missing from the negotiating process and the board decision making process, however, was any independent representation of the interests of Ridgewood's minority public stockholders. In those circumstances, there was no fair dealing, because there was no advocate committed to protect the minority's interests, and because the players were either indifferent, or had objectives adverse, to those interests."); and

- *Cole v. Kershaw*, 2000 Del. Ch. LEXIS 117, at *25-29, 2000 WL 1206672, at *7-9 (Del. Ch. Aug. 15, 2000) (awarding damages following a trial in a case involving a merger of a general partnership into a limited liability company formed and owned by all but one of the partners of the partnership, where the merger was legally valid but "equitably invalid because both the decision-making process leading up to the merger and the $2,000 merger price were unfair"; the court stated that "[p]rocedures designed to ensure fair process in the context of small enterprises may indeed differ (within limits) from those required in the context of larger corporations," but "certain 'fair process' procedures are fundamental and cannot be dispensed with," including "adequate and timely notice" permitting an investor "to seek injunctive relief or otherwise to protect his interest" and valuation not "accomplished unilaterally by self-interested parties . . . unaided by any independent or disinterested valuation advice").

The Delaware Court of Chancery's decision in *Onti, Inc. v. Integra Bank*, 751 A.2d 904 (Del. Ch. 1999), suggests that fairness under Delaware law requires fair price and fair dealing but that unfair dealing in and of itself may not result in damages. The court stated that "[i]t is hard for me to see" how shareholders "can show that the unfair dealing hurt the shareholders by more than the fair value of the company less the amount offered for their shares. *Id.* at 930 n.108. The court in *Onti* acknowledged that the Supreme Court in *Weinberger v. UOP, Inc.*, 457 A.2d 701 (Del. 1983), stated that "the factors inherent in fair dealing versus fair price . . . must be addressed together," but, according to the court in *Onti*, "where claims for unfair dealing do not rise to the level of fraud . . . the Court should primarily focus on whether the price was unfair." 751 A.2d at 930 n.108 *see also id.* (quoting *Weinberger*, 457 A.2d at 711: "in a non-fraudulent transaction we recognize that price may be the predominant consideration outweighing other features of the merger"); Chapter II, Section B 3 o (additional discussion of *Onti* decision).

Section B 3 h

Add the following at the end of footnote 1501 on page 402:

See also Strassburger v. Earley, 752 A.2d 557, 570 (Del. Ch. 2000) ("the burden of proof will shift from the defendants to the plaintiff shareholder, who must prove that the transaction is unfair . . . where minority stockholders effectively ratify the transaction").

Add the following at the end of the paragraph beginning on page 401 and concluding on page 402 (immediately after footnote 1501:

The Delaware Supreme Court reaffirmed this principle again in *Emerald Partners v. Berlin*, 726 A.2d 1215 (Del. 1999): "The burden of proof on the issue of fairness may shift . . . to the *plaintiff* to demonstrate that the transaction complained of was *not* entirely fair" by "the approval of the transaction by a *fully informed* vote of a majority of the minority shareholders." *Id.* at 1222-23.

"Although the impact of shareholder ratification differs between interested majority shareholder and interested director cases" – in interested director cases, as discussed in Chapter II, Section B 2 c, shareholder ratification triggers business judgment rule review, while in interested majority shareholder cases, as discussed above, shareholder ratification shifts the burden of proving fairness or unfairness – "in either case there arises an identical prerequisite to ratification – the duty to disclose." *In re Walt Disney Co. Derivative Litig.*, 731 A.2d

342, 369 (Del. Ch. 1998), *aff'd with leave to replead on other grounds sub nom. Brehm v. Eisner*, 746 A.2d 244 (Del. 2000). The board's duty to disclose all material facts in both the interested director and the controlling shareholder contexts is discussed in Chapter II, Sections B 2 c and Section C.

"[W]hen it comes to claiming the sufficiency of disclosure and the concomitant legal effect of shareholder ratification after full disclosure (e.g., . . . the shift of the burden of proof of entire fairness from the defendant to the plaintiff) it is defendant who bears the burden." *Solomon v. Armstrong*, 747 A.2d 1098, 1128 (Del. Ch. 1999), *aff'd*, 746 A.2d 277 (unpublished opinion, full text available at 2000 Del. LEXIS 30 and 2000 WL 140072) (Del. Jan. 26, 2000).

"[E]ntire fairness review is unaffected by shareholder ratification" where there is a controlling shareholder but no "specialized voting restrictions (e.g., class voting or majority of the minority approval)." *Id.* at 1116 n.55. "The theory is that since the controlling shareholder can force through the proposed action/transaction by virtue of his control over the franchise, shareholder ratification is self-serving and unremarkable." *Id.*

Add the following at the end of footnote 1501 on page 402:

See also Solomon, 747 A.2d at 1116 ("an informed ratification by a majority of minority shareholders of a transaction between a controlling shareholder and a corporation has the effect of shifting the burden of proof on the issue of entire fairness from the controlling shareholder to the challenging shareholder"); *In re Gen. Motors Class H S'holders Litig.*, 734 A.2d 611, 617 (Del. Ch. 1999) ("in a situation involving an 'interested cash-out merger' *and* a controlling stockholder, the effect of stockholder ratification is limited to shifting the burden of proof under the entire fairness standard from the defendants to the plaintiffs"); *Disney*, 731 A.2d at 368 ("[i]n the context of disinterested shareholder ratification of a deal between the corporation and a majority shareholder, the trial court's deference manifests itself as a shift in the burden of persuasion under the entire fairness standard from the defending directors, who normally must bear the burden, to the plaintiff shareholder, who must now show that the transaction was somehow unfair").

Section B 3 i

Add the following new footnote 1504.1 at the end of the paragraph beginning and concluding on page 402:

These rules apply to all transactions between controlling stockholders and controlled corporations, and not just transactions involving mergers between controlling shareholders and controlled corporations. *See T. Rowe Price Recovery Fund, L.P. v. Rubin*, 770 A.2d 536, 552 (Del. Ch. 2000) (discussing case law).

Add the following at the end of the paragraph beginning and concluding on page 402 (after footnote 1504.1):

As a result, Delaware law "limits an otherwise fully informed, uncoerced vote in such circumstances to having the effect of making the plaintiffs prove that the transaction was unfair. Doubtless defendants appreciate this shift, but it still subjects them to a proceeding in which the substantive fairness of their actions come under close scrutiny by the court – the type of scrutiny that is inappropriate when the business judgment rule's presumption attaches to a decision." *Harbor Fin. Partners v. Huizenga*, 751 A.2d 879, 900-01 (Del. Ch. 1999).

These rules also apply where a special committee is utilized where there is no controlling shareholder but the business judgment rule presumption is overcome and the fairness standard applies for that reason. *See, e.g., Bomarko, Inc. v. Int'l Telecharge, Inc.*, 1999 Del. Ch. LEXIS 211, at *39-43, 1999 WL 1022083, at *14-15 (Del. Ch. Nov. 4, 1999), *aff'd*, 766 A.2d 437 (Del. 2000).

Add the following at the end of the third bullet in the paragraph beginning on page 403 and concluding on page 405 (immediately after footnote 1510):

- "Once the entire fairness standard has been implicated, . . . the defendants, at least initially, bear the burden of demonstrating the two basic aspects of fair dealing and fair price. The burden of proof on the issue of fairness may shift . . . to the *plaintiff* to demonstrate that the transaction complained of was *not* entirely fair" by "an approval of the transaction by an independent committee of directors who have real bargaining power that can be exerted in dealings with a majority shareholder who does not dictate the terms of the merger." *Emerald Partners v. Berlin*, 726 A.2d 1215, 1222-23 (Del. 1999) (citation omitted); *see also id.* at 1223 n.11 (the fact that plaintiff's claims alleging lack of independence are not sufficiently particularized to excuse demand with respect to a derivative claim pursuant to the stricter pleading standard that governs derivative claims – a subject discussed in Chapter IV, Section B 5 – does not mean that the same directors constituted "a well functioning independent committee as it relates to an entire fairness review" with respect to a non-derivative claim).

Add the following at the end of footnote 1512 on page 404:

See also Strassburger v. Earley, 752 A.2d 557, 570-71 (Del. Ch. 2000) ("[W]here the terms of a conflict transaction (specifically, a parent-subsidiary merger) result from a process structured to replicate arm's length negotiations, the burden of proof will shift from the defendants to the plaintiff shareholder, who must prove that the transaction is unfair. But that burden-shifting result obtains only where minority stockholders effectively ratify the transaction or where a committee of disinterested independent directors effectively represents the interest of the minority stockholders in the negotiations. . . . To be relieved of their exacting burden of proof, the defendants would have to establish that the minority's true interests were adequately represented by advocates committed to their cause."); *Bomarko*, 1999 Del. Ch. LEXIS 211, at *43, 1999 WL 1022083, at *15 ("When the entire fairness test applies, the burden of persuasion initially lies with the defendant. The burden of proof 'may be shifted from the defendants to the plaintiff through the use of a well functioning committee of independent directors.'") (quoting *Kahn v. Tremont Corp.*, 694 A.2d 422, 428 (Del. 1997); other citations omitted).

Add the following at the end of footnote 1530 on page 408:

See also Solomon v. Armstrong, 747 A.2d 1098, 1120-21 (Del. Ch. 1999), *aff'd*, 746 A.2d 277 (unpublished opinion, full text available at 2000 Del. LEXIS 30 and 2000 WL 140072) (Del. Jan. 26, 2000) (quoting *Citron v. E.I. DuPont de Nemours & Co.*, 584 A.2d 490, 502 (Del. Ch. 1990)):

> Our cases have posited that at least one of the reasons for the imposition of heightened duties in a parent-subsidiary or a controlling-shareholder merger is the potential for coercion. The theory is that minority shareholders may vote in favor of a transaction notwithstanding their actual belief that they deserve a better deal for fear of retaliation of some kind. "For example, the controlling stockholder might decide to stop dividend payments or to effect a . . . merger at a less favorable price, for which the remedy would be time consuming and costly litigation."

Add the following at the end of footnote 1532 on page 409:

See also In re W. Nat'l Corp. S'holders Litig., 2000 Del. Ch. LEXIS 82, at *87, 2000 WL 710192, at *26 (in transactions between a corporation and a controlling shareholder when an independent special committee has bargained at arm's length on behalf of the corporation, the use of the committee shifts the burden of proving fairness but does not bring the transaction "fully within the purview of the director-protective business judgment rule because the presence of a controlling shareholder 'has the potential to influence, however subtly, the vote of [ratifying] minority stockholders in a manner that is not likely to occur in a transaction with a non-controlling party'").

Replace the period at the end of footnote 1643 on page 429 with the following:

, *quoted in Jackson Nat'l Life Ins. Co. v. Kennedy*, 741 A.2d 377, 391 n.29 (Del. Ch. 1999).

Add the following at the end of the paragraph beginning on page 428 and concluding on page 431 (immediately after footnote 1657):

- *Nebel v. Southwest Bancorp, Inc.*, 1999 Del. Ch. LEXIS 30, at *22-23, 1999 WL 135259, at *7 (Del. Ch. Mar. 9, 1999) (denying motion to dismiss and stating that "there is no legal requirement" that a merger "be approved by either an independent committee of directors or by a 'majority of the minority' shareholder vote," but also stating that this ruling "was not intended, nor should it be read, to detract from the principle that fiduciaries who stand on both sides of a merger . . . and dictate its terms have the burden to show that the merger was entirely fair," and that while "the absence of a negotiating committee of independent directors, without more, does not constitute unfair dealing as a matter of law, . . . that circumstance is evidence of unfair dealing that, when combined with other pleaded facts, may state a cognizable unfair dealing claim that the fiduciaries will ultimately have the burden to negate"); and
- *Wood v. Frank E. Best, Inc.*, 1999 Del. Ch. LEXIS 141, at *12, 1999 WL 504779, at *3 (Del. Ch. July 9, 1999) (denying motion to dismiss and stating that "the lack of a vote of the minority and the lack of an

independent advisor or financial analyst acting on the minority's behalf do not state a claim for breach of fiduciary duty" but "lack of these safeguards means that there is nothing in the record at this stage of the proceedings to indicate that the merger was fair to the public shareholders").

Section B 3 i-1

Add the following new Section B 3 i-1 at the end of the paragraph beginning on page 428 and concluding on page 431 (immediately after footnote 1657):

i-1. Digex. In re Digex, Inc. Shareholder Litigation, 2000 Del. Ch. LEXIS 171, 2000 WL 1847679 (Del. Ch. Dec. 13, 2000), involved a proposed merger between WorldCom, Inc. and Intermedia Communications, Inc., the holder of 52 percent of the outstanding stock of Digex, Inc. and 94 percent of the voting power of Digex's outstanding stock. 2000 Del. Ch. LEXIS 171, at *2, 6, 2000 WL 1847679, at *1, 2. Digex's board included eight directors, five of whom also were directors or officers of Intermedia who "stood to personally profit tremendously upon a sale of Intermedia, but to profit very little, or not at all, upon a sale of Digex" because these directors owned large numbers of Intermedia shares and stock options and much smaller numbers of or no Digex shares and stock options, and three of whom were not affiliated with Intermedia. 2000 Del. Ch. LEXIS 171, at *7 & n.5, 2000 WL 1847679, at *2 & n.5. At the time of the events underlying the decision, Intermedia faced severe financial problems, but Digex was "a rapidly growing company that was extremely attractive to potential suitors." 2000 Del. Ch. LEXIS 171, at *12, 2000 WL 1847679, at *3.

The court described the potential conflicts of interest that faced the individuals who served as directors of Intermedia and Digex "due to their dual directorships and their direct, personal financial interests in any potential transaction" involving the sale or all or part of Intermedia, Digex and/or Intermedia's ownership position in Digex as follows:

> If Intermedia sold itself (which, of course, would include its majority stake in Digex), Intermedia's shareholders stood in a position to reap a substantial premium on their shares, largely due to the acquiror's presumable desire to obtain control over Intermedia's "crown jewel," Digex. This was especially true with regard to Intermedia's officers and directors, who, as discussed above, stood to profit tremendously from a sale of Intermedia. In contrast, Digex's shareholders stood to gain comparatively little under this possibility, at least in the short term, other than a new controlling shareholder.
>
> If Intermedia sold part or all of its Digex holdings, Intermedia could expect a significant payoff to fund its own operations, but Intermedia's shareholders, and especially its officers and directors, would not personally benefit to the extent they would if Intermedia itself were sold. Under this possibility, Digex shareholders could expect to reap a significant premium if Intermedia sold its holdings to an acquiror who decided to then tender for all outstanding Digex shares.

2000 Del. Ch. LEXIS 171, at *12-13, 2000 WL 1847679, at *3-4. To address these potential conflicts of interest, Digex's board of directors appointed a special committee consisting of two of Digex's three independent directors "to participate in the transaction process and make recommendations to the full board of directors on matters where there could be a perceived conflict of interest between Intermedia and Digex." 2000 Del. Ch. LEXIS 171, at *13-14, 2000 WL 1847679, at *4. The committee retained legal counsel and a financial advisor. 2000 Del. Ch. LEXIS 171, at *14, 2000 WL 1847679, at *4.

Intermedia's financial advisor, Bear Stearns & Co., approached 30 potential suitors for Intermedia and/or Digex, and three suitors emerged: WorldCom, Exodus Communications, Inc. and Global Crossing, Ltd. 2000 Del. Ch. LEXIS 171, at *9, 2000 WL 1847679, at *3. Until August 21, 2000, Digex's special committee was involved primarily with a proposed acquisition of Digex by Exodus. On August 21, the special committee arrived at a Digex board meeting prepared to vote on an Exodus transaction, but the committee learned at the meeting that the transaction would not be presented for a vote because negotiations with Global Crossing had begun. As of August 30, Digex and Global Crossing were working toward a September 1 transaction. On August 30, however, WorldCom expressed interest to Bear Stearns in acquiring Digex at $120 per share or more and stated its intent to outbid anyone. Bear Stearns informed WorldCom that it would have to move quickly, and by late that evening a draft merger agreement providing for an acquisition by WorldCom of Digex was sent to WorldCom, and Digex's special committee was informed that the Global Crossing-Digex transaction had been changed to a WorldCom-Digex transaction. 2000 Del. Ch. LEXIS 171, at *16, 21, 2000 WL 1847679, at *4, 6.

Sometime during the afternoon of August 31, WorldCom determined to purchase Intermedia rather than Digex. During the night of August 31 and the morning of September 1, Intermedia and WorldCom negotiated a merger agreement. 2000 Del. Ch. LEXIS 171, at *17-18, 2000 WL 1847679, at *5. The court noted that the parties "hotly contest the events on August 31, 2000, that led WorldCom to switch from a purchase of Digex to a purchase of Intermedia," but stated that "[a]fter substantial discovery, the plaintiffs can point to little concrete evidence in the record to refute the defendants' claim that the decision to acquire Intermedia was solely WorldCom's decision" and that it "appears doubtful to me that the plaintiffs will be able to overcome the testimony that the decision to switch deals was WorldCom's alone." 2000 Del. Ch. LEXIS 171, at *46 n.60, 2000 WL 1847679, at *13 n.60.

Late in the evening of August 31, Digex's special committee was informed that the deal had changed again and that WorldCom was buying Intermedia, not Digex. 2000 Del. Ch. LEXIS 171, at *20-21, 2000 WL 1847679, at *6. Early in the morning of September 1, the special committee met and discussed the committee's "'belief or fear' that Intermedia had manipulated WorldCom's interest from Digex to Intermedia," the committee's belief that the proposed WorldCom-Intermedia transaction was the worst of the possible alternatives for

Digex, and the committee's options. 2000 Del. Ch. LEXIS 171, at *21-24, 2000 WL 1847679, at *6. Later that morning, the Intermedia board met, following which Digex's directors were invited to join the Intermedia board for a meeting of Digex's board. Digex's interested directors and Intermedia's financial advisor, Bear Stearns, remained in the room for the Digex board meeting. 2000 Del. Ch. LEXIS 171, at *24, 2000 WL 1847679, at *7. Digex's board was informed that Intermedia's board had considered the WorldCom and Global Crossing proposals and determined that the WorldCom proposal was better for Intermedia. *Id.*

Digex's financial advisor expressed its view that the WorldCom transaction was the worst proposal from Digex's perspective. 2000 Del. Ch. LEXIS 171, at *24-25, 2000 WL 1847679, at *7. The special committee proposed a mini-auction of Digex, pursuant to which the WorldCom transaction would be deferred for three days to allow Digex's financial advisor to solicit best and final offers from WorldCom, Exodus and Global Crossing and determine whether any other potential bidders existed. This proposal was defeated by a vote of four to three: Digex's four interested directors voted against the proposal (one interested director did not participate due to health problems), and Digex's three disinterested directors voted for the proposal. 2000 Del. Ch. LEXIS 171, at *7 n.4, 25, 2000 WL 1847679, at *2 n.4, 7. The Digex board then turned to a "brief and truncated" discussion of a request by WorldCom for a waiver from Digex's board of the protections provided by Section 203 of the Delaware General Corporation Law, which reads, in relevant part, as follows:

> (a) Notwithstanding any other provisions of this chapter, a corporation shall not engage in any business combination with any interested stockholder for a period of 3 years following the time that such stockholder became an interested stockholder, unless:
>
> (1) prior to such time the board of directors of the corporation approved either the business combination or the transaction which resulted in the stockholder becoming an interested stockholder, or

> (2) upon consummation of the transaction which resulted in the stockholder becoming an interested stockholder, the interested stockholder owned at least 85% of the voting stock of the corporation outstanding at the time the transaction commenced, excluding for purposes of determining the number of shares outstanding those shares owned (i) by persons who are directors and also officers and (ii) employee stock plans in which employee participants do not have the right to determine confidentially whether shares held subject to the plan will be tendered in a tender or exchange offer.

2000 Del. Ch. LEXIS 171, at *58-59, 2000 WL 1847679, at *16-17 (quoting Del. Gen. Corp. Law § 203). Intermedia had agreed to seek this waiver from Digex, but requested, and received in return, an agreement by WorldCom that Digex's certificate of incorporation would be amended to require independent director approval of any material transaction between WorldCom and Digex. 2000 Del. Ch. LEXIS 171, at *18, 2000 WL 1847679, at *5. The discussion was limited to the question who should vote on the waiver. After a determination that all directors should vote, the vote, "once again, was four to three, with only the interested directors . . . voting in favor of the § 203 waiver." 2000 Del. Ch. LEXIS 171, at *26, 2000 WL 1847679, at *7. The Intermedia board then reconvened and approved the Intermedia merger with WorldCom. 2000 Del. Ch. LEXIS 171, at *27, 2000 WL 1847679, at *7.

Digex shareholders alleged that Intermedia and its agents breached their fiduciary duties to Digex and its minority shareholders by waiving the protections provided by Section 203. Plaintiffs moved for a preliminary injunction, and the court held that plaintiffs demonstrated a reasonable likelihood of success on the merits of this claim.

The court explained that under Section 203, "once an entity becomes an 'interested stockholder,' § 203, subject to certain exemptions, prohibits business combinations between a Delaware corporation and that shareholder for a period of three years." 2000 Del. Ch. LEXIS 171, at *59, 2000 WL 1847679, at *17. One exemption (in Section 203(a)(1)) permits transactions by interested stockholders who become interested stockholders in a transaction in which the corporation's board waives § 203, and another exemption (in Section 203(a)(2)) permits transactions by interested stockholders who become the owner of "85% of the voting stock" of the corporation in the same transaction that resulted in the interested stockholder becoming an interested stockholder – i.e., the transaction in which the stockholder became the owner of 15 percent or more of the corporation's voting stock. Del. Gen. Corp. Law § 203(a)(1), (2), (c) (5). The parties agreed that WorldCom would become an interested stockholder in Digex as a result of the merger. 2000 Del. Ch. LEXIS 171, at *59, 2000 WL 1847679, at *17.

WorldCom, the court continued, believed that "it would come within the statutory exemption provided by § 203(a)(2) for interested stockholders holding 85% or more of the 'voting stock' of the corporation," but recognized that upon completion of the merger WorldCom would "possess well over 85% of the voting power of Digex but well under 85% of the number of outstanding voting shares of Digex" and that "the application of the § 203(a)(2) exemption in situations involving 'super-voting rights' has not been definitively ruled upon by the Delaware courts." 2000 Del. Ch. LEXIS 171, at *59-62, 2000 WL 1847679, at *17. WorldCom therefore "was not content to rely merely on the 85% shareholder exemption" in § 203(a)(2) and "sought the additional certainty that would come with a § 203(a)(1) waiver agreed to by the Digex board of directors." 2000 Del. Ch. LEXIS 171, at *59-60, 2000 WL 1847679, at *17.

The court described the issue raised by WorldCom's acquisition from Intermedia of more than 85 percent of the voting power of Digex but less than 85 percent of the voting shares of Digex as follows:

> [U]pon the completion of the merger, WorldCom will possess well over 85% of the voting power of Digex but well under 85% of the number of outstanding voting shares of Digex. The three year waiting period imposed by § 203, the Delaware anti-takeover statute, does not apply where "upon consummation of

> the transaction which resulted in the stockholder becoming an interested stockholder, the interested stockholder owned at least *85% of the voting stock* of the corporation outstanding at the time that the transaction commenced" excluding certain shares for the purposes of determining the number of shares outstanding [quoting Del. Gen. Corp. Law § 203(a)(2) (emphasis added by court)]. The interpretation of the term "voting stock," therefore, lays directly at the center of this dispute whether § 203 limitations would apply to WorldCom absent the waiver. Simply put, if "85% of the voting stock" refers to voting power, WorldCom would be exempt from § 203. If "85% of the voting stock" refers to the number of shares held in the corporation as a percentage of its outstanding number of shares, then WorldCom would need to rely on the vote of the Digex board to waive its § 203 protections.

2000 Del. Ch. LEXIS 171, at *61-62, 2000 WL 1847679, at *17.

The court concluded that "[i]rrespective of the final answer to the question of what is the proper interpretation of '85% of the voting shares' in § 203(a)(2), there is no dispute that this is a close question of Delaware law where strong arguments have been put forward by both sides," and, in any event, "a decision on WorldCom's qualification for the 85% shareholder exemption would be purely advisory at this point in time" because "[t]he plaintiffs do not challenge any conduct by WorldCom that is governed by § 203." 2000 Del. Ch. LEXIS 171, at *84-86, 2000 WL 1847679, at *23.

Plaintiffs' claim, rather, was "a fiduciary duty claim, not a statutory claim, against the interested directors of Digex" based upon "the vote to waive the protections offered by § 203, a vote that has already occurred," and had meaning "[r]egardless of how § 203 will apply to WorldCom in the future." 2000 Del. Ch. LEXIS 171, at *86-87, 2000 WL 1847679, at *23-24. The court stated that "[g]iven the difficulty and complexity" surrounding the applicability of Section 203 and "the recognition of each lawyer in this matter who advised any of the parties on the applicability of § 203" that "there was no way to definitively know at the time of the waiver vote whether WorldCom actually would qualify for the 85% exception," "there is no question that the § 203 waiver had redundant value to WorldCom" and "granted some degree of bargaining leverage to Digex." 2000 Del. Ch. LEXIS 171, at *84-85, 2000 WL 1847679, at *23.

The court then turned to the Digex directors' four-to-three decision to waive the protections provided by Section 203. Since "all four votes to waive the protections were made by directors who not only sat on both the boards of Intermedia and Digex, but also possessed substantial direct, personal financial interests in the proposed transaction," the court held that the presumption of the business judgment rule was rebutted and the directors bore the burden of establishing entire fairness. 2000 Del. Ch. LEXIS 171, at *89, 2000 WL 1847679, at *24. The court considered the two basic components of fairness: fair dealing and fair price.

Fair Dealing. The fair dealing component of fairness, the court stated, concerns "how the board action was initiated, structured, negotiated, and timed," "asks whether all of the directors were kept fully informed not only at the moment in time of the vote, but also during the relevant events leading up to the vote while negotiations were presumably occurring," and "asks how, and for what reasons, the approvals of the various directors themselves were obtained." 2000 Del. Ch. LEXIS 171, at *90, 2000 WL 1847679, at *24.

The court described "the events in question from the perspective of the independent Digex directors" (2000 Del. Ch. LEXIS 171, at *91-92, 2000 WL 1847679, at *25) as follows:

- At midday on August 30, Digex "seemed headed into a three-way merger with Global Crossing and Intermedia." 2000 Del. Ch. LEXIS 171, at *92, 2000 WL 1847679, at *25.
- At 11:00 p.m. on August 30, the special committee was informed that WorldCom had offered $120 per share for Digex. *Id.*

- At 7:00 p.m. on August 31, the special committee was informed that "(i) Intermedia, not Digex, would be sold to WorldCom, and (ii) the Global Crossing transaction was effectively dead as that company would not raise its bid in competition with WorldCom and that Intermedia preferred the WorldCom transaction." 2000 Del. Ch. LEXIS 171, at *92-93, 2000 WL 1847679, at *25. The committee "immediately suspected manipulation of the WorldCom offer by Intermedia and began to search for ways to drive the deal back to including a bid for some or all of Digex's outstanding public shares." 2000 Del. Ch. LEXIS 171, at *93, 2000 WL 1847679, at *25.
- Overnight, the special committee was "informed of negotiations between WorldCom and Intermedia over the waiver of § 203." *Id.*
- On the morning of September 1, "the independent directors at last were allowed direct contact with WorldCom, their prospective controlling shareholder who had requested the § 203 waiver," "after the price and structure of the WorldCom-Intermedia deal had been agreed upon," and "the terms of the § 203 waiver had been settled between the interested directors and WorldCom during the preceding night." *Id.* These calls occurred "only *after* Clark, Digex's legal counsel, requested them." 2000 Del. Ch. LEXIS 171, at *94, 2000 WL 1847679, at *25. Also on the morning of September 1, "the independent directors received both the advice of legal counsel on the possible applicability of § 203 and the opinion of their financial advisors regarding the benefits of each prospective deal." *Id.* The independent directors then considered their options during "the very short time they had before being called into the Intermedia board meeting to hold the Digex board meeting." *Id.*

- At the September 1 Digex board meeting, the special committee's legal counsel informed the entire board of his opinion that the board's four interested directors "should not participate in the § 203 waiver vote" and "[t]his advice was rebutted by counsel for the interested directors, and ultimately ignored." *Id.* "Later, without any debate whatsoever on the merits of the waiver or the applicability of the statute, the full Digex board voted to grant the waiver by a divided vote of four interested directors for and three independent directors against." 2000 Del. Ch. LEXIS 171, at *94, 2000 WL 1847679, at *26.

Based upon this chronology, the court reached the following conclusions:

- "[R]egardless of whether the Special Committee actually had all the information possessed by Intermedia in its negotiations with WorldCom over the § 203 issue, the four interested directors controlled the flow of all information from WorldCom to the independent Digex directors during the hectic negotiating period from the evening of August 30 to the morning of September 1." 2000 Del. Ch. LEXIS 171, at *95, 2000 WL 1847679, at *26.
- "[G]iven that WorldCom first sought the waiver of § 203 during the negotiations that took place solely between WorldCom and Intermedia during the night of August 31-September 1 and that the vote at the Digex board meeting occurred at most roughly twelve hours later, all of the Digex directors learned about WorldCom's demand for the § 203 waiver only hours before the vote granting that waiver." *Id.* "To make matters worse, because the interested directors were also directors of Intermedia, they could not even devote the little time they had before the board vote to considering their options as Digex directors and negotiating solely in the interests of

Digex." 2000 Del. Ch. LEXIS 171, at *95-96, 2000 WL 1847679, at *26. "Rather, they had to spend much, if not most, of their time considering and negotiating the terms of the merger from the perspective of Intermedia, the actual participant in the deal with WorldCom." 2000 Del. Ch. LEXIS 171, at *96, 2000 WL 1847679, at *26.

- "The waiver appears to have been agreed to, in part, in exchange for an amendment to the Digex certificate of incorporation that would require the approval of independent directors of any material transaction between WorldCom and Digex after the merger." *Id.* The court stated that it was "crystal clear" that "the independent directors, at the time of the negotiation over the § 203 waiver, had absolutely no role whatsoever" in the negotiation, but "[t]he record is silent as to exploration by the interested parties of any other options available to Digex." 2000 Del. Ch. LEXIS 171, at *96-97, 2000 WL 1847679, at *26. The court stated that the answers to these questions "remain unclear": did any of the interested directors attempt to withhold approval of the Section 203 waiver "to see what WorldCom might offer to Digex in return?"; did any of the interested directors "request concessions in addition to the certificate amendment"?; and "did the interested directors simply agree" to the Section 203 waiver "in the interests of getting the deal between Intermedia and WorldCom done and only subsequently add the provision to the merger agreement concerning the certificate amendment to create the appearance of consideration for the § 203 waiver?" *Id.*

In short, the court concluded, "the Special Committee had no legal authority to directly block Intermedia's decision to sell its shares in Digex," but the § 203 waiver negotiation was "exactly where the Special Committee should have been most relevant in this whole process." 2000 Del. Ch. LEXIS 171, at *97-98, 2000 WL 1847679, at *27. Nevertheless, there "simply was no meaningful participation by any of the independent Digex directors in the negotiations leading to the § 203 waiver, the terms of that waiver, or the vote itself." 2000 Del. Ch. LEXIS 171, at *94-95, 2000 WL 1847679, at *26. To the contrary, the special committee was "missing in action – not through any failure of its own, but as a result of the control by the conflicted directors over the process." 2000 Del. Ch. LEXIS 171, at *107, 98, 2000 WL 1847679, at *30, 27.

The court rejected the defendants' contention that the "quite short" time frame during which the decision had to be made on WorldCom's request for the Section 203 waiver was dictated by the September 1 5:00 p.m. deadline placed by Global Crossing on its proposal and that the "compressed timetable" required by Global Crossing's proposal "did not allow for a more thorough analysis of the issues on hand, including the § 203 waiver." 2000 Del. Ch. LEXIS 171, at *99, 2000 WL 1847679, at *27. The court explained that "Intermedia would not allow a sale to either Exodus or Global Crossing given the offer made by WorldCom" and thus "the 5:00 p.m. Global Crossing deadline should have been of little or no consequence in comparison to the decision to waive the anti-takeover protections afforded by § 203 and any efforts to use its leverage to explore whether WorldCom would consider a partial or full tender offer for the outstanding Digex shares." 2000 Del. Ch. LEXIS 171, at *99, 2000 WL 1847679, at *28.

According to the court, "Intermedia wanted to complete a deal with WorldCom as soon as possible," and "Intermedia placed time pressure on WorldCom throughout the negotiations, not the other way around, due to the presence of Global Crossing's offer." *Id.* The court stated that "[b]y the time of the Digex meeting when the vote to waive § 203 was undertaken, the Digex board's role had been vastly simplified": previously, Digex's board was "confronted with the sale of the corporation and all the attendant analysis that goes along with that process," but by September 1 "the only issue of any consequence before the Digex board was the rather discrete issue of whether to waive the protections afforded by § 203." 2000 Del. Ch. LEXIS 171, at *100, 2000 WL 1847679, at *28. Nevertheless, "there was absolutely *no discussion whatsoever* of the effect, purpose, or applicability of § 203 to WorldCom." *Id.*

The court summarized its findings concerning fair dealing as follows:

> In sum, as to whether the waiver can be described as the result of fair dealing, the independent directors, even if we assume that they were kept fully up to date of all material information regarding the merger negotiations, were kept powerless to affect the waiver decision in any meaningful manner. The interested directors not only participated in the negotiations, they controlled them. They also denied an independent negotiating structure involving the independent directors from participating in the WorldCom negotiations over the § 203 waiver. The powerlessness of the independent directors extended to their ability to vote down the proposal to waive § 203's applicability to WorldCom. Further, there appears to have been little substantive discussion or negotiation of the waiver by the interested directors with WorldCom and no discussion of the waiver with the independent directors. All of these factors are framed by the intense time pressure placed on Digex by its corporate parent to get the WorldCom deal done as quickly as possible regardless of any consideration of the applicability or effect of the § 203 waiver on Digex after the merger, or the bargaining leverage that the Digex board might have at that moment against not only WorldCom, but Intermedia as well.

2000 Del. Ch. LEXIS 171, at *102-03, 2000 WL 1847679, at *29.

Fair Price. The fair price component of fairness, the court stated, "relates to the economic and financial considerations of the proposed decision, including any relevant factors that affect the intrinsic or inherent value of a company's stock." 2000 Del. Ch. LEXIS 171, at *90, 2000 WL 1847679, at *24. Here, "the decision put before the Digex board was simply whether or not to grant WorldCom the § 203 waiver"; that is, "was whatever Digex was being offered for this waiver worth the granting of the waiver and could Digex negotiate for more?" 2000 Del. Ch. LEXIS 171, at *108, 2000 WL 1847679, at *30. "The trade put before the Digex board" thus "was simple: waive § 203 and give up the protections granted by the statute in exchange for a stronger corporate parent who had much to offer, the certificate amendment, and the end of the burdensome relationship with Intermedia." *Id.* The court acknowledged that the certificate amendment was "of some value to the Digex minority" but "clearly" was "not worth the same as the § 203 waiver, or WorldCom would not have insisted on the waiver in the first place." 2000 Del. Ch. LEXIS 171, at *108, 2000 WL 1847679, at *31.

The court stated that "it is impossible to say" whether this was the best deal available ("[p]erhaps Digex could have extracted something more from WorldCom, perhaps not") "[b]ecause of the manner in which the negotiating process was handled." 2000 Del. Ch. LEXIS 171, at *108, 2000 WL 1847679, at *30. In the court's view, however, "given Intermedia's admittedly poor financial condition, the independent Digex directors believed that, inevitably, Intermedia would have to sell part or all of its stake in Digex if Intermedia was to remain solvent" and "[t]ime, therefore, was strongly on the side of Digex." 2000 Del. Ch. LEXIS 171, at *109, 2000 WL 1847679, at *31. Thus, the court continued, "Digex had little to lose and should have felt no immediate time pressure to make a decision that would continue to affect the public shareholders of Digex for up to the three years following the merger." 2000 Del. Ch. LEXIS 171, at *108-09, 2000 WL 1847679, at *30. According to the court, "the only entity that really stood to lose should the Digex board decide to further analyze § 203 and vote to at least delay the grant of the waiver by a day to two was Intermedia, not Digex." 2000 Del. Ch. LEXIS 171, at *111-12, 2000 WL 1847679, at *31. The court stated that "[t]he behavior of the interested directors in controlling both the negotiations and vote over the § 203 waiver surely demonstrates, in a compelling fashion, that the waiver really did present Digex with bargaining leverage against Intermedia and WorldCom," and "[t]his leverage simply was not used – could not be used – because of the decision of the interested directors." 2000 Del. Ch. LEXIS 171, at *112, 2000 WL 1847679, at *31.

Given these "unique circumstances," the court held that "this conduct by directors acting with a clear conflict of interest is difficult to justify and would not seem appropriate." *Id.* The court accordingly concluded for the purpose of the motion for a preliminary injunction that "the defendants are not reasonably likely to meet their burden as to the entire fairness of the Digex board's decision to waive Digex's § 203 protections and, therefore, that plaintiffs have demonstrated a reasonable probability of success on the merits of their § 203 claim." *Id.*

The court nevertheless denied plaintiffs' motion for a preliminary injunction because plaintiffs failed to establish "an immediate threat of irreparable harm as to the § 203 waiver decision." 2000 Del. Ch. LEXIS 171, at *113, 2000 WL 1847679, at *32. The court explained that "plaintiffs have essentially asked the Court, via an injunction, to invalidate the September 1, 2000, vote by the Digex board to waive the applicability of § 203 . . . long *after* the action threatening harm has been taken." 2000 Del. Ch. LEXIS 171, at *114, 2000 WL 1847679, at *32. The court stated that "because the wrongful act has already occurred, no prospective injunctive order can possibly be an effective remedy." 2000 Del. Ch. LEXIS 171, at *116, 2000 WL 1847679, at *32.

Furthermore, the court added, "not only would an injunction be improper here where the wrongful conduct has already occurred, but an injunction is, in my judgment, unnecessary to fully protect the Digex minority shareholders." 2000 Del. Ch. LEXIS 171, at *116-17, 2000 WL 1847679, at *33. The court explained that "extreme uncertainty" surrounded the question "whether § 203 will apply to WorldCom if it acquires Intermedia according to the merger agreement," and this "extreme uncertainty is no different today than it was in late August when the WorldCom-Intermedia transaction was being negotiated." 2000 Del. Ch. LEXIS 171, at *117, 2000 WL 1847679, at *33. The court stated that "the uncertainty that WorldCom-Intermedia attempted to contract around, via the § 203 waiver requirement, is an uncertainty that is clearly extant today, just as it was in late August, and provides the plaintiffs with all the relief to which they are entitled." *Id.*

The court added that its conclusion that "defendants are not reasonably likely to meet their burden as to the entire fairness of the Digex board's decision to waive Digex's § 203 protections," and thus that "plaintiffs have established a likelihood of success on the merits of their claim that the defendants breached their fiduciary duties in waiving the protections afforded by § 203," created "additional uncertainties with which defendants must now be concerned as well." 2000 Del. Ch. LEXIS 171, at *112, 117, 2000 WL 1847679, at *31, 33. The court stated that "[i]f this case goes to trial, the defendants will have the burden of establishing the entire fairness of the § 203 waiver" and "[t]his will be no small burden" because "the current record strongly suggests that the § 203 waiver decision was not entirely fair to the Digex minority." 2000 Del. Ch. LEXIS 171, at *118, 2000 WL 1847679, at *33. The court concluded by stating defendants' choice as follows: to proceed or not to proceed with a WorldCom-Intermedia merger "knowing that this Court seriously questions the integrity of the § 203 waiver decision and knowing that certain of the defendant fiduciaries stand accused of faithless acts that under the stringent standard of the entire fairness test, could well give rise to a range of equitable remedies, including monetary remedies." 2000 Del. Ch. LEXIS 171, at *118-19, 2000 WL 1847679, at *33.

Section B 3 j

Add the following at the end of the paragraph beginning on page 462 and concluding on page 464 (immediately after footnote 1866):

- *Sonet v. Plum Creek Timber Co.*, 1999 Del. Ch. LEXIS 49, at *32-35 & n.49, 1999 WL 160174, at *8 & n.49 (Del. Ch. Mar. 18, 1999) (granting preliminary injunction in an action involving a limited partnership where a proxy statement stated that a special committee consisting of three independent members negotiated on behalf of unitholders, where (1) one member of the committee owned a brokerage firm that did business with the general partner and wished to continue that business relationship, a second member of the committee received compensation for serving as the chairman of the board of the general partner "plus $24,000 annually for the maintenance of a car supplied for his personal benefit," and the committee's financial advisor had served as an underwriter of a public offering by the partnership "and, with commendable candor, admitted that it desired to continue its business relationship" with the general partners of the partnership in the future," and (2) "[w]hat actually did occur . . . was not negotiation" because the committee viewed its job as "accepting or rejecting offers" and "[n]egotiation on the part of a special committee involves more than simply rejecting proposals that are deemed unacceptable");
- *Bomarko, Inc. v. International Telecharge, Inc.*, 1999 Del. Ch. LEXIS 211, at *43-57, 1999 WL 1022083, at *15-20 (Del. Ch. Nov. 4, 1999), *aff'd*, 766 A.2d 437 (Del. 2000) (holding, following a trial, that defendants had failed to carry their burden of proving the fairness of a merger pursuant to which the shares of International Telecharge, Inc. ("ITI") were cashed out and the corporation was merged into a corporation owned by Ronald J. Haan, the Chairman and chief executive officer of ITI; the court declined to shift the burden of proof with respect to proving fairness because even

assuming that the three members of a special committee were independent, Haan committed several acts of disloyalty, including not disclosing a financing proposal made by Bell Atlantic to the corporation, making a counterproposal on the corporation's letterhead to Bell Atlantic that was adverse to the corporation's interests, and "subsequent[ly] redirect[ing] Bell Atlantic away" from the corporation; the court stated that "the Special Committee proceeded unaware" and "[d]ue to Haan's misconduct, the other directors were not in a position to bargain at arms length with him" and instead "operated under the assumption that if they failed to reach agreement with Haan" with respect to the merger, then ITI "was headed directly into bankruptcy");

- *Harbor Finance Partners v. Huizenga*, 751 A.2d 879, 882, 884-85, 886-89, 891-92 (Del. Ch. 1999) (denying motion to dismiss unfair dealing claim arising out of a merger of AutoNation, Incorporated into Republic Industries, Inc., where plaintiff "pled facts that suggest that the Republic Special Committee did not function with the independence and competence necessary to command any deference," "[a]s such, the burden of proof may ultimately fall on the defendants to establish that the transaction was entirely fair to Republic and its stockholders," "plaintiff has also pled facts suggesting that the defendants may be unable to prove the financial fairness of the Merger," and the "sum total convinces me that Count I states a claim"; the claim alleged that "as of the time of the Republic Board's approval of the Merger Agreement, AutoNation was an unproven start-up company with no active operations and huge capital needs," "the total investment made by AutoNation's stockholders in the company was around $52 million" but "Republic agreed to give AutoNation's stockholders Republic stock worth five times that amount and ended up pumping another $250 million into AutoNation before the Merger closed"; the Republic special committee included three directors, two of whom had business relationships that "allegedly extend beyond Republic itself" with Wayne Huizenga, Republic's chairman and chief executive officer and "the leading mover on the other side of the deal"; the special committee allegedly "did not participate in negotiations over the Merger, but left that to management insiders subordinate to . . . Huizenga"; and the special committee's financial advisor, Merrill Lynch, had been helping Huizenga determine whether to raise capital for AutoNation through an initial public offering: "The natural inference is that Merrill Lynch did its best in that role, within the wide confines of professional valuation techniques, to justify an impressive value for AutoNation on behalf of its client, Huizenga. Merrill Lynch then turned around and began working for a client, the Special Committee, whose role was to avoid overpaying for AutoNation. Thus Merrill Lynch's professional incentives were the opposite of what they had been just months before.");

- *Strassburger v. Earley*, 752 A.2d 557, 567-68, 570-71 (Del. Ch. 2000) (finding unfairness following a trial in a case where Ridgewood Properties, Inc. repurchased a total of 83 percent of its outstanding shares from its two largest shareholders, Triton Group, Ltd. and Hesperus Limited Partners, and to finance these repurchases Ridgewood sold its principal operating assets, and as a result of the repurchases N. Russell Walden's stock ownership interest increased from 6.9 percent to 55 percent; the court held that the formation of a one man special committee, Luther A. Henderson, an "independent, unconflicted, and an astute businessman" to consider the Triton repurchase and who approved the Triton repurchase because, Henderson concluded, the Triton repurchase "would eliminate the controlling stockholder who 'clearly wanted out' and whose presence would interfere with the company's 'long term progress,'" did not shift the burden of proving fairness": "To be relieved of their exacting burden of proof, the defendants would have to establish that the minority's true interests were adequately represented by advocates committed to their cause," but here "[t]here were no such advocates and there was no adequate representation"; to the contrary, "Henderson conducted no negotiations, and although he did conclude that the Triton repurchase was in the best interests of Ridgewood and its minority stockholders, Henderson based that conclusion on an investigation that he was required to conduct practically blindfolded. Henderson's assignment and investigation was restricted solely to the Triton repurchase. It did not include any assessment of the combined Triton-Hesperus transaction. The narrow scope of Henderson's assignment was highly significant, because the effectuation of the Triton repurchase alone would not give Walden absolute control, but the combined Triton and Hesperus repurchases would. Consequently, and with all due respect for Henderson's acumen as a businessman and his good intentions, his independent committee role could not and did not provide meaningful protection for the Ridgewood minority."); and

- *T. Rowe Price Recovery Fund, L.P. v. Rubin*, 770 A.2d 536, 553-56 (Del. Ch. 2000) (granting motion for a preliminary injunction enjoining the implementation of management and shared services agreements entered into by Seaman Furniture Company, Inc. and Levitz Furniture, Inc., both which were controlled by Resurgence Asset Management, L.L.C., where a special committee of Seaman's board was established and "resisted certain . . . threats and blandishments" from Resurgence and rejected one transaction, but Seaman management then "abandoned the Special Committee and its independent legal and financial advisors" and determined to accept "the fact that a deal would be done and simply strove to arrange better terms for Seaman" and agreed to "the same 60/40 equity split in favor of Levitz" that had been "fixed unilaterally by Resurgence" in order to further Resurgence's interest in reorganizing Levitz and "salvag[e] its large investment in that bankrupt company" and that had been rejected by the special committee; the court stated that "there is nothing to suggest that the negotiation process replicated or even approximated that which would occur at arm's length").

Section B 3 k -1

Add the following new Section B 3 k-1 at the end of the paragraph beginning and concluding on page 467 (immediately after footnote 1884):

k-1. Special Committee Cases Involving a Large But Not a Controlling Shareholder. The Delaware Court of Chancery's decision in *In re Western National Corp. Shareholders Litigation*, 2000 Del. Ch. LEXIS 82, 2000 WL 710192 (Del. Ch. May 22, 2000), considers the use of a special committee in the context of a transaction between a corporation and a large – but not controlling – shareholder and holds that in this context use of a properly functioning special committee provides the transaction the protection of the business judgment rule.

Western National involved a merger between Western National Corporation and its 46 percent shareholder, American

General Corporation, both of which were large, diversified insurance and financial service companies. Western National's chairman and chief executive officer was Michael J. Poulos, who had been a senior officer of American General until 1993, when Western National became a public company. Ten months later, American General acquired 40 percent of Western National and entered into a standstill agreement with Western National. The standstill agreement prohibited American General from doing any of the following before January 1, 1999 unless American General first obtained the approval of Western National's board: (1) acquiring more than 20 percent of Western National's shares in any 12 month period, (2) owning a total of more than 79 percent of Western National's shares, (3) engaging in an extraordinary transaction with Western National, or (4) nominating more than two directors to Western National's board. 2000 Del. Ch. LEXIS 82, at *7-8 & n.1, 2000 WL 710192, at *2 & n.1.

In 1996, Western National sold an additional 6 percent of its equity to American General in order to address capital needs, but by 1997 Western National needed additional capital. American General was unwilling to commit additional capital unless it could acquire absolute control of Western National, and American General's 46 percent interest made it difficult to raise equity from third parties. 2000 Del. Ch. LEXIS 82, at *8-12, 2000 WL 710192, at *3.

In this context, Western National's board formed a special committee consisting of three outside directors, Donald G. Baker, Robert M. Hermance and Alan Richards, to explore strategic alternatives. The committee, with the assistance of its own legal and financial advisors, determined that a sale of Western National (including American General's 46 percent interest) to an unrelated third party in a merger transaction was the optimal course of action. 2000 Del. Ch. LEXIS 82, at *13, 2000 WL 710192, at *3. American General, however, was unwilling to sell its 46 percent stake in Western National. As a result, the special committee determined to attempt to negotiate a fair merger price with American General before the expiration of the standstill agreement. 2000 Del. Ch. LEXIS 82, at *13-14, 2000 WL 710192, at *4.

The special committee was informed by its financial advisor, Donaldson Lufkin & Jenrette ("DLJ"), that $30 to $31 per share represented the high end of Western National's value, and proposed a $32 per share merger price. This represented a 12 percent premium over Western National's then market price of $28.19. American General rejected that proposal, contending that Western National already was fully valued in the market and that its stock price had increased by 46 percent due to speculation of a takeover bid. 2000 Del. Ch. LEXIS 82, at *15, 80, 2000 WL 710192, at *4, 24. American General proposed $28.19 per share and a 3 percent break-up fee. The special committee rejected that offer. American General then proposed $28.75 per share and an expense reimbursement provision in lieu of its previous request for a break-up fee. The committee again rejected American General's proposal. American General responded with a $29 per share offer, subject to collar provisions that would adjust the price up or down if the price of American General stock moved outside a specified range. 2000 Del. Ch. LEXIS 82, at *15, 80, 2000 WL 710192, at *5, 24. The committee rejected this offer and countered with a $31 per share price. American General rejected the $31 per share proposal and terminated negotiations, and "all parties concerned believed the negotiations had permanently broken down." 2000 Del. Ch. LEXIS 82, at *15-16, 81, 2000 WL 710192, at *4-5, 24.

At the special committee's next meeting, the committee determined to make one last effort to jump-start the talks and asked Poulos, who previously had spent 23 years at American General, to invite American General back to the negotiating table. 2000 Del. Ch. LEXIS 82, at *82-83, 2000 WL 710192, at *25. American General agreed to return to the negotiations, but only if the special committee would agree to a $29.75 per share transaction with collar provisions. The committee determined that $29.75 per share was the highest price American General would pay and that a merger with American General at this price "was superior to other strategic alternatives then available," and, following negotiations concerning the collar provisions, DLJ opined that the proposed merger was fair from a financial point of view and the parties agreed to a merger on these terms. 2000 Del. Ch. LEXIS 82, at *6, 16-17, 83, 2000 WL 710192, at *5, 25. Following special committee and board approval, the merger was submitted to shareholders, and 99.98 percent of the 79.1 percent of shareholders who voted approved the transaction. 2000 Del. Ch. LEXIS 82, at *17, 2000 WL 710192, at *5. At closing, Western National shareholders received $30.90 per share due to the appreciation of American General stock and the collar provisions. *Id.*

As discussed in Chapter II, Section B 3 a, the court held on a motion for summary judgment that American General was not a controlling shareholder. As discussed in Chapter I, Section D 2 c, the court held that the three special committee members (but not a majority of the board, at least for the purpose of the motion for summary judgment) were disinterested and independent. The court noted that the five potentially conflicted directors on Western National's board "were not particularly involved in the merger process": there was "no evidence" that three of these directors "played *any* role whatsoever (besides considering and approving the Special Committee's recommendation)" in the merger process, and the involvement of the remaining two potentially conflicted directors in the merger process "was *de minimis*." 2000 Del. Ch. LEXIS 82, at *69-70, 2000 WL 710192, at *20. Instead, "the Special Committee, whose disinterest and independence is above reproach – and its advisors performed the bulk of the heavy lifting during the course of merger negotiations." 2000 Del. Ch. LEXIS 82, at *70, 2000 WL 710192, at *20.

The court also held that the special committee's advisors were independent and were selected "in a substantively and procedurally sound manner." 2000 Del. Ch. LEXIS 82, at *75, 2000 WL 710192, at *22. The fact that management "arranged for the committee to interview advisors that appeared qualified and did not have any connection to Western National or

American General," the court stated, did not taint the process. *Id.* The court contrasted the "markedly different" selection of advisors in *Kahn v. Tremont Corp.*, 694 A.2d 422 (Del. 1997), where "the corporation's general counsel recommended a law firm that had strong financial connections to the controlling shareholder," and in *Kahn v. Dairy Mart Convenience Stores, Inc.*, 1996 Del. Ch. LEXIS 38, 1996 WL 159628 (Del. Ch. Mar. 29, 1996), where "the attorney for the controlling shareholder recommended the advisors." 2000 Del. Ch. LEXIS 82, at *75, 2000 WL 710192, at *22; *see also* Chapter II, Section B 3 i (discussing *Tremont* decision) and B 3 j (discussing *Dairy Mart* decision).

The court rejected a claim that the committee's financial advisor, DLJ, lacked independence because DLJ had participated "as one of ten or twelve co-managers in an offering of American General debt securities at the request of Goldman Sachs, the lead underwriter, two years before the merger" and because a group of bankers employed by Union Bank of Switzerland who were providing acquisition advisory services for American General a year after the merger "transferred midstream to DLJ . . . *after* American General hired them." 2000 Del. Ch. LEXIS 82, at *72, 2000 WL 710192, at *21. The court also rejected a claim that the committee's legal counsel "improperly advised" the committee because it later served as Western National's "tax counsel." The court explained that the tax advice counsel provided to Western National "only concerned the merger" and was "consistent with" and "an integral part of" counsel's work for the committee. 2000 Del. Ch. LEXIS 82, at *73, 2000 WL 710192, at *21. The court stated that "[b]ecause the Special Committee was working on behalf of Western National's shareholders (to whom [counsel] provided its tax advice), there was obviously no conflict of interest." *Id.*

The court next rejected a contention that the special committee was not "fully informed of all material information reasonably available." 2000 Del. Ch. LEXIS 82, at *76, 2000 WL 710192, at *22. The court explained that the committee had "full access to all Company information," "could and did reasonably rely on its expert advisor to obtain and analyze the specific information needed to value the Company," and "appropriately incorporated this analysis into its overall assessment of the soundness of the merger." 2000 Del. Ch. LEXIS 82, at *77, 2000 WL 710192, at *23. The court also rejected a claim that the special committee process was tainted by the presence of two potentially interested inside directors, Poulos and Scott, "during portions of the due diligence and during one of DLJ's presentations." 2000 Del. Ch. LEXIS 82, at *78, 2000 WL 710192, at *23. The court noted that defendants "plausibly contend that management directors were present at DLJ's presentation to comment on the accuracy and soundness of its valuation" and "to make sure DLJ did not miss anything," and stated that "I am unable to find fault with some management participation or input into the Special Committee process, particularly in these circumstances where the inside directors' alleged conflicts of interest range from mild to immaterial." 2000 Del. Ch. LEXIS 82, at *78-79, 2000 WL 710192, at *23. The court added that this case did "not involve the set of concerns management buyout transactions raise where it is most vital to maintain a firewall between managers participating in the buyout group and the special committee," the record did not indicate "interested managers attempting to influence a special committee's decision-making process," and there was "no evidence to support the contention that Scott or Poulos tipped the Special Committee's hand to American General." 2000 Del. Ch. LEXIS 82, at *78-79, 2000 WL 710192, at *23.

With respect to arm's length bargaining, the court concluded that the parties' negotiations (summarized above) "reasonably imply two legally significant conclusions." 2000 Del. Ch. LEXIS 82, at *81, 2000 WL 710192, at *24. First, "the Special Committee had the power to say no," and [i]ndeed, the Special Committee said it *three* times." *Id.* Second, "the fact that American General was willing to terminate the negotiations and place Western National in a *status quo ante* posture indicates that the Special Committee had a genuine choice as to the ultimate fate of the Company" because "American General was simply not going to force a deal on Western National if the Special Committee did not accept its terms." 2000 Del. Ch. LEXIS 82, at *81-82, 2000 WL 710192, at *24. The court rejected plaintiffs' contention that "the entire exchange between the Special Committee and American General was merely a splendid dance meant only to charm a reviewing court" because "calling something a sham over and over again does not make it a sham." 2000 Del. Ch. LEXIS 82, at *82, 2000 WL 710192, at *24. The court stated that "I am no more charmed by the carefully orchestrated dance of a special committee than I am by the use of baseless innuendo and unreasonable inferences to bolster a deflated legal theory," and "plaintiffs have not pointed to record facts that would lead a court – even a naturally suspicious court – to question the conduct of an independent, disinterested special committee charged with negotiating a third party merger agreement." *Id.*

In short, the court held that "the record not only illustrates arm's length bargaining but also demonstrates that American General never improperly forced a merger transaction, one way or another, onto the Special Committee." 2000 Del. Ch. LEXIS 82, at *79-80, 2000 WL 710192, at *23. Rather, the court stated, "to the extent that Western National felt pressured to do a deal, that pressure emanated from regulatory constraints and product and capital markets, not from American General." 2000 Del. Ch. LEXIS 82, at *80, 2000 WL 710192, at *23.

The court also rejected a contention that the special committee "'abdicated' its duty to negotiate vigorously on behalf of the Company and its public shareholders" by asking Poulos – Western National's chairman and chief executive officer and a former senior employee of American General – to contact American General and invite American General back to the negotiating table. The court explained that the special committee "did not abdicate its responsibility; it simply used a negotiating tactic that plaintiffs thought unwise and unduly passive." 2000 Del. Ch. LEXIS 82, at *84, 2000 WL 710192, at *25. Even if this were correct, the court stated, "the uncontested facts indicate that the Special Committee . . . carried out the bulk (if not all) of the negotiation and, more importantly, made every *decision* in the negotiating process." *Id.* In sum, the court concluded, "[w]hen shorn of all rhetoric, plaintiffs have not alleged facts that give rise to a conclusion that this merger transaction was other then the product of arm's length bargaining between a non-controlling 46 percent shareholder and a well-functioning special committee." *Id.*

Under these circumstances, the court held, the business judgment rule rather than fairness was the appropriate standard for judicial review "for two broad reasons." 2000 Del. Ch. LEXIS 82, at *85, 2000 WL 710192, at *26. First, "Delaware law will not attach liability to decisions of independent, disinterested and informed directors." 2000 Del. Ch. LEXIS 82, at *86, 2000 WL 710192, at *26. Second, "Delaware law generally respects the committee process as a legitimate method to produce disinterested and independent decisions, where some directors on the board, but not on the committee, arguably have conflicting interests." *Id.* These two principles, the court stated, "produces a general principle that liability will not attach to disinterested, independent and informed directors sitting on a special committee who recommend a merger, even if other directors on the board may have actual or potential conflicts of interest, where the board as a whole follows and accepts the committee's good faith recommendation." *Id.*

The court stated that in transactions between a corporation and a controlling shareholder when an independent special committee has bargained at arm's length on behalf of the corporation, the use of the committee shifts the burden of proving fairness but does not bring the transaction "fully within the purview of the director-protective business judgment rule because the presence of a controlling shareholder 'has the potential to influence, however subtly, the vote of [ratifying] minority stockholders in a manner that is not likely to occur in a transaction with a non-controlling party.'" 2000 Del. Ch. LEXIS 82, at *87, 2000 WL 710192, at *26 (quoting *Kahn v.*

Lynch Communications Sys., Inc., 638 A.2d 1110, 1116 (Del. 1994)). The court stated that "[t]he policy rationale requiring some variant of entire fairness, to my mind, substantially, if not entirely, abates if the transaction in question involves a large though not controlling shareholder" because "the absence of a controlling shareholder removes the prospect of retaliation" and thus "the business judgment rule should apply to an independent special committee's good faith and fully informed recommendation." 2000 Del. Ch. LEXIS 82, at *87-88, 2000 WL 710192, at *26. The court noted that the facts in this case "hold out little if any prospect for retaliation" against Western National's public shareholders:

> If Western National's Special Committee refused to recommend the merger to the full board because they believed it was not in the best interests of the Company's public shareholders, if the board did not approve it for similar reasons, or if the shareholders voted down the merger at the special meeting, it is far from clear that American General would be able to retaliate against such refusal, even if it wished. American General did not have representatives on Western National's board, so it is difficult to understand how it would implement some onerous and oppressive policy upon the public shareholders through board action. Moreover, under the terms of the Standstill Provision, American General was barred from nominating more than two Western National directors – even if it chose to go into the open market and repurchase up to the Standstill's 79 percent limit of Western National's outstanding equity.

2000 Del. Ch. LEXIS 82, at *89, 2000 WL 710192, at *26.

The court also noted that a majority of all disinterested shareholders voted in favor of the merger, and that an overwhelming majority of all disinterested shareholders who voted cast their votes in favor of the merger. 2000 Del. Ch. LEXIS 82, at *88 n.73, 2000 WL 710192, at *26 n.73. The court stated that "[w]here the unaffiliated, majority owners of a company vote so resoundingly in favor of a transaction, and where that vote was fully informed and uncoerced (as it was here . . .), I think one could reasonably ask why a corporate plebiscite on a transaction that has no elements of fraud, waste, or other inequitable conduct, should not be determinative of the claims raised here." *Id.*

The court noted that the case was analogous to *Puma v. Marriott*, 283 A.2d 693 (Del. Ch. 1971), where the court held that a transaction between Marriott Corporation and members of the Marriott family who owned 46 percent of the corporation's stock was subject to review under the business judgment rule because the transaction was approved by five outside directors who constituted a majority of Marriott's nine member board and "there was no showing of domination of the outside directors, nor any evidence to impugn the good faith and integrity of the outside directors, and no indication that the Marriott family dictated the transaction's terms." 2000 Del. Ch. LEXIS 82, at *90-91, 2000 WL 710192, at *27; *see also* Chapter II, Section B 3 a (discussing *Puma* decision). The court stated that the "only difference between *Puma v. Marriott* and this case is that Western National deployed a special committee of three outside, independent directors (from an eight-member board) while Marriott relied on five outside, independent directors (from a nine-member board)." 2000 Del. Ch. LEXIS 82, at *92, 2000 WL 710192, at *27. The court concluded that "I do not think this variation, in the circumstances of this case, should trigger a higher review standard for the Special Committee's recommendation than the business judgment rule." *Id.*

Section B 3 l

Add the following at the end of the first sentence of the paragraph beginning on page 468 and concluding on page 469:

Maryland also has rejected the business purpose test. *See Lerner v. Lerner Corp.*, 750 A.2d 709, 720-23 (Md. 2000).

Add the following at the end of the paragraph beginning on page 469 and concluding on page 470 (immediately after footnote 1906):

An Ohio court in *Kelly v. Wellsville Foundry Inc.*, 2000 Ohio App. LEXIS 6287, 2000 WL 1809021 (Ohio App. Dec. 6, 2000), concluded, in a case involving a close corporation, that a business purpose is required for a reverse stock split pursuant to which a certificate of incorporation is amended to reduce the number of authorized shares and fractional shares are purchased by the corporation. The effect of the transaction in this case was to dilute the holdings of a 20 percent block of stock to approximately 4 percent. 2000 Ohio App. LEXIS 6287, at *3-4, 9, 2000 WL 1809021, at *1, 3. The court stated that "[i]mposition of the business purpose rule is necessary to protect the interests of the minority shareholders because "[a]dopting a fairness test would permit a majority shareholder in a close corporation to eliminate a majority shareholder based on nothing more than a whim as long as the corporation complied with the statutory formalities and offered the minority a fair value for their shares." 2000 Ohio App. LEXIS 6287, at *14, 2000 WL 1809021, at *5.

Section B 3 n

Add the following at the end of footnote 1919 on page 476:

See also Paskill Corp. v. Alcoma Corp., 747 A.2d 549, 552 (Del. 2000) (the "legislative purpose is to provide equitable relief for shareholders dissenting from a merger on grounds of inadequacy of the offering price").

Add the following at the end of the first sentence (immediately after footnote 1919) of the paragraph beginning on page 476 and concluding on page 477:

"[A]ppraisal's utility is that 'shareholders who otherwise gain from appraisal-triggering transactions will only vote in favor of those transactions if their gains more than offset the costs of compensating objectors." *In re Unocal Exploration Corp. S'holders Litig.*, 2000 Del. Ch. LEXIS 92, at *27, 2000 WL 823376, at *7 (Del. Ch. June 13, 2000) (quoting *Paskill*, 747 A.2d at 553).

Add the following at the end of footnote 1920 on page 476:

See also Paskill, 747 A.2d at 552 ("[a]n appraisal proceeding is a limited statutory remedy").

Add the following at the end of footnote 1923 on page 477:

See also Nelson v. Frank E. Best Inc., 768 A.2d 473, 479 (Del. Ch. 2000) (noting "Delaware Supreme Court case law requiring a strict construction of 8 *Del. C.* § 262 demand deadlines" for appraisal and holding that the 20 day period provided for by § 262 for a demand for appraisal means 20 days even if the twentieth day is a Sunday); *Edgerly v. Hechinger*, 1998 Del. Ch. LEXIS 177, at *3-4, 7, 1998 WL 671241, at *1-2, 3 (Del. Ch. Aug. 28, 1998) (dismissing appraisal action because only "a holder of record of stock" is entitled to pursue an appraisal action and citing *Enstar Corp. v. Senouf*, 535 A.2d 1351 (Del. 1987), for the proposition that "[t]he Supreme Court construes the statutory requirements of § 262 strictly" and "[t]he legal and practical effects of having one's stock registered in street name cannot be visited upon the issuer").

Add the following at the beginning of the paragraph beginning and concluding on page 477 (immediately after footnote 1928):

Subject to statutory restrictions, "[p]roof of value can be established by any techniques or methods that are generally acceptable in the financial community and otherwise admissible in court." *M.G. Bancorp., Inc. v. LeBeau*, 737 A.2d 513, 521 (Del. 1999); *see also id.* at 527 ("this Court has eschewed choosing any one method of appraisal to the exclusion of all others"). The Delaware Supreme Court has described appraisal actions as "highly complicated matters that the Court of Chancery is uniquely qualified to adjudicate in an equitable manner." *Id.* at 526-27.

Add the following at the end of footnote 1927 on page 477:

See also Hansen v. 75 Ranch Co., 957 P.2d 32, 42 (Mont. 1998) ("the determination of 'fair value' is an 'inexact science'"); *Lawson Mardon Wheaton, Inc. v. Smith*, 734 A.2d 738, 746 (N.J. 1999) ("[v]aluation is an art rather than a science"); *id.* at 747 ("[e]ach situation presents different elements of value which must be weighted and analyzed accordingly").

Add the following at the end of footnote 1930 on page 478:

See also Paskill, 747 A.2d at 553, 554.

Replace "In other words," in the second sentence (immediately after footnote 1929) of the paragraph beginning on page 477 and concluding on page 478 with the following:

"The underlying assumption in an appraisal valuation is that the dissenting shareholders would be willing to maintain their investment position had the merger not occurred." *Paskill*, 747 A.2d at 553. Thus,

Add the following at the end of footnote 1933 on page 478:

See also Lerner v. Lerner Corp., 750 A.2d 709, 723 n.5 (Md. 2000) (Maryland law); *Hansen*, 957 P.2d at 42-43 (Montana law); *In re 75,629 Shares of Common Stock of Trapp Family Lodge, Inc.*, 725 A.2d 927, 931 (Vt. 1999) (Vermont law).

Replace "The Delaware courts therefore have held that" in the first sentence (immediately after footnote 1933) of the

paragraph beginning on page 478 and concluding on page 479 with the following:

Fair value, as used in Delaware's appraisal statute, is "the value of the company to the stockholder as a going concern, rather than its value to a third party as an acquisition." *M.P.M. Enters., Inc. v. Gilbert*, 731 A.2d 790, 795 (Del. 1999). "'The underlying assumption in an appraisal valuation is that the dissenting shareholders would be willing to maintain their investment position had the merger not occurred.' Accordingly, the corporation must be valued as a going concern based upon the 'operative reality' of the company as of the time of the merger." *M.G. Bancorp.*, 737 A.2d at 525 (quoting *Cede & Co. v. Technicolor, Inc.*, 684 A.2d 289, 298 (Del. 1996)); *see also M.G. Bancorp.*, 737 A.2d at 520 (noting conclusion by Court of Chancery that an appraisal had been performed in a "legally improper manner" because the appraiser "had determined only the 'fair market value' of MGB's minority shares, as opposed to valuing MGB in its entirety as a going concern and determining the fair value of the minority shares as a pro rata percentage of that value").

"The dissenter in an appraisal action is entitled to receive a proportionate share of the fair value in the *going concern* on the date of the merger" (*Paskill*, 747 A.2d at 554), and thus

Add the following between "and not" and "'the sale of the firm value'" in the first sentence (between footnotes 1934 and 1935) of the paragraph beginning on page 478 and concluding on page 479:

"value that is determined on a liquidated basis" (*Paskill*, 747 A.2d at 554),

Replace the Straight Arrow citation in footnote 1936 on page 478 with the following:

Gonsalves v. Straight Arrow Publishers, Inc., 1996 Del. Ch. LEXIS 106, at *5, 1996 WL 483093, at *2 (Del. Ch. Aug. 22,

1996), *aff'd*, 701 A.2d 357 (Del. 1997), *subsequent proceedings*, 725 A.2d 442 (unpublished opinion, text available at 1999 Del. LEXIS 7 and 1999 WL 87280) (Del. Jan. 5, 1999).

Add the following at the end of the first sentence (immediately after footnote 1936) of the paragraph beginning on page 478 and concluding on page 479:

"Consequently, one of the most important factors to consider is the 'nature of the enterprise' that is the subject of the appraisal proceeding." *Paskill*, 747 A.2d at 554-55. Thus, "failure to value a company as a going concern may result in an understatement of fair value." *M.P.M.*, 731 A.2d at 795. Three types of factual findings require judicial determination:

> First, there [is] a need for findings of basic facts. Second, one or more of those basic factual findings ha[ve] to be either selected alone or combined with other basic facts to quantify the inputs that would constitute the intermediate factual mathematical components of any valuation model. Finally, a proper judicial application of those mathematical components, within the context of a legally acceptable valuation model, [leads] to the ultimate judicial factual finding: Technicolor's valuation on the merger date.

Cede & Co. v. Technicolor, Inc. ("Technicolor V"), 758 A.2d 485, 491 (Del. 2000). The same rules that govern the use of expert witnesses, including court-appointed independent expert witnesses, in other types of cases govern the use of expert witnesses in appraisal cases. *Id.* at 496-99.

Replace the Straight Arrow citation in footnote 1937 on page 478 with the following:

Gonsalves v. Straight Arrow Publishers, Inc., 701 A.2d 357, 362 (Del. 1997), *subsequent proceedings*, 725 A.2d 442 (unpublished opinion, text available at 1999 Del. LEXIS 7 and 1999 WL 87280) (Del. Jan. 5, 1999);

Add the following at the end of footnote 1937 on page 479:

See also M.G. Bancorp., 737 A.2d at 526 ("the Court of Chancery has the discretion to select one of the parties' valuation models as its general framework or to fashion its own").

Add the following at the end of footnote 1938 on page 479:

See also M.G. Bancorp., 737 A.2d at 524, 526 ("although not required to do so, it is entirely proper" for court "to adopt any one expert's model, methodology, and mathematical calculations, *in toto*, if that valuation is supported by credible evidence and withstands a critical judicial analysis on the record").

Add the following at the end of the first sentence of footnote 1941 on page 479:

See also Hansen, 957 P.2d at 40-42; *Lawson*, 734 A.2d at 748.

Add the following at the end of footnote 1941 on page 479:

See also Paskill, 747 A.2d at 557; *Metro. Life Ins. Co. v. Aramark Corp.*, 1998 Del. Ch. LEXIS 70, at *5-7 (Del. Ch. Feb. 5, 1998); see *also Paskill*, 747 A.2d at 557; *HMO-W v. SSM Health Care Sys.*, 611 N.W.2d 250, 254-58 (Wis. 2000).

Change "provisions" to "premiums" in the fifth sentence (immediately after footnote 1941) of the paragraph beginning on page 478 and concluding on page 479.

Add the following at the end of footnote 1942 on page 479:

See also M.G. Bancorp., 737 A.2d at 525 ("[b]ecause MGB held a controlling interest in its two subsidiaries, it was necessary to determine the value of those controlling interests in order to ascertain the value of MGB, as a whole, as a going concern on the Merger date").

Replace the Grimes citation in footnote 1955 on page 481 with the following:

1997 Del. Ch. LEXIS 124, 1997 WL 538676 (Del. Ch. Aug. 26, 1997), *aff'd*, 708 A.2d 630 (unpublished opinion, text available at 1998 Del. LEXIS 127 and 1998 WL 171538) (Del. Apr. 1, 1998), *cert. denied*, 525 U.S. 867 (1998).

Add the following at the end of the paragraph beginning on page 480 and concluding on page 481 (immediately after footnote 1954):

In a subsequent decision, *Cede & Co. v. Technicolor, Inc. ("Technicolor V")*, 758 A.2d 485 (Del. 2000), the court held that MAF's realization of $55.7 million in cash from asset sales during 1983 pursuant to Perelman's pre-merger plan, which "expressly contemplated the sale of certain Technicolor divisions during 1983 and forecast no less than $50 million in cash proceeds," was admissible because "the actual 1983 sale proceeds represent a timely validation of the pre-merger forecast that at least $50 million would be realized from asset sales." *Technicolor V*, 758 A.2d at 499. The Supreme Court thus held that the appraisal of Technicolor as of the date of Technicolor's merger into MAF "should incorporate a projection of no less than $50 million in cash proceeds from asset sales." *Id.* The court stated that "post merger evidence is admissible 'to show that plans in effect at the time of the merger have born fruition.'" *Id.* (quoting *Gonsalves v. Straight Arrow Publishers, Inc.*, 701 A.2d 357, 362 (Del. 1997), and citing additional cases).

Add the following at the end of the paragraph beginning on page 481 and concluding on page 482 (immediately after footnote 1957):

The Delaware Supreme Court affirmed "on the basis of and for the reasons assigned by the Court of Chancery in its well-reasoned opinion." *Grimes v. Vitalink Communications Corp.*,

708 A.2d 630 (unpublished opinion, text available at 1998 Del. LEXIS 127 and 1998 WL 171538) (Del. Apr. 1, 1998), *cert. denied*, 525 U.S. 867 (1998).

Add the following at the end of the paragraph beginning and concluding on page 482(immediately after footnote 1960):

The Delaware Supreme Court in *M.P.M. Enterprises, Inc. v. Gilbert*, 731 A.2d 790 (Del. 1999), held that the Court of Chancery did not err by not comparing the terms of a merger and of prior offers for the corporation to the value the court derived in an appraisal using "facets of the experts' competing analyses." *Id.* at 796-97. The Supreme Court acknowledged that "[v]alues derived in the open market through arms-length negotiations offer better indicia of reliability than the interested party transactions that are often the subject of appraisals" but held that "the trial court, in its discretion, need not accord any weight to such values when unsupported by evidence that they represent the going concern of the company at the effective date of the merger or consideration." *Id.* at 796. The court stated that the merger price and the prior offers were offered as part of a "buy-side analysis" that "focused on the elements of value that would arise from the merger, rather than on the going concern value of MPM without any consideration of such synergistic values." *Id.* Delaware's statute, the court emphasized, directs the determination of "fair value exclusive of any element of value arising from the accomplishment or expectation of the merger or consolidation." *Id.* (quoting Del. Gen. Corp. Law § 262(h); emphasis omitted).

The court distinguished *Van de Walle v. Unimation, Inc.*, [1990-1991 Transfer Binder] Fed. Sec. L. Rep. (CCH) ¶ 95,834 (Del. Ch. Mar. 6, 1991), a case finding that transactions such as a merger and prior offers "are the most reliable indicia of fair value" and "more reliable than expert testimony." 731 A.2d at 797; *see also id.* at 797 n.46 (quoting *Van de Walle*, [1990-1991 Transfer Binder] Fed. Sec. L. Rep. (CCH) at 99,035: "[t]he fact that a transaction price was forged in the crucible of objective market reality (as distinguished from the unavoidably subjective thought process of a valuation expert) is viewed as a strong evidence that the price is fair"). The court explained that *Van de Walle* involved a claim that directors had breached their fiduciary duties by accepting an unfair merger price rather than the best price available, but in an appraisal action "the overriding consideration" is not "fairness of the price on the open market" but rather "the going concern value of the company irrespective of the synergies involved in a merger." *Id.* at 797. Accordingly, "[a] merger price resulting from arms-length negotiations where there are no claims of collusion is a very strong indication of fair value," but "in an appraisal action, that merger price must be accompanied by evidence tending to show that it represents the going concern value of the company rather than just the value of the company to one specific buyer." *Id.* In short, "[a] fair merger price in the context of a breach of fiduciary duty claim will not always be a fair value in the context of determining going concern value." *Id.*

In *Paskill Corp. v. Alcoma Corp.*, 747 A.2d 549 (Del. 2000), the Delaware Supreme Court reversed an appraisal of Paskill Corporation's 14.6 percent minority position in Okeechobee, Inc. following Okeechobee's merger with and into Okeechobee, LLC, a limited liability company wholly owned by Alcoma Corporation. Prior to the merger, Alcoma owned 54 percent of Okeechobee's outstanding stock. The Supreme Court held that "the Court of Chancery erroneously valued Okeechobee on a liquidation basis and exacerbated that problem when it calculated Okeechobee's net asset value by deducting speculative future tax liabilities." *Id.* at 550. The Supreme Court also held that "the Court of Chancery correctly excluded speculative expenses associated with uncontemplated sales when it attempted to compute Okeechobee's net asset value." *Id.* The Supreme Court instructed that "[u]pon remand, the Court of Chancery must ascertain the exact nature of Okeechobee as an enterprise. It must then determine Okeechobee's fair value as a going concern on the date of the merger by any admissible valuation technique that is based on reliable and relevant record evidence. Paskill is then entitled to receive the fair value of its proportionate interest in that operating entity at the time of the merger without any discount at the shareholder level." *Id.* at 557.

Add the following at the end of footnote 1963 on page 483:

See also Paskill, 747 A.2d at 556-57 ("In *Weinberger,* [*v. UOP, Inc.*, 457 A.2d 701 (Del. 1983),] this Court broadened the process for determining the 'fair value' of the company's outstanding shares by including all generally accepted techniques of valuation used in the financial community. As a result of that holding in *Weinberger*, the standard 'Delaware block' or weighted average method of valuation, formerly employed in appraisal valuation cases, no longer exclusively controls such proceedings.")

Add the following at the end of footnote 1964 on page 483:

See also M.P.M., 731 A.2d at 796; *Lawson*, 734 A.2d at 746 ("[s]ince the Delaware case of *Weinberger* . . . courts and commentators have come to agree that 'an assessment of fair value requires consideration of 'proof of value by any techniques or methods which are generally acceptable in the financial community and otherwise admissible in court''") (citations omitted).

Replace the paragraph beginning and concluding on page 483 with the following (between footnotes 1965 and 1966):

While "[i]t is not unusual . . . for the same merger to be challenged in a statutory appraisal action and in a separate breach of fiduciary duty damage action," *M.G. Bancorp.*, 737 A.2d at 520, an appraisal proceeding differs from a breach of fiduciary duty proceeding in at least five important ways.

First, "§ 262 is chock-full of disadvantages for shareholders, especially ones who own relatively small blocks. Most significant, . . . a stockholder who seeks appraisal must forego all of the transactional consideration and essentially place his investment in limbo until the appraisal is resolved." *Turner v. Bernstein*, 2000 Del. Ch. LEXIS 96, at *49, 2000 WL 776893, at *14 (Del. Ch. June 6, 2000). "The unavailability of a class action and fee shifting in appraisal actions makes an unfair dealing action more attractive from the perspective of plaintiffs, thus leading to the litigation of lawsuits that require a determination of the fairness of the process used and the price paid when appraisal lawsuits addressing solely the issue of fair price would otherwise be sufficient." *Andra v. Blount*, 772 A.2d 183, 192 (Del. Ch. 2000); *see also Turner*, 2000 Del. Ch. LEXIS 96, at *49, 2000 WL 776893, at *14 ("the unavailability of the class action mechanism in appraisal also acts as a substantial disincentive for its use").

Change "First" to "Second" in the first sentence (between footnotes 1965 and 1966) of the paragraph beginning on page 483 and concluding on page 484.

Add the following at the end of footnote 1966 on page 484:

See also Cede & Co. v. Technicolor, Inc. ("Technicolor I"), 542 A.2d 1182, 1186 (Del. 1988) (in an appraisal action "the only party defendant is the surviving corporation," but a breach of fiduciary duty action "is brought against the alleged wrongdoers"), *quoted in Nagy v. Bistricer*, 770 A.2d 43, 52 (Del. Ch. 2000); *Nagy*, 770 A.2d at 52 (in an appraisal action "the only relief available is a judgment against the surviving corporation"); *Turner*, 2000 Del. Ch. LEXIS 96, at *42 n.37, 2000 WL 776893, at *12 n.37 ("[i]n an appraisal, the defendant is the resulting or surviving corporation and is bound to pay the fair value of the petitioners' shares as determined by the court"; "[i]n an equitable action, the defendants are the persons (typically the directors) who are alleged to have breached fiduciary duties owed to the plaintiffs"); *Andra*, 772 A.2d at 192 n.22 (in an appraisal action, "[t]he only party held liable is the surviving corporation"; in a breach of fiduciary duty action, "the parties from whom the recovery is sought are normally the corporation's directors and executive officers") (quoting Jack B. Jacobs, *Reappraising Appraisal: Some Judicial Reflections*, Speech at 15th Annual Ray Garrett, Jr. Corporate and Securities Law Institute, Northwestern University School of Law, at 12 (Apr. 27, 1995)).

Add the following at the end of the paragraph beginning on page 483 and concluding on page 484 (immediately after footnote 1966):

A breach of fiduciary duty action does not permit pursuit of damages from the surviving corporation in the merger and thus requires reliance upon the personal resources of alleged wrongdoers or directors' and officers' liability insurance. *Turner*, 2000 Del. Ch. LEXIS 96, at *44, 2000 WL 776893, at *13.

Replace "Second, causation" in the first sentence (immediately after footnote 1966) of the paragraph beginning and concluding on page 484 with the following:

Third, in an appraisal action "a stockholder dissenting from a merger or other triggering transaction is entitled, without having to prove wrongdoing or liability on anyone's part, to a determination of the fair value of his investment." *Andra*, 772 A.2d at 192 n.22 (quoting Jacobs, *Reappraising Appraisal: Some Judicial Reflections*). A breach of fiduciary duty action requires proof of a breach of fiduciary duty. *Turner*, 2000 Del. Ch. LEXIS 96, at *42 n.37, 2000 WL 776893, at *12 n.37. Thus, "eschewing appraisal involve[s] waiving the right to obtain a fair price without the concomitant requirement of proving a fiduciary breach." *Turner*, 2000 Del. Ch. LEXIS 96, at *44, 2000 WL 776893, at *13. Causation

Replace "Third" with "Fourth" in the first sentence (immediately after footnote 1967) of the paragraph beginning on page 484 and concluding on page 485.

Replace "Courts have held, however," in the second sentence of the paragraph (immediately after footnote 1969) beginning on page 484 and concluding on page 485 with the following:

In an appraisal action, "the measure of recovery is the fair or intrinsic value of the corporation's stock immediately before the merger," and "[p]ost-merger synergies or values are not to be considered"; in a breach of fiduciary duty action, "[t]he measure of the recovery is not limited to the statutorily appraised value, and in some cases, may include post-merger values computed as rescissory damages." *Andra*, 772 A.2d at 192 n.22 (quoting Jacobs, *Reappraising Appraisal: Some Judicial Reflections*). Unlike an appraisal action, a breach of fiduciary duty action "affords an expansive remedy" that provides "whatever relief the facts of a particular case may require," including "any damages sustained by the shareholders." *Technicolor I*, 542 A.2d at 1187, *quoted in Nagy*, 770 A.2d at 52. A court thus "has greater discretion when fashioning an award of damages in an action for a breach of the duty of loyalty than it would when assessing fair value in an appraisal action." *Int'l Telecharge, Inc. v. Bomarko*, 766 A.2d 437, 441 (Del. 2000).

Nevertheless, courts have held

Add the following at the end of footnote 1970 on page 484:

See also Bomarko, Inc. v. Int'l Telecharge, Inc., 1994 Del. Ch. LEXIS 51, at *7-8, 1994 WL 198726, at *3 (Del. Ch. May 16, 1994) ("[B]reach of fiduciary duty claims that do not arise from the merger are corporate assets that may be included in the determination of fair value. . . . Although those claims may not be litigated in this proceeding, I see no reason why petitioners should be precluded from introducing evidence as to their value. . . . I anticipate that the value of the claims, if any, will be established through expert testimony in much the same manner that evidence typically is presented as to the value of other corporate assets."), *subsequent proceedings*, 1999 Del. Ch. LEXIS 211, at *75-76, 1999 WL 1022083, at *25 (Del. Ch. Nov. 4, 1999), *aff'd*, 766 A.2d 437 (Del. 2000) (concluding, after a trial, in the context of an analysis of the proper measure of damages for breach of fiduciary duty, as follows: "I value the claim by multiplying (a) my assessment of the probability of success on the merits by (b) the likely amount of a favorable recovery, and subtracting from that result (c) the reasonable costs ITI would have incurred in prosecuting the claim. I conclude that there was a .8 probability of success on this claim. I discount the outcome only to weigh the inevitable uncertainty of litigation and the chance that the forbearance agreement might be upheld. The likely recovery was $8 million. This produces a gross potential recovery of $6.4 million. It seems to me unlikely that the Company would have to pay more than 15% of that amount in fees and expenses to secure the services of competent counsel in a case of this unusually strong merit. Thus, I arrive at a value of $5.44 million for the claim. Plaintiffs will be awarded 9.48% of this amount, or $515,712 in damages for the value of this claim. This comes to $0.24 for each of plaintiffs' 2,181,682 shares."); *HMO-W v. SSM Health Care Sys.*, 611 N.W.2d 250, 258-60 (Wis. 2000).

Add the following at the end of footnote 1972 on page 485:

See also Nagy, 770 A.2d at 56 n.23 (collecting cases); *Turner*, 2000 Del. Ch. LEXIS 96, at *43 n.38, 2000 WL 776893, at *13 n.38 (derivative claims can be valued in an appraisal); *Onti, Inc. v. Integra Bank*, 751 A.2d 904, 931 (Del. Ch. 1999) (stating that the value attributed to derivative claims must factor in the value of the claims, the defenses available in the litigation, the attorneys' fees that would be incurred, and indemnification that the corporation would be required to pay).

Add the following at the end of the paragraph beginning on page 484 and concluding on page 485 (immediately after footnote 1972):

"[B]ecause those claims are assets of the corporation being valued, the court must place a value on those assets in coming to a fair value determination." *Nagy*, 770 A.2d at 56. By contrast, "individual claims that directly relate to the fairness" of a merger "are not properly subject to valuation" in a appraisal proceeding and the surviving corporation cannot be held "responsible for paying damages as to those claims" in an appraisal proceeding. *Id.*

Replace the period at the end of footnote 1978 on page 486 with the following:

and Onti, Inc. v. Integra Bank, 751 A.2d 904, 907 (Del. Ch. 1999).

Add the following at the end of the paragraph beginning on page 485 and concluding on page 486 (immediately after footnote 1979):

Nevertheless, the collateral estoppel doctrine may prevent the relitigation of issues decided in an appraisal action in a subsequent breach of fiduciary duty action and vice versa. *M.G. Bancorp.*, 737 A.2d at 519-21. Thus, the court in *M.G. Bancorporation* held, a finding in a breach of fiduciary duty action that Alex Sheshunoff & Co. Investment Bankers had determined the "fair market value" of a corporation in "a legally improper manner" collaterally estopped the corporation from arguing in an appraisal action that Sheshunoff's determination represented fair value. *Id.* at 520. As a result, the court held, the burden was upon the corporation to demonstrate how the "purportedly proper statutory appraisal valuation" offered by the corporation's expert in the appraisal action "resulted in only a 90 cents (approximately 2%) per share increase over the legally improper Sheshunoff valuation." *Id.* at 521.

Section B 3 o

Add the following at the end of footnote 1995 on page 489:

See also Nebel v. S.W. Bancorp, Inc., 1999 Del. Ch. LEXIS 30, at *13, 1999 WL 135259, at *4 (Del. Ch. Mar. 9, 1999) ("[w]here a merger eliminates the minority shareholder interest for cash and the dispute is essentially one over value, appraisal is the exclusive remedy").

Add the following at the end of the first sentence (immediately after footnote 1995) of the paragraph beginning and concluding on page 489:

It has been said that this principle "is especially applicable in the short-form merger context," where Section 253 of the Delaware General Corporation Law "permits a parent corporation that owns 90% or more of a subsidiary's stock to cause the parent corporation's board of directors unilaterally to eliminate the minority stockholders' interest." *Nebel*, 1999 Del. Ch. LEXIS 30, at *13, 1999 WL 135259, at *4.

Add the following at the end of footnote 1996 on page 489:

See also Wood v. Frank E. Best, Inc., 1999 Del. Ch. LEXIS 141, at *11, 1999 WL 504779, at *3 (Del. Ch. July 9, 1999); *Nebel*, 1999 Del. Ch. LEXIS 30, at *13, 1999 WL 135259, at *4.

Add the following at the end of footnote 1997 on page 490:

See also Bomarko, Inc. v. Int'l Telecharge, Inc., 1999 Del. Ch. LEXIS 211, at *38, 1999 WL 1022083, at *14 (Del. Ch. Nov. 4, 1999) ("in trying this consolidated fraud and appraisal action, the Chancery Court should first evaluate the fraud claims" and "[t]he Court will determine whether the Merger was entirely fair to ITI's shareholders. If I conclude that it was entirely fair, the plaintiffs' statutory appraisal remedy will be the sole means of establishing a fair value for the shares of the dissenters. If the Merger was not entirely fair, in contrast, other forms of equitable relief are available."), *aff'd*, 766 A.2d 437 (Del. 2000).

Replace the citation to the Nebel case in footnote 1998 on page 490 with the following:

[1995 Transfer Binder] Fed. Sec. L. Rep. (CCH) ¶ 98,846 (Del. Ch. July 5, 1995), *subsequent proceedings*, 1999 Del. Ch. LEXIS 30, 1999 WL 135259 (Del. Ch. Mar. 9, 1999).

Add the following at the end of the third sentence (immediately after footnote 2002) of the paragraph beginning on page 490 and concluding on page 491:

The Court of Chancery added the following in a later decision in the same case:

> Claims based on fraud or breach of the fiduciary duty of disclosure cannot be adequately addressed in an appraisal, for the additional reason that misdisclosures or nondisclosures of material facts might warrant injunctive relief that would prevent the merger from taking place. To say it differently, disclosure-based claims cannot be resolved in an appraisal proceeding because the appropriate remedies for disclosure violations (such as rescission or its monetary equivalent) are inconsistent with the purely monetary relief that is available in a statutory appraisal.

Nebel, 1999 Del. Ch. LEXIS 30, at *14, 1999 WL 135259, at *5 (citations to *Weinberger v. UOP, Inc.*, 457 A.2d 701, 714 (Del. 1983) and *Sealy Mattress Co. v. Sealy, Inc.*, 532 A.2d 1324, 1341-42 (Del. Ch. 1987) omitted), *quoted in Onti, Inc. v. Integra Bank*, 751 A.2d 904, 930 (Del. Ch. 1999).

Add the following at the end of footnote 2004 on page 491:

See also O'Reilly v. Transworld Healthcare, Inc., 745 A.2d 902, 929 (Del. Ch. 1999) (disclosure claims "completely undermine" contention that an appraisal action is the only available remedy).

Replace the period at the end of footnote 2006 on page 491 with the following:

, *quoted in Nebel*, 1999 Del. Ch. LEXIS 30, at *15, 1999 WL 135259, at *5.

Add the following at the end of the paragraph beginning and concluding on page 491 (immediately after footnote 2007):

To determine whether unfair dealing claims are "merely claims that question judgmental factors of valuation" or are "so egregious as to make it inequitable to relegate the minority shareholders to the appraisal remedy," courts "look beyond the complaint's conclusory allegations or characterizations." *Nebel*, 1999 Del. Ch. LEXIS 30, at *15, 1999 WL 135259, at *5.

Replace the paragraph beginning and concluding on page 492 (immediately after footnote 2012) with the following:

The court in *Nebel* reached a different conclusion in a later decision involving an amended complaint. The court identified two factors as "pivotal." 1999 Del. Ch. LEXIS 30, at *22, 1999 WL 135259, at *7.

First, the court pointed to "defendants' failure to establish an independent committee of directors to represent the minority stockholders' interests." 1999 Del. Ch. LEXIS 30, at *22, 1999 WL 135259, at *7. The court acknowledged its earlier ruling that "there is no legal requirement" that a merger "be approved by either an independent committee of directors or by a 'majority of the minority' shareholder vote," but stated that this ruling "was not intended, nor should it be read, to detract from the principle that fiduciaries who stand on both sides of a merger . . . and dictate its terms have the burden to show that the merger was entirely fair." *Id.* Thus, while "the absence of a negotiating committee of independent directors, without more, does not constitute unfair dealing as a matter of law, . . . that circumstance is evidence of unfair dealing that, when combined with other pleaded facts, may state a cognizable unfair dealing claim that the fiduciaries will ultimately have the burden to negate." 1999 Del. Ch. LEXIS 30, at *22-23, 1999 WL 135259, at *7. The court's first decision, the court stated, "determined only that the plaintiffs' first amended complaint did not plead unfair dealing sufficient to withstand a motion to dismiss." 1999 Del. Ch. LEXIS 30, at *23 n.23, 1999 WL 135259, at *7 n.23.

Second, the court took judicial notice of the fact that since the court's first ruling the fair value of the plaintiffs' shares had been adjudicated in an appraisal action to be $85 per share – $44 per share more than $41 per share merger price. 1999 Del. Ch. LEXIS 30, at *23, 1999 WL 135259, at *7. The court held that this "significant gap," combined with allegations that the $41 per share merger price was arrived at in an improper manner (plaintiffs alleged that defendants "made no genuine effort to determine" the corporation's "'fair value,' as opposed to the 'fair market value' of the plaintiffs' shares") and other substantive unfairness allegations "create an inference that the Merger was the product of unfair dealing . . . sufficient to state a claim upon which relief may be granted." 1999 Del. Ch. LEXIS 30, at *21, 23-24, 1999 WL 135259, at *6, 7.

The court in *Nebel* also held that the corporation's inadvertent failure to attach a copy of Delaware's appraisal statute to the notice of merger, as required by Section 262(d)(1) of the Delaware General Corporation Law, constituted an actionable disclosure claim. *Nebel v. S.W. Bancorp, Inc.*, [1995 Transfer Binder] Fed. Sec. L. Rep. (CCH) ¶ 98,846 at 93,094-96. The court concluded, however, that "a complete remedy" for this statutory violation "would be to permit the plaintiffs either to commence an appraisal proceeding or to pursue a 'quasi-appraisal' remedy," and that "[t]o invalidate or rescind the merger (or to permit a recovery of rescissory damages) solely because of that violation would go far beyond what is needed to vindicate th[e] underlying statutory purpose." *Id.* at 93,096. The plaintiffs' remedy, the court stated, should be the same as it would be in an appraisal action – i.e., "a determination . . . of the plaintiffs' proportionate share of the statutory fair value" of the corporation. *Id.*

Wood v. Frank E. Best Inc., 1999 Del. Ch. LEXIS 141, 1999 WL 504779 (Del. Ch. July 9, 1999), describes the "current state" of the law as follows: Where "cashed out minority shareholders have pleaded facts sufficient to indicate a breach of fiduciary duty, which they seek to bring against not only the surviving corporation but against individual directors or majority shareholders as well, the plaintiffs need not demonstrate inadequacy of the appraisal remedy to survive a motion to dismiss." 1999 Del. Ch. LEXIS 141, at *20, 1999 WL 504779, at *6, *quoted in Turner v. Bernstein*, 2000 Del. Ch. LEXIS 96, at *47 n.44, 2000 WL 776893, at *14 n.44 (Del. Ch. June 6, 2000), *and Nagy v. Bistricer*, 770 A.2d 43, 53-54 (Del. Ch. 2000); *see also In re Unocal Exploration Corp. S'holders Litig.*, 2000 Del. Ch. LEXIS 92, at *42-43, 2000 WL 823376, at *11 (Del. Ch. June 13, 2000) (stating that "[t]he state of the law with respect to long-form mergers involving controlling stockholders was well described" in *Wood*).

The court in *Wood* accordingly denied a motion to dismiss in a case where plaintiffs alleged that directors "stood on both sides of the cash out merger, timed the merger so as to minimize cost to themselves at the expense of the shareholders, and failed to provide any method for determining whether the merger was entirely fair to the shareholders independent of the defendants themselves or their financial advisors whom they had hired." 1999 Del. Ch. LEXIS 141, at *17, 1999 WL 504779, at *5.

The court acknowledged that "[a]ll of the allegations of breach of duty ultimately relate to the plaintiffs' claim that the price they received was unfair" and that there was "no allegation of deception which might have misled the shareholders as to whether to pursue their appraisal rights at the time of the merger." 1999 Del. Ch. LEXIS 141, at *13, 1999 WL 504779, at *4. The court nevertheless held that plaintiffs' claim that the price resulting from defendants' unfair dealing was unfair and that as a result plaintiffs were damaged "states a claim sufficient to survive a motion to dismiss, and sufficient to put the defendants to proof that the transaction was entirely fair." 1999 Del. Ch. LEXIS 141, at *17, 1999 WL 504779, at *5.

The court relied upon the Supreme Court's decision in *Cede & Co. v. Technicolor, Inc.*, 634 A.2d 345 (Del. 1993), which held that under *Weinberger v. UOP, Inc.*, 457 A.2d 701 (Del. 1983), "the measure of any recoverable loss by [the plaintiff] under an entire fairness standard of review is not necessarily limited to the difference between the price offered and the 'true' value as determined under appraisal proceedings" and that "a party may have a legally cognizable injury regardless of whether the tender offer and cash-out price is greater than the stock's fair value as determined for statutory appraisal purposes." 1999 Del. Ch. LEXIS 141, at *14-15, 1999 WL 504779, at *4 (quoting *Technicolor*, 634 A.2d at 367, 371). Rather, "[u]nder *Weinberger*, the Chancellor may 'fashion any form of equitable and monetary relief as may be appropriate, including rescissory damages.'" 1999 Del. Ch. LEXIS 141, at *15, 1999 WL 504779, at *4 (quoting *Weinberger*, 457 A.2d at 714, and *Cede*, 634 A.2d at 371). The court also pointed to the Supreme Court's decision in *Rabkin v. Philip A. Hunt Chemical Corp.*, 498 A.2d 1099 (Del. 1985), which stated that a "narrow interpretation of *Weinberger* would render meaningless our extensive discussion of fair dealing found in that opinion." 1999 Del. Ch. LEXIS 141, at *16, 1999 WL 504779, at *5 (quoting 498 A.2d at 1104).

The court thus rejected defendants' contention that "in addition to alleging breach of fiduciary duty, to survive a motion to dismiss the plaintiffs must demonstrate that appraisal is an inadequate remedy, either because deception or fraud misled shareholders into failing to pursue appraisal, or because damages available in an appraisal would be inadequate." 1999 Del. Ch. LEXIS 141, at *17, 1999 WL 504779, at *5. In the court's view, *Technicolor* makes clear "[f]or good or ill" that "a colorable allegation of breach of entire fairness is sufficient to proceed with an equitable entire fairness action, despite the availability of appraisal as an alternative remedy." 1999 Del. Ch. LEXIS 141, at *18, 1999 WL 504779, at *5, *quoted in Turner*, 2000 Del. Ch. LEXIS 96, at *47 n.44, 2000 WL 776893, at *14 n.44, *and Nagy*, 770 A.2d at 53.

The court also rejected defendants' effort to distinguish *Nebel* on the ground that "in *Nebel*, the price per share had been demonstrated through an appraisal action to have been inadequate." 1999 Del. Ch. LEXIS 141, at *19-20, 1999 WL 504779, at *6. The court reasoned that "plaintiffs here have alleged inadequate price," "[f]or purposes of this motion, I must assume that the plaintiffs will be able to demonstrate inadequate price at trial." 1999 Del. Ch. LEXIS 141, at *20, 1999 WL 504779, at *6. The court stated that "[t]he fact that inadequate price remains an allegation here, unlike the situation in *Nebel*, cannot determine the outcome of the motion to dismiss." *Id.*

The court noted the Supreme Court's recognition in *Rabkin* that its holding in *Rabkin* "encouraged litigants to forego appraisal, with its associated risks and opportunity costs, in favor of an equitable action." 1999 Del. Ch. LEXIS 141, at *21 n.29, 1999 WL 504779, at *6 n.29. The court also noted the fact that the Supreme Court in *Rabkin* placed the burden upon the Court of Chancery "to strike a balance 'between sustaining complaints averring faithless acts, which taken as true would constitute breaches of fiduciary duties that are reasonably related to and have a substantial impact upon the price offered, and properly dismissing those allegations questioning judgmental factors of valuation.'" *Id.* (quoting 498 A.2d at 1107-08). The Court of Chancery in *Wood* noted that the Supreme Court in *Rabkin* "took comfort that this Court's 'degree of sophistication' in such matters would allow performance of such a winnowing'" but "failed to explain how such a process could proceed in cases involving allegations of self-dealing in connection with a cash-out merger." 1999 Del. Ch. LEXIS

141, at *21 n.29, 1999 WL 504779, at *6 n.29, *quoted in Turner*, 2000 Del. Ch. LEXIS 96, at *46, 2000 WL 776893, at *14 n.42.

Defendants responded to the court's decision by filing "a second motion to dismiss, asserting that plaintiffs have no standing to assert certain unfair dealing claims because plaintiffs accepted the benefits of the challenged transaction by tendering their shares and accepting the consideration offered by defendants." *Wood v. Frank E. Best, Inc.*, 1999 Del. Ch. LEXIS 184, at *1, 1999 WL 743482, at *1 (Del. Ch. Sept. 7, 1999). Defendants thus relied "on the general rule that one who participates in or acquiesces in an action has no standing in a court of equity to complain about it." 1999 Del. Ch. LEXIS 184, at *1-2, 1999 WL 743482, at *1. The court determined to treat the motion to dismiss as a motion for summary judgment because "the pleadings on their face do not support the factual predicate for defendants' second motion, namely, the assertion that all the plaintiffs have accepted 'voluntarily' the cash consideration offered in the merger transactions." 1999 Del. Ch. LEXIS 184, at *2, 1999 WL 743482, at *1. "[B]ecause of the possible factual dispute over whether some (or all) of the plaintiffs 'voluntarily' accepted the merger consideration, the court "granted plaintiffs leave to take or provide limited discovery on that discrete factual issue." *Id.*

The court in *Andra v. Blount*, 772 A.2d 183 (Del. Ch. 2000), began its analysis of the unfair dealing claim before the court in *Andra* by observing that "[o]rdinarily, one would reject . . . out of hand" defendants' contention that a shareholder alleging unfair dealing should be relegated to appraisal because following the Supreme Court's decisions in *Rabkin* and *Technicolor* "it has become nearly impossible for a judge of this court to dismiss a well-pled unfair dealing claim on the basis that appraisal is available as a remedy and is fully adequate." *Id.* at 192. The court acknowledged that "the Supreme Court has never held that this Court cannot limit a plaintiff to an appraisal remedy that is fully adequate" but stated that *Rabkin* and *Technicolor* "are reasonably read as indicating that so long as a plaintiff can state a claim for breach of fiduciary duty in connection with the merger, he can press an unfair dealing claim." *Id.* The court in *Andra*, however, then stated that the *Andra* case "test[ed] the limits" of *Rabkin* and *Technicolor* and thus made it difficult to "reject . . . out of hand" defendants' contention that plaintiff should be limited to an appraisal remedy because plaintiff had conceded in a letter to the court withdrawing a motion for a preliminary injunction that damages "equivalent to the appraised value" of plaintiff's stock would provide a "complete" remedy "for the wrongs complained of in this action." *Id.* at 192, 193.

Rabkin and *Technicolor*, the court explained, rest in large part "on the rationale that a determination of fair value in an appraisal action may not always be sufficient to address the harm caused by breaches of fiduciary duty in the context of mergers." *Id.* at 192-93. The court continued:

> Because an entire fairness action permits this court the flexibility to shape a remedy fitting to the breach (e.g., rescissory damages when justified), a plaintiff who can state a claim for breach of fiduciary duty ordinarily should not be relegated to the (implicitly less adequate) remedy of appraisal, where the only remedy is the fair value of plaintiff's stock. Otherwise, there is a risk that victims of fiduciary breaches will be less than wholly compensated for the harm done them, thus creating less than an adequate incentive for fiduciaries to comply with their "unremitting" duties of loyalty and care.

Id. These considerations, the court stated, were not raised by the case before the court because plaintiff had conceded that "an award of fair value in appraisal terms" would not be "inadequate to make Andra whole." *Id.* at 193.

Instead, "the only apparent inadequacies of the appraisal remedy" involved the advantages of an unfair dealing action (in comparison to the disadvantages of an appraisal action), which the court labeled "Litigation-Cost Benefits" and summarized as follows:

> In a class action, the plaintiff's lawyers can take their fees and expenses against any classwide recovery, whereas in an appraisal action the fees and expenses can be recovered only as

> an offset against the appraisal award to the usually far smaller group of stockholders who perfected their appraisal rights. It is much less attractive, for example, to act as an attorney for fifty-seven appraisal stockholders who own small blocks than as counsel for a class comprised of all, or at least most, of the company's stockholders.

Id. at 194.

The *Andra* case thus presented "a policy choice between two models":

> Under one model, a plaintiff should be limited to appraisal if an appraisal award would be sufficient to redress the direct harm flowing from the fiduciary breach, regardless of whether it denies the plaintiff the Litigation-Cost Benefits of an unfair dealing claim. This model would stress the primacy of appraisal (when that statutory remedy is available) and the efficiency of avoiding unnecessary determinations regarding fair process when a single inquiry into price will suffice.
>
> The other model would stress the need to provide a full and adequate remedy for fiduciary breaches and would take into account the real-world significance of procedure and litigation costs in that regard. To the extent that fiduciaries believe that they can avoid responsibility to the entire class of their stockholders and require a relatively small group of appraisal petitioners to bear (out of any recovery) the substantial costs of an action to prove an unfair price, fiduciaries may not be adequately deterred from engaging in faithless behavior. This model would also recognize that a plaintiff who has an appraisal remedy minus the costs of litigation is in fact worse off than a plaintiff without an appraisal remedy who can obtain a class-wide award of quasi-appraisal damages plus the possibility of an award of attorneys' fees paid by the defendants.

Id. The court stated that the litigation cost benefits of a class action – and "not the theoretical possibility of an award of (rarely granted) rescissory damages" – is the factor that "most often makes an unfair dealing claim so much more attractive than appraisal from a plaintiff's perspective." *Id.* "Class actions and fee shifting," the court continued, "are crucial if litigation is to serve as a method of holding corporate fiduciaries accountable to stockholders"; "[w]ithout them, collective action problems would make it economically impractical for many meritorious actions to be brought." *Id.*

The court concluded that "[a]lthough the Supreme Court has never explicitly addressed the issue in this stark manner," *Rabkin* and *Technicolor* "place a higher value on the full remediation of fiduciary breaches than they do on channeling claims into the more streamlined and confined appraisal remedy process – even when that process can make a plaintiff whole (putting litigation costs to the side)." *Id.* at 195. The court accordingly held that plaintiff "may proceed with her unfair dealing claim" because "I can discern no reasoned basis" under *Rabkin* and *Technicolor* to deny a plaintiff having access to appraisal rights "access to a potential attorneys' fee award or a class-based sharing of litigation costs when a similarly situated plaintiff without appraisal rights would have such access." *Id.* at 196. The court acknowledged that its ruling that "the unavailability of a class action and an attorneys' fee award renders appraisal an inadequate remedy for a plaintiff such as Andra who concedes that a fair value award is otherwise sufficient" creates "a clear per se rule that every well-pleaded claim that a merger is unfair as a result of fiduciary breaches may proceed on an equitable, non-statutory basis, alongside any appraisal action." *Id.* at 195.

The court in *Turner v. Bernstein*, 2000 Del. Ch. LEXIS 96, 2000 WL 776893 (Del. Ch. June 6, 2000), held that shareholders may assert a breach of fiduciary duty claim for a failure to disclose material facts in connection with a cash-out merger after accepting the merger consideration and eschewing appraisal. The court rejected a contention that "this sort of strategy is offensive to Delaware law because it invites plaintiffs to sit on disclosure claims until after a vote or stockholder choice has been made, accept the transactional consideration, and then pounce on the defendants for a disclosure violation that could have been corrected in a timely manner had the claim been pressed before closure of the transaction." 2000 Del. Ch. LEXIS 96, at *45, 2000 WL 776893, at *13. The court acknowledged "the importance of these concerns" but stated that these concerns did not provide "a basis for denying plaintiffs the opportunity to press their disclosure claims" because there was "no sound statutory basis to conclude that a statutory appraisal remedy is exclusive in this context." 2000 Del. Ch. LEXIS 96, at *45-46, 2000 WL 776893, at *13-14. The court stated that "[t]he General Assembly could easily write the language to make it so; to date, it has not," and "[a]s things stand, I see no rational way for Delaware courts to fashion a distinction between situations that should be litigated exclusively under § 262 and those that can be litigated through an equitable fiduciary duty action." 2000 Del. Ch. LEXIS 96, at *46, 2000 WL 776893, at *14. The court added that "[i]n view of the importance our law places on full disclosure, it would be difficult to reconcile allowing equitable unfair dealing cases to proceed with barring equitable actions based on an inadequate disclosures." 2000 Del. Ch. LEXIS 96, at *48, 2000 WL 776893, at *14.

The court thus concluded that "a corporate board wishing to argue that a stockholder's acceptance of the merger consideration bars any further relief must also be willing to show that it provided the stockholder with all the information she needed to make a knowing and informed decision. If the board can meet this burden . . . the stockholder will . . . lose. If a corporate board cannot meet this burden, the board will be required to defend itself against claims that it breached its fiduciary duties and be held responsible in damages for any proven breaches (usually those not exculpated by a § 102(b)(7) provision)." 2000 Del. Ch. LEXIS 96, at *51-52, 2000 WL 776893, at *14. The court stated that "[b]y enabling stockholders to hold directors accountable for such fiduciary breaches (e.g., a disclosure violation that results from disloyalty), equitable actions thus serve an independent purpose not advanced by appraisal actions." 2000 Del. Ch. LEXIS 96, at *52, 2000 WL 776893, at 14; *see also In re Marriott Hotel Props. II LP Unitholders Litig.*, 2000 Del. Ch. LEXIS 17, at *73, 2000 WL 128875, at *21 (Del. Ch. Jan. 24, 2000) (permitting shareholder who tendered limited partnership units following a denial of a motion for a preliminary injunction alleging disclosure violations to continue to challenge the transaction "notwithstanding the fact that he was admittedly aware of all or nearly all of the non-disclosures or misrepresentations about which he now complains" when he tendered his units because "[t]o rule otherwise would discourage plaintiffs and their counsel from acting promptly to litigate disclosure claims in advance of the conclusion of a transaction," a result that would be "directly at odds with the interests of the class who are best served when full and complete disclosures are made in a timely fashion").

Nagy v. Bistricer, 770 A.2d 43 (Del. Ch. 2000), involved a merger agreement entered into by Riblet Products Corporation and Coleman Cable Acquisition, Inc., both of which were controlled by David Bistricer and Nachum Stein. Bistricer and Stein, the only directors of Riblet and the owners of 85 percent of Riblet's shares, caused Riblet to approve the merger agreement without any prior notice to Riblet's sole minority shareholder, Ernest Nagy. Nagy was informed that he could accept a tentatively set number of Coleman shares in exchange for his Riblet shares (this tentative number was subject to an upward or downward adjustment by Coleman based upon the advice of Coleman's investment banker) or seek appraisal. Nagy was required to choose between Coleman shares and appraisal before knowing what the upward or downward adjustment – and thus the final merger consideration – would be, and was provided no information about "why or how Bistricer and Stein approved this strange Merger Agreement as Riblet directors, no financial information about Riblet or Coleman Acquisition, and no information regarding Bistricer's and Stein's interest in Coleman Acquisition." *Id.* at 46.

Nagy commenced a breach of fiduciary duty action and demanded appraisal, and the court rejected a contention by defendants that appraisal was Nagy's exclusive remedy. The court summarized Nagy's "substantial claims for breach of fiduciary duty 'unrelated to judgmental factors of valuation . . . '" (quoting *Rabkin,* 498 A.2d at 1100) as follows:

> [T]he Merger was a self-dealing transaction between corporations controlled by Bistricer and Stein that was designed to advantage their personal interests at the expense of Nagy. In effecting the Merger, Bistricer and Stein did not deploy any of the mechanisms traditionally used to protect minority stockholders and thus they will bear the burden to show that the transaction was entirely fair. Furthermore, Bistricer and Stein failed to provide Nagy with any material financial information regarding Coleman Acquisition or Riblet that would enable Nagy to judge whether the Tentative Merger Consideration was fair. Not only that, Bistricer and Stein delegated to Coleman Acquisition the right to adjust that consideration downward after the time by which Nagy had to seek appraisal, thus forcing Nagy to make his appraisal decision while in the dark about the ultimate price offered.

Id. at 51. In other words, the court stated, "a self-dealing merger . . . was effected without the use of any fairness mechanisms, without the disclosure of material financial information, and that delegated to the acquirior the final say on the consideration to be offered." *Id.* at 55. The court concluded that "[g]iven these allegations, it would be hasty to assume that Nagy may not be able to prove his entitlement to either rescission of the merger or rescissory damages." *Id.* at 51. The court added that the terms of Section 144 of the Delaware General Corporation Law, discussed in Chapter II, Sections B 2 a-d, "would suggest that a self-dealing transaction that falls within the statute's reach," as this transaction did, "is voidable unless, at minimum, one of the statutory categories that creates an exception to voidability" – disinterested director approval, disinterested shareholder approval, or a showing of fairness – is satisfied. *Id.* at 54 n.21.

Add the following at the end of the bullets beginning on page 492 and concluding on page 496 (immediately after footnote 2030):

Different rules govern short-form mergers completed pursuant to Section 253 of the Delaware General Corporation Law, where a 90 or more percent shareholder "unilaterally sets the merger price, passes a resolution and files a certificate of merger – all without the need to consult or *deal* with the subsidiary, its directors or other stockholders." *In re Unocal Exploration Corp. S'holders Litig.*, 2000 Del. Ch. LEXIS 92, at *24, 2000 WL 823376, at *7 (Del. Ch. June 13, 2000). Under those circumstances, appraisal is the exclusive remedy "in the absence of fraud or other illegality." 2000 Del. Ch. LEXIS 92, at *29-51, 2000 WL 823376, at *8-13. Application of a fairness analysis to a short-form merger completed pursuant to Section 253 "would gut the short-form merger statute of its meaning" because "[f]or better or worse, the legislature granted a 90% parent corporation the right to merge the subsidiary out of existence unilaterally and provided an appraisal remedy for the minority stockholders," and "[i]t is simply inconsistent with that grant of power to superimpose on its exercise, in every case, an analysis of the 'procedure' employed in fixing the terms of the merger." 2000 Del. Ch. LEXIS 92, at *50-51, 2000 WL 823376, at *13; *see also Andra*, 772 A.2d at 195 n.30 ("where a majority stockholder already holds sufficient shares to conduct a short-form merger before any of the conduct which the plaintiff attacks occurred, allowing an unfair dealing attack on the merger might well conflict with § 253 because it would require (through the burden-shifting rules applicable under our law's business judgment rule and entire fairness standards) the majority stockholder to set up a special committee or to make the merger contingent on the support of a majority vote of the minority stockholders in order to avoid the burden of proving 'entire fairness'").

There is no "nearly within § 253" exception to the rule permitting both appraisal and breach of fiduciary duty actions for "appraisal-eligible mergers effected by the votes of stockholders holding a super-majority" but not 90 percent of a corporation's shares. Under these circumstances, the shareholders holding a super-majority of the corporation's shares have sufficient votes to effect a merger under Section 251 of the Delaware General Corporation Law (Section 251 requires a majority vote) and do not need the votes of any other shareholders to approve the merger, but cannot rely upon Section 251 because Section 251 requires control over 90 percent of the corporation's shares. The court in *Nagy* stated that "there is no apparent logic that justifies judicial acceptance" of a "nearly within § 253" exception to the rule permitting both appraisal and breach of fiduciary duty actions in cases where unfair dealing is alleged but the defendants' ownership interest exceeds 50 percent but does not reach the 90 percent level necessary to effect a § 253 merger. 770 A.2d at 54. The court explained that "[t]he reason why a plaintiff may not attack a 'pure' § 253 merger in a garden variety unfair dealing action is simple: allowing such an attack would be inconsistent with the procedure-free merger method contemplated by § 253 because it would, as a practical matter, require corporations to employ procedural fairness mechanisms in order to avoid liability under the entire fairness standard." *Id.* This rationale, the court stated, "is inapposite in the context of a § 251 merger." *Id.* The court in *Nagy* also noted that the Supreme Court's decision in *Technicolor* and the Court of Chancery's decisions in *Wood*, *Andra* and *Turner* all involved mergers that "had been consummated solely by the voting power of the defendants." *Id.*

Where shareholders have both an appraisal claim and a fairness claim, the shareholders must show damages in excess of the fair value awarded in the appraisal action less the amount offered in the challenged transaction or "they will essentially fail to receive any additional damages as a result of their unfair dealing claim." *Onti Inc. v. Integra Bank*, 751 A.2d 904, 930 (Del. Ch. 1999).

The court in the *Nebel* case discussed above accordingly awarded damages equal to the difference between the value of the corporation determined in the separate appraisal action noted above ($85 per share) and the price offered in the merger (as noted above, $41 per share). 1999 Del. Ch. LEXIS 30, at *27, 1999 WL 135259, at *8.

The court noted that if the substantive unfairness claim had been dismissed, then "this lawsuit would, as a practical matter, be over . . . because the minority shareholder class will have been found entitled to damages equal to the difference between the $85 appraisal value and the $41 merger price, and the other claims would have been dismissed." 1999 Del. Ch. LEXIS 30, at *28 n.32, 1999 WL 135259, at *8 n.32. The court stated that its ruling that plaintiffs were entitled to proceed on their substantive fairness claim "implicitly acknowledges (at least in theory) the possibility of a rescissory damages recovery." *Id.* This possibility of recissory damages, the court continued, "is the only reason why this case continues." *Id.* The court accordingly stated that it would not schedule a hearing on the merits of the substantive unfairness claims until plaintiffs satisfied the court that they had "a tenable basis, in fact and law, to claim damages in excess of the 'out of pocket' measure of damages (the difference between the $41 merger price and the $85 per share appraisal value)." *Id.*

The court in *Onti v. Integra Bank*, 751 A.2d 904 (Del. Ch. 1999), noted its view that "[i]t is hard for me to see how . . . plaintiffs in any appraisal/unfair dealing case . . . can show that the unfair dealing hurt the shareholders by more than the fair value of the company less the amount offered for their shares." *Id.* at 930 n.108. The court acknowledged that the Supreme Court in *Weinberger* stated that "the factors inherent in fair dealing versus fair price . . . must be addressed together," but, according to the court in *Onti*, "where claims for unfair dealing do not rise to the level of fraud . . . the Court should primarily focus on whether the price was unfair." *Id.; see also id.* (quoting *Weinberger*, 457 A.2d at 711: "in a non-fraudulent transaction we recognize that price may be the preponderant consideration outweighing other features of the merger"). The court noted the following example:

> Consider this example: If the Court determines that a company has a fair value of $100 million and the company has offered $5 million in a cash-out merger to a ten per cent shareholder, the Court will award the shareholder an additional $5 million in an appraisal action. Now, assume that the shareholder has also filed a claim for unfair dealing, asserting that the company was really worth $150 million, but the timing of the merger

> was such that the majority shareholder captured all of the additional value once he cashed out the minority shareholders. The problem, it seems to me, is that the court has already determined the value of the company to be $100 million, so why now should a minority shareholder be allowed to assert a separate claim for unfair dealing? The shareholder's unfair dealing claims should be factored into the price that the Court has determined in the appraisal action. And the unfair price claims, or substantive fairness claims, are almost by definition included in the appraisal value determined by the Court.

Id.

Delete ", with the same exceptions provided for by Delaware decisions" at the end of the paragraph beginning on page 496 and concluding on page 497 (immediately before footnote 2035).

Add the following at the end of the paragraph beginning on page 496 and concluding on page 497 (immediately after footnote 2035):

Courts construing the laws of Maryland, Minnesota and North Carolina also have reached this result. *See Popp Telcom v. Am. Sharecom, Inc.*, 210 F.3d 928, 937-39 (8th Cir. 2000) ("the appraisal right of a frozen-out shareholder is his exclusive remedy unless the merger is 'fraudulent' to him or the corporation") (construing Minnesota law and quoting *Sifferle v. Micom Corp.*, 384 N.W.2d 503, 506 (Minn. Ct. App. 1986)); *Lerner v. Lerner Corp.*, 750 A.2d 709, 717 (Md. 2000) ("a remedy other than an appraisal proceeding is only available, however, 'under very limited circumstances,' involving allegations, and ultimately proof, of ''specific acts of fraud, misrepresentation, or other items of misconduct [demonstrating] the unfairness of the merger terms to the minority''") (quoting *Walter J. Schloss Assocs. v. Chesapeake & Ohio Ry. Co.*, 536 A.2d 147, 155 (Md. App. 1988) and *Weinberger v. UOP, Inc.*, 457 A.2d 701, 703 (Del. 1983)); *Werner v. Alexander*, 502 S.E.2d 897, 900-01 (N.C. Ct. App. 1998) (stating that "the appraisal remedy is the exclusive remedy for dissatisfied shareholders unless they can show the transaction is 'unlawful' or 'fraudulent,'" that "inadequate price alone will not support a claim for fraud," and that in this case all of plaintiffs' allegations "point to one central theme": "the plaintiffs feel the defendants have intentionally engaged in a course of conduct designed to reduce the value of NCRR's assets, which in turn will reduce the value of their shares, thereby enabling these shares to be purchased at a reduced price"; "[w]hile the plaintiffs have a legitimate concern that the defendants act in such a way as to maximize shareholder value, their complaint fails to demonstrate how the defendants' conduct amounted to a false representation or concealment of a material fact, reasonably calculated and intentionally made to deceive the plaintiffs to their detriment").

Replace footnote 2037 on page 498 with the following:

Fleming v. Int'l Pizza Supply Corp., 676 N.E.2d 1051, 1057 (Ind. 1997), *subsequent proceedings*, 707 N.E.2d 1033, 1037-39 (Ind. Ct. App. 1999) (upholding constitutionality of Indiana's statute), *transfer denied*, 1999 Ind. LEXIS 738 (Ind. Aug. 30, 1999); *see also Settles v. Leslie*, 701 N.E.2d 849, 853-54 (Ind. Ct. App. 1998).

Add the following at the end of footnote 2039 on page 498:

See also In re Lazar, 262 A.D.2d 968, 969, 692 N.Y.S.2d 539, 540 (N.Y. App. Div. 4th Dep't 1999) ("[a] narrow exception to the exclusivity rule is provided in Business Corporation Law § 623(k), which authorizes 'a dissenting stockholder to bring an 'appropriate action' in his individual capacity to remedy unlawful or fraudulent corporate conduct'"; "[a]n appropriate action is one in which there is a 'primary request' for equitable relief").

Section C

Replace "The duty" in the second sentence of the paragraph beginning on page 499 and concluding on page 500 (immediately after footnote 2042) with the following:

Although in its "earliest form" the duty of disclosure was "the simple requirement that a board seeking shareholder ratification of a self-interested transaction provide shareholders all information material to the transaction," the duty of disclosure "is now recognized whenever the Board seeks shareholder action, regardless of whether the approval sought is for an act or transaction in which the board itself is conflicted." *In re Walt Disney Co. Derivative Litig.*, 731 A.2d 342, 369 (Del. Ch. 1998), *aff'd with leave to replead on other grounds sub nom. Brehm v. Eisner*, 746 A.2d 244, 249 n.3 (Del. 2000); *see also Brown v. Perrette*, 1999 Del. Ch. LEXIS 92, at *16, 1999 WL 342340, at *5 (Del. Ch. May 14, 1999) ("the historical development of Delaware's disclosure law" begins with cases involving shareholder ratification of a board's wrongful conduct where "the plaintiff attacked the validity of the ratification by arguing that the shareholders were not fully informed of the truth of the transaction that they were asked to ratify" and in that original form "a breach of the duty of disclosure did not entitle the plaintiff to damages, but precluded ratification of the underlying transaction and subjected defendants to the possibility of damages arising from their misconduct during the underlying transaction"; over time, "the Supreme Court expanded the role of the duty of disclosure, interpreting it to track the duty found in the federal securities law to fully and fairly inform shareholders of all reasonably available information material to the issue or transaction for which the board seeks shareholder approval"). The duty today is a "specific application of the general fiduciary duty owed by directors," *Malone v. Brincat*, 722 A.2d 5, 10 (Del. 1998); *see also Skeen v. Jo-Ann Stores, Inc.*, 750 A.2d 1170, 1172 (Del. 2000) ("[t]he duty of disclosure is a specific formulation" of the "general duties" owed by directors), and

Add the following at the end of footnote 2043 on page 499:

See also McMullin v. Beran, 765 A.2d 910, 925 (Del. 2000) ("[i]n properly discharging their fiduciary responsibilities, directors of Delaware corporations must exercise due care, good faith and loyalty whenever they communicate with shareholders about the corporation's affairs"); *Malone,* 722 A.2d at 11 ("[t]he duty of directors to observe proper disclosure requirements derives from the combination of the fiduciary duties of care, loyalty and good faith"); *Crescent/Mach I Partners, L.P. v. Turner*, 2000 Del. Ch. LEXIS 145, at *60-61, 2000 WL 1481002, at *16 (Del. Ch. Sept. 29, 2000) ("The fiduciary duty of disclosure arises as a subset of a director's fiduciary duties of loyalty and care. A claim for breach of the fiduciary duty of disclosure can implicate the duty of care when the misstatement or omission was made as a result of the directors' good faith, but 'erroneous judgment' concerning the proper scope and content of the disclosure. On the other hand, an alleged violation of the duty of loyalty is implicated where the required disclosure was made in 'bad faith, knowingly or intentionally.'"); *Wolf v. Assaf*, 1998 Del. Ch. LEXIS 101, at *12, 1998 WL 326662, at *4 (Del. Ch. June 16, 1998) ("[t]he duty to disclose may arise as a product of either the fiduciary duty of loyalty or the fiduciary duty of care").

Add the following at the end of footnote 2044 on page 499:

See also McMullin, 765 A.2d at 925 ("[w]hen shareholder action is requested, directors are required to provide shareholders with all information that is material to the action being requested and 'to provide a balanced, truthful account of all matters disclosed in the communication with shareholders'") (quoting *Malone*, 722 A.2d at 10).

Add the following at the end of the second sentence of the paragraph beginning on page 499 and concluding on page 500 (immediately after footnote 2044):

Put another way, "[d]irectors of Delaware corporations have a fiduciary duty to shareholders to exercise due care, good faith and loyalty whenever they communicate publicly or directly with shareholders about the corporation's affairs," and "[w]hen stockholder action is requested, directors are required to provide shareholders with all information that is material to the action being requested and 'to provide a balanced, truthful account of all matters disclosed in the communications with shareholders.'" *Emerald Partners v. Berlin*, 726 A.2d 1215, 1223 (Del. 1999) (citing and quoting *Malone*, 722 A.2d at 10). "A board can breach its duty of disclosure under Delaware law in a number of ways – by making a false statement, by omitting a material fact, or by making partial disclosure that is materially misleading." *Walt Disney*, 731 A.2d at 376; *see also O'Reilly v. Transworld Healthcare, Inc.*, 745 A.2d 902, 916 (Del. Ch. 1999).

Add the following at the end of footnote 2045 on page 499:

See also Malone, 722 A.2d at 11 & n.21; *Oliver v. Boston Univ.*, 2000 Del. Ch. LEXIS 104, at *24, 2000 WL 1038197, at *8 (Del. Ch. July 18, 2000); *cf. In re W. Nat'l Corp. S'holders Litig.*, 2000 Del. Ch. LEXIS 82, at *95, 2000 WL 710192, at *28 (Del. Ch. May 22, 2000) (large but not controlling shareholder owes no duty of disclosure to other shareholders).

Begin a new paragraph at the end of the third sentence (immediately after footnote 2045) of the paragraph beginning on page 499 and concluding on page 500.

Add the following at the end of the fourth sentence of the paragraph beginning on page 499 and concluding on page

500 (immediately after footnote 2046) and then begin a new paragraph:

A controlling shareholder has the same duty of disclosure to directors when the controlling shareholder seeks the directors' approval of a transaction between the controlling shareholder and the corporation. *Odyssey Partners, L.P. v. Fleming Cos.*, 735 A.2d 386, 412-13 (Del. Ch. 1999).

Section C 1

Add the following at the end of footnote 2055 on page 500:

See also Malone v. Brincat, 722 A.2d 5, 9 (Del. 1998) (quoting decisions holding that "directors of Delaware corporations are under a fiduciary duty to disclose fully and fairly all material information within the board's control *when it seeks shareholder action*"); *Loudon v. Archer-Daniels-Midland Co.*, 700 A.2d 135, 137-38 (Del. 1997) ("Delaware law of the fiduciary duties of directors . . . establishes a general duty of directors to disclose to stockholders all material information reasonably available when seeking stockholder action").

Add the following at the end of footnote 2056 on page 501:

See also Malone, 722 A.2d at 11 ("[e]ven when shareholder action is sought, the provisions in the General Corporation Law requiring notice to the shareholders of the proposed action do not require the directors to convey substantive information beyond a statutory minimum").

Delete the third and fourth sentences (including footnotes 2057 and 2058) of the paragraph beginning on page 500 and concluding on page 502.

Replace "The majority view in the Court of Chancery is" in the first sentence of the paragraph beginning and concluding

on page 502 (between footnotes 2058 and 2059) with the following:

Until the Delaware Supreme Court's 1998 decision in *Malone v. Brincat*, 722 A.2d 5 (Del. 1998), the majority view in the Delaware Court of Chancery was

Replace the Malone citation in footnote 2066 on page 503 with the following:

1997 Del. Ch. LEXIS 158, 1997 WL 697940 (Del. Ch. Oct. 30, 1997), *aff'd in part and rev'd in part*, 722 A.2d 5 (Del. 1998).

Replace "has been" with "was" in the first sentence of the paragraph beginning on page 504 and concluding on page 505 (immediately after footnote 2076).

Add the following at the end of the paragraph beginning and concluding on page 505 (immediately after footnote 2085):

The Supreme Court resolved the question in *Malone v. Brincat*, 722 A.2d 5 (Del. 1998), a case involving allegations that directors made false statements about the financial condition of the corporation, which allegedly caused plaintiffs to continue to hold their shares. *Id.* at 8. The court stated that "[w]henever directors communicate publicly or directly with shareholders about the corporation's affairs, with or without a request for shareholder action, directors have a fiduciary duty to shareholders to exercise due care, good faith and loyalty." *Id.* at 10. "It follows *a fortiori* that when directors communicate publicly or directly with shareholders about corporate matters the *sine qua non* of directors' fiduciary duty to shareholders is honesty." *Id.* In other words, "[s]hareholders are entitled to rely upon the truthfulness of all information disseminated to them by the directors they elect to manage the corporate enterprise." *Id.* at 10-11. Delaware law thus "protects shareholders who receive false communications from directors even in the absence of a request for shareholder action." *Id.* at

14. Therefore, "directors who knowingly disseminate false information that results in corporate injury or damage to an individual stockholder violate their fiduciary duty, and may be held accountable in a manner appropriate to the circumstances." *Id.* at 9.

According to the court, however, where, as in this case, there is no request for shareholder action, the issue is not whether directors "breached their duty of disclosure" but rather "whether they breached their more general fiduciary duty of loyalty and good faith by knowingly disseminating to the stockholders false information about the financial condition of the company." *Id.* at 10. The court stated that when directors "are not seeking shareholder action, but are deliberately misinforming shareholders about the business of the corporation, either directly or by a public statement, there is a violation of fiduciary duty" and "[t]hat violation may result in a derivative claim on behalf of the corporation or a cause of action for damages." *Id.* at 14. The court accordingly permitted the plaintiffs in the case, if possible, to amend their complaint to allege either a derivative claim and "any damage or equitable remedy sought on behalf of the corporation" or an individual claim and "a remedy that is appropriate on behalf of the named plaintiffs individually, or a properly recognizable class." *Id.* at 14-15.

Following *Malone*, "[t]he duty of disclosure is a specific formulation" of the "general duties" of care, good faith and loyalty "that applies when the corporation is seeking stockholder action." *Skeen v. Jo-Ann Stores, Inc.*, 750 A.2d 1170, 1172 (Del. 2000). The duty of disclosure thus "is a subset of the more general duties of loyalty, 'good faith', and care and is implicated only when stockholder action is contemplated, i.e., requested or required." *O'Reilly v. Transworld Healthcare, Inc.*, 745 A.2d 902, 916 (Del. Ch. 1999). "Disclosure violations arising out of communications not contemplating stockholder action implicate the broader fiduciary duties of loyalty, 'good faith' and care." *Id.; see also id.* at 917 (noting "distinction between 'the fiduciary duty of disclosure' and disclosure violations that implicate fiduciary duties in the broad sense but do not involve communications that contemplate stockholder action").

Jackson National Life Insurance Co. v. Kennedy, 741 A.2d 377 (Del. Ch. 1999), also illustrates this principle. The *Jackson National* case involved the sale to Fort James of all of the assets of Benchmark Holdings, which was owned by Benchmark Corp., and certain of the assets of WinCup Holdings, which also was owned by Benchmark Corp. The sale of these assets was followed by the formation by Fort James and WinCup Holdings of WinCup Partnership and Fort James' sale of its interest in WinCup Partnership to Benchmark Corp.'s successor, Radnor Holdings Corp. Michael T. Kennedy was the owner of 90 percent of Benchmark Corp. and the sole director of Benchmark Corp., Benchmark Holdings and WinCup Holdings. *Id.* at 382-84. As alleged by Jackson National, a preferred shareholder in Benchmark Holdings, "Kennedy, Benchmark Corp., WinCup Holdings, the WinCup Partnership and Fort James all received millions of dollars in cash and other benefits, while Benchmark Holdings itself was stripped of its assets and Jackson National was left holding preferred stock rendered worthless in a corporate shell." *Id.* at 384.

Jackson National also alleged that Kennedy and others working with him affirmatively concealed the transaction from Jackson National in letters to Jackson National's investment advisors that "failed to mention the fact that Benchmark Holdings' assets would soon be, or had just been, sold to Fort James." *Id.* Kennedy did this, according to Jackson National, so that Jackson National would not learn that a transaction had been entered into that, according to Jackson National, triggered a "Voting Event" right under Benchmark Holdings' certificate of incorporation that allowed preferred shareholders to elect a majority of Benchmark Holdings' board of directors. *Id.* at 382, 387-88.

The court held that the alleged "claim of intentional omission of material facts under circumstances that could substantially affect the preferred's rights as stockholder" did not implicate the duty of disclosure. *Id.* at 387. The court explained that "the directors of a Delaware corporation owe a fiduciary 'duty of disclosure' to its stockholders when they seek stockholder action," but "Jackson National did not have the right to participate in any stockholder action surrounding the disputed transaction and neither Kennedy nor his controlled entities had any obligation arising out of a fiduciary relationship to inform Jackson National of circumstances that might arguably constitute a Voting Event." *Id.* at 388. The court stated that neither the Delaware General Corporation Law nor Benchmark Holdings' certificate of incorporation provided Jackson National with a right to vote on Benchmark Holdings' sale of assets to Fort James, and as a result "Kennedy had no fiduciary obligation to disclose that transaction to Jackson National." *Id.* To the contrary, "Jackson National's contract rights exist independent of any affirmative request by Benchmark Holdings' directors," and "[t]hese contractual rights are in a no way dependent upon, nor do they involve, the Benchmark Holdings incumbent directors requesting that either the preferred or common stockholders take a specific action." *Id.*

Nevertheless, the court continued, the alleged intentional failure to disclose material facts "may rightly implicate a fiduciary duty" because, under *Malone*, "[t]he duty of disclosure is merely a specific application of the more general fiduciary duty of loyalty that applies only in the setting of a transaction or other corporate event that is being presented to the stockholders for action." *Id.* at 388-89. Accordingly, "one who pleads that directors deliberately omitted information from a communication with preferred stockholders under circumstances that suggest an intent to mislead the stockholders has set forth a violation of the fiduciary duty of loyalty owed to those preferred." *Id.* at 389.

The court concluded that "[h]ere, just as in *Malone*, where the directors did not seek stockholder action but were nonetheless alleged to have deliberately issued an intentionally false communication to the stockholders, 'there is a violation of fiduciary duty'" and "'[t]hat violation may result in a derivative claim on behalf of the corporation or a cause of action for damages.'" *Id.* at 389-90 (quoting *Malone*, 722 A.2d at 14). In short, "[i]t necessarily follows from *Malone* that when directors communicate with stockholders, they must recognize their duty of loyalty to do so with honesty and fairness, regardless of the stockholders' status as preferred or common, and regardless of the absence of a request for action required pursuant to a statute, the corporation's certificate of incorporation or any bylaw provision." *Id.* at 390.

Replace the Sofamor citation in footnote 2099 on page 507 with the following:

123 F.3d 394 (6th Cir. 1997), *cert. denied*, 523 U.S. 1106 (1998).

Add the following at the end of footnote 2102 on page 507:

See also State of Wis. Inv. Bd. v. Peerless Sys. Corp., 2000 Del. Ch. LEXIS 170, at *21-22, 2000 WL 1805376, at *7 (Del. Ch. Dec. 4, 2000) ("the Company per se does not owe fiduciary duties to its shareholders").

Add the following at the end of footnote 2103 on page 508:

See also Korsinsky v. Granlund, No. 605635/99, slip op. at 11-12 (N.Y. Sup. Ct. N.Y. Co. Aug. 16, 2000).

Add the following at the end of the paragraph beginning on page 507 and concluding on page 508 (immediately after footnote 2105):

The duty of disclosure does not require directors to meet with shareholders to explain the basis for a recommended course of action for which the directors seek a shareholder vote. "[N]o Delaware authority . . . requires anything more than a timely mailed proxy statement indicating the time, place and purpose of the stockholders meeting." *Crescent/Mach I Partners, L.P. v. Turner*, 2000 Del. Ch. LEXIS 145, at *50, 2000 WL 1481002, at *13.

Section C 2

Add the following at the end of the paragraph beginning on page 509 and concluding on page 510 (immediately after footnote 2119):

- *State of Wisconsin Investment Board v. Bartlett*, 2000 Del. Ch. LEXIS 42, at *26, 2000 WL 238026, at *8 (Del. Ch. Feb. 24, 2000) ("[t]his Court does not defer to directors' judgment about what information is material"; "[i]t is a matter for the Court to determine"); and
- *Crescent/Mach I Partners, L.P. v. Turner*, 2000 Del. Ch. LEXIS 145, at *64, 2000 WL 1481002, at *17 (Del. Ch. Sept. 29, 2000) ("[t]his Court does not defer to directors' judgment about what information is material").

Add the following at the end of the paragraph beginning on page 509 and concluding on page 510 (immediately after footnote 2119):

The court in *Goodwin v. Live Entertainment, Inc.*, 1999 Del. Ch. LEXIS 5, 1999 WL 64265 (Del. Ch. Jan. 22, 1999), *aff'd*, 741 A.2d 16 (unpublished opinion, text available at 1999 Del. LEXIS 238 and 1999 WL 624128) (Del. July 23, 1999), stated that there is "some appeal" to the contention that if a director protection certificate provision adopted pursuant to a statute such as Section 102(b)(7) of the Delaware General Corporation Law bars recovery for breaches of the duty of care (*see* Chapter II, Section A 7 above), then the business judgment rule governs disclosure claims against the corporation's directors because "the outcome turns solely on the presence or absence of evidence of good faith or disloyalty" and if plaintiff does not rebut the presumption of loyalty and good faith, then any disclosure deficiency "cannot be as a result of violations of the directors' duties of good faith and loyalty." 1999 Del. Ch. LEXIS 5, at *19 n.4, 1999 WL 64265, at *7 n.4. The court stated that "there is authority and commentary which is somewhat suggestive of the desirability of that approach" but "decisions of this court (albeit in different procedural contexts) have held that the business judgment rule does not apply to disclosure claims." *Id.* The court therefore determined not to "rely exclusively on the business judgment rule analysis" but noted that "that analysis and its result – which concludes that a majority of the Board was disinterested in the merger – is strong support for the conclusion I reach that there is not sufficient evidence to support a finding that any alleged non- or misdisclosure in the Proxy Statement resulted from disloyalty or bad faith." *Id.*

Section C 3

Replace the first sentence of the paragraph beginning on page 510 and concluding on page 511 (including footnote 2120) with the following:

In order to state a claim for a violation of the duty of disclosure, "a pleader must allege that facts are missing from the proxy statement, identify those facts," and "state why they meet the materiality standard." *Loudon v. Archer-Daniels-Midland Co.*, 700 A.2d 135, 141 (Del. 1997), *quoted in Skeen v. Jo-Ann Stores, Inc.*, 750 A.2d 1170, 1173 (Del. 2000); *see also O'Reilly v. Transworld Healthcare, Inc.*, 745 A.2d 902, 920 (Del. Ch. 1999) ("[t]o state a claim for breach of the fiduciary duty of disclosure on the basis of a false statement or representation, a plaintiff must identify (1) a material statement or representation in a communication contemplating stockholder action (2) that is false"); *id.* at 926 ("[t]o state a claim for breach by omission of any duty to disclose, a plaintiff must plead facts identifying (1) material, (2) reasonably available (3) information that (4) was omitted from the proxy materials"), *quoted in Crescent/Mach I Partners, L.P. v. Turner*, 2000 Del. Ch. LEXIS 145, at *61-62, 2000 WL 1481002, at *17 (Del. Ch. Sept. 29, 2000); *Oliver v. Boston Univ.*, 2000 Del. Ch. LEXIS 104, at *24, 2000 WL 1038197, at *8 (Del. Ch. July 18, 2000); *In re Walt Disney Co. Derivative Litig.*, 731 A.2d 342, 373 (Del. Ch. 1998), *aff'd with leave to replead on other grounds sub nom. Brehm v. Eisner*, 746 A.2d 244, 249 n.3 (Del. 2000); *Wolf v. Assaf*, 1998 Del. Ch. LEXIS 101, at *4, 1998 WL 326662, at *1 (Del. Ch. June 16, 1998). Neither reliance nor causation are required elements of a fiduciary duty claim based on inadequate disclosure. *Malone v. Brincat*, 722 A.2d 5, 12 (Del. 1998); *Turner v. Bernstein*, 2000 Del. Ch. LEXIS 96, at *39, 2000 WL 776893, at *12 (Del. Ch. June 6, 2000); *see also* Chapter II, Section C 5 b (discussing need for reliance and causation where more than nominal damages are sought for inadequate disclosure). "It is Plaintiffs' burden . . . to plead facts showing each element of their omission claim." *Disney*, 731 A.2d at 373.

Add the following at the end of footnote 2121 on page 511:

See also Solomon v. Armstrong, 747 A.2d 1098, 1128 (Del. Ch. 1999) ("[a]s far as claims of material misstatements, omissions and coercion go, the law is clear that plaintiff bears the burden of proof that disclosure was inadequate, misleading, or coercive"), *aff'd*, 746 A.2d 277 (unpublished opinion, full text available at 2000 Del. LEXIS 30 and 2000 WL 140072) (Del. Jan. 26, 2000).

Add the following at the end of the third sentence (immediately after footnote 2122) of the paragraph beginning on page 510 and concluding on page 511:

"Unsupported conclusions and speculation are not a substitute for facts." *Jo-Ann Stores*, 750 A.2d at 1173.

Add the following at the end of footnote 2123 on page 511:

See also O'Reilly, 745 A.2d at 924-25; *Solomon*, 747 A.2d at 1131 n.113.

Add the following at the end of the paragraph beginning and concluding on page 511 (immediately after footnote 2124):

The law thus "does not make it easy for a board of directors to obtain 'ratification effect' from a stockholder vote" because "[t]he burden to prove that the vote was fair, uncoerced, and fully informed falls squarely on the board." *Harbor Fin. Partners v. Huizenga*, 751 A.2d 879, 899 (Del. Ch. 1999); *see also Solomon*, 747 A.2d at 1117 n.58 ("the party offering the defense of shareholder ratification bears the burden of proof of showing that the disclosure was legally sufficient"); *id.* at 1128 ("when it comes to claiming the sufficiency of disclosure and the concomitant legal effect of shareholder ratification after full disclosure (e.g., claim extinguishment, the retention of the business judgment rule presumptions, or the shift of the burden of proof of entire fairness from the defendant to the plaintiff) it is the defendant who bears the burden"); *Disney*, 731 A.2d at 369 ("[t]o obtain this Court's deference to shareholder ratification, directors and majority shareholders alike must show this Court that the shareholders possessed all information germane to the transaction at the time they voted to ratify it"); *id.* ("[w]here a board seeks shareholder action, it is charged with the obligation to provide shareholders with the requisite information"); *id.* ("the simple requirement that a board seeking shareholder ratification of a self-interested transaction provide shareholders all information material to the transaction" is "an essential component of the duty of loyalty in a situation where the board seeks to comply with its fiduciary obligations by obtaining shareholder approval for the board's otherwise potentially conflicted interests"); *id.* at 369 n.75

("[t]he burden must fall on defendants who claim ratification based on shareholder vote to establish that the shareholder approval resulted from a fully informed electorate") (quoting *Smith v. Van Gorkom*, 488 A.2d 858, 893 (Del. 1985)); *id.* at 369 n.76 ("One cannot ratify that which he does not know. The burden is on him who relies on a ratification to show that it was made with a full knowledge of all material facts.") (quoting *Cahall v. Lofland*, 114 A.224, 234 (Del. Ch. 1921)).

Section C 3 a

Add the following at the end of the paragraph beginning on page 511 and concluding on page 513 (between footnotes 2146 and 2147):

The Delaware Supreme Court again reaffirmed this standard in 1998 in *Malone v. Brincat*, 722 A.2d 5, 12 n.29 (Del. 1998), in 1999 in *O'Malley v. Boris*, 742 A.2d 845, 850 (Del. 1999), and in 2000 in *Brehm v. Eisner*, 746 A.2d 244, 259 n.49 (Del. 2000), *Skeen v. Jo-Ann Stores, Inc.*, 750 A.2d 1170, 1172 (Del. 2000), and *McMullin v. Beran*, 765 A.2d 910, 925 (Del. 2000). As stated by the Delaware Court of Chancery in *In re Walt Disney Co. Derivative Litigation*, 731 A.2d 342 (Del. Ch. 1998), *aff'd with leave to replead on other grounds sub nom. Brehm v. Eisner*, 746 A.2d 244, 249 n.3 (Del. 2000), "the relevant inquiry is whether shareholders are misled as to the corporation's significant prospects (i.e., material facts), and it is *not* a question of whether or not there was an ambiguity or misstatement that might lead shareholders to an incorrect conclusion about an insignificant or irrelevant fact which has no bearing on any other material facts." *Id.* at 376; *see also id.* at 376 n.113 ("[i]t is not enough that a statement is false or incomplete, if the misrepresented fact is otherwise insignificant") (quoting *Basic Inc. v. Levinson*, 485 U.S. 224, 238 (1988)).

Add the following at the end of the paragraph beginning and concluding on page 513 (immediately after footnote 2148):

The Delaware Court of Chancery in *Disney* explained that a "partial disclosure that is materially misleading . . . occurs where a board makes a required or even non-obligatory pronouncement on a subject that is incomplete and by which shareholders are materially misled." 731 A.2d at 376. The court stated that "[a] board that provides a partial disclosure must rectify the misleading statement with follow-up disclosure that makes the information true and complete or face the consequences of a breach of fiduciary duty." *Id.* The court then stated the elements of a partial misleading disclosure claim as follows: "Generally, to state a claim of partial, misleading disclosure, a plaintiff must plead facts identifying a (1) perhaps voluntary, but (2) materially incomplete (3) statement (4) made in conjunction with solicitation of shareholder action that (5) requires supplementation or clarification through (6) corrective disclosure of perhaps otherwise immaterial, but reasonably available information." *Id.* at 377, *quoted in O'Reilly v. Transworld Healthcare, Inc.*, 745 A.2d 902, 927 (Del. Ch. 1999).

Add the following at the end of footnote 2150 on page 513:

See also Solomon v. Armstrong, 747 A.2d 1098, 1128 (Del. Ch. 1999), *aff'd*, 746 A.2d 277 (unpublished opinion, full text available at 2000 Del. LEXIS 30 and 2000 WL 140072) (Del. Jan. 26, 2000).

Add the following at the end of the second sentence of the paragraph beginning on page 513 and concluding on page 514 (immediately after footnote 2150):

"That is, the directors are 'not required to disclose all available information.'" *Matador Capital Mgmt. Corp. v. BRC Holdings, Inc.*, 729 A.2d 280, 295 (Del. Ch. 1998) (quoting *Stroud v. Grace*, 606 A.2d 75, 85 (Del. 1992)). Undisclosed facts that "add little or nothing to the information provided" are not material. *Jo-Ann Stores*, 750 A.2d at 1173. Knowledge that a statement is materially false or misleading is not an element of a disclosure claim. *O'Reilly*, 745 A.2d at 920 n.34.

Add the following at the end of footnote 2152 on page 514:

See also State of Wis. Inv. Bd. v. Peerless Sys. Corp., 2000 Del. Ch. LEXIS 170, at *60, 2000 WL 1805376, at *17 (Del. Ch. Dec. 4, 2000) ("the materiality standard refers to the deliberations of a 'reasonable investor,' not 'the plaintiff'").

Add the following at the end of footnote 2153 on page 514:

See also Solomon, 747 A.2d at 1128 & n.97 (quoting *Zirn v. VLI Corp.*, 1995 Del. Ch. LEXIS 74, at *13-14, 1995 WL 362616, at *4 (Del. Ch. June 12, 1995), *aff'd*, 681 A.2d 1050 (Del. 1996)).

Replace the period at the end of footnote 2155 on page 514 with the following:

, *quoted in Solomon*, 747 A.2d at 1130.

Add the following at the end of the fourth sentence (immediately after footnote 2155) of the paragraph beginning on page 514 and concluding on page 515:

As a result:

> The duty to disclose, though highly important, is not all encompassing. "Some information is of such dubious significance that insistence on its disclosure may accomplish more harm than good." Balanced against the requirement of complete disclosure is the pragmatic consideration that creating a lenient standard for materiality poses the risk that corporations will "bury the shareholders in an avalanche of trivial information – a result that is hardly conductive to informed decision-making."

Skeen v. Jo-Ann Stores, Inc., 1999 Del. Ch. LEXIS 193, at *13-14, 1999 WL 803974, at *4 (Del. Ch. Sept. 27, 1999), *aff'd*,

750 A.2d 1170 (Del. 2000) (quoting *TSC Indus., Inc. v. Northway, Inc.*, 426 U.S. 438 (1976)).

Add the following at the end of footnote 2156 on page 514:

See also Goodwin v. Live Entm't, Inc., 1999 Del. Ch. LEXIS 5, at *34, 1999 WL 64265, at *12 (Del. Ch. Jan. 22, 1999), *aff'd*, 741 A.2d 16 (unpublished opinion, text available at 1999 Del. LEXIS 238 and 1999 WL 624128) (Del. July 23, 1999); *Solomon*, 747 A.2d at 1128.

Add the following between the words "Additional information" and "need not" in the sixth sentence (immediately after footnote 2156) of the paragraph beginning on page 514 and concluding on page 515:

– such as "information comparing and contrasting" a proposed transaction with a hypothetical set of circumstances –

Replace the period at the end of footnote 2157 on page 515 with the following:

, *quoted in Solomon*, 747 A.2d at 1129.

Replace the period at the end of footnote 2159 on page 515 with the following:

, *quoted in Jo-Ann Stores*, 1999 Del. Ch. LEXIS 193, at *23, 1999 WL 803974, at *7; *In re Unocal Exploration Corp. S'holders Litig.*, 2000 Del. Ch. LEXIS 92, at *70, 2000 WL 823376, at *18 (Del. Ch. June 13, 2000) (quoting *Klang v. Smith's Food & Drug Ctrs.*, 1997 Del. Ch. LEXIS 73, at *33, 1997 WL 257463, at *9 (Del. Ch. May 13, 1997), *aff'd*, 702 A.2d 150 (Del. 1997)).

Add the following at the end of the eighth sentence (immediately after footnote 2159) of the paragraph beginning on page 514 and concluding on page 515:

"[A] blow-by-blow description of events leading up to the proposed transaction" is not required. *Matador*, 729 A.2d at 295.

Replace the period at the end of footnote 2160 on page 515 with the following:

, *quoted in Solomon*, 747 A.2d at 1130 *and In re Lukens Inc. S'holders Litig.*, 757 A.2d 720, 736 n.50 (Del. Ch. 1999). "The theory goes that there is a risk of information overload such that shareholders' interests are best served by an economy of words rather than an overflow of adjectives and adverbs in solicitation statements." *Solomon*, 747 A.2d at 1128.

Delete the period at the end of the last sentence of the paragraph beginning on page 514 and concluding on page 515 (immediately before footnote 2161) and add the following immediately after footnote 2161:

and would be "practically useless." *Lukens*, 757 A.2d at 736.

Add the following at the end of the paragraph beginning on page 514 and concluding on page 515 (immediately after footnote 2161):

A recommendation of a proposed transaction where directors have a duty "reasonably to seek the transaction offering the best value reasonably available to the stockholders" under cases such as *Paramount Communications, Inc. v. QVC Network Inc.*, 637 A.2d 34, 43 (Del. 1994) (discussed in Chapter III, Sections A 3 and 4), "necessarily carries with it an implicit representation" by the directors that their actions "comported with the duty articulated in *QVC*." *Matador*, 729 A.2d at 295. "Delaware law requires directors who disclose such a recommendation also disclose such information about the background of the transaction, the process followed by them to maximize value in the sale, and their reason for approving the transaction so as to be materially accurate and complete." *Id.*

Disclosure ordinarily is not required concerning the reasons and analytical basis for a fairness opinion by a financial advisor or a range of values for the corporation derived by a financial advisor. *Id.* at 297; *see also McMullen v. Beran*, 1999 Del. Ch. LEXIS 227, at *17-18 & n.28, 1999 WL 1135146, at *5 & n.28 (Del. Ch. Dec. 1, 1999), *rev'd on other grounds*, 765 A.2d 910 (Del. 2000) (rejecting disclosure claim where an opinion letter by Merrill Lynch was provided to shareholders and in the opinion letter "Merrill Lynch detailed that it had relied on both a comparable companies approach and a comparable transactions approach in concluding the Transaction price to be fair," and stating that documents do not "become material simply because they were 'furnished to the corporation's valuation advisor'") (quoting *Nebel v. S.W. Bancorp., Inc.*, [1995 Transfer Binder] Fed. Sec. L. Rep. (CCH) ¶ 98,846, at 93,095 (Del. Ch. July 5, 1995)); *Jo-Ann Stores*, 1999 Del. Ch. LEXIS 193, at *19-20, 1999 WL 803974, at *6 (the "disclosure of methodologies and analyses used by an investment banker have generally been held by the Court of Chancery not to be material"; here, "[t]he Information Statement included a summary of DLJ's fairness opinion. It also attached a copy of that opinion, which disclosed DLJ's assumptions and procedures and the matters it considered. Delaware law did not require further disclosures on that subject."); *Live Entm't*, 1999 Del. Ch. LEXIS 5, at *33-34, 37, 1999 WL 64265, at *11, 12 ("[d]isclosure of the underlying analysis supporting a fairness opinion '[is] not ordinarily required'" and this includes "ranges bearing directly on the value of the stock corporate voters are being asked to sell") (quoting *Matador*); *Abbey v. E.W. Scripps Co.*, 1995 Del. Ch. LEXIS 94, at *11, 1995 WL 478957, at *3 (Del. Ch. Aug. 9, 1995) ("information generated by the investment banker as part of its professional work in preparation for reaching and expressing its professional opinion . . . has an attenuated claim to materiality"; "the role and opinion of a banker may usually be claimed material to a shareholder" but "all of the work and consideration that enter into the ground leading to that opinion will . . . rarely if ever be material"); *In re Dataproducts Corp. S'holders Litig.*, [1991 Transfer Binder] Fed. Sec. L. Rep. (CCH) ¶ 96,227, at 91,184 (Del. Ch. Aug. 22, 1991) ("[o]ur law rejects the proposition that disclosure of the detailed facts and specific analyses underlying a financial advisor's valuation methodology is automatically mandated in all circumstances"); *In re Genentech, Inc. S'holders Litig.*, [1990 Transfer Binder] Fed. Sec. L. Rep. (CCH) ¶ 95,317, at 96,517 (Del. Ch. June 6, 1990) (plaintiffs' assertion that "analyses produced by the financial advisors and given to the board must be given to the shareholders . . . is not . . . the law of Delaware").

Add the following at the end of the paragraph beginning on page 515 and concluding on page 516 (immediately after footnote 2165):

Information contained in an SEC filing or an amendment to an SEC filing is not presumptively material. *Frank v. Arnelle*, 1998 Del. Ch. LEXIS 176, at *34 & n.48, 1998 WL 668649, at *9 & n.48 (Del. Ch. Sept. 16, 1998), *aff'd*, 725 A.2d 441 (unpublished opinion, text available at 1999 Del. LEXIS 25 and 1999 WL 89284) (Del. Jan. 22, 1999).

Section C 3 b

Add the following at the end of footnote 2168 on page 516:

See also Crescent/Mach I Partners, L.P. v. Turner, 2000 Del. Ch. LEXIS 145, at *49, 2000 WL 1481002, at *13 (Del. Ch. Sept. 29, 2000) (where shareholders received a proxy statement 26 days before a shareholder meeting, the court rejected as a matter of law an "allegation that the directors breached their fiduciary duty of loyalty by failing to allow the stockholders reasonable time to evaluate the merger"; the court explained that "Delaware corporation law only requires that corporations provide notice of the time, place and purpose of the special meeting at least 20 days prior to the date of the meeting") (citing Del. Gen. Corp. Law § 251(c)); *State of Wis. Inv. Bd. v. Bartlett*, 2000 Del. Ch. LEXIS 22, 2000 WL 193115 (Del. Ch. Feb. 9, 2000) (ordering a 15 day delay of a shareholder vote on a merger agreement scheduled for February 10, 2000 because supplemental proxy materials were issued on January 31, 2000 and shareholders did "not have adequate time to receive, absorb and consider the supplement material and consummate a change of their vote" before February 10, 2000, where plaintiff alleged that the supplemental disclosures constituted "an implied concession" that the corporation's original proxy statement contained material misstatements and omissions, and where it was "not reasonable to expect a comprehensive and careful examination of all of the facts alleged and issues raised by plaintiff's application" before the scheduled vote), *subsequent proceedings*, 2000 Del. Ch. LEXIS 42, at *24-25, 2000 WL 238026, at *7 (Del. Ch. Feb. 24, 2000) ("the supplemental disclosure has provided sufficient time for shareholders to consider the disclosure, make an informed decision, and return the proxy card," and "[t]herefore, any disputes concerning the reasonableness of the time period to receive, consider, and act upon the supplementary proxy materials are moot"); *Mentor Graphics Corp. v. Quickturn Design Sys., Inc.*, No. 16584, Tr. at 35-36 (Del. Ch. Jan. 7, 1999) ("[t]he nature of the shareholdings of this target company suggest that those persons that are holding shares are very sophisticated and are always keeping up to date on the status of the marketplace and of the positions of the various offerors"; "under these circumstances I consider it doubtful, highly doubtful, that the shareholders would not have this information which it is claimed is so essential to a meaningful vote"); *Frank v. Arnelle*, 1998 Del. Ch. LEXIS 176, *33-35, 1998 WL 668649, at *9 (Del. Ch. Sept. 16, 1998), *aff'd*, 725 A.2d 441 (unpublished opinion, text available at 1999 Del. Ch. LEXIS 25 and 1999 WL 89284) (Del. Jan. 22, 1999) (where a tender offer is pending and thus it is "reasonable to expect" that "stockholders and brokers would pay closer attention to the media" and that information will "be disseminated to the market place quickly," the issuance of a press release is "an effective and practical means of communicating with . . . stockholders in a prompt manner"); *Toder v. Hewitt*, No. 16106, Tr. op. at 98-99 (Del. Ch. Jan. 21, 1998) ("I can't say that three full business days or trading days is an insufficient time for at least many or most of the shareholders to learn of this information or for their advisors to learn of it" because "[i]n the context of a tender offer, I think that it is reasonable to expect shareholders and brokers and others to pay closer attention to developments than is true, for example, in the context of a meeting of the corporation").

Add the following at the end of footnote 2169 on page 517:

See also O'Malley v. Boris, 742 A.2d 845, 850 (Del. 1999) ("[t]he determination of materiality is a mixed question of fact and law that generally cannot be resolved on the pleadings").

Delete the citation to the Nebel case in footnote 2171 on page 517.

Add the following at the end of footnote 2171 on page 517:

See also McMullin v. Beran, 765 A.2d 910, 926 (Del. 2000); *Crescent/Mach I Partners, L.P. v. Turner*, 2000 Del. Ch. LEXIS 145, at *61-65, 2000 WL 1481002, at *17 (Del. Ch. Sept. 29, 2000); *In re Marriott Hotel Props. II LP Unitholders Litig.*, 2000 Del. Ch. LEXIS 17, at *33-41, 67-72, 2000 WL 128875, at *10-12, 19-21 (Del. Ch. Jan. 24, 2000) (denying motion to dismiss one of several claims).

Add the following at the end of footnote 2173 on page 518:

See also In re Cencom Cable Income Partners, L.P. Litig., 2000 Del. Ch. LEXIS 90, at *21-30, 2000 WL 640676, at *6-8

(Del. Ch. May 5, 2000) (denying summary judgment on two of three disclosure claims).

Add the following at the end of footnote 2174 on page 518:

See also Rosser v. New Valley Corp., 2000 Del. Ch. LEXIS 115, at *10-21, 2000 WL 1206677, at *3-6 (Del. Ch. Aug. 15, 2000) (dismissing some claims and not dismissing some claims); *Oliver v. Boston Univ.*, 2000 Del. Ch. LEXIS 104, at *27-28, 2000 WL 1038197, at *8 (Del. Ch. July 18, 2000) (dismissing some claims); *In re Encore Computer Corp. S'holder Litig.*, 2000 Del. Ch. LEXIS 93, at *24-28, 2000 WL 823373, at *8-9 (Del. Ch. June 16, 2000); *McMillan v. Intercargo Corp.*, 768 A.2d 492, 507 n.67 (Del. Ch. 2000); *In re Frederick's of Hollywood, Inc. S'holders Litig.*, 2000 Del. Ch. LEXIS 19, at *24-28, 2000 WL 130630, at *8-9 (Del. Ch. Jan. 31, 2000); *Marriott*, 2000 Del. Ch. LEXIS 17, at *33-41, 67-72, 2000 WL 128875, at *10-12, 19-21 (granting motion to dismiss all but one claim); *In re Lukens Inc. S'holders Litig.*, 757 A.2d 720, 735-36 (Del. Ch. 1999); *Harbor Fin. Partners v. Huizenga*, 751 A.2d 879, 902-04 (Del. Ch. 1999); *In re 3COM Corp. S'holders Litig.*, 1999 Del. Ch. LEXIS 215, at *18-28, 1999 WL 1009210, at *5-8 (Del. Ch. Oct. 25, 1999); *Krim v. ProNet, Inc.*, 744 A.2d 523, 528-29 (Del. Ch. 1999); *O'Reilly v. Transworld Healthcare, Inc.*, 745 A.2d 902, 916-29 (Del. Ch. Aug. 20, 1999) (dismissing some but not all claims); *Brown v. Perrette*, 1999 Del. Ch. LEXIS 92, at *27-42, 1999 WL 342340, at *8-13 (Del. Ch. May 14, 1999); *Solomon v. Armstrong*, 747 A.2d 1098, 1127-31 (Del. Ch. 1999), *aff'd*, 746 A.2d 277 (unpublished opinion, full text available at 2000 Del. LEXIS 30 and 2000 WL 140072) (Del. Jan. 26, 2000); *In re Gen. Motors Class H S'holders Litig.*, 734 A.2d 611, 621-29 (Del. Ch. 1999); *In re Walt Disney Co. Derivative Litig.*, 731 A.2d 342, 372-79 (Del. Ch. 1998), *aff'd with leave to replead on other grounds sub nom. Brehm v. Eisner*, 746 A.2d 244, 249 n.3 (Del. 2000); *Wolf v. Assaf*, 1998 Del. Ch. LEXIS 101, at *8-19, 1998 WL 326662, at *2-5 (Del. Ch. June 16, 1998); *Nebel v. S.W. Bancorp, Inc.*, [1995 Transfer Binder] Fed. Sec.

L. Rep. (CCH) ¶ 98,846, at 93,094-96 (Del. Ch. July 5, 1995), and 1999 Del. Ch. LEXIS 30, at *18-20, 1999 WL 135259, at *6 (Del. Ch. Mar. 9, 1999) (dismissing all but one disclosure claim); *Ciullo v. Orange & Rockland Utils., Inc.*, No. 601136/98, slip op. at 16 (N.Y. Sup. Ct. N.Y. Co. Jan. 8, 1999), *aff'd*, 271 A.D.2d 369, 369, 706 N.Y.S.2d 428, 429 (N.Y. App. Div. 1st Dep't), *leave to appeal denied*, 95 N.Y.2d 760, 737 N.E.2d 952, 714 N.Y.S.2d 710 (2000).

Add the following at the end of footnote 2175 on page 518:

See also State of Wis. Inv. Bd. v. Peerless Sys. Corp., 2000 Del. Ch. LEXIS 170, at *57-64, 2000 WL 1805376, at *16-18 (Del. Ch. Dec. 4, 2000); *In re W. Nat'l Corp. S'holders Litig.*, 2000 Del. Ch. LEXIS 82, at *93-99, 2000 WL 70192, at *27-29 (Del. Ch. May 22, 2000); *Goodwin v. Live Entm't, Inc.*, 1999 Del. LEXIS 5, *17-62, 1999 WL 64265, at *6-20 (Del. Ch. Jan. 22, 1999), *aff'd*, 741 A.2d 16 (unpublished opinion, text available at 1999 Del. LEXIS 238 and 1999 WL 624128) (Del. July 23, 1999); *Frank v. Arnelle*, 1998 Del. Ch. LEXIS 176, at *11-37, 1998 WL 668649, at *3-9 (Del. Ch. Sept. 16, 1998), *aff'd,* 725 A.2d 441 (unpublished opinion, text available at 1999 Del. LEXIS 25 and 1999 WL 89284) (Del. Jan. 22, 1999); *Camden v. Kaufman*, 613 N.W.2d 335, 340-41 (Mich. Ct. App. 2000).

Add the following at the end of the paragraph beginning on page 518 and concluding on page 519 (between footnotes 2175 and 2176):

A motion for judgment on the pleadings was granted in *Weiss v. Samsonite Corp.*, 741 A.2d 366, 374-75 (Del. Ch. June 14, 1999), *aff'd*, 746 A.2d 277 (unpublished opinion, text available at 1999 Del. LEXIS 387 and 1999 WL 1254563) (Del. Nov. 12, 1999).

Add the following at the end of footnote 2176 on page 519:

See also Sonet v. Plum Creek Timber Co., 1999 Del. Ch. LEXIS 49, at *24-45, 1999 WL 160174, at *6-11 (Del. Ch. Mar. 18, 1999); *Sealy Mattress Co. v. Sealy, Inc.*, 532 A.2d 1324, 1340-41 (Del. Ch. 1987).

Add the following at the end of footnote 2177 on page 519:

See also Bomarko, Inc. v. Int'l Telecharge, Inc., 1999 Del. Ch. LEXIS 211, at *53, 1999 WL 1022083, at *18 (Del. Ch. Nov. 4, 1999), *aff'd*, 766 A.2d 437 (Del. 2000).

Delete the period at the end of the first sentence of the paragraph beginning on page 519 and concluding on page 520 and add the following immediately after footnote 2177:

and, in at least two cases, on motions for summary judgment by plaintiffs. *See Nagy v. Bristricer*, 770 A.2d 43, 58-60 (Del. Ch. 2000); *Turner v. Bernstein*, 2000 Del. Ch. LEXIS 96, at *30-34, 2000 WL 776893, at *10 (Del. Ch. June 6, 2000).

Add the following at the end of footnote 2178 on page 520:

See also Kohls v. Duthie, 765 A.2d 1274, 1286-89 (Del. Ch. 2000); *State of Wis. Inv. Bd. v. Bartlett*, 2000 Del. Ch. LEXIS 42, at *23-30, 2000 WL 238026, at *7-9 (Del. Ch. Feb. 24, 2000); *McMillan v. Intercargo Corp.*, 768 A.2d 492, 499-507 (Del. Ch. 1999); *Matador Capital Mgmt. Corp. v. BRC Holdings, Inc.*, 729 A.2d 280, 294-98 (Del. Ch. 1998); *In re Life Techs., Inc. S'holders Litig.*, No. 16513, Tr. at 12-17 (Del. Ch. Nov. 24, 1998); *Golden Cycle LLC v. Allan*, 1998 Del. Ch. LEXIS 80, at *24-32, 1998 WL 276224, at *8-10 (Del. Ch. May 20, 1998).

Add the following at the end of footnote 2179 on page 520:

See also In re Unocal Exploration Corp. S'holders Litig., 2000 Del. Ch. LEXIS 92, at *64-76, 2000 WL 823376, at *17-20 (Del. Ch. June 13, 2000).

Section C 3 c

Add the following at the end of footnote 2181 on page 521:

See also Rosser v. New Valley Corp., 2000 Del. Ch. LEXIS 115, at *13, 2000 WL 1206677, at *4 (Del. Ch. Aug. 15, 2000) ("Delaware law does not require disclosure of inherently unreliable or speculative information") (quoting *Arnold v. Soc'y for Sav. Bancorp, Inc.*, 650 A.2d 1270, 1280 (Del. 1994)); *In re W. Nat'l Corp. S'holders Litig.*, 2000 Del. Ch. LEXIS 82, at 95-96, 2000 WL 70192, at *28 (Del. Ch. May 22, 2000) (pointing to a "long line of Delaware cases holding that there is no duty to speculate in a proxy statement" and that "[a]ny attempt . . . to disclose . . . the amounts of future settlement or judgments" in pending litigation "would have been utter speculation"); *Goodwin v. Live Entm't, Inc.*, 1999 Del. Ch. LEXIS 5, at *36, 1999 WL 64265, at *12 (Del. Ch. Jan. 22, 1999), *aff'd*, 741 A.2d 16 (unpublished opinion, text available at 1999 Del. LEXIS 238 and 1999 WL 624128) (Del. July 23, 1999) ("[t]he disclosure of a hypothetical – and therefore inherently tentative – concluded market value of the Series C would not have contributed meaningful or reliably to the shareholders' consideration of whether the price they were receiving for their common stock was fair").

Add the following at the end of the first sentence of the paragraph beginning on page 521 and concluding on page 524 (immediately after footnote 2181):

"[W]orst case hypotheticals" also do not need to be disclosed. *In re Walt Disney Co. Derivative Litig.*, 731 A.2d 342, 374 (Del. Ch. 1998), *aff'd with leave to replead on other grounds sub nom. Brehm v. Eisner*, 746 A.2d 244, 249 n.3 (Del. 2000).

Add the following at the end of footnote 2182 on page 522:

See also Rosser, 2000 Del. Ch. LEXIS 115, at *13, 2000 WL 1206677, at *4 ("corporate management need not disclose ruminations regarding uncertain future value because their estimates could be as misleading as helpful").

Add the following between footnote 2187 and "or" in the first sentence following the block quote in the paragraph beginning on page 521 and concluding on page 524:

"confess wrongdoing or engage in self-flagellation" (*Oliver v. Boston Univ.*, 2000 Del. Ch. LEXIS 104, at *24, 27, 2000 WL 1038197, at *8 (Del. Ch. July 18, 2000) (quoting *Citron v. E.I. DuPont de Nemours & Co.*, 584 A.2d 490, 503 (Del. Ch. 1990)),

Add the following at the end of the paragraph beginning on page 521 and concluding on page 524 (immediately after footnote 2191):

In short, "Delaware law has long held that fiduciaries need not beat themselves up in disclosures or plead guilty to fiduciary breaches." *In re ML/EQ Real Estate P'ship Litig.*, 1999 Del. Ch. LEXIS 238, at *26-27 & n.37, 1999 WL 1271885, at *7 & n.37 (Del. Ch. Dec. 20, 1999); *see also State of Wis. Inv. Bd. v. Peerless Sys. Corp.*, 2000 Del. Ch. LEXIS 170, at *62, 2000 WL 1805376, at *17 (Del. Ch. Dec. 4, 2000) (quoting *Stroud v. Grace*, 606 A.2d 75, 84 n.1 (Del. 1992)); *RCG Int'l Investors, LDC v. Greka Energy Corp.*, 2000 Del. Ch. LEXIS 157, at *51, 2000 WL 1706728, at *15 (Del. Ch. Nov. 6, 2000); *In re Lukens Inc. S'holders Litig.*, 757 A.2d 720, 724 (Del. Ch. 1999); *Brown v. Perrette*, 1999 Del. Ch. LEXIS 92, at *20, 31, 36 n.26, 39 n.29, 1999 WL 342340, at *6, 9, 11 n.26, 12 n.29 (Del. Ch. May 14, 1999); *In re Walt Disney Co. Derivative Litig.*, 731 A.2d 342, 371, 374 nn.107 & 108, 377 (Del. Ch. 1998), *aff'd with leave to replead on other grounds sub. nom. Brehm v. Eisner*, 746 A.2d 244 (Del. 2000); *In re Talley Indus., Inc. S'holders Litig.*, 1998 Del. Ch. LEXIS 53, at *40-41, 1998 WL 191939, at *13 (Del. Ch. Apr. 13, 1998); *Live*

Entm't, 1999 Del. Ch. LEXIS 5, at *28, 59-60, 1999 WL 64265, at *9, 20; *Frank v. Arnelle*, 1998 Del. Ch. LEXIS 176, at *27, 1998 WL 668649, at *7 (Del. Ch. Sept. 16, 1998), *aff'd*, 725 A.2d 441 (unpublished opinion, text available at 1999 Del. Ch. LEXIS 25 and 1999 WL 89284) (Del. Jan. 22, 1999); *Ciullo v. Orange & Rockland Utils., Inc.*, No. 601136/98, slip op. at 16 (N.Y. Sup. Ct. N.Y. Co. Jan. 8, 1999) (dismissing claim where "the nature and status" of an action was disclosed and stating that "[a] corporation does not breach its duty to disclose by failing quantifiably to disclose its litigation liabilities"), *aff'd*, 271 A.D.2d 369, 369, 706 N.Y.S.2d 428, 429 (N.Y. App. Div. 1st Dep't), *leave to appeal denied*, 95 N.Y.2d 760, 737 N.E.2d 952, 714 N.Y.S.2d 710 (2000).

Add the following at the end of the paragraph beginning on page 523 and concluding on page 524 (immediately after footnote 2191):

Thus, for instance, there is no duty to disclose a board chairman's knowledge of improper accounting practices – a fact admitted in an answer in an on-going federal court litigation (in the answer, the chairman "downplayed the significance" of the "allegedly improper accounting practices, stating that he knew of them, but believed that they were either done legitimately or did not affect the company's financial picture") – "[u]ntil a court has formally adjudicated the underlying allegation of wrongdoing." *Wolf v. Assaf*, 1998 Del. Ch. LEXIS 101, at *11, 15-16, 1998 WL 326662, at *3-4 (Del. Ch. June 16, 1998). The court explained that requiring "a disclosure of facts disgorged in litigation when those facts and the many inconsistent inferences that would be drawn from them are hotly contested . . . would suck management into a bottomless pit of self-flagellation worthy of the imagination of Dante," including (1) disclosure of "plain, unadorned 'facts' in the seductively benign way enticed by plaintiff," (2) adding "qualifying statements denying they engaged in wrongful or improper conduct and detailing why they believed that view to be correct," and (3) "recit[ing] all potential inconsistent inferences." 1998 Del. Ch. LEXIS 101, at *14-15, 1998 WL 326662, at *4. The court stated that it would not "tread the well greased slippery slope prepared by plaintiff." 1998 Del. Ch. LEXIS 101, at *15, 1998 WL 326662, at *4. The court also rejected a claim that "the chairman's knowledge of the improper accounting practices is material to his character, competence, or fitness for office." 1998 Del. Ch. LEXIS 101, at *17, 1998 WL 326662, at *5. The court stated the following:

> Delaware law does not, however, require a proxy statement to impugn a director's character or draw negative inferences from his past business practices. It only requires a summary of his credentials and his qualifications to serve on the board as well as a description of any conflicts of interest. Nothing in our law requires a masochistic litany of management minutiae.

1998 Del. Ch. LEXIS 101, at *17-18, 1998 WL 326662, at *5, *quoted in Disney*, 731 A.2d at 377; *see also Brown*, 1999 Del. Ch. LEXIS 92, at *28 n.23, 1999 WL 342340, at *8 & n.23 (as noted in *Wolf*, "disclosure of a single unadorned fact can quickly snowball into wide-ranging disclosure of facts and opinions that otherwise would never come before the shareholders" and could "'suck management into a bottomless pit of self-flagellation worthy of the imagination of Dante'").

Add the following at the end of footnote 2194 on page 525:

See also Solomon v. Armstrong, 747 A.2d 1098, 1131 (Del. Ch. 1999), *aff'd*, 746 A.2d 277 (unpublished opinion, full text available at 2000 Del. LEXIS 30 and 2000 WL 140072) (Del. Jan. 26, 2000).

Add the words "or obvious" between the words "'known or reasonably available'" and "to shareholders" in the second sentence of the paragraph beginning on page 524 and concluding on page 525 (between footnotes 2194 and 2195).

Add the following at the end of footnote 2195 on page 525:

See also Rosser, 2000 Del. Ch. LEXIS 115, at *14, 2000 WL 1206677, at *4; *Solomon*, 747 A.2d at 1131; *Golden Cycle LLC v. Allan*, 1998 Del. Ch. LEXIS 80, at *27-28, 32, 1998 WL 276224, at *9, 10 (Del. Ch. May 20, 1998) (no obligation by corporation in a response to an offer to purchase to repeat information concerning the bidder's financing disclosed by the bidder in its offer to purchase or concerning compensation arrangements between the corporation and its directors that already are "before the stockholders as a result of the Company's filings").

Add the following at the beginning of footnote 2197 on page 525:

Noerr v. Greenwood, 1997 Del. Ch. LEXIS 121, at *24, 1997 WL 419633, at *7 (Del. Ch. July 16, 1997); *O'Reilly v. Transworld Healthcare, Inc.*, 745 A.2d 902, 924-25 (Del. Ch. 1999).

Add the following at the end of the paragraph beginning on page 524 and concluding on page 525 (immediately after footnote 2197):

A challenge to a corporation's failure to disclose information to shareholders also may be dismissed where the shareholder challenging the failure by the corporation to make the disclosure "itself, made the disclosures it complains of" in a letter to all shareholders. *Peerless*, 2000 Del. Ch. LEXIS 170, at *63-64, 2000 WL 1805376, at *17-18.

Add the following at the end of the paragraph beginning on page 524 and concluding on page 525 (immediately after footnote 2197):

A claim also is not stated by a "mere failure to organize . . . documents to meet plaintiff's best case scenario for maximizing the clarity of the information presented." *Wolf*, 1998 Del. Ch. LEXIS 101, at *9, 1998 WL 326662, at *3. Accordingly, disclosure concerning a federal securities class action lawsuit involving the corporation and its directors in a Form 10-K that was mailed with a proxy statement rather than in the proxy statement itself does not state a claim because "an inclusion of facts showing that the information was in fact delivered to shareholders in a reasonable manner so that it would be a part of the total mix to be considered by them defeats conclusory claims to the contrary." 1998 Del. Ch. LEXIS 101, at *10-11, 1998 WL 326662, at *3.

Section C 3 d

Add the following at the end of footnote 2200 on page 527:

See also In re Marriott Hotel Props. II LP Unitholders Litig., 2000 Del. Ch. LEXIS 17, at *34, 2000 WL 128875, at *11 (Del. Ch. Jan. 24, 2000).

Delete the period at the end of the second sentence of the paragraph beginning on page 526 and concluding on page 527 (immediately before footnote 2200) and add the following after footnote 2200:

or conversions of partnerships into real estate investment trusts ("REITs"). *See Sonet v. Plum Creek Timber Co.*, 1999 Del. Ch. LEXIS 49, at *24-25, 43-44, 1999 WL 160174, at *6, 11 (Del. Ch. Mar. 18, 1999). The same also has been said where directors own sufficient stock to control the outcome of a vote. *Turner v. Bernstein*, 1999 Del. Ch. LEXIS 18, at *21 n.19, 1999 WL 66532, at *5 n.19 (Del. Ch. Feb. 9, 1999).

Add the following at the end of the fourth sentence (immediately after footnote 2201) of the paragraph beginning on page 526 and concluding on page 527:

"[T]he fiduciaries responsible for the disclosures have an economic interest that is adverse to the interests of their beneficiary investors." *Plum Creek*, 1999 Del. Ch. LEXIS 49, at

*43-44, 1999 WL 160174, at *11. As a result, "the materiality standard remains unchanged, but the scrutiny of the disclosures . . . is more exacting." 1999 Del. Ch. LEXIS 49, at *25, 1999 WL 160174, at *6.

Section C 3 e

Replace "Where" in the first sentence (between footnotes 2202 and 2203) of the paragraph beginning on page 527 and concluding on page 528:

The fact that a majority shareholder controls the outcome of a vote also has been said to make "a more compelling case for the application of the recognized disclosure standards." *McMullin v. Beran*, 765 A.2d 910, 925-26 (Del. 2000). Additionally, where

Add the following at the end of footnote 2203 on page 527:

See also In re Unocal Exploration Corp. S'holders Litig., 2000 Del. Ch. LEXIS 92, at *64, 2000 WL 823376, at *17 (Del. Ch. June 13, 2000).

Add the following at the end of the first sentence (immediately after footnote 2203) of the paragraph beginning on page 527 and concluding on page 528:

In other words, "the merger decision has been made and the only decision for the minority is whether to seek appraisal." *Skeen v. Jo-Ann Stores, Inc.*, 750 A.2d 1170, 1171 (Del. 2000).

Add the following at the end of footnote 2204 on page 527:

Thus, "[t]he parent need not provide all the information necessary for the stockholder to reach an independent determination of fair value; only that information material to the decision of whether or not to seek appraisal is required." *Unocal*, 2000 Del. Ch. LEXIS 92, at *64, 2000 WL 823376, at *17.

Add the following at the end of the paragraph beginning on page 527 and concluding on page 528 (immediately after footnote 2205):

The materiality standard is the same in this context as in any other context: "Directors must disclose all material facts within their control that a reasonable stockholder would consider important in deciding how to respond to the pending transaction." *Jo-Ann Stores*, 750 A.2d at 1171. Shareholders need not be "given all the financial data they would need if they were making an independent determination of value." *Id.* at 1174; *McMullin*, 765 A.2d at 925. Instead, "only that information material to the decision of whether or not to seek appraisal is required." *Unocal,* 2000 Del. Ch. LEXIS 92, at *64, 2000 WL 823376, at *17.

Section C 4

Add the following at the end of the first paragraph beginning and concluding on page 528 (immediately after footnote 2206):

The term "shareholder ratification" is a "broad term of art 'intended to describe any approval of challenged board action by a fully informed vote of shareholders, irrespective of whether that shareholder vote is legally required for the transaction to attain legal existence." *Solomon v. Armstrong*, 747 A.2d 1098, 1113 n.40 (Del. Ch. 1999) (quoting *In re Wheelabrator Techs. Inc. S'holders Litig.*, 663 A.2d 1194, 1201 n.4 (Del. Ch. 1995)); *see also Harbor Fin. Partners v. Huizenga*, 751 A.2d 879, 900 n.78 (Del. Ch. Nov. 17, 1999) ("classic ratification" involves "the voluntary addition of an independent layer of shareholder approval in circumstances where such approval is not legally required" and it is "oxymoronical to call a necessary stockholders' vote in advance of a transaction's consummation 'advance ratification'") (quoting *Wheelabrator*, 663 A.2d at 1201 n.4 and *In re 3COM Corp. S'holders Litig.*, 1999 Del. Ch. LEXIS 215, at *10, 1999 WL 1009210, at *3 (Del. Ch. Oct. 25, 1999)).

Add the following at the end of footnote 2207 on page 528:

See also Solomon v. Armstrong, 747 A.2d 1098, 1128 (Del. Ch. 1999) ("who bears the burden of proof" depends upon "which type of disclosure claim is made by whom": "As far as claims of material misstatements, omissions and coercion go, the law is clear that plaintiff bears the burden of proof that disclosure was inadequate, misleading, or coercive. On the other hand, when it comes to claiming the sufficiency of disclosure and the concomitant legal effect of shareholder ratification after full disclosure (e.g., claim extinguishment, the retention of the business judgement rule presumptions, or the shift of the burden of proof of entire fairness from defendant to the plaintiff) it is the defendant who bears the burden.") (footnotes omitted), *aff'd*, 746 A.2d 277 (unpublished opinion, full text available at 2000 Del. LEXIS 30 and 2000 WL 140072) (Del. Jan. 26, 2000); *Solomon*, 747 A.2d at 1117 n.58.

Section C 4 b

Add the following at the end of footnote 2215 on page 530:

See also Solomon v. Armstrong, 747 A.2d 1098, 1111 & n.27 (Del. Ch. 1999) (stating that "the most powerful way to ensure that a particular class of shareholders is dealt with fairly in the face of a structural conflict is to empower it with a fully-informed non-coerced vote that conditions the consummation of a transaction on its acquiescence" because "[s]uch a vote can surround a board's action with business judgment protection notwithstanding allegations that might otherwise rebut the business judgment rule's presumptions," but "[t]his statement is *not* intended to communicate that all corporate action that is required to be put to a shareholder vote, or that corporate actions submitted for shareholder approval as a voluntary matter by the board, *must* proceed on a class-by-class basis or even on a majority of the minority basis"), *aff'd*, 746 A.2d 277 (unpublished opinion, full text available at 2000 Del. LEXIS 30 and 2000 WL 140072) (Del. Jan. 26, 2000).

Section C 5 b

Delete "but before Archer-Daniels-Midland" in the second paragraph beginning and concluding on page 535 and move that paragraph (including footnotes 2249 and 2250) to page 533, at the end of the first paragraph beginning and concluding on page 533 (immediately after footnote 2236).

Add the following at the end of footnote 2248 on page 535:

See also Solomon v. Armstrong, 747 A.2d 1098, 1110 n.21 (Del. Ch. 1999), *aff'd*, 746 A.2d 277 (unpublished opinion, full text available at 2000 Del. LEXIS 30 and 2000 WL 140072) (Del. Jan. 26, 2000) (citing *Loudon v. Archer-Daniels-Midland Co.*, 700 A.2d 135, 141 (Del. 1997), for the proposition that "under certain circumstances, injunctive relief or corrective disclosure may be the only remedy available to shareholder plaintiffs").

Add the following at the end of the first paragraph beginning and concluding on page 535 (immediately after footnote 2248):

The Delaware Supreme Court in *Malone v. Brincat*, 722 A.2d 5 (Del. 1998), stated that following *Cinerama, Inc. v. Technicolor, Inc.*, 663 A.2d 1156 (Del. 1995) (discussed in Chapter II, Section A 1), *In re Tri-Star Pictures, Inc. Litigation*, 634 A.2d 319 (Del. 1993), and *Loudon v. Archer-Daniels-

Midland Co., 700 A.2d 135 (Del. 1997), "[a]n action for a breach of fiduciary duty arising out of disclosure violations in connection with a request for stockholder action does not include the elements of reliance, causation and actual quantifiable monetary damages." *Malone*, 722 A.2d at 12; *see also State of Wis. Inv. Bd. v. Peerless Sys. Corp.*, 2000 Del. Ch. LEXIS 170, at *58, 2000 WL 1805376, at *16 (Del. Ch. Dec. 4, 2000) (same). Quoting *Loudon*, the court in *Malone* stated that "where directors have breached their disclosure duties in a corporate transaction . . . there must at least be an award of nominal damages." *Malone,* 722 A.2d at 12 n.27 (quoting *Loudon,* 700 A.2d at 142, ellipsis added by court in *Malone*); *see also O'Reilly v. Transworld Healthcare, Inc.*, 745 A.2d 902, 917 (Del. Ch. 1999) ("[a] plaintiff . . . is entitled to per se nominal damages for a breach of the duty of disclosure . . . [s]o long as the plaintiff pleads sufficiently the other specific elements of a breach of the fiduciary duty of disclosure . . . without pleading causation or actual quantifiable damages" because "[b]reaches of the duty of disclosure always impinge upon the stockholder franchise and stockholders' right to make an informed decision on corporate affairs").

Nevertheless, other than nominal damages, there is "no *per se* doctrine imposing liability with regard to the fiduciary duty to disclose" in connection with a request for shareholder action. *Peerless*, 2000 Del. Ch. LEXIS 170, at *58, 2000 WL 1805376, at 816. Rather, "[a] plaintiff who seeks more than nominal damages for breach of the duty of disclosure" in connection with a request for shareholder action must "plead causation and identify actual quantifiable damages in order to survive a motion to dismiss." *O'Reilly*, 745 A.2d at 917, *quoted in Krim v. ProNet, Inc.*, 744 A.2d 523, 528 n.20 (Del. Ch. 1999). In the case of "a communication that does not contemplate stockholder action and which implicates the broader duties of loyalty, 'good faith' and care, as opposed to the more narrow duty of disclosure," a plaintiff must "plead causation and identify actual quantifiable damages in order to plead sufficiently." *O'Reilly*, 745 A.2d at 917.

The Court of Chancery in *O'Reilly v. Transworld Healthcare, Inc.*, 745 A.2d 902 (Del. Ch. 1999), observed that the Supreme Court's decision in *Malone* "does not cite the portion of the *Loudon* opinion in which the Supreme Court addressed the pleading requirements for damages in the category of disclosure claims to which the limited *per se* rule of damages did not apply under its ruling (i.e., claims not involving stockholder approval of an improperly manipulated transaction through disclosure violations)." *Id.* at 918. In that portion of *Loudon*, the court in *O'Reilly* stated, "the Supreme Court stated that damages would be awarded in those disclosure claims only if the disclosure violation impaired stockholder voting rights or deprived stockholders of their economic interests, and the complaint contained well-pleaded allegations sufficient to warrant the remedy sought." *Id.* The court in *O'Reilly* also observed that "[i]t appears that under *Loudon*'s pleading standards even a claim for nominal damages would need to be accompanied by an allegation that the disclosure violation impaired stockholder voting rights or impaired stockholders of their economic interests." *Id* at 918 n.25. The court in *O'Reilly* acknowledged that "[t]his view . . . is inconsistent with *Malone*'s pronouncement that causation is not an element of a claim for breach of the fiduciary duty of disclosure" and stated that "*Malone*'s statement that causation and actual quantifiable damages are not elements of a claim for breach of the fiduciary duty of disclosure, and, more significantly, its citations in support of that statement, constitute a retreat to *Tri-Star*'s per se rule of damages for all violations of the fiduciary duty of disclosure." *Id.* at 918 & n.25.

The court in *O'Reilly*, however, reasoned that while this statement in *Malone* "appears to be inconsistent with *Loudon*'s limitation of the per se rule of damages and *Loudon*'s heightened pleading standard for claims of breach of the fiduciary duty of disclosure not covered by the limited per se rule of damages, any such inconsistency becomes transparent when one considers *Malone*'s contemporaneous limitation on the circumstances in which the duty of disclosure applies." *Id.*

Under *Malone*, the court in *O'Reilly* explained, "the 'duty of disclosure' is implicated only in communications that request stockholder action" and "[i]f a corporate fiduciary violates the duty of disclosure, as *Malone* now narrowly defines that duty, it is axiomatic that stockholders' voting rights are impaired" and thus "[e]ven under *Loudon*, the stockholder would be entitled to nominal damages." *Id.* Accordingly, the court in *O'Reilly* stated, "*Malone*'s explicit limitation of the duty of disclosure to those instances in which stockholder action is requested dispels the apparent dichotomy that the Supreme Court created in *Loudon* for the treatment of disclosure violations arising out of communications requesting stockholder action and disclosure violations arising out of communications that do not request stockholder action." *Id.*

The court in *O'Reilly* summarized the governing rules as follows:

First, the court in *O'Reilly* stated, "the *per se* rule of damages" for duty of disclosure violations involves only communications requesting stockholder action and "encompasses only nominal damages," and "causation and actual quantifiable damages are elements of the compensatory damages portion of a claim for breach of the fiduciary duty of disclosure." *Id.* at 919. "Presumably," the court stated, "a claim for breach of the fiduciary duty of disclosure that sufficiently pleads the other specific elements of the breach arising from a false statement, omission, or partial disclosure will support a request for nominal damages, without the need to plead causation or actual quantifiable damages." *Id.* The court added that "[s]ince *Malone* did not overrule *Loudon*, however, a plaintiff may want to allege impairment of stockholder voting rights or deprivation of stockholder economic interests in order to assure survival of even a claim limited to a request for nominal damages." *Id.*

Second, the court in *O'Reilly* stated, "[t]he *per se* rule of damages does not apply to disclosure violations that arise out of communications that do not contemplate stockholder action and that, therefore, implicate only the broader fiduciary duties of loyalty, 'good faith' and care and not the narrower fiduciary duty of disclosure." *Id.* at 919-20. The court in *O'Reilly* explained that *Loudon*, a case decided before *Malone* limited the duty of disclosure to communications contemplating stockholder action, "concluded that the *per se* rule of damages did not apply to disclosure claims arising out of communications that did not contemplate stockholder action," and "*Malone*'s more narrow characterization of the 'duty of disclosure' should have no impact on *Loudon*'s treatment of these claims." *Id.* at 920. Therefore, according to the court in *O'Reilly*, "disclosure claims arising out of communications that do not contemplate stockholder action and which implicate only the broader fiduciary duties of loyalty, 'good faith' and care, as opposed to the fiduciary duty of disclosure, must be supported, under *Loudon*, by a well-pleaded complaint with allegations sufficient to warrant the remedy sought, regardless of whether the requested remedies are for nominal damages, compensatory damages or some other type of relief." *Id.* The court stated that "[t]his rule makes sense because unlike a disclosure violation arising out of a communication contemplating stockholder action, which automatically impairs stockholder voting rights, a disclosure violation arising out of a communication that does not contemplate stockholder action neither automatically impairs stockholder voting rights nor automatically deprives stockholders of their economic interests." *Id.*

The Delaware Court of Chancery in *In re Walt Disney Co. Derivative Litigation*, 731 A.2d 342 (Del. Ch. 1998), *aff'd with leave to replead on other grounds sub nom. Brehm v. Eisner*, 746 A.2d 244, 249 n.3 (Del. 2000), a pre-*Malone* decision, noted that the "expansion of the remedy available for a board's breach of the duty of disclosure reached new ground" in the Supreme Court's decision in *Tri-Star* and "seemed to demand liability for nondisclosure of material information whenever shareholder action was solicited regardless of the board's independence, disinterestedness, or good faith efforts to reasonably and fairly inform the shareholders." *Id.* at 370-

71. The Supreme Court in *Loudon*, the court in *Disney* continued, "erased the post-*Tri-Star* doubt as to whether non-loyalty based disclosure claims required damages" but "formulated a damages requirement for shareholder plaintiffs who pled breach of the duty of disclosure." *Disney*, 731 A.2d at 371. This damages requirement does not differentiate between disclosure claims where the board is disinterested and independent" and disclosure claims where the board is not disinterested and independent, but "does distinguish between disclosure violations that negatively impact shareholder voting or economic rights and those that do not." *Id.*

Under *Loudon*, the court in *Disney* stated, disclosure violations that "negatively impact shareholder voting or economic rights" do not require proof of damages but disclosure violations that do not "negatively impact shareholder voting or economic rights . . . may be dismissed for failure to state a claim." *Id.* at 371-72. "The implication is that even if the deal is unfair and despite possible nullification of the shareholders' ratification, no damages result solely from breach of the duty of disclosure unless shareholder's economic or voting rights are implicated." *Id.* at 372. The court in *Disney* stated its view that "[o]ne would expect the same result if . . . the shareholder ratification was nullified and the underlying transaction was directly examined and passed entire fairness review," but stated that *Loudon* "treats the duty of disclosure claim as a stand-alone action" with "a damages element that adequately treats both loyalty-based and non-loyalty based disclosure claims." *Id.* A shareholder accordingly can recover "quantifiable damages, but may not expect an automatic award for every disclosure violation." *Id.* The court noted that it "is uncertain . . . whether rescissory damages would or would not be available" in a case alleging a duty of disclosure claim. *Id.* at 372 n.102.

Applying the rules stated in *Loudon*, the court in *Disney* held that a claim by Disney shareholders acting on their own behalf and challenging statements made by Disney to its shareholders in connection with a 1997 shareholder vote approving a new employment agreement for the chairman of the board and chief executive officer of Disney and a new bonus plan for Disney officers failed to plead facts showing "a quantifiable and legally cognizable harm to Disney's shareholders arising from the alleged nondisclosure." *Id.* at 375. The court explained that *Loudon*'s "mandate that a plaintiff plead quantifiable damages does not undo the well-established doctrinal division between direct shareholder claims and derivative suits": "[t]o claim damages as a shareholder, the shareholder must show that the injury was peculiar to a particular class of shareholders or peculiar to shareholder interests as opposed to the company's, i.e., that shareholders have a direct claim." *Id.* The court held that the damages caused by the adoption of the challenged compensation plans would be suffered by and result in an award of damages to Disney. *Id.* at 375-76. "[U]nder no scenario would the shareholders be the direct recipients of a damage award." *Id.* at 379.

The court also rejected a claim that shareholders were entitled to "rescissory or compensatory damages resulting from the election of directors" in the same shareholder vote. Quoting *Loudon*, the court stated that "[t]here may be circumstances under which a proxy statement soliciting votes for the election of directors is actionable under Delaware law for material misstatements or omissions" and "[i]njunctive relief in the form of corrective disclosure and resolicitation may be appropriate if the matter is addressed in time," but "[i]t is difficult to see how damages may be available in such a case." *Id.* (quoting 700 A.2d at 141).

The Court of Chancery in *Brown v. Perrette*, 1999 Del. Ch. LEXIS 92, 1999 WL 342340 (Del. Ch. May 14, 1999), a post-*Malone* decision that does not cite *Malone*, similarly stated that the Supreme Court in *Loudon* "set forth the essential elements" of the duty of disclosure and "emphasized that a plaintiff seeking recovery for breach of the duty of disclosure must set forth the shareholder's economic interest or voting right harmed by the breach and request damages commensurate with the harm." 1999 Del. Ch. LEXIS 92, at *17, 1999 WL 342340, at *5.

The *Brown* case involved the question "how to apply *Loudon*'s causation requirement in circumstances where the alleged omission was of purported wrongdoing that, if true, might give rise to relief itself." 1999 Del. Ch. LEXIS 92, at *17-18, 1999 WL 342340, at *6. The court held that "[w]here the plaintiff fails to plead prima facie facts that the nondisclosure created a cognizable harm discrete from the underlying wrongdoing, the nondisclosure claim is susceptible to dismissal for failure to plead an essential requirement of a disclosure claim under *Loudon*." 1999 Del. Ch. LEXIS 92, at *18, 1999 WL 342340, at *6. Thus, nondisclosure of wrongdoing that constitutes a breach of fiduciary duty does not "constitute a separate wrong for which relief is available" in an action seeking money damages (as opposed to "a timely request for an injunction ordering proper disclosure"). 1999 Del. Ch. LEXIS 92, at *18 & n.13, 1999 WL 342340, at *6 & n.13; *see also* 1999 Del. Ch. LEXIS 92, at *23-27, 1999 WL 342340, at *7-8 (discussing availability of injunctive relief). "The underlying fiduciary duty claim, of course, remains, but in situations where the wrongdoing's nondisclosure causes no independently remediable harm, the claim fails to satisfy *Loudon*'s causation requirement." 1999 Del. Ch. LEXIS 92, at *18-19, 1999 WL 342340, at *6. "[T]he issue of nondisclosure remains as part of the loyalty claim, failing as an independent claim only because it pleads no cognizable, discrete harm." 1999 Del. Ch. LEXIS 92, at *23, 1999 WL 342340, at *7. The issue could be raised, however, to attack any affirmative defense raised by defendants based upon shareholder ratification. "In that circumstance, . . . plaintiff could rebut the validity of the ratification by showing that the shareholders did not possess all material information at the time they voted." 1999 Del. Ch. LEXIS 92, at *35-36, 1999 WL 342340, at *11.

Applying these rules, the court dismissed claims alleging that the directors of Mr. Coffee, Inc. misleadingly described an offer by Health o Meter, Inc. as superior to a competing offer by Citicorp Venture Capital ("CVC") in a proxy statement seeking shareholder approval of a proposed merger of Mr. Coffee with Health o Meter. The court explained that "the disclosure claim's viability hinges directly upon the merits of a claim of alleged underlying wrongdoing" – a claim that Mr. Coffee's directors did not comply with their duty to maximize shareholder value under cases such as *Revlon, Inc. v. MacAndrews & Forbes Holdings, Inc.*, 506 A.2d 173 (Del. 1986). The court sated that it could not perceive how the plaintiff could prevail on her disclosure claim without winning on the merits of the *Revlon* claim or "how any additional relief above what would be awarded for the *Revlon* claim could result." 1999 Del. Ch. LEXIS 92, at *33-35, 1999 WL 342340, at *10. The court explained that "a flawed bidding process would be a material fact" but that plaintiff "must prevail on the substantive claim, that the process was flawed, before the alleged flaw becomes material." 1999 Del. Ch. LEXIS 92, at *35, 1999 WL 342340, at *11. Once plaintiff prevailed on her *Revlon* claim, the court continued, however, "the alleged disclosure claim becomes superfluous because the defendants' breach of duty becomes the wrong for which an appropriate remedy must be crafted." *Id.* In other words, plaintiff failed to allege "any cognizable harm or quantifiable damages separate from the underlying *Revlon* claim" because "[a]ny remedy for the alleged disclosure violation would be subsumed by the relief for defendants' alleged breach of fiduciary duty under *Revlon*." *Id.; see also RCG Int'l Investors, LDC v. Greka Energy Corp.*, 2000 Del. Ch. LEXIS 157, at *52 & n.54, 2000 WL 1706728, at *15 & n.54 (Del. Ch. Nov. 6, 2000) (noting that "[w]hen a disclosure claim rests entirely on a party's ability to prevail on an underlying substantive claim and there is no distinct harm caused by the alleged omission or misstatement, this court has refused to examine the claim independently under the disclosure rubric," but adding that "it may be necessary in some cases to deal with the non-disclosure of the underlying misconduct by the defendants if the defendants contend that stockholders, for example, ratified the transaction").

The court in *O'Reilly v. Transworld Healthcare, Inc.*, 745 A.2d 902 (Del. Ch. 1999), followed *Brown* but in light of *Malone*, which, as discussed above, the *O'Reilly* court read to provide a *per se* rule of nominal damages for violations of the duty of disclosure but to require causation and actual quantifiable damages as elements of "the compensatory damages portion of a claim for breach of the fiduciary duty of disclosure," stated that "in order for *Brown* to be consistent with *Malone* . . . , *Brown*'s holding on damages can only apply to compensatory damages – not both nominal *and* compensatory damages." *Id.* at 919 & n.33. Thus, "in the event that the claim for breach of the fiduciary duty of disclosure arises from the misdisclosure of wrongdoing that underlies an accompanying claim challenging the fairness of the same transaction, the plaintiff will have to plead that the breach of the duty of disclosure created a cognizable harm discrete from the harm that the underlying wrongdoing caused, as well as the requisite causation and damages to support its request for more than nominal damages." *Id.* at 917; *see also id.* at 919 ("[f]ollowing this Court's recent holding in *Brown v. Perrette, et al.*, furthermore, a well-pleaded request for more than nominal damages for breach of the duty of disclosure arising from the misdisclosure of wrongdoing that underlies an accompanying claim challenging the entire fairness of the same transaction will require a plaintiff to plead that the disclosure violation created a cognizable harm discrete from the harm caused by the underlying wrongdoing in the entire fairness claim, in order for the disclosure claim to survive a motion to dismiss").

The court in *Reilly*, like the court in *Brown*, accordingly dismissed duty of disclosure claims seeking compensatory damages. The claim in *Reilly* was asserted by shareholders of Health Management Inc. ("HMI") who alleged non-disclosure of the "true purpose" of a merger between HMI and its controlling shareholder, Transworld Healthcare, Inc. *Id.* at 922. The court explained that "[t]he alleged harm that resulted from the Defendants' violations of the duty of disclosure . . . is essentially the same as the alleged harm" that was caused by the defendants' approval of the merger: "an unfair price and a diversion to the Defendants of monies that belong to HMI." *Id.* at 922-23. As a result, plaintiff failed "to plead that the Defendants' misdisclosure of Transworld's purposes created a cognizable harm discrete from the alleged usurpation of corporate opportunity and unfair dealing that proper disclosure would have revealed" and thus "[t]he compensatory damages that the HMI stockholders could be awarded if they succeed on their claims regarding the unfairness of the Merger would compensate the HMI stockholders for the harm alleged" in the disclosure portion of the complaint as well. *Id.* at 923.

The court reached the same conclusion with respect to a statement that negotiations between Transworld and HMI were "conducted on an arms length basis." *Id.* at 925. The court explained that "[o]ne of the essential allegations" underlying plaintiff's claim that the merger was unfair was plaintiff's contention that the merger negotiations "were not 'arm's length,' and resulted in unfair dealing and a usurpation of corporate opportunity by Transworld." *Id.* at 926. The court stated that the complaint "fails to plead prima facie facts that this false statement created a cognizable harm discrete from the harm caused by the alleged unfair negotiations that honest disclosure would have revealed." *Id.*

The court in *Weiss v. Samsonite Corp.*, 741 A.2d 366 (Del. Ch. 1999), *aff'd*, 746 A.2d 277 (unpublished opinion, text available at 1999 Del. LEXIS 387 and 1999 WL 1254563 (Del. Nov. 12, 1999), also dismissed a disclosure claim due to the plaintiff's failure to plead a causal connection between alleged omissions and alleged damages. Plaintiff alleged that an offer to purchase sent to shareholders in connection with a $40 per share cash self-tender offer for the corporation's common stock did not disclose "the reasoning or 'methodology' the Board used to select the $40 self-tender price, and its calculation of 'total value.'" *Id* at 375. The offer, as announced on May 20, 1998, contemplated the purchase of 59 percent of the corporation's shares but was amended on June 9, 1998 to provide for the purchase of 51 percent of the corporation's shares. *Id.* at

369 n.1. Plaintiff allegedly suffered damages because "the Company incurred debt to fund the Offer, which drove down the price of the stock" to below its pre-offer level, and "as a result the stockholders ended up with cash and stock worth at least $2 to $3 per share less than the total value they had immediately before the Offer." *Id.* at 375.

The court rejected this claim on two grounds.

First, the court took judicial notice that the market price of the corporation's stock on the day the offer, as amended, was announced was $26-7/8 per share. *Id.* at 375 & n.26. The court stated that shareholders who tendered their shares received $40 per share in cash for half of their stock and "a 'stub security' having an initial market value of $12" per share for the other half of their stock – a total value of $26 per share, which the court described as "completely consistent" with the stock's market value on the date of the offer, as amended. *Id.* at 375-76. The court rejected plaintiff's reliance upon the pre-offer market price of $29-1/4 per share, which resulted in a $2 to $3 loss per share, because "the only relevant comparison" was to the amended offer and not to the original offer. *Id.* at 376.

Second, the court took judicial notice of stock prices that demonstrated that "during the pendency of the Offer Samsonite's stock price remained relatively stable and close to its pre-Offer level" until the amendment to the offer reduced the maximum number of shares to be purchased from 59 percent to 51 percent and thus reduced the cash payout to shareholders and corporate borrowing by $60 million, from $480 million to $420 million. *Id.* The court stated that "[u]nder the plaintiff's damage theory the stock price should have increased when the Board decided to reduce the overall amount of borrowing," but the stock's market price following the amendment demonstrated that "the opposite occurred." *Id.* For those reasons, the court concluded, "the complaint does not allege facts that show a causal connection between the disclosure omissions and any alleged damage to the class." *Id.*

Section C 5 c

Delete the period at the end of the first sentence (immediately before footnote 2266) of the paragraph beginning on page 537 and concluding on page 538 and add the following (immediately after footnote 2266):

because "a good faith erroneous judgment as to the proper scope or content of required disclosure implicates the duty of care rather than the duty of loyalty." *Zirn v. VLI Corp. ("VLI II")*, 681 A.2d 1050, 1062 (Del. 1996), *quoted in Malone v. Brincat*, 722 A.2d 5, 12 n.32 (Del. 1998).

Add the following at the end of footnote 2268 on page 538:

See also O'Reilly v. Transworld Healthcare, Inc., 745 A.2d 902, 920 n.34 (Del. Ch. 1999) (knowledge that a statement is materially false or misleading is not an element of a duty of disclosure claim but "would be relevant to a claim to exempt directors from liability for the breach of the duty of disclosure pursuant to exculpatory charter provisions authorized by 8 *Del C.* § 102(b)(7)").

Add the following at the end of footnote 2269 on page 538:

See also Turner v. Bernstein, 2000 Del. Ch. LEXIS 96, at *54, 2000 WL 776893, at *15 (Del. Ch. June 1, 2000) ("the fact that § 102(b)(7) provisions are prevalent provides a strong incentive for plaintiffs to press disclosure claims promptly because although such provisions do not bar injunctive relief for duty of care violations, they will prevent a damages award").

Add the following at the end of footnote 2272 on page 539:

See also Malone, 722 A.2d at 14 n.47 ("[a] class action may not be maintained in a purely common law or equitable fraud case since individual questions of law or fact, particularly as to the element of justifiable reliance, will inevitably predominate over common questions of law or fact") (quoting *Gaffin v. Teledyne, Inc.*, 611 A.2d 467, 474 (Del. 1992)).

Section D

Add the following at the end of the first sentence of the second paragraph beginning and concluding on page 539 (between footnotes 2273 and 2274):

A claim that a transaction such as a self-tender offer coerces shareholders to act in a certain way, such as tendering, is not "sufficient, without more, to state a valid claim" because "the relevant question is not whether a tender offer is coercive, but whether it is actionably coercive." *Weiss v. Samsonite Corp.*, 741 A.2d 366, 372 (Del. Ch. 1999), *aff'd*, 746 A.2d 277 (unpublished opinion, text available at 1999 Del. LEXIS 387 and 1999 WL 1254563) (Del. Nov. 12, 1999).

Replace the word "Wrongful" in the second sentence of the second paragraph beginning and concluding on page 539 with the following (between footnotes 2273 and 2274):

To the contrary, "[a]ll disclosure of material information may cause shareholders to vote in a particular way, and so is, in some general sense, 'coercive.' Considering the legal imperative that all shareholders be armed with all material information, it cannot be that the mere potential to influence a shareholder's vote renders disclosed information actionable." *Solomon v. Armstrong*, 747 A.2d 1098, 1131 (Del. Ch. 1999), *aff'd*, 746 A.2d 277 (unpublished opinion, full text available at 2000 Del. LEXIS 30 and 2000 WL 140072) (Del. Jan. 26, 2000).

The law thus provides that wrongful

Add the following at the end of footnote 2274 on page 539:

See also Solomon, 747 A.2d at 1131; *In re Gen. Motors Class H S'holders Litig.*, 734 A.2d 611, 620 (Del. Ch. 1999).

Add the following at the end of footnote 2275 on page 539:

See also Samsonite, 741 A.2d at 372 (quoting *Lieb v. Clark*, 13 Del. J. Corp. L. 742, 749 (Del. Ch. June 1, 1987)).

Add the following at the end of the first paragraph beginning and concluding on page 540 (immediately after footnote 2279):

A shareholder plaintiff alleging wrongful coercion bears the burden of proving wrongful coercion. *Solomon*, 747 A.2d at 1128.

Section D 1

Add the following at the end of the paragraph beginning on page 542 and concluding on page 543 (immediately after footnote 2301):

The courts in *Solomon v. Armstrong*, 747 A.2d 1098 (Del. Ch. 1999), *aff'd*, 746 A.2d 277 (unpublished opinion, full text available at 2000 Del. LEXIS 30 and 2000 WL 140072) (Del. Jan. 26, 2000), and *In re General Motors Class H Shareholders Litigation*, 734 A.2d 611 (Del. Ch. 1999) – two cases discussed in detail in Chapter II, Section E 4 – reached the same conclusion in cases where holders of General Motors Corporation tracking stocks approved transactions that included amendments to certificate of incorporation provisions that eliminated the right of the holders of the tracking stocks to receive non-tracking stock having a value equal to 120 percent of the value of their tracking stock in the event of certain types of transactions.

Solomon v. Armstrong, 747 A.2d 1098 (Del. Ch. 1999), *aff'd*, 746 A.2d 277 (unpublished opinion, full text available at 2000 Del. LEXIS 30 and 2000 WL 140072) (Del. Jan. 26, 2000), involved GM Class E stock, the performance of which was linked to the performance of Electronics Data Systems

Holding Corporation ("EDS"), a wholly-owned subsidiary of GM, and a split-off of EDS to holders of Class E stock. Two statements in a consent solicitation statement disseminated by GM to Class E shareholders were alleged by Class E shareholders to be wrongfully coercive: (1) a statement that if the proposed split-off was not approved by Class E shareholders, then GM "would seek substantial changes" to the master services agreement (the "MSA") governing GM's relationship with EDS, and (2) a statement that GM "would not consider a transaction that would trigger the Class E stockholders' right" under GM's certificate of incorporation to "receive GM stock equal to 120 percent of the ratio of the average market price per share of the Class E Stock on a specified valuation date to the average market price per share of GM stock on that same date (hereinafter referred to as the 'Exchange Rate'), in the event of a recapitalization, sale, transfer, assignment, or other disposition of EDS to any entity of which GM was not a majority owner." *Id.* at 1106, 1124.

With respect the alleged statement that if the proposed split-off was not approved by Class E shareholders, then GM "would seek substantial changes" to the master services agreement, the court stated that plaintiffs did not allege that "absent the split-off no changes to the MSA would have been negotiated" or that GM "would have forced the renegotiation of the MSA irrespective of whether such changes were in the best interests of EDS or the Class E stockholders." *Id.* at 1131. To the contrary, the court concluded, "all statements regarding the renegotiation of the MSA were an acknowledgment of a change in business climate and the concomitant need to reevaluate the existing service relationship between GM and EDS." *Id.* The court described this information as "clearly relevant" and stated that this information "may have had an effect on how shareholders voted," but "I cannot conclude that it was disclosed in order to force shareholders to vote on anything other than the merits of the transaction." *Id.* In sum, "the statements that the plaintiffs allege are coercive 'merely presented to the stockholders material information required as a matter of full disclosure so that they could determine the relative merits' of the split-off." *Id.*

With respect to the alleged statement that GM "would not consider a transaction that would trigger the Class E stockholders' right" under GM's certificate of incorporation to a 120 percent premium, the court stated that no publicly disclosed document cited by plaintiff "explicitly states that GM directors would *never* consent to a transaction that might trigger the Exchange Rate provision." *Id.* Instead, plaintiffs relied upon statements such as the following:

> In considering a divestiture of EDS, the GM Board determined that any such transaction should be one that would both be tax-free . . . and not result in a recapitalization of the Class E Common Stock . . . at the 120% exchange ratio . . . . This determination was based on the GM Board's belief that the payment by General Motors of either the 20% premium on the Class E Common Stock resulting from the exchange ratio or a material tax on an EDS divestiture would not be in the best interests of General Motors and its stockholders and that payment of the 20% premium in the context of a split-off of EDS would not be consistent with the purpose for which the 120% exchange rate provision was included in the terms of the Class E Common Stock.

Id. at 1132.

The court rejected plaintiffs' claim that this statement failed to inform shareholders concerning the reason why the 120 percent provision existed. The court stated that "shareholders have *at least* a basic understanding of the attributes of their stock and how those attributes serve to benefit the shareholders" and that the court would not accept "[p]laintiffs' assumption that shareholders are ignorant about their stockholdings." *Id.* The court also stated that "it is clear from the quoted language" – and "irrespective of the 'purpose for which the 120% exchange rate provision was included'" in GM's certificate – that "a shareholder who planned to vote in favor of the transaction would thereby forfeit some benefit to which his Class E stock would otherwise be entitled." *Id.* Accordingly, any Class E shareholder "would necessarily understand that at issue was the choice of giving up some right with an easily calculated value (a 20% premium over the stock price) in exchange for the merger consideration." *Id.* The court stated that "whether that shareholder voted for or against the transaction – he would be voting on the merits and not because this disclosure introduced some other reason." *Id.* The disclosed facts "may or may not have led some shareholders to vote in favor of the split-off," but "[s]o long as the disclosure enabled shareholders to vote on the merits of the transaction . . . no exhaustive explanation of the original purpose for the Exchange Rate was required." *Id.*

The Delaware Supreme Court affirmed "on the basis of and for the reasons assigned by the Court of Chancery in its well-reasoned decision." *Solomon v. Armstrong*, 746 A.2d 277 (unpublished opinion, full text available at 2000 Del. LEXIS 30 and 2000 WL 140072) (Del. Jan. 26, 2000).

In *In re General Motors Class H Shareholders Litigation*, 734 A.2d 611 (Del. Ch. 1999), holders of GM Class H stock, who, like the GM Class E shareholders in *Solomon*, had a right to receive GM stock worth 120 percent of the market value of their stock in the event of certain types of transactions, alleged that they were wrongfully coerced by being forced to choose between acquiescing in the elimination of their "lucrative recapitalization rights" or blocking a series of transactions referred to as the "Hughes Transactions" and "thereby squandering the potentially enhanced values realizable from those transactions." *Id.* at 615, 620. The Class H shareholders also alleged that they were coerced by being told that the Hughes Transactions were entitled to tax-free treatment but that any future transaction "structured in a manner similar to the Hughes Transactions" would be a taxable transaction due to recently enacted federal tax legislation. *Id.* at 620.

The court rejected these claims. The court held that GM's board "had no duty to structure the Hughes Transactions so as to trigger the Recap Provision, and thereby avoid asking the GMH stockholders to choose between the potential for a premium under the Recap Provision and the deal consideration." *Id.* To the contrary, GM's board was "permitted to structure the deal as they did so long as they did not strong-arm the GMH stockholders into voting for it." *Id.*

"Such strong-arming is absent here," the court concluded, for the following reasons:

> In the event that the Hughes Transactions did not receive GMH stockholder approval, the GMH stockholders would have been in precisely the same position they were in before the vote. Their tracking stock rights in Hughes would have been unimpaired as would have been their contractual protection against a sale of substantially all of the assets of Hughes. However, if the electorate decided to choose the status quo, GM informed them that they should not expect that a future transaction "structured in a manner similar to the Hughes Transactions" could be accomplished in a tax-free manner. This information was material and informed the GMH stockholders of a reality with which GM and they had to contend . . . .
>
> Thus, the GMH stockholders had a free choice between maintaining their current status and taking advantage of the new status offered by the Hughes Transactions. The opportunity to make this choice by vote carried with it a concomitant obligation on the part of the voters to accept responsibility for the outcome. Would it were that the world gave each of us the opportunity to divest the word "choose" of its close relationship to the word "between." How much of our human experience would be less trying?
>
> . . . There is much democratic wisdom in the trite phrase "you can't have your cake and eat it too." That phrase applies here. All the GMH stockholders were asked to do is to accept a new status or remain in their current status. Responsible investors must be prepared to make such choices; after all, they do so every time they buy or sell securities in the market.

Id. at 620-21.

Add the following at the end of the paragraph beginning on page 543 and concluding on page 544 (immediately after footnote 2306):

Coercion also was not found in *Hills Stores Co. v. Bozic*, 769 A.2d 88 (Del. Ch. 2000), a case challenging proxy materials distributed to shareholders by the incumbent slate of directors in a proxy contest for control of Hills Stores Company. These proxy materials informed shareholders that the election of a competing slate proposed by Dickstein Partners would trigger change in control provisions in an indenture governing senior notes and a credit agreement governing the corporation's working capital facility, that if the parties to these arrangements all exercised their rights "management estimates that a change in control could cost Hills approximately $60 to $70 million." *Id.* at 97-98. Shareholders also were informed that "the key senior executives who have been responsible for Hills' success will be able to terminate their employment and obtain substantial severance benefits," that "[t]here is no assurance that Hills' senior management would remain with the Company upon such a change in control," and that "[t]he departure of those executives would be detrimental to the value of the Hills franchise." *Id.* at 98.

The court explained that "[t]he Hills board was duty-bound to inform its stockholders of the possible financial and operational implications of a Change in Control" and that "[t]he mere fact that the stockholders knew" that voting for a change in control might trigger corporate obligations "does not by itself constitute stockholder coercion." *Id.* at 104. The court added that there was "no evidence in the record to support a claim that the Hills board purposely used the Severance lever so as to place unwarranted pressure on the Hills stockholders." *Id.* Indeed, the court observed, it would have been "absurd" for the board to do so because Dickstein Partners "had assured the electorate that it could cover the Severance, refinance the company's debt facilities and senior notes," and offer shareholders a minimum of $22 per share in cash plus a $5 debenture paying 14 percent interest. *Id.* at 105 (emphasis omitted).

Add the following at the end of the paragraph beginning on page 546 and concluding on page 547 (immediately after footnote 2326):

As stated in *Weiss v. Samsonite Corp.*, 741 A.2d 366 (Del. Ch. 1999), *aff'd*, 746 A.2d 277 (unpublished opinion, text available at 1999 Del. LEXIS 387 and 1999 WL 1254563) (Del. Nov. 12, 1999), "the offering statement issued in connection with the corporate self-tender disclosed that after the completion of the offer, management would delist the shares of shareholders who did not tender. Those disclosures were found to be wrongfully coercive, because the shareholders were in effect being told that if they did not tender they would have no reliable market for their shares." *Id.*

The court in the *GM Class H* case discussed above distinguished the findings of coercion in *Lacos Land Co. v. Arden Group, Inc.*, 517 A.2d 271 (Del. Ch. 1986), and *Eisenberg v. Chicago Milwaukee Corp.*, 537 A.2d 1051 (Del. Ch. 1987), on the ground that in *Lacos* and *Chicago Milwaukee* "the electorate was told that retribution would follow if the proposed transaction was defeated." *GM Class H*, 734 A.2d at 621. In other words, "the electorate was not given an option to remain in their current position. They were put to a choice between a new position and a compromised position." *Id.* In the *GM Class H* case, by contrast, "[t]he choice given to the GMH stockholders was markedly different from the choices given to stockholders" in *Lacos* and *Chicago Milwaukee*: "GM did not threaten to punish the GMH stockholders if they voted against the Hughes Transactions. The GMH stockholders had the freedom to choose between the status quo and the deal consideration." *Id.; see also Bomarko, Inc. v. Int'l Telecharge, Inc.*, 1999 Del. Ch. LEXIS 211, at *54 n.8, 1999 WL 1022083, at *19 n.8 (Del. Ch. Nov. 4, 1999) (rejecting a coercion claim where "statements regarding bankruptcy were presented neutrally and not in a threatening way," but adding that "blatant threats" in a proxy statement that a corporation "would file for bankruptcy if the merger did not get approved . . . would be evidence of wrongful coercion of the vote"), *aff'd on other grounds*, 766 A.2d 437 (Del. 2000).

Section D 2

Add the following at the end of the first sentence of the paragraph beginning and concluding on page 547 (between footnotes 2326 and 2327):

"A tender offer that is 'actionably' or 'wrongfully' coercive is one that either (i) threatens to extinguish or dilute a percentage ownership interest in relation to the interest of other stockholders; or (ii) induces shareholders who were the victims of inequitable action to tender for reasons unrelated to the economic merits of the offer." *Weiss v. Samsonite Corp.*, 741 A.2d 366, 372 (Del. Ch. 1999), *aff'd*, 746 A.2d 277 (unpublished opinion, text available at 1999 Del. LEXIS 387 and 1999 WL 1254563) (Del. Nov. 12, 1999).

Add the following at the end of the first paragraph beginning and concluding on page 550 (immediately after footnote 2349):

In re Life Technologies, Inc. Shareholders Litigation, No. 16513 (Del. Ch. Nov. 24, 1998), also illustrates this principle.

Add the following at the end of the second paragraph beginning and concluding on page 552 (immediately after footnote 2362):

Weiss v. Samsonite Corp., 741 A.2d 366 (Del. Ch. 1999), *aff'd*, 746 A.2d 277 (unpublished opinion, text available at 1999 Del. LEXIS 387 and 1999 WL 1254563) (Del. Nov. 12, 1999), involved a self-tender offer by Samsonite Corporation to acquire 51 percent of its common stock open on an equal basis to all shareholders at a price of $40 per share in cash, a 33 percent premium over the stock's market price at the time.

Id. at 368-69. "The objective of the Plan was to return a substantial amount of cash to stockholders." *Id.* at 369. To finance the $40 per share payment, Samsonite incurred substantial new debt: $350 million in senior notes, $175 million in senior preferred stock, and a new $300 million bank credit facility. *Id.* at 369-70. The offer to purchase "prominently disclosed" the following:

> (i) in management's view, stockholders should tender 100% of their shares to maximize the value of their holdings and to ensure the success of the Plan, (ii) the offering price would be $40 per share cash, and (iii) the premium being offered for the tendered shares would likely reduce the post-tender trading price of the shares remaining after the Offer.

Id. at 370. The court stated that "the Offer was 'coercive' in the sense that the 33% market premium embodied in the $40 per share price was intended to – and did – induce the stockholders to tender their shares." *Id.* at 371.

The court held that the two board decisions that comprised the restructuring plan – incurring substantial new debt and distributing to shareholders the cash generated as a result of the assumption of that debt – "viewed singly and collectively, are entitled to business judgment rule protection as a matter of law." *Id.* The court explained that "[i]n today's financial world, dividends and self-tender offers are viewed as conventional methods of delivering to shareholders a return on their investment," and the choices "the Board here made – to assume debt and conduct a cash self-tender offer – were classic business judgment decisions of the kind that are normally protected by the business judgment rule." *Id.* at 371-72. No facts were pleaded, the court stated, that "would displace the protection of the business judgment rule" because plaintiff's challenge to the transaction focused upon "the Board's decision to structure the transaction in the chosen manner" and plaintiff "does not allege that the Board's decision caused or threatened a change in control of the Company" and did not allege facts that, if true, would demonstrate a lack of good faith or due care. *Id.* at 372.

The court held that the fact that the offer "'coerced' shareholders into tendering" was not sufficient to state a claim because the complaint did not allege either of the two scenarios that make a tender offer "'actionably' or 'wrongfully' coercive": the tender offer "either (i) threatens to extinguish or dilute a percentage ownership interest in relation to the interest of other stockholders; or (ii) induces shareholders who were the victims of inequitable action to tender for reasons unrelated to the economic merits of the offer." *Id.* Instead, "tendering Samsonite shareholders, upon completion of the Offer, would continue to own their equity interest in the company in virtually the same percentage as before" because the offer was made on a pro rata basis. *Id.* at 373. The court also pointed to the fact that plaintiff alleged "no post-Offer threatened act that could be construed as inequitable," as in *Eisenberg v. Chicago Milwaukee Corp.*, 537 A.2d 1051 (Del. Ch. 1987), a case where "the offering statement issued in connection with the corporate self-tender disclosed that after the completion of the offer, management would delist the shares of shareholders who did not tender" and thus "the shareholders were in effect being told that if they did not tender they would have no reliable market for their shares." 741 A.2d at 373.

The court rejected a contention that the self-tender offer was wrongfully coercive because "the post-tender market price per share would likely decrease." *Id.* The court explained that this fact was "clearly disclosed" and "a partial self-tender offer at a market premium is not *per se* actionably coercive, 'even if paying that premium may adversely affect the market value of the remaining outstanding shares, *provided that the offering materials make full disclosure of such an adverse effect.*'" *Id.* (quoting *Cottle v. Standard Brands Paint Co.*, [1990 Transfer Binder] Fed. Sec. L. Rep. (CCH) ¶ 95,306, at 96,429 (Del. Ch. Mar. 22, 1990); emphasis added by court in *Samsonite*). The court also rejected a contention that the self-tender offer was wrongfully coercive because, plaintiff contended, "the effect of the large cash payment would hinder the Company's ability to pay ordinary dividends in the future." *Id.* at 373. This argument, the court explained, "boils down to the assertion that the Board made a bad or shortsighted decision concerning how to deploy the company's cash." *Id.* The court stated that "[t]he wisdom or merit of a business decision of that kind is not . . . a proper subject for judicial review." *Id.*

The Supreme Court affirmed the Court of Chancery's decision "on the basis of, and for the reasons set forth" in the Court of Chancery's opinion. *Weiss v. Samsonite Corp.*, 746 A.2d 277 (unpublished opinion, text available at 1999 Del. LEXIS 387 and 1999 WL 1254563) (Del. Nov. 12, 1999).

Add the following at the end of the first paragraph beginning and concluding on page 558 (immediately after footnote 2396):

The court added the following: "One doesn't know what the imaginative brain of counsel or of concerned clients might imagine to support or inflame 'coercion' effects, but I cannot regard as established in the record at this stage, an actual threat to the investment interests of the limited partners from the general partner's acquiring a majority of the limited partnership interests." *In re Marriott Hotel Props. II LP Unitholders Litig.*, 22 Del. J. Corp. L. 373, 387 (Del. Ch. June 12, 1996).

Add the following at the end of the second paragraph beginning and concluding on page 558 (immediately after footnote 2397):

In a later decision in the same case, *In re Marriott Hotel Properties II LP Unitholders Litigation*, 2000 Del. Ch. LEXIS 17, 2000 WL 128875 (Del. Ch. Jan. 24, 2000), the court granted a motion to dismiss the coercion claim.

The court rejected plaintiff's reliance upon the fact that "if the tender offer was successful (and the Amendments approved), nontendering Unitholders, as a group, would lose the capacity to control the vote independently of the General Partner." 2000 Del. Ch. LEXIS 17, at *64, 2000 WL 128875, at *18. The court pointed to its prior conclusion that there was no "'actual threat to the investment interests of the limited partners from the general partner's acquiring a majority' of the limited partnership's voting power" and added that "[t]ender offers for majority control regularly occur and have never been found coercive for that reason alone." *Id.* (quoting 22 Del. J. Corp. L. at 387).

The court rejected plaintiff's claim that tendering unitholders "were forced to vote for the amendments as a condition of the sale of their units even though these amendments would be irrelevant to the tendering unitholders" as "an exercise in illogic." 2000 Del. Ch. LEXIS 17, at *65, 2000 WL 128875, at *19. The court explained:

> [T]he concurrent but independent existence of the Consent Solicitation and the Offer gave Unitholders more freedom of choice rather than less. Specifically, Unitholders who wanted the Offer to fail but wanted to be bought out if it succeeded had an effective strategy. They could simultaneously tender and withhold consent. Similarly, those who wished to see the Offer succeed but did not want to sell could refuse to tender but consent to the Amendments. In theory, at least, the only group that both tendered and gave a consent were those who both wanted the Offer to succeed and wanted to participate in it. To them, the Consent Solicitation was an obstacle to the desired end, not a goad to agree to changes not otherwise in their interests.

2000 Del. Ch. LEXIS 17, at *65-66, 2000 WL 128875, at *19.

The court also rejected a contention that unitholders were coerced into tendering by being told that the refinancing of mortgage debt "could be seriously detrimental to them" because the refinancing would restrict any sale of hotels for a ten year period, prohibit pre-payment of debt, and increase future debt service. 2000 Del. Ch. LEXIS 17, at *66, 2000 WL 128875, at *19. The court stated that "plaintiff does not dispute the accuracy of these statements," and "[a]ccurate descriptions of the consequences of a successful tender offer do not amount to coercion." *Id.* The court quoted the following passage from *Williams v. Geier*, 671 A.2d 1368 (Del. 1996):

> The simple answer . . . is that the Proxy was merely stating facts which were required to be disclosed. These disclosures were neutrally stated and were not threatening in any respect. . . . The board could not couch these disclosures in vague or euphemistic language or in terms that would deprive the stockholders of their right to choose. The disclosures must be forthright and clear, and they were in this case.

2000 Del. Ch. LEXIS 17, at *66-67, 2000 WL 128875, at *19 (quoting 671 A.2d at 1383). Here, too, the court stated, the challenged statements "merely disclosed neutral, non-threatening factual possibilities that could be considered important by a Unitholder in determining whether or not to tender his or her Units." 2000 Del. Ch. LEXIS 17, at *67, 2000 WL 128875, at *19.

In sum, the court held that "the decision of each limited partner whether or not to tender entailed a weighing of the price offered against the perceived risks and rewards of continuing to hold the investment," and "[j]ust because Salter and others ultimately decided that it was in their best interest to sell, rather than continue to hold . . . , does not mean that they were 'coerced' into doing so in any legally meaningful sense." 2000 Del. Ch. LEXIS 17, at *63-64, 2000 WL 128875, at *18. The court added that the offer failed to attract a large minority of units by its initial closing date and only after the price was increased by 20 percent did the offer "succeed in attracting tenders of more than 50% of the Units and, even then, only barely so." 2000 Del. Ch. LEXIS 17, at *63, 2000 WL 128875, at *18. Under these circumstances, the court observed, "[i]t is hard to take seriously a claim that plaintiff and others were 'coerced' into tendering" and asked the following two questions: "Can it be that a non-frivolous tender offer that fails to attract tenders is, nonetheless, actionably 'coercive?' If not, can that offer become actionably coercive simply by a 20% increase in its price term?" *Id.*

The court in *In re Life Technologies, Inc. Shareholders Litigation*, No. 16513 (Del. Ch. Nov. 24, 1998), held that a tender offer by a controlling shareholder, Dexter Corporation, for any and all shares of Life Technologies stock that Dexter did not already own, was not coercive because Dexter's tender offer materials stated "an intention, after completion of the tender offer, to engage in a second-step transaction in which it will acquire the remaining shares of Life Technologies for the same price and for the same consideration made in the tender offer." *Id.*, Tr. at 9-10. The court stated that the offer was "not a two-tiered offer" and that there was "no threat that Dexter will not engage in a back-end, or that the back-end will be at a lower value than the tender offer." *Id.* at 10. The court also pointed to the fact that Dexter's offer was conditioned upon the tender of a sufficient number of shares so that after the offer Dexter would own 80 percent of Life Technologies' shares, and that "[i]f anything" the 80 percent minimum condition made plaintiffs' coercion argument "less powerful" than otherwise might be the case because the 80 percent condition "creates less of an incentive for people to tender than they would have if there were no minimum condition, because it creates greater uncertainty about the ultimate success of the offer." *Id.* at 11.

The court acknowledged that Dexter had "not absolutely promised that it will promptly engage in a second-step offer, or second-step transaction, at the same price" and that Dexter had stated that "depending on the level of tenders, it may, before doing so, engage in open-market or privately-negotiated purchases in order to reach the 90 percent level" and that "if it reaches the 90 percent level, its intention is to engage in a short-form merger." *Id.* at 10. The court stated that a contention that a claim that a tender offer was coercive for this reason had been rejected in *In re Ocean Drilling & Exploration Co. Shareholders Litigation*, [1990-1991 Transfer Binder] Fed. Sec. L. Rep. (CCH) ¶ 95,898 (Del. Ch. Apr. 30, 1991), where the court described the absence of such an assurance in an offering circular as nothing more than a reflection of "basic business reality." *Id.* at 99,436.

The court distinguished *Kahn v. United States Sugar Corp.*, 11 Del. J. Corp. L. 908 (Del. Ch. Dec. 10, 1985), a case where the court found coercion because the corporation in that case, after its tender offer was completed, would have been "a substantially different and a substantially more highly leveraged corporation" than before the tender offer was made. Tr. at 11. Under those circumstances, the court in *Life Technologies* explained, "there was a threat that if there was no back-end merger . . . people would own shares in a very different and less valuable corporation." *Id.* This was not the case in the *Life Technologies* case, the court stated, because "Dexter is not placing any debt on Life Technologies in connection with this transaction." *Id.* To the contrary, "Dexter has stated that it has no plans to change the dividend policy and that it plans to continue the management of the business as before." *Id.* at 11-12.

Section E 1

Replace "15-90 (1998)" with "15–90-91 (2000)" in the Drexler citation in footnote 2403 on page 560.

Section E 1 a

Add the following at the end of the paragraph beginning on page 567 and concluding on page 568 (immediately after footnote 2452):

The court in *Metropolitan Life Insurance Co. v. Aramark Corp.*, 1998 Del. Ch. LEXIS 70 (Del. Ch. Feb. 5, 1998), granted a preliminary injunction enjoining a stock reclassification pursuant to which different shareholders – depending upon whether they were employees and, if so, their lines of work – were treated differently, with some shareholders cashed out and other shareholders not cashed out. The court held that directors may treat different shareholders differently so long as all shareholders are treated fairly. The court stated that while "there is some logic to simply applying the entire fairness requirement" in a stock reclassification case as is done in a cash-out merger case, "the prudent course is to assume that the business judgment presumption does apply." *Id.* at *3. The court found no disabling interest on the part of directors whose holdings were "not insignificant" but did not "constitute a material personal financial interest that would necessarily disable them from acting in what they in good faith perceive is the interest of the corporation as a whole." *Id.* at *4. The court found "a rational corporate purpose in pursuing a longstanding policy of increasing employee ownership and increasing incentives by that means and also by aligning some of the employees' stock ownership with the particular line of work they do." *Id.* at *5. The court also found that the corporation's directors "carefully evaluate[ed] this business plan." *Id.*

The court, however, preliminarily enjoined the stock reclassification plan because the directors applied a private company discount in assessing the value of shares. The court explained its view of this "core issue in the case" – "whether the private company discount is permitted" – as follows:

> [D]irectors have a fiduciary duty to treat all stockholders fairly. What does that mean where minority stockholders are being cashed out by some means other than merger, where the statutes provide appraisal rights? . . . I believe that the fiduciary duty in this situation was to pay stockholders who are cashed out the fair value of their stock as that term is defined in the appraisal cases and in the breach of fiduciary duty cases in merger transactions. . . .
>
> The purpose is to give cashed-out stockholders the substantial equivalent of their share of the value of the company as a going concern. That is inconsistent not only with a minority discount but also with a marketability discount. . . . There may be situations where a discount is proper when it affects the value of the assets of the company, but I do not believe it is proper when it affects the stock of the company.

Id. at *5-7. The court thus concluded that the plaintiffs had made "a strong showing that the price they would be receiving is not fair." *Id.* at *7. This showing, the court held "overcomes the business judgment rule presumption." *Id.* The court "realize[d] that the question of whether a private company discount is permissible has not been directly decided, and in a sense one could not fault the directors for making a mistake or a poor prediction on what the courts will rule. But I do not think that it follows that they are not bound to apply Delaware law, however careful they are and however much advice they get from various kinds of experts." *Id.* at *5. The court then turned to "an analysis under the entire fairness doctrine of fair process and fair price" and concluded that "if a private company discount, which was very substantial in this case, is illegal, the price wasn't fair, and if the price wasn't fair, it doesn't matter whether the process was fair." *Id.* at *7.

Section E 1 b

Replace the first paragraph beginning and concluding on page 570 (including footnotes 2463 through 2465) with the following:

Other New York courts, including *Schwartz v. Marien*, 37 N.Y.2d 487, 335 N.E.2d 334, 373 N.Y.S.2d 122 (1975), and *In re Direct Media/DMI, Inc.*, No. 112028/96 (N.Y. Sup. Ct. N.Y. Co. June 16, 1999), have held that directors "owe a fiduciary responsibility to the shareholders in general and to individual shareholders in particular to treat all shareholders fairly and evenly" but that "departure from precisely uniform treatment of stockholders may be justified where a bona fide business purpose indicates that the best interests of the corporation would be served by such departure." *Schwartz*, 37 N.Y.2d at 491-92, 335 N.E.2d at 337-38, 373 N.Y.S.2d at 127; *Direct Media*, slip op. at 5-6. "The burden of coming forward with proof of such justification shifts to the directors where . . . a prima facie case of unequal stockholder treatment is made out." *Schwartz*, 37 N.Y.2d at 492, 335 N.E.2d at 338, 373 N.Y.S.2d at 127. As stated by courts such as *Aronson v. Crane*, 145 A.D.2d 455, 535 N.Y.2d 417 (N.Y. App. Div. 2d Dep't 1988), and *Goodman v. 225 East 74th Apartments Corp.*, N.Y.L.J., Aug. 19, 1997, at 22 (N.Y. Sup. Ct. N.Y. Co. 1997), "[a] prima facie case of unequal stockholder treatment is made out where there is a departure from precisely uniform treatment of the stockholders and a resulting violation of [the directors'] fiduciary obligation to treat stockholders fairly and evenly." *Aronson*, 145 A.D.2d at 456, 535 N.Y.S.2d at 418, *quoted in Goodman*, N.Y.L.J., Aug. 19, 1997, at 22.

Section E 2

Add the following at the end of the paragraph beginning on page 570 and concluding on page 571 (immediately after footnote 2469):

As stated in *Elliott Associates, L.P. v. Avatex Corp.*, 715 A.2d 843 (Del. 1998): "Articulation of the rights of preferred stockholders is fundamentally the function of corporate drafters. . . . Any rights, preferences and limitations of preferred stock that distinguish that stock from common stock must be expressly and clearly stated. . . . [T]hese rights, preferences and limitations will not be presumed or implied." *Id.* at 852-53; *see also id.* at 853 n.46 ("Preferential rights are contractual in nature and therefore are governed by the express provisions of a company's certificate of incorporation. Stock preferences must also be clearly expressed and will not be presumed.") (quoting *Rothschild Int'l Corp. v. Liggett Group, Inc.*, 474 A.2d 133, 136 (Del. 1984)); *Mariner LDC v. Stone Container Corp.*, 729 A.2d 267, 278-79 (Del. Ch. 1998) (quoting *Avatex* and *Rothschild*). Significantly, however, while "rights and preferences of the preferred must be explicitly set forth in the certificate, a corporation "does have some obligation of fundamental fairness in carrying out its obligation to enable preferred stockholders to effectuate rights that are made explicit in the charter," and at least under certain circumstances rights and preferences may be "explicitly set forth with sufficient specificity to enable the Court to 'fill in' the manner in which those rights are to be enforced." *W. Fin. Co. v. Contour Energy Co.*, No. 17879, Tr. at 5, 8 (Del. Ch. May 19, 2000).

Replace "Nevertheless," in the first sentence (immediately after footnote 2469) of the paragraph beginning on page 571 and concluding on page 572 with the following:

Nevertheless, while "the rights of preferred shareholders are largely governed by contract law" and "directors do not owe preferred stockholders the broad fiduciary duties belonging to common stockholders," *RCG Int'l Investors, LDC v. Greka Energy Corp.*, 2000 Del. Ch. LEXIS 157, at *54, 2000 WL 1706728, at *16 (Del. Ch. Nov. 6, 2000),

Replace the Winston citations in footnotes 2484 through 2486 on page 574 with the following:

2482. 710 A.2d 835 (Del. Ch. 1997), *appeal dismissed*, 713 A.2d 932 (unpublished opinion, text available at 1998 Del. LEXIS 226 and 1998 WL 382624) (Del. June 11, 1998).

2485. *Id.* at 839 (footnotes omitted).

2486. *Id.* at 845 (footnotes omitted).

Replace the Winston citations in footnotes 2493 through 2494 on page 576 with the following:

2493. 710 A.2d at 845.

2494. *Id.* at 836, 845.

Add the following at the end of the paragraph beginning on page 577 and concluding on page 578 (immediately after footnote 2510):

The court in *Gale v. Bershad*, 1998 Del. Ch. LEXIS 37, 1998 WL 118022 (Del. Ch. Mar. 4, 1998), dismissed as "superfluous" a breach of fiduciary duty claim that was "substantially identical" to a breach of implied contract claim. 1998 Del. Ch. LEXIS 37, at *19, 22, 1998 WL 118022, at *5. The case involved a redemption of all outstanding shares of preferred stock of Axsys Technologies, Inc. at a price of $7.70 per share. A certificate of preferred stock provided that Axsys could redeem the preferred stock either for $8.00 per share or for 110 percent of "Fair Value Per Share" – a term defined in the certificate to require the board to calculate fair value "based on closing price data obtained from one of the public trading markets specified in the Certificate, unless the Axsys Preferred is not traded in any of those markets, in which case the Board may devise its own methodology to calculate Fair Value." 1998 Del. Ch. LEXIS 37, at *4-7, 1998 WL 118022, at *1-2. Prices for preferred stock were quoted on the OTC Bulletin Board, a trading service maintained under the auspices of the NASD, but Axsys' board determined that the OTC Bulletin Board did not qualify as one of the public trading markets specified in the certificate and thus the board was not obligated to calculate fair value based upon closing price data and could devise its own methodology. 1998 Del. Ch. LEXIS 37, at *8, 1998 WL 118022, at *2.

The court reasoned as follows with respect to whether the duty owed by the corporation's directors to the preferred shareholders under these circumstances was a contractual duty or a fiduciary duty:

> [T]he Court must determine whether Gale's claimed right to a fair valuation of the Preferred arises from the Certificate provision governing the terms of the Preferred, or whether it is a right or obligation created not by virtue of any preference, and is shared equally with the Common. In this case, the claimed right to a good faith calculation of Fair Value arises from the Certificate's contractual promise that holders of Preferred shall receive "fair value" for their redeemed shares. That claim is one for a breach of the implied covenant, for which the remedy would be the difference in value between the Board's improper calculation of Fair Value and the value as adjudicated by this Court.
>
> The function of the implied covenant of good faith and fair dealing in defining the duties of parties to a contract, is analogous to the role of fiduciary law in defining the duties owed by fiduciaries. An important difference, however, is that the implied covenant specifically protects the Preferred share-

> holders' expectation that the Axsys Board will properly perform their contractual obligations under the Certificate. To allow a fiduciary duty claim to coexist in parallel with an implied contractual claim, would undermine the primacy of contract law over fiduciary law in matters involving the essentially contractual rights and obligations of preferred stockholders.

1998 Del. Ch. LEXIS 37, at *20-22, 1998 WL 118022, at *5. "Stated differently," the court concluded, "because the contract claim addresses the alleged wrongdoing by the Board, any fiduciary duty claim arising out of the same conduct is superfluous. For that reason, the Court will dismiss Gale's fiduciary claim." 1998 Del. Ch. LEXIS 37, at *22, 1998 WL 118022, at *5.

Accordingly, where a certificate provision addresses a particular benefit of a particular class of stockholders, "a board's alleged evasion or breach of a charter provision for the benefit of a particular class of stockholders could be asserted only as a contract claim, not as a claim for breach of fiduciary duty." *In re Gen. Motors Class H S'holders Litig.*, 734 A.2d 611, 619 (Del. Ch. 1999).

Add the following at the end of footnote 2496 on page 576:

See also Continental Ins. Co. v. Rutledge & Co., 750 A.2d 1219, 1234 (Del. Ch. 2000):

> The implied covenant of good faith "requires a party in a contractual relationship to refrain from arbitrary or unreasonable conduct which has the effect of preventing the other party to the contract from receiving the fruits of the contract." This doctrine emphasizes "faithfulness to an agreed common purpose and consistency with the justified expectations of the other party." The parties' reasonable expectations at the time of contract formation determine the reasonableness of the challenged conduct. I note that cases invoking the implied covenant of good faith and fair dealing should be rare and fact-intensive. Only where issues of compelling fairness arise will this Court embrace good faith and fair dealing and imply terms in an agreement.

Add the following at the end of the third sentence (immediately after footnote 2514) of the paragraph beginning on page 578 and concluding on page 579:

The court in *In re FLS Holdings, Inc. Shareholder Litigation*, 19 Del. J. Corp. L. 270 (Del. Ch. Apr. 2, 1993), *aff'd sub nom. Sullivan Money Management, Inc. v. FLS Holdings, Inc.*, 628 A.2d 84 (unpublished opinion, text available at 1993 Del. LEXIS 251 and 1993 WL 245341) (Del. June 18, 1993), rejected a proposed settlement after finding that "the absence of an independent agent negotiating on behalf of the preferred stockholders and the presence of only the 'relatively weak' procedural protection of an investment banker's *ex post* opinion that the allocation was fair . . . created a substantial issue that was fairly litigable." *Jackson Nat'l Life Ins. Co. v. Kennedy*, 741 A.2d 377, 391 (Del. Ch. 1999).

Add the following at the end of the paragraph beginning on page 578 and concluding on page 579 (immediately after footnote 2517):

The court in *Jackson National Life Insurance Co. v. Kennedy,* 741 A.2d 377 (Del. Ch. 1999), repeated these principles as follows:

> The rights of preferred stockholders are in many respects both equitable and contractual. The relationship between a corporation and its preferred stockholders is "primarily . . . contractual in nature," involving "rights and obligations created contractually by the certificate of designation." [quoting *HB Korenvaes Investments, L.P. v. Marriott Corp.*, [1993 Transfer Binder] Fed. Sec. L. Rep. (CCH) ¶ 97,728, at 97,442 (Del. Ch. June 9, 1993).] On the other hand, fiduciary duties as well may be owed to preferred stockholders in limited circumstances. A corporation's directors "are fiduciaries for the preferred stockholders, whose interests they have a duty to safeguard, consistent with the fiduciary duties owed by those directors to [the corporation's] other shareholders and to [the corporation] itself." [quoting *Eisenberg v. Chicago Milwaukee Corp.*, 537 A.2d 1051, 1062 (Del. Ch. 1987).] Whether a given claim asserted by preferred stockholders is governed by contract or fiduciary duty principles, then, depends on whether the dispute

> arises from rights and obligations created by contract or from "a right or obligation that is not by virtue of a preference but is shared equally with the common." [quoting *Moore Bus. Forms, Inc. v. Cordant Holdings Corp.*, 21 Del. J. Corp. L. 279, 289 (Del. Ch. Nov. 2, 1995).]

741 A.2d at 386-87. "[O]ne such right shared equally between the common and preferred stockholders," the court continued, is the duty of loyalty. *Id.* at 387. The court cited *Jedwab v. MGM Grand Hotels, Inc.*, 509 A.2d 584 (Del. Ch. 1986), for the proposition that directors must "' . . . distinguish between 'preferential' rights (and special limitations) on the one hand and rights associated with all stock on the other'" and pointed to the recognition in *Jedwab* that a preferred shareholder's claim "to a fair allocation of the merger proceeds 'fairly implicate fiduciary duties and ought not be evaluated wholly from the point of view of the contractual terms of the preferred stock designations.'" 741 A.2d at 387 (quoting *Jedwab*, 509 A.2d at 93-94).

The court in *Jackson National* applied these principles to a claim by preferred shareholders that the proceeds of a sale of assets were unfairly allocated. *Id.* at 387. The court denied a motion to dismiss based upon allegations that the corporation had one director, this director "received millions of dollars in cash and other benefits" while the corporation "was stripped of its assets," preferred shareholders were "left holding preferred stock rendered worthless in a corporate shell," and "the disputed transaction lacked procedural safeguards to establish its fairness to the preferred stockholders." *Id.* at 384, 391.

Quadrangle Offshore (Cayman) LLC v. Kenetech Corp., 1999 Del. Ch. LEXIS 213, 1999 WL 893575 (Del. Ch. Oct. 13, 1999), *aff'd*, 751 A.2d 878 (unpublished opinion, text available at 2000 Del. LEXIS 147 and 2000 WL 431608) (Del. Apr. 4, 2000), involved a corporation, Kenetech Corporation, that defaulted on interest payments on senior notes. As a result, the holders of these notes had a right to place Kenetech in bankruptcy and nullify the value of Kenetech's common stock. Kenetech's directors, hoping to retain some value for common shareholders, convinced the noteholders to refrain from filing an involuntary bankruptcy petition. 1999 Del. Ch. LEXIS 213, at *24, 1999 WL 893575, at *8. At the same time, preferred shareholders held securities called Preferred Redeemable Increased Dividend Equity Securities ("PRIDES") that had a right to a liquidation preference that placed them "in an economically antagonistic relationship with the common." 1999 Del. Ch. LEXIS 213, at *26, 1999 WL 893575, at *8.

The court stated that "[i]t is oft noted that a preferred shareholder's rights are those specified in the certificate of designation, but existing precedent also supports the proposition that in so far as their interests are harmonious, preferred shareholders share with common shareholders the right to demand loyalty and care from the fiduciaries entrusted with managing the corporation." 1999 Del. Ch. LEXIS 213, at *24-25, 1999 WL 893575, at *8. Here, the court stated, the interests of the holders of common stock and PRIDES were "economically antagonistic," so any liquidation rights enjoyed by the PRIDES shareholders that were preferential to those of common shareholders "must be spelled out in the Certificate." 1999 Del. Ch. LEXIS 213, at *26, 1999 WL 893575, at *8.

The court then held that Kenetech's actions to retain some value for common shareholders while raising funds for noteholders did not constitute a "'liquidation' as that term is used in the Certificate," that the PRIDES shareholders were not entitled to the liquidation preference provided for in the certificate, and that Kenetech had not "delayed a decision to liquidate in bad faith in order to frustrate the liquidation preference." 1999 Del. Ch. LEXIS 213, at *27-45, 1999 WL 893575, at *8-13. The court concluded as follows:

> This is a case where the board's strategic possibilities were restricted by the need to raise funds for the Senior Note holders. By engaging in raising capital and cost cutting activities that involved selling assets, laying off workers, and canceling new projects, Kenetech performed tasks that fall within activities commonly associated with a liquidation. But, those tasks were otherwise within the bounds of the board's authority and can be plausibly explained as an attempt to pay

> off the note holders and avoid the consequences of an involuntary liquidation.
>
> The PRIDES liquidation preference was contingent upon either a third party such as the Senior Note holders forcing Kenetech into liquidation or upon the Kenetech board approving a voluntary liquidation with shareholder approval. Neither happened. To allow Quadrangle to prevail on its claim would be to allow the PRIDES holders to usurp the decision making process contractually delegated to either third parties (such as the note holders) or the board (with shareholder approval). That would create a new right for the preferred not present in the Certificate. Plaintiffs' claim, therefore, had to be analyzed as one for breach of an implied covenant of good faith and fair dealing. Because Quadrangle's evidence of a *de facto* or constructive liquidation was equally consistent with a reasonable plan to pay off Senior Note holders and preserve equity in the corporation and because Quadrangle failed to produce convincing evidence of bad faith on the board's part, I cannot conclude that Kenetech breached the Certificate's implied covenant of good faith and fair dealing.

1999 Del. Ch. LEXIS 213, at *45-46, 1999 WL 893575, at *13.

The Delaware Supreme Court affirmed, stating the following: "[T]o the extent that (a) the issues raised on appeal are factual, the record evidence supports the trial judge's factual findings; and (b) the issues raised on appeal are legal, they are controlled by settled Delaware law, which was properly applied." *Quadrangle Offshore (Cayman) LLV v. Kenetech Corp.*, 751 A.2d 878 (unpublished opinion, text available at 2000 Del. Ch. LEXIS 147 and 2000 WL 431608) (Del. Apr. 4, 2000); *see also Kohls v. Kenetech Corp.*, 2000 Del. Ch. LEXIS 102, at *17-24, 2000 WL 1041220, at *5-6 (Del. Ch. July 26, 2000) (subsequent decision dismissing action by other preferred shareholders who "fail[ed] to distinguish their claims, either factually or legally, from those adjudicated . . . in *Quadrangle*").

Add the following at the end of the second paragraph beginning and concluding on page 581 (immediately after footnote 2533):

As stated in Continental *Insurance Co. v. Rutledge & Co.*, 750 A.2d 1219, 1235 & n.37 (Del. Ch. 2000) (citations omitted):

> This dispute highlights a defining tension between contract principles and fiduciary duties. In the limited partnership context, Delaware law resolves this conflict in favor of contract law, rendering fiduciary duties default rules. Consequently, parties to a limited partnership can enter into a contract which diminishes the general partner's fiduciary duties. In order to absolve the general partner from his duties of loyalty or care, the general partner and limited partners must make their intentions plain. Typically, parties place an explicit clause in the limited partnership agreement to that effect. Where a contract clause amends the fiduciary duties a general partner owes the limited partners, a court will give full force to the terms of the contract.
>
> Many opt for the limited partnership form in Delaware precisely in order to embrace this flexibility. Commentators considering the subject agree that limited partnerships' contract theory based structure provides incentives for parties to opt for the limited partnership over other forms of business organizations. As such, parties, otherwise unwilling to shoulder fiduciary burdens, maintain the opportunity to form limited partnerships precisely because the parties can contract around some or all of the fiduciary duties the general partner typically owes the limited partners.

Section E 4

Add the following new Section E 4 at the end of the paragraph beginning on page 589 and concluding on page 590 (immediately after footnote 2579):

4. Tracking Stock Issues

A tracking stock typically is a class of common stock that is tied to and that derives its value from particular corporate operations. Tracking stock thus is an equity instrument "characterized by a peculiar separation between the economic interest it represents and the basic governance and control over the underlying assets." *Solomon v. Armstrong*, 747 A.2d 1098, 1111 (Del. Ch. 1999), *aff'd*, 746 A.2d 277 (unpublished opinion, full text available at 2000 Del. LEXIS 30 and 2000 WL 140072) (Del. Jan. 26, 2000).

The courts in *Solomon v. Armstrong*, 747 A.2d 1098 (Del. Ch. 1999), *aff'd*, 746 A.2d 277 (unpublished opinion, full text available at 2000 Del. LEXIS 30 and 2000 WL 140072) (Del. Jan. 26, 2000), and *In re GM Class H Shareholder Litigation*, 734 A.2d 611 (Del. Ch. 1999), addressed issues arising out of a tracking stock capital structure adopted by General Motors Corporation involving three classes of GM common stock: GM \$1 2/3 common stock, Class E common stock and Class H common stock. Dividends payable to holders of GM \$1 2/3 common stock were based on GM's total income, dividends payable to holders of Class E common stock were based upon the income of one wholly-owned subsidiary of GM, Electronics Data Systems Holding Corporation ("EDS"), and dividends payable to holders of Class H common stock were based upon the income of another wholly-owned subsidiary of GM, Hughes Electronics Corporation. *Solomon*, 747 A.2d at 1106; *GM Class H*, 734 A.2d at 613-14.

As discussed below, the *Solomon* case involved a split-off in 1996 by GM of EDS to holders of Class E stock and the elimination of Class E stock. The *GM Class H* case involved a series of transactions in 1997 that split up Hughes and recapitalized Class H stock into a new Class H stock. In both cases, board decisions were made subject to the approval of shareholders voting by class. *See* Chapter II, Sections E 4 a and b.

a. The GM Class E Decision. Solomon v. Armstrong, 747 A.2d 1098 (Del. Ch. 1999), *aff'd*, 746 A.2d 277 (unpublished opinion, full text available at 2000 Del. LEXIS 30 and 2000 WL 140072) (Del. Jan. 26, 2000), involved a split-off by GM of its wholly-owned EDS subsidiary to holders of GM Class E stock. At the same time that GM's board announced its plan to pursue the split-off, GM's board also announced its intention that the transaction be tax free and the board's view that a split-off transaction would not serve the best interests of GM and its shareholders if the transaction triggered a provision in GM's certificate of incorporation that entitled Class E shareholders to receive GM $1 2/3 stock equal in value to 120 percent of the value of the Class E stock in the event of a recapitalization, sale, transfer, assignment or other disposition of EDS to any entity to which GM was not a majority owner. *Id.* at 1106. GM's Capital Stock Committee, a committee of GM's board that consisted solely of independent directors whose role was to oversee all matters affected by potential divergences of interests between GM's three classes of common stock – GM $1 2/3 stock, Class E stock and Class H stock – was charged with charting a course for the split-off. *Id.* at 1106-07, 1122.

The Capital Stock Committee proceeded by establishing two management teams to negotiate the terms and conditions of the split-off: a "GM team" consisting of GM officers (two of whom also served as EDS directors) and an "EDS team" consisting of EDS officers. The GM team was responsible for negotiating on behalf of the holders of GM $1 2/3 stock and Class H stock, was authorized to utilize the GM legal and financial staffs, and engaged outside counsel and an outside financial advisor. The EDS team was responsible for negotiating on behalf of the holders of Class E stock, was authorized to utilize the EDS legal and financial staffs, and engaged outside counsel and outside financial advisors. *Id.* at 1107.

Negotiations commenced between the GM and EDS teams on various issues and focused upon changes to existing information technology ("IT") agreements between GM and EDS. The EDS team took the position that no material changes were needed to the existing IT agreements other than those necessitated by the fact that GM and EDS were to become completely independent companies. *Id.* The GM team took the position that the existing IT agreements had to be renegotiated to provide GM improved rates. *Id.*

The two sides maintained their opposing positions, and the Capital Stock Committee determined that the negotiating teams needed "guidance" and recommended that the GM board promulgate a series of guidelines including, among others, that "GM should take over from EDS the principal role of developing and supervising GM's IT strategy and programs, and that the new IT service agreements should provide GM with greater ability to test the competitiveness of the terms of any GM-EDS contract." *Id.* at 1107-08. GM's board approved the Capital Stock Committee's guidelines. *Id.*

Negotiations progressed for three more months and the parties ultimately reached agreement upon a transaction providing for (1) a merger of a wholly-owned subsidiary of EDS into GM, with each share of Class E stock converted into one share of EDS stock, and with GM's certificate of incorporation amended to delete all provisions regarding Class E stock, including the 120 percent recapitalization provision, (2) new information technology service agreements including a new master services agreement (the "MSA") between GM and EDS, and (3) a $500 million cash payment by EDS to GM. *Id.* at 1115.

The two teams recommended the agreed upon terms of the split-off to the Capital Stock Committee, which determined that the transaction "was in the best interests of, and fair to, GM and each class of GM stock." *Id.* at 1108-09. The Capital Stock Committee then recommended the transaction to GM's board, and GM's board approved the split-off "subject to the approval of a majority of the holders of each of: 1) the GM 1-2/3 common stock, voting separately as a class; 2) the GM Class E common stock, voting separately as a class; and 3) all classes of GM common stock, voting together." *Id.* at 1109. GM and EDS disseminated a consent solicitation to shareholders and obtained the necessary consents and consummated the split-off. *Id.*

The court held that plaintiffs' complaint failed to allege facts that, if true, would rebut the presumption of the business judgment rule and granted a motion to dismiss the complaint. The court focused upon three sets of arguments by plaintiffs: claims based upon traditional business judgment rule principles, plaintiffs' analogy of the transaction to a freeze-out merger, and the effect of EDS's status as a wholly-owned subsidiary of GM.

Traditional Business Judgment Rule Principles. The court explained that eleven of the thirteen GM directors who approved and recommended the split-off were non-employee, non-management outside directors and that plaintiffs did not allege that any of these outside directors were "dominated or otherwise beholden to any individual financially interested in the split-off." *Id.* at 1117. The court also stated that plaintiffs did not allege facts demonstrating that the board did not act with due care. *Id.* Instead, "plaintiffs' "primary attack" on GM's outside directors was a claim that "because most, if not all, of the outside directors held a disproportionate number of shares of GM 1-2/3 common stock, they had a *personal* financial interest in the split-off and therefore could not consider the terms of the split-off impartially." *Id.* The court rejected this claim on two grounds.

First, the court held, "[d]irectors must often resolve conflicts among classes of stock, and the fact that a majority of the directors own more of one class than another does not necessarily implicate the directors' good faith or loyalty." *Id.* at 1118. The court pointed to "the broad legal proposition that allocation of value between and among classes of shareholders is generally considered a business judgment," and described the following reasoning in *Freedman v. Restaurant Associates Industries, Inc.*, [1987-1988 Transfer Binder] Fed. Sec. L. Rep. (CCH) ¶ 93,502 (Del. Ch. Oct. 16, 1987), as "instructive" on this subject:

> It is easy to say that a director's duty runs to the corporation and all of its shareholders, but such a statement gives faint guidance to a director when conflicts among shareholder constituencies arise, as they do. For example, when merger considerations must be apportioned between Class A and Class B

> stock directors are inevitably faced with a conflict among classes of stock and, in most such instances, such directors will themselves own more of one class than another. Does such fact alone deprive such directors of the presumptions ordinarily accorded to their good faith decisions and require them to establish the intrinsic fairness of the apportionment? And, if so, do different directors have different burdens depending upon which class of stock they happen to own more of[?] It is not my impression that this is the law.

747 A.2d at 1118 n.63, 1120 (quoting [1997-1988 Transfer Binder] Fed. Sec. Rep. (CCH) ¶ 93,502, at 97,221). The court accordingly was persuaded by defendants' contention that "Delaware courts consistently apply the business judgment rule to protect directors' business judgment, *even* when the directors making the decision have financial interests as shareholders that are opposed to the interests of one or more groups of other shareholders." *Id.* at 1117; *see also* Chapter I, Section D 2 g above (discussing additional cases).

Second, the court held, "it is well established that when a party challenges a director's action based on a claim of the director's debilitating pecuniary self-interest, that party must allege that the director's interest is material to that director." *Id.* at 1118; *see also* Chapter I, Section D 2 c (discussing cases). It therefore "is not enough for plaintiffs to plead that the outside directors held a disproportionate number of shares of GM 1-2/3 common stock. . . . [P]laintiffs must also plead that the GM director defendants held these shares in amounts that were *material* to them." *Id.* at 1117. Thus, as the court stated with respect to the GM board's Capital Stock Committee, "[a]lthough plaintiffs allege that the members of the Capital Stock Committee owned disparate holdings of Class E stock compared to the other classes, thereby implicating their personal interests, those breach of loyalty claims fail as a matter of law because plaintiffs do not allege the materiality of the holdings with reference to those particular directors." *Id.* at 1110.

The court also rejected a challenge to the GM board's loyalty based upon claims that "various factors detrimentally affected the process the board set for negotiation of the substantive terms" and "loaded the process against the Class E stockholders." *Id.* at 1118. As an example, plaintiffs alleged, "at one point during the split-off negotiations GM began to pressure the EDS team with unrelated threats, including withholding certain disputed payments under pre-existing contracts and withholding consideration of post-merger anti-takeover provisions until after negotiations progressed." *Id.* According to the court, plaintiffs did not allege that the contract disputes were "explicitly linked" to the terms of the split-off or that "the amounts in dispute were material such that non-payment might have been perceived as an implicit threat," and there was "no basis for an inference that the GM board's delay in considering post-merger anti-takeover provisions had the intent, actual effect, or even the potential of strong-arming the EDS team into settling on better terms for GM's continuing shareholders." *Id.* To the contrary, the court stated, GM's board did not object to the anti-takeover provisions EDS proposed for inclusion in EDS's post-split-off certificate of incorporation; GM's board simply waited to authorize these provisions until an agreement in principle was reached on the material terms of the split-off. *Id.* at 1108 n.13, 1118.

The court also rejected plaintiffs' reliance upon a claim that the EDS team's financial advisors, Lehman Brothers, Inc. and Morgan Stanley & Co., were chosen by GM rather than the EDS team and were beholden to GM because GM paid their fees and "would earn $6.5 million of their $7.5 million fee only upon the consummation of the split-off." *Id.* at 1117. The court held that this fee structure did not form a sufficient basis for an inference that these advisors "were willing to opine, or lean toward, better terms for GM during the negotiation of the transaction." *Id.* The court explained that GM's board "independently decided that the split-off was in the best interest of the corporation – the advisors were simply employed to aid the directors (at least indirectly through the use of the negotiating teams) in obtaining all reasonably available information and to better estimate the value attributable to each of the GM operations." *Id.* at 1119. The court pointed to the absence of allegations apart from the fee structure that these financial advisors "erred in their underlying analyses or misled the board or its agents." *Id.* The court stated that "[n]o basis exists for *assuming* wrongdoing on the banks' part (and by implication the board's part) without allegations of an actual manifestation of bias in favor of GM through the investment banks' manipulation of financial information." *Id.*

The court also rejected a challenge to the board's loyalty based upon allegations that "some members of the EDS team had an interest in assuring their continued employment by EDS following the split-off" and "wanted EDS to be split off so that they could operate independently of GM management to control the newly split-off corporation and set their own compensation." *Id.* Plaintiffs alleged that for these reasons these members of the EDS team were "prone to holding the continuing GM shareholders' interests above the Class E stockholders' interests." *Id.* The court questioned plaintiffs' assumption that the EDS team's motivation was "to gain independence and greater influence over their compensation" because "it is unrealistic to imagine that the EDS team could hijack the entire EDS governance structure for its own benefit following the split-off." *Id.* at 1120 n.66.

Even accepting this assumption, the court continued, "it still does not follow" that the EDS team "would subordinate Class E stockholders' interests." *Id.* at 1119. The court pointed to three reasons in support of this conclusion. First, "nothing in the complaint" suggested that the EDS team "had anything to do with the decision to commence the split-off in the first place." *Id.* Instead, the EDS team "only entered the picture at the point where the details of the substantive terms were negotiated." *Id.* Second, "plaintiffs' contention runs contrary to reason" because "[i]f the EDS team members were indeed consumed by self-interest, as plaintiffs allege, the only reasonable inference is that they would do whatever they could to ensure that the company they were soon to inherit had as many assets and resources as possible." *Id.* Third, "all of the terms of the post-split-off incentive plan for EDS management and employees were fully disclosed in the Consent Solicitation" and "Class E stockholders (along with all other classes) specifically approved of the amended EDS incentive plan apart from the split-off transaction." *Id.* at 1119-20. "Thus, most – if not all – of plaintiffs' fears were specifically addressed by a fully-informed shareholder vote." *Id.*

Plaintiffs' Freeze-Out Merger Analogy. Plaintiffs also contended that the business judgment rule did not protect GM's split-off of EDS because, according to plaintiffs, Class E shareholders were "akin to minority shareholders of a less-than-wholly-owned subsidiary who are essentially being frozen out of their continuing interest in the corporation." *Id.* at 1120 & n.69. The court rejected this contention as a conceptualization that "could too easily deprive the board of business judgment protection in a situation where the business judgment rule's presumptions seem appropriate." *Id.* at 1123. The court reasoned as follows.

First, the court pointed to the backdrop created by the case law discussed above holding that "value allocation decisions by boards are generally protected by the business judgment rule" and the fact that "Delaware courts consistently apply the business judgment rule to protect directors' business judgment, *even* when the directors making the decision have financial interests as shareholders that are opposed to the interests of one or more groups of other shareholders." *Id.* at 1120.

Second, the court described "the form and structure" of GM's split-off of EDS as "radically different from a parent-subsidiary freeze-out merger or any other transaction with a controlling shareholder," where "our law imposes heightened fiduciary duties on the parent corporation." *Id.* at 1123. The court explained that the "pivotal factor that distinguishes plaintiffs from minority shareholders in a less-than-wholly-owned subsidiary who are 'frozen out' of their continuing interest in a corporation is that in a classic freeze-out the minority shareholders have no choice"; rather, "by virtue of its majority control, the parent corporation can force the transaction through without the consent of the minority." *Id.* at 1120. The court pointed to the potential for coercion in a transaction involving a controlling shareholder: "The theory is that minority shareholders may vote in favor of a transaction notwithstanding their actual belief that they deserve a better deal for fear of retaliation of some kind. 'For example, the controlling stockholder might decide to stop dividend payments or to effect a . . . merger at a less favorable price, for which the remedy would be time consuming and costly litigation.'" *Id.* (quoting *Citron v. E.I. DuPont de Nemours & Co.*, 584 A.2d 490, 502 (Del. Ch. 1990)).

Here, the court concluded, there was "no basis to justify such fears" because "the GM board did *not* have the power to unilaterally effectuate a freeze-out merger on its own terms" or "retaliate against the Class E stockholders if they rejected the proposed transaction." *Id.* The court pointed to (1) certificate of incorporation provisions that protected the interests of Class E shareholders by imposing contractual limitations on the GM board's power, and (2) "independent oversight for the resolution of conflicting interests" between GM's multiple classes of common stock created by the Capital Stock Committee of GM's board. *Id.* at 1123.

With respect to GM's certificate of incorporation, the court explained that the certificate required "independent class approval on any amendment which adversely affects" the "rights, powers, or privileges as embodied in the certificate" of Class E shareholders and that the split-off transaction was conditioned on a vote by the Class E shareholders. *Id.* at 1121. "Thus, Class E stockholders effectively held a veto power as a class if they did not approve of the terms of the proposed split-off or any subsequent alternative transaction." *Id.* The court stated that "[m]ore that any other factor, this detail – by itself – sufficiently distinguishes the present case from a classic freeze-out merger." *Id.*; *see also id.* at 1123 ("without first seeking the Class E stockholders' authorization to modify the terms or altogether delete" the 120 percent recapitalization provision, there was "no way the board could set the terms of any deal that could freeze out Class E stockholders without their consent").

The court also pointed to limitations in GM's certificate of incorporation upon the GM board's discretion to declare and pay dividends. According to the court, GM's certificate "restricted the board's power to declare and pay dividends on any one of the three classes of common stock to certain preformulated amounts that were attributed to each separate class of common stock and based on GM's legally available retained earnings." *Id.* at 1121. "Thus, while the board had the discretion to pay no dividends at all, to the extent that dividends were paid to any one class, the certificate's restrictions served to preserve each class's interest in retained earnings relative to the other two classes." *Id.*

These limitations in GM's certificate of incorporation, the court stated, protected Class E shareholders against "retaliatory dividend policies against a hypothetical dissenting class." *Id.* The court stated that "[i]t would be fantastic to imagine that Class E stockholders would be in any way coerced or even fearful of the potential that GM's board (overwhelmingly comprised of outside independent directors) would take the chance of alienating each and every class of stock by restricting all dividends just to punish dissenting Class E shareholders." *Id.* at 1121-22. The court acknowledged the "theoretical" possibility that GM's board "could continue to declare and pay dividends to the other classes according to relative share (as set by the pre-determined formulas) but keep the Class E stockholders' share in retained earnings, i.e., delay or deny future dividend distributions only to Class E stockholders." *Id.* at 1122. The court, however, "decline[d] to entertain such transparent hypothetical abuses and the hypothetical fear of retribution and coercion they might induce" due to the absence of any "cognizable basis . . . for even an inference of lack of due loyalty, lack of due care, or bad faith on behalf of the GM board." *Id.*

With respect to GM's Capital Stock Committee, the court stated that this board committee was maintained pursuant to GM's certificate and was comprised entirely of independent directors whose role was "to oversee all matters affected by potential divergences of interests between any of the three classes including, among other things, all inter-company and dividend policies." *Id.* This committee, the court stated, had "responsibility for structuring fair processes and dealings among the various competing interests" and thus "provided an entirely independent review of the full board's policies and had the primary responsibility for recommending solutions to resolve conflicts." *Id.* The court stated that "[n]othing in the complaint gives rise to a reasonable inference that this committee failed to operate independently, failed to execute its role with due care, or failed to execute its oversight and conflict resolution functions in good faith." *Id.*

The Effect of EDS's Status as a Wholly-Owned Subsidiary of GM. The court also pointed to the principle that "in a parent and wholly-owned subsidiary context, the directors of the subsidiary are obligated only to manage the affairs of the subsidiary in the best interest of the parent and its shareholders." *Id.* at 1123 (quoting *Anadarko Petroleum Corp. v. Panhandle E. Corp.*, 545 A.2d 1171, 1174 (Del. 1988)). Accordingly, "if GM's board acted in a way that reasonably aimed to maximize shareholders' interests, then the business judgment rule should apply irrespective of the precise effects on the EDS operations." *Id.*

The court stated that in determining whether GM's board acted in all of the various classes' best interests, there are two legally relevant questions: "First, was the process for allocating value reasonably aimed at providing a fair result to all shareholders taken together and each and every class of shareholders taken separately? Second, even to the extent that aspects of the process may have been flawed, were all shareholders sufficiently informed about the details of the process and empowered to make an independent decision on the substantive terms of the transaction?" *Id.* at 1123-24. The court stated that "[i]f *either* question is answered in the affirmative the business judgment rule's presumptions must remain in effect." *Id.* at 1124.

With respect to the reasonableness of the process, the court held that the GM board's actions "fit squarely under business judgment rule protection." *Id.* at 1127. The court stated that "where a board's task is to allocate value between two classes of stock," Delaware law does not require the board "to set up an exacting process that actually replicates an arm's-length transaction between shareholders." *Id.* at 1124. The court explained that an "arm's-length negotiation happens when a soon-to-be-subsidiary tracking stock company is first merged into another company," and that "[d]uring that process negotiators for the prospective subsidiary can anticipate future conflicts of interest and draft appropriate provisions to deal with them under the certificate of incorporation." *Id.* The court described this as "clearly a more efficient method of coping with potential divergences of interest between shareholder groups than having courts adapt procedural mechanisms (e.g., special committees, burden shifts, etc.) that are unnecessary or poorly adapted to new contexts." *Id.* Here, the court stated, the negotiations that occurred when the Class E stock was created resulted in certificate of incorporation provisions that provided "powerful procedural protections for all classes of stock." *Id.* Under these circumstances, the court concluded, it was "inappropriate for a court to impose unhelpful requirements in the name of common law fiduciary duties." *Id.*

The court then turned to the question whether the process provided for in GM's certificate of incorporation had operated as intended. The court defined the question to be decided on a motion to dismiss to be "whether plaintiffs have alleged facts from which it might be inferred that the directors or their agents did not follow the certificate's provisions: 1) in good faith; 2) employing a rational (i.e., non-arbitrary) basis for making the allocation; 3) on a reasonably informed basis (i.e., with due care); or 4) in the shareholders' interests, as opposed to the directors' or anyone else's personal profit or betterment, (i.e., that they acted with due loyalty)." *Id.* at 1124-25. The court stated that "[i]f no basis exists for such an inference, then the business judgment rule should protect the board's allocation determination." *Id.* at 1125.

Here, the court concluded, plaintiffs did not allege facts permitting the court to infer that GM's directors did not follow any provisions in GM's certificate of incorporation. The court explained that GM's board, through its Capital Stock Committee, attempted to resolve the questions raised by the process of splitting GM into two separate companies, one of which would be an independent EDS, by creating negotiating teams and "trying to approximate an arm's length transaction." *Id.* at 1125. These questions included "precisely who owned what, which corporation should maintain control over which business decisions, and to what extent was a wealth transfer necessary in order to ensure that each corporation received value in exchange for rights that it had previously enjoyed." *Id.* The court stated that "[i]n most respects the GM board and the Capital Stock Committee went about this task the right way: 1) the negotiations persisted for quite some time; 2) the two teams seemed to come close to impasse before the GM board stepped in; 3) all of the relevant groups retained highly reputable legal counsel; and 4) disclosure of the events surrounding the transaction appears to have been thorough." *Id.*

While there were "a few details" that gave the court "reason to pause," the court held that these details did "not compromise the application of the business judgment rule." *Id.* The court pointed to the following four guidelines given by the Capital Stock Committee (with the board's approval) to the negotiating teams after the teams reached a deadlock concerning the substantive teams of the transaction:

> (i) an appropriate, long-term IT supply contract should be developed for the proposed split-off to achieve the respective business goals of GM and EDS; (ii) the terms of any such contract should take into account and further the legitimate interests and expectations of all GM stockholders; (iii) GM should resume the principal role in developing and supervising its IT strategy and programs, while still drawing on EDS's

> expertise; and (iv) since following any split-off the Capital Stock Committee would no longer be able to review the terms on which EDS provides IT services to GM and would therefore have to rely on contractual protections, the IT Services Agreements should provide GM with greater ability to test the competitiveness of the terms of which EDS would provide such services to GM, including through the opportunity to competitively bid limited portions of GM's IT service needs and to award such bids to suppliers other than EDS when appropriate.

Id. at 1125-26. The court stated that the third and the fourth directives "are clearly statements that push the negotiating teams towards discussions aimed at furthering GM's, and not EDS's, corporate policies." *Id.* at 1126. Accordingly, "[t]he communication of these guidelines, while not conclusive, is a reasonable basis for an inference of lack of arm's-length negotiations" because in "unrelated party arm's-length negotiations, there is simply no entity with overriding authority to dictate terms that benefit one side over the other." *Id.*

The court concluded, however, that "while the GM board may have dictated certain items, to the extent that those terms represented a transfer of value from EDS to GM, the effects of that transfer could be balanced by the remaining issues." *Id.* The court explained that the items underlying these guidelines "were not the only items on the negotiation table between the two teams" because "the two most substantive issues" to be resolved by the two teams – the new terms of the MSA and the amount of a payment by EDS to GM – were not yet settled. *Id.* The court also stated that there was "no indication" that GM's board "acted in bad faith, arbitrarily, carelessly, or selfishly" in dictating the terms that were dictated. *Id.* To the contrary, the court concluded, "it seems perfectly reasonable for the GM board to decide that the GM corporation should be in charge of its own IT systems and that, absent the Capital Stock Committee's oversight powers, there should be some new fairness mechanism to regulate the working relationship between EDS and GM after the split-off." *Id.* at 1127.

The court also rejected plaintiffs' contention that in "dictating" terms "the GM board was motivated by an improper personal self-interest in that the directors sought to procure better terms for continuing GM shareholders because they would continue to serve those shareholders after the transaction." *Id.* at 1126. The court described "the nexus between the theoretical benefit that the GM directors might achieve for the continuing shareholders and the directors' theoretically related entrenchment motivation" as "simply too tenuous." *Id.* at 1127. The court reasoned that "[i]n most circumstances Delaware law routinely rejects the notion that a director's interest in maintaining his office, by itself, is a debilitating factor." *Id.* at 1126. "Even in the more extreme situation where directors allegedly engage in defensive actions to thwart the advances of a hostile bidder (e.g., the *Unocal* context)," the court continued, "the business judgment rule is not automatically rebutted"; instead, the court "merely engages in an additional inquiry, i.e., heightened scrutiny." *Id.; see also* Chapter III, Section A 2 (discussing *Unocal Corp. v. Mesa Petroleum Co.*, 493 A.2d 946 (Del. 1985) and its progeny). Here, the court stated, "the 'entrenchment fear' must *at least* be an order of magnitude less severe" than in the case of directors who engage in defensive actions: "unlike the *Unocal* scenario where directors' offices are potentially imminently threatened (i.e., if a proxy contest occurs the incumbent directors may be out of a job), none of GM's directors would lose their position after the consummation (or failure) of the split-off." *Id.* Indeed, the court added, "even if the GM directors negotiated an extraordinarily lousy deal for the continuing shareholders they would not suffer any immediate threat to their corporate office." *Id.* at 1126-27.

Finally, the court held that "even to the extent that aspects of the process may have been flawed," shareholders were "sufficiently informed about the details of the process and empowered to make an independent decision on the substantive terms of the transaction." *Id.* at 1124. The shareholders' vote thus operated "as an independent foundation for the application of the business judgment rule." *Id.*; *see also id.* at 1127 (rejecting disclosure claims based upon alleged false or misleading statements in GM's consent solicitation); *id.* at 1131-33 (rejecting coercion claims based upon alleged coercive statements in the consent solicitation); Chapter II, Section D 1 (discussing coercion claims).

The Delaware Supreme Court affirmed "on the basis of and for the reasons assigned by the Court of Chancery in its well-reasoned decision." *Solomon v. Armstrong*, 746 A.2d 277 (unpublished opinion, full text available at 2000 Del. LEXIS 30 and 2000 WL 140072) (Del. Jan. 26, 2000).

b. The GM Class H Decision. In re General Motors Class H Shareholders Litigation, 734 A.2d 611 (Del. Ch. 1999), involved a series of transactions completed in 1997 that split up another wholly-owned subsidiary of GM, Hughes Electronics Corporation. Before this series of transactions – known as the Hughes Transactions – GM had two classes of common stock, GM $1 2/3 common stock, which was paid dividends based upon GM's total income, and GM Class H stock, which was paid dividends based upon the income of Hughes Electronics. Before the Hughes Transactions, Hughes Electronics consisted of three businesses: (1) Hughes Defense, a defense and aerospace company, (2) Hughes Telecom, a space and telecommunications business, and (3) Delco Electronics Co., a manufacturer of electronic systems and parts. *Id.* at 612-13. Together, Hughes Defense and Hughes Telecom functioned as parts of a business collectively known as Hughes Aircraft Company. *Id.* The Hughes Transactions included the following:

- A spin off of Hughes Defense to GM $1 2/3 common stock and GMH shareholders.
- A subsequent merger of Hughes Defense with Raytheon Corp., leaving the GMH and GM $1 2/3 stockholders as owners of $5.2 billion worth of newly issued Class A Raytheon shares. Approximately 58.7% of the Raytheon shares went to GMH holders and 41.3% went to GM $1 2/3 holders.

- The GMH and GM $1 2/3 stockholders received 100% of the Raytheon Class A shares, constituting 30% of the total equity of Raytheon. However, the voting rights of the Class A comprised 80% of the voting power in Raytheon board of director elections.
- In the merger, Raytheon assumed responsibility for $4.3 billion worth of Hughes Defense debt.
- A transfer of Delco to GM, after which Delco became a part of GM's Delphi Automotive Systems business.
- A net infusion of $1.0 billion to Hughes Telecom for investment in its business, as a result of certain financing arrangements between GM and Raytheon.
- A recapitalization of the GMH stock into a new GMH common stock linked to the performance of Hughes Telecom, but not Delco.

Id. at 613-14. The "end result" was that "GMH shareholders ended up with (i) a large economic interest as direct stockholders in Raytheon, the purchaser of Hughes Defense; (ii) a 'tracking interest' in Hughes Telecom as holder of the recapitalized GMH shares; and (iii) a more tenuous economic interest in Delco, now a division of GM." *Id.* at 614.

The GM board's approval of the Hughes Transactions was subject to the approval of GM's two classes of common stock, GM $1 2/3 stock and GMH stock, voting separately. *Id.* Prior to the Hughes Transactions, GM's certificate of incorporation included a "Recap Provision" granting holders of GMH stock the right to receive GM $1 2/3 stock with 120 percent of the market value of their GHM stock under certain circumstances. *Id.* The Consent Solicitation GM used to secure shareholder consents in favor of the Hughes Transactions informed shareholders that the Hughes Transactions included an amendment of GM's certificate "to eliminate any possible application of the recapitalization provision to the Hughes Transactions." *Id.*

Plaintiffs alleged that "the GM directors breached their fiduciary duties of care and loyalty by: using an unfair process to establish the terms of the Hughes Transactions and to apportion the consideration between the GMH and GM $1 2/3 stockholders; failing to inform themselves about the value of and rights attached to GMH stock; coercing the GMH stockholders to vote for the Hughes Transactions; and attempting in bad faith to deprive the GMH stockholders of their right to a premium under the Recap Provision." *Id.* at 616. The court dismissed these claims on three grounds.

First, the court held that plaintiffs' claims were barred because the Hughes Transactions were approved by GM's shareholders, voting by class. The court explained that "[b]ecause the shareholders were afforded the opportunity to decide for themselves on accurate disclosures and in a non-coercive atmosphere, the business judgment rule applies." *Id.; see also id.* at 621-22 (rejecting disclosure claims based upon alleged false or misleading statements in GM's consent solicitation); *id.* at 620-21 (rejecting coercion claims based upon alleged coercive statements in the consent solicitation); Chapter II, Section D 1 (discussing coercion claims).

The court rejected a contention that "the effect of stockholder ratification is limited to shifting the burden of proof under the entire fairness standard from the defendants to the plaintiffs" because, plaintiffs contended, "the structure of GM's ownership interest in Hughes gives rise to concerns about 'implied coercion' such as has been found to exist where a controlling stockholder dominates the corporation." *Id.* at 617. The court stated that "[t]his is not such a situation" because "[t]he disapproval of the Hughes Transactions would not have displeased a controlling stockholder, from whom the GMH stockholders might reasonably fear retaliation." *Id.*

The court also rejected a contention that "the board breached its fiduciary duties by failing to provide structural protections for the GMH stockholders because of the potential divergence between the interests of GMH and GM $1 2/3 stockholders." *Id.* at 616 n.2. The court stated that "[w]here a board of directors offers a group of stockholders the ultimate procedural protection – the right to affirm or veto the decision at the corporate ballot box – and where that vote is untainted by misleading disclosures or improper coercion, I do not believe that plaintiffs can state a claim that the failure to employ lesser protections, such as a special committee mechanism, constitutes, in and of itself, a breach of fiduciary duty." *Id.*

Second, the court held that "plaintiffs' challenge to the independence of the members of GM's Board," which was based upon an allegation that GM's directors owned "substantially more GM $1 2/3 shares than GMH shares," was "too weak to state a claim that the business judgment rule does not apply to the Board's approval of the Hughes Transactions." *Id.* at 617. The court explained that to show that a director's independence was compromised by his or her ownership of greater amounts of GM $1 2/3 stock than GMH stock, "the plaintiffs must plead that the amount of such holdings and the predominance of such holdings over GMH holdings was of a sufficiently material importance, in the context of the director's economic circumstances, as to have made it improbable that the director could perform her fiduciary duties to the GMH shareholders without being influenced by her overriding personal interest in the performance of the GM $1 2/3 shares." *Id.*

Here, the court continued, plaintiffs' complaint was "devoid of any alleged facts supporting the materiality of the GM $1 2/3 holdings to the directors" or "an inference that the GM directors' holdings of GM $1 2/3 stock were so substantial as to have rendered it improbable that those directors could discharge their fiduciary obligations in an even-handed manner." *Id.* at 618. To the contrary, the court explained, the GM directors' ownership of more GM $1 2/3 shares than GMH shares was "wholly unsurprising" because there were seven times as many GM $1 2/3 shares on the market than GMH shares. *Id.* The court also relied upon the ownership by GM's directors of a greater proportion of the outstanding GMH shares than of the outstanding GM $1 2/3 shares (0.9 percent versus 0.4 percent) and the fact that "the potentially divergent interests of the GMH and GM $1 2/3 shareholders in the context of the Hughes Transactions was heavily balanced by their shared interest in obtaining the highest possible price from Raytheon." *Id.*

The court thus concluded that plaintiffs' duty of loyalty claim "hinges" upon a belief that where two shareholder groups have potentially divergent interests, a duty of loyalty claim may be stated "merely by alleging that the Board treated one group unfairly – even if it was for reasons unrelated to director self-interest." *Id.* The court stated that "that is not the law." *Id.* "Rather, the plaintiffs must plead facts from which one could infer disloyalty or bad faith on the part of GM's directors, in the sense that the directors acted for reasons inimical to their fiduciary responsibilities." *Id.* Accordingly, "an allegation that properly motivated directors, for no improper personal reason, advantaged one class of stockholders over the other in apportioning transactional consideration does not state a claim for breach of the duty of loyalty." *Id.* The fact that GMH shareholders had "tracking" interests in Hughes, the court added, "does not distinguish this case from those in which boards had to balance the interests of different classes of common and/or preferred stockholders." *Id.* at 619; *see also* Chapter II, Section E 2 (discussing this principle).

Third, the court held that plaintiffs' claim that "the GM directors attempted in bad faith to deprive them of the premium under the Recap Provision" was a "contractual rather than fiduciary" claim. *Id.* The court stated that "a board's alleged evasion or breach of a charter provision for the benefit of a particular class of stockholders" can be asserted "only as a contract claim, not as a claim for breach of fiduciary duty." *Id.; see also* Chapter II, Section E 2 (discussing this principle in the context of preferred shareholders).

The court in *Harbor Finance Partners v. Huizenga*, 751 A.2d 879 (Del. Ch. 1999), explained that "[i]n evaluating whether to accord business judgment rule protection to a decision of the General Motors board" in the *Class H* case, "I recently weighed whether the members of the General Motors board owned so much more of one class of GM's stock than the other as to render it improbable that they could evaluate the transaction impartially." *Id.* at 888 n.28. The court stated that "I engaged in the weighing analysis rather than assume that the necessity of decisionmaking in such circumstances renders it proper for the court to blind itself totally to the directors' economic motivations." *Id.* The court noted its view that this analysis "was beneficial to the stockholders in that case because it recognized that a board's personal economic circumstances might make it impossible for them to act as impartial broker between classes of the corporation's stockholders in a zero-sum transaction." *Id.* The court added that "[u]se of the weighing analysis in such cases encourages directors to avoid acting unilaterally in situations where their disinterestedness might be reasonably questioned and to employ procedural protections such as class-specific votes or special committees to ensure fairness." *Id.*

Section F 1

Add the following at the end of the paragraph beginning and concluding on page 591 (immediately after footnote 2585):

Accordingly, as stated by the Delaware Court of Chancery in *Geyer v. Ingersoll Publications Co.*, 621 A.2d 784 (Del. Ch. 1992), "the general rule is that directors do not owe creditors duties beyond the relevant contractual terms." *Id.* at 787; *see also Quadrangle Offshore (Cayman) LLC v. Kenetech Corp.*, 1999 Del. Ch. LEXIS 213, at *23, 1999 WL 893575, at *7 (Del. Ch. Oct. 13, 1999), *aff'd*, 751 A.2d 878 (unpublished opinion, text available at 2000 Del. LEXIS 147 and 2000 WL 431608) (Del. Apr. 4, 2000) ("As a general principle, a board owes fiduciary duties towards its shareholders, not its debt holders. The rights of debt holders are restricted to those provided in the instrument creating the debtor/creditor relationship."). A bankruptcy court in Illinois construing Delaware law in *In re Ben Franklin Retail Stores, Inc.*, 225 B.R. 646 (Bankr.

N.D. Ill. 1998), *aff'd on this ground and rev'd on other grounds*, 2000 U.S. Dist. LEXIS 276, 2000 WL 28266 (N.D. Ill. Jan. 12, 2000), summarized the law as follows:

> Under Delaware law, directors of solvent corporations owe fiduciary duties to shareholders, but not to creditors. The shareholders, after all, own the corporation and management of the corporate assets is vested in the directors. The directors are therefore entrusted with the control and management of the property of others. As frequently happens when a person is so entrusted with the property of others, the law imposes fiduciary obligations on that person. Creditors, on the other hand, deal with corporations by entering into contracts. Satisfaction of their claims against the corporate assets requires only compliance with their contracts. So long as the corporation is solvent, they require no additional protection; by definition, a solvent corporation, no matter how badly managed otherwise, is able to satisfy its contractual obligations.
>
> In economic terms, this rule of "managerial allegiance [to shareholders] is justified by the status of shareholders as the residual claimants on the corporation's cash flow. So long as the corporation is solvent, business decisions made by managers directly affect the income of the shareholders." The value of the creditors' claims to corporate earnings and assets, however, is fixed by contract. The business decisions of managers will therefore have no affect on the income of creditors.

Id. at 652-53 (citation and footnote omitted). This ruling was affirmed by a federal district court in *In re Ben Franklin Retail Stores, Inc.*, 2000 U.S. Dist. LEXIS 276, at *12, 2000 WL 28266, at *4 (N.D. Ill. Jan. 12, 2000).

Add the following at the end of the paragraph beginning on page 593 and concluding on page 594 (immediately after footnote 2607):

A fourth federal district court in New York also reached this conclusion in *Benjamin v. Kim*, 1999 U.S. Dist. LEXIS 6089, 1999 WL 249706 (S.D.N.Y. Apr. 27, 1999). Applying Delaware law and citing *Simons v. Cogan*, 549 A.2d 300 (Del. 1988), and *Metropolitan Securities v. Occidental Petroleum Corp.*, 705 F. Supp. 134 (S.D.N.Y. 1989), the court stated that "absent fraud or other special circumstances, a convertible debenture holder lacks standing to bring a claim for breach of fiduciary duty." 1999 U.S. Dist. LEXIS 6089, at 42-43, 1999 WL 249706, at *13. The court explained that "a convertible debenture represents a contractual entitlement to the repayment of debt and does not represent an equitable interest in the issuing corporation necessary for the imposition of a trust relationship with concomitant fiduciary duties." 1999 U.S. Dist. LEXIS 6089, at *43, 1999 WL 249706, at *13. The court accordingly held that "[a]s it is undisputed that no plaintiff ever converted his notes into shares of GMR stock, the foregoing disposes of plaintiffs' breach of fiduciary claim" against a director and officer against whom no viable claim for fraud had been stated. The court also held, however, that "because plaintiffs have asserted a viable claim of fraud" against a second director and officer, "they do have standing to assert a breach of fiduciary duty claim" against that director and officer. 1999 U.S. Dist. LEXIS 6089, at *44-45, 1999 WL 249706, at *13.

Section F 2

Replace the Cooper citation in footnote 2623 on page 597 with the following:

Cooper v. Parsky, 1997 U.S. Dist. LEXIS 4391, at *68-69, 1997 WL 242534, at *22 (S.D.N.Y. Jan. 8, 1997), *magistrate judge's report and recommendation adopted by district court*, 1997 U.S. Dist LEXIS 3665, 1997 WL 150934 (S.D.N.Y. Mar. 27, 1997), *aff'd and rev'd on other grounds*, 140 F.3d 433 (2d Cir. 1998);

Add the following at the end of footnote 2623 on page 596:

See also Technic Eng'g, Ltd. v. Basic Envirotech, Inc., 53 F. Supp. 2d 1007, 1011 (N.D. Ill. 1999); *Mussetter v. Lyke*, 10 F. Supp. 2d 944, 964 (N.D. Ill. 1998), *aff'd*, 202 F.3d 274 (unpublished opinion, text available at 1999 U.S. App. LEXIS

30220 and 1999 WL 1054602) (7th Cir. Nov. 17, 1999); *In re Toy King Distribs., Inc.*, 256 B.R. 1, 166-67 (Bankr. M.D. Fla. 2000); *In re Ben Franklin Retail Stores, Inc.*, 225 B.R. 646, 653 (Bankr. N.D. Ill. 1998), *aff'd on this ground and rev'd on other grounds*, 2000 U.S. Dist. LEXIS 276, at *8, 2000 WL 28266, at *3 (N.D. Ill. Jan. 12, 2000); *In re Main, Inc.*, 1999 U.S. Dist. LEXIS 9312, at *41-42, 43-44, 1999 WL 424296, at * 14, 15 (E.D. Pa. June 23, 1999); *Odyssey Partners, L.P. v. Fleming Cos.*, 735 A.2d 386, 417 (Del. Ch. 1999); *St. James Capital Corp. v. Pallet Recycling Assocs. of N. Am., Inc.*, 589 N.W. 2d 511, 514-15 (Minn. Ct. App. 1999).

Add the following at the end of the paragraph beginning on page 596 and concluding on page 597 (immediately after footnote 2624):

As stated in *In re Ben Franklin Retail Stores, Inc.*, 225 B.R. 646 (Bankr. N.D. Ill. 1998), *aff'd on this ground and rev'd on other grounds*, 2000 U.S. Dist. LEXIS 276, 2000 WL 28266 (N.D. Ill. Jan. 12, 2000), and *In re Toy King Distributors, Inc.*, 256 B.R. 1 (Bankr. M.D. Fla. 2000):

> The economic rationale for the "insolvency exception" is that the value of creditors' contract claims against an insolvent corporation may be affected by the business decisions of managers. At the same time, the claims of the shareholders are (at least temporarily) worthless. As a result it is the creditors' who "now occupy the position of residual owners."

Ben Franklin, 225 B.R. at 653, *quoted in Toy King*, 256 B.R. at 167. For a claim to exist against directors under this theory, insolvency must exist at the time of the alleged breach of fiduciary duty; it is insufficient that the corporation later becomes insolvent. *Benjamin v. Kim*, 1999 U.S. Dist. LEXIS 6089, at *43 & n.14, 1999 WL 249706, at *13 & n.14 (S.D.N.Y. Apr. 27, 1999).

Replace "1990 & Supp. 1997" with "2000" in the Fletcher citation in footnote 2625 on page 597.

Add the following at the end of footnote 2625 on page 597:

See also Fleming, 735 A.2d at 417.

Add "and" between footnote 2634 and "In re Xonics" and delete "and Gans v. MDR Liquidating Corp.," and footnote 2636 in the third sentence of the paragraph beginning and concluding on page 598.

Delete the Gans citation in footnote 2637 on page 598.

Add the following at the end of the paragraph beginning and concluding on page 598 (immediately after footnote 2637):

The courts in Delaware follow the latter approach, speaking in terms of duties to "the entire corporate enterprise rather than any single group interested in the corporation at a point in time when shareholders' wishes should not be the directors' only concern." *Fleming*, 735 A.2d at 417 (quoting *Geyer v. Ingersoll Publ'ns Co.*, 621 A.2d 784, 789 (Del. Ch. 1992)); *see also Credit Lyonnais Bank Nederland, N.V. v. Pathe Communications Corp.*, 17 Del. J. Corp. L. 1099, 1155 n.55, 1157 (Del. Ch. Dec. 30, 1991) (discussing "community of interests"; discussed in Chapter II, Section F 3); *Gans v. MDR Liquidating Corp.*, 1990 Del. Ch. LEXIS 3, at *24, 1990 WL 2851, at *8 (Del. Ch. Jan. 10, 1990); *In re Ben Franklin Retail Stores, Inc.*, 225 B.R. 646, 655-56 (Bankr. N.D. Ill. 1998), *aff'd on this ground and rev'd on other grounds*, 2000 U.S. Dist. LEXIS 276, at *10-14, 2000 WL 28266, at *3-4 (N.D. Ill. Jan. 12, 2000).

Section F 2 a

Add the following at the end of the paragraph beginning and concluding on page 600 (immediately after footnote 2653):

A bankruptcy court construing Texas law in *In re Performance Nutrition, Inc.*, 239 B.R. 93 (Bankr. N.D. Tex. 1999), similarly stated that "the business judgment rule may be wholly inapplicable in a case where the corporation is insolvent" and that "[t]he officers and directors of a debtor in possession owe the same fiduciary duties as a trustee in bankruptcy." *Id.* at 111.

Section F 2 b

Add the following at the end of the paragraph beginning on page 603 and concluding on page 604 (immediately after footnote 2674):

The Delaware Court of Chancery in *Odyssey Partners, L.P. v. Fleming Cos.*, 735 A.2d 386 (Del. Ch. 1999), addressed a determination by ABCO Holding, Inc.'s board to approve the purchase by Fleming Companies, ABCO's majority shareholder, of the senior loan and security interest in ABCO in a transaction that made Fleming the sole secured creditor of the corporation and that would be followed by Fleming noticing a foreclosure sale of ABCO's assets. At the foreclosure, Fleming bid $66 million, the exact amount of the indebtedness being foreclosed, for all of the collateral identified in the notice of sale. All secured and unsecured creditors were paid in full, and ABCO's shareholders received nothing. *Id.* at 405. The foreclosure sale thus "resulted in ABCO's 50.1% stockholder (Fleming) owning 100% of its assets, while ABCO's other stockholders ended up holding shares worth nothing." *Id.* at 406. Because ABCO's certificate of incorporation included a director protection provision barring recovery for money damages for breaches of the duty of care, the court analyzed the ABCO board's conduct "only in the context of plaintiffs' allegations of breach of the duties of loyalty or good faith." *Id.* at 416.

The court stated that ABCO's directors "correctly understood that ABCO was insolvent": "[i]t needed cash to continue operating but no stockholder or other person stood ready to provide such funding." *Id.* at 418. The court pointed to Fleming's undertaking "to pay all of ABCO's unsecured debt obligations, regardless of the outcome of the foreclosure sale" and the fact that Fleming had conditioned this undertaking on the directors' agreement to proceed with the foreclosure sale. *Id.* The court stated that Fleming's willingness to pay all of ABCO's unsecured debt obligations "protected the interests of ABCO's general creditors" and "protected the interests of the stockholders and the corporate enterprise by providing a mechanism to keep ABCO supplied and operating during the interim period leading up to the foreclosure sale." *Id.* The court noted that "everyone understood that ABCO would be worth more as an operating concern than not." *Id.*

The court rejected "the plaintiffs' argument that the directors' failure to pursue the alternative of a bankruptcy filing evidences their disloyalty or bad faith." *Id.* The court stated that "the record shows that the directors acted properly in considering and rejecting this possible course of action" as not being a viable option because, the directors believed, "a bankruptcy filing would produce negative returns for all of the ABCO constituencies, including its stockholders." *Id.* at 418-20. The court pointed to the board's obligation "to consider and protect interests other than those of the stockholders" and stated that "[w]hen bankruptcy and foreclosure are compared, and the effects of both on the shareholders, creditors and other corporate constituencies balanced, the decision to proceed with the foreclosure cannot be said to have been made in bad faith or a manner that was disloyal to ABCO, taken as a whole." *Id.* at 419-20.

Under these circumstances, the court concluded, "I find no evidence of disloyalty or bad faith to ABCO's stockholders." *Id.* at 418. To the contrary, the court found that "most of the directors perceived (correctly) that ABCO's debt load was greater than the fair market value of its assets and that there were, as a practical matter, no viable alternatives to the threatened foreclosure." *Id.*

The court in *In re Ben Franklin Retail Stores, Inc.*, 225 B.R. 646 (Bankr. N.D. Ill. 1998), *aff'd on this ground and rev'd on other grounds*, 2000 U.S. Dist. LEXIS 276, 2000 WL 28266 (N.D. Ill. Jan. 12, 2000), a decision by a bankruptcy court in Illinois construing Delaware law, rejected a claim that directors of an insolvent corporation breached their fiduciary duty to creditors by "prolong[ing] the debtors' corporate lives" and "sink[ing] the debtors deeper into insolvency." *Id.* at 656. The court explained that there was no allegation that "any assets were dissipated or diverted or put at undue risk for the benefit of shareholders or preferred creditors" or that the corporation "did not get full value for the debts they incurred, or that they did not use that value in an effort to restore the corporation to financial health." *Id.* There was, in other words, no allegation that the corporation's directors "did not use the corporate assets in 'an informed, good faith effort to maximize the corporation's long-term wealth creating capacity.'" *Id.* (quoting *Credit Lyonnais Bank Nederland, N.V. v. Pathe Communications Corp.*, 17 Del. J. Corp. L. 1099, 1157 (Del. Ch. Dec. 30, 1991)).

In *St. James Capital Corp. v. Pallet Recycling Associates of North America, Inc.*, 589 N.W.2d 511 (Minn. Ct. App. 1999), a court applying Minnesota law held that "Minnesota has never adopted the trust fund doctrine, which provides that the assets of an insolvent corporation are to be held in trust for the corporation's creditors." *Id.* at 515-16. The court stated that "the directors and officers of a corporation, once it becomes insolvent, are not transformed into a trust relationship and do not owe a legal duty to liquidate corporate assets in such a way as to minimize losses incurred by the corporation's creditors." *Id.* at 517.

The court accordingly dismissed a breach of fiduciary duty claim against the directors of Pallet Recycling Association of North America, Inc. ("PRANA"), a corporation that (1) failed to complete a securities placement it was obligated to complete pursuant to the terms of a $1.5 million bridge loan due to financial problems, and then (2) after becoming insolvent and receiving an offer from PalEx, a competitor, to purchase the corporation for approximately $10 million, failed to comply with a confidentiality agreement concerning the negotiations with PalEx and the terms of PalEx's offer. As a result, PalEx withdrew the offer and the corporation's assets were liquidated and sold at book value or less, with the corporation receiving less than the value PalEx had offered to pay for the assets. *Id.* at 513-14. These claims, the court stated, "simply put, are criticisms of the subjective business judgment made by PRANA's corporate directors and officers on how best to proceed with the proposed takeover by PalEx, and the placement of debt or equity securities on behalf of PRANA," and "[u]nder the business judgment rule, we do not 'second-guess the business decisions of corporate professionals.'" *Id.* at 515 (citation omitted).

The court stated that to hold that creditors are owed a duty by an insolvent corporation's directors and officers to minimize any loss that may occur as a result of the corporation's insolvency "would allow creditors of a corporation, solvent or insolvent, to interfere unduly and interject themselves in the day-to-day management of the corporation." *Id.* at 516. The court described it as "axiomatic that creditors have the right to be repaid" but added that "it is equally true that they do not have the right, absent an agreement to the contrary, to dictate what course of action the directors and officers of a corporation shall take in managing the company, or, as in this case, to direct how the assets of the corporation shall be disposed of to satisfy the debts of the corporation." *Id.* The court emphasized that the corporation's directors and officers were not alleged to have "preferred themselves" or engaged in "self-dealings to the detriment of other creditors." *Id.* at 515, 517.

Section F 2 c

Add the following at the end of the paragraph beginning on page 604 and concluding on page 605 (immediately after footnote 2682):

In *In re Toy King Distributors, Inc.*, 256 B.R. 1 (Bankr. M.D. Fla. 2000), a bankruptcy court in Florida similarly denied business judgment rule protection where a creditors' committee proved facts overcoming the business judgment rule presumption with respect to both the duties of care and loyalty. *Id.* at 168-74.

Replace "A fourth case" with "An additional case" in the first sentence (immediately after footnote 2682) in the paragraph beginning and concluding on page 605.

Add the following at the end of the paragraph beginning and concluding on page 605 (immediately after footnote 2685):

Another case – *Quadrangle Offshore (Cayman) LLC v. Kenetech Corp.*, 1999 Del. Ch. LEXIS 213, 1999 WL 893575 (Del. Ch. Oct. 13, 1999), *aff'd*, 751 A.2d 878 (unpublished opinion, text available at 2000 Del. LEXIS 147 and 2000 WL 431608) (Del. Apr. 4, 2000) – involved a corporation, Kenetech Corporation, that defaulted on interest payments on senior notes. As a result, the holders of these notes had a right to place Kenetech in bankruptcy and nullify the value of Kenetech's common stock. Kenetech's directors, hoping to retain some value for common shareholder, convinced the noteholders to refrain from filing a bankruptcy petition. 1999 Del. Ch. LEXIS 213, at *24, 1999 WL 893575, at *8. The dispute before the court was a dispute between common shareholders and preferred shareholders and is discussed in Chapter II, Section E 2. In the course of the court's decision resolving that dispute, the court stated that the board's actions "were reasonable in light of Kenetech's situation and comported with the board's fiduciary duties towards its common shareholders." 1999 Del. Ch. LEXIS 213, at *24, 1999 WL 893575, at *8, *quoted in Kohls v. Kenetech Corp.*, 2000 Del. Ch. LEXIS 102, at *20, 2000 WL 1041220, at *5 (Del. Ch. July 26, 2000) (subsequent decision by other preferred shareholders raising same claims as *Quadrangle* decision).

Section F 3

Add the following at the end of the second paragraph beginning and concluding on page 619 (immediately after footnote 2766):

The Delaware Court of Chancery in *Francotyp-Postalia AG & Co. v. On Target Technology*, 1998 Del. Ch. LEXIS 234, 1998 WL 928382 (Del. Ch. Dec. 24, 1998), declined to define insolvency as the situation where "a company's liabilities exceed its assets" because this definition "ignores the realities of the business world in which corporations incur significant debt in order to seize business opportunities" and "could lead to a flood of litigation arising from alleged insolvencies and to premature appointments of custodians and potential corporate liquidations." 1998 Del. Ch. LEXIS 234, at *16, 1998 WL 928382, at *5. Instead, the court defined insolvency as "a corporation's inability to meet its debts as they fall due in the ordinary course of business." 1998 Del. Ch. LEXIS 234, at *16-17, 1998 WL 928382, at *5. The court stated that "[d]efining insolvency as a corporation's inability to meet its debts as they fall due in the ordinary course of business is consistent with this Court's precedents" and pointed to *Siple v. S & K Plumbing & Heating, Inc.*, 1982 Del. Ch. LEXIS 553, 1982 WL 8789 (Del. Ch. Apr. 13, 1982), a case stating that insolvency "may consist of a deficiency of assets below liabilities with no reasonable prospect that the business can be continued in the face thereof, or it may consist of an inability to meet recurring obligations as they fall due in the ordinary course of business." 1998 Del. Ch. LEXIS 234, at *17, 1998 WL

928382, at *5 (quoting 1982 Del. Ch. LEXIS 553, at *5, 1982 WL 8789, at *2). The court stated that "[e]ven the *Siple* Court's version of insolvency based on liabilities in excess of assets requires the additional element that there is no reasonable prospect that the business can be continued in the face of that condition, suggesting that liabilities in excess of assets, alone, does not constitute insolvency." 1998 Del. Ch. LEXIS 234, at *17, 1998 WL 928382, at *5.

Add the following at the end the first paragraph beginning and concluding on page 620 (between footnotes 2768 and 2769):

A third decision by the Court of Chancery addressing this subject is *Odyssey Partners, L.P. v. Fleming Cos.*, 735 A.2d 386 (Del. Ch. 1999).

Add the following at the end of the second paragraph beginning and concluding on page 620 (immediately after footnote 2773):

The board's "obligation to the community of interest that sustain[s] the corporation" is "to exercise judgment in an informed, good faith effort to maximize the corporation's long-term wealth creating capacity." *Credit Lyonnais Bank Nederland, N.V. v. Pathe Communications Corp.*, 17 Del. J. Corp. L. 1099, 1155 (Del. Ch. Dec. 30, 1991).

Add the following at the end of the paragraph beginning on page 623 and concluding on page 624 (immediately after footnote 2787):

The court in *Odyssey Partners, L.P. v. Fleming Cos.*, 735 A.2d 386 (Del. Ch. 1999), similarly held that "[a]n insolvent corporation is one that is 'unable to pay its debts as they fall due in the usual course of business.'" *Id.* at 417 (quoting *Geyer v. Ingersoll Publ'ns Co.*, 621 A.2d 784, 789 (Del. Ch. 1992)). The court held that this standard of insolvency was met where the corporation had defaulted on loan obligations, notices of default had been given, the corporation's debts exceeded the fair market value of its assets, and the evidence "strongly suggest[ed]" that the corporation's equity value was less than zero. *Id.* at 417, 420, 423-24. The court quoted the statement in *Ingersoll* that "[t]he existence of the fiduciary duties at the moment of insolvency may cause directors to choose a course of action that best serves the entire corporate enterprise rather than any single group interested in the corporation at a point in time when shareholders' wishes should not be the directors' only concern." *Id.* at 417 (quoting 621 A.2d at 789).

A bankruptcy court in Illinois construing Delaware law in *In re Ben Franklin Retail Stores, Inc.*, 225 B.R. 646 (Bankr. N.D. Ill. 1998), *aff'd on this ground and rev'd on other grounds*, 2000 U.S. Dist. LEXIS 276, 2000 WL 28266 (N.D. Ill. Jan. 12, 2000), similarly stated that Delaware law "requires directors to take creditor interests into account, but not necessarily to give those interests priority." *Id.* at 655. The directors' duty "is to serve the interests of the corporate enterprise, encompassing all of its constituent groups, without preference to any. . . . [I]t is not a duty to liquidate and pay creditors when the corporation is near insolvency, provided that in the directors' informed, good faith judgment there is an alternative. Rather, the scope of that duty to the corporate enterprise is 'to exercise judgment in an informed, good faith effort to maximize the corporation's long-term wealth creating capacity.'" *Id.* (quoting *Credit Lyonnais*, 17 Del. J. Corp. L. at 1155).

This ruling was affirmed by a federal district court in *In re Ben Franklin Retail Stores, Inc.*, 2000 U.S. Dist. LEXIS 276, at *10-14, 2000 WL 28266, at *3-4 (N.D. Ill. Jan. 12, 2000). As in *Ingersoll* and *Fleming*, the district court in *Ben Franklin* stated that "fiduciary duties at the moment of insolvency may cause directors to choose a course of action that best serves the entire corporate enterprise rather than any single group interested in the corporation at a point in time when shareholders' wishes should not be the directors' only concern." 2000 U.S. Dist. LEXIS 276, at *12-13, 2000 WL 28266, at *4 (quoting 621 A.2d at 789 and 735 A.2d at 417).

The court in *Francotyp-Postalia AG & Co. v. On Target Technology, Inc.*, 1998 Del. Ch. LEXIS 234, 1998 WL 928382 (Del. Ch. Dec. 24, 1998), addressed the definition of insolvency in a different context: a request for the appointment of a corporate receiver under Section 226(a)(2) of the Delaware General Corporation Law, which permits the appointment of a custodian or, if the corporation is insolvent, a receiver, when "[t]he business of the corporation is suffering or is threatened with irreparable injury because the directors are so divided respecting the management of the affairs of the corporation that the required vote for action by the board of directors cannot be obtained and the stockholders are unable to terminate this division." 1998 Del. Ch. LEXIS 234, at *11, 1998 WL 928382, at *3-4 (quoting Del. Gen. Corp. Law § 226(a)(2)).

The court defined insolvency "in the circumstances of this case to be when a corporation is unable to meet its debts as they fall due in the usual course of business," and rejected a claim that insolvency occurs "when a company's liabilities exceed its assets." 1998 Del. Ch. LEXIS 234, at *16, 1998 WL 928382, at *5. The court stated that "[i]t is all too common, especially in the world of start-up companies . . . for a Delaware corporation to operate with liabilities in excess of assets for that condition to be the sole indicia of insolvency." *Id.* Therefore, the court stated, "[d]efining insolvency to be when a company's liabilities exceed its assets ignores the realities of the business world in which corporations incur significant debt in order to seize business opportunities." *Id.* In the court's view, "I cannot accept that definition as a 'bright line' rule as it could lead to a flood of litigation arising from alleged insolvencies and to premature appointments of custodians and potential corporate liquidations." *Id.*

The court noted the discussion of insolvency in *Geyer* and the statement in that decision that "[a]n entity is insolvent when it is unable to pay its debts as they fall due in the usual course of business" and "an entity is insolvent when it has liabilities in excess of a reasonable market value of assets held." 1998 Del. Ch. LEXIS 234, at *17 n.8, 1998 WL 928382, at *5 n.8 (quoting *Geyer*, 621 A.2d at 789). The court in *Francotyp-Postalia* stated that the court in *Geyer* "was presented with the issue of whether a director becomes a fiduciary of a creditor on account of the corporation's insolvency only after bankruptcy proceedings have been instituted, or whether a director becomes a fiduciary at some earlier time." 1998 Del. Ch. LEXIS 234, at *17 n.8, 1998 WL 928382, at *5 n.8. According to the court in *Francotyp-Postalia*, the court in *Geyer* cited the definitions of insolvency quoted above "in support of its finding that no authority exists indicating that the ordinary meaning of the word insolvency is the institution of statutory proceedings." *Id.* The court in *Francotyp-Postalia* stated its view that "I do not believe the *Geyer* Court, in its discussion of insolvency, was advancing a precise definition that this Court is to use in determining whether, in fact, an entity is insolvent." *Id.*

Add the following at the end of footnote 2807 on page 626:

See also Mussetter v. Lyke, 10 F. Supp. 2d 944, 964 (N.D. Ill. 1998), *aff'd*, 202 F.3d 274 (unpublished opinion, text available at 1999 U.S. App. LEXIS 30220 and 1999 WL 1054602) (7th Cir. Nov. 17, 1999) (fiduciary duties to corporation's creditors "arise upon the fact of insolvency, not upon the commencement of insolvency proceedings").

Add the following at the end of the second paragraph beginning and concluding on page 626 (immediately after footnote 2807):

In another decision, *Weaver v. Kellogg*, 216 B.R. 563 (S.D. Tex. 1997), the court denied a motion for summary judgment by the defendants in an action challenging numerous corporate transactions that occurred prior to a bankruptcy filing; according to plaintiffs, the corporation had been "an undercapitalized company that was in fact insolvent for a number of years before it filed for bankruptcy." *Id.* at 569. The court held that "under both Delaware law and Texas law, corporate insiders . . . may have a fiduciary duty to the corporation's creditors" if the corporation was, at the time of a challenged transaction, in "the vicinity of insolvency" or if the transaction "led" to the corporation's insolvency. *Id.* at 583-84. Applying this principle, the court concluded that factual issues precluded a determination as a matter of law. *Id.* at 584. The court in *Technic Engineering, Ltd. v. Basic Envirotech*, 53 F. Supp. 2d 1007 (N.D. Ill. 1999), similarly denied a motion for summary judgment by the defendants in a case where a creditor "presented sufficient evidence" that directors and officers of Basic Environmental Engineering, Inc. "planned and effected the transfer of substantially all of Environmental's assets to another Basic family company" at a time when the plaintiff in the case was a creditor of Environmental and "Environmental was generally not paying debts as they came due" and "its debts exceeded its assets at fair market value" and thus Environmental was insolvent. *Id.* at 1011-12.

CHAPTER III

Introduction

Add the following at the end of footnote 1 on page 631:

See also Quickturn Design Sys., Inc. v. Shapiro, 721 A.2d 1281, 1290 (Del. 1998).

Section A 1

Add the following at the end of footnote 18 on page 635:

See also Chesapeake Corp. v. Shore, 771 A.2d 293, 328 (Del. Ch. 2000) ("[i]t is quite different for a corporate board to determine that the owners of the company should be barred from selling their shares than to determine what products the company should manufacture"); *In re Gaylord Container Corp. S'holders Litig.*, 747 A.2d 71, 78 n.10 (Del. Ch. 1999) ("the power of even a well-intentioned board to take corporate action solely to prevent otherwise willing stockholders from receiving sales offers is quite different from the power to decide whether the corporation should manufacturer buggies or electric cars" because "[t]he former power arguably stretches the theoretical limits of fiduciary power by having the (at least quasi-) agents (i.e., the directors) influence or, in some instances, dictate whether the principals (i.e., the stockholders) can sell the enterprise").

Add the following at the end of footnote 22 on page 635:

See also Strassburger v. Earley, 752 A.2d 557, 572-76 (Del. Ch. 2000).

Add the following at the end of footnote 25 on page 636:

See also Hills Stores Co. v. Bozic, 769 A.2d 88, 106 n.59 (Del. Ch. 2000) (noting "the proven willingness of Delaware courts to strike down purposely entrenching board action and even well-intentioned board action that has the primary purpose of thwarting a stockholder vote"); *Strassburger*, 752 A.2d at 572-73 ("it is improper to cause the corporation to repurchase its stock for the sole or primary purpose of maintaining the board in control" and "[i]n such a case the purchase is deemed unlawful even if the purchase price is fair").

Section A 2

Add the following at the end of the paragraph beginning on page 638 and concluding on page 639 (immediately after footnote 68):

This standard again was reaffirmed by the Delaware Supreme Court in *Quickturn Design Systems, Inc. v. Shapiro*, 721 A.2d 1281, 1290 (Del. 1998).

Add the following at the end of footnote 70 on page 639:

See also In re Gaylord Container Corp. S'holders Litig., 753 A.2d 462, 474 n.32, 485 n.80 (Del. Ch. 2000).

Add the following at the end the second sentence (immediately after footnote 74) of the paragraph beginning on page 639 and concluding on page 640:

Thus, "Delaware law does not require a board to wait until the eve of battle to consider the erection of sound defensive barriers" and "recognizes that such a requirement would encourage haste rather than due care." *Gaylord*, 753 A.2d at 478.

Add the following at the end of the paragraph beginning on page 639 and concluding on page 640 (immediately after footnote 76):

Nevertheless, "Delaware case law has assured stockholders that the fact that the court has approved a board's decision to put defenses in place on a clear day does not mean that the board will escape its burden to justify its use of those defenses in the heat of battle under the *Unocal* standard." *Hills Stores Co. v. Bozic*, 769 A.2d 88, 106-07 (Del. Ch. 2000).

Section A 2 a

Replace the words "the initial burden lies with" in the fourth sentence (immediately after footnote 82) of the paragraph beginning on page 640 and concluding on page 642 with the following:

"the board is not afforded the immediate presumption of propriety under the business judgment rule," and instead "an additional inquiry" is required by the court. *Solomon v. Armstrong*, 747 A.2d 1098, 1112 (Del. Ch. 1999), *aff'd*, 746 A.2d 277 (unpublished opinion, full text available at 2000 Del. LEXIS 30 and 2000 WL 140072) (Del. Jan. 26, 2000); *see also id.* at 1126 ("the business judgment rule is not automatically rebutted"; "[t]he court merely engages in an additional inquiry, i.e., heightened scrutiny"). An initial burden is placed upon

Add the following at the end of footnote 83 on page 642:

See also Quickturn Design Sys., Inc. v. Shapiro, 721 A.2d 1281, 1290 (Del. 1998).

Replace "In other words" in the first sentence (between footnotes 83 and 84) following the bullets in the paragraph beginning on page 640 and concluding on page 642 with the following:

This "enhanced judicial scrutiny requires an evaluation of the board's justification for each contested defensive measure and its concomitant results." *Quickturn*, 721 A.2d at 1290; *see also Unitrin, Inc. v. Am. Gen. Corp.*, 651 A.2d 1361, 1387 (Del. 1995) (court must "evaluate the board's overall response, including the justification for each contested defensive measure, and the results achieved thereby," and "[w]here all of the target board's defensive actions are inextricably related, the principles of *Unocal* require that such actions be scrutinized collectively as a unitary response to the perceived threat"); *In re Gaylord Container S'holders Litig.*, 753 A.2d 462, 480 (Del. Ch. 2000) (where defensive measures are adopted "as an integrated package, 'the principles of *Unocal* require that [they] be scrutinized collectively as a unitary response to the perceived threat'") (quoting *Unitrin*). Thus, for each contested defensive measure,

Add the following at the end of the first block quote (immediately after footnote 84) in the paragraph beginning on page 640 and concluding on page 642:

The Court of Chancery, however, has noted that "[t]he use of the term 'reasonableness test' to describe the first *Unocal* prong is a bit confusing, because both prongs hinge on reasonableness." *Gaylord*, 753 A.2d at 474 n.35. The court noted that "[t]he first prong is essentially an inquiry into whether the board used a reasonable process to identify a legitimate threat to the corporation." *Id.*

Add the following at the end of footnote 91 on page 643:

See also Chesapeake Corp. v. Shore, 771 A.2d 293, 330 (Del. Ch. 2000); *Gaylord*, 753 A.2d at 477.

Add the following at the end of the second paragraph beginning and concluding on page 643 (immediately after footnote 91):

The Delaware Court of Chancery has stated that "[a]ny determination of a reasonable investigation . . . , at minimum, would require that the board be apprised of all relevant and reasonably available facts" and that if a board approves a challenged transaction based on materially false or misleading information "it would seem very hard for defendants to argue that the board's response was made after a reasonable investigation." *In re Dairy Mart Convenience Stores, Inc. Derivative Litig.*, 1999 Del. Ch. LEXIS 94, at *54, 1999 WL 350473, at *15 (Del. Ch. May 24, 1999). The Court of Chancery also has stated that "[w]ithout a clear understanding of the defendants' motivations, it is difficult to determine whether the board had sufficient information to act in a way that could be said to fall within a range of reasonableness." 1999 Del. Ch. LEXIS 94, at *56-57, 1999 WL 350473, at *15.

Add the following at the end of footnote 92 on page 644:

See also Quickturn, 721 A.2d at 1290; *Gaylord*, 753 A.2d at 475, 488; *Dairy Mart*, 1999 Del. Ch. LEXIS 94, at *41, 1999 WL 350473, at *11.

Add the following at the end of the paragraph beginning and concluding on page 644 (immediately after footnote 94):

The *Unocal* standard of review thus "enables the court to do something that it ordinarily cannot do under Delaware corporate law: examine the substantive reasonableness of the decisions of a board of directors. Not only that, *Unocal* requires the board of directors to bear the burden of justifying the reasonableness of its actions." *Gaylord*, 753 A.2d at 474.

Add the following at the end of footnote 96 on page 644:

See also In re First Interstate Bancorp Consolidated S'holder Litig., 1999 Del. Ch. LEXIS 178, at *32, 1999 WL 693165, at *10 (Del. Ch. Aug. 26, 1999) (noting that plaintiffs' claims had survived a motion to dismiss "in substantial measure, only because so-called *Unocal* claims generally involve 'questions of fact to be decided at trial, not on the pleadings'"), *aff'd sub. nom. First Interstate Bancorp v. Williamson*, 755 A.2d 388 (unpublished opinion, text available at 2000 Del. LEXIS 165 and 2000 WL 949652) (Del. Apr. 19, 2000) (quoting *Wells Fargo & Co. v. First Interstate Bancorp*, 21 Del. J. Corp. L 818, 830 (Del. Ch. Jan. 18, 1996)); *Carmody v. Toll Bros., Inc.*, 723 A.2d 1180, 1194-95 (Del. Ch. 1998) (the enhanced scrutiny required by *Unocal* "is, by its nature, fact-driven and requires a factual record" and "[f]or that reason, as the Supreme Court recently observed, enhanced scrutiny 'will usually not be satisfied by resting on a defense motion merely attacking the pleadings'"; "[o]nly 'conclusory complaints without well-pleaded facts [may] be dismissed early under Chancery Rule 12'") (quoting *In re Sante Fe Pac. Corp. Shareholder Litig.*, 669 A.2d 59, 72 (Del. 1995)); *Flake v. Hoskins*, 55 F. Supp. 2d 1196, 1217 (D. Kan. 1999) (following *Santa Fe* in case governed by Missouri law and stating that "[i]n *Santa Fe*, the Delaware Supreme Court noted that claims under *Unocal* can rarely be disposed of on a motion to dismiss").

Add the following at the end of footnote 100 on page 645:

See also Hills Stores Co. v. Bozic, 769 A.2d 88, 109 (Del. Ch. 2000) ("Under *Unocal*, it putatively remains open to the plaintiffs to show that board action that has been found to be proper under heightened scrutiny is, nonetheless, invalid because if resulted from breaches of the duty of care or loyalty by the board"); *Chesapeake Corp. v. Shore*, 771 A.2d 293, 333, 334

(Del. Ch. 2000); *Gaylord*, 753 A.2d at 476; *Solomon*, 747 A.2d at 1112; *Dairy Mart*, 1999 Del. Ch. LEXIS 94, at *41, 1999 WL 350473, at *11.

Add the following at the end of the paragraph beginning and concluding on page 645 (immediately after footnote 101):

A transaction governed by *Unocal*, however, may for other reasons be a self-dealing transaction requiring review to ensure that the transaction was entirely fair to the corporation and its shareholders. *Diary Mart*, 1999 Del. Ch. LEXIS 94, at *61, 1999 WL 350473, at *17.

The Delaware Court of Chancery has noted that "[i]n the absence of evidence of bad faith," placing the burden of establishing entire fairness on directors while a board is exploring alternatives to a tender offer "would be inconsistent with the interests of the Company, and potentially destructive of stockholder interest in value maximization." *Golden Cycle LLC v. Allan*, 1998 Del. Ch. LEXIS 80, at *35 n.10, 1998 WL 276224, at *11 n.10 (Del. Ch. May 20, 1998); *see also Golden Cycle LLC v. Allan*, 1998 Del. Ch. LEXIS 237, at *35-39, 1998 WL 892631, at *12-13 (Del. Ch. Dec. 10, 1998) (entire fairness standard not triggered by approval of a merger agreement by directors, none of whom were outside or independent directors, notwithstanding claims that (1) the bidder with whom the merger agreement had been entered into had agreed to honor stock options and compensation packages previously granted by the directors to themselves, while another bidder had threatened litigation over these payments, (2) the bidder with whom the merger agreement had been entered into had "a policy of retaining key management" (the court stated that there was no showing "of an offer of employment, written or otherwise, or even discussions regarding post-transaction employment"), and (3) the directors felt "personal affront at having been the target of an unsolicited tender offer and a consent solicitation to remove them from office" (the court stated that there was "no evidence that the Board harbors any untoward hostility" toward the complaining bidder or discriminated against that bidder "as a result of this alleged 'animus'").

As noted by the Court of Chancery in *Hills Stores Co. v. Bozic*, 769 A.2d 88 (Del. Ch. 2000).

> To date, Delaware law has not taken the position that a board of directors' decision to oppose a takeover is subject to the entire fairness standard simply because a majority of the board has an "interest" in continuing to remain in control. Rather, the potential conflict always inherent in a challenge to a board's control is the very foundation for the *Unocal* standard of review itself. In the application of that standard, the court is to consider whether a majority of the directors have a financial or personal "interest" in securing the continuation of the incumbent board's control of the corporation, but the presence of a majority of directors "interested" in this sense does not trigger the entire fairness standard of review unless the defensive measure under challenge is subject to fairness review by virtue of the application of 8 *Del. C.* § 144. A credible argument can be made, of course, that a board's decision to take steps to maintain itself in office is an inherently self-interested decision that invariably ought to be evaluated under the exacting entire fairness standard. But the extremity of this approach might well inhibit defensive action that is in fact stockholder-protective and act as a disincentive for qualified businesspeople to serve on boards. The current Delaware approach avoids these costs while providing stockholders with sufficient protection from improper entrenching tactics – so long as our courts apply *Unocal* with the appropriate rigor and sanction only well-justified and proportionate defensive measures.

Id. at 106 (footnotes omitted).

Add the following at the end of the paragraph beginning and concluding on page 647 (immediately after footnote 112):

As stated in *Chesapeake Corp. v. Shore*, 771 A.2d 293 (Del. Ch. 2000), "*Unitrin* mandates that the court afford a reasonable degree of deference to a properly functioning board that identifies a threat and adopts proportionate defenses after a careful and good faith inquiry." *Id.* at 329. The court must consider "the actual substantive reasonableness of defensive measures and whether a board in fact made a good faith and informed business judgment in adopting those measures," but also must "give some reasonable deference to the considered business judgment of a board" and "should not quibble around the margins if a board determined that a measure was reasonable after informed and good faith deliberations." *Id.* at 333-34; *see also Hills*, 769 A.2d at 107 ("*Unocal* is not intended to lead to a standard, mechanistic, mathematical exercise") (quoting *Unitrin*, 651 A.2d at 1373).

Add the following at the end of the paragraph beginning on page 647 and concluding on page 648 (immediately after footnote 118):

The Court of Chancery in *In re Gaylord Container Corp. Shareholders Litigation*, 753 A.2d 462 (Del. Ch. 2000), offered the following additional observations concerning the *Unocal* analysis:

> In itself, the *Unocal* test is a straightforward analysis of whether what a board did was reasonable. But *Unocal*'s purpose and application have been cloaked in a larger, rather ill-fitting doctrinal garment. Once the court applies the *Unocal* test, its job is, as a technical matter, not over. If, upon applying *Unocal*, the court finds that the defendants have met their burden of demonstrating the substantive reasonableness of their actions, the court must then go on to apply the normal review appropriate in cases that do not implicate *Unocal*. In essence, the court must reimpose on the plaintiffs the burden of showing "'by a preponderance of the evidence'" that the business judgment rule is inapplicable. Of course, the business judgment rule exists in large measure to prevent the business decisions of a board of directors from being judicially examined for their substantive reasonableness – an eventuality that has, in the *Unocal* context, already taken place.
>
> Thus after the defendants have met their burden to show that they acted reasonably – a showing that is materially enhanced by the presence of a majority of outside independent directors – in response to a legitimate corporate threat, the plaintiffs must be afforded the opportunity to show that the board's decision should be overturned because it was the product of a breach of one of the traditional duties of loyalty and care. It is not at all apparent how a plaintiff could meet this burden in a

> circumstance where the board met its burden under *Unocal*. To the extent that the plaintiff has persuasive evidence of disloyalty (for example, that the board acted in a self-interested or bad-faith fashion), this would fatally undercut the board's *Unocal* showing. Similarly, it is hard to see how a plaintiff could rebut the presumption of the business judgment rule by demonstrating that the board acted in a grossly careless manner in a circumstance where the board had demonstrated that it had acted reasonably and proportionately. Least of all could a plaintiff show that the board's actions lacked a rational business purpose in a context where the board had already demonstrated that those actions were reasonable, i.e., were rational.
>
> Likewise, it has been held that a board that fails to meet its *Unocal* burden may still prevail by demonstrating that its actions satisfied the exacting entire fairness test. This back-end window is more plausible, because one could posit a scenario where a board's threat analysis (the first *Unocal* prong) was deficient (e.g., it simply adopted defensive measures without conducting a threat analysis) but where the defensive measures it adopted were not draconian, were within the range of reasonableness, and were proportionate to market threats that objectively faced the company. In that scenario, there might be a basis for refusing to enjoin the measures. But in a situation where the board failed to demonstrate that the measures themselves were reasonable and not draconian, it seems extraordinarily unlikely that those measures could be deemed "fair."
>
> Fortunately, in practice, the back end of the *Unocal* analysis rarely is an issue. Practitioners recognize that the front end largely disposes of all issues and therefore focus nearly all their energies on the *Unocal* test itself.

Id. at 474-77 (footnotes omitted).

Add the following at the end of footnote 119 on page 648:

See also In re IXC Communications, Inc. S'holders Litig., 1999 Del. Ch. LEXIS 210, at *29, 1999 WL 1009174, at *10 (Del. Ch. Oct. 27, 1999). *But see ACE Ltd. v. Capital Re Corp.*, 747 A.2d 95, 108 (Del. Ch. 1999) (suggesting that a board decision "designed to prevent another bidder, through a tender offer or rival stock-for-stock bid, from preventing the consummation of a transaction" would be subject to enhanced judicial scrutiny under *Unocal* rather than deference under the business judgment rule).

Section A 2 b (ii)

Add the following at the end of the paragraph beginning on page 658 and concluding on page 659 (immediately after footnote 201):

A federal court in California construing Delaware law also rejected a contention that *Unocal* governed board conduct in *McLachlan v. Simon*, 31 F. Supp. 2d 731 (N.D. Cal. 1998), a case involving a proposed merger of a mutual fund into another fund and the replacement of the fund's investment advisor. The court stated that the proposed merger was "not similar to the possibility of a corporate takeover" and thus *Unocal* had no applicability. *Id.* at 738. The court also relied upon its conclusion that "the main concern of courts in such takeover situations is that the directors will frustrate or completely disenfranchise the shareholders' right to vote" but that here shareholders were allowed to vote on the proposed merger and replacement of the fund's investment advisor. *Id.*

Section A 2 b (iii)

Add the following at the end of the paragraph beginning and concluding on page 662 (immediately after footnote 219):

The court in *In re Gaylord Container Corp. Shareholders Litigation*, 1996 Del. Ch. LEXIS 149, 1996 WL 752356 (Del. Ch. Dec. 19, 1996), *subsequent proceedings*, 753 A.2d 462 (Del. Ch. 2000), considered a package of defensive measures including (1) a shareholder rights plan and (2) charter and bylaw amendments (i) eliminating shareholders' right to act by written consent or call special shareholders' meetings, (ii) requiring that board nominations be made during a period beginning 90 days and ending 60 days before Gaylord's annual meeting, and (iii) requiring a supermajority vote to change these provisions. *Id.* at 463, 469. The charter and bylaw provisions, but not the shareholder rights plan, were adopted with shareholder approval. *Id.*

On a motion to dismiss written by former Vice Chancellor Bernard Balick, the court determined to review the "combined effect" of the rights plan and the charter and bylaw amendments under *Unocal*. 1996 Del. Ch. LEXIS 149, at *11, 1996 WL 752356 at *3. In a subsequent decision on a motion for summary judgment written by Vice Chancellor Leo E. Strine, Jr., the court noted that the Delaware Supreme Court's decision in *Williams v. Geier*, 671 A.2d 1368, 1377 (Del. 1996), holds that *Unocal* does not apply to shareholder approved defensive measures and thus that "only the Rights Plan, and not the stockholder-approved amendments, were properly subject to *Unocal* review." 753 A.2d at 474 n.32. According to Vice Chancellor Strine, Vice Chancellor Balick's prior decision appeared to hold that the purpose of the shareholder approved bylaws "'was to increase to effectiveness of the shareholder rights plan' and therefore 'the board's unilateral adoption of the shareholder rights plan is subject to enhanced scrutiny,' with that scrutiny considering 'the effect of the rights plan in combination with the amendments.'" *Id.* (quoting 1996 Del. Ch. LEXIS 149, at *10, 1996 WL 752356, at *3). Vice Chancellor Strine stated that Vice Chancellor Balick's decision was the law of the case and found the board's conduct survived scrutiny under *Unocal*, but added that "to the extent Vice Chancellor Balick's opinion leaves this option open to me, I note that *Williams v. Geier* also supports the result I reach as to the Amendments." 753 A.2d at 474 n.32.

Section A 2 c (i)

Replace heading (i) in the paragraph beginning on page 663 and concluding on page 664 (between footnotes 222 and 223) with the following:

(i) Structural Coercion.

Add the following at the end of the paragraph beginning on page 663 and concluding on page 664 (immediately after footnote 227):

A federal court construing Missouri law in *Flake v. Hoskins*, 55 F. Supp. 2d 1196 (D. Kan. 1999), held that offers for a large block of ESOP shares suggested "a potential for a two-tiered takeover" but that this "mere potential" was "not sufficient to meet defendants' burden of showing a reasonable fear." *Id.* at 1217. Directors can overcome this burden, the court stated, only by showing that "they conducted a reasonable investigation to develop their fear." *Id.* The court denied a motion to dismiss, stating that "[n]othing in the complaint hints at any investigation into the offers, let alone a reasonable investigation to determine whether the threat required defensive measures and if so, which ones." *Id.*

Section A 2 c (ii)

Add the following at the end of footnote 239 on page 666:

See also In re Gaylord Container Corp. S'holders Litig., 753 A.2d 462, 478 (Del. Ch. 2000) (the Supreme Court has held that "a board may even act to protect stockholders from the threat of having their shares purchased at a sub-optimum price through a fully financed, all cash, all shares (i.e., non-structurally coercive) acquisition offer" and that "the directors of a Delaware corporation have the prerogative to determine that the market undervalues its stock and to protect its stockholders from offers that do not reflect the long-term value of the corporation under its present management plan") (citing *Paramount Communications, Inc. v. Time Inc.*, 571 A.2d 1140, 1152-53 (Del. 1990) and *Unitrin, Inc. v. Am. Gen. Corp.*, 651 A.2d 1361, 1376 (Del. 1995)); *NiSource Capital Mkts. Inc. v. Columbia Energy Group*, 1999 Del. Ch. LEXIS 198, at *6, 1999 WL 959183, at *2 (Del. Ch. Sept. 24, 1999) ("an offer price exceeding the defendants' internal valuation of its stock may not be dispositive of the lack of a threat" because "[t]he threat necessarily need not be financial inadequacy"; "[a]s opposed to an inadequate offer, the bidder's proposal might instead threaten the target's long-term business plan").

Add the following at the end of footnote 251 on page 669:

See also Gaylord, 753 A.2d at 478-79 n.56:

> Reasonable minds can and do differ on whether it is appropriate for a board to consider an all cash, all shares tender offer as a threat that permits any response greater than that necessary for the target board to be able to negotiate for or otherwise locate a higher bid and to provide stockholders with the opportunity to rationally consider the views of both management and the prospective acquiror before making the decision to sell their personal property. But it is settled law that a board of directors may view such an offer as requiring a far more substantial response that, depending on the particular circumstances, may pass muster under *Unocal. See Time*, 571 A.2d at 1152-53 (specifically distancing itself from Court of Chancery opinions such as *City Capital Associates v. Interco, Inc.*, Del. Ch., 551 A.2d 797 (1988), suggesting that all cash, all shares bids posed a limited threat to stockholders and could justify only measured and time-limited uses of poison pills and other defensive options).

Add the following at the end of the paragraph beginning on page 670 and concluding on page 671 (immediately after footnote 264):

The Delaware Court of Chancery's decision in *Chesapeake Corp. v. Shore*, 771 A.2d 293 (Del. Ch. 2000), similarly held that $16.50 and $17.25 all cash for all shares tender offers by Chesapeake Corporation for Shorewood Packaging Corporation were "inadequate from a price perspective" but that the threat posed to Shorewood by these offers was not "a particularly dangerous one": "there was nothing structurally coercive" about the offers because they were not "front-end loaded" or "two-tiered," a poison pill rights plan was in place, the bidder had no ability to call a special shareholders' meeting and instead had to present its offer "through the more deliberative Consent Solicitation process," and "[e]ven after a successful Consent Solicitation, the Tender Offer could not go forward until a new Shorewood board was seated and redeemed the pill after proper deliberations." *Id.* at 331. The court also relied upon the fact that "Chesapeake had indicated that its Offer was negotiable" and upon the Shorewood board's determination to "cloak[ ] itself in the business strategy privilege" and thus "cut off any ability of the court to assess how inadequate the Chesapeake offer really is." *Id.*

Section A 2 c (iii)

Replace heading (iii) in the second paragraph beginning and concluding on page 672 (immediately after footnote 272) with the following:

(iii) Substantive Coercion and Shareholder Confusion.

Add the following at the end of the second paragraph beginning and concluding on page 672 (between footnotes 272 and 273):

This threat – "the risk that shareholders will mistakenly accept an underpriced offer because they disbelieve management's representations of intrinsic value" – has been labeled "substantive coercion." *See, e.g., Unitrin, Inc. v. Am. Gen. Corp.*, 651 A.2d 1361, 1384 (Del. 1995); *Paramount Communications Inc. v. Time Inc.*, 571 A.2d 1140, 1153 n.17 (Del. 1990) (each quoting Gilson & Kraakman, *Delaware's Intermediate Standard for Defensive Tactics: Is There Substance to Proportionality Review?*, 44 Bus. Law. 247, 267 (1989)). "Substantive coercion" thus differs from what has been termed "structural coercion" – "the risk that disparate treatment of non-tendering shareholders might distort shareholders' tender decisions." *Unitrin*, 651 A.2d at 1384.

Delete the second sentence (including footnote 277) of the paragraph beginning on page 673 and concluding on page 674.

Add the following at the end of the second paragraph beginning and concluding on page 676 (immediately after footnote 296):

The Delaware Court of Chancery in *Mentor Graphics Corp. v. Quickturn Design Systems, Inc.*, 728 A.2d 25 (Del. Ch.), *aff'd sub nom. Quickturn Design Systems, Inc. v. Shapiro,* 721 A.2d 1281 (Del. 1998), similarly found that the board of Quickturn Design Systems, Inc. "reasonably perceived a cognizable threat" in an offer for all of Quickturn's shares by Mentor Graphics Corporation that represented an approximately 50 percent premium over Quickturn's pre-offer price. *Id.* at 33. This threat, the court explained, was a "concern that Quickturn shareholders might mistakenly, in ignorance of Quickturn's true value, accept Mentor's inadequate offer, and elect a new board that would prematurely sell the company before the new board could adequately inform itself of Quickturn's fair value and before the shareholders could consider other options." *Id.* at 46, *quoted in* 721 A.2d at 1290. The court pointed to the Quickturn board's belief that Mentor's offer was "timed to strike at Quickturn while its stock price was at a temporary low" and stated that "[t]he board, aided by the advice of Quickturn's management and financial advisors, had sufficient opportunity to evaluate" the corporation's prospects "before concluding that Quickturn's then-current market price (and Mentor's offer) did not reflect the company's intrinsic worth." *Id.* at 46-47. The court stated that "[b]ecause the shareholders as a group did not have a similar foundation of knowledge or opportunity for reflection, there is a basis in the record for the board to have regarded the risk of shareholder ignorance of Quickturn's intrinsic value as an element of the threat posed by Mentor's hostile bid." *Id.* at 47.

Add the following at the end of the paragraph beginning and concluding on page 677 (immediately after footnote 299):

The Delaware Court of Chancery in *Chesapeake Corp. v. Shore*, 771 A.2d 293 (Del. 2000), offered several observations concerning cases concluding that "a corporate board may consider a fully-financed all-cash, all-shares premium to market value offer a threat to stockholders" because "the board believes that the company's present strategic plan will deliver more value than the premium offer, the stock market has not yet bought that rationale, the board may be correct, and therefore there is a risk that 'stockholders might tender . . . in ignorance or based on a mistaken belief . . . .'" *Id.* at 324 (quoting *Unitrin*, 651 A.2d at 1384).

First, the *Chesapeake* court observed, "[o]ne might imagine that the response to this particular type of threat might be time-limited and confined to what is necessary to ensure that the board can tell its side of the story effectively." *Id.* The court explained that "the threat is defined as one involving the possibility that stockholders might make an erroneous investment or voting decision" and thus "the appropriate response would seem to be one that would remedy that problem by providing the stockholders with adequate information." *Id.* at 325. Additionally, the court continued, "it may be that the corporate board acknowledges that an immediate value-maximizing transaction would be advisable but thinks that a better alternative than the tender offer might be achievable," and thus "[a] time period that permits the board to negotiate for a better offer or explore alternatives would also be logically proportionate to the threat of substantive coercion." *Id.*

The court acknowledged, however, that "our law has, at times, authorized defensive responses" to threats of this type "that arguably go far beyond these categories." *Id.* As an example, the court cited *Unitrin*, where, the *Chesapeake* court stated, "the Supreme Court held that it was not necessarily a disproportionate response" to an all cash for all shares premium tender offer that shareholders "were susceptible to accepting . . . ignorantly or mistakenly" for Unitrin's board "to buy its stock in a selective repurchase program at a price comparable to the tender offer price (thus arguably 'substantively coercing' participants itself) even though the selective repurchase program thereby increased the percentage of the company's stock in directors' hands to as much as 28%." *Id.* (footnote omitted). The *Unitrin* decision – and the *Chesapeake* court's discussion of the *Unitrin* decision – is discussed more fully in Chapter III, Section E 1 d.

Second, the *Chesapeake* court observed, "the importance to stockholders of a proper *Unocal* analysis can hardly be overstated in a case where a corporate board relies upon a threat of substantive coercion as its primary justification for defensive measures." *Id.* at 327. The court stated that "it is important to recognize that substantive coercion can be invoked by a corporate board in almost every situation" because "[t]here is virtually no CEO in America who does not believe that the market is not valuing her company properly." *Id.* Moreover, the court continued, "one hopes that directors and officers can always say that they know more about the company than the company's stockholders – after all, they are paid to know more." *Id.* As a result, the court stated, "the threat that stockholders will be confused or wrongly eschew management's advice is omnipresent." *Id.* Accordingly, "the use of this threat as justification for aggressive defensive measures could easily be subject to abuse." *Id.*

The court continued:

> The only way to protect stockholders is for courts to ensure that the threat is real and that the board asserting the threat is not imagining or exaggerating it. In this respect, it bears

> emphasis that one of corporate management's functions is to ensure that the market recognizes the value of the company and that the stockholders are apprised of relevant information about the company. This informational responsibility would include, one would think, the duty to communicate the company's strategic plans and prospects to stockholders as clearly and understandably as possible. If management claims that its communication efforts have been unsuccessful, shouldn't it have to show that its efforts were adequate before using the risk of confusion as a reason to deny its stockholders access to a bid offering a substantial premium to the company's market price? [Or denying stockholders the ability to vote for a new board that will afford them such access?] Where a company has a high proportion of institutional investors among its stockholder ranks, this showing is even more important because a "relatively concentrated percentage of [such] stockholdings would facilitate [management's] ability to communicate the merits of its position." [*Unitrin,* 651 A.2d at 1383, n.33.]
>
> This confusion rationale should be tested against the information currently available to investors. The proliferation of computer technology and changes in the broadcast media industry have given investors access to abundant information about the companies in which they invest. The capability of corporations to communicate with their stockholders has never been greater. And the future promises even easier and more substantial information flows.
>
> Our law should also hesitate to ascribe rube-like qualities to stockholders. *If stockholders are presumed competent to buy stock in the first place, why are they not presumed competent to decide when to sell in a tender offer after an adequate time for deliberation has been afforded them?*

Id. at 327-28 & nn. 76, 77.

Third, the *Chesapeake* court also observed, "corporate boards that rely upon substantive coercion as a defense are unwilling to bear the risk of their own errors." *Id.* at 328. The court explained that "Corporate America would rightfully find it shocking if directors were found liable because they erroneously blocked a premium tender offer, the company's shares went into the tank for two years thereafter, and a court held the directors liable for the investment losses suffered by stockholders the directors barred from selling." *Id.* The court stated that "because directors are not anxious to bear *any* of the investment risk in these situations, courts should hesitate before enabling them to make such fundamental investment decisions for the company's owners." *Id.* In the courts words:

> It is quite different for a corporate board to determine that the owners of the company should be barred from selling their shares than to determine what products the company should manufacture. Even less legitimate is a corporate board's decision to protect stockholders from erroneously turning the board out of office.

Id. (footnotes omitted).

Fourth, the *Chesapeake* court described it as "interesting" that "the threat of substantive coercion seems to cause a ruckus in boardrooms most often in the context of tender offers at prices constituting a substantial premium to prior trading levels" but not in the context of "day-to-day sales of small blocks." *Id.* The court stated that "[t]he stockholder who sells in a depressed market for the company's stock without a premium is obviously worse off than one who sells at a premium to that depressed price in a tender offer," but "it is only in the latter situation" – where "the premium situation usually involves a possible change in management" – "that corporate boards commonly swing into action with extraordinary measures." *Id.*

For all of these reasons, the *Chesapeake* court concluded that "[a]s *Unocal* recognized, the possibility that management might be displaced if a premium-producing tender offer is successful creates an inherent conflict between the interests of stockholders and management." *Id.* According to the *Chesapeake* court, "[a]llowing such directors to use a broad substantive coercion defense without a serious examination of the legitimacy of that defense would undercut the purpose the *Unocal* standard of review was established to serve." *Id.* at 329.

Applying these principles, the *Chesapeake* court held that the board of Shorewood Packaging Corporation, faced with an all cash for all shares offers by Chesapeake Corporation, failed to demonstrate "an informed, good faith judgment that the Shorewood electorate would be confused about Shorewood's value and vote with Chesapeake as a result of confusion, rather than informed, self-interest" or that "such a threat of confusion actually exists." *Id.* at 333. The court described this claim as "a post hoc, litigation-inspired rationale" and stated that the board's reliance upon this threat "slighted, if not totally disregarded key issues." *Id.* at 332-33. These "key issues" included the following:

- institutional investors and management holders comprised over 80% of the Shorewood electorate;
- Shorewood was followed by analysts from several major brokerage houses that were regularly briefed by Shorewood management on the company's strategy and initiatives;
- Shorewood had disclosed information about all of the strategic issues that supposedly were not understood by the market;
- analysts had factored these issues into their reports on Shorewood's value;
- Shorewood's board had the opportunity to address the confusion issue through more complete and consistent disclosures to its stockholders; and
- Shorewood's management believed it had strong credibility on Wall Street and felt that it could communicate effectively about key corporate issues if given the time and resources.

Id. at 332. Nor, the court continued, did the board "conduct any sort of informal survey of its largest stockholders or the analyst community to see if they were befuddled" – a task that the court stated "would not have been difficult, given the fact that several analysts follow Shorewood and given the concentrated institutional investor holdings in Shorewood." *Id.* The court added that Shorewood's board continued to rely upon the purported threat of shareholder confusion even after less than 1 percent of Shorewood's shareholders tendered their shares to Chesapeake, even after analysts valued Shorewood at a higher price than the Chesapeake offers, and even after "the board had discussed all the issues the market could not understand in the company's own 14D-9." *Id.*

Section A 2 d

Add the following at the end of the paragraph beginning and concluding on page 681 (immediately after footnote 325):

The defensive action must be (1) "a statutorily authorized form of business decision which a board of directors may routinely make in a non-takeover context" and (2) an action that is "limited and corresponded in degree or magnitude to the degree or magnitude of the threat (i.e., assuming the threat was relatively 'mild', was the response relatively 'mild'?)." *Unitrin v. Am. Gen. Corp.*, 651 A.2d 1361, 1389 (Del. 1995); *Chesapeake Corp. v. Shore*, 771 A.2d 293, 342-43 (Del. Ch. 2000).

Add the following at the end of footnote 328 on page 682:

See also Mentor Graphics Corp. v. Quickturn Design Sys., Inc., 728 A.2d 25, 40 (Del. Ch.) ("the guiding principle is reasonableness, not perfection" and "[s]o long as a reviewing Court finds that the defensive measure (assuming it is neither coercive nor preclusive) was objectively reasonable when adopted, the measure must be upheld even if hindsight later reveals other choices that arguably were better or wiser"), *aff'd on other grounds sub nom. Quickturn Design Sys., Inc. v. Shapiro,* 721 A.2d 1281 (Del. 1998).

Add the following at the end of footnote 331 on page 682:

See also In re Gaylord Container Corp. S'holders Litig., 753 A.2d 462, 485 (Del. Ch. 2000) ("the fact that one might have decided" the need for a particular defensive measure "differently than the board did is not sufficient to create a genuine issue for trial unless one believes that the facts would support a finding that the board's contrary judgment was outside the range of reasonable responses to the circumstances"; "[t]his type of quibbling with a board's decisions seems inconsistent with the more deferential *Unocal* analysis articulated in *Unitrin*").

Add the following at the end of the second sentence (immediately after footnote 334) of the paragraph beginning and concluding on page 682:

The court noted the origins of the word "draconian" and a dictionary definition of draconian including the words "barbarously severe", "harsh" and "cruel." *Unitrin*, 651 A.2d at 1384 n.34; *see also McMillan v. Intercargo Corp.*, 768 A.2d 492, 506 n.61 (Del. Ch. 2000) (noting association of the word "draconian" in *Unitrin* with "barbarous severity" and "cruelty").

Add the following at the end of the first sentence (immediately after footnote 349) of the second paragraph beginning and concluding on page 684:

A defensive measure is coercive if "it will improperly influence the shareholder vote" and is preclusive if "it would unduly delay, and thereby ultimately prevent" the completion of an offer. *Quickturn,* 728 A.2d at 47.

Add the following at the end of footnote 350 on page 684:

See also Gaylord, 753 A.2d at 480 (footnotes omitted):

> The key inquiry under this prong of *Unocal* is whether the defensive measures are "draconian," in the sense of being preclusive or coercive. A defensive measure is preclusive when its operation precludes an acquisition of the company. A defensive measure is coercive when it operates to force management's preferred alternative upon the stockholders. When defensive measures are neither preclusive or coercive, they

will be upheld if they fall within the "range of reasonableness.'"

Add the following at the end of footnote 353 on page 684:

See also In re Dairy Mart Convenience Stores, Inc., 1999 Del. Ch. LEXIS 94, at *40-41, 1999 WL 350473, at *11 (Del. Ch. May 24, 1999) ("the board must show that it implemented a defensive response that was proportional to the threat perceived in that it (i) fell within a range of reasonableness; (ii) was not preclusive of a third-party proxy contest; and (iii) was not coercive in the sense that the board 'crammed down' on its shareholders a management-sponsored transaction").

Add the following at the end of the second paragraph beginning and concluding on page 684 (immediately after footnote 353):

The Delaware Court of Chancery has stated that "an adjudication that a board's action falls within a range of reasonableness, at minimum, would require that the board be apprised of all relevant and reasonably available facts," and that "where a board does not have a basic understanding of its own actions or the consequences of its actions, at minimum, those actions cannot be deemed a reasonable response to a perceived threat under a *Unocal/Unitrin* analysis." *In re Dairy Mart Convenience Stores, Inc.*, 1999 Del. Ch. LEXIS 94, at *54, 51 n.46, 1999 WL 350473, at *14 & n.46 (Del. Ch. May 24, 1999). The court also has stated that "[w]ithout a clear understanding of the defendants' motivations, it is difficult to determine whether the board had sufficient information to act in a way that could be said to fall within a range of reasonableness." *Dairy Mart*, 1999 Del. Ch. LEXIS 94, at *56-57, 1999 WL 350473, at *15.

As stated by the Court of Chancery in *Chesapeake Corp. v. Shore*, 771 A.2d 293 (Del. Ch. 2000), "*Unitrin* mandates that the court afford a reasonable degree of deference to a properly functioning board that identifies a threat and adopts proportionate defenses after a careful and good faith inquiry." *Id.* at 329.

The court must consider "the actual substantive reasonableness of defensive measures and whether a board in fact made a good faith and informed business judgment in adopting those measures," but also must "give some reasonable deference to the considered business judgment of a board" and "should not quibble around the margins if a board determined that a measure was reasonable after informed and good faith deliberations." *Id.* at 333-34.

Add the following new footnote 353.1 at the end of the first sentence of the paragraph beginning on page 684 and concluding on page 685:

See Quickturn, 728 A.2d at 40 ("a determination of this kind is fact specific and not constrained by any prescribed formula").

Section A 2 e

Add the following at the end of footnote 369 on page 686:

See also Flake v. Hoskins, 55 F. Supp. 2d 1196, 1214 (D. Kan. 1999).

Add the following at the end of footnote 372 on page 686:

See also Safety-Kleen Corp. v. Laidlaw Envtl. Servs., Inc., 1999 WL 601039, at *10 (N.D. Ill. Feb. 4, 1998), *subsequent proceedings*, No. 97 C 3003, Tr. at 33, 34 (N.D. Ill. Mar. 5, 1998).

Replace "The Second Circuit, unlike Unocal, has" with "The Second Circuit and other courts construing New York law, unlike Unocal, have" in the first sentence (between footnotes 374 and 375) of the paragraph beginning and concluding on page 687.

Add the following at the end of footnote 375 on page 687:

See also Minzer v. Keegan, 1997 U.S. Dist. LEXIS 16445, at *32 (E.D.N.Y. Sept. 22, 1997); *Steiner v. Lozyniak*, 261 A.D.2d 131, 132, 687 N.Y.S.2d 256, 256-57 (N.Y. App. Div. 1st Dep't 1999); *Rand v. Crosby*, No. 400063/98, slip op. at 4-6 (N.Y. Sup. Ct. N.Y. Co. May 17, 1999).

Add "Maryland," between "Indiana," and "New Jersey" in the first sentence (between footnotes 382 and 383) of the paragraph beginning on page 688 and concluding on page 689.

Add the following at the end of the second sentence (immediately after footnote 383) of the paragraph beginning on page 688 and concluding on page 689:

Maryland's statute states that "[t]he duty of the directors of a corporation does not require them to . . . [a]ccept, recommend, or respond on behalf of the corporation to any proposal by an acquiring person" – a term defined to mean "a person who is seeking to acquire control of a corporation" – or "[a]ct or fail to act solely because of: (i) [t]he effect the act or failure to act may have on an acquisition or potential acquisition of control of the corporation; or (ii) [t]he amount or type of any consideration that may be offered or paid to stockholders in an acquisition." Md. Gen. Corp. Law §§ 2-405.1(d)(1), (5), 3-801. The statute states that "[a]n act of a director of a corporation is presumed to satisfy" the standards by which directors are required to act. *Id.* § 2-405.1(e). The statute also states that "[a]n act of a director relating to or affecting an acquisition or a potential acquisition of control of a corporation may not be subject to a higher duty or greater scrutiny than is applied to any other act of a director." *Id.* § 2-405.1(f).

Add the following at the end of the third sentence (immediately after footnote 384) of the paragraph beginning on page 688 and concluding on page 689:

The court in *IBS Financial Corp. v. Seidman & Associates, L.L.C.*, 136 F.3d 940 (3d Cir. 1998), thus stated that "unlike Delaware, New Jersey has chosen not to apply heightened scrutiny to director action taken in defense against a proposed acquisition." *Id.* at 949. The court concluded, however, that New Jersey's statute applies only where a board of directors is "faced with 'any proposal or offer to acquire the corporation,'" and in the absence of a "proposal or offer to acquire the corporation" New Jersey's statute "does not insulate the board's action from judicial scrutiny" where the board acts in a manner "intended to hamper the exercise by some shareholders of their franchise." *Id.* (quoting N.J. Bus. Corp. Act § 14A.6-1(3)).

Add the following at the end of the paragraph beginning and concluding on page 692 (immediately after footnote 404):

The court in *AMP Inc. v. Allied Signal Inc.*, 1998 U.S. Dist. LEXIS 15617, 1998 WL 778348 (E.D. Pa. Oct. 8, 1998), reached the same conclusion in a case challenging a decision by the board of AMP Incorporated, a Pennsylvania corporation, to amend its shareholder rights plan in response to an unsolicited tender offer by Allied Signal, Inc. for all shares of AMP common stock at $44.50 per share in cash, to be followed by a second step merger pursuant to which Allied Signal would acquire all remaining shares of AMP common stock at the same $44.50 per share price. 1998 U.S. Dist. LEXIS 15617, at *2-3, 1998 WL 778348, at *1. At the same time, Allied Signal commenced a consent solicitation seeking to amend AMP's bylaws to expand AMP's board from 11 directors to 28 directors and elect individuals nominated by Allied Signal to fill the newly created vacancies on AMP's board and thus give Allied Signal control over a majority of AMP's board. The court stated that the individuals nominated by Allied Signal were directors and officers of Allied Signal "who would cause

AMP to accept Allied Signal's takeover bid." 1998 U.S. Dist. LEXIS 15617, at *3-4, 1998 WL 778348, at *1-2.

As discussed in more detail in Section G 2 d of this Chapter, the court relied upon the protection provided by Pennsylvania's statute to "the actions of a majority board of disinterested directors in resisting unsolicited takeovers by retaining the ordinary business judgment rule with respect to the adoption of defensive measures." 1998 U.S. Dist. LEXIS 15617, at *14, 1998 WL 778348, at *5. The court held that "it cannot be said . . . that the action of the directors" challenged in this case – an amendment of AMP's shareholder rights plan to make the rights non-redeemable "if the disinterested majority loses control of the board" – "was done in bad faith and breach of fiduciary duty to AMP, where the objective is to resist a takeover by Allied Signal, where AMP had rejected Allied Signal's merger bid prior to the present consent solicitation as contrary to AMP's best interests, and where AMP's board has determined that its own previously adopted business plan is superior to Allied Signal's merger plan for the future growth of AMP." 1998 U.S. Dist. LEXIS 15617, at *16, 21, 1999 WL 778348, at *6, 8.

The court also enjoined Allied Signal's consent solicitation seeking to expand the size of AMP's board and elect new directors "until the duty of directors is stated as being solely to the corporation and each nominee undertakes to be bound personally by that duty, if elected." 1998 U.S. Dist. LEXIS 15617, at *30, 1999 WL 778348, at *11. The court explained that "[i]f Allied Signal's directors and officers are elected to AMP's board of directors, they will have an inherent conflict" with their fiduciary duties to Allied Signal that "will necessarily put them at risk of violating Pennsylvania's fiduciary duty standard." 1998 U.S. Dist. LEXIS 15617, at *27, 1998 WL 778348, at *10. The court stated that Allied Signal's nominees "have fiduciary duties to Allied Signal's board's merger directives that may be completely antithetical to the interests of AMP." 1998 U.S. Dist. LEXIS 15617, at *28, 1998 WL 778348, at *10. The court accordingly required Allied Signal to state "unequivocally that its director nominees have a fiduciary duty solely to AMP under Pennsylvania law" and to include "a statement from each nominee affirmatively committing personally to that duty." 1998 U.S. Dist. LEXIS 15617, at *34, 1998 WL 778348, at *12. The court stated that it could not "speculate that interested directors will not respect their fiduciary duty," but "it is imperative that the nominees state that each is committed to discharging that duty, which is solely to AMP." 1998 U.S. Dist. LEXIS 15617, at *27-28, 1998 WL 778348, at *10.

Otherwise, the court stated, "[t]he foreseeable practical consequence of electing Allied Signal's nominees . . . is to embroil some court continually in determining whether, in voting on matters of corporate governance, let alone corporate independence, the interested Allied Signal nominees have breached their fiduciary duties, as a group or individually." 1998 U.S. Dist. LEXIS 15617, at *25-26, 1998 WL 778348, at *9. In the court's view, "AMP shareholders have a right to elect Allied Signal's nominees as a majority to AMP's board to attempt to consummate a merger for the profit objectives of Allied Signal and AMP shareholders," but "the public should be satisfied, before its courts may become the regular final arbiters of disputes about fiduciary duty, that AMP shareholders have knowingly chosen that path." 1998 U.S. Dist. LEXIS 15617, at *26, 1998 WL 778348, at *9.

Section A 3

Replace the semi-colon in footnote 414 on page 694 with the following:

, *quoted in McMullin v. Beran*, 765 A.2d 910, 918 (Del. 2000).

Add the following at the end of footnote 414 on page 694:

See also Emerald Partners v. Berlin, 726 A.2d 1215, 1224 (Del. 1999) ("when a corporation undertakes a transaction that will cause a change in corporate control, the responsibility of the directors is to obtain the 'best value reasonably available for the stockholders'") (quoting *Paramount Communications Inc. v. QVC Network Inc.*, 637 A.2d 34, 46, 48 (Del. 1994)).

Add the following at the end of the first sentence (immediately after footnote 414) of the paragraph beginning on page 694 and concluding on page 695:

This is "a different type of heightened scrutiny" that focuses "on the directors' duty to take care to achieve the highest and best price for shareholders in the context of a change of control," and "[a]ny failure to take 'extra' care in achieving the highest and best price can arise out of any combination of lack of due care or disloyalty on the directors' behalf." *Solomon v. Armstrong*, 747 A.2d 1098, 1112 n.31 (Del. Ch. 1999), *aff'd*, 746 A.2d 277 (unpublished opinion, full text available at 2000 Del. LEXIS 30 and 2000 WL 140072) (Del. Jan. 26, 2000). Put another way, in "a final-stage transaction for all shareholders" (such as "a proposed 'all shares' tender offer that is to be followed by a cash-out merger"), "the time frame for the board's analysis is immediate value maximization for all shareholders." *McMullin*, 765 A.2d at 918. "In pursuing that objective, the directors must be especially diligent." *Id.*

Add the following at the end of footnote 427 on page 698:

See also In re Lukens Inc. S'holders Litig., 757 A.2d 720, 731 (Del. Ch. 1999) ("'*Revlon* duties' refer only to a director's performance of his or her duties of care, good faith and loyalty in the unique factual circumstance of a sale of control over the corporate enterprise" and "[a]lthough this court and the Supreme Court may use the term to categorize certain claims, 'there are no special and distinct '*Revlon* duties'''").

Add the following at the end of footnote 469 on page 704:

See also Crescent/Mach I Partners, L.P. v. Turner, 2000 Del. Ch. LEXIS 145, at *57-58, 2000 WL 1481002, at *15-16 (Del. Ch. Sept. 29, 2000) ("Generally, when a board of directors is considering a single offer fairness requires a canvass of the market to determine if higher bids can be elicited. However, if the directors possess a body of reliable evidence with which to evaluate the fairness of the transaction they are permitted to approve the transaction without conducting a canvass of the market. . . . [P]laintiffs' Complaint fails to indicate how the directors abdicated their fiduciary duties by failing to accumulate a reliable body of evidence with which to evaluate the fairness of the transaction.") (footnote omitted).

Section A 3 b

Add the following at the end of the paragraph beginning and concluding on page 708 (immediately after footnote 491):

In short, a special duty is triggered where "an asset belonging to public stockholders (a control premium) is being sold and may never be available again." *Paramount Communications Inc. v. QVC Network Inc.*, 637 A.2d 34, 45 (Del. 1994), *quoted in McMullen v. Beran*, 1999 Del. Ch. LEXIS 227, at *12 n.16, 1999 WL 1135146, at *3 n.16 (Del. Ch. Dec. 1, 1999), *rev'd on other grounds*, 765 A.2d 910 (Del. 2000).

Add the following at the end of the first paragraph beginning and concluding on page 712 (immediately after footnote 507):

McMullin v. Beran, 765 A.2d 910 (Del. 2000), involved a suit by a shareholder of ARCO Chemical Company ("Chemical"), challenging an agreement by Chemical's board providing for an acquisition by Lyondell Petrochemical Company of Chemical's shares at a price of $57.75 per share pursuant to (1) a tender offer for all shares, with Chemical's 80 percent shareholder, Atlantic Richfield Company, obligated to tender its shares, and (2) a second-step merger at the same price. *Id.* at 914-15. The court acknowledged that this case does "not involve a 'change of control' of Chemical, as that concept has been described in the prior decisions of this Court," but stated that the Chemical board's approval of the transaction nevertheless "implicated the directors' ultimate fiduciary duty that was described in *Revlon* and its progeny – to focus on whether shareholder value has been maximized" – "because, rather than selling only its own 80% interest, ARCO negotiated for, with the Chemical Board's approval, the entire sale of Chemical to Lyondell." *Id.* at 920 (footnote omitted); *cf. In re Digex, Inc. S'holder Litig.*, 2000 Del. Ch. LEXIS 171, at *55 & n.70, 2000 WL 1847679, at *15 & n.70 (Del. Ch. Dec. 13, 2000) (distinguishing *McMullin* and finding no *Revlon* duties on the part of a corporation's board when a controlling shareholder sells either itself or its controlling interest in the corporation).

Replace the Parnes citation in footnote 511 on page 713 with the following:

1997 Del. Ch. LEXIS 70, 1997 WL 257435 (Del. Ch. May 12, 1997), *rev'd on other grounds*, 722 A.2d 1243 (Del. 1999).

Add the following at the end of the first paragraph beginning and concluding on page 713 (immediately after footnote 514):

The Delaware Court of Chancery stated again in *Krim v. ProNet, Inc.*, 744 A.2d 523 (Del. Ch. 1999), that the duty to maximize shareholder value under cases such as *Revlon, Inc. v. MacAndrews & Forbes Holdings, Inc.*, 506 A.2d 173 (Del. 1986), *Paramount Communications, Inc. v. QVC Network, Inc.*, 637 A.2d 34 (Del. 1994), *Arnold v. Society for Savings Bancorp, Inc.*, 650 A.2d 1270 (Del. 1994), and *In re Santa Fe Pacific Corp. Shareholder Litigation*, 669 A.2d 59 (Del. 1995), "does not apply to stock-for-stock strategic mergers of publicly traded companies, a majority of the stock of which is dispersed in the market" – i.e., "when ownership remains with the public shareholders and no change of control results." *Krim*, 744 A.2d at 528. The court in *In re Delta & Pine Land Co. Shareholders Litigation*, 2000 Del. Ch. LEXIS 91, 2000 WL 875421 (Del. Ch. June 21, 2000), likewise held that a duty to maximize shareholder value under *Revlon* is not triggered by "a stock-for-stock transaction between two widely-held public companies" or an announcement following the termination of such a transaction that "the board continues to explore all strategic alternatives in order to maximize value for its shareholders." 2000 Del. Ch. LEXIS 91, at *28-31, 2000 WL 875421, at *8-9.

The court in *In re Lukens Inc. Shareholders Litigation*, 757 A.2d 720 (Del. Ch. 1999), observed that "although there is no case directly on point" the court "cannot understand" how directors could not be obligated "to seek out the best price reasonably available" before entering into a merger agreement providing for receipt of a combination of cash and stock, with 62 percent of the total consideration being cash. *Id.* at 725, 732 n.25. The court stated that "[t]he Supreme Court has not set out a black line rule explaining what percentage of the consideration can be cash without triggering *Revlon*," but reasoned that "a cash offer for 95% of a company's shares, for example, even if the other 5% will be exchanged for the shares of a widely held corporation, will constitute a change of corporate control" and stated that "[u]ntil instructed otherwise, I believe that purchasing more than 60% achieves the same result." *Id.* at 732 n.25. The court stated that "[w]hether 62% or 100% of the consideration was to be in cash, the directors were obligated to take reasonable steps to ensure that the shareholders received the best price available because, in any event, for a substantial majority of the then-current shareholders, 'there is no long run.'" *Id.* (quoting *In re TW Servs., Inc. S'holder Litig.*, [1989 Transfer Binder] Fed. Sec. L. Rep. (CCH) ¶ 94,334, at 92,179 (Del. Ch. Mar. 2, 1989)).

Section A 3 c

Add the following at the end of footnote 536 on page 716:

See also Crescent/Mach I Partners, L.P. v. Turner, 2000 Del. Ch. LEXIS 145, at *58 & n.64, 2000 WL 1481002, at *16 & n.64 (Del. Ch. Sept. 29, 2000).

Add the following at the end of the paragraph beginning and concluding on page 716 (immediately after footnote 539):

The Delaware Supreme Court's more recent decision in *McMullin v. Beran*, 765 A.2d 910 (Del. 2000) – discussed in Chapter III, Section A 3 b above – holds that *Revlon* and its progeny require directors to obtain the best price available for all shareholders in a merger with a third party proposed by a controlling shareholder. 765 A.2d at 920. The *McMullin* decision cites *Bershad v. Curtiss-Wright Corp.*, 535 A.2d 840 (Del. 1987), favorably in another context (for the proposition that directors faced with a controlling shareholder who opposes a transaction have no fiduciary responsibility to engage in a futile exercise) (*id.* at 920 n.40), but does not explain why *Revlon* duties requiring directors to obtain the best price available for all shareholders apply in the context of a merger with a third party (as in *McMullin*) but not a merger with the controlling shareholder (as in *Bershad*).

The Delaware Court of Chancery's decision in *Odyssey Partners, L.P. v. Fleming Cos.*, 735 A.2d 386 (Del. Ch. 1999), illustrates that "*Revlon* duties do not arise where the directors do not have the power to control the terms on which a sale of the company takes place." *Id.* at 416, *quoted in In re Digex, Inc. S'holders Litig.*, 2000 Del. Ch. LEXIS 171, at *55, 2000 WL 1847679, at *16 (Del. Ch. Dec. 13, 2000). The *Fleming* case involved an insolvent corporation, ABCO Holding, Inc., whose majority shareholder, Fleming Companies, (1) purchased the senior loan and security interest in ABCO previously held by Chemical Bank, thus making Fleming both a majority shareholder and the sole secured creditor of ABCO, and (2) noticed a foreclosure sale at which it bid $66 million, the exact amount of the indebtedness being foreclosed, for all of the collateral identified in the notice of sale. *Id.* at 405. Following the foreclosure sale, ABCO paid all of its secured and unsecured creditors in full, and the owners of ABCO equity received nothing. *Id.* The foreclosure sale thus "resulted in ABCO's 50.1% stockholder (Fleming) owning 100% of its assets, while ABCO's other stockholders ended up holding shares worth nothing." *Id.* at 406.

Under these circumstances, the court in *Fleming* held, "[t]he special fiduciary duties described in *Revlon* and its progeny never arose." *Id.* at 416. Citing *Arnold v. Society for Savings Bancorp., Inc.*, 650 A.2d 1270 (Del. 1994), which, in turn, stated the test previously announced in *Paramount Communications, Inc. v. QVC Network, Inc.*, 637 A.2d 34 (Del. 1994), the court stated that "the *ABCO board* did not 'initiate an active bidding process,' did not 'seek an alternative transaction involving a break-up of the company' and did not approve a transaction resulting in 'a sale or change of control' of ABCO." *Fleming*, 735 A.2d at 416 (quoting *Arnold v. Soc'y for Sav. Bancorp., Inc.*, 650 A.2d 1270, 1289-90 (Del. 1994)). Instead, the court explained, "*Fleming* initiated a statutory process that led to a sale at auction" of the corporation's assets. *Id.* at 416. "That process was, as a matter of law, controlled by Fleming, not ABCO." *Id.* Moreover, the court added, "the process did not result in a change in the share ownership or control of ABCO." *Id.* The court thus rejected "engrafting *Revlon* duties upon a process initiated by a creditor and that is legally beyond the directors' control." *Id.*

Replace the period at the end of the Marriott citation in footnote 586 on page 723 with the following:

, *subsequent proceedings*, 2000 Del. Ch. LEXIS 17, 2000 WL 128875 (Del. Ch. Jan. 24, 2000).

Replace the period at the end of the Marriott citation in footnote 587 on page 723 with the following:

; 2000 Del. Ch. LEXIS 17, at *21-22 & n.20, 49-50, 2000 WL 128875, at *7 & n.20, 14.

Add the following new footnote 593.1 at the end of the paragraph beginning on page 723 and concluding on page 724:

1996 Del. Ch. LEXIS 100, at *48, 1996 WL 483086, at *15.

Add the following at the end of the paragraph beginning on page 723 and concluding on page 724 (immediately after new footnote 593.1):

The Delaware Court of Chancery's decision in *Brown v. Perrette*, 1999 Del. Ch. LEXIS 92, 1999 WL 342340 (Del. Ch. May 14, 1999), notes another open issue under *Revlon* and *QVC*: whether, following the completion of a bidding contest, a "post-bidding renegotiation of a winning bidder's offer reinvokes the acquiree board's duty to shop the company." 1999 Del. Ch. LEXIS 92, at *34, 1999 WL 342340, at *10. The court stated that "I have reservations about this proposition" but assumed for the purpose of the motion before the court that plaintiff had pled a prima facie *Revlon* claim. *Id.*

Replace "Finally, the" with "The" in the first sentence (between footnotes 601 and 602) of the second paragraph beginning and concluding on page 725.

Add the following at the end of the second paragraph beginning and concluding on page 725 (immediately after footnote 603):

The Delaware Court of Chancery's decision in *In re IXC Communications, Inc. Shareholders Litigation*, 1999 Del. Ch. LEXIS 210, 1999 WL 1009174 (Del. Ch. Oct. 27, 1999), rejected a contention that a board that entered into a stock for stock merger agreement that did not trigger enhanced scrutiny under *Revlon* and *QVC* did so "in order to serve its 'self-interest' in avoiding duties under *Revlon*." 1999 Del. Ch. LEXIS 210, at *18, 1999 WL 1009174, at *7. The court pointed to the fact that the board included "three of the largest individual shareholders in the corporation and the largest single institutional investor" in the corporation and stated that it would be "a serious factual stretch" to conclude that such a board "would completely ignore the best economic interests of the shareholders in order to avoid so-called 'onerous' *Revlon* duties found in Delaware common law." 1999 Del. Ch. LEXIS 210, at *19, 1999 WL 1009174, at *7. The court stated that "I simply cannot accept a scenario that suggests that such a twisted self interest could even exist; namely, so intense a desire to avoid an artifice of perceived legal duties (duties which in actuality this Court determines from the context, *after the fact*) that the directors would actively shirk their fiduciary obligations *and* in the process ignore their own economic self-interests." 1999 Del. Ch. LEXIS 210, at *19, 1999 WL 1009174, at *7.

Section A 3 d

Add the following at the end of the paragraph beginning and concluding on page 726 (immediately after footnote 609):

A court construing Wisconsin law in *Safety-Kleen Corp. v. Laidlaw Environmental Services, Inc.*, 1999 WL 601039 (N.D. Ill. Feb. 4, 1998), also evaluated board conduct on the basis of the rules announced in *Revlon* and *QVC*.

Add the following at the end of the paragraph beginning on page 726 and concluding on page 727 (immediately after footnote 616):

A Michigan court in *Camden v. Kaufman*, 613 N.W.2d 335 (Mich. Ct. App. 2000), following the Delaware Supreme

Court's decision in *Bershad v. Curtis-Wright Co.*, 535 A.2d 840 (Del. 1987) (discussed in Chapter III, Section A 3 c), rejected a claim that a majority shareholder cashing out minority shareholders had a fiduciary duty to obtain "maximum value" for the stock of the minority. 613 N.W.2d at 340.

Add the following at the end of the first paragraph beginning and concluding on page 729 (immediately after footnote 635):

A federal court construing Missouri law in *Flake v. Hoskins*, 55 F. Supp. 2d 1196 (D. Kan. 1999), also adopted the principles articulated in *Revlon* and its progeny. *Id.* at 1213-14. The court then applied these principles in the context of a merger agreement entered into by J.C. Nichols Company ("JCN") and Highwoods Properties, Inc. The agreement provided for Highwoods to acquire all shares of JCN stock in exchange for cash or Highwoods stock, at the option of the holder of JCN stock, with the cash payment being limited to 40 percent of the total consideration and thus, if more than 40 percent of JCN's shareholders elected to receive cash, then those shareholders would receive proportionate amounts of cash and Highwoods stock. The merger agreement was entered into following a series of escalating bids for a large block (over 30 percent) of JCN shares held by an employee stock ownership plan. Following completion of the merger, former JCN shareholders owned less than 10 percent of Highwoods stock. *Id.* at 1205-07, 1212.

The court held that the merger agreement was not subject to enhanced scrutiny under *Revlon*. The court pointed to the three circumstances under which *Revlon* duties arise under Delaware law:

> (1) "when a corporation initiates an active bidding process seeking to sell itself or to effect a business reorganization involving a clear break-up of the company," (2) "where, in response to a bidder's offer, a target abandons its long-term strategy and seeks an alternative transaction involving the break-up of the company," or (3) when approval of a trans-

> action results in a "sale or change of control." In the latter situation, there is no "sale or change in control" when "'[c]ontrol of both [companies] remain[s] in a large, fluid, changeable and changing market.'"

Id. at 1213 (quoting *In re Sante Fe Pac. Corp. S'holder Litig.*, 669 A.2d 59, 71 (Del. 1995) and *Arnold v. Soc'y for Sav. Bancorp, Inc.*, 650 A.2d 1270, 1290 (Del. 1994), and omitting citations).

With respect to the first category, the court held that plaintiff's complaint "does not allege an active bidding process." *Id.* at 1214. Instead, plaintiff alleged only that JCN's board "specifically sought a white knight buyer." *Id.* The court stated that "[t]he record contains no allegation that JCN received or solicited other bids." *Id.* The court also stated that the receipt of bids for the block of shares held by JCN's employee stock ownership plan did not "place plaintiff within the first category." *Id.*

With respect to the second category, the court held that "[p]laintiff does not allege that defendants sought a transaction that would break up the corporation." *Id.* at 1215. To the contrary, the court stated, "plaintiff alleges the opposite – that defendants sought a transaction that would keep JCN intact and thus enable JCN executives to maintain their management portions." *Id.* "To allege a break up of a corporation," the court stated, "plaintiff must allege that defendant's actions end the corporate existence of the company." *Id.* at 1214.

With respect to the third category, the court held that plaintiff failed to allege a "sale or change in control" because there is no sale or change of control when control of two companies "'remain[s] in a large, fluid, changeable and changing market.'" *Id.* at 1215 (quoting *Arnold*, 650 A.2d at 1289). Here, the court stated, "[b]efore the Highwoods acquisition, a large, fluid market held control over JCN," and "[a]fter the acquisition, a large, fluid market held control over Highwoods." *Id.* The court rejected plaintiff's reliance upon the dilution of voting power suffered by JCN shareholders that reduced the JCN shareholders' position from owners of 100 percent of JCN before the acquisition to the position of minority shareholders in Highwoods after the acquisition. The court reasoned that "[t]his fact alone is not sufficient to constitute a change of control" because "a dilution of shares occurs in every stock-for-stock transaction." *Id.* The court also rejected plaintiff's contention that a change of control occurred because the merger involved "cash and Highwoods stock for JCN stock" rather than a stock for stock merger. *Id.* The court stated that "[p]laintiff cites no case law which makes such a distinction," and "the Court fails to see the difference." *Id.* at 1215. In support of this conclusion, the court reasoned that "JCN shareholders had the ability to choose a straight stock for stock merger if they so desired," "[t]he dilution of stock is not sufficient to establish a change of control," "[a]ny other reduction that shareholders suffered as a result of the cash/stock alternative was at their own discretion," and "[a] shareholder cannot accept the partial cash buy-out and then complain that his or her power as a shareholder has been wrongfully reduced as a result of that choice." *Id.* at 1215-16.

Add the following at the end of the second paragraph beginning and concluding on page 729 (immediately after footnote 638):

In New York, *Revlon* and its progeny have not been adopted as the law. *See Minzer v. Keegan*, 1997 U.S. Dist. LEXIS 16445, at *31 (E.D.N.Y. Sept. 22, 1997). As discussed in Chapter III, Section A 6 b, "[a] New York statute provides instead that in actions involving change of control, . . . directors . . . are free to consider not only short-term considerations such as merger price, but long-term factors as well." 1997 U.S. Dist. LEXIS 16445, at *31. As a result, "[i]n New York, whether the defendants' conduct complied with their obligations turns not on the price at which they arrived, but on whether their actions complied with the business judgment rule." 1997 U.S. Dist. LEXIS 16445, at *32.

The Missouri decision in *Flake* discussed above reached the opposite result with respect to Missouri's non-shareholder constituency statute. According to the court in *Flake*, the duties of a corporate board under Missouri's non-shareholder constituency statute (Mo. Gen. & Bus. Corp. Law § 351.347) "are not truly different" from a board's duties under cases such as *Revlon*. The court explained that "*Revlon* does not require a board to accept the highest offer regardless of any other considerations. Rather, the board must simply accept the best alternative for shareholders, all things considered." *Flake*, 55 F. Supp. 2d at 1214. The court stated that "[t]he only noticeable difference" between "[t]he possible factors to consider under *Revlon*" and the factors listed in the Missouri statute is that Missouri's statute "allows the board to consider the effect of the sale on other constituencies, without expressly requiring a link to general shareholder interests." *Id.* The court stated that "[t]his difference does not appear to be significant, however, because in all business actions, a corporate board of directors owes a fiduciary duty to shareholders and must generally operate for their benefit," and "[a]ny consideration of other constituencies must therefore have at least a reasonable relationship to the general interests of shareholders." *Id.*

Add "Maryland," between "Indiana," and "New Jersey" in the first sentence (between footnotes 638 and 639) of the paragraph beginning and concluding on page 730.

Add the following at the end of footnote 639 on page 730:

See also Md. Gen. Corp. Law § 2-405.1(f).

Section A 4

Replace the period at the end of the footnote 645 on page 730 with the following:

, *quoted in McMullin v. Beran*, 765 A.2d 910, 918 (Del. 2000).

Replace "Id." with "QVC, 637 A.2d" in footnote 646 on page 730.

Delete the "and" in footnote 647 on page 730 and replace the period at the end of footnote 647 with the following:

and McMullin v. Beran, 765 A.2d 910, 918 (Del. 2000).

Section A 4 a

Add the following at the end of footnote 663 on page 733:

See also Golden Cycle LLC v. Allan, 1998 Del. Ch. LEXIS 237, at *41, 1998 WL 892631, at *13 (Del. Ch. Dec. 10, 1998); *Matador Capital Mgmt. Corp. v. BRC Holdings, Inc.*, 729 A.2d 280, 290 (Del. Ch. 1998) (both quoting *Paramount Communications, Inc. v. QVC Network Inc.*, 637 A.2d 34, 45 (Del. 1994)).

Add the following at the end of footnote 664 on page 733:

See also Golden Cycle, 1998 Del. Ch. LEXIS 237, at *41, 1998 WL 892631, at *13; *Matador*, 729 A.2d at 290 (both quoting *QVC*, 637 A.2d at 45).

Add the following at the end of the paragraph beginning and concluding on page 733 (immediately after footnote 664):

The directors' responsibility "[i]n determining which alternative provides the best value for the stockholders" is to "analyze the entire situation and evaluate in a disciplined manner the consideration being offered" and "assess a variety of practical considerations relating to each alternative, including: [an offer's] fairness and feasibility; the proposed or actual financing for the offer, and the consequences of that financing; questions of illegality; . . . the risk of non-consummation; . . . the bidder's identity, prior background and other business venture experiences; and the bidder's business plans for the corporation and their effects on stockholder interests." *QVC*, 637 A.2d at 44 (quoting *Mills Acquisition Co. v. Macmillan, Inc.*, 559 A.2d 1261, 1282 n.29 (Del. 1989)); *see also Golden Cycle*, 1998 Del. Ch. LEXIS 237, at *40-41, 1998 WL 892631, at *13; *Matador*, 729 A.2d at 291 (both quoting *QVC*). "While the assessment of these factors may be complex, the board's goal is straightforward: Having informed themselves of all material information reasonably available, the directors must decide which alternative is most likely to offer the best value reasonably available to the stockholders." *QVC*, 637 A.2d at 44-45.

Add the following at the end of footnote 667 on page 734:

See also Golden Cycle, 1998 Del. Ch. LEXIS 237, at *41-42, 1998 WL 892631, at *14; *Matador*, 729 A.2d at 290-91 (both quoting *QVC*, 637 A.2d at 45).

Add the following at the end of the paragraph beginning on page 733 and concluding on page 734 (immediately after footnote 667):

Thus, "the Court's responsibility is not to second-guess the decision-making process of the directors." *Golden Cycle*, 1998 Del. Ch. LEXIS 237, at *41, 1998 WL 892631, at *14; *Matador*, 729 A.2d at 290.

Add the following at the end of footnote 673 on page 735:

See also In re Lukens Inc. S'holders Litig., 757 A.2d 720, 731 (Del. Ch. 1999) ("'*Revlon* duties' refer only to a director's performance of his or her duties of care, good faith and loyalty in the unique factual circumstances of a sale of control over the corporate enterprise" and "[a]lthough this court and the Supreme Court may use the term to categorize certain claims, there are no special and distinct '*Revlon* duties'").

Add the following at the end of the paragraph beginning on page 735 and concluding on page 736 (immediately after footnote 680):

"[W]hile a board may not favor one bidder over another for selfish or inappropriate reasons, it may do so if 'in good faith and advisedly it believes shareholder interests would be thereby advanced.'" *Golden Cycle*, 1998 Del. Ch. LEXIS 237, at *42-43, 1998 WL 892631, at *14 (quoting *In re Fort Howard Corp. S'holders Litig.*, 14 Del. J. Corp. L. 699, 722 (Del. Ch. Aug. 8, 1988)).

Section A 4 b

Add the following at the end of footnote 719 on page 743:

See also State of Wis. Inv. Bd. v. Bartlett, 2000 Del. Ch. LEXIS 42, at *4 n.1, 18, 2000 WL 238026, at *1 n.1, 6 (Del. Ch. Feb. 24, 2000) (rejecting reliance upon *Mills Acquisition Co. v. Macmillan, Inc.*, 559 A.2d 1261 (Del. 1989), in a case challenging a board decision to allow the board's chairman, who the corporation had agreed would receive 0.75 percent of the aggregate value of the consideration to be paid in any strategic alliance entered into by the corporation, to negotiate a merger agreement; the court explained that "[i]n *Macmillan*, the negotiators were also active bidders," while here the board chairman who negotiated the transaction had no ties to any potential acquiror and "[h]is charge was to negotiate the best business deal he could" and he "undertook that mission incentivized by a fee tied to the best result he could obtain for all shareholders").

Section A 4 c

Add the following at the end of footnote 790 on page 755:

See also Crescent/Mach I Partners, L.P. v. Turner, 2000 Del. Ch. LEXIS 145, at *58-60, 2000 WL 1481002, at *16 (Del. Ch. Sept. 29, 2000); *McMillan v. Intercargo Corp.*, 768 A.2d 492, 502-07 (Del. Ch. 2000); *State of Wis. Inv. Bd. v. Bartlett*, 2000 Del. Ch. LEXIS 42, at *15-19, 2000 WL 238026, at *4-6 (Del. Ch. Feb. 24, 2000); *Matador Capital Mgmt. Corp. v. BRC Holdings, Inc.*, 729 A.2d 280, 290-94 (Del. Ch. 1998); *Golden Cycle, LLC v. Allan*, 1998 Del. Ch. LEXIS 80, at *32-35, 1998 WL 276224, at *11 (Del. Ch. May 20, 1998), *subsequent proceedings*, 1998 Del. Ch. LEXIS 237, at *39-53, 1998 WL 892631, at *13-17 (Del. Ch. Dec. 10, 1998); *In re Talley Indus., Inc. S'holder Litig.*, 1998 Del. Ch. LEXIS 53, at *33-38, 1998 WL 191939, at *11-12 (Del. Ch. Apr. 13, 1998); *Am. Bus. Info., Inc. v. Faber*, No. 16265, Tr. at 123 (Del. Ch. Mar. 27, 1998), *interlocutory appeal refused*, 711 A.2d 1227 (unpublished opinion, text available at 1998 Del. LEXIS 137 and 1998 WL 188550) (Del. Apr. 2, 1998).

Add the following at the end of footnote 791 on page 755:

See also Safety-Kleen Corp. v. Laidlaw Envtl. Servs., Inc., 1999 WL 601039, at *9-19 (N.D. Ill. Feb. 4, 1998), *subsequent proceedings*, No. 97 C 3003, Tr. at 29-35 (N.D. Ill. Mar. 5, 1998).

Add the following at the end of footnote 795 on page 757:

See also Safety-Kleen, 1999 WL 601039, at *1-2; *Crescent*, 2000 Del. Ch. LEXIS 145, at *59, 2000 WL 1481002, at *16; *McMillan*, 768 A.2d at 501, 505 n.55; *Wis. Inv. Bd.*, 2000 Del. Ch. LEXIS 42, at *16-17, 2000 WL 238026, at *5; *Goodwin v. Live Entm't, Inc.*, 1999 Del. Ch. LEXIS 5, at *6-7, 66-68, 1999 WL 64265, at *2, 22 (Del. Ch. Jan. 22, 1999), *aff'd*, 741 A.2d 16 (unpublished opinion, text available at 1999 Del. LEXIS 238 and 1999 WL 624128) (Del. July 23, 1999); *Talley*, 1998 Del. Ch. LEXIS 53, at *6-9, 35, 1998 WL 191939, at *2-3, 11.

Add the following at the end of footnote 796 on page 758:

See also Safety-Kleen, 1999 WL 601039, at *2-3; *Goodwin*, 1999 Del. Ch. LEXIS 5, at *6-12, 65-66, 1999 WL 64265, at *2-3, 22; *Golden Cycle*, 1998 Del. Ch. LEXIS 237, at *5-31, 1998 WL 892631, at *2-10; *Matador*, 729 A.2d at 292-93; *Talley*, 1998 Del. Ch. LEXIS 53, at *35-37, 1998 WL 191939, at *11-12.

Add the following at the end of footnote 797 on page 758:

See also Golden Cycle, 1998 Del. Ch. LEXIS 237, at *46-48, 1998 WL 892631, at *15-16.

Add the following at the end of footnote 798 on page 758:

See also Golden Cycle, 1998 Del. Ch. LEXIS 237, at *31, 49, 1998 WL 892631, at *10, 16.

Add the following at the end of footnote 802 on page 759:

See also Golden Cycle, 1998 Del. Ch. LEXIS 237, at *31, 49, 1998 WL 892631, at *10, 16.

Add the following at the end of footnote 803 on page 759:

See also Golden Cycle, 1998 Del. Ch. LEXIS 237, at *31, 49, 1998 WL 892631, at *31, 49.

Add the following at the end of footnote 804 on page 759:

See also Golden Cycle, 1998 Del. Ch. LEXIS 237, at *49, 1998 WL 892631, at *16; *Matador*, 729 A.2d at 292.

Add the following at the end of footnote 807 on page 759:

See also Golden Cycle, 1998 Del. Ch. LEXIS 237, at *49, 1998 WL 892631, at *11.

Add the following new bullet between the seventh and eighth bullets (immediately after footnote 807) in the paragraph beginning on page 754 and concluding on page 760:

- the limited number of potential acquirors (*Wis. Inv. Bd.*, 2000 Del. Ch. LEXIS 42, at *18, 2000 WL 238026, at *6),

Add the following immediately after footnote 809 in the eighth bullet in the paragraph beginning on page 754 and concluding on page 760:

"frustrate any deal" by making the corporation appear "over-shopped" (*Wis. Inv. Bd.*, 2000 Del. Ch. LEXIS 42, at *17-18, 2000 WL 238026, at *5),

Add the following at the end of footnote 810 on page 760:

See also In re IXC Communications, Inc. S'holders Litig., 1999 Del. Ch. LEXIS 210, at *15, 1999 WL 1009174, at *5 (Del. Ch. Oct. 27, 1999) (upholding, in a case governed by the business judgment rule rather than enhanced scrutiny under *Revlon* and *QVC*, board decisions made in a search for a strategic partner based upon a "perceived need to combine in a strategic deal with long term value rather than engage in an auction for questionable short term gain" and in an effort "to avoid the appearance of a company in trouble" and "a 'fire sale' atmosphere that, in the board's judgment, would not be in the best interest of the shareholders").

Delete the comma at the end of the eighth bullet (immediately before footnote 810) and add the following between footnote 810 and "and" in the paragraph beginning on page 754 and concluding on page 760:

("[w]hether it is wiser for a disinterested board to take a public approach to selling a company versus a more discrete approach relying upon targeted marketing by an investment banker is the sort of business strategy question Delaware courts ordinarily do not answer" (*McMillan*, 768 A.2d at 505)),

Replace the period at the end of the last bullet in the paragraph beginning on page 754 and concluding on page 760 (immediately before footnote 811) with "or other constituencies."

Add the following at the end of footnote 811 on page 760:

See also Safety-Kleen, 1999 WL 601039, at *12, 15.

Add the following at the end of the last bullet in the paragraph beginning on page 754 and concluding on page 760 (immediately after footnote 811):

- whether a bidder has determined not to participate in the process established by the corporation's directors to sell the corporation. *See Safety-Kleen*, 1999 WL 601039, at *16; *Golden Cycle*, 1998 Del. Ch. LEXIS 237, at *45-46, 50, 1998 WL 892631, at *15, 17.

Add the following at the end of the paragraph beginning on page 754 and concluding on page 760 (immediately after footnote 812):

The higher "price per share" thus is not "always better than a differently structured lower 'price per share.'" *McMullen v. Beran*, 1999 Del. Ch. LEXIS 227, at *9 n.12, 1999 WL 1135146, at *3 n.12 (Del. Ch. Dec. 1, 1999), *rev'd on other grounds*, 765 A.2d 910 (Del. 2000).

Add a comma immediately before footnote 840 in the second sentence of the paragraph beginning on page 765 and concluding on page 767, delete "and" immediately after footnote

840, and add the following between footnote 841 and "there is 'no single blueprint' . . . '" in the same sentence:

and *McMullin v. Beran*, 765 A.2d 910 (Del. 2000),

Add the following at the end of footnote 842 on page 765:

See also McMullin, 765 A.2d at 918.

Add the following at the end of the bullets in the paragraph beginning on page 765 and concluding on page 767 (immediately after footnote 861):

- *In re Talley Industries, Inc. Shareholders Litigation*, 1998 Del. Ch. LEXIS 53, at *34, 1998 WL 191939, at *11 (Del. Ch. Apr. 9, 1998) ("there 'is no single blueprint' that a board authorizing a sale of the corporate enterprise must follow to fulfill its fiduciary duties") (quoting *Barkan v. Amsted Indus., Inc.*, 567 A.2d 1279, 1286 (Del. 1989));
- *Golden Cycle, LLC v. Allan*, 1998 Del. Ch. LEXIS 80, at *33, 1998 WL 276224, at *11 (Del. Ch. May 20, 1998) and 1998 Del. Ch. LEXIS 237, *40, 1999 WL 892631, at *13 (Del. Ch. Dec. 10, 1998) ("[i]n Delaware, it is well established that there 'is no single blueprint' that a board must follow, in the context of a sale of the company, in order to fulfill its fiduciary duties") (quoting *Barkan*, 567 A.2d at 1286);
- *Goodwin v. Live Entertainment, Inc.*, 1999 Del. Ch. LEXIS 5, at *63, 1999 WL 64265, at *21 (Del. Ch. Jan. 22, 1999), *aff'd*, 741 A.2d 16 (unpublished opinion, text available at 1999 Del. LEXIS 238 and 1999 WL 624128) (Del. July 23, 1999) ("there is no single blueprint that a board must follow to fulfill its [*Revlon*] duties"); and

- *McMillan v. Intercargo Corp.*, 768 A.2d 492, 502 (Del. Ch. 2000) ("there is no single blueprint that a board must follow to fulfill its [*Revlon*] duties").

Add the following at the end of the paragraph beginning on page 768 and concluding on page 769 (immediately after footnote 875):

The court in *Golden Cycle, LLC v. Allan*, 1998 Del. Ch. LEXIS 237, 1998 WL 892631 (Del. Ch. Dec. 10, 1998), upheld the conduct of the directors of Global Motorsport Group, Inc. notwithstanding the following "strikingly unusual aspect" of the case: "the Global board twice approved merger agreements without contacting Cycle, a party known to be interested in acquiring Global, and offering it an opportunity to bid higher." 1998 Del. Ch. LEXIS 237, at *44, 1998 WL 892631, at *14. The court acknowledged that "[a]t first glance, it seems incongruous to conclude that directors can fulfill their *Revlon* duties without contacting a known interested party who might be willing to offer more." *Id.* The court concluded, however, that Cycle had "made a strategic decision" not to deal directly with Global's board and not to participate in the process adapted by the board for the sale of the corporation and instead "to appeal directly to the stockholders" with a consent solicitation seeking to replace the board. 1998 Del. Ch. LEXIS 237, at *22, 45, 50, 1998 WL 892631, at *7, 15, 16. "In effect," the court stated, "Cycle went AWOL but now seeks leave to criticize the actions taken by the Board to compensate for Cycle's refusal to participate." *Id.*

These considerations, the court stated, "seriously undermine[d] the credibility" of Cycle's "broadside attack at what it characterizes as the Board's selective, preferential and exclusive dealing" with another bidder and left the court "unable to give much weight or credence to Cycle's attacks on the Board process." 1998 Del. Ch. LEXIS 237, at *45-46, 1998 WL 892631, at *15. The court also pointed to the fact that the terms of the merger agreement entered into by the board did not preclude further bidding. 1998 Del. Ch. LEXIS 237, at *44, 1998 WL 892631, at *14. Under these "peculiar circumstances," the court held, Global's directors did not have "a duty to call Cycle to inquire if it was ready to raise its bid" and satisfied their *Revlon* duties "without contacting a known interested party who might be willing to offer more." 1998 Del. Ch. LEXIS 237, at *44, 49, 1998 WL 892631, at *14, 16; *see also* 1998 Del. Ch. LEXIS 237, 1998 WL 892631, at *15 (also discussing court's reliance upon Golden Cycle's "strategic decision . . . to disengage from the Board's process").

The court also pointed to the fact that Golden Cycle's "strategic decision . . . to disengage from the Board's process . . . deprived this proceeding (or at least important aspects of it) of a firm grounding in reality" because "[w]e do not know what would have happened if Cycle had signed the confidentiality agreement" Global's board asked Cycle to sign in return for confidential information about Global and "[w]e do not know what would have happened if Cycle had made a nonbinding indication of interest to the Board at a price above $18 per share." 1998 Del. Ch. LEXIS 237, at *45-46, 1998 WL 892631, at *15. Additionally, "[b]ecause Cycle did not sign the confidentiality agreement or pursue the issue with Global," there was no record permitting the court to judge whether Cycle was "treated differently" by being asked to show evidence of financing as a precondition of due diligence and, if so, "whether the difference in treatment was or was not appropriate." 1998 Del. Ch. LEXIS 237, at *47 n.14, 1998 WL 892631, at *15 n.14.

The court stated that "[i]nstead of presenting a factual record on these matters, Cycle asks me to join it in speculating that, if Cycle had signed the confidentiality agreement . . . Global nevertheless would have erected barriers to Cycle's due diligence and its participation in the Board-created process." 1998 Del. Ch. LEXIS 237, at *46, 1998 WL 892631, at *15. In the court's view, it is not "appropriate to adjudicate questions relating to the Board's satisfaction of its *Revlon* duties in such a hypothetical way." *Id.* The court accordingly concluded that

Golden Cycle's "decision to disengage from the Board's process" thus "seriously undermine[d] the credibility of Cycle's arguments" and left the court "unable to give much weight or credence to Cycle's attacks on the Board process." 1998 Del. Ch. LEXIS 237, at *45-46, 1998 WL 892631, at *15.

The court in *Safety-Kleen Corp. v. Laidlaw Environmental Services, Inc.*, 1999 WL 601039 (N.D. Ill. Feb. 4, 1998), likewise relied heavily upon a determination by one bidder, Laidlaw Environmental Services, Inc., not to participate in a bidding process for Safety-Kleen Corporation established by Safety-Kleen's board. The process asked bidders to sign a confidentiality and standstill agreement and then, after being provided confidential non-public information about the corporation, to submit bids. *Id.* at *2-3. Safety-Kleen's board determined to favor a bid by a group led by Philip Services Corporation over a bid by Laidlaw where the two bids were "reasonably financially equivalent in terms of their short term shareholder value." *Id.* at *9. The board based its decision upon the board's belief that the Philip group's bid would better serve the interests of non-shareholder constituencies and upon the board's doubts concerning the synergies Laidlaw expected to achieve following a combination of Safety-Kleen and Laidlaw and thus the value of the Laidlaw stock that Laidlaw had offered Safety-Kleen shareholders. *See* Chapter III, Section G 2 a (discussing this aspect of the decision in more detail).

With respect to Laidlaw's determination not to participate in the bidding process established by Safety-Kleen's board, the court stated its view that Laidlaw's refusal to sign a standstill agreement was "one of the major obstacles to its success" and that the board's unwillingness to redeem Safety-Kleen's rights plan and let shareholders choose between the two bids themselves could not be "viewed in isolation from the whole process the Board put in motion." *Id.* at *16. The court explained that the board's reservations about the synergies Laidlaw expected following a combination of Safety-Kleen and Laidlaw reflected (1) Laidlaw's determination not to enter into a confidentiality agreement and thus not to perform due diligence, and (2) Laidlaw's determination not to provide Safety-Kleen information Safety-Kleen requested about the synergies anticipated by Laidlaw. *Id.* at *16. The court acknowledged that Laidlaw was "free to decline to enter into a confidentiality and standstill agreement" and was "free to decline to provide information requested by Safety-Kleen," but stated that Laidlaw's actions "made it difficult for the board to evaluate the Laidlaw proposal in as much depth as it could evaluate the competition, and in all likelihood deprived Laidlaw of useful if not important information about Safety-Kleen." *Id.* Without evidence of bias, interest or corruption, the court stated, "it has to assume" that if Laidlaw had entered into the process provided for by Safety-Kleen's board, then Laidlaw's bid "would have been evaluated exactly as the competition was evaluated, and had the Board found it superior, Laidlaw's offer would have been recommended." *Id.*

The court emphasized that "[t]his is not a case of an entrenched board trying to fend off a hostile bid to save the status quo, but a case in which a board has embarked upon a process in which it has asked bidders to negotiate with it and satisfy it that the bidder's offer is the best available." *Id.* at *18. The court stated that a board acting in good faith can structure a bidding process in this manner and that once the board is prepared to recommend one proposal to shareholders the board need not "scuttle its process and let all bidders submit their proposals to the shareholders" simply because one bidder would prefer that course. *Id.* Requiring boards to allow all bidders to submit their proposals to shareholders," the court stated, "would be to choose as a policy preference unrestricted shareholder choice as a more important value than the board's ability to exercise its business judgment in good faith to establish a process that potential acquirors know they must take seriously." *Id.*

In sum, the court concluded, the refusal by Safety-Kleen's board to waive Safety-Kleen's rights plan in order to allow Laidlaw to present its offer to Safety-Kleen's shareholders was "part of a fair and consistent auction process which required any bidder who wanted the lifting of impediments to negotiate with the Board and persuade the Board that its offer was the best." *Id.* at *19. No principle of law, the court concluded, "says that Laidlaw should be able at this eleventh hour to get all the advantages that fell to the winner of the auction process without assuming the risks of entering into the process that other bidders took." *Id.*

Add the following at the end of the paragraph beginning and concluding on page 770 (immediately after footnote 887):

The fact that a court "would have negotiated this deal differently" does not mean that the board "should have negotiated this deal differently" or that the court should "throw a judicial monkey wrench into it." *Am. Bus. Info., Inc. v. Faber*, No. 16265, Tr. at 144 (Del. Ch. Mar. 27, 1998), *interlocutory appeal refused*, 711 A.2d 1227 (unpublished opinion, text available at 1998 Del. LEXIS 137 and 1998 WL 188550) (Del. Apr. 2, 1998).

Add the following at the end of footnote 892 on page 771:

See also McMillan v. Intercargo Corp., 1999 Del. Ch. LEXIS 95, at *9 n.6, 1999 WL 288128, at *3 n.6 (Del. Ch. May 3, 1999) (rejecting *Revlon* claim where "[t]he record shows that the currently proposed $12 price is the highest value currently available and there is no evidence to the contrary").

Section A 4 f

Add the following at the end of the paragraph beginning and concluding on page 773 (immediately after footnote 905):

The Delaware Court of Chancery in *Golden Cycle, LLC v. Allan*, 1998 Del. Ch. LEXIS 80, 1998 WL 276224 (Del. Ch. May 20, 1998), reached the same conclusion. Following receipt of an unsolicited $18 per share tender offer from

Golden Cycle, LLC, the board of Global Motorsport Group, Inc. determined that the tender offer was inadequate and should be opposed. The board also determined, "purportedly without making any decision to sell the Company or to engage in a business combination with another Company, to explore alternatives available to it to maximize stockholder value." 1998 Del. Ch. LEXIS 80, at *10, 1998 WL 276224, at *3. This process included "permitting persons expressing interest in acquiring the Company to perform due diligence." 1998 Del. Ch. LEXIS 80, at *13, 1998 WL 276224, at *4. All persons seeking to perform due diligence were required to sign a form Confidentiality and Standstill Agreement providing that

> for a period of two years neither that person nor any of its affiliates will, unless invited by the Board: (i) acquire or offer to acquire Global stock; (ii) make or solicit proxies or consents; (iii) participate in a "group" with regard to Global securities; (iv) assist anyone in any of the prohibited activities; or (v) request that Global waive the provisions of the Standstill.

1998 Del. Ch. LEXIS 80, at *14, 1998 WL 276224, at *4. Global offered to make the same information available to Golden Cycle on the condition that it sign the Confidentiality and Standstill Agreement. Golden Cycle refused and sued, contending that Global's refusal to provide Golden Cycle information unless Golden Cycle agreed to the terms of the Confidentiality and Standstill Agreement "prevent[ed] the maximization of stockholder value." 1998 Del. Ch. LEXIS 80, at *33, 1998 WL 276224, at *11.

The court held that "[e]ven assuming the plaintiff is correct and *Revlon* duties are implicated at this time, the plaintiff is still not entitled to the relief it requests." 1998 Del. Ch. LEXIS 80, at *33, 1998 WL 276224, at *11. The court explained that Global's board, "in the face of what it perceives to be an inadequate offer, is engaged in a process of examining alternatives to Golden Cycle's $18 offer." 1998 Del. Ch. LEXIS 80, at *34, 1998 WL 276224, at *11. The court stated that "as long as the Board acts with care and in the good faith pursuit of shareholder interest, it may tilt the playing filed, and, at least for some period of time, keep Golden Cycle at arms-length." *Id.* The court acknowledged that its decision was, "of course, based on the premise that the Board is acting in good faith," and stated that "[t]o date, there has been only limited discovery into the facts surrounding the Board's exploration of alternatives to Golden Cycle's $18 offer" and that "[a]s events unfold, closer examination into these issues may become necessary and appropriate." 1998 Del. Ch. LEXIS 80, at *35, 1998 WL 276224, at *11.

Subsequently, Global offered "to enter into a confidentiality agreement with no standstill provisions at all." *Golden Cycle, LLC v. Allan*, 1998 Del. Ch. LEXIS 237, *21, 1998 WL 892631, at *7 (Del. Ch. Dec. 10, 1998). Global advised Golden Cycle as follows:

> Potential buyers, including Golden Cycle after signing a confidentiality agreement, can receive a confidential offering memorandum prepared in conjunction with management and Cleary Gull [Global's financial advisor]. That offering memorandum has significant non-public data that would allow Golden Cycle to formulate a fair proposal. In addition to the offering memorandum, Golden Cycle will be provided with updated financial results and projections. The package will also include a draft form bid letter that has been and will be provided to all interested parties. Based on any revised acceptable proposal and satisfactory evidence of financing we will give you, your lenders, and advisors access to the Company's senior management team and data room to further revise your bid and continue due diligence. We have and are using this process with past and current interested parties.
>
> If Golden Cycle has a bona fide interest in purchasing the Company at a fair price, we are confident that the foregoing procedures will enable it to do so. Please have Golden Cycle's financial advisors contact Cleary Gull if there is interest in proceeding as outlined above.

1998 Del. Ch. LEXIS 237, at *21-22, 1998 WL 892631, at *7.

Golden Cycle did not respond to Global's invitation to participate in the process established by Global's board because Golden Cycle believed that "as a condition to accessing due diligence beyond the Offering Memorandum" it would be required "to present an 'acceptable' nonbinding proposal" and "offer evidence of financing at the stage of making a non-binding proposal." 1998 Del. Ch. LEXIS 237, at *22-23, 1998 WL 892631, at *7. Golden Cycle also believed that Global's board "would never deal with us in good faith." 1998 Del. Ch. LEXIS 237, at *23, 1998 WL 892631, at *8. As stated by Golden Cycle's president: "It was obvious to me that we would never receive meaningful due diligence from Global. If we signed the confidentiality agreement and made a bid, they would never find our bid acceptable. If they did, they would not accept our evidence of financing." *Id.* Golden Cycle accordingly determined "to stop wasting our time and to appeal directly to shareholders" through a consent solicitation seeking to replace the board. 1998 Del. Ch. LEXIS 237, at *22, 1998 WL 892631, at *7

A short time later, Global entered into a merger agreement with Stonington Acquisition Corporation pursuant to which Stonington would acquire all of Global's shares for $19.50 per share. 1998 Del. Ch. LEXIS 237, at *12-17, 1998 WL 892631, at *4-6. The agreement permitted Global's board "to consider and negotiate a bona fide acquisition proposal from a third party where the Board concludes that the outside proposal is a financed offer more favorable than Stonington's and that the failure to do so would violate its fiduciary duties." 1998 Del. Ch. LEXIS 237, at *16, 1998 WL 892631, at *5. The merger agreement also permitted Global's board "to provide nonpublic information to such a competing bidder upon the execution of a confidentiality agreement comparable to that signed by Stonington" and "to terminate the Stonington agreement in favor of a better offer." *Id.*

The court denied a motion by Golden Cycle seeking an order "requiring the Board to give Golden Cycle access to all confidential information made available to Stonington." 1998 Del. Ch. LEXIS 237, at *3 n.1, 1998 WL 892631, at *1 n.1. The court held that directors "are entitled to establish the process best adapted to the sale of their company," and "[i]f a potential purchaser chooses to disregard this process" the directors "can make a good faith decision to treat it differently" if doing so "is in the best interests of the stockholders." 1998 Del. Ch. LEXIS 237, at *48, 1998 WL 892631, at *16. The court stated that "[t]his includes differentiating between a bidder who refuses to sign a confidentiality agreement and one who does not." *Id.*

Here, the court explained, Global's board "developed a two-step process for disseminating nonpublic information to potential acquirors; first, the Offering Memorandum, which was given upon execution of a confidentiality agreement and second, upon provision of an acceptable indication of price, full access to management and advisors for due diligence purposes." 1998 Del. Ch. LEXIS 237, at *46-47, 1998 WL 892631, at *15. The court stated that "[t]he record shows that the Board followed this process for all of the acquirors interested in negotiating a sale with Global." *Id.* The court added that "[i]n one respect, at least, Cycle was treated more favorably than others – Global offered it the opportunity to sign a confidentiality agreement with greatly reduced standstill provisions, and later with no standstill provision at all." *Id.*

Section A 4 f-1

Add the following new section "f-1" at the end of the paragraph beginning on page 776 and concluding on page 777 (immediately after footnote 924):

f-1. Controlling Shareholder Considerations. The principles discussed above apply "[i]n the context of an entire sale, and in the absence of an extant majority shareholder." *McMullin v. Beran*, 765 A.2d 910, 918 (Del. 2000). Different principles apply to the fiduciary responsibilities of directors to minority shareholders "in the specific context of evaluating a proposal for a sale of the entire corporation to a third party at the behest of the majority shareholder." *Id.* at 919. Under these circumstances, the majority shareholder "has the right to vote its shares in favor of the . . . transaction it proposed for the board's consideration," and the corporation's board is "powerless to out-vote" the majority shareholder and thus "cannot realistically *seek* any alternative." *Id.; see also* Chapter II, Section B 3 b (discussing right of controlling shareholder to vote and tender its shares according to its own self-interest).

The controlled corporation's directors, however, still have the obligation "to make an informed and deliberate judgment, in good faith, about whether the sale to a third party that is being proposed by the majority shareholder will result in a maximization of value for the minority shareholders," and, when the proposed transaction consists of a tender offer and a merger, to determine whether shareholders should accept the tender offer or merger consideration or seek an appraisal. *Id.* Where the controlled corporation itself is not being sold (for example, where the controlling shareholder is selling itself or its interest in the controlled corporation), there is no duty on the part of the controlled corporation's board to maximize shareholder value under *Revlon* and its progeny. *In re Digex Inc. S'holders Litig.*, 2000 Del. Ch. LEXIS 171, at *54-55, 2000 WL 1847679, at *15 (Del. Ch. Dec. 13, 2000).

McMullin v. Beran, 765 A.2d 910 (Del. 2000), illustrates these principles. The facts underlying the decision began on February 17, 1998, when Atlantic Richfield Company ("ARCO"), the owner of 80 percent of the shares of ARCO Chemical Company ("Chemical"), received an unsolicited call from Lyondell Petrochemical Company expressing an interest in acquiring Chemical. From February to June 1998, ARCO and its financial advisor, Solomon Smith Barney, contacted potential competing bidders to determine their interest in participating in a bidding process. In mid-March, ARCO informed Chemical's board that it "had received indications of interest for an acquisition" of all of Chemical's outstanding common shares. Chemical's directors authorized ARCO to explore a sale of the entire company. *Id.* at 915.

Lyondell made a series of bids that ultimately reached $57.75 per share in cash. Following negotiations, Lyondell submitted a merger agreement and other related contracts providing for a tender offer by Lyondell for all Chemical shares at $57.75 per share, with ARCO obligated to tender its shares and Lyondell obligated following the tender offer to complete a second-step merger in which all untendered shares would be cashed out at the same $57.75 per share offered in the tender offer. *Id.* at 915-16. On June 18, 1998, Chemical's board approved Lyondell's proposal after hearing presentations from representatives of ARCO, Solomon, and Chemical's own financial advisor, Merrill Lynch. On June 24, 1998, Lyondell commenced its tender offer and 99 percent of Chemical's shares were tendered to Lyondell. A short time later Lyondell completed the second-step merger. *Id.* at 916.

The plaintiff in the case, a minority shareholder of Chemical, acknowledged that ARCO had received the same consideration in amount and form per share as all other shareholders but alleged that ARCO had initiated the transaction at a time when ARCO needed cash. *Id.* at 921. According to the plaintiff, more consideration could have been obtained by using consideration other than cash or not selling the corporation at this particular time. Plaintiff thus alleged that ARCO "gained financial advantage from the immediate all-cash Transaction with Lyondell, at the expense of the minority shareholders, by sacrificing some of the value of Chemical, which might have been realized in a differently timed or structured agreement." *Id.*

The court stated that "[w]hen a board is presented with the majority shareholder's proposal to sell the entire corporation to a third party, the ultimate focus on value maximization is the same as if the board itself had decided to sell the corporation to a third party," and "the directors are obliged to make an informed and deliberate judgment, in good faith, about whether the sale to a third party that is being proposed by the majority shareholder will result in a maximization of value for the minority shareholders." *Id.* at 919. Where a sale to a third party is "proposed, negotiated and timed by a majority shareholder, however, the board cannot realistically *seek* any alternative because the majority shareholder has the right to vote its shares in favor of the third-party transaction it proposed for the board's consideration." *Id.* Accordingly, "because the minority shareholders of Chemical were powerless to out-vote ARCO, they had only one decision to make: whether to accept the tender offer from Lyondell or to seek an appraisal value of their shares in the ensuing merger." *Id.* Chemical's directors "did not have the ability to *act* on an informed basis to *secure* the best value reasonably available for all shareholders in any alternative to the third-party transaction with Lyondell that ARCO had negotiated," but Chemical's directors did "have the duty to act on an informed basis to independently ascertain how the merger consideration being offered in the third party Transaction with Lyondell compared to Chemical's value as a going concern" and thus Chemical's appraisal value. *Id.* In the court's words:

> [O]nce having assumed the position of directors of [Chemical], a corporation that had stockholders other than [ARCO], [the directors] become fiduciaries for the minority shareholders, with a concomitant affirmative duty to protect the interests of the minority, as well as the majority, stockholders. Thus, the [Chemical] Board, in carrying out its affirmative duty to protect the interests of the minority, could not abdicate its obligation to make an informed decision on the fairness of the merger by simply deferring to the judgment of the controlling shareholder . . . .

Id. at 919-20 (quoting *Sealy Mattress Co. v. Sealy, Inc.*, 532 A.2d 1324, 1338 (Del. Ch. 1987)).

The court stated that "[e]ffective representation of the financial interests of the minority shareholders" thus "imposed upon the Chemical Board an affirmative responsibility to protect those minority shareholders' interests." *Id.* at 920. This responsibility "required the Chemical Board to: first, conduct a critical assessment of the third-party Transaction with Lyondell that was proposed by the majority shareholder; and second, make an independent determination whether that transaction maximized value for all shareholders." *Id.* Chemical's directors "had a duty to fulfill this obligation faithfully and with due care so that the minority shareholders would be able to make an informed decision about whether to accept the Lyondell Transaction tender offer price or to seek an appraisal of their shares." *Id.*

The court held that the plaintiff's complaint "passed judicial muster" under the standard governing motions to dismiss. *Id.* at 917. The court explained that plaintiff had alleged facts that, if true, would overcome the presumption of the business judgment rule and trigger the entire fairness standard on two separate and independent grounds.

First, the court held that plaintiff's allegations, if true, "suggest that the directors of Chemical breached their duty of care by approving the merger with Lyondell without adequately informing themselves about the transaction and without determining whether the merger consideration equaled or exceeded Chemical's appraisal value as a going concern." *Id.* at 922. The court pointed to plaintiff's allegations that "the Chemical Board met only once to consider the Transaction negotiated by ARCO with Lyondell" and "approved the Transaction with Lyondell at that one meeting on the basis of the disclosures made to them by ARCO's financial advisor" (significantly, it should be noted, Chemical's financial advisor also attended the meeting, made a presentation and expressed its opinion that $57.75 per share was fair to Chemical's stockholders, other than ARCO, from a financial point of view). *Id.* at 915-16, 922. The court stated that "[t]he imposition of time constraints on a board's decision-making process may compromise the integrity of its deliberative process" and that "[h]istory has demonstrated" that "boards 'that have failed to exercise due care are frequently boards that have been rushed.'" *Id.* at 922. The court concluded that "[o]ne can reasonably infer from the factual allegations" in the complaint "that the Chemical Board compromised its deliberative process by seeking to accommodate ARCO's immediate need for cash." *Id.*

The court agreed that Chemical's board "could properly rely on the majority shareholder to conduct preliminary negotiations," but stated that the board had the "ultimate" duty "to make an informed and independent decision on whether to recommend approval of the third-party Transaction with Lyondell to the minority shareholders" or to urge minority shareholders not to tender their shares to Lyondell and to pursue an appraisal action during the second step of the transaction. *Id.* at 924. Based upon plaintiff's allegations that "ARCO unilaterally initiated, structured and negotiated the Transaction to sell all of Chemical" and that the Chemical Board "made no determination of Chemical's entire value as a going concern before making its expedited decision to recommend approval of ARCO's proposed third-party Transaction with Lyondell," the court stated that "[o]ne can reasonably infer" that "Chemical's minority shareholders might have received more than $57.75 cash in an appraisal proceeding, if the Chemical Directors had fulfilled their fiduciary duties to *ascertain* whether the proposed sale to Lyondell maximized value for all shareholders." *Id.* at 924-25.

Second, the court held that plaintiff's allegation that "a majority of Chemical's board of directors was dominated by ARCO" was a "well-pled" allegation of a breach of the duty of loyalty: six of twelve Chemical directors were ARCO officers and two additional Chemical directors had prior affiliations with ARCO as officers of ARCO subsidiaries. *Id.* at 923. The court stated that "none of those eight 'ARCO controlled' Chemical Directors abstained from the discussions or the vote concerning the proposed transaction between Chemical and Lyondell" and that "these ARCO connections caused the Chemical Board to enter into the third-party Transaction with Lyondell." *Id.* The court also pointed to plaintiff's allegation that "if the Chemical Directors had analyzed the sale of Chemical to Lyondell with the goal of maximizing value for all shareholders and not just to accommodate ARCO, the Chemical board would have concluded that the minority shareholders would have fared better in an appraisal than the Lyondell Transaction that it recommended to them." *Id.*

Section A 4 g

Add the following at the end of the paragraph beginning and concluding on page 781 (immediately after footnote 954):

In *In re Frederick's of Hollywood, Inc. Shareholders Litigation*, 1998 Del. Ch. LEXIS 111, 1998 WL 398244 (Del. Ch. July 9, 1998), the court similarly rejected a claim that the directors of Frederick's of Hollywood breached their fiduciary duties in a bidding contest between Knightsbridge Capital Corporation and Veritas Capital Fund, L.P. During the bidding contest, Knightsbridge acquired control of a majority of Frederick's shares, and the plaintiffs in the case alleged that Frederick's directors breached their fiduciary duties by not granting Veritas an option permitting Veritas to purchase newly issued shares of the Frederick's stock in order to dilute Knightsbridge's stock interest. Citing *Mendel v. Carroll*, 651 A.2d 297 (Del. Ch. 1994), the court stated that this claim "would appear to be contrary to Delaware law." 1998 Del. Ch. LEXIS 111, at *11 & n.9, 1998 WL 398244, at *3 & n.9.

The court also dismissed a claim by shareholders that Knightsbridge tortiously interfered with prospective contractual relations between the corporation and Veritas. Citing *Mendel* again, the court stated that "the limited case law on this subject indicates that except where the majority stockholder is acting to maintain corporate control or is threatening to exploit the vulnerability of the minority stockholders, the issuance of a 'dilutive option' would constitute a breach of fiduciary duty in violation of Delaware law." 1998 Del. Ch. LEXIS 111, at *20, 1998 WL 398244, at *6. Thus, the court concluded, "plaintiffs have not pled that a valid business expectancy existed, because the complaint reveals no lawful way that Frederick's could have circumvented Knightsbridge's power (and, as the majority shareholder, its right) to vote down any transaction it did not favor." *Id.; see also In re Frederick's of Hollywood, Inc. S'holders Litig.*, 2000 Del. Ch. LEXIS 19, at *26-27 & n.19, 2000 WL 130630, at *8 & n.19 (Del. Ch. Jan. 31, 2000) (dismissing claim that consent solicitation statement falsely stated that one of the board's reservations about accepting an offer made by Veritas was that the Veritas offer was conditioned on the grant of a dilutive option because, according to plaintiffs, Veritas was willing to negotiate the size of the option; the court explained that "[e]ven if Veritas was willing to negotiate the size of the dilutive option, it does not follow that the Board had no reason to be concerned about its legality").

Section A 4 i

Add the following new Section A 4 i at the end of the paragraph beginning on page 789 and concluding on page 790 (immediately after footnote 1008):

i. Director Protection Statutes. The court in *Goodwin v. Live Entertainment, Inc.*, 1999 Del. Ch. LEXIS 5, 1999 WL 64265 (Del. Ch. Jan. 22, 1999), *aff'd*, 741 A.2d 16 (unpublished opinion, text available at 1999 Del. LEXIS 238 and 1999 WL 624128) (Del. July 23, 1999), stated that there is "some appeal" to the contention that if a director protection certificate provision adopted by shareholders pursuant to a statute such as Section 102(b)(7) of the Delaware General Corporation Law bars recovery for breaches of the duty of care (*see* Chapter II, Section A 7), then the business judgment rule governs claims under cases such as *Revlon* and *QVC*. The court determined not to adopt this rule, however, "in view of the heightened scrutiny (and concomitant burden shifting) required in the context of a merger involving a change of control." 1999 Del. Ch. LEXIS 5, at *19, 1999 WL 64265, at *7. The court instead reviewed "independently whether any failure of the Board in the sale process can be attributed to disloyal or bad faith acts." *Id.* The court noted, however, that its determination that plaintiff "has not rebutted the business judgment rule's presumption of loyalty supports the conclusion that the sale process was not compromised by disloyalty or bad faith since a finding that a majority of the Board was disinterested is strong evidence that the Board was 'motivated by a good faith desire to achieve the best available transaction.'" *Id.* (quoting *Equity-Linked Investors, L.P. v. Adams*, 705 A.2d 1040, 1055 (Del. Ch. 1997)).

The court in *In re Lukens Inc. Shareholders Litigation*, 757 A.2d 720 (Del. Ch. 1999), went one step further and relied upon a Section 102(b)(7) certificate provision to dismiss a claim that the directors of Lukens Inc. did not act in accordance with their responsibilities under *Revlon* and *QVC* in connection with a bidding contest between Bethlehem Steel Corporation and Allegheny Ludlum Corporation for Lukens that ended with an agreement between Bethlehem and Allegheny pursuant to which Bethlehem acquired Lukens and sold the Lukens assets sought by Allegheny to Allegheny. *Id.* at 726.

The court stated that "[a] corporate board's failure to obtain the best value for its stockholders may be the result of illicit motivation (bad faith), personal interest divergent from shareholder interest (disloyalty) or a lack of due care." *Id.* at 731. According to the court, "[i]f a complaint merely alleges that the directors were grossly negligent in performing their duties in selling the corporation, without some factual basis to suspect their motivations, any subsequent finding of liability will, necessarily, depend on finding breaches of the duty of care, not loyalty or good faith." *Id.* at 731-32. Here, the court stated:

> The well-pleaded allegations of the Complaint typify only a claim of negligence or gross negligence. For example, the Complaint accuses the Director Defendants of failing to act, as follows: to determine the interests of other potential acquirers; to consider the value of a break-up of the Company in numerous sale transactions instead of the sale of the Company as a whole; to include provisions in the merger agreement that protected Lukens and its stockholders from collusion among Bethlehem and other interested bidders; to use "the leverage provided by the Allegheny offer to seek to modify or eliminate the termination fee or any other provisions" of the merger agreement; to negotiate directly with Allegheny with respect to raising its offer; to adequately canvass the market; and so on.

Id. at 728. Due to the absence of an adequate allegation that the directors acted in bad faith or with disloyalty, the court held, the court only could find that the directors "breached their duty of care and nothing more." *Id.* at 732. Accordingly, the court concluded, plaintiffs' claim that the directors did not act in accordance with their responsibilities under *Revlon* and *QVC* should be dismissed pursuant to the corporation's Section 102(b)(7) certificate provision. *Id.* at 732-34.

The court in *In re Frederick's of Hollywood, Inc. Shareholders Litigation*, 2000 Del. Ch. LEXIS 19, 2000 WL 130630 (Del. Ch. Jan. 31, 2000), also relied upon a Section 102(b)(7) certificate provision to dismiss a claim that directors breached their duty to obtain the best value reasonably available to the stockholders. Quoting *Lukens*, the court stated that "[a] corporate board's failure to obtain the best value for its stockholders may be the result of illicit motivation (bad faith), personal interest divergent from shareholder interest (disloyalty) or a lack of due care." 2000 Del. Ch. LEXIS 19, at *16-17, 2000 WL 130630, at *5 (quoting *Lukens*, 757 A.2d at 731). The court concluded that the complaint alleged violations of the board's duty of care and loyalty in conclusory terms but pleaded facts that, if true, would constitute "only a breach of the duty of care – a claim that is not cognizable because of the exculpatory clause in Frederick's charter." 2000 Del. Ch. LEXIS 19, at *17, 2000 WL 130630, at *5.

The court in *McMillan v. Intercargo Corp.*, 768 A.2d 492 (Del. Ch. 2000), similarly relied upon a Section 102(b)(7) certificate provision to dismiss a claim that the approval by the directors of Intercargo Corporation of a merger agreement pursuant to which XL America, Inc. acquired all of Intercargo's shares for $12 per share constituted a breach of fiduciary duty. The court explained that "[b]ecause the plaintiffs may not recover damages for a breach of the duty of care by the defendant directors" due to the corporation's Section 102(b)(7) provision, "the court's focus is necessarily upon whether the complaint alleges facts that, if true, would buttress a conclusion that the defendant directors breached their duty of loyalty or otherwise engaged in conduct not immunized by the exculpatory charter provision." *Id.* at 501. The court stated that "[t]he fact that a corporate board has decided to engage in a change of control transaction invoking so-called *Revlon* duties does not change the showing of culpability a plaintiff must make in order to hold the directors liable for monetary damages." *Id.* at 502. Accordingly, "if a board unintentionally fails, as a result of gross negligence and not of bad faith or self-interest, to follow up on a materially higher bid and an exculpatory charter provision is in place, then the plaintiff will be barred from recovery, regardless of whether the board was in *Revlon*-land." *Id.* The court found that plaintiffs failed to state a claim that "the defendant directors – as a result of bad faith, self-interested, or other intentional misconduct rising to the level of a breach of the duty of loyalty failed to seek the highest attainable value for Intercargo's stockholders." *Id.; see also id.* ("the defendant directors are entitled to dismissal unless the plaintiffs have pled facts that, if true, support the conclusion that the defendant directors failed to secure the highest attainable value as a result of their own bad faith or otherwise disloyal conduct").

Section A 5

Add the following at the end of the paragraph beginning on page 790 and concluding on page 791 (immediately after footnote 1020):

"Because the test is so exacting . . . whether it applies comes close to being outcome-determinative in and of itself." *Chesapeake Corp. v. Shore*, 771 A.2d 293, 319-20 (Del. Ch. 2000); *see also State of Wis. Inv. Bd. v. Peerless Sys. Corp.*, 2000 Del. Ch. LEXIS 170, at *26-27, 2000 WL 1805376, at *8 (Del. Ch. Dec. 4, 2000) ("the choice of the applicable test to judge director action often determines the outcome of the case," and this is "particularly true" in a case involving a shareholder vote "because the two possible tests provide for vastly different levels of review": (1) "deferential business judgment review," where "an attack on a fully informed majority decision to ratify a disputed action or transaction 'normally must fail,'" versus (2) *Blasius* review, where defendants bear "the 'quite onerous' burden of demonstrating a compelling justification for their actions") (quoting *Stroud v. Grace*, 606 A.2d 75, 90 (Del. 1992) and *Williams v. Geier*, 671 A.2d 1368, 1376 (Del. 1996)).

Section A 5 b

Add the following at the end of the paragraph beginning and concluding on page 794 (immediately after footnote 1044):

The Delaware Court of Chancery in *Carmody v. Toll Brothers, Inc.*, 723 A.2d 1180 (Del. Ch 1998), denied a motion to dismiss a claim that the adoption of a dead hand shareholder rights plan poison pill provision was subject to review under the *Blasius* standard. The dead hand provision in *Toll Brothers* prevented "any directors of Toll Brothers, except those who were in office as of the date of the Rights Plan's adoption (June 12, 1997) or their designated successors, from redeeming the Rights until they expire on June 12, 2007." 723 A.2d at 1184. As a result, "only a specific, defined category of directors – the 'Continuing Directors' –" could redeem the rights. *Id.* The challenge to the dead hand provision rights plan stated a claim under *Blasius*, the court held, because the complaint alleged that "the 'dead hand' provision will either preclude a hostile bidder from waging a proxy contest altogether, or, if there should be a contest, it will coerce those shareholders who desire the hostile offer to succeed to vote for those directors who oppose it – the incumbent (and 'Continuing') directors." *Id.* at 1194; *see also* Chapter III, Section G 2 d (discussing *Toll Brothers* decision in greater detail).

The Court of Chancery in *Golden Cycle, LLC v. Allan*, 1998 Del. Ch. LEXIS 80, 1998 WL 276224 (Del. Ch. May 20,

1998), held that the *Blasius* standard of review did not apply to a March 30, 1998 determination by the board of Global Motorsport Group, Inc. to set a March 30, 1998 record date for a consent solicitation by Golden Cycle LLC. Seven days earlier, on March 23, Golden Cycle had sent Global a letter offering to purchase all outstanding shares of Global stock and informing Global that if Global's board did not wish to proceed with negotiations or provide Golden Cycle an opportunity to conduct due diligence, then Golden Cycle would consider attempting to replace Global's board and elect directors committed to selling Global to the highest bidder. The following day, March 24, Golden Cycle filed preliminary consent solicitation materials with the Securities and Exchange Commission. On March 27, Golden Cycle sent a second letter to Global stating Golden Cycle's disappointment that Global refused to meet with Golden Cycle to negotiate the terms of a transaction. On March 30, as stated above, Global's board set a March 30 record date for Golden Cycle's consent solicitation. On April 1, a press release announcing the record date was issued. 1998 Del. Ch. LEXIS 80, at *6-8, 1998 WL 276224, at *2.

The court stated that "[t]he situation presented by the Board's action in fixing the March 30 record date is critically different than the action under attack in *Blasius*," where "the Board's actual purpose in adding two new directors was to preclude 'the stockholders of a majority of [Atlas'] shares from placing a majority of new directors on the board through Blasius' consent solicitation'" – an act of "preclusive character." 1998 Del. Ch. LEXIS 80, at *22, 1998 WL 276224, at *7 (quoting 564 A.2d at 655). The court acknowledged that "the early and unannounced setting of the record date has had some effect (i) in disenfranchising persons who purchased shortly before or after March 30, and (ii) in creating some confusion among nominee holders over the identity of their beneficial holders as of that date" because nominees lacked notice of the need to generate lists of beneficial owners as of March 30 on that date and in some cases were unable to reconstruct complete lists of beneficial owners as of March 30. 1998 Del. Ch.

LEXIS 80, at *8-9, 22, 1998 WL 276224, at *3, 7. The court concluded, however, that "there is no suggestion in the record that these problems will preclude or even substantially interfere with the ability of the Global stockholders to remove and replace the entire board, should they choose to do so." 1998 Del. Ch. LEXIS 80, at *22, 1998 WL 276224, at *7. For these reasons, the court held there was "nothing about the action" taken by Global's board "remotely comparable to the action taken in *Blasius*" and that application of the *Blasius* standard therefore was unwarranted. 1998 Del. Ch. LEXIS 80, at *22-23, 1998 WL 276224, at *7.

The Court of Chancery in *Apple Computer, Inc. v. Exponential Technology, Inc.*, 1999 Del. Ch. LEXIS 9, 1999 WL 39547 (Del. Ch. Jan. 21, 1999), held that a sale of patents constituting substantially all of a corporation's assets without obtaining shareholder approval, where the corporation's directors did not realize that Section 271 of the Delaware General Corporation Law requires a shareholder vote where a corporation sells all or substantially all of its assets, did not trigger enhanced judicial scrutiny under *Blasius* rather than judicial review under the business judgment rule. The court explained that "*Blasius* and similar cases involve tactical maneuvers by incumbent boards seeking to ward off hostile acquirers and defeat dissident slates." 1999 Del. Ch. LEXIS 9, at *14, 1999 WL 39547, at *4. A result of "the potential for entrenchment in the face of a hostile acquisition," the courts in those cases have "carefully scrutinized board action implicating shareholder franchise rights . . . because of the inherent possibility that the board will frustrate a shareholder vote in order to protect itself." 1999 Del. Ch. LEXIS 9, at *15, 1999 WL 39547, at *4. Here, by contrast, Exponential's sale of patents "could not serve as an opportunity for entrenchment" and "did not invoke either a traditional duty of loyalty conflict or an inherently suspect defense against a hostile bid or election of an insurgent slate." 1999 Del. Ch. LEXIS 9, at *17, 1999 WL 39547, at *5. The court held that "[i]n the absence of a hostile acquirer or some other motivation for disenfranchising the shareholders," a board's unintentional failure to fulfill its obligations under Section 271 by approving a sale of substantially all of a corporation's assets without obtaining shareholder approval does not trigger enhanced scrutiny under *Blasius*. *Id.*

The Court of Chancery in *In re Gaylord Container Corp. Shareholders Litigation*, 753 A.2d 462 (Del. Ch. 2000), held that a board decision to time a shareholder vote on charter and bylaw amendments to occur just before a dual class voting structure was to expire – and thus while one shareholder "still had voting control" but just before that shareholder would lose voting control and it thus would become "more difficult" to secure a favorable shareholder vote – did not require "a compelling justification under *Blasius*." *Id.* at 484, 486. The court stated that the charter and bylaw amendments adopted in this manner were "nonpreclusive and noncoercive in the traditional *Unocal* sense and within the range of reasonable responses" to the threat of an inadequate and/or coercive tender offer following the expiration of the corporation's dual class voting structure. *Id.* at 486. Under these circumstances, the court stated, it would be "incongruous" to hold that these defensive measures were "invalid because the board chose the swiftest and surest method of securing their implementation." *Id.* To the contrary, "by securing the speedy enactment of those measures, the board cannot be said to have 'acted for the primary purpose of thwarting the exercise of a shareholder vote.'" *Id.* (quoting *Blasius*, 564 A.2d at 660). The court emphasized that "the prototypical case implicating so-called *Blasius* review involves a situation where: i) a stockholder vote or action by stockholder consent is imminent or threatened; and ii) the board purposely thwarts the opportunity for that vote or action to take place or takes steps to reverse the likely result (e.g., by reducing the voting power of a particular stockholder)." *Id.* at 487. "Neither situation," the court stated, "is present here." *Id.*

The court also rejected plaintiffs' contention that "the mere fact that the Amendments included a supermajority provision making it difficult for stockholders to undo them in the future" raised "an issue distinct from the core *Unocal* analysis." *Id.* The court explained that "[s]upermajority provisions are common and lawful features of corporate charters," and "all supermajority provisions, of course, make it more difficult for stockholders to act together to change company policy." *Id.* As a result, "a principled basis for invalidating such a provision, unless its primary purpose is disenfranchisement or its effects on stockholder voting power reach a level beyond the pale of *Unocal*, is not readily apparent." *Id.*

State of Wisconsin Investment Board v. Peerless Systems Corp., 2000 Del. Ch. LEXIS 170, 2000 WL 1805376 (Del. Ch. Dec. 4, 2000), involved a postponement of the closing of the polls at an annual meeting and the reconvening of the meeting 30 days later, at which time a proposal that trailed in the polls when the meeting was postponed received enough votes to pass by a slim margin.

The court "reaffirm[ed] the fundamental importance of the voting rights of shareholders in Delaware law" and stated that "[n]o one should doubt that '[t]here exists in Delaware a general policy against disenfranchisement' as '[t]he shareholder franchise is the ideological underpinning upon which the legitimacy of directorial power rests.'" 2000 Del. Ch. LEXIS 170, at *23, 2000 WL 1805376, at *7 (quoting *Blasius*, 564 A.2d at 659, 669). The court described the *Blasius* test as "a relatively simple, yet extremely powerful, two-part test based on the duty of loyalty." 2000 Del. Ch. LEXIS 170, at *27, 2000 WL 1805376, at *8. First, "the plaintiff must establish that the board acted for the primary purpose of thwarting the exercise of a shareholder vote." *Id.* Second, "the board has the burden to demonstrate a compelling justification for its actions," and "even where the Court finds that the action taken by the board was made in good faith, it may still constitute a violation of the duty of loyalty" if the board does not overcome its burden of demonstrating "a compelling justification for its actions." *Id.* Thus, "*Blasius* does not apply in all cases where a board of directors has interfered with a shareholder vote." 2000 Del. Ch. LEXIS 170, at *28, 2000 WL 1805376, at *8. The court stated that "[i]n the absence of a finding that the primary purpose of the board's action was to interfere with or impede exercise of the shareholder franchise, the business judgment rule presumption applies," and "with a fully informed shareholder approval of the proposal in question, the burden of proof remains squarely with the plaintiff to prove . . . that the board action was not properly taken or that the action was the product of fraud, manipulation, or other inequitable conduct." 2000 Del. Ch. LEXIS 170, at *32, 2000 WL 1805376, at *9. The court's application of the *Blasius* test in *Peerless* is discussed in Chapter III, Section H 1 a.

Add the following at the end of the paragraph beginning on page 797 and concluding on page 799 (immediately after footnote 1063):

- *Starkman v. United Parcel Services of America, Inc.*, No. 17747, Tr. at 28-29 (Del. Ch. Oct. 18, 1999) (rejecting contention that a *Blasius* claim was stated where a board allegedly "proposed a merger rather than an amendment to the certificate of incorporation for an improper purpose; that is, for the purpose of depriving the stockholder group as a whole of the ability or the opportunity to exercise a supermajority vote"; the court stated that "[i]f, as I have found, the board was perfectly in its right to propose a merger, the fact that it did so because it didn't wish to comply with the supermajority vote requirement and face either the higher obstacle of getting those votes or, as the board would have it, the extra time required to do so" is not sufficient to state a claim: "Certainly the *Blasius* case provides no support. In *Blasius* the issue was that the board of directors, in the middle of an effort by outsiders to exercise their franchise, acted to pack the board and preempt the ability of those stockholders to use their vote to elect directors. There is nothing of the sort present here.").

Section A 5 c

Add the following at the end of the paragraph beginning on page 804 and concluding on page 805 (immediately after footnote 1105):

The Court of Chancery in *Chesapeake Corp. v. Shore*, 771 A.2d 293 (Del. Ch. 2000), also addressed the extent to which the *Blasius* standard of review is a viable standard of review separate and apart from *Unocal* in a case where *Unocal* otherwise would be the standard of review. The court noted that "[i]n the wake of *Blasius*, Delaware courts have struggled with how broadly the case should be applied" and that "it is not easy in most cases to determine whether the *Blasius* standard should be invoked." *Id.* at 319-20.

The court explained that it was "undisputed in *Blasius* that the board's actions precluded the election of a new board majority and that the board intended that effect." *Id.* at 320. The court in *Blasius* thus "had no difficulty in concluding that the 'board acted for the primary purpose of thwarting the exercise of a shareholder vote.'" *Id.* (quoting *Blasius*, 564 A.2d at 660). By contrast, "[i]n the more typical case involving board actions touching upon the electoral process," the court continued, "the question of whether the board's actions are preclusive is usually hotly contested," and "the preclusion question and the issue of the board's 'primary purpose' are not easily separable." *Id.* As a result, the court "must be rather deep in its analysis before it can ever determine if the *Blasius* standard properly applies" because "[t]he line between board actions that influence the electoral process in legitimate ways (e.g., delaying the election to provide more time for deliberations or to give the target board some reasonable breathing room to identify alternatives) and those that preclude effective stockholder action is not always luminous," and "[a]bsent confessions of improper purpose, the most important evidence of what a board intended to do is often what effects its actions have." *Id.* "Put another way, rather than the standard of review determining how the court looks at the board's actions, how the court looks at the board's actions influences in an important way what standard of review is to apply." *Id.*

The court also noted that the Supreme Court's opinions in *Stroud v. Grace*, 606 A.2d 75 (Del. 1992), and *Unitrin v. American General Corp.*, 651 A.2d 1361 (Del. 1995), have "recognized the high degree of overlap between the concerns animating the *Blasius* standard of review and those that animate *Unocal*":

> For example, in *Stroud v. Grace*, the Delaware Supreme Court held that *Unocal* must be applied to any defensive measure touching upon issues of control, regardless of whether that measure also implicates voting rights. In so ruling, the Court noted that "[b]oard action interfering with the exercise of the franchise often ar[ises] during a hostile contest for control where an acquiror launch[es] both a proxy fight and a tender offer. When a case involves defensive measures of such a nature, the trial court is not to ignore the teaching of *Blasius* but must "recognize the special import of protecting the shareholders' franchise within *Unocal*'s requirement that any defensive measure be proportionate and 'reasonable in relation to the threat posed.'" Therefore, a "board's unilateral decision to adopt a defensive measure touching upon issues of control that purposely disenfranchise its shareholders is strongly suspect under *Unocal*, and cannot be sustained without a compelling justification."
>
> The Supreme Court's *Unitrin* opinion seems to go even further than *Stroud* in integrating *Blasius*'s concern over manipulation of the electoral process into the *Unocal* standard of review. . . . [T]he Court emphasized the "assiduous[ness of] its concern about defensive actions designed to thwart the essence of corporate democracy by disenfranchising shareholders" and its acceptance of the "'basic tenets'" of *Blasius*. Because the board's actions came in the face of a tender offer coupled with a proxy fight, the Court cited extensively to *Stroud*'s discussion of the interrelationship of *Blasius* and *Unocal* in such circumstances.

771 A.2d at 320-21 (quoting *Stroud*, 606 A.2d at 82, 92 n.3 and *Unitrin*, 651 A.2d at 1378) (footnotes omitted).

Nevertheless, the court in *Chesapeake* stated, "when it came time to assess whether . . . the repurchase program" in *Unitrin* "was invalid . . . the Supreme Court appeared to eschew any application of the compelling justification test." 771 A.2d at 321. According to the court in *Chesapeake*, the Supreme Court "did start its analysis with a sentence stating: 'We begin our examination of Unitrin's Repurchase Program mindful of the special import of protecting the shareholder's franchise within *Unocal*'s requirement that a defensive response be reasonable and proportionate.'" *Id.* (quoting 651 A.2d at 1379). The Supreme Court, however, "never cited to *Blasius* after that point in its opinion, never referenced or applied the compelling justification standard, and, to the contrary, emphasized the latitude a board of directors must be given to adopt reasonable defensive measures in its business judgment." *Id.*

Thus, the court in *Chesapeake* stated, *Stroud* and *Unitrin* "left unanswered the question most important to litigants: when will the compelling justification test be used, whether within the *Unocal* analysis or as a free-standing standard of review?" *Id.* The court continued:

> Assuming the compelling justification language is to be taken seriously, whether that language applies could, of course, tilt the outcome of a *Unocal* analysis in an important way. After *Unitrin*, this question became even more consequential, because that opinion appeared to accord target boards of directors quite a bit of leeway to take defensive actions that made it more difficult for an insurgent slate to win a proxy fight.

Id.

The court then surveyed a series of Court of Chancery decisions illustrating that "it is often impossible to distinguish the inquiry of whether a measure fails to pass muster under *Unocal* from the inquiry necessary to determine whether the *Blasius* standard of review even applies," including (1) cases where a "finding of non-preclusiveness" resulted in holdings that "a defensive measure affecting the electoral process was not preclusive and therefore did not trigger *Blasius*" and were "within the range of reason under the *Unocal* test" and (2) cases where a defensive measure "forced stockholders to vote for the incumbent directors in the election" and thus was coercive and "[a]s a result, the complaint stated a claim under both *Unocal* and *Blasius*." *Id.* at 322-23 & nn.57, 58 (citing, in the first category, *Stahl v. Apple Bancorp, Inc.*, 579 A.2d 1115 (Del. Ch. 1990), *Commonwealth Assocs. v. Providence Health Care, Inc.*, 1993 Del. Ch. LEXIS 321, 1993 WL 432779 (Del. Ch. Oct. 22, 1993), *Kidsco Inc. v. Dinsmore*, 674 A.2d 483 (Del. Ch. 1995), *aff'd*, 670 A.2d 1338 (unpublished opinion, text available at 1995 Del. LEXIS 426 and 1995 WL 715886) (Del. Nov. 29, 1995), *H.F. Ahmanson & Co. v. Great W. Fin. Corp.*, 1997 Del. Ch. LEXIS 84, 1997 WL 305824 (Del. Ch. June 3, 1997), and *Golden Cycle, LLC v. Allan*, 1998 Del. Ch. LEXIS 80, 1998 WL 276224 (Del. Ch. May 20, 1998), and, in the second category, *Carmody v. Toll Bros., Inc.*, 723 A.2d 1180 (Del. Ch. 1998), and *Mentor Graphics Corp. v. Quickturn Design Sys., Inc.*, 728 A.2d 25 (Del. Ch.), *aff'd sub nom. Quickturn Design Sys., Inc. v. Shapiro*, 721 A.2d 1281 (Del. 1998)).

On this basis, the court observed, "[i]n reality, invocation of the *Blasius* standard of review usually signals that the court will invalidate the board action under examination," and "[f]ailure to invoke *Blasius*, conversely, typically indicates that the board action survived (or will survive) review under *Unocal*." 771 A.2d at 323. For this reason, the court stated, "one might reasonably question to what extent the *Blasius* 'compelling justification' standard of review is necessary as a lens independent of or to be used within the *Unocal* frame." *Id.* The court continued:

> If *Unocal* is applied by the Court with a gimlet eye out for inequitably motivated electoral manipulations or for subjectively well-intentioned board action that has preclusive or coercive effects, the need for an additional standard of review is substantially lessened. Stated differently, it may be optimal simply for Delaware courts to infuse our *Unocal* analyses with the spirit animating *Blasius* and not hesitate to use our remedial powers where an inequitable distortion of corporate

> democracy has occurred. This is especially the case when a typical predicate to the invocation of *Blasius* is the court's consideration of *Unocal* factors, such as the board's purpose and whether the board's actions have preclusive or coercive effects on the electorate.

Id.

The court concluded, however, that "I must apply the law as it exists," and "[t]hat means that *Unocal* must be applied" because the case before the court involved a supermajority bylaw that was adopted as a defensive measure and "[t]o the extent that I further conclude that the Supermajority Bylaw was adopted for the primary purpose of interfering with or impeding the stockholder franchise, the Bylaw cannot survive a *Unocal* review unless it is supported by a compelling justification." *Id.* at 323-24. To apply this approach in a reasoned manner, the court first examined the bylaw "employing purely the *Unocal* standard," and then, "[a]fter examining the defendant's justifications for the Bylaw and whether the Bylaw is a proportionate response under *Unocal*," the court then considered "whether the compelling justification standard of *Blasius* is implicated." *Id.* at 324. The court acknowledged that "this order of examination may seem backwards" but explained that the "threat justification under the first prong of *Unocal*" and the effect of the bylaw on the consent solicitation being mounted in the case "as considered under the second prong of *Unocal* . . . both bear on whether I can conclude that the defendants' ''primary purpose'' was 'to interfere with or impede exercise of the shareholder franchise.'" *Id.* (quoting *Stroud*, 606 A.2d at 92 n.3).

Hills Stores Co. v. Bozic, 769 A.2d 88 (Del. Ch. 2000), involved a claim by Hills Stores Company ("Hills") and its Hills Department Stores Company ("HDS") subsidiary against former directors of Hills following a successful proxy contest led by Dickstein Partners, an investment fund that had promised either to purchase all Hills shares for $22 in cash plus a $5 payable-in-kind bond per share or to sell Hills to the highest bidder in an auction. During the proxy contest, Dickstein assured Hills shareholders that Dickstein had the ability to finance the acquisition and cover the costs that would accompany a change of control, including severance payments to Hills executives pursuant to employment agreements granting the executives the right to resign and receive severance in the event of any change in control not approved by the Hills board. The agreements had been entered into during a previous Dickstein-initiated control contest, and claims by Dickstein challenging the validity of the agreements previously had been settled. *Id.* at 89-90.

During the days leading up to the election, the Hills board authorized the creation of "rabbi trusts" into which funds sufficient to pay the severance and other benefits due under the employment agreements were deposited. These funds would be paid automatically upon the occurrence of events giving the covered executives the right to payment under the employment agreements. *Id.* at 99. On the day before the election, the Hills board rejected a demand by Dickstein that the board vote to approve the change in control solely for the purpose of ensuring that the employment agreements would not be triggered. The board based this determination upon its belief that a change in control was "a serious threat to Hills" and that Hills "had promised the covered executives severance in such a situation." *Id.* at 90. After Dickstein took control of Hills, the covered executives resigned and received their severance, the corporation's creditors terminated their debt agreements with Hills, and Dickstein failed to consummate its acquisition effort or conduct an auction. Instead, Dickstein caused Hills to sue the former Hills board based upon a claim that "the payment of severance resulted from breaches of fiduciary duty and contract by the former Hills directors." *Id.*

The court rejected Dickstein's contention that the *Blasius* compelling justification standard of review governed the board's decision not to approve the change of control for the purpose of ensuring that the employment agreements would not be triggered. The court explained that there was no evidence (and Dickstein was estopped from arguing due to the settlement it previously had agreed to) that the Hills board adopted the employment agreements "as a method of placing pressure on the Hills electorate to vote against a Change in Control." *Id.* at 103. To the contrary, the court stated, the employment agreements "were executed as an incentive for current management to remain at Hills in the face of a takeover threat from Dickstein" and "a double trigger" – requiring not just a "single trigger" change in control, but also a demotion or termination or a change in control not approved by the pre-change in control directors – "was put in place to give the Hills board negotiating leverage with potential acquirors and to assuage the company's creditors." *Id.* at 92, 103.

The court also explained that the employment agreements were not "the sort of corporate action that directly affects the electoral rules or process." *Id.* at 103. Instead, the court stated, the employment agreements had only "the incidental effect of coercing or placing an undue toll on the free exercise of the shareholder vote" by exacting "a financial penalty on the company and therefore the stockholders if they vote for an unapproved Change in Control." *Id.* The court rejected plaintiffs' contention that this "incidental effect" was "sufficient to trigger *Blasius* review" because, the court stated, "this is an argument that the *Blasius* standard is triggered because the Employment Agreements fail the proportionality prong of *Unocal*, which already proscribes coercive defensive measures." *Id.*

The court acknowledged that "our case law often determines whether *Blasius* applies by examining whether the challenged action is coercive or preclusive of electoral action, an exercise that is duplicative of *Unocal*," but concluded that "[r]ather than extend this unwieldy and redundant practice to corporate action that is not directed specifically at the electoral process, I believe that it is more rational and efficient to apply the more flexible, but still exacting, *Unocal* standard in situations like this, but with a sharp eye out for electoral coercion." *Id.* at 103-04. A different approach, the court stated, "could subject a variety of measures commonly reviewed under

Unocal to *Blasius* scrutiny." *Id.* at 104. For example, the court noted, a termination fee payable in the event of a shareholder vote against a merger "places the same sort of economic toll on the franchise" as employment agreements payable in the event of a change of control. *Id.* Because the *Unocal* standard (and, in appropriate cases, the *Revlon* standard) can "be applied to strike down termination fees or severance payments that coerce stockholders," the court stated, "there is no need to layer *Blasius* on top of them." *Id.*

Section A 6 a

Replace the heading in the paragraph beginning on page 808 and concluding on page 809 (between footnotes 1134 and 1135) with the following:

a. Case Law Decided Without Reference to State Statutes.

Add the following at the end of footnote 1150 on page 810:

See also Safety-Kleen Corp. v. Laidlaw Envtl. Servs., Inc., 1999 WL 601039, at *12, 15, 18 (N.D. Ill. Feb. 4, 1998) (decision construing statute discussed in Chapter III, Section A 6 b).

Add the following at the end of the paragraph beginning on page 811 and concluding on page 812 (immediately after footnote 1159):

As stated by the Court of Chancery in *Chesapeake Corp. v. Shore*, 771 A.2d 293 (Del. Ch. 2000), the interests of constituencies such as "employees or communities that might be adversely affected by a change of control" are "of little, if no relevance, under Delaware corporate law." *Id.* at 328 & n.82.

Section A 6 b

Add the following at the end of footnote 1161 on page 813:

See also In re Bakalis, 220 B.R. 525, 536 (Bankr. E.D.N.Y. 1998) (noting board's duties in light of this statute).

Add the following at the end of the paragraph beginning on page 813 and concluding on page 814 (immediately after footnote 1172):

A federal court construing Wisconsin law in *Safety-Kleen v. Laidlaw Environmental Services, Inc.*, 1999 WL 601039 (N.D. Ill. Feb. 4, 1998) – a case discussed in Chapter III, Section G 2 a – held that Wisconsin's non-shareholder constituency statute (Wis. Bus. Corp. Law § 180.0827) – "clearly establishes . . . that Wisconsin corporate directors may legitimately and without breaching their fiduciary duties to shareholders take into consideration in exercising their business judgment the impact of their decisions on non-shareholder constituencies." 1999 WL 601039, at *12. Under this statute, "maximizing short term shareholder value, that is, getting the highest price" in a tender offer, is not "the only interest the board may legitimately pursue." *Id.* In the case before the court, which involved "financially equivalent offers" for Safety-Kleen by two bidders (Philip, Apollo Advisors L.P. and Laidlaw Environmental Services, Inc.), the court concluded that Safety-Kleen's board did not act unreasonably in determining that "Philip's stated intention to keep Safety-Kleen's headquarters in operation and continue Safety-Kleen's charitable commitments and community involvement was preferable to Laidlaw's plans to move the company to South Carolina." *Id.* at *9, 12. The court stated that "there is no question that under Wisconsin law the Board could take into consideration its view that the Laidlaw proposal would be significantly deleterious to other constituencies such as the community where for many years Safety-Kleen has done business and to its employees." *Id.* at *15; *see also id.* at *18 ("Wisconsin law explicitly allows" directors to consider non-shareholder interests). The court, however, added that if directors ignore "a clearly better offer simply because of their commitment to the interests of other constituencies, their conduct might be cause for great concern, because the directors have fiduciary duties to the shareholders which cannot be ignored." *Id.* at *12.

A federal court construing Missouri law in *Flake v. Hoskins*, 55 F. Supp. 2d 1196 (D. Kan. 1999), stated that the duties of a corporate board under Missouri's non-shareholder constituency statute (Mo. Gen. & Bus. Corp. Law § 351.347) "are not truly different" from a board's duties under cases such as *Revlon*. The court explained that "*Revlon* does not require a board to accept the highest offer regardless of any other considerations. Rather, the board must simply accept the best alternative for shareholders, all things considered." *Flake*, 55 F. Supp. 2d at 1214. The court stated that "[t]he only noticeable difference" between "[t]he possible factors to consider under *Revlon*" and the factors listed in the Missouri statute is that Missouri's statute "allows the board to consider the effect of the sale on other constituencies, without expressly requiring a link to general shareholder interests." *Id.* The court stated that "[t]his difference does not appear to be significant, however, because in all business actions, a corporate board of directors owes a fiduciary duty to shareholders and must generally operate for their benefit," and "[a]ny consideration of other constituencies must therefore have at least a reasonable relationship to the general interests of shareholders." *Id.*

By contrast, a federal court construing New York law in *Minzer v. Keegan*, 1997 U.S. Dist. LEXIS 16445 (E.D.N.Y. Sept. 22, 1997), stated that the *Revlon* doctrine "has never been adopted by the New York courts" and that New York's non-shareholder constituency statute "provides instead that in actions involving change of control, . . . directors . . . are free to consider not only short-term considerations such as merger price, but long-term factors as well." 1997 U.S. Dist. LEXIS 16445, at *31; *see also Rand v. Crosby*, No. 400063/98, slip op. at 4 (N.Y. Sup. Ct. N.Y. Co. May 17, 1999) ("a board of directors' determination of what price to sell a company's shares falls squarely within the business judgment rule").

Add the following at the end of the paragraph beginning and concluding on page 814 (immediately after footnote 1174):

Maryland's statute authorizes the adoption of a certificate of incorporation provision that "allows the board of directors, in considering a potential acquisition of control of the corporation, to consider the effect of the potential acquisition of control on (i) [s]tockholders, employees, suppliers, customers, and creditors of the corporation; and (ii) [c]ommunities in which offices or other establishments of the corporation are located." Md. Gen. Corp. Law § 2-104(b)(9). The statute states that "[t]he inclusion or omission of a provision in the charter that allows the board of directors to consider the effect of a potential acquisition of control" on the person or entities specified in the statute "does not create an inference concerning factors that may be considered by the board of directors regarding a potential acquisition of control." *Id.* § 2-104(c).

Add "Maryland," between "Indiana," and "North Carolina" in the first sentence (between footnotes 1184 and 1185) of the paragraph beginning on page 816 and concluding on page 817.

Add the following at the end of footnote 1185 on page 816:

See also Md. Gen. Corp. Law § 2-405.1(f).

Section A 7

Add the following at the end of footnote 1215 on page 824:

See also In re Gaylord Container Corp. S'holders Litig., 753 A.2d 462, 477 (Del. Ch. 2000).

Add the following at the end of the first sentence (immediately after footnote 1215) of the paragraph beginning on page 823 and concluding on page 824:

The Delaware Supreme Court in *Unitrin, Inc. v. American General Corp.*, 651 A.2d 1361 (Del. 1995), also held that "the presence of a majority of outside independent directors will materially enhance" the proof offered by a board of directors in support of its initial burden of demonstrating good faith and a reasonable investigation. *Id.* at 1375; *see also Hills Stores Co. v. Bozic*, 769 A.2d 88, 107 (Del. Ch. 2000); *Chesapeake Corp. v. Shore*, 771 A.2d at 293, 330 n.86 (Del. Ch. 2000). The court in *Unitrin* noted that "[a]n 'outside' director has been defined as a non-employee and non-management director" and "[i]ndependence 'means that a director's decision is based on the corporate merits of the subject before the board rather than extraneous considerations or influences.'" *Id.* (quoting *Grobow v. Perot*, 539 A.2d 180, 184 n.2 (Del. 1988), and *Aronson v. Lewis*, 473 A.2d 805, 816 (Del. 1984)).

Add the following at the end of footnote 1219 on page 824:

See also Chesapeake, 771 A.2d at 330 (concluding that "six of the nine members of the Shorewood board cannot be considered outside, independent directors" and "[t]herefore, the board's actions are entitled to less deference").

Add the following at the end of the paragraph beginning on page 823 and concluding on page 824 (immediately after footnote 1222):

The Court of Chancery in *Chesapeake Corp. v. Shore*, 771 A.2d 293 (Del. Ch. 2000), noted that it has been "stated unequivocally" that "[t]he presence of a majority of outside independent directors will materially enhance" a board's ability to meet its burden "as to the first prong of *Unocal*," which requires a showing that the board had reasonable grounds to perceive a threat to corporate policy and effectiveness, but "it is less certain that the Supreme Court believes it to be relevant to the second prong," which requires that the defensive measures adopted were reasonable in relation to the threat posed. *Id.* at 330 & n.86. The court in *Chesapeake* stated its view that the presence of a majority of outside independent directors is relevant to both prongs of *Unocal* "because what a board does is as important as why a board claims it decided to do it." *Id.* at 330 n.86. According to the court in *Chesapeake*, "[t]he absence or presence of an outside majority might be a factor leading a court to conclude that particular defensive options were selected in good or bad faith." *Id.*

Add the following at the end of the paragraph beginning on page 826 and concluding on page 827 (immediately after footnote 1233):

Kohls v. Duthie, 765 A.2d 1274 (Del. Ch. 2000), a case involving a management buyout of Kenetech Corporation sponsored by a third party venture capital fund, also illustrates this point. Mark D. Lerdal, the corporation's chief executive officer, participated in the buyout by contributing his shares to the purchaser in exchange for equity. The transaction was negotiated by a special committee of two outside directors, the committee was advised by independent legal and financial experts, and the committee acted "deliberately and in a fully informed manner"; indeed, the court stated, the committee "met more than twenty times and approved the final merger proposal at the conclusion of a two-day meeting at which it received reports from both its legal and financial advisors," relied upon an opinion from its financial advisor stating that the transaction price was fair to shareholders other than Lerdal from a financial point of view, "bargained for and obtained terms in the merger agreement that allow for an effective post-announcement market check," and "had the power to 'say no' and appears to have exercised that power during the course of vigorous arm's-length negotiations." *Id.* at 1277, 1285. Under these circumstances, the court concluded, the transaction was subject to review under "the deferential business judgment standard of review" rather than the entire fairness standard of review. *Id.*

Section A 8

Add the following at the end of the paragraph beginning on page 833 and concluding on page 834 (immediately after footnote 1273):

The Delaware Court of Chancery in *In re Gaylord Container Corp. Shareholders Litigation*, 747 A.2d 71 (Del. 1999), stated that "settled case law indicates that a potential acquiror may bring an individual action to challenge defensive actions impeding its bid. *Id.* at 81. The court noted that "[t]here are very sound practical, value-enhancing reasons for the case law according bidders standing, even though the practice of according *bidders standing as stockholders* leads to a certain amount of undeniable doctrinal incoherence." *Id.* at 81 n.14. The court also noted that "[t]here are also very sound doctrinal reasons for recognizing that defensive measures primarily affect stockholders as prospective sellers and bidders (regardless of stockholder status) as prospective buyers, and enabling each to bring individual actions to protect their legitimate interests in being able to deal with each other without improper (i.e., not fiduciarily compliant) interference by corporate boards." *Id.*

One commentator has summarized the law as follows:

> [A]t a minimum, the factors a court will consider will include: (i) the relationship between the potential acquiror's standing and the merits of the dispute; (ii) the interests of the parties and the public in resolving the controversy; (iii) the investment of effort and resources by the parties in the litigation; and (iv) the presence of shareholder plaintiffs who are also challenging the target board's actions, regardless of whether the shareholder plaintiffs raise claims paralleling those of the potential acquiror. This list is not exhaustive, and other factors certainly will be relevant depending on the context of the case. Where

these factors support a judicial decision on the merits, the potential acquiror's *Unocal* claim will go forward.

Laster, *The Line Item Veto and Unocal: Can a Bidder Qua Bidder Pursue Unocal Claims Against a Target Corporation's Board of Directors?*, 53 Bus. Law. 767, 797 (1998).

Section B 1 a

Add the following at the end of the paragraph beginning on page 845 and concluding on page 846 (immediately after footnote 1337):

- *BBC Capital Markets, Inc. v. Carver Bancorp, Inc.*, No. 17743, Tr. at 3-4, 9-10 (Del. Ch. Feb. 16, 2000) (refusing to grant a preliminary injunction enjoining Carver Bancorp from counting votes of shares held by Morgan Stanley & Co. Incorporated and Provender Opportunities Fund, L.P. where, plaintiffs alleged, Carver entered into "business relationships with Morgan Stanley and Provender, timed by Carver's CEO, and her friends at Morgan Stanley and Provender to grant them voting shares in exchange for infusions of capital by the record date" for a shareholder meeting at which plaintiff sought to elect two directors to Carver's eight member board in an election alleged to threaten the CEO's status as CEO; the court stated that "I cannot grant what is tantamount to summary judgment on the merits to the plaintiff in the face of unresolved credibility issues," and "since granting the plaintiff's application today would result in full, final and complete relief, the harm done to defendants by issuing the preliminary injunction today, a legal declaration that Carver may not count Morgan Stanley and Provender votes at the annual meeting, would far outweigh the harm done to plaintiff by denying the relief").

Section B 2 d

Add the following at the end of footnote 1529 on page 877:

See also Matador Capital Mgmt. Corp. v. BRC Holdings, Inc., 729 A.2d 280, 298-300 (Del. Ch. 1998) (rejecting contention that acquisition of BRC by ACS by means of a tender offer and merger was barred by Section 203 because ACS had entered into an agreement with a 20 percent shareholder of BRC pursuant to which the 20 percent shareholder agreed to tender her shares to ACS within five days after the commencement of the ACS tender offer; the court found no basis to conclude that ACS reached an "agreement, arrangement or understanding" with the 20 percent shareholder that was not approved in advance by the BRC board").

Section B 2 e

Replace the Unisys citation in footnote 1538 on page 879 with the following:

In re Unisys Sav. Plan Litig., 1997 U.S. Dist. LEXIS 19198, at *67-75, 1997 WL 732473, at *22-25 (E.D. Pa. Nov. 24, 1997), *aff'd*, 173 F.3d 145, 153-54 (3d Cir.), *cert. denied*, 528 U.S. 950 (1999) (same);

Add the following at the end of the paragraph beginning and concluding on page 886 (immediately after footnote 1573):

Flake v. Hoskins, 55 F. Supp. 2d 1196 (D. Kan. 1999), involved claims that directors had breached fiduciary duties under ERISA in a case involving a plan instrument providing that directors were fiduciaries with respect to "(1) plan administration, (2) the issuance of advisory opinions regarding disposition of the trust assets, and (3) removing the trustee." *Id.* at 1219. The court held that allegations that implicated the fiduciary duties specified in the plan instrument, including claims that the directors failed to render an advisory opinion regarding offers for ESOP stock and provided holders of ESOP shares misleading information, stated a claim for breach of defendants' fiduciary duty under ERISA. *Id.* at 1221. "Most of plaintiff's allegations," the court also held, however, "revolve around the disposition of the ESOP shares" and plaintiff's contention that the corporation's directors acted "for the sole purpose of preventing" the ESOP's trustee "from selling the ESOP shares" to various offerors. *Id.* at 1221. These allegations did not state a claim for breach of fiduciary duty under ERISA, the court stated, because under the governing plan instrument "defendants were not fiduciaries regarding the actual disposition of trust assets." *Id.* at 1219.

Replace the NationsBank citation in footnote 1602 on page 892 with the following:

126 F.3d 1354 (11th Cir. 1997), *reh'g denied*, 135 F.3d 1409 (11th Cir.), *cert. denied*, 525 U.S. 816 (1998).

Replace the NationsBank citation in footnote 1616 on page 894 with the following:

1995 U.S. Dist. LEXIS 5328, 1995 WL 316550 (N.D. Ga. Mar. 29, 1995), *amended*, 1995 WL 389614 (N.D. Ga. May 10, 1995), *aff'd in part and rev'd in part sub nom. Herman v. NationsBank Trust Co.*, 126 F.3d 1354 (11th Cir. 1997), *reh'g denied,* 135 F.3d 1409 (11th Cir.), *cert. denied*, 525 U.S. 816 (1998).

Add the following at the end of the paragraph beginning on page 900 and concluding on page 901 (immediately after footnote 1652):

NationsBank petitioned for rehearing, and took issue with the court's holding that the Polaroid ESOP participants were not given sufficient notice that they were fiduciaries with respect to the unallocated shares. *Herman v. NationsBank N.A.*,

135 F.3d 1409, 1410 (11th Cir.), *cert. denied*, 525 U.S. 816 (1998). The court pointed to the "Summary Plan Description ('SPD') provided to all the participants after the ESOP was established in July 1998" as the "best piece of evidence NationsBank presents" on this subject. *Id.* The SPD stated the following:

> Will I Be Contacted In the Event of a Tender Offer? . . .
>
> In the event of a tender offer, Polaroid shareholders and Stock Equity Plan members [i.e., the participants] would be asked if they want to sell or 'tender' their shares.
>
> Important: If a plan member does not respond, that plan member is assumed to be deciding *against* the tender offer.
>
> Unallocated stock will be tendered in the same proportion as the allocated shares.
>
> Example: If 10% of the allocated shares are tendered by plan members, 10% of the unallocated shares also would be tendered.

Id. According to NationsBank, this statement put participants "on notice that their actions in regard to the allocated shares would control the tendering of the unallocated shares, and as a result the participants were fiduciaries with regard to the unallocated shares." *Id.*

The court disagreed. The court explained that the most the SPD demonstrated was that "at the time the SPD was distributed the participants had notice that, in the event of a tender offer, their actions in regard to the allocated shares would control the tendering of the unallocated shares." *Id.* This fact, the court concluded, "is not enough to put the participants on notice that they were fiduciaries with regard to the unallocated shares." *Id.* The court reasoned as follows:

> The participants could not be fiduciaries with regard to the unallocated shares in the absence of explicit notice that they could be held liable for their actions with regard to the unallocated shares. We emphasized that point in our previous opinion when we stated that the possibility of the participants being subject to liability as fiduciaries for their actions with regard to the unallocated shares was "unacceptable . . . where participants are not adequately informed of the responsibilities

> they possess *and* the liability that could go hand in hand with those responsibilities." Nothing in the SPD or in the materials NationsBank sent the participants concerning the tender offer put the participants on notice that they could be held liable as fiduciaries for their actions with regard to the unallocated shares.

Id. (citing *Herman v. NationsBank Trust Co.*, 126 F.3d 1354, 1367 (11th Cir. 1997), *reh'g denied*, 135 F.3d 1409 (11th Cir.), *cert. denied*, 525 U.S. 816 (1998); emphasis added in decision denying petition for rehearing).

This conclusion, the court added, made it "unnecessary for us to address the broader question of whether ESOP participants can under any circumstances be named fiduciaries for unallocated shares." *Id.* at 1410-11. The court quoted from its prior decision:

> "[B]ecause ESOP participants could conceivably face liability to other persons and entities if they were named fiduciaries with regard to unallocated shares, we are not sure that such status could be forced upon participants even with sufficient notice. A plan might be required to give participants a chance to opt-out from such responsibilities and liabilities. However, we need not and do not decide that matter."

Id. at 1411 (quoting 126 F.3d at 1367 n.11).

Section D 1

Add the following at the end of the paragraph beginning on page 908 and concluding on page 909 (between footnotes 1702 and 1703):

The Delaware Court of Chancery in *McMillan v. Intercargo Corp.*, 768 A.2d 492 (Del. Ch. 2000), explained that deal protection provisions such as stock options, no shop provisions and termination fee provisions are governed by the standard of judicial review provided for in *Unocal*:

> Under a "duck" approach to the law, "deal protection" terms self-evidently designed to deter and make more expensive alternative transactions would be considered defensive and

> reviewed under the *Unocal Corp. v. Mesa Petroleum Co.*, Del. Supr., 493 A.2d 946 (1985) standard. The word "protect" bears a close relationship to the word "from." Provisions of this obviously defensive nature (e.g., no-shops, no-talks, termination fees triggered by the consummation of an alternative transaction, and stock options with the primary purpose of destroying pooling treatment for other bidders) primarily "protect" the deal and the parties thereto *from* the possibility that a rival transaction will displace the deal. Such deal protection provisions accomplish this purpose by making it more difficult and more expensive to consummate a competing transaction and by providing compensation to the odd company out if such an alternative deal nonetheless occurs. Of course, the mere fact that the court calls a 'duck" a "duck" does not mean that such defensive provisions will not be upheld so long as they are not draconian.

768 A.2d at 506 n.62. In the sale of control context, the standard of judicial review provided for in cases such as *Revlon, Inc. v. MacAndrews & Forbes Holdings, Inc.*, 506 A.2d 173 (Del. 1986) and *Paramount Communications, Inc. v. QVC Network Inc.*, 637 A.2d 34 (Del. 1994), also may apply. *McMillan*, 768 A.2d at 506.

The court in *McMillan* added that the law does not require that merger agreements "contain only such 'deal protection' measures as will not deter the timid or those potential acquirors unwilling to bear the costs that may result from the law's acknowledgment that parties to executory contracts have legitimate, although constrained, contract rights." *Id.* at 506 n.65.

The court in *McMillan* also noted that the absence of an allegation that a board refused to consider a higher bid or that merger agreement provisions prevented a competing bidder from presenting a superior offer during the time period between the announcement of a merger and the closing of the merger is a fact that weighs heavily in favor of dismissal of a case challenging a board's adoption of a deal protection measure. *Id.* at 506-07. The court in *McMillan* accordingly dismissed a case where "[i]n contrast to the usual *Revlon/Unocal* case involving defendants who have resisted a sale," the complaint "attempts to state a claim against a board with a disinterested majority that engaged an investment banker to search for strategic buyers, that consummated a merger agreement with a third-party purchaser, and that put up no insuperable barriers to a better deal." *Id.* at 507.

Section D 1 a

Add the following at the end of the paragraph beginning and concluding on page 910 (immediately after footnote 1707):

The same result was reached by another federal court construing New York law in *Minzer v. Keegan*, 1997 U.S. Dist. LEXIS 16445 (E.D.N.Y. Sept. 22, 1997). This case involved a determination by The Greater New York Savings Bank to enter into a merger agreement with Astoria Financial Corporation rather than with North Fork Bancorporation and to include an option in the merger agreement permitting Astoria to purchase 19 percent of Greater New York's common stock if Greater New York merged with anyone other than Astoria. 1997 U.S. Dist. LEXIS 16445, at *4-10. The court held that "plaintiffs are not likely to convince a trier of fact that The Greater's decision to prefer a community-oriented bank" over "a more one size fits all institution" was "so beyond the pale of corporate decision-making as to be an invalid business judgment." 1997 U.S. Dist. LEXIS 16445, at *35. The court rejected challenges to the lock-up option on the grounds that "New York courts have condoned the routine practice of giving financial incentives to a preferred suitor" and "[p]laintiffs are not likely to convince a trier of fact" that the lock-up option (and a break-up agreed to at the same time) were "anything other than the products of a second valid business judgment following the original valid business judgment to prefer one suitor over another." 1997 U.S. Dist. LEXIS 16445, at *35-36.

Add the following at the end of the first sentence (immediately after footnote 1721) of the paragraph beginning on page 912 and concluding on page 913:

The Delaware Court of Chancery also upheld a stock option in *State of Wisconsin Investment Board v. Bartlett*, 2000 Del. Ch. LEXIS 42, at *22-23 & nn. 16, 24, 2000 WL 238026, at *7 & nn. 16, 24 (Del. Ch. Feb. 24, 2000).

Add the following at the end of the paragraph beginning on page 912 and concluding on page 913 (immediately after footnote 1723):

The court in *Wisconsin Investment Board* stated that "Delaware law permits lock-ups and related agreements 'where their adoption is untainted by director interest or other breaches of fiduciary duty.'" 2000 Del. Ch. LEXIS 42, at *30, 2000 WL 238026, at *9 (quoting *Revlon, Inc. v. MacAndrews & Forbes Holdings, Inc.*, 506 A.2d 173, 176 (Del. 1986)). Accordingly, "in the absence of breach of fiduciary duty in agreeing to the lock-up devices, these provisions are reviewable as business judgments and are, thus, granted deference." 2000 Del. Ch. LEXIS 42, at *30, 2000 WL 238026, at *9. The court added that the stock option in this case was not used as a defensive mechanism "instituted to respond to a perceived threat from a potential acquiror making a competing bid." 2000 Del. Ch. LEXIS 42, at *31, 2000 WL 238026, at *9.

Section D 3

Add the following at the end of the second paragraph beginning and concluding on page 935 (between footnotes 1869 and 1870):

Merger agreements have included not just "no shop" provisions that prohibit the target corporation's board from soliciting interest or new bids after the merger agreement has been entered into, but also "no talk" provisions that prohibit the target corporation's board from talking to third parties who express an interest in making a higher bid for the corporation except under stated conditions. No talk provisions are discussed in Chapter III, Section D 7.

Add the following at the end of the second paragraph beginning and concluding on page 940 (immediately after 1907):

The Court of Chancery in *State of Wisconsin Investment Board v. Bartlett*, 2000 Del. Ch. LEXIS 42, 2000 WL 238026 (Del. Ch. Feb. 24, 2000), also upheld a no shop provision. The court stated that "Delaware law permits lock-ups and related agreements 'where their adoption is untainted by director interest or other breaches of fiduciary duty.'" 2000 Del. Ch. LEXIS 42, at *30, 2000 WL 238026, at *9 (quoting *Revlon, Inc. v. MacAndrews & Forbes Holdings, Inc.*, 506 A.2d 173, 176 (Del. 1986)). Accordingly, "in the absence of breach of fiduciary duty in agreeing to the lock-up devices, these provisions are reviewable as business judgments and are, thus, granted deference." 2000 Del. Ch. LEXIS 42, at *30, 2000 WL 238026, at *9. The court added that the no shop provision in this case was not used as a defensive mechanism "instituted to respond to a perceived threat from a potential acquiror making a competing bid." 2000 Del. Ch. LEXIS 42, at *31, 2000 WL 238026, at *9.

Section D 3 b

Add the following between "Window shop provisions" and "are promises" in the first sentence of the paragraph beginning on page 942 and concluding on page 943 (between footnotes 1921 and 1922):

– often called no shop provisions –

Add the following at the end of the second sentence (immediately after footnote 1922) in the paragraph beginning on page 942 and concluding on page 943, and then begin a new paragraph:

The Delaware Court of Chancery in *McMillan v. Intercargo Corp.*, 768 A.2d 492 (Del. Ch. 2000), stated that "a rather standard no shop provision" in a merger agreement that permits a board "to consider an unsolicited proposal that the board determined was likely to be consummated and more favorable" to shareholders than the merger agreement is "hardly indicative" of a breach of fiduciary duty. *Id.* at 506. As stated by the Court of Chancery in *ACE Ltd. v. Capital Re Corp.*, 747 A.2d 95 (Del. Ch. 1999), a no shop provision prohibiting directors from "playing footsie with other potential bidders or . . . stirring up an auction . . . is perfectly understandable, if not necessary, if good faith business transactions are to be encouraged." *Id.* at 106, *quoted in Intercargo*, 768 A.2d at 506 n.63.

Add the following at the end of the paragraph beginning and concluding on page 944 (immediately after footnote 1934):

The Delaware Court of Chancery's decision in *Matador Capital Management Corp. v. BRC Holdings, Inc.*, 729 A.2d 280 (Del. Ch. 1998), involved a merger agreement provision stating that BRC Holdings, Inc. "shall not, directly or indirectly, through any officer, director, employee, representative, or agent of the Company or any of its subsidiaries, solicit or encourage (including by way of furnishing information) the initiation of any inquiries or proposals regarding a Third Party Acquisition." *Id.* at 288-89. The provision also restricted BRC's ability to provide a third party with information and consider a third party bid unless BRC first received "an unsolicited bona fide written Acquisition Proposal" and BRC's board determined "in good faith, after consultation with, and the receipt of advice from, outside counsel" that the proposal "may reasonably result in a transaction more favorable to the

Company's stockholders than the transaction [currently] contemplated." *Id.* at 289.

The court rejected plaintiffs' contention that "these 'defensive' measures serve to prevent not only negotiations, but even the dissemination of information, between BRC and other potential bidders." *Id.* at 291. The court reasoned as follows:

> Plaintiffs interpret these measures entirely too broadly. Contrary to plaintiffs' suggestion, these measures do not foreclose other offers, but operate merely to afford some protection to prevent disruption of the Agreement by proposals from third parties that are neither bona fide nor likely to result in a higher transaction. Quite simply, these do not appear to prevent a third party from making a bona fide offer at a price higher than that offered by ACS.
>
> Similarly, these measures do not prevent the BRC board "from even responding to unsolicited inquiries" as plaintiffs contend, but instead restrict such a response to situations where the board has made a good faith determination that the unsolicited offer "may reasonably result in a transaction more favorable to [BRC's] stockholders" than the Agreement.

Id. The court also pointed to testimony by BRC's chairman that "[i]f someone wants to come in and pay a higher price, we would welcome him and we would sell our shares to the highest bidder." *Id.* Citing *Yanow v. Scientific Leasing, Inc.*, [1987-1988 Transfer Binder] Fed. Sec. L. Rep. (CCH) ¶ 93,660 (Del. Ch. Feb. 5, 1988), the court stated that "[s]uch provisions do not preclude 'post-agreement market checks' and may comport with the board's fiduciary duties." 729 A.2d at 291.

The Delaware Court of Chancery's decision in *Golden Cycle, LLC v. Allan*, 1998 Del. Ch. LEXIS 237, 1998 WL 892631 (Del. Ch. Dec. 10, 1998), upheld a provision in a merger agreement entered into by Global Motorsport Group, Inc. and Stonington Acquisition Corporation that permitted Global's board "to consider and negotiate a bona fide acquisition proposal from a third party where the Board concludes that the outside proposal is a financed offer more favorable than Stonington's and that the failure to do so would violate its fiduciary duties." 1998 Del. Ch. LEXIS 237, at *16, 1998 WL 892631, at *5. The merger agreement also permitted Global's board "to provide nonpublic information to such a competing bidder upon the execution of a confidentiality agreement comparable to that signed by Stonington" and "to terminate the Stonington agreement in favor of a better offer." *Id.* The court stated that "Delaware law recognizes the propriety in appropriate circumstances" of this type of provision and that a competing bidder's objection to the window shop provision was "based entirely on the fact" that it "cannot now enter into a confidentiality agreement with Global without the same two-year standstill agreed to by Stonington." 1998 Del. Ch. LEXIS 237, at *51-52, 1998 WL 892631, at *17. This objection came "with ill grace," the court observed, because the competing bidder repeatedly had "refused to accept a confidentiality agreement without any standstill provisions at all" before Global's board entered into its merger agreement with Stonington. *Id.*

Section D 3 c

Add the following new footnote 1940.1 at the end of the first sentence of the paragraph beginning on page 945 and concluding on page 946:

Cf. Golden Cycle, LLC v. Allan, 1998 Del. Ch. LEXIS 237, at *53 n.16, 1998 WL 892631, at *17 n.16 (Del. Ch. Dec. 10, 1998) (rejecting claim that board did not obtain the "best available alternative" because it "did not undertake an appropriate post-agreement market check," where the board had conducted "a seven-month, 79 company exploration" before entering the challenged merger agreement).

Section D 4 a

Add the following at the end of the paragraph beginning and concluding on page 958 (immediately after footnote 2028):

The Delaware Court of Chancery also has upheld termination fees and expense reimbursement provisions in *Matador Capital Management Corp. v. BRC Holdings, Inc.*, 729 A.2d 280 (Del. Ch. 1998), *Golden Cycle, LLC v. Allan*, 1998 Del. Ch. LEXIS 237, 1998 WL 892631 (Del. Ch. Dec. 10, 1998), *In re IXC Communications, Inc. Shareholders Litigation*, 1999 Del. Ch. LEXIS 210, 1999 WL 1009174 (Del. Ch. Oct. 27, 1999), *Goodwin v. Live Entertainment, Inc.*, 1999 Del. Ch. LEXIS 5, 1999 WL 64265 (Del. Ch. Jan. 22, 1999), *aff'd*, 741 A.2d 16 (unpublished opinion, text available at 1999 Del. LEXIS 238 and 1999 WL 624128) (Del. July 23, 1999), *State of Wisconsin Investment Board v. Bartlett*, 2000 Del. Ch. LEXIS 42, 2000 WL 238026 (Del. Ch. Feb. 24, 2000), and *McMillan v. Intercargo Corp.*, 768 A.2d 492 (Del. 2000). A termination fee also was upheld by a federal court construing New York law in *Minzer v. Keegan*, 1997 U.S. Dist. LEXIS 16445 (E.D.N.Y. Sept. 22, 1997).

Add the following at the beginning of the paragraph beginning and concluding on page 965 (immediately after footnote 2077):

The court stated that "[t]ermination or cancellation fees are not unusual in corporate sale or merger contexts" and "are used to reimburse the prospective buyer for expenditures in pursuing the transaction and also for lost opportunities." *Kysor Indus. Corp. v. Margaux, Inc.*, 674 A.2d 889, 897 (Del. Super. 1996).

Add the following at the end of the third sentence (immediately after footnote 2079) of the paragraph beginning and concluding on page 965:

The court noted that "[c]ommentators have expressed the view that liquidated damage provisions in the one-to-five percent range of the proposed acquisition price are within a reasonable range." *Kysor*, 674 A.2d at 897.

Add the following at the end of the paragraph beginning and concluding on page 965 (immediately after footnote 2081):

The Delaware Court of Chancery upheld a $10 million termination fee (in addition to a $3 million expense reimbursement provision) in *Matador Capital Management Corp. v. BRC Holdings, Inc.*, 729 A.2d 280 (Del. Ch. 1998). The case involved a merger agreement entered into by BRC Holdings, Inc. and Affiliated Computer Services, Inc. ("ACS"), pursuant to which ACS would acquire BRC. The fee was payable to ACS if the merger agreement was terminated for any of the following "reasons relating to the negotiation or arrangement of another offer":

> (1) a third party makes a bona fide offer for BRC and, as a result, the Board determines that its fiduciary duties obligate it to terminate the agreement; (2) ACS terminates the agreement because BRC negotiates with or enters into an agreement, letter of intent, or arrangement with a third party with respect to that party's acquisition of the Company or more than 19.9% of the assets or outstanding shares of the Company; or (3) ACS terminates the agreement because the Board withdraws or modifies "in a manner adverse to the Purchaser its approval or recommendation of the Offer, this Agreement, or the Merger or has recommended another offer, or has adopted any resolution to effect any of the foregoing."

Id. at 289.

The court stated that the termination fee was "not invoked by the board's receipt of another offer, nor is it invoked solely because the board decides to provide information, or even negotiates with another bidder." *Id.* at 291 n.15. As a result, the court stated, the provision "can hardly be said" to bar the corporation "'' . . . from negotiating with 'prior bidders . . . or those that expressed interest,' as plaintiffs suggest." *Id.* Citing *Kysor*, the court stated that "this measure is commonplace . . .

and can be within the boundaries established by case law." *Id.* (noting reference in *Kyser* to the fact that "commentators find liquidated damages provisions in the range of one to five percent of the proposed acquisition price reasonable").

The Court of Chancery upheld a $3 million termination fee and a $1 million expense reimbursement provision in *Golden Cycle, LLC v. Allan*, 1998 Del. Ch. LEXIS 237, 1998 WL 892631 (Del. Ch. Dec. 10, 1998). The court stated that "Delaware law recognizes the propriety in appropriate circumstances of reasonable and proportionate termination fee / expense reimbursement" provisions, and that the provisions in this case, which amounted to less than 3 percent of the transaction value, were "within the boundaries established by law," resulted from a demand made by the corporation's merger partner, Stonington Acquisition Corporation, and were less than the amounts expended by Stonington in connection with the transaction. 1998 Del. Ch. LEXIS 237, at *51-52, 1998 WL 892631, at *17. The court also pointed to the fact that the competing bidder that was challenging the termination fee and expense reimbursement provisions was waging a consent solicitation to replace Global's board and if it "can obtain the necessary consents representing a majority of the voting power of the Company before the Stonington tender offer closes, its nominees will be elected to the board of directors and can act to terminate the merger agreement and repudiate the offensive termination fee provisions." 1998 Del. Ch. LEXIS 237, at *54, 1998 WL 892631, at *17. The court stated that "[t]he availability of this self-help strongly suggests that there is no need for injunctive relief" and distinguished the situation presented where a "lock-up at a grossly unfair price precluded further competitive bidding." *Id.*

The Court of Chancery in *In re IXC Communications, Inc. Shareholders Litigation*, 1999 Del. Ch. LEXIS 210, 1999 WL 1009174 (Del. Ch. Oct. 27, 1999), upheld a $105 million termination fee where the parties disagreed with respect to "exactly what percentage of the total merger deal that this termination fee comprises." 1999 Del. Ch. LEXIS 210, at *7,

28-29, 1999 WL 1009174, at *6, 10. The court relied upon the business judgment rule due to "the absence of a showing of disloyalty or lack of care in agreeing to the termination fee" and stated that "enhanced judicial scrutiny does not apply" because the termination fee was not a defensive mechanism "instituted to respond to a perceived threat to a potential acquiror." 1999 Del. Ch. LEXIS 210, at *29, 1999 WL 1009174, at *10. The court stated its view that it is "nearly impossible" to evaluate termination fees "independently" without considering other provisions of the merger agreement because "the fees are likely part of a careful balance of consideration from each side and the result of a give and take process." 1999 Del. Ch. LEXIS 210, at *28, 1999 WL 1009174, at *10. Thus, the court continued, "for this Court to interject itself into a battle over whether the termination fees are excessive would require a wholesale evaluation of the fairness of all of the terms of the Merger Agreement, as well as the process which brought them about, in order to decide whether the termination fee implicates a potential unconscionable expenditure based upon a percentage of the value of the deal." *Id.*

The Delaware Court of Chancery in *Goodwin v. Live Entertainment, Inc.*, 1999 Del. Ch. LEXIS 5, 1999 WL 64265 (Del. Ch. Jan. 22, 1999), *aff'd*, 741 A.2d 16 (unpublished opinion, text available at 1999 Del. LEXIS 238 and 1999 WL 624128) (Del. July 23, 1999), similarly described a termination fee as "commonplace" and stated that a 3.125 percent fee was "within the range of reasonableness approved by this court in similar contexts." 1999 Del. Ch. LEXIS 5, at *69, 1999 WL 64265 at *23.

The Court of Chancery in *State of Wisconsin Investment Board v. Bartlett*, 2000 Del. Ch. LEXIS 42, 2000 WL 238026 (Del. Ch. Feb. 24, 2000), stated that "Delaware law permits lock-ups and related agreements 'where their adoption is untainted by director interest or other breaches of fiduciary duty.'" 2000 Del. Ch. LEXIS 42, at *30, 2000 WL 238026, at *9 (quoting *Revlon, Inc. v. MacAndrews & Forbes Holdings, Inc.*, 506 A.2d 173, 176 (Del. 1986)). Accordingly, "in the absence of breach of fiduciary duty in agreeing to the lock-up devices, these provisions are reviewable as business judgments and are, thus, granted deference." 2000 Del. Ch. LEXIS 42, at *30, 2000 WL 238026, at *9. The court added that the termination fee in this case was not used as a defensive mechanism "instituted to respond to a perceived threat from a potential acquiror making a competing bid." 2000 Del. Ch. LEXIS 42, at *31, 2000 WL 238026, at *9.

The Court of Chancery in *McMillan v. Intercargo Corp.*, 768 A.2d 492 (Del. Ch. 2000), upheld a 3.5 percent termination fee in a merger agreement entered into by Intercargo Corporation and XL America, Inc. pursuant to which XL would acquire all Intercargo shares for $12 per share. The court stated that "[a]lthough in purely percentage terms, the termination fee was at the high end of what our courts have approved, it was still within the range that is generally considered reasonable." *Id.* at 505. Equally important, the court continued, the fee was structured so that "the fee would be payable only if the stockholders were to get a better deal," and thus ensured that shareholders "would not cast their vote in fear that a 'no' vote alone would trigger the fee." *Id.* at 505 & n.60. The court stated that "[f]rom the preclusion perspective, it is difficult to see how a 3.5% fee would have deterred a rival bidder who wished to pay materially more for Intercargo." *Id.* at 505. The court acknowledged that "[n]o doubt the presence of the fee would rebuff a bidder who wished to top XL's bid by a relatively insignificant amount that would not have been substantially more beneficial to Intercargo's stockholders," but stated that "to call such an insubstantial obstacle 'draconian' is inconsistent with the very definition of the term." *Id.* at 506.

Add the following at the end of the paragraph beginning on page 970 and concluding on page 971 (immediately after footnote 2112):

The court in *Minzer v. Keegan*, 1997 U.S. Dist. LEXIS 16445 (E.D.N.Y. Sept. 22, 1997), also construing New York law, upheld a $5 million break-up fee in a merger agreement entered into by The Greater New York Savings Bank with Astoria Financial Corporation. The court stated that "New York courts have condoned the routine practice of giving financial incentives to a preferred suitor" and that "[p]laintiffs are not likely to convince a trier of fact" that the break-up fee (and an option agreed to at the same time, pursuant to which Astoria could purchase 19 percent of Greater New York's stock if Greater New York entered into a merger agreement with any other party) were "anything other than the products of a second valid business judgment following the original valid business judgment to prefer one suitor over another." 1997 U.S. Dist. LEXIS 16445, at *35-36.

Section D 4 b

Add the following between footnote 2141 and "and the Sixth Circuit" in the first sentence in the paragraph beginning on page 974 and concluding on page 975:

and *Phelps Dodge Corp. v. Cyprus Amax Minerals Co.*, 1999 Del. Ch. LEXIS 202, 1999 WL 1054255 (Del. Ch. Sept. 27, 1999)

Add the following at the end of the paragraph beginning on page 976 and concluding on page 977 (immediately after footnote 2159):

The Delaware Court of Chancery in *Phelps Dodge Corp. v. Cyprus Amax Minerals Co.*, 1999 Del. Ch. LEXIS 202, 1999 WL 1054255 (Del. Ch. Sept. 27, 1999), concluded that the plaintiffs in a case challenging a 6.3 percent termination fee had established "a reasonable probability of success on the merits." 1999 Del. Ch. LEXIS 202, at *5, 1999 WL 1054255, at *2. The court stated that the 6.3 percent termination fee "certainly seems to stretch the definition of range of reasonableness," the test by which defensive measures are judged under cases such as *Unocal* and *QVC*, and "probably stretches the definition beyond its breaking point." 1999 Del. Ch. LEXIS 202, at *5, 1999 WL 1054255, at *2. The court denied a motion for a preliminary injunction, however, due to the absence of irreparable harm. *Id.*

Section D 6

Replace "1996" with "Supp. 1998/99" in the Model Act § 11.03 citation in footnote 2193 on page 983.

Add the following at the end of footnote 2194 on page 983:

See also In re Lukens Inc. S'holders Litig., 757 A.2d 720, 725 (Del. Ch. 1999) (describing a "customary 'fiduciary out'" provision "allowing the board to adequately inform itself and take action on any unsolicited 'superior proposal' from a third party"); *Golden Cycle, LLC v. Allan*, 1998 Del. Ch. LEXIS 237, at *16, 1998 WL 892631, at *5 (Del. Ch. Dec. 10, 1998) ("[t]he final Merger Agreement contains a window-shop provision that acts as a fiduciary out and allows the Board to consider and negotiate a bona fide acquisition proposal from a third party where the Board concludes that the outside proposal is a financed offer more favorable than Stonington's and that the failure to do so would violate its fiduciary duties").

Section D 6 a

Change "decision" to "decisions" in the first sentence (between footnotes 2197 and 2198) of the paragraph beginning on page 984 and concluding on page 985 and in the same sentence delete the comma between "Inc." and footnote 2198 and add "and Quickturn Design Systems, Inc. v. Shapiro, 721 A.2d 1281 (Del. 1998)," between footnote 2198

and "the Colorado and Nebraska Supreme Court's decisions".

Add the following at the end of the paragraph beginning and concluding on page 985 (immediately after footnote 2211):

The Delaware Supreme Court's decision in *Quickturn Design Systems, Inc. v. Shapiro*, 721 A.2d 1281 (Del. 1998) – as discussed in Chapter III, Section G 2 d – involved a delayed redemption poison pill shareholder rights plan that did not permit the redemption of rights for six months following the replacement of a majority of the corporation's directors. The court held that this rights plan provision was invalid under Section 141(a) of the Delaware General Corporation Law, which "confers upon any newly elected board of directors *full* power to manage and direct the business and affairs of a Delaware corporation." 721 A.2d at 1292. The court stated that a delayed redemption provision "would prevent a newly elected board of directors from *completely* discharging its fundamental management duties to the corporation and its stockholders for six months . . . in an area of fundamental importance to the shareholders – negotiating a possible sale of the corporation." *Id.* at 1291-92. According to the court, "no defensive measure can be sustained which would require a new board of directors to breach its fiduciary duty." *Id.* at 1292. The court repeated – and added emphasis to the words "or not act" in – its statement in *Paramount Communications Inc. v. QVC Networks, Inc.*, 637 A.2d 34 (Del. 1994), that "[t]o the extent that a contract, or a provision thereof, purports to require a board to act *or not act* in such a fashion as to limit the exercise of fiduciary duties, it is invalid and unenforceable." 721 A.2d at 1292 (quoting 637 A.2d at 51; emphasis added in *Quickturn*).

Add "and Quickturn" between "QVC" and "did not" in the first sentence (between footnotes 2211 and 2212) of the paragraph beginning on page 985 and concluding on page 987.

Section D 6 c

Add the following at the end of the paragraph beginning on page 1001 and concluding on page 1002 (immediately after footnote 2307):

The Delaware Court of Chancery in *ACE Limited v. Capital Re Corp.*, 747 A.2d 95 (Del. Ch. 1999), described a claim by a merger partner against a later bidder for tortious interference with the merger agreement "a la the famous or infamous (depending on your point of view) *Pennzoil* case" as a "theoretical impossibility." *Id.* at 101 n.16. The case involved a merger agreement entered into by Capital Re Corporation and ACE Limited and a later offer by XL Capital Ltd. The court reasoned that "a claim that XL Capital was legally forbidden from making such an offer seems far-fetched, if not outrageous" because the merger agreement "specifically contemplates that Capital Re could entertain other offers and in some circumstances could validly discuss such offers and abandon the Merger Agreement if such an offer were 'superior' and unmatched by ACE." *Id.* The court stated that "[i]f such a claim is plausible, then the fiduciary out in the contract is, of course, useless." *Id.*

Section D 7

Add the following new Section D 7 at the end of the paragraph beginning and concluding on page 1002 (immediately after footnote 2298):

7. No Talk and Restrictive Fiduciary Out Provisions

Four Delaware Court of Chancery decisions issued during 1999 and 2000 – written by Chancellor William B. Chandler III in *Phelps Dodge Corp. v. Cyprus Amax Minerals Co.*, 1999 Del. Ch. LEXIS 202, 1999 WL 1054255 (Del. Ch. Sept. 27, 1999), Vice Chancellor Leo E. Strine, Jr. in *ACE Limited v.*

Capital Re Corp., 747 A.2d 95 (Del. Ch. 1999), and Vice Chancellor (and now Justice) Myron T. Steele in *In re IXC Communications, Inc. Shareholders Litigation,* 1999 Del. Ch. LEXIS 210, 1999 WL 1009174 (Del. Ch. Oct. 27, 1999) and *State of Wisconsin Investment Board v. Bartlett*, 2000 Del. Ch. LEXIS 42, 2000 WL 238026 (Del. Ch. Feb. 24, 2000) – address (1) restrictive no talk provisions in merger agreements that limit the target corporation's board to talk to third parties who express an interest in making a higher bid for the corporation and (2) restrictive fiduciary out provisions that limit the board's right to consider later better offers even if the board's fiduciary duties otherwise would require consideration of those offers. Two of the decisions *(Phelps Dodge* and *Capital Re)* view such provisions as troublesome and suggest that they are permissible only under narrow circumstances; the other two decisions *(IXC* and *Bartlett)* appears more willing to accept such provisions.

Phelps Dodge, *Capital Re*, *IXC* and *Bartlett* all involved stock for stock merger agreements entered into under circumstances where there was no sale of control and no duty under cases such as *Revlon, Inc. v. MacAndrews & Forbes Holdings, Inc.*, 506 A.2d 173 (Del. 1986), and *Paramount Communications, Inc. v. QVC Network, Inc.*, 637 A.2d 34 (Del. 1994), "to seek the transaction offering the best value reasonably available to the stockholders." *QVC*, 637 A.2d at 43.

Phelps Dodge. Chancellor Chandler's decision in *Phelps Dodge Corp. v. Cyprus Amax Minerals Co.*, 1999 Del. Ch. LEXIS 202, 1999 WL 1054255 (Del. Ch. Sept. 27, 1999), involved a stock for stock merger agreement entered into by Cyprus Amax Mineral Company and Asarco Inc. A no talk provision prevented Cyprus Amax and Asarco from encouraging or learning about any later proposals. The court's ruling does not mention a fiduciary out provision, but the merger agreement included a fiduciary out provision that permitted the board to recommend shareholder disapproval of the merger if the board determined "in good faith, based on advice of outside counsel, that its failure to do so would constitute a breach of its fiduciary duties." *The Clause At Issue, in* Corporate Control Alert, Oct. 1999, at 10.

The court denied a motion for a preliminary injunction in an action brought by a competing bidder, Phelps Dodge Corporation, due to the absence of irreparable harm but held that "the plaintiffs have demonstrated a reasonable probability of success on the merits of this litigation." 1999 Del. Ch. LEXIS 202, at *2, 1999 WL 1054255, at *1. The court described no talk provisions as "troubling" because "[a] target can refuse to negotiate" but "the decision not to negotiate . . . must be an informed one" and no talk provisions "prevent a board from meeting its duty to make an informed judgment with respect to even considering whether to negotiate with a third party." 1999 Del. Ch. LEXIS 202, at *3-4, 1999 WL 1054255, at *1. The court stated that there was no requirement that Cyprus or Asarco negotiate with Phelps Dodge, but Cyprus and Asarco "should not have completely foreclosed the opportunity to do so, as this is the legal equivalent of willful blindness, a blindness that may constitute a breach of a board's duty of care; that is, the duty to take care to be informed of all material information reasonably available." 1999 Del. Ch. LEXIS 202, at *4-5, 1999 WL 1054255, at *2.

At a minimum, *Phelps Dodge* teaches that strict no talk provisions, with or without a fiduciary out provision, will be scrutinized closely.

Capital Re. Vice Chancellor Strine's decision in *ACE Limited v. Capital Re Corp.*, 747 A.2d 95 (Del. Ch. 1999), involved a stock for stock merger agreement entered into by Capital Re Corporation with ACE Limited. Two noteworthy facts distinguished the facts in this case from the facts in most cases. First, ACE owned 12.3 percent of Capital Re's stock. Second, ACE had voting agreements with shareholders holding an additional 33.5 percent of Capital Re's shares that obligated votes in favor of the merger. As a result, ACE controlled nearly 46 percent of the vote and thus "the Capital Re board knew when it executed the Merger Agreement that unless it terminated the Merger Agreement, ACE would have, as a virtual certainty, the votes to consummate the merger even if a materially more valuable transaction became available." *Id.* at 98.

The merger agreement included a no talk provision that prohibited Capital Re from "participating in *discussions* or negotiations with or even providing information to a third party." *Id.* A fiduciary out provision permitted Capital Re's board to consider other offers if the board concluded "in good faith . . . based on the written advice of its outside legal counsel, that participating in such negotiations or discussions or furnishing such information is required in order to prevent the Board of Directors of the Company from breaching its fiduciary duties to its stockholders." *Id.*

Before entering into the merger agreement, the board had "not explored the marketplace with confidence." *Id.* at 107 n.36. Between the announcement of the merger agreement and a vote on the merger by Capital Re's shareholders, the market value of the ACE stock offered as merger consideration dropped from $17 per share to less than $10 per share, and XL Capital Ltd. made a higher and all cash offer. *Id.* at 97, 99. Capital Re's counsel advised the board in writing that discussions with XL Capital would be "consistent with" their fiduciary duties, but this written advice did not say, as required by the literal terms of the merger agreement, that discussions with XL Capital were "required" in order to fulfill the board's fiduciary duties. *Id.* at 98. Capital Re's board nevertheless determined that "it was duty-bound to enter discussions with XL Capital" and, in accordance with the merger agreement, sent ACE a written notice stating that it intended to terminate Capital Re's merger agreement with ACE unless ACE increased the merger consideration within five business days. *Id.* at 100.

In an action brought by ACE, the court denied a motion for a temporary restraining order enjoining Capital Re from terminating the merger agreement. The court held that "ACE is unlikely to be able to convince a court on final hearing that Capital Re breached a valid contractual provision by entering into discussions with XL Capital." *Id.*

The court began by finding that "the probable better interpretation of the contract" is that the no talk and fiduciary out provision required the board to "'base' its judgment on the 'written advice' of outside counsel" but that "the ultimate 'good faith' judgment about whether the board's fiduciary duties required it to enter discussions with XL Capital" belonged to the board itself. *Id.* at 103. The court reasoned that "it seems likely that in the end a fact-finder will conclude that the board had a good faith basis for determining that it must talk with XL Capital and not simply let the Capital Re stockholders ride the merger barrel over the financial falls." *Id.*

In the alternative, the court acknowledged that the merger agreement could be interpreted in accordance with ACE's contention that ACE "specifically bargained for the language requiring the Capital Re board to 'base' its judgment on the 'written advice' of outside counsel so as to lock up the merger as tightly as legally permissible." *Id.* at 104. The court also acknowledged that ACE's contention that the court could find that Capital Re's counsel "did not have a sufficient good faith belief that discussions with XL Capital were legally mandated to issue a written opinion to that effect . . . might ultimately be proven correct." *Id.*

The court concluded in its alternative ruling, however, that "even it ACE is correct about what the Merger Agreement means," ACE still was "unlikely to prevail on the merits" because ACE's interpretation of the contract was unenforceable for public policy reasons. *Id.* at 106. The court explained that one of the "circumstances in which the high priority our society places on the enforcement of contracts between private parties gives way to even more important concerns . . . is when the trustee or agent of certain parties enters into a contract containing provisions that exceed the trustee's or agent's authority." *Id.* at 104. The court continued: "[T]he Delaware law of mergers and acquisitions has given primacy to the interests of stockholders in being free to maximize value from their ownership of stock without improper compulsion from executory contracts entered into by boards – that is, from contracts that essentially disable the board and the stockholders from doing anything other than accepting the contract even if another much more valuable opportunity comes along." *Id.* at 104-05.

The court then offered the following additional thoughts concerning no talk provisions accompanied by restrictive fiduciary out provisions of the type ACE contended it had bargained for and received. According to the court, "[i]t is one thing" – and "perfectly understandable, if not necessary, if good faith business transactions are to be encouraged" – "for a board of directors to agree not to play footsie with other potential bidders or to stir up an auction." *Id.* at 106. By contrast, "[i]t is quite another thing for a board of directors to enter into a merger agreement that precludes the board from considering any other offers unless a lawyer is willing to sign an opinion indicating that his client board is 'required' to consider that offer." *Id.* A provision of this type, the court stated, "involves an abdication by the board of its duty to determine what its own fiduciary obligations require at precisely that time in the life of the company when the board's own judgment is most important." *Id.* According to the court, "[a] ban on considering such a proposal, even one with an exception where legal counsel opines in writing that such consideration is 'required,' comes close to self-disablement by the board." *Id.* at 107.

The court then analyzed the issue under two potential standards of judicial review: business judgment rule principles and the enhanced scrutiny Delaware courts use to review defensive measures under *Unocal.* "Examined under either doctrinal rubric," the court in *Capital Re* concluded, the fiduciary out provision "as construed by ACE is of quite dubious validity." *Id.* 747 A.2d at 109.

Under business judgment rule principles, the court stated, the board's "bedrock duties of care and loyalty" in a context "where the board is making a critical decision affecting stockholder ownership and voting rights" make it "especially important" that the board "negotiate with care and retain sufficient flexibility to ensure that the stockholders are not unfairly coerced into accepting a less than optimal exchange for their shares." *Id.* at 108-09. The court then quoted the *Phelps-Dodge* court's statement that no talk provisions are "troubling" because they "prevent a board from meeting its duty to make an informed judgment with respect to even considering whether to negotiate with a third party." *Id.* at 109 (quoting *Phelps-Dodge*, 1999 Del. Ch. LEXIS 202, at *4, 1999 WL 1054255, at *1-2).

Under *Unocal*, the court continued, enhanced scrutiny may be required of stock for stock merger agreement provisions that are "designed to prevent another bidder, through a tender offer or rival stock-for-stock bid, from preventing the consummation of a transaction." *Id.* at 108. In the view of the court in *Capital Re*, if a merger agreement precludes board consideration of alternative favorable offers, then the board's approval of the merger agreement is "as formidable a barrier to another offer as a non-redeemable poison pill." *Id.* Accordingly, "it might therefore be possible to construct a *plausible* argument that a no-escape Merger Agreement that locks up the necessary votes constitutes an unreasonable preclusive and coercive defensive obstacle within the meaning of *Unocal*." *Id.*

At a minimum, *Capital Re* holds that where there has been no market canvass and the shareholder vote on the merger agreement is foreordained, a no talk provision without a fiduciary out provision – or with a fiduciary out provision requiring a lawyer to sign an opinion stating that the board is required to consider that offer – is unenforceable.

IXC and Bartlett. Vice Chancellor Steele's decision in *In re IXC Communications, Inc. Shareholders Litigation*, 1999 Del. Ch. LEXIS 210, 1999 WL 1009174 (Del. Ch. Oct. 27, 1999), involved a stock for stock merger agreement entered into by IXC Communications, Inc. with Cincinnati Bell, Inc.

("CBI"), with IXC shareholders receiving CBI stock. A no talk provision "prevent[ed] the parties from entertaining other potential deals." 1999 Del. Ch. LEXIS 210, at *7, 1999 WL 1009174, at *2. A fiduciary out provision "permit[ted] the board of IXC to ultimately oppose the merger, should it see fit." *Id.* The merger agreement later was amended (apparently in reaction to the *Phelps Dodge* decision) to permit either party to consider "superior proposals." 1999 Del. Ch. LEXIS 210, at *9, 1999 WL 1009174, at *3.

The merger agreement followed an announcement six months before the agreement was reached that IXC had retained Morgan Stanley Dean Witter to consider possible merger or sale options. The announcement was intended "to send a message to the 'universe' of players in the telecommunications market that IXC was interested in potential partners or acquirors" and "to send a message that parties with enough interest could approach them for possible strategic partnering." 1999 Del. Ch. LEXIS 210, at *4, 1999 WL 1009174, at *1. The announcement also was intended not to announce a sale or make IXC appear "desperate to sell." *Id.* In the following months, "IXC had various contacts with interested parties" including "a who's who of telecommunications players," but no offer superior to the CBI offer ever was received. *Id.*

The court denied a motion for a preliminary injunction in an action brought by IXC shareholders. Unlike the court in *Phelps Dodge*, the court in *IXC* described "no talk" provisions as "common in merger agreements" and stated that they "do not imply some automatic breach of fiduciary duty." 1999 Del. Ch. LEXIS 210, at *17, 1999 WL 1009174, at *6. According to the court, "the plaintiff alleges nothing about the genesis of this proposed merger, whether in the negotiations or in the proposed terms, to lead me to conclude that the actions of the board as a whole (as well as the self-interest of the director-shareholders) were not in alignment with the interests of all IXC shareholders." 1999 Del. Ch. LEXIS 210, at *18, 1999 WL 1009174, at *6.

The no talk provision here did not trouble the court for two reasons. First, the provision "emerged late in the process," after "the IXC board met its duty of care by informing itself over the nearly six months lasting from the February 5 public announcement to the late July approval of the IXC-CBI merger." *Id.* Second, the provision later was retracted and a fiduciary out provision permitted the board "to hear any proposals it sees fit" and "would have allowed the board to entertain any proposal superior to CBI's." *Id.* The court accordingly held that the board's determination to enter into a merger agreement with CBI was protected by the business judgment rule presumption that a board acts "with care, loyalty, and in 'good faith,'" and that the court therefore was "obligated to defer to the board's substantive business judgment and allow the shareholders to pass ultimate judgment on their actions" when the shareholders voted on the merger agreement. 1999 Del. Ch. LEXIS 210, at *13, 1999 WL 1009174, at *4.

Vice Chancellor Steele's decision in *State of Wisconsin Investment Board v. Bartlett*, 2000 Del. Ch. LEXIS 42, 2000 WL 238026 (Del. Ch. Feb. 24, 2000), involved a merger between Medco Research Inc. and King Pharmaceuticals protected by a "no talk/no shop provision." 2000 Del. Ch. LEXIS 42, at *21 n.16, 2000 WL 238026, at *6 n.16. The court stated that Medco's board had retained Hambrecht & Quist, LLC ("H & Q"), an investment banking firm "with considerable experience in the pharmaceutical industry and with Medco in particular" to assist "its effort to 'shop' the company," and that H & Q "aggressively sought out suitors who might benefit from Medco's existing drug pipeline and income stream." 2000 Del. Ch. LEXIS 42, at *3, 16, 2000 WL 238026, at *1, 5. The court also stated that "[n]otwithstanding plaintiff's allegations, it seems apparent to me that the evidence equally supports the view that Medco's board proceeded with the King merger because its efforts had failed to find a viable combination with other suitors," that the merger with King "appeared to be a viable and preferable option to going it alone," and that Medco's board "reasonably relied upon their investment banker's advice and appropriately apprised the fear that appearing 'over-shopped' could frustrate any deal." 2000 Del. Ch. LEXIS 42, at *17-18, 2000 WL 238026, at *5.

Without discussing whether the merger agreement contained a fiduciary out provision, the court stated that "the facts do not support a conclusion that the Medco directors acted inconsistently with what they believed to be the best interest of the Medco shareholders." 2000 Del. Ch. LEXIS 42, at *20, 2000 WL 238026, at *6. The court stated that "Delaware law permits lock-ups and related agreements 'where their adoption is untainted by director interest or other breaches of fiduciary duty.'" 2000 Del. Ch. LEXIS 42, at *30, 2000 WL 238026, at *9 (quoting *Revlon, Inc. v. MacAndrews & Forbes Holdings, Inc.*, 506 A.2d 173, 176 (Del. 1986)). Accordingly, "in the absence of breach of fiduciary duty in agreeing to the lock-up devices, these provisions are reviewable as business judgments and are, thus, granted deference." *Id.* The court added that the no talk provision was not used as a defensive mechanism "instituted to respond to a perceived threat from a potential acquiror making a competing bid." 2000 Del. Ch. LEXIS 42, at *31, 2000 WL 238026, at 9. The court also quoted the following passage from *IXC*: "[T]he plaintiff alleges nothing about the genesis of this proposed merger, whether in negotiations or in the proposed terms, to lead me to conclude that the actions of the board as a whole (as well as the self-interest of the director-shareholders) were not in alignment with the interests of all [Medco] shareholders." 2000 Del. Ch. LEXIS 42, at *20, 2000 WL 238026, at *6 (quoting 1999 Del. Ch. LEXIS 210, at *18, 1999 WL 1009174, at *6).

At a minimum, *IXC* holds that no talk provisions that are entered into following a market test (though not necessarily a *Revlon* market test) and that permit a board to consider new proposals as the board "sees fit" are enforceable. As noted above, the court in *Bartlett* did not directly discuss whether the merger agreement in *Bartlett* contained a fiduciary out provision. The *IXC* and *Bartlett* decisions post-date but do not discuss the *Phelps Dodge* or *Capital Re* decisions.

Phelps Dodge, Capital Re, IXC and Bartlett Read Together. Read together, the *Phelps Dodge, Capital Re, IXC* and *Bartlett* decisions suggest that a no talk provision, while potentially troublesome, is not impermissible as a matter of law if it is accompanied by a meaningful fiduciary out provision. The debate that has followed these decisions centers around the required breadth of the fiduciary out provision.

At one end of the spectrum, a fiduciary out provision can permit a board that has entered into a merger agreement to act as it believes appropriate after receiving any later expression of interest and determine whether that expression of interest warrants talking or negotiation (and providing access to nonpublic information) and possibly an agreement to enter into a new merger agreement with the later bidder. At the other end of the spectrum, a fiduciary out provision can permit a board that has entered into a merger agreement to talk or negotiate with (and provide access to nonpublic information to) a later bidder only if the later bidder has made a written and clearly superior offer, and only after giving the board's original merger partner notice of the superior offer and an opportunity to top the superior offer. Any number of permutations in between these two ends of the spectrum are possible.

Another potentially important variable is whether the fiduciary out provision permits the board itself to terminate the original merger agreement in the event of a later better offer or requires the board to allow shareholders to vote on the original merger agreement in accordance with the terms of that agreement (with shareholders being told about any subsequent proposal). The court in *Capital Re* noted that a shareholder vote in *Capital Re* was meaningless because the result of the vote was a virtual certainty due to ACE's control over nearly 46 percent of the vote, and distinguished the result in *Kontrabecki Group, Inc. v. Triad Park, LLC*, 1998 Del. Ch. LEXIS 246 (Del. Ch. Mar. 18, 1998), on this ground. The court in *Triad Park* granted a temporary restraining order (1) enjoining termination by the board of Triad Park, LLC of a merger agreement entered into by Triad with The Kontrabecki Group despite the Triad board's receipt of what it believed to be a superior proposal (the court stated that Kontrabecki had alleged a colorable claim that the new proposal did not constitute a superior proposal) and (2) requiring a shareholder vote on the merger agreement after shareholders were informed concerning the new proposal. 747 A.2d at 110; *Kontrabecki*, 1998 Del. Ch. LEXIS 246, at *1-3. The *Capital Re* decision thus suggests that courts may be more willing to uphold restrictive no talk and fiduciary out provisions where shareholders have the ultimate authority to decide whether to approve the merger agreement and the shareholders' vote is not locked up at the time the merger agreement is signed. *See also IXC,* 1999 Del. Ch. LEXIS 210, at *2, 1999 WL 1009174, at *1 (denying motion for preliminary injunction enjoining a shareholder vote on a merger agreement where the vote "will be part of a democratic governance process: (1) in which shareholders are adequately informed; and, (2) in which shareholders will be free to exercise their judgment based upon their individual assessment of their own economic interests").

The court in *Capital Re* acknowledged that there are "limited circumstances in which a board could prudently place itself in the position of not being able to entertain and consider a superior proposal to a transaction dependent on a stockholder vote" and offered the following example: "where a board has actively canvassed the market, negotiated with various bidders in a competitive environment, and believes that the necessity to close a transaction requires that the sales contest end." 747 A.2d at 107. At the same time, however, the court in *Capital Re* suggested that a board decision "designed to prevent another bidder, through a tender offer or rival stock-for-stock bid, from preventing the consummation of a transaction" would be subject to enhanced judicial scrutiny under *Unocal* rather than deference under the business judgment rule. *Id.* at 108. The court in *Capital Re* did not address the Delaware Supreme Court's statement in *Unitrin v. American General Corp.*, 651 A.2d 1361 (Del. 1995), that board responses to offers to merge are governed by the business judgment rule rather than *Unocal* because "a statutory prerequisite . . . to a merger transaction is approval by the Board before any stockholder action." *Id.* at 1376 n.16 (citing Del. Gen. Corp. Law § 251(b)). The court in *ICX*, unlike the court in *Capital Re*, held that *Unocal* was not applicable because merger agreement provisions are not "defensive mechanisms instituted to respond to a perceived threat to a potential acqurior." 1999 Del. Ch. LEXIS 210, at *29, 1999 WL 1009174, at *10.

Section E 1

Add the following at the end of the second paragraph beginning and concluding on page 1003 (between footnotes 2309 and 2310):

"In today's financial world, dividends and self-tender offers are viewed as conventional methods of delivering to shareholders a return on their investment" and are "classic business judgment decisions of the kind that are normally protected by the business judgment rule." *Weiss v. Samsonite Corp.*, 741 A.2d 366, 371-72 (Del. Ch. 1999), *aff'd*, 746 A.2d 277 (unpublished opinion, text available at 1999 Del. LEXIS 387 and 1999 WL 1254563) (Del. Nov. 12, 1999).

Replace "1998" with "2000" in the Drexler citation in footnote 2311 on page 1004.

Replace the Folk citation in footnote 2311 on page 1004 with the following:

I Rodman Ward, Jr., Edward P. Welch & Andrew J. Turezyn, *Folk on the Delaware General Corporation Law* §§ 160.1-.12 (4th ed. Supp. 2001-2);

Replace the Securities Law Techniques citation in footnote 2311 on page 1004 with the following:

Johnston, *Repurchases of Shares – State of State Law, in* 5 *Securities Law Techniques* § 69 (A.A. Sommer, Jr. ed. 2001).

Section E 1 a

Replace 6-74 with 6-79 and replace "1998" with "2001" in the Balotti citation in footnote 2331 on page 1007.

Section E 1 d

Add "(i.e., substantive coercion)" between "stock" and the period immediately before footnote 2457 at the end of the second sentence of the first paragraph beginning and concluding on page 1025.

Add the following at the end of the paragraph beginning and concluding on page 1030 (immediately after footnote 2484):

The Court of Chancery in *Chesapeake Corp. v. Shore*, 771 A.2d 293 (Del. Ch. 2000), discussing *Unitrin, Inc. v. American General Corp.*, 651 A.2d 1361 (Del. 1995), observed that assuming a 90 percent turnout American General had to win 64.12 percent of the unaligned votes to elect directors (a majority of a quorum was required to elect directors) and 74.73 percent of the unaligned votes to complete a merger (a majority of outstanding shares was required to approve a merger). *Id.* at 325. The court in *Chesapeake* described these required majorities as "a rather formidable and, one might daresay, preclusive barrier to the insurgent." *Id.* at 326.

According to the *Chesapeake* court, "three reasons seemed to underline the Supreme Court's conclusion that the repurchase program might not be preclusive," that "the Chancery Court's determination that a successful proxy contest was not a realistic possibility could not be sustained," and that the matter should be remanded for further findings: (1)

"Unitrin's stockholder base was heavily concentrated within a small number of institutional investors," which "'facilit[ed the] bidder's ability to communicate the merits of its position'"; (2) "the fact that the insurgent would have to receive majorities from disinterested voters uncommon in hotly contested elections in republican democracies was of '*de minimis*' importance 'because 42% of Unitrin's stock was owned by institutional investors'" and "it is hard to imagine a company more readily susceptible [than Unitrin] to a proxy contest concerning a pure issue of dollars"; and (3) "the Supreme Court was unwilling to presume that the directors' block" of 28 percent of Unitrin's shares "– which was controlled almost entirely by non-management directors – would not sell for the right price or vote themselves out of office to facilitate such a sale." *Id.* (citing and quoting *Unitrin*, 651 A.2d at 1381 n.27, 1383 & n.33).

The Supreme Court's first two premises, the *Chesapeake* court stated, were "somewhat contradictory" to the Supreme Court's "acceptance of substantive coercion as a rationale" for Unitrin's "sweeping defensive measures against the American General bid." *Id.* The court explained:

> On the one hand, a corporate electorate highly dominated by institutional investors has the motivation and wherewithal to understand and act upon a proxy solicitation from an insurgent, such that the necessity for the insurgent to convince over 64% of the non-aligned votes to support its position in order to prevail is not necessarily preclusive. On the other hand, the same electorate must be protected from substantive coercion because it (the targeted board thinks) is unable to digest management's position on the long-term value of the company, compare that position to the view advocated by the tender offeror, and make an intelligent (if not risk free) judgment about whether to support the election of a board that will permit them to sell their shares of stock.

Id. The court in *Chesapeake* then observed that the Supreme Court's opinion in *Unitrin* "did not ultimately validate the Unitrin defensive repurchase program"; "[r]ather, the Supreme Court remanded the case to the Chancery Court to conduct a further examination of the repurchase program, using the refined *Unocal* analysis the Court set forth," which emphasized "the need for trial courts to defer to well-informed corporate boards that identify legitimate threats and implement proportionate defensive measures addressing those threats." *Id.* at 326-27. The court in *Chesapeake* stated that "[it] was open for the court" in Unitrin "on remand to conclude, after considering the relevant factors articulated by the Supreme Court, that the repurchase program was invalid." *Id.* at 327.

As discussed later in this Chapter, the court in *Chesapeake* held that a supermajority bylaw was preclusive and not a proportionate response to the threat posed by an all cash for all shares tender offer. *See* Chapter III, Section H 2 f-1. The court in *Chesapeake* acknowledged that "I cannot deny that there is some tension between some of my analysis and the reasoning in *Unitrin*," but concluded that "my ultimate conclusion can be reconciled with that decision for several reasons." 771 A.2d at 344.

First, the court stated, the supermajority bylaw invalidated in the *Chesapeake* case set "a much higher barrier than the repurchase program in *Unitrin*": assuming a 90 percent turnout, 88% of disinterested votes were required in order for Chesapeake to amend the bylaws of the target corporation, Shorewood Packaging Corporation, whereas only 64% of disinterested votes were required to change the board in *Unitrin*. Since there was "no reliable evidence" suggesting that the required 88% of disinterested votes was "'realistically' attainable," the court concluded, the bylaw was preclusive. *Id.*

Second, the court stated, "the substantive coercion rationale cannot be wielded as imprecisely by the Shorewood board as was done by the defendants in *Unitrin* because the facts do not bear that rationale out in this case." *Id.* The fact that less than 1 percent of Shorewood's shareholders tendered their shares in response to Chesapeake's tender offer, the court stated, suggested "very little risk of voter confusion." *Id.* The corporation's "sophisticated stockholder and analyst base," the court added, also "undercut the need for any defense so extreme." *Id.*

Third, the court continued, "[i]n *Unitrin*, the directors had no material financial interests in the company other than as stockholders" and thus "had no financial incentive to vote their shares simply to remain as directors." *Id.* "The opposite" was true in the case of Shorewood's directors: "six of the nine Shorewood directors have substantial monetary reasons to vote to keep themselves in control" and, "[i]ndeed, they ha[d] already announced their intention to oppose Chesapeake" at the time they adopted the supermajority bylaw challenged in *Chesapeake* case. *Id.*

Finally, the court concluded, "*Unitrin* emphasized the need for deference to boards that make reasoned judgments about defensive measures" but "in no way suggests that the court ought to sanction a board's adoption of very aggressive defensive measures when the board has given little or no consideration to relevant factors and less preclusive alternatives." *Id.* In *Chesapeake*, the court stated, "the level of attention the Shorewood board paid to the relevant issues was grossly insufficient." *Id.*

Section E 2

Add "1" at the beginning of the Drexler citation in footnote 2540 on page 1039 and replace "1997" with "1999" in the same citation.

Add the following at the end of footnote 2541 on page 1039:

See also Maul v. Kirkman, 637 A.2d 928, 938 (N.J. Super. Ct. App. Div. 1994) ("[t]he question of whether or not a dividend is to be declared . . . is exclusively a matter of business judgment for the board of directors") (quoting what now appears at 3A William M. Fletcher, *Cyclopedia of the Law of Private Corporations* § 1041.20, at 59 (1994 & Supp. 2000)).

Add the following at the end of footnote 2542 on page 1039:

See also Smith v. Smitty McGee's, Inc., 1998 Del. Ch. LEXIS 87, at *32, 1998 WL 246681, at *8 (Del. Ch. May 8, 1998) (quoting *Eshleman v. Keenan*, 194 A. 40, 43 (Del. Ch. 1937), *aff'd*, 2 A.2d 904 (Del. 1938)) (footnotes omitted):

> Generally, whether or not a corporation should declare a dividend rests within the sound discretion of the board of directors, and the decision is protected by the business judgment rule. A plaintiff may allege wrongdoing against the board of directors, however, that causes them to lose the protection of the business judgment rule. A court may compel a corporation to pay a dividend where "the corporation's affairs are in a condition justifying the declaration of the dividend as a matter of prudent business management and that the withholding of it is explicable only on the theory of an oppressive or fraudulent abuse of discretion."

Add the following at the end of the paragraph beginning and concluding on page 1039 (immediately after footnote 2542):

"In today's financial world, dividends and self-tender offers are viewed as conventional methods of delivering to shareholders a return on their investment" and are "classic business judgment decisions of the kind that are normally protected by the business judgment rule." *Weiss v. Samsonite Corp.*, 741 A.2d 366, 371-72 (Del. Ch. 1999), *aff'd*, 746 A.2d 277 (unpublished opinion, text available at 1999 Del. LEXIS 387 and 1999 WL 1254563) (Del. Nov. 12, 1999).

Section F

Replace "1996" with "Supp. 1998/99" in the Model Act § 6.01 and 7.21 citation in footnote 2631 on page 1052.

Replace "6-114" with "6-120" and replace "1998" with "2001" in the Balotti citation in footnote 2633 on page 1053.

Add the following at the end of footnote 2634 on page 1053:

See also Browning, *Heard on the Street: As Hot New Issues Increase So Does Supervoting Stock*, Wall St. J., Apr. 24, 1996, at C1.

Add the following at the end of footnote 2636 on page 1054:

See also Chapter II, Section E 4 above (discussing tracking stock).

Section F 1

Add the following at the end of the paragraph beginning on page 1054 and concluding on page 1055 (immediately after footnote 2642):

As stated in *In re Digex, Inc. Shareholders Litigation*, 2000 Del. Ch. LEXIS 171, 2000 WL 1847679 (Del. Ch. Dec. 13, 2000):

> [S]uper-voting rights are certainly not a new invention under Delaware law . . . . The DGCL has long recognized that, with respect to corporations authorized to issue stock, voting rights of that stock may be varied by the certificate of incorporation as between classes and as between series within a class. Thus, the right to vote certain shares may be denied entirely, may be limited to certain matters, more or less than one vote may be given to the shares of any class or series, and the separate vote of a class or series may be required as a prerequisite to specified corporate actions.

2000 Del. Ch. LEXIS 171, at *82-83, 2000 WL 1847679, at *22.

Section F 3

Add the following at the end of footnote 2749 on page 1077:

See also Starkman v. United Parcel Serv. of Am., Inc., No. 17747, Tr. at 10-12, 23-28 (Del. Ch. Oct. 18, 1999) (denying a motion for a preliminary injunction seeking to enjoin a transaction creating a super-voting common stock structure based upon a claim that the certificate of incorporation required a supermajority vote to implement the super-voting common stock structure; the court also observed that plaintiff had little likelihood of success on the merits of an entrenchment claim because in the context of the corporation's existing capital structure "I find very little in the proposal" to create a super-voting common stock "that differentiates the likely outcome from the situation that exists today").

Section G

Replace "1700" with "2300" in the second sentence (immediately after footnote 2798) of the paragraph beginning on page 1085 and concluding on page 1086.

Replace "See generally" and the Bryan citation in footnote 2799 on page 1085 with the following:

See Leonard Loventhal Account v. Hilton Hotels Corp., 2000 Del. Ch. LEXIS 149, at *15, 2000 WL 1528909, at *4 (Del. Ch. Oct. 10, 2000); Joy M. Bryan, *Corporate Anti-Takeover Defenses: The Poison Pill Device* App. A–1-76 (alphabetical list of corporations that adopted rights plans from 1991 through December 15, 1999), App. B–1-122 (alphabetical list of corporations that adopted rights plans from 1986 through 1990) & App. C–1-69 (list of corporations that have adopted poison pills by state of incorporation) (2000).

Add the following at the end of the third sentence (immediately after footnote 2800) of the paragraph beginning on page 1085 and concluding on page 1086:

As stated by the Delaware Court of Chancery in 2000:

> The Delaware courts first examined and upheld the right of a board of directors to adopt a poison pill rights plan fifteen years ago in *Moran v. Household International, Inc.* [, 490 A.2d 1059 (Del. Ch.), *aff'd*, 500 A.2d 1346 (Del. 1985).] Since that decision, others have followed which affirmed the validity of a board of directors' decision to adopt a poison pill rights plan. Today, rights plans have not only become commonplace in Delaware, but there is not a single state that does not permit their adoption.
>
> *   *   *
>
> As the popularity of the poison pill defense has grown among Delaware directors over the past fifteen years, plans once described as "novel and complicated" [quoting *Household*, 490 A.2d at 1065] have become increasingly commonplace and rudimentary. Presently, practitioners can look to numerous corporation law guides and treatises for examples and explanations of the basic provisions and forms of this popular takeover defense mechanism.

Hilton, 2000 Del. Ch. LEXIS 149, at *1-2, 6, 2000 WL 1528909, at *1, 2.

Add the following at the end of the paragraph beginning on page 1085 and concluding on page 1086 (immediately after footnote 2801):

"Delaware courts have authorized the adoption of a poison pill in many cases." *In re Gaylord Container Corp. S'holders Litig.*, 753 A.2d 462, 481 (Del. Ch. 2000).

Add the following at the end of footnote 2801 on page 1086:

See also Gaylord, 753 A.2d at 483 n.72 (discussing empirical evidence that rights plans do not "present an unreasonable barrier to acquisition offers").

Replace "As a general rule, most shareholder rights plans involve" in the first sentence (immediately after footnote

2801) of the paragraph beginning and concluding on page 1087 with the following:

"The primary purpose of a poison pill is to enable the target board of directors to prevent the acquisition of a majority of the company's stock through an inadequate and/or coercive tender offer. The pill gives the target board leverage to negotiate with a would-be acquiror so as to improve the offer as well as the breathing room to explore alternatives to and examine the merits of an unsolicited bid." *Gaylord*, 753 A.2d at 481.

Most shareholder rights plans accomplish this by means of

Add the following at the end of the paragraph beginning on page 1087 and concluding on page 1088 (immediately after footnote 2803):

The Delaware Court of Chancery described this process with respect to the "standard model" rights plan provisions in a plan adopted by Toll Brothers, Inc. as follows:

> The dilutive mechanism of the Rights is "triggered" by certain defined events. One such event is the acquisition of 15% or more of Toll Brothers' stock by any person or group of affiliated or associated persons. Should that occur, each Rights holder (except the acquiror and its affiliates and associates) becomes entitled to buy two shares of Toll Brothers common stock or other securities at half price. That is, the value of the stock received when the Right is exercised is equal to two times the exercise price of the Right. In that manner, this so-called "flip in" feature of the Rights Plan would massively dilute the value of the holdings of the unwanted acquiror.
>
> The Rights also have a standard "flip over" feature, which is triggered if after the Stock Acquisition Date, the company is made a party to a merger in which Toll Brothers is not the surviving corporation, or in which it is the surviving corporation and its common stock is changed or exchanged. In either event, each Rights holder becomes entitled to purchase common stock of the acquiring company, again at half-price, thereby impairing the acquiror's capital structure and drastically diluting the interest of the acquiror's other stockholders.

> The complaint alleges that the purpose and effect of the company's Rights Plan, as with most poison pills, is to make any hostile acquisition of Toll Brothers prohibitively expensive, and thereby to deter such acquisitions unless the target company's board first approves the acquisition proposal. The target board's "leverage" derives from another critical feature found in most rights plans: the directors' power to redeem the Rights at any time before they expire, on such conditions as the directors "in their sole discretion" may establish.

Carmody v. Toll Bros., Inc., 723 A.2d 1180, 1183-84 (Del. Ch. 1998).

Add the following at the end of footnote 2805 on page 1089:

See also Golden Cycle, LLC v. Allan, 1998 Del. Ch. LEXIS 80, at *5, 1998 WL 276224, at *2 (Del. Ch. May 20, 1998) and 1998 Del. Ch. LEXIS 237, at *8, 1999 WL 892631, at *3 (Del. Ch. Dec. 10, 1998) (describing a rights plan having both flip-in and flip-over features and a 15 percent acquisition trigger as being "of the type normally adopted by corporations wishing to protect against unsolicited and unwanted takeover attempts").

Add the following at the end of the paragraph beginning on page 1088 and concluding on page 1089 (immediately after footnote 2805):

Emeritus Corp. v. ARV Assisted Living, Inc., No. 793420 (Cal. Super. Ct. Orange Co. June 30, 1999), illustrates a court decision finding that a shareholder rights plan had been triggered and awarding damages.

The case involved a contest for control of ARV Assisting Living, Inc. between Emeritus Corporation and Prometheus Assisted Living. On July 10, 1997, Emeritus proposed an acquisition of all outstanding shares of ARV's common stock at $14 per share at a time when the stock's market value was $10.25 per share. On July 14, ARV entered into a stock purchase agreement with Prometheus, pursuant to which Prometheus acquired 16 percent of ARV's common stock at a price of $14 per share, and pursuant to which Prometheus could acquire up to a total of 49.9 percent of ARV's common stock at the same $14 per share price if the stock purchase agreement received shareholder approval. At the same time, ARV directors and officers who, with related family trusts and partnerships, owned substantial blocks of ARV stock, entered into a stockholders' voting agreement with Prometheus. The shareholders who entered into the voting agreement agreed to vote their shares in support of the board's and Prometheus's respective nominees to ARV's board. *Id.*, slip op. at 4-5.

Also on July 14, 1997, ARV's board adopted a rights plan that would be triggered if Prometheus became the beneficial owner – a defined term – of 50 percent or more of ARV's stock or if any other shareholder became the beneficial owner of 10 percent or more of ARV's stock. Upon the occurrence of either of those triggering events, the plan obligated ARV to distribute rights certificates to all shareholders of ARV except the shareholder who triggered the plan. Holders of the rights certificates would have the right to purchase newly issued ARV shares at half of the then current market price of ARV shares. *Id.* at 3-4.

On October 12, 1997, Emeritus again offered to purchase all outstanding shares of ARV's common stock, this time for $16.50 per share in cash. On October 13, 1997, ARV's board rejected the offer. On October 29, 1997, after being advised by ARV's proxy consultant that shareholders likely would vote against the July 14, 1997 stock purchase agreement and the further purchases of ARV stock at $14 per share by Prometheus provided for by that agreement, ARV and Prometheus terminated the stock purchase agreement and entered into a new set of agreements that were not subject to shareholder approval. These new agreements permitted Prometheus to retain the 16 percent block of stock it had acquired under the July 14, 1997 stock purchase agreement, permitted Prometheus to acquire a total of up to 49.9 percent of ARV's shares, as had been permitted under the stock purchase agreement, and provided for the purchase by Prometheus of $60 million worth of notes from ARV that could be converted by ARV into ARV common stock at $14 per share. These notes permitted ARV, at its discretion, to place 23 percent of ARV's stock in Prometheus's hands. *Id.* at 5. At the same time, a second shareholder voting agreement was entered into with provisions similar to the first shareholder voting agreement. *Id.* at 5-6.

On November 24, 1997, Emeritus commenced a tender offer for ARV at a price of $17.50 per share and filed proxy materials with the Securities and Exchange Commission stating Emeritus's intent to field a slate of candidates to run for election to ARV's board at ARV's annual meeting on January 28, 1998. On December 5, 1997, ARV converted the notes held by Prometheus into common stock. The combination of Prometheus' ownership of shares and control over the voting of shares under the stockholders' voting agreement gave Prometheus control over the votes of 48 percent of ARV's common stock. During January 1998, Prometheus purchased another 8.7 percent of ARV's common stock. The admitted purpose of these purchases was "to ensure that the Emeritus slate was defeated" at ARV's annual meeting on January 28, 1998. *Id.* at 6.

Following a trial, the court held that Prometheus's acquisitions of ARV stock made Prometheus the beneficial owner of 50 percent or more of ARV's stock as the term beneficial owner was defined in the rights plan and thus triggered the rights plan. Accordingly, the court held, rights certificates should have been distributed to all shareholders other than Prometheus on January 30, 1998. *Id.* at 6-13.

The court rejected Prometheus's reliance upon a plan provision protecting an acquiring person who inadvertently triggered the plan where (1) ARV's board determines in good faith that the triggering of the plan was "inadvertent," (2) ARV's board determines in good faith that the purchase of shares that triggered the plan was made "without any intention of changing or influencing control," and (3) the acquiring person sells a sufficient number of shares "as promptly as practical" in order to reduce its holdings below the trigger level. *Id.* at 14. According to the court, none of these three conditions occurred in this case. The court acknowledged that ARV's board "passed a resolution that mirrored the language of the inadvertence clause of the Agreement," but the court found that the board never determined whether the actions by Prometheus in fact were inadvertent. *Id.* The court also found that the purchases were made with an "intention of . . . influencing control" and that "Prometheus did not sell a sufficient number of shares to fall beneath its 50% trigger level 'as promptly as practicable'" in order to reduce its holdings below the trigger level because "Emeritus informed Prometheus by letter dated January 26, 1998 of its view that the Agreement had been triggered" but "[w]ith the crucial shareholders' vote at the January 28, 1998 meeting imminent, Prometheus took no immediate steps to divest itself of the appropriate amount of stock." *Id.* at 15. Thus, the court concluded, far from being inadvertent, "Prometheus's actions that precipitated the triggering event . . . were part of a deliberate strategy." *Id.* at 14.

The court held that Emeritus could not be made whole simply by ordering ARV to issue the rights certificates that should have been distributed on January 30, 1998 because ARV's stock price had dropped from $12.875 on January 30, 1998 to approximately $4 per share as of the June 30, 1999 date of the court's decision. The court stated that the exercise price of the rights issued on January 30, 1998 would have been $7.58 per share, which was $5.29 less than ARV's $12.87 per share stock price at that time, and thus the rights, if they had been issued as required, could have been used on January 30, 1998 to purchase ARV shares at a $5.29 per share savings. As a result of the subsequent drop of ARV's stock price to $4 per share, however, rights issued on June 30, 1999 would have "an effective exercise price substantially *higher* than the current trading price" and thus "would be of correspondingly limited value." *Id.* at 18.

The court accordingly determined to "adjust the terms of its injunctive relief" to account for the decline in ARV's stock value or else "ARV would be the direct beneficiary of its own refusal to distribute the Rights." *Id.* at 18-19. Based upon expert testimony, the court concluded that the value of the rights to which Emeritus was entitled in January 30, 1998 was $5,405,482, and the court awarded damages in that amount. *Id.* at 21-23.

Add the following new footnote 2806.1 at the end of the third sentence of the paragraph beginning on page 1090 and concluding on page 1091:

See Carmody v. Toll Bros., Inc., 723 A.2d 1180, 1185 (Del. Ch. 1998) ("[T]he relevant history begins in the early 1980s with the advent of the 'poison pill' as an antitakeover measure. That innovation generated litigation focused upon the issue of whether any poison pill rights plan could validly be adopted under state corporation law. The seminal case, *Moran v. Household International, Inc.* [, 490 A.2d 1059 (Del. Ch.), *aff'd*, 500 A.2d 1346 (Del. 1985)], answered that question in the affirmative.").

Add the following new footnote 2806.2 at the end of the fourth sentence of the paragraph beginning on page 1090 and concluding on page 1091:

See Toll Bros., 723 A.2d at 1186 ("It being settled that a corporate board could permissibly adopt a poison pill, the next litigated question became: under what circumstances would the directors' fiduciary duties require the board to redeem the rights in the face of a hostile takeover proposal? That issue was litigated, in Delaware and elsewhere, during the second half of the 1980s.").

Section G 1 a

Add the following at the end of the paragraph beginning on page 1094 and concluding on page 1095 (immediately after footnote 2830):

The Delaware Court of Chancery in *Leonard Loventhal Account v. Hilton Hotels Corp.*, 2000 Del. Ch. LEXIS 149, 2000 WL 1528909 (Del. Ch. Oct. 10, 2000), rejected a challenge to a rights plan having "a structure similar to many other poison pill rights plans" (2000 Del. Ch. LEXIS 149, at *7, 2000 WL 1528909, at *2) adopted since *Moran v. Household International, Inc.*, 500 A.2d 1346 (Del. 1985). The court in *Hilton* summarized the rights plan in the *Hilton* case as follows:

> Under the Rights Plan, each shareholder receives in the form of a dividend authorized by the Hilton Board one preferred share purchase right (a "Right" held by a "Right Holder") for each share of common stock outstanding as of November 30, 1999. Initially, the Rights attach to Hilton's outstanding common shares (the "Hilton common shares"), and each Right entitles the holder to purchase for $80 one one-hundredth of a share of Series A Junior Participating Preferred Stock (the "Preferred Stock") having the rights, powers and preferences set forth in the Certificate of Designations. Upon the occurrence of certain triggering events, including the acquisition of 20 percent or more of Hilton common stock by any person or affiliated group, the Rights entitle the Right Holder to purchase two shares of Hilton common stock or other securities at half-price. This is designed to massively dilute the holdings of the unwanted, potential acquiror.

2000 Del. Ch. LEXIS 149, at *7-8, 2000 WL 1528909, at *2. The court held that the *Household* decision "considered and upheld the basic concept of a stockholder rights plan, including its core elements and the manner in which it operates" and that "[n]early identical challenges to fundamental attributes of rights plans that existed in the Household rights plan are foreclosed by the powerful effect" of the *Household* decision and the doctrine of stare decisis. 2000 Del. Ch. LEXIS 149, at *15,

2000 WL 1528909, at *4. The court acknowledged that since *Household*, "corporate boards have inserted new provisions into rights plans that require judicial scrutiny," but stated that "no substantive factual difference exists between the relevant aspects of the Household rights plan and the Hilton Rights Plan" and that the doctrine of stare decisis cannot be overcome simply by asserting "legal theories not considered or determined" in *Household*. 2000 Del. Ch. LEXIS 149, at *24, 2000 WL 1528909, at *6-7.

The court then "re-affirm[ed] the principle set forth in *Household*" that directors are not insulated from liability for decisions with respect to whether or not to redeem rights. 2000 Del. Ch. LEXIS 149, at *43, 2000 WL 1528909, at *12. The court quoted *Household* as follows:

> The Rights Plan is not absolute. When the Household Board of Directors is faced with a tender offer and a request to redeem the Rights, they will not be able to arbitrarily reject the offer. They will be held to the same fiduciary standards any other board of directors would be held to in deciding to adopt a defensive mechanism, the same standard as they were held to in originally approving the Rights Plan.

Id. (quoting 500 A.2d at 1354).

Add the following new footnote 2837.1 at the end of the paragraph beginning and concluding on page 1095:

See also Hilton, 2000 Del. Ch. LEXIS 149, at *2 & n.3, 2000 WL 1528909, at *1 & n.3 (noting jurisdictions other than Delaware that have followed *Household* and stating that "[t]oday, rights plans have not only become commonplace in Delaware, but there is not a single state that does not permit their adoption").

Section G 1 b

Add the following at the end of the first paragraph beginning and concluding on page 1103 (immediately after footnote 2878):

Decisions discussing the standard of judicial review applied by New York courts construing this statute are discussed in Chapter III, Section G 2 e.

Section G 1 c (i)

Add the following at the end of the first paragraph beginning and concluding on page 1107 (between footnotes 2904 and 2905):

As stated by a New York court in *Rand v. Crosby*, No. 400063/98 (N.Y. Sup. Ct. N.Y. Co. May 17, 1999), "[t]he adoption of a shareholders' rights plan to ward off undesired takeover attempts is a practice that has been sanctioned by the courts." *Id.*, slip op. at 4.

Section G 1 c (iii)

Add the following at the end of the paragraph beginning and concluding on page 1118 (immediately after footnote 2964):

The court subsequently dismissed the case on a motion for summary judgment in *In re Gaylord Container Corp. Shareholders Litigation*, 753 A.2d 462 (Del. Ch. 2000). The court described the rights plan as "a garden-variety poison pill" and stated that "Delaware courts have authorized the adoption of a poison pill in many cases." *Id.* at 481. The court stated that the adoption of the rights plan was "proportionate to the legitimate threats identified by the Gaylord board" – the threat of an inadequate and/or coercive tender offer following the expiration of the corporation's dual class voting structure. *Id.* As stated by the court: "The primary purpose of a poison pill is to enable the target board directors to prevent the acquisition of a majority of the company's stock through an inadequate and/or coercive tender offer," and "[t]he pill gives the target board leverage to negotiate with a would-be acquiror so as to improve the offer as well as the breathing room to explore alternatives to and examine the merits of an unsolicited bid." *Id.*

The court acknowledged that "a poison pill absolutely precludes a hostile acquisition so long as the pill remains in place," but still "is not in itself preclusive" because "in the event of a concrete battle for corporate control, the board's decision to keep the pill in place in the face of an actual acquisition offer will be scrutinized again under *Unocal*." *Id.* Additionally, the court stated, "the pill may be redeemed by a new board elected after a successful proxy fight by an acquiror at the Gaylord annual meeting" because "[a]ll an acquiror needs is the necessary votes to elect a new board, which can redeem the pill and allow the offer to go forward." *Id.* The charter and bylaw amendments, the court continued, were "necessary if the Gaylord board was to address the threats it identified" in order to "force an acquiror seeking to obtain control of Gaylord to do so at the annual stockholders' meeting after giving stockholders adequate time to consider the platforms and qualifications of the contending director slates." *Id.* at 482. The charter and bylaw amendments thus limited the corporation's "exposure to a proxy fight outside of the company's annual meeting" – "hardly," the court stated, a "show-stopper." *Id.* at 484; *see also* Chapter II, Sections H 2 Introduction, H 2 a, H 2 d and H 2 f-1 (also discussing Gaylord's charter and bylaw amendments).

Add the following at the end of the paragraph beginning on page 1120 and concluding on page 1121 (immediately after footnote 2979):

A federal court construing Missouri law in *Flake v. Hoskins*, 55 F. Supp. 2d 1196 (D. Kan. 1999), denied a motion to dismiss a complaint challenging a rights plan adopted following offers for a large block of shares held by the corporation's employee stock ownership plan. The rights plan granted shareholders the right to purchase one share of common stock for each share owned, at half of market price, if an acquiror acquired 15 percent or more of the corporation's stock without board approval. *Id.* at 1206. According to plaintiffs, "[t]he board thereby discriminated against unfriendly offerors and tilted the playing field to favor those bidders who were willing to make an offer which benefited defendants." *Id.* The court stated that "Missouri looks to Delaware law in examining corporate actions," that Delaware's *Unocal* standard applies to Missouri corporations, and that under Delaware law "claims under *Unocal* can rarely be disposed of on a motion to dismiss." *Id.* at 1214, 1217. Here, the court stated, "[n]othing in the complaint hints at any investigation into the offers" by the corporation's board, "let alone a reasonable investigation to determine whether the threat required defensive measures and if so, which ones." *Id.* at 1217. "Clearly," the court continued, "the complaint does not require the Court to find that defendants implemented the shareholder rights plan in good faith." *Id.* at 1217-18.

Section G 2

Add the following at the end of the paragraph beginning and concluding on page 1146 (between footnotes 3141 and 3142):

As a result, "the mere adoption of a garden-variety pill" that "absolutely precludes a hostile acquisition so long as the pill remains in place . . . is not in itself preclusive under Delaware law . . . because in the event of a concrete battle for corporate control, the board's decision to keep the pill in place in the face of an actual acquisition offer will be scrutinized again under *Unocal*." *In re Gaylord Container Corp. S'holders Litig.*, 753 A.2d 462, 481 (Del. Ch. 2000).

Replace the period at the end of footnote 3145 on page 1147 with the following:

, *quoted in Leonard Loventhal Account v. Hilton Hotels Corp.*, 2000 Del. Ch. LEXIS 149, at *44, 2000 WL 1528909, at *12 (Del. Ch. Oct. 10, 2000) (and adding that this statement "remains as true today as the day it was written").

Add the following at the end of the paragraph beginning on page 1148 and concluding on page 1149 (immediately after footnote 3163):

The Delaware Court of Chancery in *Carmody v. Toll Brothers, Inc.*, 723 A.2d 1180 (Del. Ch. 1998), surveyed the case law and concluded that courts are "extremely reluctant to order the redemption of poison pills on fiduciary grounds" because "the prudent deployment of the pill" has proven "largely beneficial to shareholder interests" and often has "resulted in a bidding contest that culminated in an acquisition on terms superior to the initial hostile offer." *Id.* at 1186.

Add the following at the end of the first paragraph beginning and concluding on page 1150 (immediately after footnote 3168):

The Delaware Court of Chancery also followed *In re Sante Fe Pacific Corp. Shareholder Litigation*, 669 A.2d 59 (Del. 1995), in *Toll Brothers,* a case challenging the adoption of a dead hand shareholder rights plan provision, and denied a motion to dismiss on this basis. 723 A.2d at 1194-95; *see also* Chapter III, Section G 2 d (discussing *Toll Brothers*).

Section G 2 a

Add the following at the end of the paragraph beginning on page 1157 and concluding on page 1158 (immediately after footnote 3220):

The Delaware Court of Chancery in *Golden Cycle, LLC v. Allan*, 1998 Del. Ch. LEXIS 80, 1998 WL 276224 (Del. Ch. May 20, 1998), denied a motion for a preliminary injunction seeking to require the directors of Global Motorsport Group, Inc. to redeem the rights or render a rights plan inapplicable to an $18 per share tender offer by Golden Cycle LLC. The court stated that "the relief requested is wholly unwarranted and unnecessary at this time" because "the market price of Global's common stock remains more than $2.00 higher than Global Cycle's tender offer and, as a result of this fact, virtually no shares have been tendered into Golden Cycle's offer." 1998 Del. Ch. LEXIS 80, at *36, 1998 WL 276224, at *12. Under these circumstances, the court reasoned, "there is no basis on which I could conclude that the Rights Plan . . . is having any effect on Golden Cycle's ability to attract tenders" and "[n]or will it do so unless Golden Cycle raises its offer, or unless changes in market conditions render its $18 offer competitive." *Id.*

The court also pointed to the fact that Global's board was not a classified or staggered board, no charter restrictions prevented shareholder action by written consent, and ownership of common stock was "concentrated in the hands of a small number of institutional investors not affiliated with the Company" – factors that "combine to give the common stockholders of Global an unusual degree of practical control over the outcome of this contest." 1998 Del. Ch. LEXIS 80, at *4, 1998 WL 276224, at *1. The court stated that "there is every reason to conclude that the stockholders are fully empowered to remedy" any impediment to any offer posed by Global's rights plan because "[t]hey have the immediately exercisable power (not shown to be materially impacted by any action taken by the Board) to remove the directors and replace them with others committed to redeeming the Rights." 1998 Del. Ch. LEXIS 80, at *19-20, 1998 WL 276224, at *6. Accordingly, "[n]o injunction is needed to accomplish these objectives once the stockholders decide it is in their best interest so to act." 1998 Del. Ch. LEXIS 80, at *20, 1998 WL 276224, at *6.

The court reached the same conclusion in a second decision, this one following a merger agreement entered into by Global and Stonington Acquisition Corporation that required Global to amend its rights plan to make it inapplicable to Stonington's tender offer and prohibited Global's board from redeeming or further amending the rights plan without Stonington's consent. *Golden Cycle, LLC v. Allan*, 1998 Del. Ch. LEXIS 237, at *51 n.15, 1998 WL 892631, at *17 n.15 (Del. Ch. Dec. 10, 1998). The court explained that the merger agreement contained "a window-shop provision that acts as a fiduciary out and allows the Board to consider and negotiate a bona fide acquisition proposal from a third party where the Board concludes that the outside proposal is a financed offer more favorable than Stonington's," and "the rights plan 'lock-up' . . . goes away the moment the Stonington Merger Agreement terminates." 1998 Del. Ch. LEXIS 237, at *16, 52, 1998 WL 892631, at *5, 17. Accordingly, the court held, the rights plan provides "no impediment to either the existing directors or any other board of directors entering into a higher price transaction with Cycle." 1998 Del. Ch. LEXIS 237, at *52, 1998 WL 892631, at *17.

A federal court construing Wisconsin law in *Safety-Kleen Corp. v. Laidlaw Environmental Services, Inc.*, 1999 WL 601039 (N.D. Ill. Feb. 4, 1998), denied a motion for a preliminary injunction seeking to require the directors of Safety-Kleen Corporation to redeem rights and allow Safety-Kleen's shareholders to choose between two bids that were "reasonably financially equivalent in terms of their short term shareholder value." *Id.* at *9.

The case involved the culmination of a process that began during the summer of 1997 when Safety-Kleen's board asked its financial advisor, William Blair & Company, to contact third parties that Safety-Kleen and Blair thought might be interested in acquiring Safety-Kleen. A total of 94 parties expressed an interest, and, of these 94 parties, 50 agreed to sign a confidentiality and standstill agreement that precluded an offer to acquire Safety-Kleen stock without the approval of

Safety-Kleen's board for a period of 18 to 24 months. These 50 potential acquirors were provided confidential non-public information about Safety-Kleen. *Id.* at *2. Five potential buyers ultimately were asked "to submit their best and highest written offer, including the price per share, proposed transaction structure, and amounts and sources of funds" and to comment upon a draft merger agreement by November 14, 1997. *Id.* at *3.

One bidder, Laidlaw Environmental Services, Inc., refused to sign the confidentiality and standstill agreement because Laidlaw "wanted to make sure that any bid it decided to make would be put before Safety-Kleen shareholders." *Id.* On November 3, 1997, Laidlaw offered to purchase all shares of Safety-Kleen stock for $14 in cash and 2.4 shares of Laidlaw stock, which then was trading at $4.88 per share – a total market value of $25.71 per share. The offer was not subject to due diligence or financing contingencies. *Id.* Safety-Kleen and Laidlaw representatives met to discuss Laidlaw's offer and plans for the company in the event of an acquisition of Safety-Kleen by Laidlaw – an important consideration to Safety-Kleen's board because Laidlaw's offer included stock in the combined Laidlaw-Safety-Kleen entity. Laidlaw believed that approximately $100 million in synergies would be achieved by moving Safety-Kleen's headquarters from Elgin, Illinois to South Carolina, where Laidlaw's headquarters were located, and by closing various additional Safety-Kleen facilities. Safety-Kleen believed that a combination of Safety-Kleen and Laidlaw would result in at most $30 to $40 million in synergies. Safety-Kleen requested further information about Laidlaw's proposal and estimate concerning synergies that could be achieved by the combination. Laidlaw refused to provide this information. *Id.* at *4.

On November 7, another bidder, Philip Services Corporation, which had signed a confidentiality and standstill agreement, informed Blair that it was prepared to pay at least $26 per share in cash and Philip stock but that Philip would submit a proposal only if Safety-Kleen agreed to negotiate exclusively with Philip. *Id.* On November 14, after Philip had stated a willingness to increase its offer to $27 per share in cash and with Laidlaw's proposal valued at $25.70 using Laidlaw's then current stock price, Safety-Kleen's board determined to authorize exclusive negotiations with Philip. *Id.* at *6.

On November 20, Safety-Kleen and Philip entered into a merger agreement providing for Philip to pay Safety-Kleen's shareholders $27 per share in cash. *Id.* at *7. The merger agreement included a fiduciary out clause that prohibited solicitation by Safety-Kleen of other proposals but provided that "in the case of proposals not solicited by Safety-Kleen the Board could negotiate with persons or entities concerning an acquisition proposal if it concluded in good faith after consultation with its financial advisors that such person or entity made or was reasonably likely to make a bona fide acquisition proposal for a transaction more favorable to the company's shareholders from a financial point of view than the transaction proposed with Philip." *Id.* at *6. The merger agreement also included a $50 million termination fee and provided for reimbursement of up to $25 million in expenses if Safety-Kleen failed to complete the merger. *Id.* Under Wisconsin law, a vote in favor of the merger agreement by two-thirds of Safety-Kleen's shareholders was required. *Id.* at *9, 17.

Also on November 20, and in response to the announcement of the $27 per share merger agreement entered into by Safety-Kleen and Philip, Laidlaw increased it offer to (1) $15 per share in cash, subject to reductions for expenses Safety-Kleen incurred in connection with its merger agreement with Philip, and (2) Laidlaw common stock having a market value of $15 per share, with a "collar" providing that no fewer than 2.8 shares and no more than 3.5 shares would be exchanged. *Id.* at *7-8.

Safety-Kleen's board concluded, and the court agreed, that the $27 all cash offer by Philip and the $30 cash and stock offer by Laidlaw were "reasonably financially equivalent in terms of their short term shareholder value" because "the contingencies inherent in the stock portion of the Laidlaw offer and the slightly lower value of the Philip cash offer balance[d] out" and thus "the Laidlaw offer, although possibly facially worth more, also could be worth less." *Id.* at *9.

In the face of these more or less financially equivalent offers, Safety-Kleen's board determined that "the Philip proposal stood a better chance of serving the interests of non-shareholder constituencies" because Philip's stated intention but not contractual obligation was "to keep Safety-Kleen as a stand-alone business, to maintain Safety-Kleen's principal offices in Elgin, Illinois, and to maintain Safety-Kleen's charitable and community commitments," while Laidlaw's intention was "to close the Elgin headquarters facility, substantially reduce the number of Safety-Kleen employees, and radically reduce Safety-Kleen's separate ongoing operations." *Id.* at *6, 7, 13. Safety-Kleen's board also determined that "the Laidlaw offer was not good for the stock's long-term prospects" because, in addition to uncertainties involving the stock portion of Laidlaw's offer, the board perceived "enormous potential environmental liabilities stemming from Laidlaw's incineration and landfill disposal methods" and these potential liabilities would be shifted to Safety-Kleen's shareholders if Laidlaw's offer was accepted. *Id.* at *6, 8, 13.

Laidlaw sought a mandatory injunction requiring that Safety-Kleen's board "lift its poison pill . . . so that the shareholders could choose between the Board's recommended transaction and the Laidlaw bid." *Id.* at *9. Laidlaw did not challenge the independence of Safety-Kleen's directors, only one of whom was an officer or employee of Safety-Kleen, and the court found the board to be "an independent board whose financial interests are aligned with those of the other shareholders." *Id.* at *11. The court explained that "[m]ost of the directors are substantial Safety-Kleen shareholders with one Board member owning 10 percent of the company and another 1 percent." *Id.* The court stated that none of the board members stood "to gain any personal consideration in the form of employment, payment, or anything else from the Philip merger," and that there was nothing in the record that "suggests that self-interest or entrenchment was a factor present in any respect." *Id.* The court also stated that the directors were "well-informed," "met frequently in long meetings to assess the alternatives available to them," had "highly reputable" legal and financial advisors, and had engaged in "a long and scrupulously deliberate auction process." *Id.* at *11, 15; *see also id.* at *19 (the board "has made a business judgment" and "[n]othing has been shown to suggest" that the board is acting "because of any conflict of interest or based on inadequate information or for any illegitimate reason").

Laidlaw also did not challenge the board's decision to enter into an exclusive bargaining arrangement with Philip before attempting to negotiate a better offer with Laidlaw. The court stated that the evidence supported Safety-Kleen's contention that "as of November 20, with Philip the only serious bidder other than Laidlaw, who had declined to sign the confidentiality and standstill agreement, the Board was legitimately concerned that it would lose the opportunity to enter into a $27 offer with Philip if it did not agree to Philip's exclusivity request." *Id.* at *13.

The "key issue" raised by Laidlaw's motion thus was whether a disinterested and informed board faced with "probably financially equivalent" bids is compelled to redeem a shareholder rights plan and allow shareholders to choose between the two bids for themselves. *Id.* The court stated that "there is no question that under Wisconsin law the Board could take into consideration its view that the Laidlaw proposal would be significantly deleterious to other constituencies such as the community where for many years Safety-Kleen has done business and to its employees." *Id.* at *15. Likewise, the court continued, the board could take into consideration its view that Laidlaw's proposal "was not in the long-term interests of shareholders because Laidlaw's synergy estimates displayed a lack of knowledge of key aspects of Safety-Kleen's business, a judgment that becomes important when shareholders are getting a mixture of stock and cash rather than cash alone." *Id.* at *15.

The court stated its view that Laidlaw's refusal to sign a standstill agreement was "one of the major obstacles to its success" and that the court did not believe that the board's unwillingness to redeem Safety-Kleen's rights plan "can be viewed in isolation from the whole process the Board put in motion." *Id.* at *16. The court explained that the board's reservations about the synergies Laidlaw expected following a combination of Safety-Kleen and Laidlaw reflected Laidlaw's determinations (1) not to enter into a confidentiality agreement and thus not to perform due diligence, and (2) not to provide Safety-Kleen with information requested by Safety-Kleen concerning synergies anticipated by Laidlaw. *Id.* at *16. The court stated that Laidlaw was "free to decline to enter into a confidentiality and standstill agreement" and was "free to decline to provide information requested by Safety-Kleen, but Laidlaw's actions made it difficult for the board to evaluate the Laidlaw proposal in as much depth as it could evaluate the competition, and in all likelihood deprived Laidlaw of useful if not important information about Safety-Kleen." *Id.* Without evidence of bias, interest or corruption, the court stated, "it has to assume" that if Laidlaw had entered into the process provided for by Safety-Kleen's board, then Laidlaw's bid "would have been evaluated exactly as the competition was evaluated, and had the Board found it superior, Laidlaw's offer would have been recommended." *Id.*

The court also pointed to the fact that Safety-Kleen's rights plan had "over a long period of time" served its "appropriate function of enhancing shareholder value." *Id.* The court stated that Laidlaw repeatedly had made offers and asked Safety-Kleen to lift the rights plan with respect to those offers. The court stated that if Safety-Kleen had lifted its rights plan when Laidlaw made its first offer, "it is highly unlikely that Laidlaw would have made the succession of improved offers" that Laidlaw ultimately made and "Philip may have walked away from the negotiations process with Safety-Kleen and not offered its all cash $27 offer." *Id.* The court stated that "this kind of bidding history demonstrates how defensive measures serve a legitimate stockholder interest in maximizing the value of shareholders' shares." *Id.* The court stated that Safety-Kleen's board, without a rights plan, would have "no leverage to use in its future negotiations with Laidlaw and others" and if Safety-Kleen's shareholders voted against the merger of Safety-Kleen and Philip at $27 per share in cash that Safety-Kleen's board had recommended to the shareholders, then the bidding would not be over and "the Board will need considerable leverage to keep a Laidlaw bid equivalent to $27." *Id.* The court added that it had "doubt" concerning Laidlaw's contention that it had made its "final and best offer." *Id.*

The court rejected Laidlaw's suggestion that Safety-Kleen's board could set aside its rights plan "conditionally, just long enough for the shareholders to vote on the two proposals." *Id.* The court reasoned that "Laidlaw's conditional exemption proposal serves the purpose of getting Laidlaw's bid before the shareholders and is appealing because it would serve the end of giving shareholders a choice, but it depends on a finding by this court that when the bidding stops, even when the Board has been acting in a careful and informed manner, with no conflicts of interest, anyone with a reasonably equivalent bid can have a court set aside defensive measures." *Id.* If that were the law, the court stated, it would be "hard to see why anyone would bid in a controlled auction and why anyone would take defensive measures seriously" because the better strategy would be "to let someone else negotiate, make an equivalent proposal and get an injunction to remove defensive measures." *Id.* In the court's view, "[i]n the long run, that would be bad for shareholders because it would leave boards with substantially reduced negotiating leverage." *Id.*

The court thus held that "a well-informed board, acting pursuant to expert advice, with no conflicts of interest" does not breach its fiduciary duties "by recommending one proposal to the shareholders and leaving defensive measures in place as to others." *Id.* at *18. This is "even more the case," the court concluded, where "the directors have considered non-shareholder interests that Wisconsin law explicitly allows them to take into consideration and have made a judgment in view of the stock portion of the Laidlaw bid that Laidlaw's anticipated prospects for the surviving entity are doubtful, and further have found in view of these interests that the recommended offer is superior." *Id.*

The court emphasized that "[t]his is not a case of an entrenched board trying to fend off a hostile bid to save the status quo, but a case in which a board has embarked upon a process in which it has asked bidders to negotiate with it and satisfy it that the bidder's offer is the best available." *Id.* The court stated that a board acting in good faith can structure a bidding process in this manner and that once the board is prepared to recommend one proposal to shareholders the board need not "scuttle its process and let all bidders submit their proposals to the shareholders." *Id.* Requiring boards to allow all bidders to submit their proposals to shareholders, the court stated, "would be to choose as a policy preference unrestricted shareholder choice as a more important value than the board's ability to exercise its business judgment in good faith to establish a process that potential acquirors know they must take seriously." *Id.*

In sum, the court concluded, the refusal by Safety-Kleen's board to waive Safety-Kleen's rights plan was "part of a fair and consistent auction process which required any bidder who wanted the lifting of impediments to negotiate with the Board and persuade the Board that its offer was the best." *Id.* at *19. No principle of law, the court concluded, "says that Laidlaw should be able at this eleventh hour to get all the advantages that fell to the winner of the auction process without assuming the risks of entering into the process that other bidders took." *Id.*

A second decision in the case one month later, *Safety-Kleen Corp. v. Laidlaw Environmental Services, Inc.*, No. 97 C 3003 (N.D. Ill. Mar. 5, 1998), involved an increased offer by Ladilaw: (1) $18 per share in cash, subject to reductions for expenses Safety-Kleen incurred in connection with its merger agreement with Philip, with these reductions capped at $75 million, and (2) $12 per share in stock, with a collar. 1999 WL 601039, at *9; Mar. 5, 1998 Tr. at 29. This time, Safety-Kleen's financial advisor opined that it was more likely than not that Laidlaw's offer would have a value at closing in excess of Philip's $27 per share all cash offer. Tr. at. 29-30.

Laidlaw sought another preliminary injunction, which was heard less than two business days before Safety-Kleen's shareholders were scheduled to vote on the Safety-Kleen merger with Philip. *Id.* at 35. Laidlaw focused upon Blair's "current opinion adverse to the opinion of the Board" and "quoted statements from Board members suggesting an unwillingness to negotiate with Laidlaw" even if Safety-Kleen's shareholders reject the proposed Safety-Kleen merger with Phillip. *Id.* at 32-33.

The court stated that there was "no question" that Blair's opinion and the quoted statements from Safety-Kleen's directors "raise questions both as to the Board's adherence to *Unocal* standards and the possibility that the Board may be using the pill to suggest to shareholders that Philip may be their only option." *Id.* at 33. The court concluded, however, that Blair's opinion addressed only "the comparative value of the two offers at closing," that "[t]he Board is normally entitled to consider a broad range of factors," and that the fact that "Laidlaw has raised questions does not mean that Laidlaw has established either a breach of *Unocal* duties or that the shareholders are being coerced." *Id.* at 32, 33. Rather, the court stated, "[i]t means that there is a basis for a more searching inquiry." *Id.*

The court pointed to the limited record before it and the lack of time before the shareholder meeting for "a hearing at which the Board's rationale could be examined in light of the opinions of the various financial advisors and experts retained by the parties." *Id.* at 32. The court stated that "Safety-Kleen has represented to this court that if the Philip offer is approved by the Safety-Kleen shareholders, no merger will take place for one week." *Id.* The court concluded that "[i]f the directors' refusal to lift the defensive measures is a breach of fiduciary duty today, it will be a breach of fiduciary duty as of next week," and "[w]hatever power the court has to enjoin these defensive measures now, it will have next week." *Id.* at 33-34. The court also pointed to the fact that "the entry of an injunction at this point would irreparably taint the possibility of a fair vote on the Philip merger." *Id.* at 34-35.

The court accordingly denied Laidlaw's motion for a preliminary injunction but scheduled a hearing to take place after the shareholder vote. The court stated that "[i]f the Laidlaw offer is sufficiently superior so that the Board can be said to have violated its fiduciary duty in keeping the defensive measures in place, . . . the Court will be able to enjoin the defensive measurers as well as the consummation of the Philip merger." *Id.* at 34-35.

Subsequently, Safety-Kleen's shareholders did not approve the proposed merger with Philip by the required two-thirds vote, Laidlaw increased the cash portion of its offer to $18.30 per share, and Safety-Kleen's board agreed to remove its rights plan. *Safety-Kleen Approves Takeover Offer from Laidlaw*, N.Y. Times, Mar. 17, 1998, at D4.

Section G 2 d

Replace the heading at the beginning of the paragraph beginning and concluding on page 1184 (immediately after footnote 3386) with the following:

d. "Continuing Director", "Dead Hand" and "No Hand" Restrictions Upon the Authority of Future Boards to Redeem Rights.

Add the following at the end of the paragraph beginning and concluding on page 1184 (between footnotes 3386 and 3387):

"No hand" provisions, once triggered, do not permit any directors to redeem rights.

Shareholder rights plans of this type have "the potential to deter a proxy contest altogether" and thus be a "show stopper" because "if only the incumbent directors or their designated successors could redeem the pill" then "it would make little sense for shareholders or the hostile bidder to wage a proxy contest to replace the incumbent board" with new directors. *Carmody v. Toll Bros., Inc.*, 723 A.2d 1180, 1186-87 (Del. Ch. 1999). This "eliminate[s] from the scene the only group of persons having the power to give the hostile bidder and target company shareholders what they desired: control of the target company (in the case of the hostile bidder) and the opportunity to obtain an attractive price for their shares (in the case of the target company stockholders)." *Id.* at 1187.

Replace the first sentence of the paragraph beginning and concluding on page 1186 (including footnote 3395) with the following:

The Delaware courts addressed dead hand rights plan provisions for the first time in the Court of Chancery's decision in *Carmody v. Toll Brothers, Inc.* 723 A.2d 1180 (Del. Ch. 1998).

The dead hand provision in *Toll Brothers*, like other dead hand provisions, authorized "only a specific, defined category of directors – the 'Continuing Directors' – to redeem the Rights" provided for by the corporation's rights plan. *Id.* at 1184. The term "Continuing Director" was defined as follows:

> (i) any member of the Board of Directors of the Company, while such person is a member of the Board, who is not an Acquiring Person, or an Affiliate [as defined] or Associate [as defined] of an Acquiring Person, or a representative or nominee of an Acquiring Person or of any such Affiliate or Associate, and was a member of the Board prior to the date of this agreement, or (ii) any Person who subsequently becomes a member of the Board, while such Person is a member of the Board, who is not an Acquiring Person, or an Affiliate [as defined] or Associate [as defined] of an Acquiring Person, or a

> representative or nominee of an Acquiring Person or of any such Affiliate or Associate, if such Person's nomination for election or election to the Board is recommended or approved by a majority of the Continuing Directors.

Id. The plan thus prevented "any director of Toll Brothers, except those who were in office as of the date of the Rights Plan's adoption (June 12, 1997) or their designated successors, from redeeming the Rights until they expire on June 12, 2007." *Id.*

The court denied a motion to dismiss claims alleging that the adoption of this dead hand provision by Toll Brothers violated Delaware statutory law and constituted a breach of fiduciary duty. On both of these grounds, the court held, "the complaint states legally cognizable claims for relief" and thus "the pending motion to dismiss must be denied." *Id.* at 1182.

With respect to Delaware statutory law, the court pointed to Sections 141(a) and (d) of the Delaware General Corporation Law.

Section 141(a) provides that "[t]he business and affairs of every corporation . . . shall be managed by or under the direction of a board of directors." 723 A.2d at 1191 (quoting Del. Gen. Corp. Law § 141(a)). The court stated that "[t]he 'dead hand' poison pill is intended to thwart hostile bids by vesting shareholders with preclusive rights that cannot be redeemed except by the Continuing Directors." *Id.* at 1191. The dead hand provision thus "would jeopardize a newly-elected future board's ability to achieve a business combination by depriving that board of the power to redeem the pill without obtaining the consent of the 'Continuing Directors,' who (it may be assumed) would constitute a minority of the board." *Id.* As a result, "the 'dead hand' provision would interfere with the board's power to protect fully the corporation's (and its shareholders') interests in a transaction that is one of the most fundamental and important in the life of a business enterprise." *Id.*

Section 141(d) provides that a "certificate of incorporation may confer upon holders of any class or series of stock the right to elect 1 or more directors who shall serve for such term, and have such voting powers as shall be stated in the certificate of incorporation" and that "[t]he terms of office and voting powers of the directors elected in the manner so provided in the certificate of incorporation may be greater than or less than those of any other director or class of directors." *Id.* at 1191 (quoting Del. Gen. Corp. Law § 141(d)). Thus "under § 141(d), the power to create voting power distinctions among directors exists only where there is a classified board, and where those voting power distinctions are expressed in the certificate of incorporation." *Id.* at 1190. In other words, "if one category or group of directors is given distinctive voting rights not shared by the other directors, those distinctive voting rights must be set forth in the certificate of incorporation." *Id.* at 1191. In the case of a dead hand rights plan, the court stated, however, distinctive voting rights are created among directors in a rights plan rather than in the certificate of incorporation. *Id.*

Additionally, the statutory "'right to elect 1 or more directors who shall . . . have such [greater] voting powers' is reserved to the stockholders, not to the directors or a subset thereof." *Id.* Thus, "[a]bsent express language in the charter, nothing in Delaware law suggests that some directors of a public corporation may be created less equal than other directors, and certainly not by unilateral board action." *Id.* According to the court, "[v]esting the pill redemption power exclusively in the Continuing Directors transgresses the statutorily protected shareholder right to elect the directors who would be so empowered." *Id.*

The court rejected a contention that "the 'dead hand' provision is tantamount to a delegation to a special committee, consisting of the Continuing Directors, of the power to redeem the pill." *Id.* at 1192. The court explained that "[i]n adopting the Rights Plan, the board did not, nor did it purport to, create a special committee having the exclusive power to redeem the pill." *Id.* The court added that "[t]he analogy also ignores fundamental structural differences between the creation of a special board committee and the operation of the 'dead hand' provision of the Rights Plan" because "[t]he creation of a special committee would not impose long term structural power-related distinctions between different groups of directors of the same board" and "[t]he board that creates a special committee may abolish it at any time, as could any successor board." *Id.* By contrast, a "'dead hand' provision, if legally valid, would embed structural power-related distinctions between groups of directors that no successor board could abolish until after the Rights expire." *Id.*

With respect to Delaware fiduciary duty law, the court focused upon claims under the *Unocal* and *Blasius* doctrines, discussed earlier in this Chapter. *See* Chapter III, Sections A 2 (*Unocal)* and 5 (*Blasius*).

Unocal requires enhanced judicial scrutiny of defensive measures – scrutiny that "is, by its nature, fact-driven" and "[f]or that reason . . . 'will usually not be satisfied by resting on a defense motion merely attacking the pleadings.'" *Id.* at 1194 (quoting *In re Santa Fe Pac. Corp. S'holder Litig.*, 669 A.2d 59, 72 (Del. 1995)). As a result, "[o]nly 'conclusory complaints without well-pleaded facts [may] be dismissed early.'" *Id.* at 1194-95 (quoting *Santa Fe,* 669 A.2d at 72). Here, the court stated, the complaint was "far from conclusory." *Id.* at 1195.

First, the court explained, "[t]he complaint alleges that the 'dead hand' provision 'disenfranchises shareholders by forcing them to vote for incumbent directors or their designees if shareholders want to be represented by a board entitled to exercise its full statutory prerogatives.'" *Id.* If true, the court stated, this allegation would render the dead hand provision coercive and thus disproportionate and unreasonable under *Unocal. Id.*

Second, the court continued, "[t]he complaint also alleges that that provision 'makes an offer for the Company much more unlikely since it eliminates use of a proxy contest as a possible means to gain control . . . [because] . . . any directors elected in such a contest would still be unable to vote to redeem the pill'" and thus "'renders future contests for corporate control of Toll Brothers prohibitively expensive and effectively impossible.'" *Id.* If true, the court stated, this allegation would render the dead hand provision preclusive and thus disproportionate and unreasonable under *Unocal. Id.*

Blasius requires that "[a] board's unilateral decision to adopt a defensive measure touching 'upon issues of control' that purposefully disenfranchises its shareholders is strongly suspect under *Unocal*, and cannot be sustained without a 'compelling justification.'" *Id.* at 1193 (quoting *Stroud v. Grace*, 606 A.2d 75, 92 n.3 (Del. 1992)). The court stated that "[a] claim that the directors have unilaterally 'create[d] a structure in which shareholder voting is either impotent or self-defeating' is necessarily a claim of purposeful disenfranchisement." *Id.* at 1193. The challenge to the dead hand provision rights plan stated a claim under *Blasius*, the court thus held, because the complaint alleged that "the 'dead hand' provision will either preclude a hostile bidder from waging a proxy contest altogether, or, if there should be a contest, it will coerce those shareholders who desire the hostile offer to succeed to vote for those directors who oppose it – the incumbent (and 'Continuing') directors." *Id.* at 1194.

The court pointed to "the Supreme Court's rational for upholding the validity of the poison pill" in *Moran v. Household International, Inc.*, 500 A.2d 1346 (Del. 1985), and "the primacy of the shareholder vote in our scheme of corporate jurisprudence." 723 A.2d at 1193. The court reasoned as follows:

> In *Moran*, the Supreme Court upheld the adoption of a poison pill, in part because its effect upon a proxy contest would be "minimal," but also because if the board refused to redeem the plan, the shareholders could exercise their prerogative to remove and replace the board. In *Unocal* the Supreme Court reiterated that view – that the safety valve which justifies a board being allowed to resist a hostile offer a majority of shareholders might prefer, is that the shareholders always have their ultimate recourse to the ballot box. Those observations reflect the fundamental value that the shareholder vote has

> primacy in our system of corporate governance because it is the "ideological underpinning upon which the legitimacy of directorial power rests."

Id. (footnotes omitted).

The court also pointed to *Sutton Holding Corp. v. DeSoto, Inc.*, [1991 Transfer Binder] Fed. Sec. L. Rep. (CCH) ¶ 96,012 (Del. Ch. May 14, 1991), a decision not involving a shareholder rights plan, in which the court assumed but did not hold that provisions barring any amendment to the corporation's existing pension plans for a period of five years following a change in control (which was defined as the acquisition of 35 percent or more of the corporation's outstanding shares without prior approval of two-thirds of the corporation's board and a majority of "continuing directors") constituted a breach of the duty of loyalty. *Id.* at 90,064-65. The court stated that "[w]hen the . . . board injected this provision in the Company's pension plans, its dominant motivation was doubtlessly not to create a valuable economic right" but instead to deter a change in control. *Id.* at 90,064.

The court in *Toll Brothers* quoted the following statement by the court in *Sutton*:

> Provisions in corporate instruments that are intended principally to restrain or coerce the free exercise of the stockholder franchise are deeply suspect. The shareholder vote is the basis upon which an individual serving as a corporate director must rest his or her claim to legitimacy. Absent quite extraordinary circumstances, in my opinion, it constitutes a fundamental offense to the dignity of this corporate office for a director to use corporate power to seek to coerce shareholders in the exercise of the vote.

723 A.2d at 1194 (quoting [1991 Transfer Binder] Fed. Sec. L. Rep. (CCH) at 90,064). Applying this principle, the court in *Toll Brothers* stated, the court in *Sutton* recognized that the purpose of the challenged provisions in *Sutton* was "to foreclose a 'raider' from financing any part of a takeover by resorting to the company's excess pension funding while permitting that fund to be available to directors approved by the incumbents ('continuing directors') for any corporate purpose" and

"observed that the '. . . most critical defect, in my opinion, is the fact that the 'enemy' here, the raider, includes anyone that the shareholders elect but that the board has not nominated.'" 723 A.2d at 1194 (quoting [1991 Transfer Binder] Fed. Sec. L. Rep. (CCH) at 90,064-65 n.3). The court in *Toll Brothers* stated that "[t]hat same 'defect' is complained of here" in connection with the dead hand rights plan provision. 723 A.2d at 1194.

The court in *Toll Brothers* accordingly held that plaintiff's "*Blasius*-based breach of fiduciary duty claim" challenging the dead hand provision "was cognizable under Delaware law." *Id.* at 1194.

The court noted that "the 'dead hand' provision at issue here is of unlimited duration" and that "nothing in this Opinion should be read as expressing a view or pronouncement" concerning "'a dead hand' provision of limited duration (e.g., six months)." *Id.* at 1195 n.52.

A short time later, in *Mentor Graphics Corp. v. Quickturn Design Systems, Inc.*, 728 A.2d 25 (Del. Ch.), *aff'd sub nom. Quickturn Design Systems, Inc. v. Shapiro,* 721 A.2d 1281 (Del. 1998), the Court of Chancery was faced with the issue left open in *Toll Brothers*: a rights plan precluding redemption only for a six month period. The plan in this case was adopted by Quickturn Design Systems, Inc., the target of an unwanted bid by Mentor Graphics Corporation. At the time Mentor commenced its bid, Quickturn had in place a "dead hand" rights plan. After determining that Mentor's offer was inadequate, Quickturn's board replaced the plan's dead hand feature with a "no hand" delayed redemption provision providing that if a majority of Quickturn's directors were replaced by shareholder action, then for six months no directors could redeem the rights "if such redemption is reasonably likely to have the purpose or effect of facilitating a Transaction with an Interested Person." 721 A.2d at 1287 n.15. The term "Interested Person" was defined to include anyone who would acquire a majority of the corporation's stock as a result of the transaction and who "directly or indirectly proposed, nominated or financially supported" the election of a director to the board – a definition that included Mentor. *Id.* The effect "would be to delay the ability of a newly-elected, Mentor-nominated board to redeem the Rights Plan or 'poison pill' for six months, in any transaction with an Interested Person" – that is, Mentor. *Id.* at 1287-88.

At the same time, Quickturn's board amended a bylaw provision that permitted holders of 10 percent or more of Quickturn's stock to call a special shareholders meeting. *Id.* at 1287. The bylaw was amended because it previously "did not explicitly state who would be responsible for determining the time, place and record date for the meeting" and "arguably would have allowed a hostile bidder holding the requisite number of shares to call a special stockholders meeting on minimal notice and stampede the shareholders into making a decision without time to become adequately informed." *Id.* at 1288-89. As amended, the bylaw provided that "the corporation (Quickturn) would fix the record date for, and determine the time and place of, that special meeting, which must take place not less than 90 days nor more than 100 days after the receipt and determination of the validity of the shareholders' request." *Id.* at 1287; *see also id.* at 1288. The effect of the bylaw amendment was to delay a shareholder-called special meeting for three months. *Id.* at 1288. The combined effect of the bylaw amendment and the rights plan amendment was "to delay any acquisition of Quickturn by Mentor for at least nine months." *Id.*

Following a trial, the Court of Chancery upheld Quickturn's bylaw amendment (this portion of the ruling was not appealed) but invalidated Quickturn's no hand provision without addressing the "higher level" statutory validity question. 728 A.2d at 52 n.105. Instead, the Court of Chancery decided the case by holding that Quickturn's no hand provision could not survive the "enhanced" judicial scrutiny standard applied under *Unocal:* "[f]or a target board's actions to be entitled to business judgment rule protection, the target board must first establish that it had reasonable grounds to believe that the hostile bid constituted a threat to corporate policy and effectiveness; and second, that the defensive measures adopted were 'proportionate,' that is, reasonable in relation to the threat that the board reasonably perceived." 721 A.2d at 1290.

With respect to the first prong of the *Unocal* test, the Court of Chancery found that Quickturn's board "reasonably perceived a cognizable threat": a "concern that Quickturn shareholders might mistakenly, in ignorance of Quickturn's true value, accept Mentor's inadequate offer, and elect a new board that would prematurely sell the company before the new board could adequately inform itself of Quickturn's fair value and before the shareholders could consider other options." *Id.* at 1290; 728 A.2d at 46; *see also* Chapter III, Section A 2 c (iii) (discussing this aspect of *Quickturn* decision).

With respect to the second prong of the *Unocal* test, however, the Court of Chancery found that Quickturn's no hand provision was a disproportionate response to the threat the board perceived. The court cited three bases for this conclusion.

First, the Court of Chancery explained that the board's rationale for adopting the delayed redemption provision was "to force any newly elected board (as distinguished from only a Mentor-nominated board) to take sufficient time to become familiar with Quickturn and its value, and to provide shareholders the opportunity to consider alternatives, before selling Quickturn to any acquiror." *Id.* at 50. According to the court, the delayed redemption provision "does not create a six month pill redemption delay in all cases where a newly elected, Mentor-nominated board seeks to sell the company to any bidder." *Id.* Instead, the delayed redemption provision "creates such a delay only if a newly elected board seeks to sell Quickturn to an 'Interested Person,' which in this case is Mentor" and permits a new board to "sell the company to anyone other than Mentor on its very first day in office, or at any time during the six month nonredemption period." *Id.* The court held that the plan thus "cannot be reconciled with the directors' stated justification for adopting it," and as a result "the board has not carried its burden of demonstrating that the [plan] is reasonable in relation to the perceived threat." *Id.* at 51.

Second, the Court of Chancery found that the directors were "unable to articulate a cogent reason why a six month delay is reasonable." *Id.* According to the directors, they "settled on six months because that period was 'reasonable' and the 'minimum' time a newly elected board would need to become sufficiently informed about Quickturn, based upon their own experience as to how long they, as directors, needed to learn about the company." *Id.* (footnote omitted) The court acknowledged that "a board is entitled to rely upon its experience when making a business decision" but added that "when the decision is of a kind that is subject to enhanced judicial scrutiny, the board must articulate a reason more specific and nonconclusory than a statement such as 'six months was reasonable.'" *Id.* Here, the court stated, "the board has offered no justification that is anchored to any objective fact or criterion." *Id.*

Third, the Court of Chancery found that the board's "articulated purpose – to give a newly elected board time to inform itself of Quickturn's value – would already have been achieved by the conclusion of the three month delay period imposed by the By-Law Amendment." *Id.* The court explained that the purpose of the bylaw amendment was to provide shareholders 90 to 100 days to make an informed decision between two slates of directors and that "the subject matter about which the shareholders would be informing themselves" during the three month bylaw amendment period and "the subject about which a new board would be informing itself" during the six month nonredemption period was the same: "should the company be sold and, if so, when and at what price?" *Id.* The court asked: "If three months is an adequate time for shareholders to become informed, why should a new board require six months?," and "why would the Mentor director nominees be unable to inform themselves on that issue (as the Quickturn shareholders must) during the three month period imposed by the Amended By-Law?" *Id.* at 51-52. The court held that "[t]he conclusion that must be drawn is that the board has failed to show why the additional six month delay . . . is necessary to achieve the board's stated purpose" for adopting the no hand provision. *Id.* at 52.

The Court of Chancery reached its conclusion that the plan fell "outside the range of reasonable responses" despite its finding that the plan was neither coercive nor preclusive. *Id.* at 47. The court acknowledged that "in different circumstances a delayed redemption provision of the kind at issue here might have . . . coercive or preclusive effects" but stated that this case involved "unique circumstances" that made it unlikely that the plan would "operate in a manner that is coercive or preclusive in this particular case," and, as a result, the "cloud cast" by the delayed redemption plan seemed "relatively insignificant." *Id.* at 48. The "unique circumstances" relied upon by the court included the following: (1) the holders of a majority of Quickturn's shares had tendered their shares to Mentor, (2) recent court decisions enforcing emulation product patents owned by Quickturn and enjoining Mentor from selling certain emulation products in the United States required Mentor to "acquire Quickturn's patents or the power to direct their nonenforcement, which means that Mentor must acquire Quickturn" in order "[t]o ensure Mentor's ability to grow in the emulation market (and not incur damage liability for patent infringement)," (3) Mentor had obtained "a secure financing commitment that is effective for three years – a period far longer than the six month delay" created by the delayed redemption provision, and (4) "a newly elected board could, immediately after taking office, cause Quickturn to enter into a legally binding agreement with Mentor to acquire Quickturn in a transaction that would close six months later." *Id.* at 48-49. The court stated that "[g]iven these unique circumstances, it is far from certain" that a six month delay would "preclude Mentor from acquiring Quickturn if Mentor's nominees become the new board majority." *Id.* at 49.

The Supreme Court affirmed the Court of Chancery's decision on the "higher level" statutory validity question that the Court of Chancery had relied upon in *Toll Brothers* but that the Court of Chancery had not reached in *Quickturn* (728 A.2d at 52 n.105): Section 141(a) of the Delaware General Corporation Law – one of the sources, according to the Delaware Supreme Court's decision in *Household*, of a board's authority to enact rights plans. *Quickturn*, 721 A.2d at 1291; *Household*, 500 A.2d at 1353. The Supreme Court in *Quickturn* did not address or rely upon Section 141(d) of the Delaware General Corporation Law, which the Court of Chancery had relied upon in addition to Section 141(a) in *Toll Brothers*.

The Supreme Court in *Quickturn* stated that "[o]ne of the most basic tenets of Delaware corporate law is that the board of directors has the ultimate responsibility for managing the business and affairs of a corporation." *Quickturn*, 721 A.2d at 1291. This "basic tenet" is codified in Section 141(a): "The business and affairs of every corporation . . . shall be managed by or under the direction of a board of directors, except as may be otherwise provided . . . in its certificate of incorporation." *Id.* at 1291 & n.37 (quoting Del. Gen. Corp. Law § 141(a)). Section 141(a) thus "requires that any limitation on the board's authority be set out in the certificate of incorporation." *Id.* at 1291.

Quickturn's certificate of incorporation, the court stated, "contains no provision purporting to limit the authority of the board in any way." *Id.* The court accordingly held that Quickturn's rights plan "is invalid under Section 141(a), which confers upon any newly elected board of directors *full* power to manage and direct the business and affairs of a Delaware corporation" where no certificate provision provides otherwise. *Id.* at 1292. To the contrary, the court stated, the plan "prevents a newly elected board of directors from *completely* discharging its fiduciary duties to the corporation and its stockholders for six months." *Id.* The court acknowledged that this suspension of the rights plan "limits the board of directors' authority in only one respect" but stated that it "restricts the board's power in an area of fundamental importance to the shareholders – negotiating a possible sale of the corporation." *Id.*

In sum, the court concluded, the delayed redemption provision "would prevent a new Quickturn board of directors from managing the corporation by redeeming the Rights Plan to facilitate a transaction that would serve the stockholders' best interests, even under circumstances where the board would be required to do so because of its fiduciary duty to the Quickturn stockholders." *Id.* at 1292-93. The provision thus "impermissibly circumscribes the board's statutory power under Section 141(a) and the directors' ability to fulfill their concomitant fiduciary duties." *Id.* at 1293. The court added that "no defensive measure can be sustained which would require a new board of directors to breach its fiduciary duty." *Id.* at 1292.

The Supreme Court's decision in *Quickturn* involved a no hand delayed redemption rights plan. The court's reasoning, however, makes clear that all types of dead hand and no hand poison pill rights plans now are prohibited in Delaware unless authorized by a certificate of incorporation provision.

A federal court construing Georgia law reached a different result and denied a motion for a preliminary injunction enjoining utilization of a continuing director rights plan adopted by Healthdyne Technologies, Inc. in *Invacare Corp. v. Healthdyne Technologies, Inc.*, 968 F. Supp. 1578 (N.D. Ga. 1997).

Add the following at the end of the first paragraph beginning and concluding on page 1189 (immediately after footnote 3412):

The Delaware Court of Chancery in *Toll Brothers* distinguished the *Invacare* decision as follows:

> In *Invacare*, the United States District Court for the Northern District of Georgia, applying Georgia law, upheld a "continuing director" provision of a target company's rights plan. It was argued that the continuing director provision was invalid because it imposed significant limitations upon the board's

> powers that should have been, but were not, included in the articles of incorporation or the bylaws, as Georgia's corporation statute required. The court rejected that argument. Distinguishing [*Bank of New York Co. v. Irving Bank Corp.* 139 Misc. 2d 665, 528 N.Y.S.2d 482 (N.Y. Sup. Ct. N.Y. Co. 1988)] the court held that the Georgia Business Corporation Code had no statutory requirement mandating that limitations on the directors' powers be expressed in the certificate of incorporation. That court noted that the Georgia statute gave the board "sole discretion" to determine the terms and conditions of a rights plan, and that the Official Comment stated that the board's discretion is limited only by its fiduciary obligations to the corporation. The court also found that the Georgia Fair Price statutory provision, which required unanimous approval by the "continuing directors" or recommendation by at least two thirds of the "continuing directors" and approval by a specified percentage of shareholder votes, supported the conclusion that "Georgia corporate law embraces the concept of continuing directors as part of a defense against hostile takeovers." 968 F.Supp at 1580. The relevant Delaware corporate statutory scheme, like New York's, differs materially from that of Georgia.

723 A.2d at 1192 n.38.

AMP Inc. v. Allied Signal Inc., 1998 U.S. Dist. LEXIS 15617, 1998 WL 778348 (E.D. Pa. Oct. 8, 1998), involved a tender offer announced on August 4, 1998 by Allied Signal, Inc., for all shares of common stock of AMP Incorporated, a Pennsylvania corporation, at $44.50 per share in cash, to be followed by a second step merger pursuant to which Allied Signal would acquire all remaining shares of AMP common stock at the same $44.50 per share price. 1998 U.S. Dist. LEXIS 15617, at *2-3, 1998 WL 778348, at *1. At the same time, Allied Signal commenced a consent solicitation to amend AMP's bylaws to expand AMP's board from 11 directors to 28 directors and elect Allied Signal nominees to fill the newly created vacancies on AMP's board and thus give Allied Signal control over a majority of AMP's board. The court stated that Allied Signal's nominees were directors and officers of Allied Signal "who would cause AMP to accept Allied Signal's takeover bid." 1998 U.S. Dist. LEXIS 15617, at *3-4, 1998 WL 778348, at *1-2.

At the time Allied Signal announced its tender offer and consent solicitation, AMP's board had a shareholder rights plan with a 20 percent trigger and "a 'dead hand' provision which provided that, if a new majority was elected, only the directors who were on the board prior to the change in majority could vote to redeem the poison pill." 1998 U.S. Dist. LEXIS 15617, at *5, 1998 WL 778348, at *2. On August 20, 1998, in response to Allied Signal's tender offer and consent solicitation, AMP's board amended AMP's rights plan "to remove the 'dead hand' provision and to make the rights non-redeemable and non-amendable should AMP's disinterested board majority be replaced as a result of the acquisition of control of the board by a majority of directors nominated by an unsolicited acquiring company." 1998 U.S. Dist. LEXIS 15617, at *5-6, 1998 WL 778348, at *2. The plan would remain non-redeemable and non-amendable until November 6, 1999, the date of the plan's expiration. The board adopted a resolution stating that the plan would not be renewed for at least six months following its expiration. 1998 U.S. Dist. LEXIS 15617, at *6, 1998 WL 778348, at *2.

On September 14, 1998, Allied Signal amended its consent solicitation to add a proposal asking AMP's shareholders to amend AMP's bylaws to remove all power, rights and duties with respect to the rights plan from AMP's board and assign this authority to a three person board committee. 1998 U.S. Dist. LEXIS 15617, at *6, 1998 WL 778348, at *3. On September 17, 1998, AMP amended its rights plan to drop the plan's trigger from 20 percent to 10 percent and to provide that the plan would become non-redeemable and non-amendable if Allied Signal's three person committee proposal was implemented. 1998 U.S. Dist. LEXIS 15617, at *7, 1998 WL 778348, at *3. As of September 14, 1998, 72 percent of AMP's shares has been tendered in response to Allied Signal's tender offer. 1998 U.S. Dist. LEXIS 15617, at *6, 1998 WL 778348, at *2.

The court held that a transfer of power by shareholders with respect to AMP's rights plan from the corporation's board to a three person board committee would violate Pennsylvania law. The court explained that Section 2513 of Pennsylvania's Business Corporation Law grants directors "broad power to adopt shareholder rights plans" and permits rights plans to include "'such terms as are fixed by the board of directors,' including but not limited to, 'conditions that preclude or limit any person or persons owning or offering to acquire a specified number or percentage of the outstanding common shares . . . from exercising, converting, transferring or receiving the shares.'" 1998 U.S. Dist. LEXIS 15617, at *14-15, 1998 WL 778348, at *4, 5 (quoting Pa. Bus. Corp. Law § 2513). The only exception, the court continued, occurs where the corporation opts out of Section 2513 by a certificate of incorporation provision – something AMP had not done. 1998 U.S. Dist. LEXIS 15617, at *10, 1998 WL 778348, at *4. The court held that AMP's shareholders thus were bound by Section 2513 and had "no power to take away the board's authority" under Section 2513 through an amendment of AMP's by-laws. 1998 U.S. Dist. LEXIS 15617, at *15, 1998 WL 778348, at *5. The court added that "the attempted adoption of a by-law to this effect by Allied Signal or AMP shareholders constitutes an attempt to propose an amendment to AMP's articles of incorporation" and "[t]his cannot be done by shareholders." 1998 U.S. Dist. LEXIS 15617, at *16, 1998 WL 778348, at *6.

The court also held that AMP's directors did not breach their fiduciary duties by amending AMP's rights plan to provide that rights issued pursuant to the plan would become non-redeemable and non-amendable "if the disinterested majority loses control of the board following receipt of an unsolicited acquisition proposal or if the shareholders take action to transfer authority relating to AMP's poison pill to persons outside of the board." 1998 U.S. Dist. LEXIS 15617, at *16, 1998 WL 778348, at *6. The court relied upon Sections 2513, 1715 and 2538 of Pennsylvania's Business Corporation Law.

Section 2513, as noted above, permits the adoption of rights plans with "such terms as are fixed by the board of directors." 1998 U.S. Dist. LEXIS 15617, at *16-17, 1998 WL 778348, at *6 (quoting Pa. Bus. Corp. Law § 2513). Section 1715(c) provides that "[d]irectors are not required to redeem any rights under a shareholder rights plan adopted under § 2513 or to act as the board solely because of the effect such action might have on a potential or proposed acquisition of control of the corporation." 1999 U.S. Dist. LEXIS 15617, at *13-14, 17, 1998 WL 778348, at *5, 6. Section 1715(c) also provides that directors are not required to act "solely because of the consideration that might be offered or paid to shareholders in such an acquisition." 1998 U.S. Dist. LEXIS 15617, at *14, 17, 1998 WL 778348, at *5, 6. On the basis of these statutory provisions, the court concluded that "in amending the poison pill and fixing it as non-amendable and non-redeemable, AMP did not act beyond the scope of its statutory authority." 1998 U.S. Dist. LEXIS 15617, at *17, 1998 WL 778348, at *6.

Section 1715(a)(3) of Pennsylvania's statute, the court continued, permits directors to "consider the resources, intent and conduct (past, stated or potential) of any person seeking to acquire control of the corporation." 1998 U.S. Dist. LEXIS 15617, at *17-18, 1998 WL 778348, at *6. The court explained that "[t]he stated intent of Allied Signal is to acquire control of AMP" by nominating for seats on AMP's board "directors and executive officers of Allied Signal who are bound by Allied Signal's corporate decision to acquire AMP" and to seek "to induce shareholder support" for AMP's "interested nominees and other parts of its takeover plan with premium payments for AMP shares." 1998 U.S. Dist. LEXIS 15617, at *18, 1998 WL 778348, at *7. The court concluded that "[t]he totality of the conduct of Allied Signal is such that the existing AMP board could reasonably anticipate that, if elected, the action of Allied Signal's interested director majority with respect to the poison pill would be tantamount to a vote on merger." *Id.* The court added its view that "[d]espite Allied Signal's statements that if elected its interested majority would fulfill their director responsibilities, the present disinterested AMP board is not required to disregard experience and believe that a Trojan Horse brought within their walls is intended as a gift to corporate governance." 1998 U.S. Dist. LEXIS 15617, at *18-19, 1998 WL 778348, at *7.

Section 1715(d) of Pennsylvania's statute, the court then stated, "protects the actions of a majority board of disinterested directors in resisting unsolicited takeovers by retaining the ordinary business judgment rule with respect to the adoption of defensive measures." 1998 U.S. Dist. LEXIS 15617, at *14, 1998 WL 778348, at *5. The court held that "it cannot be said . . . that the action of the directors in amending the poison pill to its present form until November 6, 1999, was done in bad faith and breach of fiduciary duty to AMP, where the objective is to resist a takeover by Allied Signal, where AMP had rejected Allied Signal's merger bid prior to the present consent solicitation as contrary to AMP's best interests, and where AMP's board has determined that its own previously adopted business plan is superior to Allied Signal's merger plan for the future growth of AMP." 1998 U.S. Dist. LEXIS 15617, at *21, 1999 WL 778348, at *8. The court stated that the non-redemption and non-amendable provisions of AMP's rights plan were finite in time and thus "must be viewed in light of the ordinary business judgment that is allowed directors, as well as the presumptions of good faith for disinterested majorities in Section 1715(d) in matters dealing with potential or proposed acquisition of control of the corporation." 1998 U.S. Dist. LEXIS 15617, at *20-21, 1998 WL 778348, at *8. If the non-redemption and non-amendable provisions were not finite in time, the court added, "it would mitigate towards a finding of lack of good faith or self-dealing." 1998 U.S. Dist. LEXIS 15617, at *20, 1998 WL 778348, at *8.

Section 2538(b) of Pennsylvania's statute, the court also stated, does not permit interested directors to vote on a merger transaction with an interested shareholder and defines interested directors for this purpose as "persons who are 'directors or officers of, or have a material equity interest in, the interested shareholder,' or persons who have been 'nominated for election by the interested shareholder, and first elected as a director, within 24 months of the date of the vote of the proposed transaction.'" 1998 U.S. Dist. LEXIS 15617, at *19, 1998 WL 778348, at *7 (quoting Pa. Bus. Corp. Law § 2538(b)). The court stated that "[a]ll of Allied Signal's nominees to AMP's board of directors meet the definition of interested director under Section 2538(b)" and that the restrictions imposed by AMP's rights plan were comparable to the restrictions imposed by Section 2538. 1998 U.S. Dist. LEXIS 15617, at *19-20, 1998 WL 778348, at *7. The court described the disinterested director concept as an integral part of Pennsylvania's "permitted statutory defense against hostile takeovers" and concluded that "the AMP board's importation of the disinterested director concept into the redemption of its poison pill is not contrary to the public policy of Pennsylvania." 1998 U.S. Dist. LEXIS 15617, at *20, 1998 WL 778348, at *7.

A Maryland statute provides that "[t]he board of directors of a corporation may, in its sole discretion . . . [s]et the terms and conditions of rights, options, or warrants under a stockholder rights plan." Md. Gen. Corp. Law § 2-201(c)(1). These rights, options, or warrants "may, in the sole discretion of the board of directors, include any limitation, restrictions or condition that (i) [p]recludes, limits, invalidates, or voids the exercise, transfer, or receipt of the rights, options, or warrants by designated persons or classes of persons in specified circumstances; or (ii) limits for a period not to exceed 180 days the power of a future director to vote for the redemption, modification, or termination of the rights, options, or warrants." *Id.* § 2-201(c)(2).

Delete the second and third paragraphs beginning and concluding on page 1189 and the first paragraph beginning and concluding on page 1190 (including footnotes 3413 through 3417).

Section G 2 e

Add "Maryland," between "Statutes in" and "New York" in the first sentence (between footnotes 3417 and 3418) of the second paragraph beginning and concluding on page 1190.

Add the following at the end of the first sentence of the second paragraph beginning and concluding on page 1190 (immediately after footnote 3418):

Maryland also has adopted a statute addressing board redemption of shareholder rights plans.

Replace the Steiner citation in footnote 3420 on page 1190 with the following:

N.Y.L.J., June 19, 1997, at 29 (N.Y. Sup. Ct. N.Y. Co. 1997), *subsequent proceedings*, No. 601661/97 (N.Y. Sup. Ct. N.Y. Co. Mar. 17, 1998), *aff'd*, 261 A.D.2d 131, 687 N.Y.S.2d 256 (N.Y. App. Div. 1st Dep't 1999).

Replace the Steiner citation in footnote 3425 on page 1191 with the following:

N.Y.L.J., June 19, 1997, at 29 (N.Y. Sup. Ct. N.Y. Co. 1997), *subsequent proceedings*, No. 601661/97 (N.Y. Sup. Ct. N.Y. Co. Mar. 17, 1998), *aff'd*, 261 A.D.2d 131, 687 N.Y.S.2d 256 (N.Y. App. Div. 1st Dep't 1999).

Add the following at the end of the paragraph beginning and concluding on page 1193 (immediately after footnote 3435):

The state court in the *Steiner* action subsequently dismissed that action pursuant to the business judgment rule. The court stated that plaintiff simply "alleges in a conclusory fashion that defendants breached their fiduciary duties by failing to obtain the best price for the shareholders" but "[p]laintiff has failed to allege, much less establish, any facts of fraud or bad faith" and "[i]n the absence of bad faith or fraud, the business judgment rule bars judicial inquiry into actions taken by corporate directors." *Steiner v. Lozyniak*, No. 601661/97, slip op. at 2 (N.Y. Sup. Ct. N.Y. Co. Mar. 17, 1998), *aff'd*, 261 A.D.2d 131, 687 N.Y.S.2d 256 (N.Y. App. Div. 1st Dep't 1999). The court pointed to the federal court's conclusion in *Dynamics Corp. of America v. WHX Corp.*, 967 F. Supp. 59 (D. Conn. 1997), that "[a]ll of the evidence . . . leads this Court to conclude that the value of the combined consideration of cash and CTS stock still exceeds the WHX offer" and held that "[c]ontrary to plaintiff's assertion and as noted by [the federal court], the facts clearly indicate that the directors accepted the offer with the highest total value." *Steiner*, slip op. at 2-3. An appellate court "agree[d] with the motion court that plaintiff fails to make a meritorious showing of self-dealing or bad faith by defendants such as would warrant judicial inquiry into their decisions with respect to the subject merger in derogation of the business judgment rule." *Steiner v. Lozyniak*, 261 A.D.2d 131, 132, 687 N.Y.S.2d 256, 256-57 (N.Y. App. Div. 1st Dep't 1999).

The court in *Rand v. Crosby*, No. 400063/98 (N.Y. Sup. Ct. N.Y. Co. May 17, 1999), similarly held that "a board of directors' determination of what price to sell a company's shares falls squarely within the business judgment rule." *Id.*, slip op. at 4. Accordingly, the court stated, "[t]he adoption of a shareholder rights' plan to ward off undesired takeover attempts is a practice that has been sanctioned by the courts." *Id.* The court continued:

> It is within the business judgment of the board to amend such a plan to allow the company to be sold to a particular purchaser. To hold otherwise, would require the court to substitute its judgment for that of the company's board as to whether it is wiser to accept the offer that has been received (the bird in the hand), or to speculate on the possibility of another better offer which might be obtained (the two in the bush). The "business judgment rule" precludes the court from making such judgments.

Id. at 5. The court held that none of plaintiff's allegations "are adequately pleaded so as to constitute a *prima facie* showing that puts the good faith of the directors in issue such that the business judgment rule should not be invoked." *Id.* at 6. The court accordingly granted summary judgment in favor of directors alleged to have breached their fiduciary duty by entering into a merger agreement. *Id.*

Add the following at the end of the paragraph beginning on page 1193 and concluding on page 1194 (immediately after footnote 3438):

The court in *AMP Inc. v. Allied Signal Inc.*, 1998 U.S. Dist. LEXIS 15617, 1998 WL 778348 (E.D. Pa. Oct. 8, 1998), a decision discussed in more detail in Chapter III, Section G 2 d, stated that Pennsylvania's statute does not require that directors redeem rights under a shareholder rights plan "solely because of the effect such action might have on a potential or proposed acquisition of control of a corporation" and "protects the actions of a majority board of disinterested directors in resisting unsolicited takeovers by retaining the ordinary business judgment rule with respect to the adoption of defensive measures." 1998 U.S. Dist. LEXIS 15617, at *13-14, 1998 WL 778348, at *5.

Maryland's statute provides that "[t]he duty of directors of a corporation does not require them to . . . [a]uthorize the corporation to redeem any rights under, modify, or render inapplicable, a stockholder rights plan." Md. Gen. Corp. Law § 2-405.1(d)(2). The statute states that "[t]he duty of the directors of a corporation does not require them to . . . [a]ccept, recommend, or respond on behalf of the corporation to any proposal by an acquiring person" – a term defined to mean "a person who is seeking to acquire control of a corporation" – or "[a]ct or fail to act solely because of: (i) [t]he effect the act or failure to act may have on an acquisition or potential acquisition of control of the corporation; or (ii) [t]he amount or type of any consideration that may be offered or paid to stockholders in an acquisition." *Id.* §§ 2-405.1(d)(1), (5), 3-801. The statute also states that "[a]n act of a director of a corporation is presumed to satisfy" the standards by which directors are required to act, and that "[a]n act of a director relating to or affecting an acquisition or a potential acquisition of control of a corporation may not be subject to a higher duty or greater scrutiny than is applied to any other act of a director." *Id.* §§ 2-405.1(e), (f).

As noted in Chapter III, Section G 2 d, Maryland's statute also provides that "[t]he board of directors of a corporation may, in its sole discretion . . . [s]et the terms and conditions of rights, options, or warrants under a stockholder rights plan" and these rights, options, or warrants "may, in the sole discretion of the board of directors, include any limitation, restrictions or condition that (i) [p]recludes, limits, invalidates, or voids the exercise, transfer, or receipt of the rights, options, or warrants by designated persons or classes of persons in specified circumstances; or (ii) limits for a period not to exceed 180 days the power of a future director to vote for the redemption, modification, or termination of the rights, options, or warrants." *Id.* §§ 2-201(c)(1), (2).

Section G 3

Replace "Intro–1-2 (1988) with "Intro–1-7 (2000)" in the Bryan citation in footnote 3444 on page 1195.

Replace the paragraph beginning on page 1196 and concluding on page 1197 through the second paragraph beginning and concluding on page 1199 (including footnotes 3448 through 3463) with the following:

The Oklahoma Supreme Court in *International Brotherhood of Teamsters General Fund v. Fleming Cos.*, 975 P.2d 907 (Okla. 1999), held that Oklahoma law does not restrict the authority to create and implement shareholder rights plans exclusively to a corporation's board of directors, and that shareholders may propose resolutions requiring that shareholder rights plans be submitted to shareholders for a vote. In the court's words:

> We hold under Oklahoma law there is no exclusive authority granted boards of directors to create and implement shareholder rights plans, where shareholder objection is brought and passed through official channels of corporate governance. We find no Oklahoma law which gives exclusive authority to a corporation's board of directors for the formulation of shareholder rights plans and no authority which precludes shareholders from proposing resolutions or bylaw amendments regarding shareholder rights plans. We hold shareholders may propose bylaws which restrict board implementation of shareholder rights plans, assuming the certificate of incorporation does not provide otherwise.

Id. at 908.

The case arose out of a bylaw proposed in connection with the 1997 annual meeting of shareholders of Fleming Companies, Inc. by the International Brotherhood of Teamsters General Fund, an owner of Fleming stock. The proposed bylaw required that any shareholder rights plan implemented or maintained by Fleming be approved by a majority of Fleming's shareholders. The Teamsters' resolution read, in full, as follows:

> Resolved, That shareholders hereby exercise their right under 18 O.S.A. Sec. 1013 to amend the bylaws of Fleming Companies, Inc. to add the following Article:
>
> Article X
>
> Poison Pills (Shareholder Rights Plans)
>
> A. The Corporation shall not adopt or maintain a poison pill, shareholder rights plan, rights agreement or any other form of "poison pill" which is designed or has the effect of making acquisition of large holdings of the Corporation's shares of stock more difficult or expensive (such as the 1986 "Rights Agreement"), unless such plan is first approved by a majority shareholder vote. The Company shall redeem any such rights now in effect. The affirmative vote of a majority of shares voted shall suffice to approve such a plan.

> B. This article shall be effective immediately and automatically as of the date it is approved by the affirmative vote of the holders of a majority of the shares, present, in person or by proxy at a regular or special meeting of shareholders.
>
> C. Notwithstanding any other provision of these bylaws, this Article may not be amended, altered, deleted or modified in any way by the Board of Directors without prior shareholder approval.

Id. at 909. "The proposal was essentially a ratification procedure wherein the shareholders would force the board to formulate a rights plan both the board and shareholders could agree on or do away with such a plan altogether." *Id.*

Fleming refused to include the resolution in its proxy statement because, Fleming contended, the proposal was not a proper subject for shareholder action under Oklahoma law. *Id.* at 909-10. The Teamsters commenced litigation in the United States District Court for the Western District of Oklahoma. On January 14, 1997, the court held that Fleming was required to include the resolution in its proxy statement. *Int'l Bhd. of Teamsters Gen. Fund v. Fleming Cos.*, No. CIV-96-1650, Tr. (W.D. Okla. Jan. 14, 1997), *reprinted in The Word from Oklahoma*, Corporate Control Alert, Mar. 1997, at 11, and 1997 U.S. Dist. LEXIS 2980 (W.D. Okla. Jan. 24, 1997). In a later ruling, the district court refused to stay its order pending an appeal. *Int'l Bhd. of Teamsters Gen. Fund v. Fleming Cos.*, 1997 U.S. Dist. LEXIS 2979, 1997 WL 996768 (W.D. Okla. Feb. 19, 1997). The court acknowledged that "the issues presented by this case are novel," and held that the appeal would not be mooted by requiring inclusion of the proposal in Fleming's proxy statement while the appeal was pending. 1997 U.S. Dist. LEXIS 2979, at *2, 1997 WL 996768, at *1. The court reasoned as follows:

> The vote of shareholders is subject to defeasance by the Court of Appeals. If this Court is reversed by the Court of Appeals, the shareholder vote will be nullified. Fleming has made no claim of specific harms to be suffered by the corporation. There has been no showing that the stock price will be affected or that the shareholders, who are, in fact, the corporation, will suffer any harm.

Id. The court added that it considered "the operation of shareholder democracy to be very much in the public interest." *Id.* Fleming responded by terminating its rights plan. Shareholders then voted in favor of the resolution. *Fleming Cos.: Net Income Declines 11% as Sales Decrease by 8.1%*, Wall St. J., May 1, 1997 (available only in Dow Jones News/Retrieval Publications Library).

Fleming appealed to the United States Court of Appeals for the Tenth Circuit, which certified the following issue as an "unsettled question of state law" to the Oklahoma Supreme Court:

> Does Oklahoma law [A] restrict the authority to create and implement shareholder rights plans exclusively to the board of directors, or [B] may shareholders propose resolutions requiring that shareholder rights plans be submitted to the shareholders for vote at the succeeding annual meeting?

Int'l Bhd. of Teamsters Gen. Fund v. Fleming Cos., Nos. 97-6037, 97-6132 (10th Cir. Sept. 23, 1997), *reprinted in* 13 Corporate Officers & Directors Liability Litig. Rptr. No. 7, Feb. 9, 1998, at D1.

The Oklahoma Supreme Court "answer[ed] the first part of the question in the negative and the second part affirmatively." *Int'l Bhd. of Teamsters Gen. Fund v. Fleming Cos.*, 975 P.2d 907, 908 (Okla. 1999). The court's decision focused upon sections 1013 and 1038 of the Oklahoma General Corporation Act (which correspond to sections 109 and 157 of the Delaware General Corporation Law). Sections 1013 and 1038 provide as follows:

> *Section 1013*: "The bylaws may contain any provision, not inconsistent with law or with the certificate of incorporation, relating to the business of the corporation, the conduct of its affairs, and its rights or powers or the rights or powers of its shareholders, directors, officers or employees."
>
> *Section 1038*: "Subject to any provisions in the certificate of incorporation, every corporation may create and issue . . . rights or options entitling the holders thereof to purchase from the corporation any shares of its capital stock . . . such rights or options to be evidenced by or in such instrument or instru-

> ments as shall be approved by the board of directors. The terms upon which . . . and the price . . . at which any such shares may be purchased from the corporation upon the exercise of any such right . . . shall be such as shall be stated in the certificate of incorporation, or in a resolution adopted by the board of directors providing for the creation and issue of such rights . . . ."

Okla. Gen. Corp. Act §§ 1013, 1038. According to the Teamsters, section 1013 "gives shareholders of a publicly traded corporation, such as Fleming, the authority to adopt bylaws addressing a broad range of topics from a corporation's business, corporate affairs, and rights and powers of shareholders and directors." *Fleming*, 975 P.2d at 910. According to Fleming, section 1038 "gives the board of directors authority to create and issue shareholder rights plans, subject only to limits which might exist in the corporation's certificate of incorporation; and that shareholders cannot through bylaws restrict the board's powers to implement a rights plan." *Id.*

The court resolved the "apparent conflict" between these statutes by stating that "[w]hile this Court would agree with Fleming that a corporation may create and issue rights and options within the grant of authority given it" by section 1038, "it does not automatically translate that the board of directors of that corporation has in itself the same breadth of authority." *Id.* The court also pointed to the fact that a shareholder rights plan "is essentially a variety of stock option plan" and stated that "[t]here is authority supporting shareholder ratification of stock option plans." *Id.* The court cited the Delaware Supreme Court's decision in *Michelson v. Duncan*, 407 A.2d 211 (Del. 1979), a case where "shareholders ratified a stock option package, curing a voidable act of the corporation's board of directors" and that "explains that shareholder approval can cure the invalidity of an otherwise voidable act of the company's board." *Fleming*, 975 P.2d at 911 (citing 407 A.2d at 218-20). The court also cited provisions in the Internal Revenue Code providing for certain tax treatment of incentive stock options and employee stock purchase plans that are "approved by the stockholders of the granting corporation." 26 U.S.C.

§§ 422(b)(1), 423(b)(2). The court stated that the Internal Revenue Code's recognition of shareholder approval of stock options, like *Michelson*, "reveals stock option plans are not exempt from shareholder approval or ratification." *Fleming*, 975 P.2d at 912.

The court contrasted Oklahoma's statute to statutes enacted in what the court described as "at least twenty-four states" that include provisions intended to "ensure their domestic corporations, and in many instances the board of directors itself, are able to implement shareholder rights plans." *Id.* The court quoted the following examples of statutes adopted in Idaho, Illinois, Indiana, Kentucky and Nevada, respectively:

> Nothing contained in this chapter is intended or shall be construed in any way to limit, modify or restrict an issuing public corporation's authority to take any action *which the directors may appropriately determine* to be in furtherance of the protection of the interests of the corporation and its shareholders, *including without limitation* the authority to adopt or enter into plans, arrangements or instruments that deny rights, privileges, power or authority to the holder or holders of at least a specified number of shares or percentage of share ownership or voting power in certain circumstances.
>
> [E]xcept as otherwise provided in the articles of incorporation, a corporation may create and issue, whether or not in connection with the issue and sale of its shares or bonds, rights or options entitling the holders thereof to purchase from the corporation, *upon such consideration, terms and conditions as may be fixed by the board*, shares of any class or series, whether authorized but unissued shares, treasury shares or shares to be purchased or acquired, notes of the corporation or assets of the corporation. The terms and conditions of such rights or options may include, without limitation, restrictions or conditions that preclude or limit the exercise, transfer or receipt of such rights or options by any person or persons owning or offering to acquire a specified number or percentage of the outstanding common shares or other securities of the corporation, or any other transferee or transferees of any such person or persons, or that invalidate or void such rights or options held by any such person or persons or any such transferee or transferees.

> Without limiting the generality of the foregoing, *directors are not required* to render inapplicable any of the provisions of IC 23-1-43, to redeem any rights under or to render inapplicable a shareholder rights plan adopted pursuant to IC 23-1-26-5, or to take or decline to take any other action under this article, solely because of the effect such action might have on a proposed acquisition of control of the corporation or the amounts that might be paid to shareholders under such an acquisition.
>
> [T]he *board of directors of a corporation may . . . create and issue rights or options . . . which may contain provisions which adjust the option price* or number of shares issuable under such rights or options in the event of an acquisition of shares or a reorganization, merger, consolidation, sale of assets or other occurrence involving such corporation.
>
> [T]he *directors of an issuing corporation* [are not restricted] from taking action to protect the interests of the corporation and its stockholders, including, but not limited to, adopting or executing plans, arrangements or instruments that deny rights, privileges, power or authority to a holder of a specified number of shares or percentage of share ownership or voting power.

Id. at 912-13 (quoting Idaho Bus. Corp. Act § 30-1706(1), Ill. Bus. Corp. Act § 5/6.05(f), Ind. Bus. Corp. Law § 23-1-35-1(f), Ky. Bus. Corp. Act § 271B.12-210(5), and Nev. Gen. Corp. Law § 78.378(3) (emphasis added by court). These examples, the court stated, "illustrate how a board of directors can operate with relative autonomy when a rights plan endorsement statute applies." *Id.* at 913.

The court thus rejected Fleming's reliance upon section 1038 of Oklahoma's statute for the proposition that "only the certificate of incorporation can limit the board's authority to implement such a plan" and held that nothing in Oklahoma's General Corporation Act or existing case law indicates that shareholder rights plans are "somehow exempt from shareholder adopted bylaws." *Id.* at 912. The court acknowledged that a certificate of incorporation provision that precludes bylaw amendments concerning shareholder rights plans could preclude a bylaw of the type proposed by the Teamsters. *Id.* The court concluded, however, that nothing in Fleming's certificate "speaks in any way to the board's authority or shareholder constraints regarding shareholder rights plans." *Id.* A certificate of incorporation that is silent concerning shareholder rights plans, the court stated, does not preclude shareholder enacted bylaws regarding the implementation of rights plans. *Id.*

In sum, the court held, without the authority granted in a statute endorsing rights plans such as the statutes quoted above, rights plans may be enacted but "the board may well be subject to the general procedures of corporate governance, including the enactment of bylaws which limit the board's authority to implement rights plans." *Id.* at 913. The court emphasized that its holding was limited to a finding that where the certificate of incorporation does not address shareholder rights plans "shareholders may, through the proper channels of corporate governance, restrict the board of directors' authority to implement shareholder rights plans." *Id.* The court also emphasized that "we do not suggest all shareholder rights plans are required to submit to shareholder approval, ratification or review." *Id.*

Replace the paragraph beginning on page 1201 and concluding on page 1202 (including footnotes 3472 and 3473) with the following:

To date, the Delaware courts have not directly addressed the issue, although the Delaware Supreme Court in *Quickturn Design Systems, Inc. v. Shapiro*, 721 A.2d 1281 (Del. 1998) – in the context of a rights plan precluding redemption for a six month period following a change in control (*see* Chapter III, Section G 2 d) – has stated that Section 141(a) of the Delaware General Corporation Law "requires that any limitation on the board's authority be set out in the certificate of incorporation." 721 A.2d at 1291. The Oklahoma Supreme Court in *Fleming* stated that "Oklahoma and Delaware have substantially similar corporation acts" (*Fleming*, 975 P.2d at 911), but most (but not all) Delaware commentators appear to agree that binding shareholder resolutions are likely to be held invalid under Delaware law. *See, e.g.*, Alexander, *Teamsters v. Fleming:*

Delaware's Different Approach, LXX Corporation Bulletin No. 7 (Apr. 1, 1999); Richards & Stearn, *Shareholder By-Laws Requiring Boards of Directors to Dismantle Rights Plans are Unlikely to Survive Scrutiny under Delaware Law*, 54 Bus. Law. 607 (1999); Hamermesh, *Corporate Democracy and Stockholder-Adopted Bylaws: Taking Back the Street?*, 73 Tulane L. Rev. 409 (1998); *Experts Comment on Fleming Decision*, Bank and Corporate Governance Law Reporter, Feb. 1999, at 1102-48.

The Delaware Court of Chancery declined to address this issue in the context of a motion for expedited proceedings in *General Datacomm Industries, Inc. v. State of Wisconsin Investment Board*, 731 A.2d 818 (Del. Ch. 1999), a case challenging the validity of a similar type of shareholder resolution but involving the repricing of stock option plans rather than a poison pill rights plan. The resolution sought adoption of the following bylaw by General Datacomm Industries, Inc. ("GDC"):

> **Option Repricing**. [GDC] shall not reprice any stock options already issued and outstanding to a lower strike price at any time during the term of such option, without the prior approval of the shareholders.

Id. at 818. According to GDC, the case required "prompt resolution so that GDC is not required to suffer a facially invalid bylaw and its directors are not impaired in the management of [GDC's] incentive compensation program for recruitment and retention of key employees due to uncertainty, as long as this dispute remains unresolved, over their authority to act without stockholder approval." *Id.* The court rejected this contention but stated that "in the event that the Repricing Bylaw is adopted by the GDC stockholders, I will promptly, upon renewed application by GDC, consider whether a schedule for expedited proceedings to address the issues raised by its complaint should be put in place." *Id.* at 819.

Relying upon *Diceon Electronics Inc. v. Calvary Partners, L.P.*, 1990 Del. Ch. LEXIS 209, 1990 WL 237089 (Del. Ch. Dec. 27, 1990) – a case discussed in Chapter III, Section

H 2 g below – the court explained that GDC shareholders could cast an informed vote if the proxy materials disclosed the existence of "differing views concerning the validity of the Repricing Bylaw," that GDC's proxy materials did "state GDC's view that the Repricing Bylaw is invalid," and that "a post-meeting adjudication would not unduly disrupt the corporation's affairs." 731 A.2d at 821. Rather, the court continued:

> At most, the Repricing Bylaw will inhibit the GDC board's ability to reprice options in the event that in the board's business judgment such repricing becomes necessary in the period between the Repricing Bylaw's adoption at the annual meeting (if that occurs) and a post-adoption adjudication of its validity by this court. The speculative nature of these eventualities, the availability of prompt injunctive relief, and the fact that this court has committed to consider promptly a request to expedite a post-adoption adjudication eliminates any necessity for a pre-adoption adjudication of the Repricing Bylaw's validity.

Id.

The court also stated that "lack of urgency cuts against the need to determine a potentially important issue of Delaware law in haste," and noted the court's "reluctance to encourage corporations to seek advisory opinions about important issues of Delaware corporation law as a method of shaping their annual proxy materials." *Id.* The court explained that "[i]f this option were routinely available, this court could find itself playing a parallel role to the SEC, which is regularly involved, pursuant to its statutory and regulatory authority, in the proxy preparation process." *Id.* at 822. The court stated that its "traditional commitment to prompt justice should ordinarily be sufficient to address any legitimate corporate interests threatened by the adoption by stockholders of an invalid bylaw," and that "[a]bsent an imminent threat of irreparable injury, there seems to be no need and much risk for this court to step into the void when the SEC concludes," as it had in this case, that state law was "not clear enough" to permit exclusion of the proposal from proxy materials. *Id.* The court stated that "[t]he SEC's judgment in such a situation would suggest that the issue involved is of a difficult nature and that it deserves careful scrutiny: that is, that the issue is of precisely the sort about which this court should be reluctant to opine until the issue is ripe for judicial resolution." *Id.*

In language equally applicable to shareholder resolutions requiring shareholder votes on poison pill rights plans, the court summarized the legal issues "worthy of careful consideration" and "the difficulties this subject generally raises" as follows:

> Just as this nascent effort to shift the balance of corporate power from directors to stockholders through the use of stockholder-adopted by-law provisions is gaining momentum, however, it has exposed a critical dearth of precedent. For while stockholders have unquestioned power to adopt by-laws covering a broad range of subjects, it is also well established in corporate law that stockholders may not directly manage the business and affairs of the corporation, at least without specific authorization either by statute or in the certificate or articles of incorporation. There is an obvious zone of conflict between these precepts: in at least some respects, attempts by stockholders to adopt by-laws limiting or influencing director authority inevitably offend the notion of management by the board of directors. However, neither the courts, the legislators, the SEC, nor legal scholars have clearly articulated the means of resolving this conflict and determining whether a stockholder-adopted by-law provision that constrains director managerial authority is legally effective.
>
> Related to this gap in legal authority is a less substantive but nearly as important area of legal uncertainty. Even if the stockholders could validly initiate and adopt a by-law limiting the authority of the directors, such a by-law amendment would accomplish little or nothing if the board of directors could simply repeal it after the stockholders adopted it. In some jurisdictions, of course, there is no question that such repeal can be prevented. Under many statutory schemes, the board of directors may not repeal a stockholder-adopted by-law if that by-law expressly prohibits such repeal. In other jurisdictions, however, notably Delaware and New York, the corporation statutes allow the board of directors to amend the by-laws if the certificate or articles of incorporation so provide and place no express limits on the application of such director amendment authority to stockholder-adopted by-laws. The second significant legal uncertainty, therefore, is whether, in the

> absence of an explicitly controlling statute, a stockholder-adopted by-law can be made immune from repeal or modification by the board of directors.

Id. at 821-22 & n.2 (quoting Hamermesh, 73 Tul. L. Rev. at 415-17).

Section H

Add the following at the end of the paragraph beginning and concluding on page 1203 (between footnotes 3473 and 3474):

As the Delaware Court of Chancery explained in *Carmody v. Toll Brothers, Inc.*, 723 A.2d 1180 (Del. Ch. 1998), the ability of a hostile offeror "to effect an 'end run' around the poison pill" by making "a tender offer coupled with a solicitation for shareholder proxies to remove and replace the incumbent board with the acquiror's nominees who, upon assuming office, would redeem the pill" necessitates counter-strategies by target company boards. *Id.* at 1186; *see also In re Gaylord Container Corp. S'holders Litig.*, 753 A.2d 462, 482 (Del. Ch. 2000) ("Market participants are remarkably adaptive. When poison pills became prevalent, would-be acquirors resorted to proxy contests as a method of obtaining indirectly that which they could no longer get through a tender offer. By taking out the target company's board through a proxy fight or a consent solicitation, the acquiror could obtain control of the board room, redeem the pill, and open the way for consummation of its tender offer.") (footnote omitted).

The court in *Toll Brothers* observed that counter-strategies generally are successful where the intent is "to delay the process to enable the board to develop alternatives to the hostile offer" but are "largely unsuccessful" where the intent is "to stop the proxy contest (and as a consequence, the hostile offer) altogether." *Id.* The court pointed to the following examples:

> For example, in cases where the target board's response was either to (i) amend the by-laws to delay a shareholders meeting to elect directors, or (ii) delay an annual meeting to a later date

> permitted under the bylaws, so that the board and management would be able to explore alternatives to the hostile offer (but not entrench themselves), those responses were upheld. On the other hand, where the target board's response to a proxy contest (coupled with a hostile offer) was (i) to move the shareholders meeting to a later date to enable the incumbent board to solicit revocations of proxies to defeat the apparently victorious dissident group, or (ii) to expand the size of the board, and then fill the newly created positions so the incumbents would retain control of the board irrespective of the outcome of the proxy contest, those responses were declared invalid.
>
> Another statutorily permissible defensive device – the "staggered" or classified board – was useful, but still of limited effectiveness. Because only one third of a classified board would stand for election each year, a classified board would delay – but not prevent – a hostile acquiror from obtaining control of the board, since a determined acquiror could wage a proxy contest and obtain control of two thirds of the target board over a two year period, as opposed to seizing control in a single election.

Id. at 1186 & nn.16-17 (citing *Stahl v. Apple Bancorp, Inc.*, 579 A.2d 1115 (Del. Ch. 1990) (discussed in Chapter III, Section H 1 b), *Kidsco Inc. v. Dinsmore*, 674 A.2d 483 (Del. Ch.), *aff'd*, 670 A.2d 1338 (unpublished opinion, text available at 1995 Del. LEXIS 426 and 1995 WL 715886) (Del. Nov. 29, 1995) (discussed in Chapter III, Section H 2 d), *Aprahamian v. HBO & Co.*, 531 A.2d 1204 (Del. Ch. 1987) (discussed in Chapter III, Section H 1 a) and *Blasius Indus., Inc. v. Atlas Corp.*, 564 A.2d 651 (Del. Ch. 1988) (discussed in Chapter III, Sections A 5 a and H 2 c).

This litigation experience, the court in *Toll Brothers* concluded, has "taught that a target board, facing a proxy contest joined with a hostile tender offer, could, in good faith, employ non-preclusive defensive measures to give the board time to explore transactional alternatives" but that a target board cannot "erect defenses that would either preclude a proxy contest altogether or improperly bend the rules to favor the board's continued incumbency." 723 A.2d at 1186-87.

Section H 1 a

Add the following at the end of the paragraph beginning and concluding on page 1217 (immediately after footnote 3561):

State of Wisconsin Investment Board v. Peerless Systems Corp., 2000 Del. Ch. LEXIS 170, 2000 WL 1805376 (Del. Ch. Dec. 4, 2000), involved a postponement of the closing of the polls at an annual meeting and the reconvening of the meeting 30 days later, at which time a proposal that trailed in the polls when the meeting was postponed received enough votes to pass by a slim margin.

The facts underlying the decision began on May 20, 1999 with the issuance by Peerless Systems Corporation of a proxy statement in connection with its June 17, 1999 annual meeting. The proxy statement described three proposals to be voted upon at the meeting: Proposal 1, seeking to re-elect each of Peerless's four incumbent directors; Proposal 2, seeking to increase by 1,000,000 the number of Peerless shares available for issuance through the corporation's existing stock option plan; and Proposal 3, seeking to ratify the board's selection of an auditor. 2000 Del. Ch. LEXIS 170, at *4-5, 2000 WL 1805376, at *2. The State of Wisconsin Investment Board ("SWIB") informed Peerless that SWIB opposed Proposal 2, retained a proxy solicitor to solicit against Proposal 2, and sent a letter to all Peerless shareholders asking them to vote against Proposal 2. 2000 Del. Ch. LEXIS 170, at *6, 2000 WL 1805376, at *2.

Just prior to the annual meeting, Peerless held a special shareholders meeting to consider a proposed merger with Auco, Inc. At the special meeting, shareholders approved the merger by a vote of 5,697,037 for and 352,539 against, with 9,600 abstentions. A total of 6,059,176 votes were cast out of a possible 11,286,967 votes. This meant that approximately 54 percent of Peerless shares were voted and that 50.47 percent of Peerless's outstanding shares were voted in favor of the merger. 2000 Del. Ch. LEXIS 170, at *7, 2000 WL 1805376, at *2.

At the annual meeting on June 17, 1999, Edward A. Galvadon, Peerless's chairman, chief executive officer and president, closed the polls on Proposals 1 and 3, both of which passed easily: on Proposal 1, each director received at least 9,300,000 votes and no more than 209,983 votes were withheld for any of the directors, and Proposal 3 received 9,480,908 votes for and 30,821 votes against, with 3,400 abstentions. 2000 Del. Ch. LEXIS 170, at *9, 2000 WL 1805376, at *3.

For Proposal 2, however, Galvadon adjourned the meeting for 30 days without closing the polls. If the polls had been closed, Proposal 2 would have been defeated by a vote of 3,605,191 (31.94 percent of outstanding shares) to 2,920,925 shares (25.88 percent of outstanding shares), with 7,000 shares abstaining. The total number of shares casting votes on Proposal 2 as of the adjournment of the meeting was 6,533,116 or 57.88 percent of the total number of outstanding shares – more than the approximately 54 percent of Peerless shares voted in connection with the Auco merger. 2000 Del. Ch. LEXIS 170, at *10-11, 2000 WL 1805376, at *4.

According to Peerless, the primary reason for the adjournment was the low voter turnout on Proposal 2 in contrast to Proposals 1 and 3 – a difference accounted for, Peerless stated, by (1) New York Stock Exchange rules that permit brokers and other agents to vote on routine matters such as Proposals 1 and 3 without instructions from beneficial owners but that require the vote of beneficial owners on non-routine matters such as Proposal 2, (2) the fact that over 2,000,000 shares of Peerless stock (approximately 17.7 percent of the outstanding shares entitled to vote) were held by European investors, many of whom "[e]vidently . . . experienced certain difficulties in voting because their agents were not familiar with American voting procedures," (3) the possibility that shareholders may have discarded their proxy materials without reading them, believing that they had received a duplicate mailing of the proxy statement for the special meeting to vote on the Auco merger, and (4) the fact that Peerless management "devoted a significant amount of time soliciting in favor of the Auco merger at the expense of any efforts they may have made to solicit for Proposal 2." 2000 Del. Ch. LEXIS 170, at *11-14, 2000 WL 1805376, at *4.

Following the adjournment, Peerless continued to solicit votes on Proposal 2 and admittedly "devoted more time to contacting shareholders who were more likely to support management and vote in favor of Proposal 2." 2000 Del. Ch. LEXIS 170, at *14-15, 2000 WL 1805376, at *5. Peerless did not issue a press release or supplementary proxy materials informing shareholders that the meeting had been adjourned after the polls were closed on Proposals 1 and 3 but before the polls were closed on Proposal 2, that Proposal 2 would have been defeated if the polls had been closed, why the meeting was adjourned, or that Peerless planned to continue its efforts to solicit the votes of certain shareholders. 2000 Del. Ch. LEXIS 170, at *14, 2000 WL 1805376, at *5. SWIB, however, sent a letter to all Peerless shareholders that "questioned the propriety of the adjournment and urged shareholders to vote against proposal 2." 2000 Del. Ch. LEXIS 170, at *16, 2000 WL 1805376, at *5.

The meeting was reconvened on July 16, 1999, and Proposal 2 passed by a vote of 3,874,380 for (34.33 percent of outstanding shares) to 3,653,310 against (32.37 percent of outstanding shares) – a margin of just 221,070 votes (1.96 percent of outstanding shares). *Id.* The total number of votes cast on Proposal 2 equaled 7,527,690 (66.69 percent of outstanding shares). 2000 Del. Ch. LEXIS 170, at *16-17, 2000 WL 1805376, at *5. From the time of the adjournment on June 17 to the closing of the polls on July 16, 953,455 shares were voted for Proposal 2 and 48,119 shares were voted against Proposal 2. 2000 Del. Ch. LEXIS 170, at *17, 2000 WL 1805376, at *5.

SWIB commenced litigation, and the case reached the court in the context of cross-motions for summary judgment on a claim that Peerless and Galvadon breached fiduciary duties to shareholders by inequitably interfering with and manipulating voting and depriving Peerless shareholders of their voting rights. 2000 Del. Ch. LEXIS 170, at *1-2, 17, 2000 WL 1805376, at *1, 6.

The court began by rejecting a claim that SWIB lacked standing to challenge the adjournment of the meeting because, according to Peerless, SWIB did not attend the meeting or the reconvened meeting and did not object to the adjournment at either meeting. 2000 Del. Ch. LEXIS 170, at *19, 2000 WL 1805376, at *6. The court stated that it was "aware of no Delaware case or statute that holds that a shareholder must attend a shareholders meeting and record an objection or lose its ability to challenge the propriety of a shareholder vote." 2000 Del. Ch. LEXIS 170, at *19-20, 2000 WL 1805376, at *6. The court also pointed to "very strong policy rationales" explaining why an "attendance and objection requirement simply cannot be the law of Delaware." 2000 Del. Ch. LEXIS 170, at *20, 2000 WL 1805376, at *6.

First, the court stated, the proxy solicitation system "works in large part because shareholders are not required to attend meetings to protect their rights" and "values the widespread ownership and distribution of corporate securities that is enabled by the proxy instrument." *Id.*

Second, the court stated, "the proxy system helps both the large investor who is spared the impracticalities and costs of attending all of the shareholder meetings of companies in a heavily diversified portfolio as well as the small investor who may not have the time, money, or other resources necessary to attend the shareholder meetings of the companies in which that individual chooses to invest." *Id.* The court stated that "[n]either the large nor the small investor should have to sacrifice its rights to challenge improper actions by directors and officers simply because they have not attended a shareholders meeting." *Id.*

Third, the court continued, "where there is fraud, abuse, or some other inequitable conduct affecting the propriety of a shareholder vote, if the improper act or the effects of that act are not exposed until after the shareholders meeting," an "attendance and objection requirement" would "bar shareholders from having the ability to challenge improprieties that they could not have possibly known about at the time of the shareholders meeting." 2000 Del. Ch. LEXIS 170, at *21, 2000 WL 1805376, at *6.

The court also rejected a claim that Peerless owed no fiduciary duty to SWIB and thus was not a proper defendant in the case. The court acknowledged that Peerless "per se does not owe fiduciary duties to its shareholders," but stated that "Peerless took action through its CEO, director, and co-defendant, Galvadon" and that "the decision to adjourn was only made after consultation with, and approval by, the other Peerless directors." 2000 Del. Ch. LEXIS 170, at *22, 2000 WL 1805376, at *7.

The court then turned to the principal issue dividing the parties: did Peerless and Galvadon breach the fiduciary duty of loyalty by adjourning Peerless's annual meeting on June 17, 1999 without closing the polls on Proposal 2? The court began its discussion of this issue and the standard established for cases involving interference with voting rights in *Blasius Industries, Inc. v. Atlas Corp.*, 564 A.2d 651 (Del. Ch. 1988), by "reaffirm[ing] the fundamental importance of the voting rights of shareholders in Delaware law" and stating that "[n]o one should doubt that '[t]here exists in Delaware a general policy against disenfranchisement' as '[t]he shareholder franchise is the ideological underpinning upon which the legitimacy of directorial power rests.'" 2000 Del. Ch. LEXIS 170, at *23, 2000 WL 1805376, at *7 (quoting *Blasius*, 564 A.2d at 659, 669); *see also* Chapter III, Section A 5 (discussing *Blasius* standard).

The court described the *Blasius* test as "a relatively simple, yet extremely powerful, two-part test based on the duty of loyalty." 2000 Del. Ch. LEXIS 170, at *27, 2000 WL 1805376, at *8. First, "the plaintiff must establish that the board acted for the primary purpose of thwarting the exercise of a shareholder vote." *Id.* Second, "the board has the burden to demonstrate a compelling justification for its actions," and "even where the Court finds that the action taken by the board was made in good faith, it may still constitute a violation of the duty of loyalty." *Id.* Thus, "*Blasius* does not apply in all cases where a board of directors has interfered with a shareholder vote." 2000 Del. Ch. LEXIS 170, at *28, 2000 WL 1805376, at *8. "The court stated that "[i]n the absence of a finding that the primary purpose of the board's action was to interfere with or impede exercise of the shareholder franchise, the business judgment rule presumption applies," and "with a fully informed shareholder approval of the proposal in question, the burden of proof remains squarely with the plaintiff to prove . . . that the board action was not properly taken or that the action was the product of fraud, manipulation, or other inequitable conduct." 2000 Del. Ch. LEXIS 170, at *32, 2000 WL 1805376, at *9.

The court reviewed the evidence placed before it on the parties' cross-motions for summary judgment and held that "the primary purpose behind the adjournment was to ensure the passage of Proposal 2 by interfering with the shareholder vote and allowing Proposal 2 to have more time to gain votes." 2000 Del. Ch. LEXIS 170, at *39, 2000 WL 1805376, at *11. "[T]he simple truth," the court found, "is that the adjournment only occurred because Proposal 2 did not have enough votes to pass on the date of the Annual Meeting." 2000 Del. Ch. LEXIS 170, at *40, 2000 WL 1805376, at *12. This finding, the court noted, "in no way indicates that the defendants acted in bad faith in calling for the adjournment," and, indeed, the court stated that "I assume that the defendants acted in good faith at all times." 2000 Del. Ch. LEXIS 170, at *40-41, 2000 WL 1805376, at *12. Nevertheless, the court continued, "I may still find that the defendants violated the fiduciary duty of loyalty." 2000 Del. Ch. LEXIS 170, at *41, 2000 WL 1805376, at *12. The court distinguished between "purpose" and "justification":

> [I]nquiries into *purpose* as opposed to *justification* are two separate analyses that must remain distinct. The question of *purpose* asks for what ultimate ends were the acts committed. Purpose is defined as "[a]n objective, goal, or end." The concept of *justification* concerns the rationale behind the search for that end. *Justification* is defined as "[a] lawful or sufficient reason for one's acts or omissions."

2000 Del. Ch. LEXIS 170, at *38-39, 2000 WL 1805376, at *11 (quoting *Black's Law Dictionary* 1250, 870-81 (7th ed. 1999)).

The court then reviewed Peerless's "plethora of justifications for their decision to adjourn the meeting" and considered "their persuasiveness both individually and collectively." 2000 Del. Ch. LEXIS 170, at *42, 2000 WL 1805376, at *12.

First, Peerless contended that the *Blasius* standard should not apply because "the facts of this case are quite different from the typical *Blasius* case that involves entrenchment or control issues in which a clear conflict exists between the board and the shareholders." *Id.* The court acknowledged that this fact "makes it more problematic to subject the adjournment to heightened *Blasius* scrutiny" but concluded that "*Blasius* does not only apply in cases involving hostile acquirers or directors wishing to retain their position against the will of the shareholders." 2000 Del. Ch. LEXIS 170, at *43-44, 2000 WL 1805376, at *12-13. In the court's words:

> The derivation of board power from shareholders, as well as the allocation of power with respect to governance of the corporation, are broad structural concerns within the corporate form that are present in any shareholder vote. The fiduciary duty of loyalty between a board of directors and the shareholders of a corporation is always implicated where the board seeks to thwart the action of the company's shareholders.

2000 Del. Ch. LEXIS 170, at *44, 2000 WL 1805376, at *13.

The court noted SWIB's allegations that Peerless's directors, especially Galvadon, had a personal financial interest in the decision to adjourn the vote on Proposal 2. Galveston, SWIB alleged, received a substantial portion of his compensation in the form of stock options and knew he could receive options from the 1,000,000 shares that were the subject of Proposal 2. *Id.* The court, however, also noted Peerless's contentions that Proposal 2 did not grant options to any director, officer, or employee and did not vary the terms on which any options were granted pursuant to the corporation's existing option plan, that "any interest created by the directors' status as potential recipients of options in the normal course of business is too remote and attenuated to pose a conflict of interest under these circumstances," that "the outside directors received all their options according to a pre-existing fixed formula," and that "any option grant made to Galvadon would first have to be approved by a committee of outside directors." 2000 Del. Ch. LEXIS 170, at *45, 2000 WL 1805376, at *13. The court concluded that "the factual record on this issue is insufficiently developed to enable me to come to any clear conclusions" on this subject in the context of the pending motions for summary judgment. 2000 Del. Ch. LEXIS 170, at *46, 2000 WL 1805376, at *13.

Second, Peerless contended that no act of disenfranchisement occurred because the adjournment provided all Peerless shareholders "a full and fair opportunity to vote." 2000 Del. Ch. LEXIS 170, at *47, 2000 WL 1805376, at *13. Peerless reasoned that "because Proposal 2 ultimately passed at the Reconvened Meeting, albeit with the support of less than a majority of outstanding Peerless shares . . . the adjournment allowed for the expression of a *greater number* of shareholders and concurrently effectuated the true, overall will of the Peerless shareholders." *Id.* The court described this claim as "essentially" an argument that "the post-adjournment ratification of Proposal moots SWIB's claims." 2000 Del. Ch. LEXIS 170, at *47, 2000 WL 1805376, at *14. The court assumed that "the adjournment was made in the interests of the Company and therefore was a voidable act that may be cured" by ratification and not a void act that could not be cured by ratification, but stated that "[t]he parties hotly dispute whether the defendants solicited votes in favor of Proposal 2 during the adjournment or rather simply solicited votes without illustrating a bias either way" and thus concluded "it is far from clear whether the ratification was 'fairly effected and intrinsically valid.'" 2000 Del. Ch. LEXIS 170, at *48, 2000 WL 1805376, at *14 (quoting *Michelson v. Duncan*, 407 A.2d 211, 220 (Del. 1979)).

Third, Peerless pointed to the low vote count on Proposal 2 at the moment of adjournment and contended that "a need for a higher vote count justified the adjournment." 2000 Del. Ch. LEXIS 170, at *49, 2000 WL 1805376, at *14. The court stated that "I know of no Delaware case or statute that supports this rationale where a quorum is present" and that "one is hard pressed to understand why this particular low vote count required adjournment, while other similarly low vote counts do not." *Id.* The court also found this argument unpersuasive in light of the lack of an adjournment of the special meeting to vote on the Auco merger (more shares were voted at the annual meeting prior to adjournment than at the special meeting) or the reconvened meeting (where the margin of votes in favor of Proposal 2 was 1.96 percent with 33.33 percent of shareholders not voting). *Id.* The court added that "[t]he lack of any informational disclosures aimed at increasing the vote count . . . further attest to the unimportance of this factor." 2000 Del. Ch. LEXIS 170, at *50, 2000 WL 1805376, at *14.

Fourth, Peerless described "the troubles of their European shareholders in unsuccessfully attempting to vote their proxies." *Id.* The court acknowledged that "[g]enerally, this Court is very lenient in enabling shareholders to vote by proxy" but concluded that "[u]ltimately, the European shareholders, not Peerless, must bear responsibility for entering into the proxy relationship, choosing their own custodial bankers, and making sure their chosen agent is competent enough to vote these proxies on time." 2000 Del. Ch. LEXIS 170, at *50-51, 2000

WL 1805376, at *14. These requirements, the court stated, "represent the absolute bare minimum expected of shareholders who choose not to attend a shareholder meeting and vote by proxy." 2000 Del. Ch. LEXIS 170, at *51, 2000 WL 1805376, at *14. The court stated that "[p]erhaps I would be slightly more sympathetic to the European shareholders' plight if the circumstances were different" but emphasized that "we are dealing here with sophisticated investors." 2000 Del. Ch. LEXIS 170, at *52, 2000 WL 1805376, at *15. The court added that "even at the outermost boundary of accommodation, the Company might believe it has some responsibility to help sophisticated European investors properly vote their shares in compliance with the governing voting procedures," but here "Peerless asks this Court, in effect, to make the shareholders who voted on time bear responsibility for the inability of other shareholders and the chosen agents of those shareholders to properly file their proxies on time." 2000 Del. Ch. LEXIS 170, at *52-53, 2000 WL 1805376, at *15. This, the court stated, "is inappropriate." 2000 Del. Ch. LEXIS 170, at *53, 2000 WL 1805376, at *15.

Fifth, Peerless contended that the adjournment was "lawfully consistent with its by-laws." *Id.* The court rejected this contention on the ground that "inequitable action does not become permissible simply because it is legally possible." *Id.* (quoting *Schnell v. Chris-Craft Indus., Inc.*, 285 A.2d 437, 439 (Del. 1971)).

Sixth, Peerless contended that the alternative to adjourning the meeting "would have been to admit defeat on Proposal 2 and resubmit the proposal for a new vote at a subsequent shareholders meeting" and that this course would have entailed "substantial cost and some delay." 2000 Del. Ch. LEXIS 170, at *53-54, 2000 WL 1805376, at *15. The court stated that "I am not blind to the practicalities of shareholder votes" but concluded that "this justification, perhaps vitally important in the minds of management in terms of cost and efficiency analyses, is not a compelling reason to forego the legally required procedures." 2000 Del. Ch. LEXIS 170, at *54, 2000 WL 1805376, at *15.

The court concluded that "it is doubtful that at the end of the day, based on the factual record presently before me, the defendants will have provided a compelling justification for their actions" but added that "[t]he justifications offered by Peerless *collectively* provide some hope or reasonable possibility for satisfying the onerous compelling justification burden." 2000 Del. Ch. LEXIS 170, at *55, 2000 WL 1805376, at *15. The court accordingly "confess[ed] discomfort, at the summary judgment stage, in deciding whether the defendants had a compelling justification when calling for the adjournment" and thus held that "defendants acted with the primary purpose of interfering with the shareholder vote on Proposal 2 (and therefore *Blasius* does apply)" but left "for another day the question whether defendants acted with a compelling justification." *Id.* This issue, the court stated, "requires further argument and factual development" and "[a]ccordingly, I deny both the plaintiff's and the defendants' motions for summary judgment." *Id.*

The court ended its decision with the following observations emphasizing "the importance of the shareholder franchise as the bedrock foundation upon which the legitimacy of directorial power rests":

> Any efforts by those controlling the vote to alter the results of that vote, even where there is no clear conflict of interest between the directors and the shareholders, must be undertaken with extreme caution so as not to undermine the legitimacy of the corporate structure itself. In this case, it is not clear at this point whether the defendants exercised this high degree of caution embodied in the "compelling justification" standard. It is clear, however, that adjournments that are specifically aimed at interfering with the results of a valid shareholder vote will bestir deep judicial suspicion.
>
> In sum, although the defendants would appear to have a difficult road ahead of them if they are to demonstrate a compelling justification for their actions, I am nevertheless not prepared to declare, as a matter of law, that Peerless cannot satisfy the compelling justification burden. Therefore, I deny

> both the plaintiff's and the defendants' motions for summary judgment.

2000 Del. Ch. LEXIS 170, at *68, 2000 WL 1805376, at *19.

Section H 1 d

Add the following at the end of the second paragraph beginning and concluding on page 1241 (between footnotes 3717 and 3718):

Additional decisions include *Golden Cycle, LLC v. Allan*, 1998 Del. Ch. LEXIS 80, 1998 WL 276224 (Del. Ch. May 20, 1998), and *AMP Inc. v. Allied Signal Inc.*, 1998 U.S. Dist. LEXIS 15617, 1998 WL 778348 (E.D. Pa. Oct. 8, 1998).

Add the following at the end of the second paragraph beginning and concluding on page 1245 (immediately after footnote 3740):

Golden Cycle, LLC v. Allan, 1998 Del. Ch. LEXIS 80, 1998 WL 276224 (Del. Ch. May 20, 1998), involved a record date set by the board of Global Motorsport Group., Inc. for a consent solicitation by Golden Cycle, LLC. On March 23, 1998, Golden Cycle sent Global a letter offering to purchase all outstanding shares of Global stock and informing Global that if Global's board did not wish to proceed with due diligence or provide Golden Cycle an opportunity to conduct due diligence, then Golden Cycle would consider attempting to replace Global's board and elect directors committed to selling Global for the highest price reasonably available. On March 24, Golden Cycle filed preliminary consent solicitation materials with the Securities and Exchange Commission. On March 27, Golden Cycle sent a second letter to Global stating Golden Cycle's disappointment that Global refused to meet with Golden Cycle to negotiate the terms of a transaction. On March 30, Global's board, acting by unanimous written consent without a meeting, set a March 30 record date for Golden

Cycle's consent solicitation. On April 1, a press release announcing the record date was issued. 1998 Del. Ch. LEXIS 80, at *6-8, 1999 WL 276224, at *2.

The court held that the board's decision to set the record date was not governed by the *Blasius* "compelling justification" standard of review for the reasons discussed in Chapter III, Section A 5 b. The court stated that it was "an interesting question" and that there was "reason to doubt" whether the "enhanced duty" *Unocal* standard provided the appropriate standard of review for "the act of fixing a record date, essentially a ministerial act." 1998 Del. Ch. LEXIS 80, at *23, 1998 WL 276224, at *8. The court, however, found it "unnecessary to decide" whether *Unocal* applied because there was no basis in the record to conclude that the March 30 record date was "materially interfering with the stockholders' franchise or Golden Cycle's ability to solicit consents." 1998 Del. Ch. LEXIS 80, at *23, 1998 WL 276224, at *8. The court added that "the significantly concentrated ownership of Global's common stock" (47% of the common shares (or approximately 52% of the shares held by persons other than Global)" was "held by eleven institutional investors and another 19% by arbitrageurs") "strongly suggest[ed] that whatever effects the setting of the March 30 record date may have, it will not, as a practical matter, interfere with the ability of the stockholders as a whole to remove the directors." 1998 Del. Ch. LEXIS 80, at *4, 23, 1998 WL 276224, at *1, 8.

The court acknowledged "the haste with which the Board acted to fix the record date" and the fact that "the Company's failure to give prompt notice of its establishment . . . suggest that the director defendants, or their advisors, thought their actions would limit or interfere with Golden Cycle's ability to solicit consents." 1998 Del. Ch. LEXIS 80, at *23 n.7, 1998 WL 276224, at *8 n.7. The court concluded, however, that "a record date was needed, the Board had the power to fix it, and there is an insufficient record from which to conclude that the date actually fixed will interfere with Golden Cycle's consent solicitation in a material respect." *Id.*

AMP Inc. v. Allied Signal Inc., 1998 U.S. Dist. LEXIS 15617, 1998 WL 778348 (E.D. Pa. Oct. 8, 1998), involved a tender offer announced on August 4, 1998 by Allied Signal, Inc., a Delaware corporation, for all shares of common stock of AMP Incorporated, a Pennsylvania corporation, at $44.50 per share in cash, to be followed by a second step merger pursuant to which Allied Signal would acquire all remaining shares of AMP common stock at the same $44.50 per share price. 1998 U.S. Dist. LEXIS 15617, at *2-3, 1998 WL 778348, at *1. At the same time, Allied Signal commenced a consent solicitation seeking to amend AMP's bylaws to expand AMP's board from 11 directors to 28 directors and elect Allied Signal nominees to fill the newly created vacancies and thus give Allied Signal control over a majority of AMP's board. The court stated that the Allied Signal nominees were directors and officers of Allied Signal "who would cause AMP to accept Allied Signal's takeover bid." 1998 U.S. Dist. LEXIS 15617, at *3-4, 1998 WL 778348, at *1-2.

As discussed in more detail in Chapter III, Section G 2 d, AMP responded by amending its shareholder rights plan "to make the pill non-redeemable and non-amendable should AMP's disinterested board majority be replaced as a result of the acquisition of control of the board by a majority of directors nominated by an unsolicited acquiring company." 1998 U.S. Dist. LEXIS 15617, at *5-6, 1998 WL 778348, at *2. The rights plan would remain non-redeemable and non-amendable until November 6, 1999, the date of the rights plan's expiration. 1998 U.S. Dist. LEXIS 15617, at *3, 1998 WL 778348, at *1. At the same time, AMP's board set October 15, 1998 as the record date for Allied Signal's consent solicitation proposals. *Id.* On September 14, 1998, Allied Signal amended its consent solicitation to add a proposal asking AMP's shareholders to amend AMP's bylaws to remove all power, rights and duties with respect to the rights plan from AMP's board and assign this authority to a three person board committee. 1998 U.S. Dist. LEXIS 15617, at *6, 1998 WL 778348, at *3. AMP's board then set November 16, 1998 as the record date for the amended consent solicitation. 1998 U.S. Dist. LEXIS 15617, at *6-7, 1998 WL 778348, at *3.

The court held that the AMP board's decision to set a November 16, 1998 record date for Allied Signal's consent solicitation proposal to transfer the AMP board's authority relating to AMP's rights plan to a board committee – one month later than the October 15, 1998 record date set for Allied Signal's earlier consent solicitation proposals – was neither illegal nor inequitable. 1998 U.S. Dist. LEXIS 15617, at *30-31, 1998 WL 778348, at *11. The court explained that AMP's decision to set a November 16, 1998 record date did not violate Pennsylvania's statute, which required that a record date be not more than ninety days prior to a shareholder meeting, or AMP's bylaws, which required that "a record date must be fixed by the board within ten days of a request to fix a record date, but do not restrict the date a board may choose." 1998 U.S. Dist. LEXIS 15617, at *31, 1998 WL 778348, at *11-12.

The court then pointed to Section 1715(d) of the Pennsylvania Business Corporation Law, which "protects the actions of a majority board of disinterested directors in resisting unsolicited takeovers by retaining the ordinary business judgment rule with respect to the adoption of defensive measures" and requires "clear and convincing evidence" that disinterested directors have not acted "in good faith after reasonable investigation" in order to impose liability in cases "relating to or affecting an acquisition or potential or proposed acquisition of control of the corporation." 1998 U.S. Dist. LEXIS 15617, at *14, 1998 WL 778348, at *5; Pa. Bus. Corp. Law § 1715(d). The court stated that "Allied Signal has not demonstrated by clear and convincing evidence, that the AMP board's actions in setting the record date did not satisfy the directors' fiduciary duty standard," and added that "[u]nder Section 1715(d), because the record date relates to a proposed acquisition, AMP's board is entitled to the presumption that its actions were in the best interests of the corporation." 1998 U.S. Dist. LEXIS 15617, at *31-32, 1998 WL 778348, at *12.

Section H 2

Replace "1996" with "Supp. 1998/99" in the Model Act § 2.06 citation in footnote 3741 on page 1245.

Add the following at the end of footnote 3743 on page 1246:

See also Carmody v. Toll Bros., Inc., 723 A.2d 1180, 1186 n.17 (Del. Ch. 1998) (describing staggered or classified board as "useful, but still of limited effectiveness": "Because only one third of a classified board would stand for election each year, a classified board would delay – but not prevent – a hostile acquiror from obtaining control of the board, since a determined acquiror could wage a proxy contest and obtain control of two thirds of the target board over a two year period, as opposed to seizing control in a single election").

Add the following at the end of the paragraph beginning on page 1246 and concluding on page 1247 (immediately after footnote 3746):

The court in *In re Gaylord Container Corp. Shareholders Litigation*, 753 A.2d 462 (Del. Ch. 2000), upheld the adoption of charter and bylaw provisions adopted by the directors of Gaylord Container Corporation providing that shareholder action only could be taken at a shareholder meeting and not by written consent, and providing that special shareholder meetings only could be called by the corporation's chairman or its board of directors. *Id.* at 469. The court explained that these "garden-variety" provisions "force an acquiror seeking to obtain control of Gaylord to do so at the annual stockholders' meeting" and thus "limit Gaylord's exposure to a proxy fight outside of the company's annual meeting." *Id.* at 464, 482. The court acknowledged that "there is no doubt that acquirors would prefer to operate on their own timetables and to take over a board whenever they can muster the necessary votes," but concluded that "the fact that the Amendments force an acquiror to fight its battle at the annual meeting hardly makes them 'show stopper[s].'" *Id.* at 482.

The court also relied upon the fact that an acquiror could ask Gaylord's board to schedule a special meeting and stated that the board's "decision whether to accede to such a request would be reviewable under the particular circumstances then presented." *Id.* at 483. "Put differently," the court stated, "the Amendments do not divest the Gaylord board and its Chairman of their fiduciary duties in exercising their now exclusive power to schedule special stockholder meetings. If the board were to refuse such a request without properly informing itself or for reasons inimical to the interests of the Gaylord stockholders, it could open itself up to a successful application for injunctive relief." *Id.*

The court thus concluded that Gaylord's charter and bylaw provisions were "not an ineffectual corporate Maginot Line . . . [b]ut nor are they insurmountable or impossible to outflank." *Id.* at 482. The court noted, however, that "the conclusion that the adoption of this approach by a disinterested board on a clear day was proper does not necessarily validate, for example, similar action by an interested board designed to preclude a particular bidder from mounting a proxy fight or consent solicitation effort under the electoral rules that existed when the bidder made its intentions known." *Id.* at 482 n.70.

Add the following at the end of footnote 3748 on page 1247:

See also Gaylord, 753 A.2d at 464, 482 (describing advance notice provision as a "garden-variety" defensive measure requiring that an acquiror give shareholders "adequate time to consider the platforms and qualifications" of contending director slates); *see also* Chapter III, Section H 2 d (discussing *Gaylord* and other decisions).

Add the following between "supermajority provisions, which" and "'take various forms . . . '" in the first sentence of the

second paragraph beginning and concluding on page 1247 (between footnotes 3748 and 3749):

are "common and lawful features of corporate charters" (*Gaylord*, 753 A.2d at 487; *cf. Chesapeake Corp. v. Shore*, 771 A.2d 293, 343 & n.113 (Del. Ch. 2000) (declining to decide whether "a board of directors may not, by bylaw, require a supermajority vote to amend the bylaws" and describing this question as "a novel and important issue of Delaware corporation law")) and

Add the following at the end of the second paragraph beginning and concluding on page 1247 (immediately after footnote 3751):

Due to the "general policy against disenfranchisement . . . , 'high vote requirements which purport to protect minority shareholders by disenfranchising the majority, must be clear and unambiguous. There must be no doubt that the shareholders intended that a supermajority would be required. When a provision which seeks to require the approval of a supermajority is unclear or ambiguous, the fundamental principle of majority rule will be held to apply.'" *Starkman v. United Parcel Serv. of Am., Inc.*, No. 17747, Tr. at 17 (Del. Ch. Oct. 18, 1999) (quoting *Centaur Partners, IV v. Nat'l Intergroup, Inc.*, 582 A.2d 923, 927 (Del. 1990)). "[W]here a board is presented with a situation in which it can proceed one way which requires a supermajority vote or it can proceed in accordance with the law another way which does not, the fact that the board chooses to proceed with the low-vote mechanism, even if it is done because it fears it cannot obtain the high vote, . . . is certainly not something that would justify the issuance of an injunction or a finding of breach of duty." *Id.* at 30; *see also Frankino v. Gleason*, 1999 Del. Ch. LEXIS 219, at *1-3, 11-17, 1999 WL 1032773, at *1, 3-5 (Del. Ch. Nov. 5, 1999) (upholding two actions taken by written consent by a 55 percent shareholder – first, elimination of a supermajority voting provision in Article IX of the corporation's bylaws requiring an 80 percent vote to amend Article III of the corporation's bylaws, which regulated board size, and second, an expansion of the corporation's board from six to thirteen members and election of the 55 percent shareholder's nominees to the seven newly created board seats; the court relied upon a provision in Article II of the bylaws stating that "a simple majority vote is effective to resolve any issue unless a different vote is required by '*express provision* of the statutes or the Certificate of Incorporation or . . . these Bylaws'"; the court described this bylaw provision as "consistent with Delaware's 'general policy against disenfranchisement'" (quoting *Blasius Indus., Inc. v. Atlas Corp.*, 564 A.2d 651, 669 (Del. Ch. 1988)) and rejected a contention that allowing Article IX to be amended by a simple majority vote "would render nugatory the supermajority vote requirement in Article IX of the bylaws because the case involved "director-only approved bylaw amendments" and not "shareholder-approved supermajority requirements in both the charter and bylaws"), *subsequent proceedings*, 1999 Del. Ch. LEXIS 218, at *6, 1999 WL 1063071, at *2 (Del. Ch. Nov. 12, 1999) (describing earlier decision as "a straightforward application of the contract law principles employed when interpreting bylaw provisions"), *aff'd sub nom. McNamara v. Frankino*, 744 A.2d 988 (unpublished opinion, text available at 1999 Del. LEXIS 418 and 1999 WL 1319365) (Del. Dec. 9, 1999).

Section H 2 a

Add the following at the end of the paragraph beginning on page 1252 and concluding on page 1253 (immediately after footnote 3784):

The Delaware Court of Chancery in *In re Gaylord Container Corp. Shareholders Litigation*, 753 A.2d 462 (Del. Ch. 2000), on a motion for summary judgment, upheld a series of charter and bylaw provisions approved by the shareholders of Gaylord Container Corporation eliminating shareholders' right to act by written consent or call special shareholders' meetings, requiring that board nominations be made in the period beginning 90 days and ending 60 days before Gaylord's annual meeting, and requiring a supermajority vote to change these provisions. *Id.* at 463, 469. The court tested each of these provisions in accordance with the *Unocal* doctrine, but added that the Supreme Court in *Williams v. Geier*, 671 A.2d 1368 (Del. 1996) stated that "[a] *Unocal* analysis should be used only when a board unilaterally (i.e., without stockholder approval) adopts defensive measures in reaction to a perceived threat" (*id.* at 1377) and "[u]nder the *Williams* approach" the charter and bylaw amendments "are not subject to heightened scrutiny because they were approved by a stockholder vote." 753 A.2d at 485 n.80.

The court rejected a claim that the shareholder vote on the charter and bylaw amendments was "inherently wrongful" because the board caused the vote to occur just before a dual class voting structure was to expire and thus while one shareholder "still had voting control and could ensure their passage." *Id.* at 484. The court explained that the Gaylord board faced a legitimate threat of an inadequate and/or coercive tender offer following the expiration of the dual class voting structure and, if the defensive measures adopted to address this threat were – as the court determined they were – "neither coercive, preclusive, or unreasonable in their effect," then "the mere fact that the board chose to put them in place rapidly through a vote it knew would succeed does not render the board's response disproportionate." *Id.* at 485. To the contrary, the court stated, "[t]his type of quibbling" is inconsistent with *Unocal. Id.* The court continued as follows:

> [T]he board's decision to put into place seamless defensive coverage efficiently cannot be deemed an unreasonable approach to the situation it faced. Nor was the board bound, if it believed an earlier vote was advisable, effectively to accelerate the expiration of the dual class voting structure by timing any action on the Amendments to occur after the expiration of that structure. The board's decision to take the most expedient and certain route to ensuring the adoption of Charter and

> Bylaw Amendments it deemed in the best interests of Gaylord and the company's stockholders does not constitute an independent basis for invalidating the board's action.

Id. The court acknowledged that a vote on the charter and bylaw amendments "may not have been necessary" at the time the board determined to schedule to vote – i.e., before expiration of the dual class voting structure – "[b]ut the fact that one might have decided that question differently than the board did is not sufficient to create a genuine issue for trial unless one believes that the facts would support a finding that the board's contrary judgment was outside the range of reasonable responses to the circumstances." *Id.*

Section H 2 c

Replace the paragraph beginning and concluding on page 1255 through the paragraph beginning on page 1256 and concluding on page 1257 (including footnotes 3798 through 3807) with the following:

The Third Circuit, construing New Jersey law in *IBS Financial Corp. v. Seidman & Associates, L.L.C.*, 136 F.3d 940 (3d Cir. 1998), invalidated a determination by the board of IBS Financial Corp. ("IBSF") to amend the corporation's bylaws to reduce its size from seven to six directors in July 1996. The board made this determination after one of the two IBSF directors slated to run for reelection in 1996 announced that he intended to step down as an IBSF director, and at a time when "it was generally expected" that a group calling itself the IBSF Committee to Maximize Shareholder Value would seek two board seats at IBSF's annual meeting in December 1996, as it unsuccessfully had done at IBSF's annual meeting in December 1995. *Id.* The IBSF board's reduction of its size from seven to six directors left only one seat open for election at IBSF's annual meeting in 1996. *Id.*

IBSF directors testified that "the board acted for three reasons in reducing the board's size from seven to six":

(1) "the board thought that its work could be performed as well with one fewer member, because most of the decisions affecting IBSF – a holding company – were made by the board of IBSF's operating subsidiary, Interboro Savings & Loan Association," (2) "the board thought a smaller size would provide more flexibility if IBSF should in the future undertake acquisitions of other companies," and (3) "the board wished to hinder the Committee's attempt to gain a substantial presence on the board." *Id.* The district court found that "the first two proferred reasons were 'suspiciously pretextual'" and that the third rationale was "the primary motivation behind the IBSF board's decision." *Id.* (quoting *IBS Fin. Corp. v. Seidman & Assocs.*, 954 F. Supp. 980, 985 (D.N.J. 1997), *aff'd on this ground and rev'd on other grounds*, 136 F.3d 940 (3d Cir. 1998)).

The Third Circuit concluded that "New Jersey shares Delaware's interest in providing significant protection to a shareholder's right to vote" and that New Jersey courts would look to *Blasius Industries, Inc. v. Atlas Corp.*, 564 A.2d 651 (Del. Ch. 1988), for guidance in assessing the propriety of a board's reduction of its size. 136 F.3d at 950. *Blasius*, the court continued, "requires that a board's action primarily motivated by a desire to frustrate shareholder franchise be justified by a compelling interest." *Id.* at 949. The court stated that there was "substantial support in the record" for the trial court's finding that "the board's primary motivation in reducing its size was to hinder the Committee's proxy solicitation" and "to foreclose the Committee from electing two directors." *Id.* at 950-51. The Third Circuit accepted the district court's finding that the board's "other reasons for reducing board size – 1) flexibility to add board members in case of an acquisition, and 2) efficiency" were "pretextual in light of the ability of the board to accommodate up to fifteen members in the event of an acquisition, and the lack of documentation of discussions of flexibility or efficiency gains from a reduction in board size at prior board meetings." *Id.* at 950. These other rationales, the court added, "arose for the first time in depositions taken after the litigation had commenced and in all but one instance after the Court alerted the parties to the viability of such case law applicable to defendants' first counterclaim." *Id.* at 951 n.9.

The Third Circuit rejected a contention that "even if the board was primarily motivated by a desire to prevent the Committee from gaining two seats on the board, the board's action does not fall within the *Blasius* rubric because at the time the board reduced its size there was no chance that the Committee could take control of the board." *Id.* at 951. The court explained that it was enough that "the anticipated 1996 election represented a step toward control of the board by the Committee" and that a contest for "outright control of the board" was not required "in order to trigger *Blasius*." *Id.* The court also rejected a contention that "*Blasius* and the cases following it" require that "the proxy process be 'engaged'" before judicial scrutiny under *Blasius* is required. *Id.* at 951 n.10. The court explained that Delaware courts "consider the degree to which the proxy process has been invoked in determining whether action taken by a board is primarily motivated by a desire to impair the shareholder franchise" but have not established "a hard line rule that a proxy contest must be engaged in order for *Blasius* to apply." *Id.* (citing *Stahl v. Apple Bancorp, Inc.*, 579 A.2d 1115 (Del. Ch. 1990) (discussed in Chapter III, Section H 2 d), *Kidsco v. Dinsmore*, 674 A.2d 483 (Del. Ch. 1995), *aff'd*, 670 A.2d 1338 (unpublished opinion, text available at 1995 Del. LEXIS 426 and 1995 WL 715886 (Del. Nov. 29, 1995) (discussed in Chapter III, Section H 2 d), and *Dolgoff v. Projectavision*, 21 Del. J. Corp. L. 1128 (Del. Ch. Feb. 29, 1996) (discussed in Chapter III, Section H 1 b)). Here, the court stated, "it was . . . generally expected, following the Committee's failure to elect directors of its choice in December 1995, that the Committee would resume its campaign in 1996; thus when the board acted, in the summer of 1996, to eliminate the Lockhart seat as of the 1996 election, the proxy process had, realistically, been 'engaged' ever since the fall of 1995." *Id.*

The Third Circuit thus concluded as follows:

> *Blasius* dictates that actions taken for the purpose of interfering with the shareholder franchise must be supported by compelling justification. The board did not establish a compelling justification in the district court and does not urge such a justification in this appeal. Because we uphold the district court's finding that the board reduced its size in order to frustrate the Committee's attempt to gain a substantial presence on the board, and because the board has not articulated a compelling justification for its action, the district court's invalidation of the reduction in the board will be sustained.

Id. at 951.

Section H 2 d

Replace the heading and "The leading case addressing" following the heading in the beginning of the paragraph beginning and concluding on page 1257 (immediately after footnote 3807) with the following:

d. Bylaws Regulating Board Nominations, Shareholder Resolutions, Calling of Shareholder Meetings and Voting at Shareholder Meetings. The Delaware Court of Chancery in *In re Gaylord Container Corp. Shareholders Litigation*, 753 A.2d 462 (Del. Ch. 2000), upheld a bylaw amendment adopted by the board of Gaylord Container Corporation that required that nominations for election to Gaylord's board be made between 60 and 90 days before the corporation's annual meeting. The board adopted this bylaw shortly before a dual class voting structure was about to expire and "thereby expose the Gaylord's stockholders for the first time to the potential duress of an inadequate and/or coercive acquisition offer." *Id.* at 464. The court described this bylaw as a "garden-variety" defensive measure requiring that an acquiror give shareholders "adequate time to consider the platforms and qualifications" of contending director slates. *Id.* at 464, 482. The court stated that "the fact that an acquiror must make its nominations at least sixty days in advance of the meeting merely lengthens the electoral contest in a way that strikes a reasonable balance between the electorate's need to hear out all participants in the debate and the acquiror's need for an adequate opportunity to line up a slate before the meeting." *Id.* at 482. The court noted that this provision was "far less preclusive than a staggered board provision, which can delay an acquiror's ability to take over a board for several years." *Id.* The court added, however, that "the conclusion that the adoption of this approach by a disinterested board on a clear day was proper does not necessarily validate, for example, similar action by an interested board designed to preclude a particular bidder from mounting a proxy fight or consent solicitation effort under the electoral rules that existed when the bidder made its intentions known." *Id.* at 482 n.70.

The leading case invalidating

Add the following at the end of the first paragraph beginning and concluding on page 1268 (immediately after footnote 3876):

The Delaware Court of Chancery's decision in *Mentor Graphics Corp. v. Quickturn Design Systems, Inc.*, 728 A.2d 25 (Del. Ch.), *aff'd on other grounds sub nom. Quickturn Design Systems, Inc. v. Shapiro*, 721 A.2d 1281 (Del. 1998), upheld a bylaw amendment adopted by Quickturn Design Systems, Inc., in response to an offer by Mentor Graphics Corporation that Quickturn's board had determined was inadequate. This bylaw amendment addressed Section 2.3 of Quickturn's bylaws, which prior to the amendment, permitted holders of 10 percent or more of Quickturn's stock to call a special shareholders meeting. The amendment to Section 2.3 provided that "if any such special meeting is requested by shareholders, the corporation (Quickturn) would fix the record date for, and determine the time and plan of, that special meeting, which must take place not less than 90 days nor more than 100 days after the receipt and determination of the validity of the shareholders' request. *Id.* at 35; *see also id.* at 38-39 (quoting bylaw provision). The court found that "the board amended the By-

Law because (i) the original § 2.3 was incomplete: it did not explicitly state who would be responsible for determining the time, place, and record date for the meeting; and (ii) the original by-law language arguably would have allowed a hostile bidder holding the requisite percentage of shares to call a special stockholders meeting on minimal notice and stampede the shareholders into making a decision without time to become adequately informed." *Id.* at 39. The bylaw amendment "responded to those concerns by explicitly making the board responsible for fixing the time, place, record date, and notice of the special stockholders meeting; and by mandating a 90 to 100 day period of delay for holding the meeting after the validity of the shareholder's meeting request is determined." *Id.* The effect of the bylaw amendment was to delay a shareholder-called special meeting for three months. *Id.* at 36.

At the same time, Quickturn's board adopted a poison pill shareholder rights plan provision that precluded redemption of Quickturn's rights plan for six months after the replacement of a majority of Quickturn's directors by shareholder action. 721 A.2d at 1287-88; *see also* Chapter III, Section G 2 d (discussing this aspect of *Quickturn* decision). The combined effect of the bylaw amendment and the delayed redemption rights plan provision was "to delay any acquisition of Quickturn by Mentor for at least nine months." *Id.*

The court focused its analysis of the bylaw amendment upon the three month delay provided for by the amendment "on a 'standalone' basis" and not "as part of a combined package" consisting of the bylaw amendment and the delayed redemption rights plan provision because the court separately had determined that the delayed redemption rights plan provision was invalid on grounds unrelated to the bylaw. *Id.* at 39 & n.56; *see also* Chapter III, Section G 2 d (discussing this aspect of *Quickturn* decision). The court noted that if it had upheld the rights plan provision, then it would have scrutinized the bylaw amendment together with the delayed redemption rights plan provision "as a collective unitary response to the perceived threat." *Id.* at 39 n.56.

The court stated that the threat in response to which Quickturn's board adopted the challenged bylaw amendment resulted from the incompleteness of the original bylaw, which "permitted stockholders having the requisite number of voting shares to call a special stockholders meeting 'at any time,' yet failed to specify who would determine the time, place, and record date for the meeting" and thus created the possibility that" a hostile bidder seeking to replace the board would . . . call a special meeting on minimal notice, and thereby force Quickturn's shareholders to decide which director slate should be elected without adequate time to become properly informed." *Id.* at 40. The issue thus was whether the 90 to 100 day delay interval chosen by the Quickturn board was reasonable in relation to its purpose: "to afford shareholders sufficient time to make an informed decision" – i. e., "to give the shareholders a reasonable opportunity to inform themselves about the issues presented, particularly when the election is contested." *Id.* at 41.

According to plaintiffs, the 90 to 100 day period was too long and thus was disproportionate to the perceived threat and the bylaw amendment's purpose. "[M]ost proxy contests," plaintiffs reasoned, "are completed within 35 days, and the sophisticated insider and institutional investors who hold a large percentage of Quickturn's stock do not need a period three times that long to become informed." *Id.* at 41. The court stated that "even if that is true, surely that cannot be the exclusive measure or determinant of what delay is reasonable in this context." *Id.* The court explained that "[s]ome proxy contests may, because of their internal dynamics, be more protracted than others" and thus "may require more than 35 days to conclude," and that "not all shareholders are insiders, institutions, or arbitrageurs" and "some shareholders may need more time than others to become informed and to reflect upon the information provided to them." *Id.* The court stated that the choice between a 35 day bylaw – which plaintiffs conceded a board reasonably could adopt – and a bylaw providing for a longer period "is necessarily and inherently judgmental" and "requires a reasoned, good faith effort by the board to select a delay period that will remedy the information problem without improperly deterring a dissenting shareholder from exercising its right to wage a proxy contest." *Id.*

Here, the court found, "the 90 to 100 day interval chosen by the Quickturn board . . . arguably may approach the outer limit of reasonableness," but it "struck a proper balance in this specific case." *Id.* at 41-42. The court pointed to the board's consideration of several alternatives, including "(i) repealing altogether the original by-law that entitled shareholders to call a special meeting, (ii) leaving that by-law unchanged, and (iii) amending the by-law to provide for a longer (120 to 150 day) – or shorter (30 day) – delay interval." *Id.* at 42. The court stated that the board selected "90 to 100 days because that period corresponded to the mandated delay period in the pre-existing 'advance notice' bylaw" in Section 2.5 of Quickturn's bylaws, which required that "stockholders who seek to nominate directors at an annual or special meeting must, at least 90 days in advance of the meeting, inform the corporation of that fact and submit specified information about the stockholder-nominated slate." *Id.* The alignment of these two bylaws was reasonable, the court concluded, for two reasons.

First, the court stated, the purpose of Quickturn's pre-existing advance notice bylaw in Section 2.5 was "to give the corporation at least 90 days' prior notice of any impending proxy contest, together with information about the proposed opposition slate, in advance of any annual or special meeting called by the board," and the amendment to § 2.3 of Quickturn's bylaws "furthered that purpose." *Id.* at 42. The court explained that "Section 2.3 as originally drafted, stood as an apparent exception to that 90 day advance notice requirement in cases where a special meeting is called for by stockholders representing 10% of the voting shares . . . because the original § 2.3 permitted shareholders to call a special stockholders meeting 'at any time,' which arguably allowed a special stockholders meeting to be called on less than 90 days' notice" and "[i]n that event it would be impossible for the dissident shareholders to comply with the advance notice by-law." *Id.* The court stated that the bylaw amendment "eliminated that apparent exception by mandating a 90 to 100 day delay period for shareholder-requested special meetings to elect directors." *Id.*

The court described that judgment as "reasonable, because the need for advance notice and information in the case of a contested election of directors called by shareholders under § 2.3, and the need for such notice and information in cases covered by the advance notice by-law (§ 2.5), is the same." *Id.* Indeed, the court stated, "[t]he board could reasonably conclude that it made no sense to require 90 to 100 days advance notice of a proxy contest for all shareholders meetings, except special meetings requested by shareholders who would likely be the very persons initiating the proxy contest." *Id.* at 42 n.66. In short, "[b]y creating a delay period in § 2.3 that is essentially identical to the advance notice period prescribed by § 2.5, the board ensured that shareholders requesting a special meeting under § 2.3 would have sufficient time to comply with the advance notice requirement." *Id.* at 42.

Second, the court described advance notice bylaws mandating a 90 day notice period as "commonplace." *Id.* The court cited expert testimony presented by both sides in the litigation and an "uncontroverted" 1998 study by the Investor Responsibility Research Corporation finding that "of 1922 large publicly traded companies, 880 (46%) have some form of advance notice by-law" and "[o]f those by-laws, the most common notice period (adopted by 335 companies) is 50 to 70 days, and the second most common notice period (adopted by 223 companies) is 75 to 100 days." *Id.* at 42-43.

The court added that the record did not disclose any basis upon which the court could conclude that the minimum advance notice requirement in Section 2.5 of Quickturn's bylaws was unreasonable, and "[b]y parity of reasoning, it therefore follows that the 90 to 100 day provision of the By-Law Amendment" to Section 2.3 of Quickturn's bylaws "falls within a range of reasonable responses to the threat perceived by the Quickturn board." *Id.* at 43.

The court noted that its conclusion "should not be regarded as a pronouncement that a by-law mandated 90 to 100 day interval between the request for and the holding of a shareholder-initiated special meeting is invariably reasonable as a mater of law" and "should not be read as a rule of broad general application" because "[c]onceivably a 90 to 100 day delay might not be found reasonable in other circumstances." *Id.* at 43 n.70. According to the court, "it is impossible to draw a line that categorically separates mandatory delay periods which have a basis in reason, from those that so manifestly burden or impede the election process that they can only be characterized as intended to entrench the incumbent board." *Id.* As a result, the court observed, "attorneys who represent corporate boards would best serve their clients well by counseling caution and restraint in this area, rather than seeking continually to push the time-delay envelope outwards to test its fiduciary duty limits." *Id.*

Quickturn appealed the Court of Chancery's ruling preliminarily enjoining the delayed redemption shareholder rights plan to the Delaware Supreme Court, but Mentor did not cross-appeal the Court of Chancery's ruling refusing to enjoin enforcement of Quickturn's bylaw amendment. 721 A.2d at 1289. The Supreme Court's decision in the case accordingly did not address the bylaw amendment. *Id.*

Section H 2 f-1

Add the following at the end of the paragraph beginning on page 1277 and concluding on page 1278 (immediately after footnote 3936):

f-1. The Gaylord and Chesapeake Supermajority Provisions. The Delaware Court of Chancery in *In re Gaylord Container Corp. Shareholders Litigation*, 753 A.2d 462 (Del. Ch.

2000), upheld a shareholder approved supermajority provision requiring a 66 2/3 percent shareholder vote to amend charter or bylaw provisions that eliminated the right Gaylord Container Corporation shareholders had before the charter and bylaw amendments to act by written consent and to call special meetings and that required that board nominations be made in the period beginning 90 days and ending 60 days before the corporation's annual meeting. *Id.* at 464, 469.

The "most critical fact supporting this conclusion," the court stated, "is the reality that an effective fight over board control can occur once a year, rendering the supermajority provision an insubstantial barrier to an acquisition." *Id.* at 483-84. The court recognized that the supermajority provision "makes it very difficult" to amend the corporation's bylaws without board support and that a 66 2/3 percentage voting requirement "is no trivial hurdle given the likelihood that less that a 100% turnout can be expected." *Id.* at 484. The necessary vote, however, was "theoretically achievable" because Gaylord's founder, largest shareholder, chief executive officer and board chairman, Marvin Pomerantz, "holds only 12% of the vote and is not in a position to block the electorate." *Id.* at 465, 484. The court acknowledged that "other directors and Gaylord management hold another 8% of the stock," but stated that the directors' share of that percentage (a percentage that none of the parties had specified) "cannot be lumped together with Pomerantz's shares because none of those directors is a manager or has an interest (beyond mere board service) conflicting with the interests of Gaylord's stockholders." *Id.* at 484. The court stated that "[i]n the absence of countervailing evidence, these stockholder-directors 'are presumed to act in their own best economic interest when they vote . . . .'" *Id.* (quoting *Unitrin Inc. v. Am. Gen. Corp.*, 651 A.2d 1361, 1380-81 (Del. 1995)).

The court noted that the Delaware Supreme Court's decision in *Unitrin* held that "the fact that a repurchase program would place as much as 28% of the stock in directors' hands did not necessarily preclude a successful proxy fight in a vote requiring a majority of the outstanding shares, assuming a 90% turnout," and thus "[a]fter *Unitrin*, it is not clear" that Gaylord's supermajority provision and distribution of voting power "can be deemed preclusive." *Id.* The court held that it need not reach this question, however, "because the supermajority provision does not subject *all* charter changes to a 66 2/3% stockholder vote." *Id.* Rather, "[o]nly those provisions that were part of the defensive measures are subject to the supermajority requirement," and "the supermajority requirement for bylaw changes only applies to stockholder-initiated bylaw amendments." *Id.*

As a result, the court stated, it was "not clear . . . why the supermajority provision would hamper the ability of a new board to manage the company with the necessary flexibility." *Id.* The court explained that "[i]f such a board wished to amend any of the bylaws, it could do so itself without a stockholder vote," and "if a new board wished to restore the stockholders' ability to act by written consent, for example, it could propose a charter amendment and solicit proxies in connection with the annual meeting if it wished to do so efficiently." *Id.* In sum, the court concluded, "because a majority of the stockholders can elect a new insurgent board at the annual meeting without impairment by the supermajority provision and because that board will have the necessary managerial flexibility to run the company efficiently," the supermajority provision "simply reinforces the elimination of the option of removing the board by written consent" and "has little additional defensive bite." *Id.*

By contrast, the Delaware Court of Chancery in *Chesapeake Corp. v. Shore*, 771 A.2d 293 (Del. Ch. 2000), invalidated a series of bylaw amendments adopted by the board of Shorewood Packaging Corporation shortly after receiving an unwanted $16.50 per share all cash offer by Chesapeake Corporation, which held 14.9 percent of Shorewood's shares, for all other shares of Shorewood stock. The bylaws "were designed to make it more difficult" for Chesapeake to amend the Shorewood bylaws to eliminate Shorewood's classified board structure and install a new board willing to approve Chesapeake's offer. The bylaws eliminated the ability of shareholders to call special meetings, remove directors without cause or fill board vacancies, adopted procedures regulating the consent solicitation process that gave the board "significant leeway" to determine a record date for a consent solicitation, and raised the number of votes required to amend the bylaws from 50 percent to a 66 2/3 percent – a percentage lowered shortly before trial to a 60 percent – supermajority. *Id.* at 296-97. The court found that "[b]ecause Shorewood's management controls nearly 24% of the company's stock, the 66 2/3% Supermajority Bylaw made it mathematically impossible for Chesapeake to prevail in a Consent Solicitation without management's support, assuming a 90% turnout." *Id.* at 297.

Shorewood's bylaw amendments first were discussed during a 30 minute telephone board meeting on March 18, 1999 and were considered individually without consideration of their "cumulative impact." *Id.* at 305. The bylaw amendments were not provided to the board in writing prior to the meeting. *Id.* The court described the board's deliberations concerning the supermajority bylaw as "quite truncated and perfunctory" and found that the information presented to the board concerning this subject was "grossly inadequate." *Id.* According to the court, the board "failed to even discuss, among other things, much less give adequate consideration to the following factors":

- the likely voter turnout in the event of a consent solicitation;
- the composition of the Shorewood electorate, including the proportion of Shorewood shares held by institutional investors and by Shorewood insiders;
- whether it was reasonable to expect that anyone could obtain 66 2/3% of the outstanding shares in a consent solicitation without the support of the Shore

family shares and the other shares controlled by Shorewood insiders; and

- whether the Shorewood board faced a realistic prospect of losing a consent solicitation battle with Chesapeake without a supermajority bylaw.

Id. at 305-06. Shorewood's directors also did not consider "whether the perquisites of their positions might lead the management-stockholders to vote differently than stockholders without any other financial relationship with Shorewood." *Id.* at 306.

Shorewood's board "supposedly voted to approve the bylaw amendments at their phone meeting on November 18" but "subsequently executed a written consent confirming the adoption of the bylaw amendments." *Id.* at 310. Even at the time the directors were asked to execute the consent "the directors had not been provided with a text of the amendments," but they "signed anyway." *Id.*

On December 3, 1999, Chesapeake announced a tender offer for all shares of Shorewood stock and a consent solicitation seeking to amend Shorewood's bylaws to eliminate Shorewood's classified board structure, remove Shorewood's directors, and elect a new board. On the same day, Chesapeake commenced litigation seeking to enjoin the supermajority bylaw. *Id.* at 312.

On January 5, 2000, after early returns showed that less than 1 percent of Shorewood's shares had been tendered to Chesapeake, Shorewood's board, "obviously motivated" by the litigation, met by telephone and during this meeting determined to reduce the supermajority voting requirement from 66 2/3 percent to 60 percent. *Id.* at 314. Shorewood's directors were not given prior notice that this subject would be discussed at the meeting, the discussion of this subject lasted only approximately 45 minutes, and the only professional advisor who spoke to the board, Arthur Crozier of Innisfree M&A Incorporated, Shorewood's proxy solicitor, participated for "5 minutes. Not even." *Id.* Crozier told the board "that, based on his experience as a proxy solicitor, Shorewood could expect a 95% turnout" in the consent solicitation commenced by Chesapeake. *Id.* The board asked no questions about the basis for Crozier's opinion, which, the court stated, was "superficial compared to that which he and his company usually rely upon to advise their clients." *Id.* The board "never considered whether it was reasonably practicable for Chesapeake or any other third party opposed to the board to win under these rules" and "received no advice regarding that issue." *Id.* at 315.

As discussed in Chapter III, Sections A 5 c, the court reviewed the supermajority bylaw under the *Unocal* standard because the bylaw was adopted as a defensive measure but added that under the *Blasius* standard "[t]o the extent that I further conclude that the Supermajority Bylaw was adopted for the primary purpose of interfering with or impeding the stockholder franchise, the Bylaw cannot survive a *Unocal* review unless it is supported by a compelling justification." 771 A.2d at 324. The court thus first examined the bylaw "employing purely the *Unocal* standard" and then determined "whether the compelling justification of *Blasius*" was implicated. *Id.* The court acknowledged that "this order of examination may seem backwards" but explained that the "threat justification under the first prong of *Unocal*" and the effect of the bylaw "as considered under the second prong of *Unocal* . . . both bear on whether I can conclude that the defendants' ''primary purpose'' was 'to interfere with or impede exercise of the shareholder franchise.'" *Id.* (quoting *Stroud v. Grace*, 606 A.2d 75, 92 n.3 (Del. 1992)).

Applying *Unocal*, the court held that the supermajority bylaw provision was not a proportionate response to the threats facing Shorewood: price inadequacy (in this case not "a particularly dangerous" threat, for the reasons discussed in Chapter III, Section A 2 c (ii)), and substantive coercion and shareholder confusion (not a threat at all, the court concluded, for the reasons discussed in Chapter III, Section A 2 c (iii)).

Under *Unocal*, the court stated, a defensive measure is a proportionate response to a threat if the measure (1) is not preclusive, and (2) is within the range of reasonable defensive responses to the threat. 771 A.2d at 333.

With respect to preclusion, the court held that Shorewood's directors failed to demonstrate that the supermajority bylaw was not preclusive because the directors did not demonstrate that it was "'realistically' attainable for Chesapeake to prevail in a Consent Solicitation to amend the Shorewood bylaws." *Id.* (quoting *Unitrin*, 651 A.2d at 1389). Rather, the court concluded, "the Shorewood board simply made no judgment at all whether it was 'realistically' attainable for Chesapeake to amend the Shorewood bylaws in the face of either the 66 2/3% Supermajority Bylaw or the final 60% Supermajority Bylaw," and, indeed, the board "did not even discuss this issue." *Id.* at 334. The court described the fact that it was "'mathematically impossible' for Chesapeake to prevail in a consent solicitation involving a 90% turnout, assuming that the Shorewood board followed its announced intention to oppose such a Solicitation," as "[a]n indication of how blind the Shorewood board was to the relevance of whether the Supermajority Bylaw was preclusive." *Id.* Even at the time the board lowered the requirement to 60 percent, the court continued, the board "again ignored whether Chesapeake could 'realistically' attain the necessary votes to amend the Shorewood bylaws if the Shorewood board continued to oppose that endeavor." *Id.*

The court also pointed to the "host of other relevant issues" that Shorewood's board failed to consider, including "the historical turnout in Shorewood elections, the composition of the Shorewood electorate, and the self-interest of the management holders." *Id.* The board's "impoverished deliberations," the court continued, "were only once supplemented by expertise, and that consisted of less than five minutes of input from Crozier of Innisfree, who opined without much preparation that 95% of the electorate would vote" but was "asked no questions and never was asked to advise whether an insurgent could realistically attain victory in the face of the Supermajority Bylaw." *Id.* The court thus concluded that "nothing in the Shorewood board's deliberations is sufficient to help them carry the day" with respect to whether the supermajority bylaw provision was a proportionate response to any threat facing Shorewood, and that Shorewood's board "breached its duty of care in adopting the Supermajority Bylaw on a grossly uninformed basis." *Id.* at 334 & n.100.

Shorewood's proof at trial regarding preclusion, the court stated, "[a]t most" demonstrated that it was "theoretically possible for Chesapeake, given ideal circumstances, to meet the 60% threshold." *Id.* at 340. No "real-world evidence," however, demonstrated that "such ideal circumstances have ever come to pass for an insurgent in Chesapeake's position facing the concerted opposition of management holders controlling over 20% of the vote." *Id.* The court also pointed to the percentages of participating disinterested shares (i.e., shares other than the 14.9 percent block held by Chesapeake and the 24 percent block held by management) Chesapeake would be required to win in order to prevail in the consent solicitation under the following "extremely optimistic turnout assumptions": (1) assuming a 90 percent turnout rate, 88 percent of disinterested shares would be needed by Chesapeake to win, and (2) assuming a 95 percent turnout, 80 percent of disinterested shares would be needed by Chesapeake to win. *Id.* at 341.

The court then considered how these percentages would change if the court assumed that an over 5 percent block of Shorewood stock held by Ariel Capital Management, Inc. was included with Chesapeake's 14.9 percent block. Ariel had sold 14.9 percent of its more than 20 percent block to Chesapeake for $17.25 per share plus the difference between $17.25 and any winning Chesapeake bid or the difference between $17.25 and the midpoint between Chesapeake's highest bid and any other party's winning bid, thus giving Ariel an incentive to vote in favor of the highest bid over $17.25 even if the highest bid was not a Chesapeake bid. Based upon the assumption that Ariel would vote its shares with Chesapeake, Chesapeake would be required to obtain the following "extremely high" percentage of participating disinterested shares: (1) assuming a 90 percent turnout, 86.5 percent of disinterested shares would be needed by Chesapeake to win, and (2) assuming a 95 percent turnout, 78 percent of disinterested shares would be needed by Chesapeake to win. *Id.* at 311-12, 315, 342.

Under any of these scenarios, the court stated, "[t]he required disinterested majorities are more commonly associated with sham elections in dictatorships than contested elections in genuine republics" and are "unattainably high." *Id.* at 342.

With respect to whether the supermajority bylaw was within the range of reasonable defensive responses to the threat posed by Chesapeake, the court held that Shorewood's directors failed to demonstrate that the supermajority bylaw was a proportionate response. The reasonableness of a response to a threat, the court explained, turns upon "whether the defensive measure at issue 'is a statutorily authorized form of business decision which a board of directors may routinely make in a non-takeover context' and is 'limited and corresponded in degree or magnitude to the degree or magnitude of the threat . . . .'" *Id.* at 342-43 (quoting *Unitrin*, 651 A.2d at 1389). Here, the court stated, "[b]oth questions must be answered in the negative." *Id.* at 343.

First, the court held, "the decision to adopt a supermajority bylaw is not one 'routinely' made in the 'non-takeover' context." *Id.* "Rather, such bylaws are almost always a method of minimizing the ability of stockholders to interfere with the board's control or management of the company." *Id.* The court thus did not reach Chesapeake's argument that "a board of directors may not, by bylaw, require a supermajority vote to amend the bylaws" – a contention that the court described as "a novel and important issue of Delaware corporation law." *Id.* at 343 & n.113.

Second, the court also held, the supermajority bylaw was "an extremely aggressive and overreaching response to a very mild threat." *Id.* at 343. The court explained:

> The board already had a poison pill in place that gave it breathing room and precluded the Tender Offer. The Defensive Bylaws had eliminated Chesapeake's ability to call a special meeting, at which a majority of a quorum could act. This forced Chesapeake to proceed through the slower route of a Consent Solicitation with the minimum support of a majority of the outstanding shares. The Shorewood board controlled, per the Defensive Bylaws, the record date. This guaranteed adequate time for communications and counter-solicitation efforts, as well as for the board to develop and consider strategic alternatives.
>
> Given these factors, the board could have addressed the threat at hand through an aggressive communications plan. The board could have also taken Chesapeake up on its offer to negotiate price and structure, if the board truly believed that price inadequacy was the problem. It never considered these less extreme and more proportionate options.
>
> Instead, the board adopted a Supermajority Bylaw that can only be surmounted by obtaining over 88% of the disinterested votes, assuming a 90% turnout. Yet the board has been unable to demonstrate that such an outcome can be achieved. . . .
>
> Finally, the board did not even achieve its desired objective of vesting control in a majority of the disinterested shares. It most likely vested control of the vote in 88% of the disinterested shares. This is pretty wide of the target at which the board aimed. Even crediting that the board thought that more than a bare majority of disinterested stockholders should decide the question, the board could have selected a level within the realm of reason understandable by citizens of a republican democracy.

Id. at 343-44 (footnote omitted).

With respect to the *Blasius* standard of review, the court concluded that Shorewood's directors "clearly acted to 'interfere with or impede . . . [the exercise of] the shareholder franchise.'" *Id.* at 345 (quoting *Williams v. Geier*, 671 A.2d 1368, 1376 (Del. 1996)). The court stated that Shorewood's board adopted the supermajority bylaw "as a way of reducing the voting power of Chesapeake and Ariel" and that the "primary purpose for this action was to impair Chesapeake's ability to win a Consent Solicitation by increasing the required majority Chesapeake needed to obtain to preclusive levels." *Id.*

at 344-45. The court described "[t]he fact that the defendants originally raised the bar to a level where it was mathematically impossible for Chesapeake to win, assuming a 90% turnout" and "their failure to consider whether Chesapeake had a reasonable chance to succeed under the ultimate 60% Supermajority Bylaw" as "strong evidence" of the directors' "intent to preclude any consent solicitation by Chesapeake that would threaten their control." *Id.* at 345.

The *Blasius* compelling justification standard therefore applied, the court held, and the "mild threat" posed to Shorewood by Chesapeake's all cash for all shares tender offer and consent solicitation did not provide a compelling justification for the supermajority bylaw. *Id.* To the contrary, the court stated, the Shorewood directors' "belief that – because of their superior access to company information – they 'know[ ] better than . . . the stockholders' about 'who should comprise the board of directors' provides no legitimate justification at all." *Id.* (quoting *Blasius*, 564 A.2d at 662-63).

Finally, the court noted that it did not reach, but did not reject, Chesapeake's contention that the supermajority bylaw also was invalid under *Schnell v. Chris-Craft Industries, Inc.*, 285 A.2d 437 (Del. 1971), which holds that "inequitable action does not become permissible simply because it is legally possible." *Id.* at 439; *see also* Chapter III, Section H 1 a (discussing *Schnell* decision). The court stated that there was "ample evidence of entrenchment motives on the part of Shorewood's management . . . out to protect their lucrative offices, rather than the Shorewood stockholders." 771 A.2d at 345 n.123.

Section H 2 g

Add the following at the end of the second paragraph beginning and concluding on page 1287 (immediately after footnote 3999):

The Delaware Court of Chancery in *Diceon Electronics, Inc. v. Calvary Partners, L.P.*, 1990 Del. Ch. LEXIS 209, 1990 WL 237089 (Del. Ch. Dec. 27, 1990), similarly denied a request that an action seeking a declaratory judgment invalidating proposed bylaw amendments, scheduled to be voted upon at an annual meeting, be decided before the meeting. The bylaws, if adopted, would have imposed director qualifications that most or all of the corporation's incumbent directors could not meet and thus potentially could have forced their removal. 1990 Del. Ch. LEXIS 209, at *1, 1990 WL 237089, at *1. The court stated that "where (as here) the Court is asked to adjudicate the validity of a proposed measure that has not been – and may never be – adopted, compelling reasons to justify judicial intervention must be shown." 1990 Del. Ch. LEXIS 209, at *7, 1990 WL 237089, at *2. Applying this test, the court reasoned as follows:

> No such compelling reasons are shown here. Despite Diceon's contrary assertion, its shareholders do not need an adjudication of the by-law proposal's validity in order to cast an informed vote. The requisite information can be provided by the parties themselves, by disclosing in their proxy materials their respective positions concerning the legality of the proposal. Nor has Diceon shown that a post-meeting adjudication would unduly risk disrupting the corporation's affairs such that earlier intervention is mandated as a matter of practical necessity. Any adjudication (whether in a § 225 action or otherwise) would occur on an expedited schedule consistent with the Court's other commitments. And any claim of potential disruption occasioned by two groups of directors, each claiming to be lawfully in office, is speculative at this point and can be controlled by this Court's injunctive processes.

1990 Del. Ch. LEXIS 209, at *7-8, 1990 WL 237089, at *3. The Court of Chancery followed *Diceon* in *General Datacomm Industries, Inc. v. State of Wisconsin Investment Board*, 731 A.2d 818 (Del. Ch. 1999), a case involving a shareholder resolution requiring shareholder approval of any repricing of stock options. The *General Datacomm* case is discussed in Chapter III, Section G 3.

Section H 3 c

Replace the Silverman citation in footnote 4098 on page 1307 with the following:

N.Y.L.J., Mar. 17, 1997, at 27 (N.Y. Sup. Ct. N.Y. Co.), *aff'd*, 248 A.D.2d 332, 670 N.Y.S.2d 95 (N.Y. App. Div. 1st Dep't 1998).

Add the following at the end of the paragraph beginning and concluding on page 1308 (immediately after footnote 4101):

An appellate court affirmed on the ground that the trial court "correctly concluded that plaintiff did not have standing to prosecute a derivative action on behalf of the corporate defendant Loral Space and Communications Limited since the claims plaintiff sought to bring in a derivative capacity were not properly the claims of Loral Space but rather those of the Loral Corporation, an entity of which plaintiff is no longer a stockholder, her shares therein having been previously tendered for cash in the course of the Loral Corporation's merger with the Lockheed Corporation." *Silverman v. Schwartz*, 248 A.D.2d 332, 670 N.Y.S.2d 95 (N.Y. App. Div. 1st Dep't 1998). The court added that "even if plaintiff had standing, the complaint would have been properly dismissed on the ground that the documentary evidence offered by defendants conclusively establishes that the Loral Corporation was contractually bound to make the payment to which plaintiff objects." *Id.*

Section H 3 g

Replace the paragraph beginning and concluding on page 1329 through the paragraph beginning on page 1331 and concluding on page 1332 (including footnotes 4242 through 4259) with the following:

The Delaware Court of Chancery in *Hills Stores Co. v. Bozic*, 1997 Del. Ch. LEXIS 47, 1997 WL 153823 (Del. Ch. Mar. 25, 1997), denied a motion to dismiss a claim that the directors of Hills Stores Company breached their fiduciary duties by establishing and funding trusts to provide for the immediate payment of more than $30 million in severance benefits for six key executives and a consultant pursuant to employment agreements providing for these payments in the event of a change of control not approved by the corporation's board. 1997 Del. Ch. LEXIS 47, at *7-11, 1997 WL 153823, at *2-3.

Plaintiffs alleged that the employment agreements providing for these severance benefits had been adopted in August 1994, three days after Dickstein Partners, Inc. had commenced a consent solicitation, and that the benefits would be triggered by any change in control of Hills Department Stores Company, a regional retailer owned by Hill Stores that operated 156 stores. Litigation challenging the employment agreements was commenced by shareholders shortly after the employment agreements were entered into and settled with the consent of Dickstein, which agreed as part of the settlement to terminate its consent solicitation. 1997 Del. Ch. LEXIS 47, at *4-5, 1997 WL 153823, at *1-2. In May 1995, Dickstein commenced another consent solicitation. According to plaintiffs' complaint, the funding trusts were created after the directors concluded that Dickstein's consent solicitation would succeed and that Dickstein would elect a new slate of directors, who then would approve an offer by Dickstein to purchase all shares of Hills Stores. 1997 Del. Ch. LEXIS 47, at *5-6, 1997 WL 153823, at *2. At the same time that the funding trusts were established, the directors refused to approve Dickstein's proposed change in control, and amended the employment agreements to provide for severance payments upon a change of control not just of Hills Department Stores but also Hill Stores itself. This change was made, according to the directors, "simply to correct a clerical error in the agreements." 1997 Del. Ch. LEXIS 47, at *6, 1997 WL 153823, at *2. Plaintiffs alleged that the creation and funding of the trusts caused Hills Department Stores to breach certain loan covenants and impair the relationships Hills Stores and Hills Department Stores Company had with these lenders. *Id.*

Plaintiffs also alleged that the last business day before the results of the proxy contest were to be certified, the trustee was provided with a schedule of payments greater than the payments provided for in the employment agreements, and on the day the results were certified the key executives who were the beneficiaries of the employment agreements resigned from their positions and received their severance benefits. *Id.* Two weeks later, Dickstein announced that it would not acquire (or seek to sell) Hills Stores stock due to the costs of the change of control. *Id.*

The directors contended that the terms of the employment agreements required that they not approve any proposed change in control that was the result of a contested election, and that as a result the decision not to approve the change of control was a proper exercise of business judgment. 1997 Del. Ch. LEXIS 47, at *7, 1997 WL 153823, at *2. The court, however, held that this contract interpretation issue could not be decided in the context of a motion to dismiss. 1997 Del. Ch. LEXIS 47, at *8, 1997 WL 153823, at *3.

The court also held that "[e]ven if the former directors' interpretation of the agreements is correct, or they had a good faith belief that it was, it is questionable how amending the agreements to apply to a change in control of Hill Stores or establishing trusts for the purpose of immediately paying the severance benefits were in the interest of the corporation." *Id.* The court rejected the directors' contention that the amendment to the agreement simply corrected a clerical error as "a matter of proof that cannot be decided on the face of the complaint." *Id.* The court rejected the directors' contention that "it was surely proper to provide for the performance of the agreements" because "that does not answer the plaintiffs' allegation that establishing the trusts harmed the interest of the corporation by causing it to breach covenants and depriving the new board of an opportunity to persuade the key executives to remain with the corporation." 1997 Del. Ch. LEXIS 47, at *8-9, 1997 WL 153823, at *3.

The court added that the challenged acts were defensive in nature, and thus "it is likely that some or all of the defendants' conduct at issue in this case will be subject to enhanced scrutiny" pursuant to the *Unocal* doctrine. 1997 Del. Ch. LEXIS 47, at *9, 1997 WL 153823 at *3. This enhanced scrutiny, the court stated, "cannot be given on a motion to dismiss for failure to state a claim upon which relief can be granted." 1997 Del. Ch. LEXIS 47, at *9, 1997 WL 153823, at *3; *see also* 1997 Del. Ch. LEXIS 47, at *3, 1997 WL 153823, at *1 (same); Chapter III, Section A 2 a (discussing this aspect of *Unocal* doctrine). Additionally, the court stated, "[e]ven if the business judgment presumption applies," the plaintiffs' allegation that the directors acted for an improper purpose was sufficient to defeat the motion to dismiss. 1997 Del. Ch. LEXIS 47, at *10, 1997 WL 153823, at *3. The court reasoned as follows with respect to this conclusion:

> Directors must always act in what they believe in good faith to be in the best interest of the corporation. The plaintiffs allege that the defendants acted in bad faith. It may turn out that the plaintiffs' proof does not overcome the presumption that the former directors acted in good faith. But on a motion to dismiss, the court assesses the legal sufficiency of the complaint, not the probability of success. The plaintiffs have pled sufficient factually specific allegations to create a fair inference that in reacting to their defeat by the Dickstein Partners' nominees the former directors might have been motivated by concerns other than the best interest of the corporation and its stockholders.

1997 Del. Ch. LEXIS 47, at *10-11, 1997 WL 153823, at *3 (footnote omitted).

In a subsequent decision on a motion for summary judgment, the court found that undisputed facts warranted dismissed of most of plaintiffs' claims. *Hills Stores Co. v. Bozic*, 769 A.2d 88 (Del. Ch. 2000). The facts, as stated by the court in its summary judgment opinion – as opposed to the facts alleged in plaintiffs' complaint, which had been accepted as true for the purpose of the previously decided motion to dismiss – were as follows.

In August 1994, Dickstein Partners Inc. commenced a consent solicitation seeking to remove four members of the Hills Stores Company board and replace them with Dickstein nominees pledged to support a stock repurchase program proposed by Dickstein. After obtaining advice from outside counsel and financial advisors, the Hills board determined to oppose Dickstein's proposal and to enter into employment agreements with seven of the corporation's top executives and a full-time consultant who also was the corporation's chief merchant. These employment agreements were intended to provide their recipients, who had other employment options, "enough security to allow them to focus on their jobs without distraction by Dickstein's overtures." *Id.* at 91.

A "double trigger" approach was utilized: the right to severance was triggered not just by a "single trigger" change in control, but by one of two "double triggers": (i) a change in control followed by a demotion or termination, or (ii) a change in control not approved by a majority of the corporation's continuing directors, with the term continuing director defined to include any of the corporation's directors at the time the plan was adopted and any successor to a continuing director recommended for election or elected to succeed a continuing director by a majority of the continuing directors then serving the corporation's board, so long as the continuing director was not affiliated with the acquiring person. *Id.* at 92. The court stated that the primary reason motivating the double trigger approach was the ability to use the double trigger as negotiating leverage in a way that could not be accomplished with a single trigger. The court explained:

> [T]he double trigger approach gave the Hills board the ability to "deliver management" to a friendly acquiror in a negotiated transaction. The flip side of this ability was that the board could refuse to approve the Change in Control "if the prospec-

> tive acquiror didn't seem to be offering sufficiently for the company . . . ." That is, the Hills board could use the double trigger as negotiating leverage. If an acquiror agreed to the board's terms, the board could approve the Change in Control and allow the acquiror the opportunity to keep the Covered Executives or, at the very least, avoid the Severance. If an acquiror did not agree to the board's terms, the board could protect the expectations of the Covered Executives and deter the unwanted overture by failing to approve the Change in Control. This guaranteed the Covered Executives their Severance while increasing the potential acquiror's cost of acquisition.

Id. (quoting deposition testimony).

Litigation challenging the employment agreements was commenced by shareholders shortly after the employment agreements were entered into and then settled with the consent of Dickstein. The settlement ended Dickstein's 1994 consent solicitation and resulted in a release of "all claims . . . that arise now or hereafter out of . . . the Employment Agreements" that "had been brought or could have been brought" by Hills or Hills shareholders. *Id.* at 93-94. After the settlement was signed but before it was approved by the court, Hills adopted a Supplemental Executive Retirement Plan (the "SERP") covering twenty top executives at Hills. Unlike the employment agreements, the SERP benefits vested automatically upon a change in control. *Id.* at 94.

In May 1995, Dickstein proposed an acquisition of all outstanding Hills shares in exchange for $22 per share in cash plus a $5 payment in kind ("PIK") bond. At the same time, Dickstein nominated a slate of directors for election at the corporation's annual meeting on June 23, 1995. The Hills board, again acting with the advice of outside counsel and financial advisors, "determined that the offer was inadequate and shakily financed and that Dickstein's proposed strategy for the company was harmful. Rather than erecting substantial defensive measures, however, the Hills board decided to let the stockholders decide whether to accept the Dickstein offer for themselves in a board election contest at the Hills annual meeting." *Id.* at 89-90. In June 1995, the Hills board mailed proxy materials to shareholders that explained the board's reason for rejecting Dickstein's proposal, recommended against the election of the Dickstein slate, and informed shareholders that a change in control could trigger the employment agreements and could require Hills to refinance senior notes and its working capital credit facility at a cost of approximately $60 to $70 million. *Id.* at 97-98. Dickstein's proxy materials "acknowledged the same potential effects" and assured Hills' stockholders that Dickstein "had the wherewithal to refinance the company's debt and bear the other costs associated with a Change of Control (including the Severance and SERP obligations) and to acquire all the shares of the company for $22 in cash plus $5 in PIK." *Id.* at 98, 101.

During the days leading up to the vote, the Hills board authorized the creation of "rabbi trusts" and funded those trusts using funds from the corporation's revolving credit facility. These trusts ensured that all amounts due pursuant to the employment agreements would be paid automatically upon the occurrence of events giving the covered executives the right to payment under the terms of the employment agreements. *Id.* at 99. The Hills board also corrected an error in the employment agreements that triggered the right to severance upon an unapproved change of control of Hills' wholly owned Hills Department Stores Company subsidiary rather than of Hills. The court rejected a challenge to this reformation of the employment agreements on the ground that "[i]f ever there was a clear case of scrivener's error justifying reformation, this was it." *Id.* at 94 n.29.

On June 22, 1995, the day before the election, at a time when "the board knew that it was probable that Dickstein would win the election," the Hills board met in response to a demand by Dickstein that the board vote to approve the Dickstein change in control solely for the purpose of not triggering the employment agreements. "[A]fter receiving advice from legal counsel, the members of the Hills board without an interest in that decision unanimously decided not to approve the Dickstein change in control" because they believed that the change in control was "a serious threat to Hills" and because Hills "had promised the covered executives severance in such a situation." *Id.* at 89-90, 99-101.

Dickstein won the election, and the "known and foreseeable risks" Dickstein had assumed occurred: the covered executives resigned and received their severance, the company's creditors terminated their debt agreements, and Dickstein was forced to refinance the corporation's debt. *Id.* at 90, 101. "Despite the fact that Dickstein had assured Hills' stockholders it had the wherewithal to refinance the company's debt and bear the other costs associated with a Change in Control" and acquire all shares for $22 in cash per share plus a $5 PIK bond, Dickstein "never consummated its acquisition offer nor did it conduct an auction." *Id.* Instead, Dickstein determined to manage the company and, in September 1995, caused Hills to sue the former Hills board for breach of fiduciary duty, breach of contract and unjust enrichment. *Id.*

The court held that the decision not to approve the change in control solely for the purpose of not triggering the employment agreements was a defensive measure subject to review under *Unocal*'s heightened scrutiny. The court stated that "[a]lthough the Employment Agreements are not so self-evidently defensive as a poison pill, their origin and purpose convince me that they have objectively defensive characteristics justifying heightened scrutiny." *Id.* at 106. The agreements, the court explained, "were concededly adopted as a 'reaction to a perceived 'threat to corporate policy and effectiveness which touches upon issues of control''": the board "feared that it would lose management in the face of Dickstein's 1994 overtures" and determined to adopt a "double trigger approach" in order to provide the board "negotiating leverage in the context of a change of control battle" because the contractual change in control approval process provision could be used "as an incentive to a friendly transaction, as a tool to extract a higher bid from a potential acquiror, or as a financial barrier to an acquisition bid the board believed was inadvisable." *Id.* (quoting

Stroud v. Grace, 606 A.2d 75, 82 (Del. 1992) and *Gilbert v. El Paso Co.*, 575 A.2d 1131, 1144 (Del. 1990)).

Delaware law, the court stated, "has assured stockholders that the fact that the court has approved a board's decision to put defenses in place on a clear day does not mean that the board will escape its burden to justify its use of those defenses in the heat of battle under the *Unocal* standard." *Id.* at 106-07. To the contrary, the court continued, "[t]he 'omnipresent specter that a board may be acting primarily in its own interests'" that underlies the *Unocal* standard "is if anything, more ominously haunting when a board is faced with an actual contest for control, such as was the case here, and must decide how to deploy its defensive arsenal." *Id.* at 107 (quoting *Unocal*, 493 A.2d at 954).

The court also rejected a contention that the business judgment rule rather than *Unocal* provided the appropriate standard of judicial review because, according to the Hills directors, they "let the stockholders decide who should run the company in a fair election" and thus "there was no evidence that the Hills board decided to trigger the Severance in order to deter the Dickstein Change in Control." *Id.* The court pointed to "the concededly defensive capabilities the double trigger gave the Hills board" and stated that "Dickstein all but invited the board to sit down with it and negotiate an increase in its bid in exchange for a board decision not to trigger the Severance." *Id.* The board thus "had the chance to exercise the sort of negotiating leverage the double trigger was intended to give it" and the board's "decision how to exercise that leverage in an actual conflict is entitled to no more deference than its original decision to give itself that leverage." *Id.*

Turning to the application of the *Unocal* standard, the court described "the board's prior decision to promise the Covered Executives severance in the context of a non-Approved Change in Control and the plaintiffs' waiver of the right to challenge that basic promise" in the settlement of the case challenging that decision as "critically important foundational facts" in evaluating the board's conduct under *Unocal* that "greatly restrict the court's ability to second-guess the board's decision to trigger the Severance if the court concludes that the board has met its burden to demonstrate that it made a good faith and informed judgment that the Dickstein Change in Control was a threat to Hills and its stockholders." *Id.* at 108. The court explained that as a result of the waiver of the right to challenge the validity of the employment agreements, plaintiffs "cannot in good faith claim that the Severance is a disproportionate response to a situation where the Hills board, on a good faith and informed basis, concluded that a Change in Control was adverse to the interests of Hills and its stockholders." *Id.* at 107-08. "[T]o find otherwise," the court stated, "would be to say that the plaintiffs waived nothing when they agreed not to challenge the adoption of the Employment Agreements." *Id.* at 107.

The court then found that a majority of the Hills board had no self-interest in the employment agreements, that plaintiffs "produced no evidence rebutting the board's showing that the Dickstein Change in Control was reasonably considered by it to be dangerous," and that the directors' determination to trigger the obligation to make severance payments under the agreements because "they believed that the Dickstein Change in Control was a harmful threat and because they believed that the company should live up to its contractual commitments was a reasonable decision." *Id.* at 109. The court added that in assessing the reasonableness of the board's decision it was "[n]otable . . . that if Dickstein had been capable of doing what it assured the Hills stockholders it could do – consummating an acquisition of Hills that required the payment of the Severance and the refinancing of the company's debt and senior notes – this case would not be here." *Id.*

The court rejected "the narrow prism through which the plaintiffs would have me view the board's actions" – i.e., the duty of the Hills directors on June 22, 1995 "to consider the narrow question of whether, if the Dickstein slate prevailed, as the board thought likely, it was in the best interests of Hills to trigger the Severance rights of the Covered Executives." *Id.* at 108. According to plaintiffs' view of the case, the court stated, the board was to ignore the fact that "the Covered Executives had remained loyal employees during a period of corporate turbulence and had resisted the opportunity to go to work for other employers," the fact that "the Covered Employees had signed contracts that gave them the right to Severance unless the board *affirmatively approved* a Change in Control," the fact that these contracts "were subject to an implied covenant of good faith and fair dealing," and the fact that the board "had in good faith and with the advice of outside financial and legal advisors reached the judgment that the Dickstein Change in Control was adverse to the interests of the company and its stockholders." *Id.* The court continued:

> [T]he logic of this approach escapes my comprehension. Unless the Employment Agreements are read as containing a wholly illusory promise of Severance when the board does not approve a Change of Control, the plaintiffs' approach is baffling. Because I do not believe that a responsible board could read the Employment Agreements as providing the Covered Executives with an essentially phony promise, I do not accept the plaintiffs' approach.

Id. Rather, the court concluded, the Hills board "would have exercised bad faith under the Employment Agreements if it had voted to approve the Change in Control simply so as to avoid triggering the Covered Executives' right to Severance." *Id.* at 109. The court observed that "[a]fter one party to a contract has given its consideration for a promised payment, it is often in the other party's narrow, selfish interest to accept that consideration and avoid the promised payment." *Id.* "Acting on that interest," the court stated, "is commonly referred to as a breach of contract." *Id.*

The court then noted the possibility that board action found to be proper under heightened scrutiny nonetheless may be invalid because it resulted from breaches of the duty of care or loyalty, but held that "plaintiffs have not come close to generating a triable issue" on either of these theories. *Id.*

With respect to the duty of care, the court stated that the plaintiffs' contention that the Hills board "ignored or gave inadequate weight to certain factors" simply "rehashes their view that on June 22, 1995 the board was supposed to blind itself to its contractual obligations and its previous good-faith determination that the Dickstein Change to Control was inadvisable." *Id.* at 110. The evidence, the court stated, was "clear": "the board believed that the departure of the Covered Executives would hurt the company; knew that at least some, if not all, of the covered executives were likely to depart if granted Severance; and understood the size of the payments to be made to the Covered Executives." *Id.* This evidence, the court held, "simply will not support a finding of gross negligence in the face of the substantial evidence of the board's careful consideration of the merits of the Dickstein Change in Control, the board's decision to allow the stockholders to choose that Change in Control in a fair election, and the board's reliance upon advice from respected outside advisors." *Id.* The court added that the four directors who were named as defendants in the case who were not beneficiaries of the challenged employment agreements also were protected from liability for money damages by an exculpatory charter provision adopted under Section 102(b)(7) of the Delaware General Corporation Law. *Id.* at 110 n.73.

With respect to the duty of loyalty, the court stated that the majority of the Hills board had no financial interest in the challenged employment agreements, that there was no evidence that the three interested directors on the Hills board "either possessed the capability to or in fact did exercise undue influence on the disinterested majority," and that "the board's unrebutted showing that it legitimately opposed the Change of Control for good faith reasons makes any inference of a loyalty breach impossible." *Id.* at 109.

The court, however, denied defendants' motion for summary judgment and granted summary judgment in plaintiffs' favor on breach of contract and unjust enrichment claims. The court found that the three members of the Hills board who received employment agreement payments were paid amounts in excess of the amounts required by the employment agreements because Hills mistakenly included discretionary non-mandatory "special bonuses" paid in 1995 in its calculation of the severance payments owed under the employment agreements. The court stated that the employment agreements clearly and unambiguously required payment only of amounts that covered employees "would have been entitled" to receive if they remained employed and the "special bonuses" were not bonuses to which the covered employees would have been entitled to receive if they had remained employed. *Id.* at 111-12.

Section H 4

Replace "5th ed. 1995" with "6th ed. 2000" in the Fleischer citation in footnote 4305 on page 1339.

Section H 5

Replace 6-120 with 6-125 and replace "1998" with "2001" in the Balotti citation in footnote 4326 on page 1343.

Section H 6

Add the following at the end of footnote 4330 on page 1344:

See also Apple Computer, Inc. v. Exponential Tech., Inc., 1999 Del. Ch. LEXIS 9, at *38, 1999 WL 39547, at *10 (Del. Ch. Jan. 21, 1999) ("[p]ursuit of a legal claim in court is well within the range of acceptable – one may even say, common – activities in which corporations engage").

Replace "5th ed. 1995" with "6th ed. 2000" in the Fleischer citation in footnote 4334 on page 1345.

Replace "1997" with "2000" in the Lipton citation in footnote 4334 on page 1345.

Add the following at the end of the bullets in the paragraph beginning on page 1345 and concluding on page 1347 (immediately after footnote 4348):

- *Safety-Kleen Corp. v. Laidlaw Environmental Services, Inc.*, No. 97 C 3003, Tr. at 34 (N.D. Ill. Mar. 5, 1998) ("the entry of an injunction at this point would irreparably taint the possibility of a fair vote"); and
- *BBC Capital Markets, Inc. v. Carver Bancorp, Inc.*, No. 17743, Tr. at 10-11 (Del. Ch. Feb. 16, 2000) ("[f]urther comment by the Court on the merits of the issue and the factual dispute would be inappropriate, in my view, and could be misused by either party in support of their positions taken with the Carver shareholders").

Section I 1 a

Add the following at the end of footnote 4400 on page 1356:

See also Strassburger v. Earley, 752 A.2d 557, 572 (Del. Ch. 2000) ("[t]he corporation may . . . lawfully repurchase shares of particular stockholders selectively, without being required to offer to repurchase the shares of all stockholders generally").

CHAPTER IV

Section A

Add the following at the end of footnote 1 on page 1380:

See also Elf Atochem N. Am., Inc. v. Jaffari, 727 A.2d 286, 293 & n.39 (Del. 1999) ("the derivative form of action permits an individual shareholder to bring 'suit to enforce a corporate cause of action against officers, directors and third parties'") (quoting *Kamen v. Kemper Fin. Servs., Inc.*, 500 U.S. 90, 95 (1991) (citation omitted)); *id.* at n.39 ("in derivative action, shareholder 'stands in the shoes' of the corporation") (quoting *Schleiff v. Baltimore & Ohio R.R. Co.*, 130 A.2d 321, 327 (Del. Ch. 1955)).

Add the following at the end of footnote 4 on page 1380:

See also Parnes v. Bally Entm't Corp., 722 A.2d 1243, 1245 (Del. 1999) ("[a] derivative claim is one that is brought by a stockholder, on behalf of the corporation, to recover for harms done to the corporation"; "a stockholder suing derivatively is bringing a corporate claim, not a personal one"); *In re Trump Hotels S'holder Derivative Litig.*, 2000 U.S. Dist. LEXIS 13550, at *16-17, 2000 WL 1371317, at *5 (S.D.N.Y. Sept. 21, 2000); *Pace v. Jordan*, 999 S.W.2d 615, 622 (Tex. App. 1999).

Add the following at the end of footnote 5 on page 1380:

See also McDermott, Will & Emery v. Superior Court, 83 Cal. App. 4th 378, 382, 99 Cal. Rptr. 2d 622, 625 (Cal. Ct. App. 2000) ("A derivative action . . . does not transfer the cause of action from the corporation to the shareholders. Rather, the cause of action in a shareholder derivative suit belongs to and remains with the corporation.").

Add the following at the end of footnote 7 on page 1381:

See also McDermott, 83 Cal. App. 4th at 382, 99 Cal. Rptr. 2d at 625.

Add the following at the end of the paragraph beginning on page 1380 and concluding on page 1381 (immediately after footnote 7):

"Any claim belonging to the corporation may, in appropriate circumstances, be asserted in a derivative action," including claims that do and do not involve corporate mismanagement or breach of fiduciary duty. *Midland Food Servs., LLC v. Castle Hill Holdings V, LLC*, 1999 Del. Ch. LEXIS 162, at *28, 1999 WL 550360, at *9 (Del. Ch. July 16, 1999).

Add the following at the end of footnote 9 on page 1381:

See also Parnes, 722 A.2d at 1245.

Add the following at the end of footnote 10 on page 1381:

See also Parnes, 722 A.2d at 1245; *Trump Hotels*, 2000 U.S. Dist. LEXIS 13550, at *16-17, 2000 WL 1371317, at *5.

Add the following at the end of footnote 11 on page 1381:

See also McDermott, 83 Cal. App. 4th at 382, 99 Cal. Rptr. 2d at 625.

Add the following at the end of footnote 13 on page 1382:

See also Weber v. King, 110 F. Supp. 2d 124, 133 (E.D.N.Y. 2000) (collecting cases); *Trump Hotels*, 2000 U.S. Dist. LEXIS 13550, at *17, 2000 WL 1371317, at *5; *Trabucco v. Carlile*, 57 F. Supp. 2d 1074, 1076 (D. Or. 1999).

Replace "7-257" with "7-252" and replace "1996" with "Supp. 1998/99" in the Model Act § 7.40-7.47 citation in footnote 23 on page 1384.

Section A 1

Add the following at the end of footnote 31 on page 1386:

See also IM2 Merchandising & Mfg., Inc. v. Tirex Corp., 2000 Del. Ch. LEXIS 156, at *19, 2000 WL 1664168, at *6 (Del. Ch. Nov. 2, 2000); *Ash v. McCall*, 2000 Del. Ch. LEXIS 144, at *38, 2000 WL 1370341, at *1 (Del. Ch. Sept. 15, 2000); *Leung v. Schuler*, 2000 Del. Ch. LEXIS 41, at *25-26, 2000 WL 264328, at *7 (Del. Ch. Feb. 29, 2000).

Add the following at the end of the paragraph beginning and concluding on page 1386 (immediately after footnote 33):

A shareholder may challenge a stock issuance authorized before the person became a shareholder but not completed until after the person became a shareholder, *Leung*, 2000 Del. Ch. LEXIS 41, at *25-28, 2000 WL 264328, at *8, but a shareholder who purchases stock in an initial public offering may not challenge a board decision prior to the offering to sell stock to board members in the initial public offering at a price lower than the price offered to the public. *7547 Partners v. Beck*, 682 A.2d 160, 162-63 (Del. 1996).

Replace "1996" with "Supp. 1998/99" in the Model Act § 7.41 citation in footnote 34 on page 1386.

Replace "7-340" with "7-332" in the Model Act § 7.41 citation in footnote 35 on page 1387.

Replace "1998" with "2001" in the Wright citation in footnote 45 on page 1388.

Add the following at the end of the paragraph beginning and concluding on page 1389 (immediately after footnote 47):

The owner of a debenture (including a convertible debenture) is not a shareholder and does not have standing to bring a derivative claim on behalf of the corporation. *Benjamin v. Kim*, 1999 U.S. Dist. LEXIS 6089, at *45 n.15, 1999 WL 249706, at *13 n.15 (S.D.N.Y. Apr. 27, 1999) (citing *Brooks v. Weiser*, 57 F.R.D. 491, 493 (S.D.N.Y. 1972) and what now appears at 19 Am. Jur. 2d Corps. § 2347 (1986 & Supp. 2001)).

Section A 2

Add the following at the end of footnote 49 on page 1389:

See also Kona Enters., Inc. v. Estate of Bishop, 179 F.3d 767, 769-70 (9th Cir. 1999); *Button v. Hodapp*, 1999 U.S. Dist. LEXIS 13966, at *2-4, 1999 WL 46635, at *1-2 (S.D.N.Y. Feb. 1, 1999) (citing additional cases); *Lichtenberg v. Besicorp Group Inc.*, 43 F. Supp. 2d 376, 387 (S.D.N.Y. 1999); *Parnes v. Bally Entm't Corp.*, 722 A.2d 1243, 1244-45 (Del. 1999); *Grimes v. Donald*, 2000 Del. Ch. LEXIS 162, at *8 & n.6, 2000 WL 1788784, at *3 & n.6 (Del. Ch. Nov. 30, 2000); *IM2 Merchandising & Mfg., Inc. v. Tirex Corp.*, 2000 Del. Ch. LEXIS 156, at *19, 2000 WL 1664168, at *6 (Del. Ch. Nov. 2, 2000); *Ash v. McCall*, 2000 Del. Ch. LEXIS 144, at *38, 2000 WL 1370341, at *11 (Del. Ch. Sept. 15, 2000); *Oliver v. Boston Univ.*, 2000 Del. Ch. LEXIS 104, at *17 & n.6, 2000 WL 1038197, at *6 & n.6 (Del. Ch. July 18, 2000); *Turner v. Bernstein*, 1999 Del. Ch. LEXIS 18, at *36-37, 45, 1999 WL

66532, at *10, 11 (Del. Ch. Feb. 9, 1999); *In re First Interstate Bancorp Consol. S'holder Litig.*, 729 A.2d 851, 867 (Del. Ch. 1998), *aff'd sub nom. Bradley v. First Interstate Corp.*, 748 A.2d 913 (unpublished opinion, text available at 2000 Del. LEXIS 113 and 2000 WL 383788) (Del. Mar. 21, 2000); *Ciullo v. Orange & Rockland Utils., Inc.*, 271 A.D.2d 369, 369, 706 N.Y.S.2d 428, 429 (N.Y. App. Div. 1st Dep't), *leave to appeal denied*, 95 N.Y.2d 760, 737 N.E.2d 952, 714 N.Y.S.2d 710 (2000); *Silverman v. Schwartz*, 248 A.D.2d 332, 670 N.Y.S.2d 95 (N.Y. App. Div. 1st Dep't 1998).

Add the following at the end of footnote 53 on page 1390:

See also Ash, 2000 Del. Ch. LEXIS 144, at *47 & n.48, 2000 WL 1370341, at *13 & n.48; *Lewis v. Ward*, 2000 Del. Ch. LEXIS 126, at *1-2, 2000 WL 1336721, at *1 (Del. Ch. Apr. 25, 2000); *First Interstate*, 729 A.2d at 867. *But see Lichtenberg*, 43 F. Supp. 2d at 387 n.9 ("there is no indication that New York courts would recognize such an exception").

Add the following at the end of footnote 82 on page 1395:

See also Prof'l Mgmt. Assocs., Inc. v. Coss, 598 N.W.2d 406, 413 (Minn. Ct. App. 1999), *review denied*, 1999 Minn. LEXIS 780 (Minn. Nov. 23, 1999) (following *Blasband v. Rales*, 971 F.2d 1034 (3d Cir. 1992), and holding under Delaware law that a shareholder of a corporation that is merged into another corporation in a stock-for-stock merger and that becomes a wholly owned subsidiary of the second corporation has standing to continue a derivative suit brought on behalf of the first corporation before the merger, but the suit must be amended to allege that it is on behalf of the second corporation).

Add the following at the end of the paragraph beginning of page 1394 and concluding on page 1395 (immediately after footnote 82):

The Delaware Court of Chancery in *First Interstate* stated that the Third Circuit's ruling in *Blasband* was "inconsistent with the clear holding" of *Lewis v. Anderson*, 477 A.2d 1040 (Del. 1984). 729 A.2d at 868 & n.18. The Delaware Supreme Court affirmed, stating that plaintiff's claims were derivative claims and "[a]ccordingly, Appellant lacks standing to assert those claims." *Bradley v. First Interstate Corp.*, 748 A.2d 913 (unpublished opinion, text available at 2000 Del. LEXIS 113, at *1 and 2000 WL 383788, at *1) (Del. Mar. 21, 2000) (citing *Andersen*); *see also Golaine v. Edwards*, 1999 Del. Ch. LEXIS 237, at *11, 1999 WL 1271882, at *4 (Del. Ch. Dec. 21, 1999) (stating, in case involving a stock-for-stock merger, that "plaintiff Golaine and all the other Duracell stockholders lost their status as Duracell stockholders and therefore their standing to sue derivatively on behalf of Duracell").

The Court of Chancery in *Ash v. McCall*, 2000 Del. Ch. LEXIS 144, 2000 WL 1370341 (Del. Ch. Sept. 15, 2000), in a decision written by Chancellor William B. Chandler III, stated that "*First Interstate* clearly expressed the Delaware Courts' rejection of the Third Circuit's holding in *Blasband v. Rales* that the combination of a direct pre-merger equity interest (in the subsidiary) and a direct but diluted post-merger equity interest (in the surviving corporation) is sufficient to meet the common law continuous ownership requirement necessary to prosecute pre-merger derivative claims." 2000 Del. Ch. LEXIS 144, at *45, 2000 WL 1370341, at *13. Thus, "[t]he Third Circuit's view . . . is not the law in Delaware." 2000 Del. Ch. LEXIS 144, at *45-46, 2000 WL 1370341, at *13. Chancellor Chandler, however, noted that he found the Third Circuit's view "persuasive" and "consistent with basic economic principles, as well as fundamental principles of equity and fairness," but stated that in light of *Andersen* "I am not free to follow" *Blasband* and that any change of the law in Delaware on this subject "will have to come from the Delaware Supreme Court." 2000 Del. Ch. LEXIS 144, at *46 n.47, 2000 WL 1370341, at *13 n.47.

Replace the Drain citation in footnote 83 on page 1395 with the following:

685 A.2d 119 (Pa. Super. 1996), *aff'd on other grounds*, 712 A.2d 273 (Pa. 1998).

Add the following at the end of the paragraph beginning and concluding on page 1395 (immediately after footnote 87):

On an appeal to the Supreme Court of Pennsylvania, the defendants in the case "abandoned the argument made below that the policyholders cannot bring suit on behalf of a corporation that no longer exists after a merger." *Drain v. Covenant Life Ins. Co.*, 712 A.2d 273, 278 (Pa. 1998).

Add the following at the end of footnote 95 on page 1396:

See also First Interstate, 729 A.2d at 868 (rejecting the result in *Gaillard v. Natomos Co.*, 173 Cal. App. 3d 410, 219 Cal. Rptr. 74 (Cal. Ct. App. 1985), in favor of the "clear and controlling . . . teaching of the Delaware Supreme Court in *Lewis v. Anderson*").

Add the following at the end of the third sentence (immediately after footnote 95) in the paragraph beginning on page 1396 and concluding on page 1397:

A federal court construing California law in *In re General Instrument Securities Litigation*, 23 F. Supp. 2d 867 (N.D. Ill. 1998), followed *Gaillard* and held that "where a plaintiff loses his ownership as a result of the alleged wrongdoing" California law is not "strictly construed to prevent such a plaintiff from maintaining a derivative action." *Id.* at 872.

Replace "7-341" with "7-333" and replace "1996" with "Supp. 1998/99" in the Model Act § 7.41 citation in footnote 101 on page 1397.

Section A 3

Add the following at the end of footnote 122 on page 1400:

See also In re Fuqua Indus., Inc. S'holder Litig., 752 A.2d 126, 129 n.2 (Del. Ch. 1999) ("Unlike Rule 23.1 of the Federal Rules of Civil Procedure, Court of Chancery Rule 23.1 does not explicitly include an adequacy requirement. In *Katz v. Plant Industries*, the Court held that the adequacy requirement of Federal Rule 23.1 also applies to Court of Chancery Rule 23.1 as the adequacy language of the federal rule made explicit what was already 'implicitly a part of the federal as well as Delaware rule.' *Katz v. Plant Industries, Inc.*, Del. Ch., C.A. No. 6407, Marvel, C. (Oct. 27, 1981).").

Add the following at the end of the first sentence (immediately after footnote 130) of the paragraph beginning on page 1400 and concluding on page 1401:

Additional examples of Delaware decisions discussing the requirement that a derivative plaintiff must fairly and adequately represent the interests of the corporation include *In re Dairy Mart Convenience Stores, Inc. Derivative Litigation*, 1999 Del. Ch. LEXIS 94, at *25-35, 1999 WL 350473, at *7-10 (Del. Ch. May 24, 1999), and *In re Fuqua Industries, Inc. Shareholder Litigation*, 752 A.2d 126 (Del. Ch. 1999).

Add the following at the end of the second sentence (immediately after footnote 136) of the paragraph beginning on page 1400 and concluding on page 1401:

Another case discussing the fair and adequate requirement in a state court outside of Delaware is *Robbins v. Tweetsie Railroad, Inc.*, 486 S.E.2d 453, 455-57 (N.C. Ct. App. 1997).

Add the following at the end of footnote 139 on page 1402:

See also Fuqua, 752 A.2d at 130; *Dairy Mart*, 1999 Del. Ch. LEXIS 94, at *26, 1999 WL 350473, at *8.

Add the following at the end of the second sentence (immediately after footnote 142) after the block quote in the paragraph beginning on page 1401 and concluding on page 1402:

"[W]hile many courts have cited them, it is far from clear how many factors must be present to find a representative plaintiff inadequate and how the factors should be weighed." *Fuqua*, 752 A.2d at 130.

Replace "1996" with "Supp. 1998/99" in the Model Act § 7.41 citation in footnote 146 on page 1403.

Section A 4

Add the following at the end of footnote 154 on page 1404:

See also Lushbough v. Merchants Group, Inc., No. 115600/93, slip op. at 7-8 (N.Y. Sup. Ct. N.Y. Co. Apr. 7, 1997); *Alphin v. Cotter*, 1998 Phila. Cty. Rptr. LEXIS 69 (Pa. Common Pleas Ct. Phila. Cty. June 18, 1998) (requiring posting of $50,000 bond at start of litigation but denying motion for an award of attorneys' fees after plaintiff "determined not to proceed further with his derivative claims" and directing that the full amount held as security be returned to plaintiff's counsel), *aff'd mem.*, 737 A.2d 1266 (Pa. Super. Ct.), *petition for allowance of appeal denied*, 740 A.2d 1143 (Pa. 1999).

Replace "§ 7.46" with "§ 7.46(2)" and replace "1996" with "Supp. 1998/99" in the Model Act § 7.46 citation in footnote 159 on page 1406.

Section A 7

Replace "1996" with "Supp. 1998/99" in the Model Act § 7.45 citation in footnote 173 on page 1408.

Replace the Seinfeld citation in footnote 191 on page 1410 with the following:

172 Misc. 2d 159, 162, 656 N.Y.S.2d 707, 709 (N.Y. Sup. Ct. N.Y. Co. 1997), *rev'd on other grounds*, 246 A.D.2d 291, 676 N.Y.S.2d 579 (N.Y. App. Div. 1st Dep't 1998).

Add the following at the end of the first sentence (immediately after footnote 192) of the paragraph beginning on page 1409 and concluding on page 1410:

Another example of a federal court decision approving a settlement of derivative litigation is *In re Ikon Office Solutions, Inc. Securities Litigation*, 194 F.R.D. 166, 188-91 (E.D. Pa. 2000).

Section A 8

Add the following at the end of footnote 203 on page 1411:

See also Weber v. King, 110 F. Supp. 2d 124, 132 (E.D.N.Y. 2000) ("we examine the nature of the wrongs alleged in the complaint, and not the Plaintiffs' stated intention and characterization of their claims"); *Rubenstein v. Skyteller, Inc.*, 48 F. Supp. 2d 315, 323 (S.D.N.Y. 1999) ("In determining whether a complaint states an individual or a derivative cause of action, the Court is not bound by the designation employed by the plaintiff. Rather, the nature of the action is determined from the body of the complaint.") (quoting *Moran v. Household Int'l Inc.*, 490 A.2d 1059, 1069-70 (Del. Ch.), *aff'd*, 500 A.2d 1346 (Del. 1985)); *Golaine v. Edwards*, 1999 Del. Ch. LEXIS 237, at *10, 1999 WL 1271882, at *3 (Del. Ch. Dec. 21, 1999) ("the court must look to "the body of the complaint, not to the plaintiff's designation or stated intention'"") (quoting *Kramer v. Western Pac. Indus., Inc.*, 546 A.2d 348, 352 (Del. 1998) and *Lipton v. News Int'l, Plc.*, 514 A.2d 1075, 1078 (Del. 1986)); *Fischer v. Fischer*, 1999 Del. Ch. LEXIS 217, at *9, 1999 WL 1032768, at *3 (Del. Ch. Nov. 4, 1999); *Turner v. Bernstein*, 1999 Del. Ch. LEXIS 18, at *38 n.41, 1999 WL 66532, at *10 n.41 (Del. Ch. Feb. 9, 1999) (quoting *Kramer*).

Add the following at the end of footnote 204 on page 1412:

See also Atkins v. Hibernia Corp., 182 F.3d 320, 323 (5th Cir. 1999); *Marquit v. Dobson*, 1999 U.S. Dist. LEXIS 19964, at *2, 2000 WL 4155, at *1 (S.D.N.Y. Dec. 29, 1999), *aff'd on other grounds*, 225 F.3d 1135 (unpublished opinion, text available at 2000 U.S. App. LEXIS 25695 and 2000 WL 1529918) (2d Cir. Oct 13, 2000)); *Green v. Nuveen Advisory Corp.*, 186 F.R.D. 486, 489 (N.D. Ill. 1999).

Add "mergers," between "context of" and "defensive actions" in the second sentence of the paragraph beginning and concluding on page 1412 (between footnotes 205 and 206).

Replace the semicolon in footnote 206 on page 1412 with the following:

, *quoted in In re Gaylord Container Corp. S'holders Litig.*, 747 A.2d 71, 76 (Del. Ch. 1999);

Add the following at the end of footnote 206 on page 1412:

See also Golaine, 1999 Del. Ch. LEXIS 237, at *12, 1999 WL 1271882, at *4 (noting "expressions of frustration by our courts with the individual-derivative claim distinction in merger settings"); *Turner*, 1999 Del. Ch. LEXIS 18, at *39, 1999 WL 66532, at *10 ("a thin gray line often marks the difference between derivative and individual claims that arise in the merger context"); *Carmody v. Toll Bros., Inc.*, 723 A.2d 1180, 1188 (Del. Ch. 1998) ("in litigation involving a challenge to defensive takeover tactics, the line between derivative and individual actions is often vague").

Add the following at the end of the paragraph beginning and concluding on page 1412 (immediately after footnote 206):

As a result, application of the governing rule "has yielded less than predictable results," some of which, it has been said, "seem to flow from whether the plaintiff cited the correct magic words, rather than from any real distinction between the relief sought or the injury suffered." *Gaylord*, 747 A.2d at 75; *see also id.* at 77-83 (suggesting reasons why "there may be value to rethinking the derivative-individual claim distinction in the area of defensive measures").

Replace "1997" with "1999" in the Cary citation in footnote 207 on page 1413.

Add the following at the end of footnote 212 on page 1414:

See also Parnes v. Bally Entm't Corp., 722 A.2d 1243, 1245 (Del. 1999) (stating that "[a] stockholder who directly attacks the fairness or validity of a merger alleges an injury to the stockholders, not the corporation" and adding that "it is often difficult to determine whether a stockholder is challenging the merger itself, or alleged wrongs associated with the merger, such as the award of golden parachute employment contracts").

Add the following at the end of the paragraph beginning on page 1413 and concluding on page 1414 (immediately after footnote 214):

As stated by the Second Circuit, "[t]he general rule, applicable in New York and elsewhere, [is] that where an injury is suffered by a corporation and the shareholders suffer solely through depreciation in the value of their stock, only the corporation itself, its receiver, if one has been appointed, or a stockholder suing derivatively in the name of the corporation may maintain an action against the wrongdoer." *Vincel v. White Motor Corp.*, 521 F.2d 1113, 1118 (2d Cir. 1975), *quoted in Marquit v. Williams*, 229 F.3d 1135 (unpublished opinion, text available at 2000 U.S. App. LEXIS 25695 and 2000 WL 1529918) (2d Cir. Oct. 13, 2000).

Add the following at the end of footnote 215 on page 1415:

See also In re Cencom Cable Income Partners, L.P. Litig., 2000 Del. Ch. LEXIS 10, at *21, 2000 WL 130629, at *6 (Del. Ch. Jan. 27, 2000).

Section A 9

Add the following at the end of footnote 216 on page 1415:

See also Silver v. Allard, 16 F. Supp. 2d 966, 967 n.2, 968 (N.D. Ill. 1998); *Flocco v. State Farm Mut. Auto. Ins. Co.*, 752 A.2d 147, 154 (D.C. 2000); *Prof'l Mgmt. Assocs., Inc. v. Coss*, 598 N.W.2d 406, 413 (Minn. Ct. App. 1999), *review denied*, 1999 Minn. LEXIS 780 (Minn. Nov. 23, 1999).

Add the following at the end of the first sentence (immediately after footnote 216) in the second paragraph beginning and concluding on page 1415:

Put another way, "a double derivative action is ultimately brought 'in the right of' the subsidiary, not the parent." *Cochran v. Stifel Fin. Corp.*, 2000 Del. Ch. LEXIS 58, at *48, 2000 WL 286722, at *14 (Del. Ch. Mar. 8, 2000).

Replace "1997" with "2000" in the Fletcher citation in footnote 218 on page 1416.

Add the following at the end of footnote 218 on page 1416:

See also Ash v. McCall, 2000 Del. Ch. LEXIS 144, at *48-49, 2000 WL 1370341, at *13 (Del. Ch. Sept. 15, 2000); *Cochran*, 2000 Del. Ch. LEXIS 58, at *47, 2000 WL 286722, at *13; *Flocco*, 752 A.2d at 152 n.6; *Prof'l Mgmt.*, 598 N.W.2d at 413.

Add the following at the end of the first paragraph beginning and concluding on page 1416 (immediately after footnote 218):

This rule "implicitly recognize[s] the presumptive independence of the subsidiary board." *Cochran*, 2000 Del. Ch. LEXIS 58, at *47, 2000 WL 286722, at *13. Both the parent corporation and the subsidiary corporation(s) are indispensable parties. *See Ash*, 2000 Del. Ch. LEXIS 144, at *49, 2000 WL 1370341, at *13; *Carlton Invs. v. TLC Beatrice Int'l Holdings, Inc.*, 1996 Del. Ch. LEXIS 47, at *25, 1996 WL 189435, at *8 (Del. Ch. Apr. 16, 1996); *Flocco*, 752 A.2d at 154.

Add the following at the end of the second paragraph beginning and concluding on page 1416 (immediately after footnote 220):

The Delaware Court of Chancery in *Shaev v. Wyly*, 1998 Del. Ch. LEXIS 2, 1998 WL 13858 (Del. Ch. Jan. 6, 1998), *motion for reargument denied*, 1998 Del. Ch. LEXIS 33, 1998 WL 118200 (Del. Ch. Mar. 6, 1998), *aff'd*, 719 A.2d 490 (unpublished opinion, text available at 1998 Del. LEXIS 356 and 1998 WL 764168) (Del. Oct. 1, 1998), held that where a shareholder plaintiff "(1) currently owns shares in two independent corporations that used to stand in a parent/wholly-owned subsidiary relationship and (2) once had legal standing as a shareholder of the parent to bring a double derivative action on behalf of the former subsidiary for its directors' alleged breach of fiduciary duty but (3) lost that standing when the parent 'spun-off' the subsidiary, plaintiff nonetheless has equitable standing to bring a derivative action on behalf of the former subsidiary to recover for the alleged breach of fiduciary duty, even though the challenged actions occurred before plaintiff could have owned shares in the subsidiary." 1998 Del. Ch. LEXIS 2, at *1, 1998 WL 13858, at *1.

The court stated that the principle codified in Section 327 of the Delaware General Corporation Law, which provides that

> [i]n any derivative suit instituted by a stockholder of a corporation, it shall be averred in the complaint that the plaintiff was a stockholder of the corporation at the time of the transaction of which he complains or that his stock devolved upon him by operation of law,

did not bar the action. 1998 Del. Ch. LEXIS 2, at *9-10, 1998 WL 13858, at *3 (quoting Del. Gen. Corp. Law § 327); *see also* Chapter IV, Sections A 1 and 2 (discussing this principle). The court explained that the plaintiff had not purchased his shares in the parent corporation "to bring suit for actions taken before he was a shareholder." 1998 Del. Ch. LEXIS 2, at *13, 1998 WL 13858, at *4. Accordingly, the court concluded, "the sole aim of section 327" – "'to prevent what has been considered an evil, namely, the purchasing of shares in order to maintain a derivative action designed to attack a transaction which occurred prior to the purchase of the stock'" – "would not be served by denying plaintiff standing to sue." 1998 Del. Ch. LEXIS 2, at *13 & n.19, 1998 WL 13858, at *4 & n.19 (quoting *Rosenthal v. Burry Biscuit Corp.*, 60 A.2d 106, 111 (Del. Ch. 1948)). To the contrary, the court stated, "to deny standing on these facts would insulate defendants from potential liability for their alleged misdeeds." 1998 Del. Ch. LEXIS 2, at *13, 1998 WL 13858, at *4.

In an opinion denying a motion for reconsideration, the court added the following: "[t]he rationale behind section 327, its contemporaneous ownership requirement, and its policy to prevent specious challenges by those without an equitable basis for complaint simply does not demand closing the door on all potentially meritorious claims." 1998 Del. Ch. LEXIS 33, at *4, 1998 WL 118200, at *1. The court continued:

> Here, plaintiff lost his chance to file a double derivative action because, after the spin-off, Software and Commerce were no longer in a parent/subsidiary relationship. Were this Court to apply section 327 strictly, plaintiff would also be barred from filing a derivative action. Under those circumstances, I refuse, as I believe one charged with the duty to apply equitable principles must, to adhere blindly to a technical legal rule and to allow thereby an alleged corporate wrongdoer to thumb his nose at the possibility of redress. Thus, I found that plaintiff has *equitable* standing to bring a derivative action on Commerce's behalf, notwithstanding the fact that the challenged actions occurred before he owned any Commerce shares. I reconsidered my finding in light of the defendants' repeated arguments and reexamined my role as a member of a court charged to see that equity be done, and I decline to alter my conclusion on this issue.

1998 Del. Ch. LEXIS 33, at *6, 1998 WL 118200, at *2.

The court rejected defendants' reliance upon *Anadarko Petroleum Corp. v. Panhandle Eastern Corp.*, 545 A.2d 1171 (Del. 1988), a case holding that (1) "a parent does not owe a fiduciary duty to its wholly-owned subsidiary," (2) "in a parent and wholly-owned subsidiary context, the directors of the subsidiary are obligated only to manage the affairs of the subsidiary in the best interests of the parent and its shareholders," and (3) a parent and the directors of a wholly-owned subsidiary do not owe fiduciary duties to the prospective stockholders of the subsidiary by reason of having set a record date for a spin-off of the subsidiary and establishing a market before the spin-off for the subsidiary's shares on a when-issued basis. 1998 Del. Ch. LEXIS 2, at *7-8, 1998 WL 13858, at *2 (quoting 545 A.2d at 1174). According to the court in *Shaev*, the plaintiff in *Shaev* did not claim that the subsidiary's directors owed plaintiff a duty as a prospective shareholder of the to be spun-off subsidiary. 1998 Del. Ch. LEXIS 2, at *8, 1998 WL 13858, at *3; 1998 Del. Ch. LEXIS 33, at *3, 1998 WL 118200, at *1. Rather, the claim was that the subsidiary's directors owed plaintiff a duty as a current shareholder of the parent. 1998 Del. Ch. LEXIS 33, at *3, 1998 WL 118200, at *1. "Unlike Anadarko," the court added, "the spin-off in the present action had not been announced, and may not even have been contemplated, at the time the events now challenged as a breach of fiduciary duty took place." 1998 Del. Ch. LEXIS 2, at *8, 1998 WL 13858, at *3. The court concluded: "*Anadarko* did not contemplate the contemporaneous ownership requirement of section 327 at all, much less whether, *as a matter of equity*, section 327 should apply to deny a plaintiff standing under the circumstances presented . . . in this case." 1998 Del. Ch. LEXIS 33, at *5-6, 1998 WL 118200, at *2.

The Supreme Court affirmed the Court of Chancery's decision "on the basis of and for the reasons assigned by the Court of Chancery." *Wyley v. Shaev*, 719 A.2d 490 (unpublished opinion, text available at 1998 Del. LEXIS 356 and 1998 WL 764168) (Del. Oct. 1, 1998).

The Ninth Circuit in *Batchelder v. Kawamoto*, 147 F.3d 915 (9th Cir.), *cert. denied*, 525 U.S. 982 (1998), rejected a claim that California law and public policy would be offended by applying Japanese law to bar a double derivative action by the holder of American Depository Receipts ("ADRs"), each of which represented ownership of ten shares of stock in Honda Japan, a Japanese corporation that was the sole shareholder of American Honda, a California corporation, against the directors of Honda Japan, American Honda and third parties. The court stated that "California has never expressly recognized double derivative suits" and "[i]ndeed, one decision even suggests that California would bar such suits." *Id.* at 920 (citing *Gaillard v. Natomas Co.*, 173 Cal. App. 3d 410, 419, 219 Cal. Rptr. 74, 80 (1985), a case suggesting, according to the court in *Batchelder*, that there is no double derivative action in California "because Cal. Corp. Code § 800 requires contemporaneous ownership of shares in corporation on behalf of which suit was brought").

Section A 10

Replace "1998" with "2001" in the Wright, Miller & Cooper citation in footnote 222 on page 1417.

Add to the following at the end of the first paragraph beginning and concluding on page 1421 (immediately after footnote 256):

The same result was reached in *Trabucco v. Carlile*, 57 F. Supp. 2d 1074, 1077 (D. Or. 1999).

Section B 1

Add the following at the end of footnote 296 on page 1427:

See also Emerald Partners v. Berlin, 726 A.2d 1215, 1223 (Del. 1999) (noting that "stricter pleading standard" applies to derivative claims); *Malone v. Brincat*, 722 A.2d 5, 14 (Del. 1998) (Delaware law "requires pre-suit demand or cognizable and particularized allegations that demand is excused"); *Leung v. Schuler*, 2000 Del. Ch. LEXIS 41, at *23, 2000 WL 264328, at *7 (Del. Ch. Feb. 29, 2000) (the "special pleading requirements for derivative actions . . . are more stringent than the notice pleading requirements" that govern other pleadings); *Greenwald v. Batterson*, 1999 Del. Ch. LEXIS 158, at *12, 1999 WL 596276, at *4 (Del. Ch. July 26, 1999); *Lewis v. Austen*, 1999 Del. Ch. LEXIS 125, at *31 n.33, 1999 WL 378125, at *8 n.33 (Del. Ch. June 2, 1999).

Add the following at the end of the paragraph beginning and concluding on page 1427 (immediately after footnote 296):

As stated by the Delaware Supreme Court in 2000 in *Brehm v. Eisner*, 746 A.2d 244 (Del. 2000):

> Pleadings in derivative suits are governed by Chancery Rule 23.1 . . . . Those pleadings must comply with stringent requirements of factual particularity that differ substantially from the permissive notice pleadings governed solely by Chancery Rule 8(a). Rule 23.1 is not satisfied by conclusory statements or mere notice pleading. On the other hand, the pleader is not required to plead evidence. What the pleader must set forth are particularized factual statements that are essential to the claim. Such facts are sometimes referred to as "ultimate facts," "principal facts" or "elemental facts." Nevertheless, the particularized factual statements that are required to comply with the Rule 23.1 pleading rules must also comply with the mandate of Chancery Rule 8(e) that they be "simple, concise and direct."
>
> * * *
>
> There is a very large – though not insurmountable – burden on stockholders who believe they should pursue the remedy of a derivative suit instead of selling their stock or seeking to reform or oust the[ir] directors from office.

Id. at 254, 267. "A prolix complaint larded with conclusory language . . . does not comply with these fundamental pleading mandates." *Id.*

Replace the first "and" in footnote 299 on page 1428 with a comma and replace the first semi-colon in this footnote with the following:

and *Pace v. Jordan*, 999 S.W.2d 615, 621 (Tex. App. 1999);

Section B 2

Add the following at the end of the paragraph beginning on page 1443 and concluding on page 1444 (immediately after footnote 402):

- *Brehm v. Eisner*, 746 A.2d 244, 257 (Del. 2000) ("a claim of the corporation should be evaluated by the board of directors to determine if pursuit of the claim is in the corporation's best interests").

See also Flocco v. State Farm Mut. Auto Ins. Co., 752 A.2d 147, 151 (D.C. 2000) ("'The directors of a corporation and not its shareholders manage the business and affairs of the corporation.' . . . 'The decision to bring a law suit or to refrain from litigating a claim on behalf of a corporation is a decision concerning the management of the corporation.'") (quoting *Levine v. Smith*, 591 A.2d 194, 200 (Del. 1991), and *Spiegel v. Buntrock*, 791 A.2d 767, 773 (Del. 1990)).

Add the following at the end of footnote 413 on page 1446:

See also Harhen v. Brown, 730 N.E.2d 859, 865 (Mass. 2000) ("[t]he rationale behind the demand requirement is that, as a basic principle of corporate governance, the board of directors or majority of shareholders should set the corporation's business policy, including the decision whether to pursue a lawsuit").

Add the following at the end of footnote 415 on page 1446:

See also In re Ikon Office Solutions, Inc. Sec. Litig., 194 F.R.D. 166, 190 (E.D. Pa. 2000) ("[t]he board of directors has the primary authority to file a lawsuit on behalf of the corporation") (quoting *Drage v. Procter & Gamble*, 694 N.E.2d 479, 482 (Ohio Ct. App. 1997)).

Add the following at the end of the second sentence (immediately after footnote 417) after the block quote in the paragraph beginning on page 1445 and concluding on page 1446:

An intermediate appellate court in Texas in *Pace v. Jordan*, 999 S.W.2d 615 (Tex. App. 1999), similarly stated that "[a] corporation's directors, not its shareholders, have the right to control litigation of corporate causes of action" and thus "the corporation, through its board of directors, determines whether the chances for a successful suit, the costs of maintaining a suit, and other factors militate in favor of instituting such an action." *Id.* at 622-23.

Add the following at the end of footnote 418 on page 1446:

See also McDermott, Will & Emery v. Superior Court, 83 Cal. App. 4th 378, 383, 99 Cal. Rptr. 2d 622, 625 (Cal. Ct. App. 2000) ("whether or not a corporation shall seek to enforce in the courts a cause of action for damages, is like other business questions, ordinarily a matter of internal management, and is left to the discretion of the directors") (quoting *United Copper Sec. Co. v. Amalgamated Copper Co.*, 244 U.S. 261, 263-64 (1917)); *Einhorn v. Culea*, 612 N.W.2d 78, 83 (Wis. 2000) (derivative litigation "undermines the basic principle of corporate governance that the decisions of the corporation, including the decision to initiate litigation, should be made by the board of directors").

Replace the semi-colon following the Grimes citation in footnote 423 on page 1447 with the following:

, *quoted in Brehm v. Eisner*, 746 A.2d 244, 255 (Del. 2000);

Add the following at the end of footnote 423 on page 1447:

See also Einhorn, 612 N.W.2d at 83 ("the board of directors or majority shareholders of a corporation, not the courts or minority shareholders, should resolve internal conflicts").

Replace the period at the end of footnote 425 on page 1448 with the following:

and *Brehm*, 746 A.2d at 255.

Add the following at the end of footnote 426 on page 1448:

See also White v. Panic, 2000 Del. Ch. LEXIS 14, at *17-18, 2000 WL 85046, at *5 (Del. Ch. Jan. 19, 2000) ("[t]he purpose for the demand requirement and concomitant heightened pleading standard is to 'effectively distinguish between strike suits motivated by the hope of creating settlement leverage through the prospect of expensive and time-consuming litigation discovery and suits reflecting a reasonable apprehension of actionable director malfeasance that the sitting board cannot be expected to objectively pursue on the corporation's behalf").

Add the following at the end of footnote 434 on page 1450:

See also In re Delta & Pine Land Co. S'holders Litig., 2000 Del. Ch. LEXIS 91, at *25, 2000 WL 875421, at *7 (Del. Ch. June 21, 2000) ("[i]n forming their business judgment about whether to sue, Delta's board should consider all adverse consequences that might result from bringing suit, such as the cost of litigation, the potential to temporarily paralyze the company and, as in this case, the possibility that such a suit will strain existing contractual relations").

Add the following at the end of footnote 444 on page 1452:

See also Wilson v. Tully, 243 A.D.2d 229, 236, 676 N.Y.S.2d 531, 537 (N.Y. App. Div. 1st Dep't 1998) ("[a]s a practical matter, where, as plaintiffs allege, Merrill Lynch is named as a defendant in at least 10 separate actions and class actions, its board of directors, who would be important witnesses for the corporation in those suits as well as in this derivative suit, could reasonably conclude, on the advice of counsel, that it is in the best interests of Merrill Lynch and its stockholders to vigorously defend or even settle those suits, rather than pursuing this diametrically opposed derivative suit").

Add the following at the end of the paragraph beginning on page 1453 and concluding on page 1454 (immediately after footnote 451):

As stated by a federal court construing Illinois law in *In re Abbott Laboratories Derivative Shareholder Litigation*, 126 F. Supp. 2d 535 (N.D. Ill. 2000), "it appears to be recognized by all concerned that it is highly unlikely that a demand here would lead to a decision to initiate litigation, because the necessary allegations would seriously compromise the defense of the various securities cases filed in the wake of the consent decree," but "[t]he issue is not, however, what the directors would do, so long as the decision was arguably an appropriate business judgment, but whether they can act without being influenced by improper considerations." *Id.* at 536.

Section B 3

Add the following at the end of footnote 458 on page 1455:

See also Ash v. McCall, 2000 Del. Ch. LEXIS 144, at *16, 2000 WL 1370341, at *6 (Del. Ch. Sept. 15, 2000) ("[a] shareholder's right to bring a derivative action does not arise until he has made a demand on the board of directors to institute such action directly, such demand has been wrongfully refused, or until the shareholder has demonstrated, with particularity, the reasons why pre-suit demand would be futile"); *Greenwald v. Batterson*, 1999 Del. Ch. LEXIS 158, at *12-13, 1999 WL 596276, at *4 (Del. Ch. July 26, 1999) ("[t]he right to bring a derivative action does not come into existence until the plaintiff shareholder has made a demand on the corporation to institute such an action or until the shareholder has demonstrated that demand would be futile") (quoting *Kaplan v. Peat, Marwick, Mitchell & Co.*, 540 A.2d 726, 730 (Del. 1988)).

Section B 4 a

Delete the Silicon Graphics citation in footnote 472 on page 1458.

Add the following at the end of footnote 472 on page 1458:

See also In re Silicon Graphics Inc. Sec. Litig., 183 F.3d 970, 990 (9th Cir. 1999); *In re Trump Hotels S'holder Derivative Litig.*, 2000 U.S. Dist. LEXIS 13550, at *18, 2000 WL 1371317, at *6 (S.D.N.Y. Sept. 21, 2000); *In re Oxford Health*

Plans, Inc., 192 F.R.D. 111, 113 (S.D.N.Y. 2000); *In re Cendant Corp. Derivative Action Litig.*, 96 F. Supp. 2d 394, 399 (D.N.J. 2000); *Ash v. Alexander*, 2000 U.S. Dist. LEXIS 171, at *3, 2000 WL 20704, at *1 (S.D.N.Y. Jan. 12, 2000); *Silver v. Allard*, 16 F. Supp. 2d 966, 968-69 (N.D. Ill. 1998); *Reimel v. MacFarlane*, 9 F. Supp. 2d 1062, 1065 n.2 (D. Minn. 1998); *In re Cendant Corp. Derivative Action Litig.*, 189 F.R.D. 117, 128 (D.N.J. 1999); *In re General Instrument Corp. Sec. Litig.*, 23 F. Supp. 2d 867, 873 n.5 (N.D. Ill. 1998); *Strougo v. Bassini*, 1 F. Supp. 2d 268, 273 (S.D.N.Y. 1998); *Edge Partners, L.P. v. Dockser*, 944 F. Supp. 438, 442 (D. Md. 1996).

Replace "1996" with "Supp. 1998/99" in the Model Act § 7.47 citation in footnote 473 on page 1458.

Replace the Teachers' Retirement citation in footnote 474 on page 1459 with the following:

Teachers' Retirement Sys. v. Welch, 244 A.D.2d 231, 232, 664 N.Y.S.2d 38, 40 (N.Y. App. Div. 1st Dep't 1997);

Add the following at the end of footnote 474 on page 1459:

See also In re First Interstate Bancorp Consol. S'holder Litig., 729 A.2d 851, 865-66 (Del. Ch. 1998), *aff'd sub nom. Bradley v. First Interstate Corp.*, 748 A.2d 913 (unpublished opinion, text available at 2000 Del. LEXIS 113 and 2000 WL 383788) (Del. Mar. 21, 2000); *Flocco v. State Farm Mut. Auto. Ins. Co.*, 752 A.2d 147, 151 (D.C. 2000); *Wilson v. Tully*, 243 A.D.2d 229, 232, 676 N.Y.S.2d 531, 534 (N.Y. App. Div. 1st Dep't 1998).

Section B 5 a

Add the following at the end of footnote 540 on page 1469:

See also Flocco v. State Farm Mut. Auto. Ins. Co., 752 A.2d 147, 152 & n.6 (D.C. 2000) (demand not excused by press release issued by corporation that characterized plaintiff's claims as "absurd" and "wholly lacking in merit").

Add the following at the end of footnote 542 on page 1470:

See also Mizel v. Connelly, 1999 Del. Ch. LEXIS 157, at *16 & n.5, 1999 WL 550369, at *5 & n.5 (Del. Ch. July 22, 1999).

Add the following at the end of the paragraph beginning on page 1470 and concluding on page 1471 (immediately after footnote 543):

The same is true in a case where demand is excused but a special litigation committee consisting of independent directors is formed to consider whether litigation of a shareholder claim will serve the best interests of the corporation (*see* Chapter IV, Section C). As explained in *Finley v. Superior Court*, 80 Cal. App. 4th 1152, 96 Cal. Rptr. 2d 128 (2000):

> The premise of plaintiffs' argument is that the "sole purpose" of the defense "is to dispose of meritless shareholder 'strike suits' without the need for a full trial." The defense, however, has consistently been viewed as a confluence of the business judgment rule and the demand requirement. As such, its main purpose, like theirs, is to further the fundamental principle that those best suited to make decisions for a corporation – including the decision to file suit on its behalf – are its directors, not its stockholders or the courts. [citations omitted]. To serve this purpose, the defense must be allowed whenever a committee of disinterested directors acting in good faith has determined a derivative action is not in the best interests of the corporation – if possible, on motion, but if necessary, in a full trial.

Id. at 1163, 96 Cal. Rptr. 2d at 135-36.

Section B 5 b

Replace "1998" with "2000" in the Drexler citation in footnote 550 on page 1472.

Replace "in 1993 and" with "in 1993," in the first sentence of the paragraph beginning on page 1472 and concluding on page 1473 (between footnotes 557 and 558).

Replace the period at the end of the first sentence of the paragraph beginning on page 1472 and concluding on page 1473 (between footnotes 557 and 558) with the following:

and *Brehm v. Eisner*, 746 A.2d 244 (Del. 2000).

Add the following at the end of footnote 560 on page 1473:

See also Brehm, 746 A.2d at 253, 256.

Add the following between footnote 564 and "a lack of independence" in the fourth sentence of the paragraph beginning on page 1473 and concluding on page 1474:

"[i]ndependence means that a director's decision is based on the corporate merits of the subject before the board rather than extraneous considerations or influences" (*Brehm*, 746 A.2d at 256 n.31 (quoting *Aronson v. Lewis*, 473 A.2d 805, 814 (Del. 1984)), and

Add the following at the end of the paragraph beginning on page 1473 and concluding on page 1474 (immediately after footnote 565):

Thus, "the issues of disinterestedness and independence involved in the first prong of *Aronson* are whether a majority of the . . . Board . . . in office when plaintiffs filed th[eir] action . . . was disinterested and independent. That is, were they incapable, due to personal interest or domination and control, of objectively evaluating a demand, if made, that the Board assert the corporation's claims that are raised by plaintiffs or otherwise remedy the alleged injury?" *Brehm*, 746 A.2d at 257.

Add the following at the end of footnote 570 on page 1474:

See also In re Cendant Corp. Derivative Action Litig., 96 F. Supp. 2d 394, 401 (D.N.J. 2000).

Add the following at the end of footnote 587 on page 1477:

See also In re Cooper Cos. S'holders Derivative Litig., 2000 Del. Ch. LEXIS 158, at *15 n.5, 2000 WL 1664167, at *5 n.5 (Del. Ch. Oct. 31, 2000) ("the term 'reasonable doubt' means, 'reason to doubt'").

Add the following at the end of the second sentence (immediately after footnote 591) of the paragraph beginning and concluding on page 1477:

The Delaware Court of Chancery in *Beneville v. York*, 769 A.2d 80 (Del. Ch. 2000), also held that demand is required only if there is "a sufficient number of impartial directors who can cause the corporation to act favorably on a demand" and that "[i]f the members of the board who cannot impartially consider the demand have the corporate power to prevent the corporation from bringing suit, then our law considers demand futile, whether it is because the conflicted directors command a majority or because they have equal voting power with the impartial directors." *Id.* at 82. The court added that "[u]nder traditional rules of board governance, an equally divided vote on a motion to bring suit has the same effect as a vote in which the motion is defeated by a one vote majority," and "[g]iven this reality, it would be logically incoherent for Delaware courts to refuse to excuse demand where half of the board cannot impartially consider a demand but to excuse demand where a bare majority cannot act impartially." *Id.* The Delaware

Court of Chancery reached the same conclusion in *Kohls v. Duthie*, 2000 Del. Ch. LEXIS 103, at *19 n.30, 26-27, 2000 WL 1041219, at *5 n.30, 7 (Del. Ch. July 26, 2000).

Add the following at the end of the paragraph beginning on page 1478 and concluding on page 1479 (immediately after footnote 602):

The court in *Beneville* noted another possibility: a corporation, by certificate or bylaw, having "a standing litigation committee comprised solely of non-management, independent directors who are empowered to accept demands without involvement by the other board members." 769 A.2d at 87 n.16. The court stated that "[w]ithout deciding the question, I assume that Delaware courts would give careful consideration to a claim by the defendants that demand must be made in such circumstances." *Id.*

Section B 5 c

Add a comma after "Rales v. Blasband" in the first sentence of the paragraph beginning and concluding on page 1479, delete "and" immediately following footnote 608, and add the following immediately following footnote 609:

and *Brehm v. Eisner*, 746 A.2d 244 (Del. 2000)

Add the following at the end of footnote 610 on page 1479:

See also Brehm, 746 A.2d at 253, 256.

Add the following at the end of the paragraph beginning and concluding on page 1479 (immediately after footnote 611):

With respect "to the so-called second prong of *Aronson*," "[t]he issue is whether plaintiffs have alleged particularized facts creating a reasonable doubt that the actions of the defendants were protected by the business judgment rule." *Brehm*, 746 A.2d at 255.

Add the following at the end of the paragraph beginning on page 1480 and concluding on page 1481 (immediately after footnote 613):

The Supreme Court added the following with respect to the second prong of *Aronson* in *Brehm v. Eisner*, 746 A.2d 244 (Del. 2000): Demand will be excused "only if the Court of Chancery in the first instance, and this Court in its de novo review, conclude that the particularized facts in the complaint create a reasonable doubt that the informational component of the directors' decisionmaking process, measured by concepts of gross negligence, included consideration of all material information reasonably available." *Id.* at 259. This analytical framework is applied "to the particularized facts pleaded, juxtaposed with the presumption of regularity of the Board's process." *Id.*

Replace the period at the end of footnote 616 on page 1481 with the following:

, *quoted in Greenwald v. Batterson*, 1999 Del. Ch. LEXIS 158, at *12, 1999 WL 596276, at *4 (Del. Ch. July 26, 1999), *and Lewis v. Austen*, 1999 Del. Ch. LEXIS 125, at *31 n.33, 1999 WL 378125, at *8 n.33 (Del. Ch. June 2, 1999).

Replace the period at the end of footnote 617 on page 1482 with the following:

and *In re Trump Hotels S'holder Derivative Litig.*, 2000 U.S. Dist. LEXIS 13550, at *17, 2000 WL 1371317, at *6 (S.D.N.Y. Sept. 21, 2000).

Add the following at the end of the paragraph beginning on page 1481 and concluding on page 1482 (immediately after footnote 621):

As stated by the Supreme Court in *Brehm*: "Plaintiffs are entitled to all reasonable factual inferences that logically flow from the particularized facts alleged, but conclusory allegations are not considered as expressly pleaded facts or factual inferences." *Brehm*, 746 A.2d at 255.

Add the following at the end of the paragraph beginning and concluding on page 1482 (immediately after footnote 623):

Appellate review of the trial court's exercise of its discretion, however, is "de novo and plenary" and "not a deferential review that requires us to find an abuse of discretion." *Brehm*, 746 A.2d at 253. The scope of appellate review is the same as any other ruling assessing the legal sufficiency of a pleading and granting or denying a motion to dismiss. *Id.*

Section B 5 c (i)

Add the following at the end of the paragraph beginning on page 1482 and concluding on page 1483 (between footnotes 628 and 629):

Brehm v. Eisner, 746 A.2d 244 (Del. 2000), discussed in Chapter II, Section B 2 g, illustrates another application of the *Arsonson* test requiring demand.

Add the following at the end of the first paragraph of footnote 657 on page 1488:

See also In re Silicon Graphics Inc. Sec. Litig., 183 F.3d 970, 990 (9th Cir. 1999); *Brehm*, 746 A.2d at 257 n.34; *Kohls v. Duthie*, 2000 Del. Ch. LEXIS 103, at *13, 2000 WL 1041219, at *4 (Del. Ch. July 26, 2000).

Add the following at the end of the second paragraph of footnote 657 on page 1488:

See also Ash v. Alexander, 2000 U.S. Dist. LEXIS 171, at *4-5, 2000 WL 20704, at *2 (S.D.N.Y. Jan. 12, 2000) (New York law); *Reimel v. MacFarlane*, 9 F. Supp. 2d 1062, 1066 (D. Minn. 1998) (Minnesota law); *Strougo v. Bassini*, 1 F. Supp. 2d 268, 273 (S.D.N.Y. 1998) (Maryland law); *Pace v. Jordan*, 999 S.W.2d 615, 624 (Tex. App. 1999) (Texas law).

Add the following at the end of the second sentence (immediately after footnote 658) of the paragraph beginning on page 1488 and concluding on page 1490:

Instead, the complaint must allege "specific facts establishing that 'the potential for liability is not 'a mere threat' but instead may rise to 'a substantial likelihood''" of liability. *Kohls*, 2000 Del. Ch. LEXIS 103, at *14, 2000 WL 1041219, at *4 (quoting Donald J. Wolfe, Jr. & Michael A. Pittenger, *Corporate and Commercial Practice in the Delaware Court of Chancery* § 9-2(b)(3)(iii), at 570 (1998), *Rales v. Blasband*, 634 A.2d 927, 934 (Del. 1993), and *Aronson v. Lewis*, 473 A.3d 805, 815 (Del. 1984)). This rule "flow[s] from the premise that, where business judgment protection is available, a mere threat of personal liability resulting from one's participation as a director in approving a transaction should not suffice to sterilize a director's discretion." *Kohls*, 2000 Del. Ch. LEXIS 103, at *14, 2000 WL 1041219, at *4.

Add the following at the end of the second paragraph of footnote 661 on page 1490:

See also Brehm, 746 A.2d at 257 n.34; *Pace*, 999 S.W.2d at 624.

Replace the Silicon Graphics citation in the first paragraph of footnote 662 on page 1492 with the following:

In re Silicon Graphics Inc. Sec. Litig., [1996-1997 Transfer Binder] Fed. Sec. L. Rep. (CCH) ¶ 99,325, at 95,968 (N.D. Cal. Sept. 25, 1996), *aff'd*, 183 F.3d 970 (9th Cir. 1999).

Replace the Drain citation in the second paragraph of footnote 662 on page 1492 with the following:

Drain v. Covenant Life Ins. Co., 685 A.2d 119, 128 (Pa. Super. Ct. 1996), *aff'd on other grounds*, 712 A.2d 273 (Pa. 1998) (Pennsylvania law).

Replace the Weinstock citation in the first paragraph of footnote 662 on page 1492 with the following:

Weinstock v. Bromery, N.Y.L.J., Mar. 28, 1996, at 29 (N.Y. Sup. Ct. N.Y. Co.), *aff'd sub nom. Teachers' Retirement Sys. v. Welch*, 244 A.D.2d 231, 664 N.Y.S.2d 38 (N.Y. App. Div. 1st Dep't 1997).

Add the following at the end of the second paragraph of footnote 662 on page 1492:

See also In re Abbott Labs. Derivative S'holder Litig., 126 F. Supp. 2d 535, 536 (N.D. Ill. 2000) (Illinois law); *Silver v. Allard*, 16 F. Supp. 2d 966, 970-71 (N.D. Ill. 1998) (Illinois law); *Pace*, 999 S.W.2d at 623.

Add the following at the end of the first paragraph of footnote 663 on page 1493:

See also In re Walt Disney Co. Derivative Litig., 731 A.2d 342, 354-55 n.18 (Del. Ch. 1998), *aff'd with leave to replead on other grounds sub nom. Brehm v. Eisner*, 746 A.2d 244 (Del. 2000).

Add the following at the end of the first paragraph of footnote 664 on page 1493:

See also Disney, 731 A.2d at 354-55 n.18.

Replace the parenthetical in the second bullet on page 1493 with the following (immediately before footnote 665):

(several courts construing Maryland law, however, have held in actions brought on behalf of investment funds that service on the boards of multiple investment funds managed by the same investment advisor may be sufficient to excuse demand; a subsequently enacted Maryland statute overrules these decisions)

Add the following at the end of footnote 665 on page 1493:

See also Strougo v. BEA Assocs., 2000 U.S. Dist. LEXIS 346, at *13, 2000 WL 45714, at *5 (S.D.N.Y. Jan. 19, 2000); *Strougo v. Bassini*, 1 F. Supp. 2d at 273-74; *cf. Marquit v. Dobson*, 1999 U.S. Dist. LEXIS 19964, at *6-7, 2000 WL 4155, at *2 (S.D.N.Y. Dec. 29, 1999) (distinguishing *Strougo v. Scudder, Stevens & Clark, Inc.*, 964 F. Supp. 783 (S.D.N.Y. 1997), because under Maryland law "a shareholder demand would not be futile if the fund had at least two disinterested directors" and in the case of the three funds before the court, unlike the case of the fund before the court in *Strougo*, two of the three funds had more than two disinterested directors having no association with any other fund managed by the funds' advisor, and the third fund had "no director who does not serve on the board of at least one other fund" managed by the funds' advisor but "more than two of these serve only on one other board and there is no allegation that their compensation is so substantial that it would have an impact on their independence"; the court added its view that "[i]t is doubtful that the mere fact that a director serves on the board of two funds would be sufficient to compel the conclusion that he was not disinterested"), *aff'd on other grounds*, 225 F.3d 1135 (unpublished opinion, text available at 2000 U.S. App. LEXIS 25695 and 2000 WL 1529918) (2d Cir. Oct. 13, 2000); *see also* Md. Gen. Corp. Law § 2-405.3 ("[a]

director of a corporation who with respect to the corporation is not an interested person, as defined by the Investment Company Act of 1940, shall be deemed to be independent and disinterested when making any determination or taking any action as a director"); *BEA Assocs.*, 2000 U.S. Dist. LEXIS 346, at *13, 2000 WL 45714, at *5 (holding that Md. Gen. Corp. Law § 2-405.3 does not change result reached in *Strougo v. Bassini*; discussed in Chapter I, Section D 2 e).

Add the following at the end of the second paragraph of footnote 666 on page 1493:

See also Flocco v. State Farm Mut. Auto. Ins. Co., 752 A.2d 147, 152 n.6 (D.C. 2000); *Ash*, 2000 U.S. Dist. LEXIS 171, at *4-5, 2000 WL 20704, at *2.

Add the following at the end of the first paragraph of footnote 670 on page 1494:

See also White v. Panic, 2000 Del. Ch. LEXIS 14, at *25, 2000 WL 85046, at *7 (Del. Ch. Jan. 19, 2000).

Add the following at the end of the first paragraph of footnote 671 on page 1495:

See also Ash v. McCall, 2000 Del. Ch. LEXIS 144, at *19-22, 2000 WL 1370341, at *6-7 (Del. Ch. Sept. 15, 2000); *In re Delta & Pine Land Co. S'holders Litig.*, 2000 Del. Ch. LEXIS 91, at *21-22, 2000 WL 875421, at *7 (Del. Ch. June 21, 2000); *Disney*, 731 A.2d at 355 & n.19, 356-60 (discussed in Chapter I, Section D 2 c); *Elliman v. Elliman*, No. 603377/96, slip op. at 11 (N.Y. Sup. Ct. N.Y. Co. Apr. 7, 1999) (Delaware law).

Replace the Woolworth citation in the first paragraph of footnote 674 on page 1496 with the following:

In re Woolworth Corp. Shareholder Derivative Litig., No. 109465/94, slip op. at 4-5 (N.Y. Sup. Ct. N.Y. Co. May 3, 1995), *aff'd*, 240 A.D.2d 189, 658 N.Y.S.2d 869 (N.Y. App. Div. 1st Dep't 1997) (New York law);

Add the following at the end of the first paragraph of footnote 674 on page 1496:

See also White, 2000 Del. Ch. LEXIS 14, at *25-26, 2000 WL 85046, at *7; *Disney*, 731 A.2d at 355 & n.18, 360.

Add the following at the end of the second paragraph of footnote 674 on page 1496:

See also Abbott Labs., 126 F. Supp. 2d at 537.

Add the following at the end of footnote 677 on page 1497:

Cf. Solomon v. Armstrong, 747 A.2d 1098, 1126 (Del. Ch. 1999) (stating in a case not involving the demand requirement that "Delaware law routinely rejects the notion that a director's interest in maintaining his office, by itself, is a debilitating factor"), *aff'd*, 746 A.2d 277 (unpublished opinion, full text available at 2000 Del. LEXIS 30 and 2000 WL 140072) (Del. Jan. 26, 2000).

Add the following at the end of footnote 680 on page 1497:

See also Greenwald v. Batterson, 1999 Del. Ch. LEXIS 158, at *13-15, 1999 WL 596276, at *5 (Del. Ch. July 26, 1999) (rejecting "paper-thin allegations of entrenchment" where there was no "allegation that the directors believed themselves vulnerable to removal from office" and no "allegation that an actual threat to the directors' positions on the board existed").

Add the following at the end of the first paragraph of footnote 682 on page 1498:

See also Lewis v. Austen, 1999 Del. Ch. LEXIS 125, at *31 n.33, 1999 WL 378125, at *8 n.33 (Del. Ch. June 2, 1999) (same quote without the words "such as entrenchment").

Add the following at the end of the first paragraph of footnote 687 on page 1499:

See also Wilson v. Tully, 243 A.D.2d 229, 235, 676 N.Y.S.2d 531, 536 (N.Y. App. Div. 1st Dep't 1998).

Add the following between "directors" and "'consistently . . .'" in the first sentence of the paragraph beginning on page 1501 and concluding on page 1502 (between footnotes 695 and 696):

"made a prior decision" (*Ash v. McCall*, 2000 Del. Ch. LEXIS 144, at *33, 2000 WL 1370341, at *10 (Del. Ch. Sept. 15, 2000)),

Add the following at the end of the first sentence (immediately after footnote 698) of the paragraph beginning on page 1501 and concluding on page 1502:

"That, in hindsight, such action or inaction may turn out to be controversial, unpopular or even wrong is insufficient to excuse plaintiffs' failure to make a demand." *Wilson*, 243 A.D.2d at 238, 676 N.Y.S.2d at 538.

Add the following at the end of the first sentence (immediately after footnote 700) of the paragraph beginning and concluding on page 1502:

Nor does the fact that claims are "obviously serious and troubling" alter "the board's role in determining how and when to address claims." *White*, 2000 Del. Ch. LEXIS 14, at *34, 2000 WL 85046, at *9.

Add the following at the end of the paragraph beginning and concluding on page 1502 (immediately after footnote 701):

Of course, "the existence of a board-initiated action 'conclusively defeats any claim that demand would have been futile. Indeed, there is something to be said for the idea that this Court should inquire no further if it finds that the corporate directors are litigating the same claims advanced in the derivative action.'" *Delta & Pine*, 2000 Del. Ch. LEXIS 91, at *17-18, 2000 WL 875421, at *6 (quoting *Silverzweig v. Unocal Corp.*, 1989 Del. Ch. LEXIS 4, at *11-12, 1989 WL 3231, at *4 (Del. Ch. Jan. 19, 1989), *aff'd*, 561 A.2d 993 (unpublished opinion, text available at 1989 Del. LEXIS 151 and 1989 WL 68307) (Del. May 19, 1989)).

Where a shareholder alleges a lack of due care and an expert has advised the board in its decision-making process, "the complaint must allege particularized facts (not conclusions)" that, if proved, would overcome the business judgment rule presumption by showing, for example, that

> (a) the directors did not in fact rely on the expert; (b) their reliance was not in good faith; (c) they did not reasonably believe that the expert's advice was within the expert's professional competence; (d) the expert was not selected with reasonable care by or on behalf of the corporation, and the faulty selection process was attributable to the directors; (e) the subject matter (in this case the cost calculation) that was material and reasonably available was so obvious that the board's failure to consider it was grossly negligent regardless of the expert's advice or lack of advice; or (f) that the decision of the Board was so unconscionable as to constitute waste or fraud.

Brehm, 746 A.2d at 262; *see also Ash*, 2000 Del. Ch. LEXIS 144, at *31-32, 2000 WL 1370341, at *9:

> The McKesson board is entitled to the presumption that it exercised proper business judgment, including proper reliance on experts. Plaintiffs have not rebutted the presumption with particularized facts creating reason to believe that the McKesson board's conduct was grossly negligent. That is, plaintiffs have not alleged particularized facts (in contrast with conclusions) that, if proved, would show that (1) the directors in fact did not rely on the expert, or (2) that their reliance was

not in good faith, or (3) that they did not reasonably believe that the experts' advice was within the experts' professional competence, or (4) that the directors were at fault for not selecting experts with reasonable care, or (5) that the issue (here, alleged accounting deficiencies in HBOC's financial records) was so obvious that the board's failure to detect it was grossly negligent regardless of the experts' advice, or (6) that the board's decision was so unconscionable as to constitute waste or fraud. [citing *Brehm*, 746 A.2d at 262.] This complaint is devoid of particularized allegations along these lines and is, therefore, incapable or surviving a motion to dismiss.

Section B 5 c (ii)

Add the following at the end of the paragraph beginning on page 1507 and concluding on page 1512 (immediately after footnote 765):

- *Benerofe v. Cha*, 1998 Del. Ch. LEXIS 28, at *5-6, 10, 1998 WL 83081, at *2, 3 (Del. Ch. Feb. 20, 1998) (excusing demand in a case challenging contracts entered into by a corporation, Inorganic Coatings, Inc. ("ICI"), and its controlling shareholder, Kun Sul Painting Industries, Co., Ltd. ("KSP"), where ICI's board included three directors, one of whom, Jung Woong Cha, was the president of KSP, and another of whom, Chang Kim, was the president and chief executive officer of ICI and a designee of KSP, provided ICI "day to day full-time management" and had "bought a house in suburban Philadelphia, near ICI's offices, and moved his principal residence there so he could live near his place of work," and received compensation for his services to ICI in an amount that was not public information but that "has been and is his principal source of financial support");
- *Smith v. Smitty McGee's, Inc.*, 1998 Del. Ch. LEXIS 87, at *26-29, 1998 WL 246681, at *7 (Del. Ch.

May 8, 1998) (excusing demand due to the lack of disinterestedness on the part of the sole director of the corporation with respect to claims against her former husband that sought restitution of assets her former husband had obtained through alleged wrongdoing and transferred to her; the court reached this conclusion notwithstanding the fact that the director's former husband had agreed to indemnify her and to renegotiate their property settlement if she were found liable in the action because "the re-opening of an otherwise final property division is, itself, potentially disadvantageous");

- *Mizel v. Connelly*, 1999 Del. Ch. LEXIS 157, at *1-4, 6-14, 1999 WL 550369, at *1-2, 3-4 (Del. Ch. July 22, 1999) (excusing demand in an action challenging a transaction entered into by President Casinos, Inc. and a corporation owned by John E. Connelly, the chairman, chief executive officer and 32.7 percent shareholder of President Casinos, where the corporation's five member board included (1) Connelly, (2) John S. Aylsworth, the president and chief operating officer of President Casinos, who received more than $620,000 in annual compensation from the corporation, and (3) Terrence L. Wirginis, the vice president and vice chairman of the board of President Casinos, who received more than $239,000 in annual compensation from the corporation, and who also was Connelly's grandson; the court reasoned that (1) Connelly "as their boss . . . exerts 'considerable influence' over Aylsworth and Wirginis" and "[s]ince Aylsworth and Wirginis each derive their principal income from their employment at President Casinos, it is doubtful that they can consider the demand on its merits without also pondering whether an affirmative vote would endanger their continued employment," (2) Connelly's ownership of 32.7 percent of President Casino's stock and the fact that he was the corporation's largest shareholder "undoubtedly . . . may not be sufficient to constitute control for certain corporation law purposes" but "great weight" should be attached "to the practical power wielded by a stockholder controlling such a block and to the impression of such power likely to be harbored by the stockholder's fellow directors," and (3) the fact that Wirginis is Connelly's grandson is "of great consequence" because "[t]he existence of a very close family relationship between directors should, without more, generally go a long (if not the whole) way toward creating a reasonable doubt" sufficient to excuse demand);

- *Harbor Finance Partners v. Huizenga*, 751 A.2d 879, 882 (Del. Ch. 1999) (excusing demand in a case challenging an acquisition by Republic Industries, Inc. of AutoNation, Incorporated allegedly entered into for the benefit of Republic directors who owned a substantial block of AutoNation shares and on terms that allegedly were unfair to Republic, where three of Republic's seven directors, Wayne Huizenga, George D. Johnson, Jr. and John J. Melk, were conceded to have held enough AutoNation shares before the merger to render them interested in the transaction – Huizenga received 6,397,757 Republic shares worth $235 million in exchange for over 29,375,000 AutoNation shares, Johnson received 544,490 Republic shares worth over $20 million in exchange for his 2.5 million AutoNation shares, and Melk received 179,681 Republic shares worth over $6.6 million in exchange for his 825,000 AutoNation shares – and a fourth director, Harris W. Hudson, received Republic shares worth $825,000 in exchange for his AutoNation shares in the merger; the court stated that "at this pleading stage, it would be difficult for me to infer other than that Hudson desired to receive the highest possible price for his AutoNation shares" but acknowledged that "economic evidence might ultimately persuade me that it would have been irrational for Hudson to seek unfair economic advantage in the Merger for AutoNation stockholders at the expense of Republic, because any such advantage would cause more than offsetting harm to him" due to his ownership of 10.1 percent of Republic's shares; the court also relied upon a "longstanding pattern of mutually advantageous business relations" between Hudson and Huizenga, Republic's chairman and chief executive officer, and the fact that Hudson and Huizenga were brothers-in-law);

- *Grace Brothers, Ltd. v. UniHolding Corp.*, 2000 Del Ch. LEXIS 101, at *1-3, 25-34, 2000 WL 982401, at *1, 8-10 (Del. Ch. July 12, 2000) (excusing demand in suit against the directors of UniHolding Corporation ("UniHolding") and Unilabs Holdings, SA ("Unilabs"), a 41.6 percent shareholder of UniHolding, for allowing Unilabs Group Limited ("UGL"), a wholly-owned subsidiary of Unilabs, to assume control over UniHolding's primary asset, a 54 percent stake in Unilabs, SA ("ULSA"), by means of an issuance by UGL of a controlling block of UGL stock to Unilabs and Unilabs affiliates in exchange for their UniHolding shares and leaving UniHolding with no assets other than a minority interest in UGL, a British Virgin Island corporation whose shares were not listed on any stock exchange and that provided minority shareholders no liquidity and substantially reduced informational rights, and following which UniHolding defaulted on federal securities law disclosures and UniHolding was delisted, causing, plaintiffs alleged, "UniHolding stockholders to find themselves with delisted stock that is valued at one-sixth of its worth in 1997, even though its former controlled subsidiary, ULSA, is prospering"; UniHolding's six member board included (1) Edgar Zwirn, the chairman of the board of UniHolding, Unilabs and USLA and the "dominant player in Unilabs" who "orchestrated the Challenged Transactions and directed the other UniHolding board members to assent"; the court stated that "UniHolding had the option of restructuring through a merger in which it would have had to ensure that the Minority Stockholders received fair consideration or through a distribution of its controlling interest in ULSA directly to its stockholders on a pro rata basis," but "[i]nstead UniHolding chose to effect a transaction that enabled the Controlling Group to continue to use the Minority Stockholders' equity to help them exercise firm majority control over ULSA while decreasing the Minority Shareholders' liquidity and informational rights," and "[i]t is thus implausible that Zwirn – who indirectly owns over 23% of Unilabs – had no financial interest in the Challenged Transactions"; (2) Enrico Gherardi and Alessandra van Gemerden, who were uncle and nephew and together owned 13 percent of Uniholding's stock before the challenged transactions and who converted their UniHolding shares into UGL shares in the challenged transactions, and one of whom served on the ULSA board, the other of whom served on boards of two other UniHolding subsidiaries, and both of whom were affiliated with a company that received over $2.5 million in consulting fees from UniHolding and another UniHolding subsidiary during the 1997 to 1999 period; under these circumstances, the court stated, "Gherardi's and van Gemerden's involvement in the Unilabs' family of companies was so extensive and apparently lucrative" that it created "a reasonable doubt about their ability to act adversely to Zwirn's interests" because "Zwirn is clearly positioned to exert substantial influence over decisions regarding Gherardi's and van Gemerden's roles at and remuneration from Unilabs-affiliated companies," and (3) Tobias Fenster, Zwirn's brother-in-law and the chief executive officer of ULSA's Spanish subsidiary and a director of other Unilabs-related companies).

- *In re Cooper Cos. Shareholders Derivative Litigation*, 2000 Del. Ch. LEXIS 158, at *17-21, 2000 WL 1664167, at *6-7 (Del. Ch. Oct. 31, 2000) (excusing demand where a ten member board included (1) three directors, Gary, Steven and Brad Singer, who lacked disinterestedness because they were alleged to have profited from a wrongful scheme, (2) one director, Joseph C. Feghali, who lacked independence because he was Steven Singer's father-in-law, a family relationship "sufficient to create a reason to doubt" Feghali's ability to consider a demand, and (3) two directors, Robert S. Weiss, the corporation's chief financial officer and treasurer, and Robert S. Holcombe, the corporation's vice president and general counsel. With respect to Weiss and Holcombe, the court held "it is reasonable to infer from the fact that Gary Singer was Messrs. Weiss's and Holcombe's corporate superior, that he (Gary) was in a position to exercise 'considerable influence' over them" and that "[t]hat inference, coupled with the allegation that Messrs. Weiss and Holcombe were among the directors who (along with the Singers) absented themselves" from – and thus ensured the lack of a quorum and therefore no corporate action at – an emergency board meeting called by two independent directors to consider how the corporation should respond to guilty pleas by two individuals who identified Gary Singer as a participant in criminal conduct was sufficient to create a doubt concerning the disinterestedness or independence of Weiss and Holcombe and thus excuse demand);

- *Professional Management Associates, Inc. v. Coss*, 574 N.W.2d 107, 110-11 (Minn. Ct. App. 1998), *review denied*, 1998 Minn. LEXIS 196 (Minn. Apr. 14, 1998) (excusing demand under Delaware law in an action alleging that the board of Green Tree Financial Corporation was liable for corporate waste for approving a compensation agreement with Lawrence M. Coss, Green Tree's chief executive officer and the chairman of Green Tree's board, where Green Tree's board consisted of five directors, one of whom was Coss and two of whom were corporate officers who lacked independence from Coss because "[t]he bonus component of the officers' compensation is determined by the compensation committee on the basis of Coss's recommendation" and "the record demonstrates that even though Evans's and Pott's employment and compensation do not hinge solely on their relationship with Coss, Coss as chief executive officer and chairman of the board is in a position to exert considerable influence over Evans and Potts"); and

- *In re Trump Hotels Shareholder Derivative Litigation*, 2000 U.S. Dist. LEXIS 13550, at *20-30, 2000 WL 1371317, at *7-10 (S.D.N.Y. Sept. 21, 2000) (excusing demand under Delaware law in an action filed by shareholders of Trump Hotels & Casino Resorts, Inc. ("THCR") challenging a sale of Trump's Castle by Donald Trump to THCR; the court held that a demand upon THCR's five member board was excused because the board included (1) Trump, who indisputably was interested in the transaction, (2) Nicholas A. Ribis, who served as THCR's president and chief executive officer and also served on the boards of eleven other companies or subsidiaries controlled by Trump for which he received millions of dollars in compensation, and (3) Wallace B. Askins, Peter M. Ryan and Don M. Thomas, who served on one or more boards of THCR subsidiaries and "knew that successful service on the board of THCR and its subsidiaries might lead to future positions on other Trump-controlled entities as it had for Ribis." With respect to Askins, the court also pointed to the fact that Askins served on the boards of Trump's Castle and TC/GP, the company that owned 37.5 percent of Castle Associates, the Trump entity that owned and operated Trump's Castle before the sale of Trump's Castle to THCR, with Trump and Ribis, "the two THCR board members most interested in transaction"; the court stated that "Askins' prior board membership on the very property sold to THCR as well as his directorship in TC/GP necessarily provided him with additional information, which arguably made him a less than neutral decision-maker," and the court added that "Askins' history of personally beneficial affiliation with Trump-controlled entities, and specifically with Trump and Ribis, both clearly interested THCR Board leaders, diminishes the possibility that Askins had only the corporation's interests in mind when evaluating the transaction." With respect to Thomas, the court also pointed to the fact that Thomas was Senior Vice President of Corporate Affairs of the Pepsi-Cola Bottling Company, which, one year after Thomas joined the THCR board was awarded an exclusive contract to supply Pepsi beverages to Trump's Taj Mahal Casino, a THCR subsidiary, which provided approximately $500,000 in annual revenues to Pepsi; the court stated that "the presence of the contract alone is insufficient to raise a reasonable doubt" concerning Thomas' independence because

> "[a]t best, Thomas may have received increased compensation or influence from Pepsi for his role in securing the contract" but "any link to Trump is attenuated at best," but held that "the presence of the contract as well as the possibility of future contracts, given the totality of the circumstances raises a reasonable doubt as to Thomas' independence from Trump.")

Cf. In re Delta & Pine Land Co. S'holders Litig., 2000 Del. Ch. LEXIS 91, at *26, 2000 WL 875421, at *8 (Del. Ch. June 21, 2000) (describing the following "consistent theme running through" cases where demand is excused: a complaint alleging "particularized facts showing influence or control over the employment, the livelihood, or the financial interests of the directors on an individual and personal basis," and requiring demand in a case where this element was "glaringly absent").

Add the following at the end of the paragraph beginning and concluding on page 1513 (immediately after footnote 771):

As a result, demand will be excused "[s]o long as the plaintiff states a claim implicating the heightened scrutiny required by *Unocal*," and "[t]he derivative-individual claim distinction" thus has "no practical importance at the pre-transaction stage of corporate litigation." *In re Gaylord Container Corp. S'holders Litig.*, 747 A.2d 71, 81 (Del. Ch. 1999).

Replace "Pre-Santa Fe, Wells Fargo and Gaylord" with "Other" in the first sentence of the paragraph beginning and concluding on page 1514 (between footnotes 778 and 779).

Add the following at the end of the paragraph beginning and concluding on page 1514 (between footnotes 778 and 779):

To plead entrenchment, a plaintiff "must allege facts sufficient to demonstrate that the 'sole or primary purpose' of the challenged board action was to perpetuate the directors in control of the corporation." *Greenwald v. Batterson*, 1999 Del. Ch. LEXIS 158, at *14, 21, 1999 WL 596276, at *5, 7 (Del. Ch. July 26, 1999) (quoting *Green v. Phillips*, 22 Del. J. Corp. L. 360, 369 (Del. Ch. June 19, 1996)).

Add the following at the end of the first sentence (immediately after footnote 780) of the paragraph beginning on page 1514 and concluding on page 1515:

The same result was reached in *Carmody v. Toll Brothers, Inc.*, 723 A.2d 1180 (Del. Ch. 1998). The complaint in that case alleged "in a particularized way" that directors "acted for entrenchment purposes" by adopting a dead hand poison pill shareholder rights plan provision that had a "deterrent effect upon the shareholders' interests, in particular, the shareholders' present entitlement to receive and consider takeover proposals and to vote for a board of directors capable of exercising the full array of powers provided by statute, including the power to redeem the poison pill." *Id.* at 1188-89; *see also* Chapter III, Section G 2 d (discussing *Toll Brothers* decision).

Add the following at the end of footnote 790 on page 1516:

But see Reimel v. MacFarlane, 9 F. Supp. 2d 1062, 1065-67 (D. Minn. 1998) (declining, in a case governed by Minnesota law, to follow *In re Chrysler Corp. S'holders Litig.*, 18 Del. J. Corp. L. 237 (Del. Ch. Mar. 25, 1992), which excused demand based upon "allegations of directors perpetuating themselves in office"; the court held that the adoption of a poison pill rights plan does not excuse demand because the "board members – whether they originally intended to entrench themselves or adopted the Plan in a good faith attempt to prevent a hostile takeover – may now be willing to revisit their previous actions and resolve this dispute through alternative means").

Add the following at the end of footnote 814 on page 1519:

See also Greenwald, 1999 Del. Ch. LEXIS 158, at *20, 1999 WL 596276, at *7 ("[p]laintiff faces a substantial burden, as the second prong of the *Aronson* test is 'directed to extreme cases in which despite the appearance of independence and disinterest a decision is so extreme or curious as to itself raise a legitimate ground to justify further inquiry and judicial review'") (quoting *Kahn v. Tremont*, 1994 Del. Ch. LEXIS 41, at *21, 1994 WL 162613, at *6 (Del. Ch. Apr. 21, 1994), *subsequent proceedings*, 1996 Del. Ch. LEXIS 40, 1996 WL 145452 (Del. Ch. Mar. 21, 1996), *rev'd on other grounds*, 694 A.2d 422 (Del. 1997)); *Lewis v. Austen*, 1999 Del. Ch. LEXIS 125, at *31 n.33, 1999 WL 378125, at *8 n.33 (Del. Ch. June 2, 1999) ("*Aronson*'s second prong is 'directed to extreme cases in which despite the appearance of independence and disinterest a decision is so extreme or curious as to itself raise a legitimate ground to justify further inquiry and judicial review' and the test 'is thus necessarily high, similar to the legal test for waste'").

Add the following at the end of the paragraph beginning on page 1520 and concluding on page 1521 (immediately after footnote 824):

Demand also was excused on this ground in *Sanders v. Wang*, 1999 Del. Ch. LEXIS 203, 1999 WL 1044880 (Del. Ch. Nov. 8, 1999). The plaintiffs in *Sanders* alleged that a shareholder approved key employee stock ownership plan permitted a board compensation committee to grant up to 6,000,000 shares of common stock to plan participants but the committee increased the 6,000,000 number to more than 20,000,000 in order to reflect stock splits. 1999 Del. Ch. LEXIS 203, at *5-7, 1999 WL 1044880, at *2. The court held that the 6,000,000 share ceiling was clear and unambiguous and that the award of more than 6,000,000 shares was a "clear violation" of the plan "without any legal justification." 1999 Del. Ch. LEXIS 203, at *17-31, 1999 WL 104880, at *6-9. These alleged facts, the court held, "raise doubt that the board's actions resulted from a valid exercise of business judgment" and thus were sufficient to excuse demand. 1999 Del. Ch. LEXIS 203, at *13-14, 1999 WL 1044880, at *5.

Kohls v. Duthie, 2000 Del. Ch. LEXIS 103, 2000 WL 1041219 (Del. Ch. July 26, 2000), involved an action challenging the sale by the Hillman Company, the largest holder of Kenetech Corporation common stock, of Hillman's 12.8 million shares, constituting over 30 percent of the corporation's outstanding shares, to Mark D. Lerdal, Kenetech's president and chief executive officer, for $1,000. According to the plaintiffs, Lerdal's purchase of these shares at this nominal price constituted a usurpation of a corporate opportunity. 2000 Del. Ch. LEXIS 103, at *1, 2000 WL 1041219, at *1. The court held that demand was excused because one member of Kenetech's four member board at the time the suit was filed, Lerdal, clearly was conflicted, and a second member of the member board, Charles Christenson, although "neither interested in the challenged transaction nor beholden to Lerdal," was "interested in the decision to bring the litigation" and "conflicted from impartially evaluating a demand" due to "a 'substantial threat' of personal liability." 2000 Del. Ch. LEXIS 103, at *22, 2000 WL 1041219, at *6. The other two directors at the time of the alleged wrongdoing had been replaced on the board by outside, independent directors. 2000 Del. Ch. LEXIS 103, at *4, 2000 WL 1041219, at *1.

The court focused upon the following "highly unusual set of facts":

> The complaint does not allege merely the opportunity to repurchase shares of stock at market price. Rather, the complaint alleges the forfeiture or usurpation of an opportunity for the corporation to realize a substantial windfall for the benefit of its stockholders.
>
> - The company's CEO learned that its 30% shareholder was anxious to sell its position and was willing to do so for next to nothing. The CEO wanted to buy the shares *himself*. The other members of the board of directors also learned of this opportunity and jointly considered purchasing it, *in their personal capacities*.

- The CEO consulted with counsel and gave the other directors a series of reasons why the company could not buy the shares. The complaint alleges (in a conclusory fashion) that these reasons were false on their face and could not have been believed by the others, including Christenson. Moreover, it is alleged that Christenson (and, I infer, the board as a whole) "failed to obtain competent legal, financial or accounting advice." The CEO then convinced the others to let him take the deal alone. *Those shares were allegedly worth many times the price paid for them, and are now worth over 8,000 times their cost to the CEO.*

2000 Del. Ch. LEXIS 103, at *23-24, 2000 WL 1041219, at *6 (footnote omitted). "Put simply," plaintiffs asserted, "no properly motivated director could have perceived this corporate opportunity and not thoroughly inquired into the company's ability to exploit it." 2000 Del. Ch. LEXIS 103, at *24-25, 2000 WL 1041219, at *7. The court concluded that "the allegations of the complaint, if true, would establish that Christenson faces a 'substantial likelihood' of personal liability for breach of fiduciary duty and aiding and abetting Lerdal's breach of duty." 2000 Del. Ch. LEXIS 103, at *25, 2000 WL 1041219, at *7. The court rejected a contention that it could "simply require Lerdal to transfer the shares to the company as a remedy" and thus "Christenson does not face personal liability"; according to the court, the complaint "requests, to the extent the stock cannot be transferred, that all of the defendants be held jointly and severally liable to Kenetech." 2000 Del. Ch. LEXIS 103, at *25 n.40, 2000 WL 1041219, at *7 n.40.

In a subsequent decision, *Kohls v. Duthie*, 765 A.2d 1274 (Del. Ch. 2000), the court denied a motion for a preliminary injunction enjoining a management buy-out transaction sponsored by a third party venture capital firm that would cause plaintiffs to lose standing to pursue their derivative corporate opportunity claim. The court stated that "the evidence now in the record strongly suggests that the likelihood of success on the merits of the derivative claim is remote" due to testimony that the seller of the shares, Hillman, "did not offer and would not have sold its shares to Kenetech due to Kenetech's distressed financial condition and Hillman's need for a certain and final sale to meet its tax planning objectives." *Id.* at 1277, 1284. "Not only does the record suggest the overall weakness of the derivative claim," the court continued, "but it also appears more clearly that the remedy available to plaintiffs on that claim is the cancellation of the shares acquired by Lerdal." *Id.* at 1284. As a result, the court stated, "[t]he possibility of a money judgment against Christenson and the other director defendants in the derivative litigation is exceedingly remote." *Id.*

Add the following at the end of the paragraph beginning and concluding on page 1524 (immediately after footnote 849):

Indeed, it is "axiomatic that a corporate act cannot be a product of sound business judgment and also constitute waste." *Ash v. McCall*, 2000 Del. Ch. LEXIS 144, at *23, 2000 WL 1370341, at *7 (Del. Ch. Sept. 15, 2000); *see also Leung v. Schuler*, 2000 Del. Ch. LEXIS 41, at *34, 2000 WL 264328, at *10 (Del. Ch. Feb. 29, 2000) ("[i]f a cognizable claim of waste is alleged, that would deprive the challenged conduct of the protection of the business judgment rule and, consequently, would excuse demand").

Replace "Allegations of waste that are not" in the first sentence of the paragraph beginning on page 1527 and concluding on page 1528 (between footnotes 875 and 876) with the following:

"[A]llegations of waste must nevertheless comply with the Rule 23.1 demand requirements" and be

Add the following new footnote 875.1 at the end of the first sentence (immediately after footnote 875) of the paragraph beginning on page 1527 and concluding on page 1528:

875.1. *Ash*, 2000 Del. Ch. LEXIS 144, at *23, 2000 WL 1370341, at *7.

Add the following at the end of the paragraph beginning on page 1528 and concluding on page 1529 (immediately after 892):

In a later decision in the case, however, the court held that demand was excused because plaintiffs pleaded "the previously missing allegation that ICI sold its products to KSP at prices less than ICI was able to obtain in the open market for similar products and similar quantities." *Benerofe v. Cha*, 1998 Del. Ch. LEXIS 28, at *12-13, 1998 WL 83081, at *4 (Del. Ch. Feb. 20, 1998). This allegation, the court held, supported "a claim that the prices charged to KSP by ICI for its products (prices that ICI is alleged to have had the ability to increase at any time) were so inadequate that 'no person of ordinary, sound business judgment would deem it' a reasonable decision." 1998 Del. Ch. LEXIS 28, at *13, 1998 WL 83081, at *4.

The court in *Apple Computer, Inc. v. Exponential Technology, Inc.*, 1999 Del. Ch. LEXIS 9, 1999 WL 39547 (Del. Ch. Jan. 21, 1999), refused to excuse demand based upon an allegation that the approval of litigation support agreements by the board of Exponential Technology, Inc. constituted waste. The agreements were entered into by Exponential with Exponential's chairman, Gordon Campbell, its chief financial officer, Stephanie Dorris, and one other corporate officer, Donald Shriner. The agreements provided for these three corporate officers to perform services that would assist Exponential's pursuit of a litigation alleging that Apple Computer had forced Exponential out of business by breach of contract, breach of fiduciary duty, and intentional and negligent interference with contractual relations and prospective economic advantage. 1999 Del. Ch. LEXIS 9, at *4-8, 1999 WL 39547, at *1-2. The agreements entitled Exponential to a total of 342 to 502 hours of work per month from these three officers. All three would perform litigation support services, and one, Ms. Dorris, also would assist Exponential's winding up process. The cost of the agreements would be a minimum of $23,200 and a maximum of $66,000 per month, depending upon the number of hours worked. 1999 Del. Ch. LEXIS 9, at *8-9, 1999 WL 39547, at *3.

The court assumed that Campbell, Dorris and Shriner would receive the $66,000 per month maximum amount permitted by the agreements and that in return Exponential would receive 502 hours of work. 1999 Del. Ch. LEXIS 9, at *43, 1999 WL 39547, at *11. The court pointed to the absence of any "credible allegations that this compensation will bankrupt Exponential" or that Campbell, Dorris and Shriner "lack the ability or intent to provide their support services." *Id.* The court stated that the "exact pecuniary value" of the services Exponential would receive is "hard to measure, but 502 hours of service per month falls well within the range of reasonable value to receive in exchange for consulting fees of $66,000." 1999 Del. Ch. LEXIS 9, at *43-44, 1999 WL 39547, at *11. The court added that it "need not evaluate the merits" of the action brought by Exponential against Apple Computer "to conclude that the lawsuit's existence constitutes a reasonable business purpose for entering into the litigation support agreement, and Exponential's undisputed shutdown merits employ of Dorris' efforts to wind up Exponential's operations." 1999 Del. Ch. LEXIS 9, at *44, 1999 WL 39547, at *11.

The court rejected a "general waste" claim by Apple Computer based upon a contention that Exponential's assets were dwindling. The court stated that "[e]xcept for the litigation support agreements, Apple does not document what assets were traded away or what inadequate consideration might have been received." 1999 Del. Ch. LEXIS 9, at *45, 1999 WL 39547, at *12. According to the court, "[t]he issue is not the size of the Exponential assets conveyed in contrast to the amount of assets remaining in Exponential, but the size of Exponential assets conveyed in comparison to the value received in exchange." *Id.*

Add the following at the end of the paragraph beginning and concluding on page 1529 (immediately after footnote 895):

An additional case rejecting waste allegations and refusing to excuse demand on this ground is *Ash v. McCall*, 2000 Del. Ch. LEXIS 144, at *23-26, 2000 WL 1370341, at *7-8 (Del. Ch. Sept. 15, 2000).

Section B 5 d

Add the following at the end of the first paragraph beginning and concluding on page 1530 (immediately after footnote 902):

Under these circumstances, "'the absence of any action or decision on the part of the board to which the demand would be addressed 'makes it impossible to perform the essential inquiry contemplated by *Aronson*'' – whether the presumption of the business judgment rule applied to the challenged transaction." *Kohls v. Duthie*, 2000 Del. Ch. LEXIS 103, at *15-16, 2000 WL 1041219, at *4 (Del. Ch. July 26, 2000) (quoting Donald J. Wolfe, Jr. & Michael A. Pittenger, *Corporate and Commercial Practice in the Delaware Court of Chancery* § 9-2(b)(3)(iii) (1998), and *Rales v. Blasband*, 634 A.2d 927, 933 (Del. 1993)).

Add the following at the end of footnote 904 on page 1530:

See also Kohls, 2000 Del. Ch. LEXIS 103, at *16 n.25, 2000 WL 1041219, at *4 n.25 (stating that "the *Aronson* test cannot be applied 'where a business decision was made by the board of a company, but a majority of the directors making that decision have been replaced' by the time the complaint is filed" (quoting *Rales v. Blasband*, 634 A.2d 927, 934 (Del. 1993)), but holding that "[h]ere, only 2 of the 4 directors have been replaced" and "[t]hus, all other things being equal, the *Aronson* test could still be applied"); *Smith v. Smitty McGee's, Inc.*, 1998 Del. Ch. LEXIS 87, at *3-4, 26-27, 1998

WL 246681, at *1, 7 (Del. Ch. May 8, 1998) (applying *Rales* test where sole director resigned and was replaced by new sole director).

Add the following at the end of footnote 905 on page 1531:

See also Kohls, 2000 Del. Ch. LEXIS 103, at *16, 2000 WL 1041219, at *4.

Add the following at the end of footnote 906 on page 1531:

See also In re Walt Disney Co. Derivative Litig., 731 A.2d 342, 379 (Del. Ch. 1998), *aff'd with leave to replead on other grounds sub nom. Brehm v. Eisner*, 746 A.2d 244 (Del. 2000) (stating that *Rales* "establishes the standard for pre-suit demand where, as here, the conduct challenged, i.e., breach of contract, is something other than a decision of the board of directors" and dismissing a contract claim belonging to corporation against a former corporate officer).

Add the following at the end of footnote 907 on page 1531:

See also Ash v. McCall, 2000 Del. Ch. LEXIS 144, at *36 & n.33, 2000 WL 1370341, at *10 & n.33 (Del. Ch. Sept. 15, 2000)

Add the following at the end of footnote 908 on page 1531:

See also Ash, 2000 Del. Ch. LEXIS 144, at *36 *n.33, 2000 WL 1370341, at 10 & n.33.

Add the following at the end of footnote 909 on page 1531:

See also Kohls, 2000 Del. Ch. LEXIS 103, at *16 n.25, 2000 WL 1041219, at *4 n.25.

Add the following at the end of footnote 916 on page 1533:

See also In re Abbott Labs. Derivative S'holder Litig., 126 F. Supp. 2d 535, 536 (N.D. Ill. 2000) ("[w]hen the Certificate of Incorporation exempts the directors from liability for acts or omissions other than violations of their duty of loyalty or acts not in good faith or involving intentional misconduct or knowing violations of law, the complaint must plead non-exempt conduct with sufficient particularity to permit the court reasonably to determine from the face of the complaint whether there is a substantial likelihood of liability").

Delete the second sentence (including footnote 917) in the paragraph beginning and concluding on page 1533.

Replace the Weinstock citation in footnote 968 on page 1541 with the following:

N.Y.L.J., Mar. 28, 1996, at 29 (N.Y. Sup. Ct. N.Y. Co.) and No. 100151/95 (N.Y. Sup. Ct. N.Y. Co. Oct. 30, 1996), *aff'd sub nom. Teachers' Retirement Sys. v. Welch*, 244 A.D.2d 331, 664 N.Y.S.2d 38 (N.Y. App. Div. 1st Dep't 1997).

Replace the Teachers' Retirement citation in footnote 976 on page 1543 with the following:

Teachers' Retirement Sys. v. Welch, 244 A.D.2d 231, 232, 664 N.Y.S.2d 38, 40 (N.Y. App. Div. 1st Dep't 1997).

Add the following at the end of the paragraph beginning on page 1542 and concluding on page 1543 (immediately after footnote 976):

In *Wilson v. Tully*, 243 A.D.2d 229, 676 N.Y.S.2d 531 (N.Y. App. Div. 1st Dep't 1998), another New York court construing Delaware law reached the same result, this time in a case where plaintiffs alleged breaches of fiduciary duty by the directors of Merrill Lynch & Co., Inc. in connection with Merrill Lynch's dealings with Orange County, California.

Plaintiffs alleged that a Merrill Lynch broker, Michael Stamenson, acted as an investment advisor to Orange County's Treasurer-Tax Collector and caused Orange County to purchase $4.9 billion in derivative instruments from Merrill Lynch. Interest rate increases in late 1993 and early 1994 caused the the value of Orange County's portfolio to decline sharply, and Orange County alleged that as a result it sustained approximately $2 billion in losses. *Id.* at 231, 676 N.Y.S.2d at 533-34.

The court rejected plaintiffs' contention that demand was excused because Merrill Lynch's directors "either wittingly or unwittingly permitted the allegedly illegal course of conduct to develop and continue to the point where Merrill Lynch was exposed to enormous legal liability." *Id.* at 234, 676 N.Y.S.2d at 535. Plaintiffs alleged that "[i]n so doing" Merrill Lynch's directors "violated their fiduciary duty to monitor Merrill Lynch's corporate affairs." *Id.*

Citing the Delaware Court of Chancery's decision in *In re Caremark International, Inc. Derivative Litigation*, 698 A.2d 959, 967 (Del. Ch. 1996), the court stated that "[i]t has been said that such a claim is possibly the most difficult theory in corporation law upon which a plaintiff might hope to win a judgment." 243 A.D.2d at 234, 676 N.Y.S.2d at 535. Here, the court concluded, plaintiffs had failed to overcome their pleading burden because "[n]owhere in their 68-page complaint do plaintiffs point to any specific conduct of the individual directors or board resolution relating to Orange County, but rely upon conclusory allegations that the defendant directors 'knew or recklessly disregarded' or 'knew or were reckless in not knowing' of Merrill Lynch's perilous course of conduct, thereby exposing the Company to numerous lawsuits and substantial damages." *Id.* at 234, 676 N.Y.S.2d at 536.

The court rejected an allegation that Merrill Lynch's board had knowledge of the alleged illegality of Merrill Lynch's dealings with Orange County because the directors "knew or recklessly disregarded Stamenson's history of selling highly leveraged, inappropriate investment products to municipal customers, '*potentially* in violation of federal and state law.'" *Id.* (emphasis added by court). The court pointed to the fact that "elsewhere in the complaint, in quoting a 1994 newspaper article," plaintiffs "acknowledge that five bills approved by the California Legislature since 1987 'widened counties' authority to put local tax money into more exotic investments' and that 'Merrill Lynch was quick to take advantage of the relaxed investment guidelines [it] fought so hard to achieve.'" *Id.* Thus, the court stated, "any illegality . . . had apparently been remedied consciously by Merrill Lynch, not by stopping such sales, but by lobbying to have legislation passed, which plaintiffs admit permitted Orange County's investment in such exotic investments." *Id.* at 237, 676 N.Y.S.2d at 537. The court added that "[e]ven assuming the possible illegality of Merrill Lynch's dealings with Orange County, demand would still not be excused absent specific allegations of self-dealing or bias on the part of a majority of the board." *Id.* at 235, 676 N.Y.S.2d at 536. To the contrary, the court quoted the Second Circuit's decision in *Lewis v. Graves*, 701 F.2d 245 (2d Cir. 1983), for the following proposition:

> Derivative suits are almost invariably directed at major, allegedly illegal, corporate transactions. By virtue of their offices, directors ordinarily participate in the decision making involved in such transactions. . . . Excusing demand on the mere basis of prior board acquiescence, therefore, would obviate the need for demand in practically every case.

243 A.D.2d at 235, 676 N.Y.S.2d at 536 (quoting 701 F.2d at 248).

The court also pointed to press reports of "internal squabbling regarding Merrill Lynch's aggressive sales practices toward Orange County" and that "top Merrill Lynch & Co. executives battled fiercely with one another over whether to rein in their business with the county." *Id.* According to plaintiffs, Merrill Lynch's directors "made a conscious decision to authorize or permit" the alleged wrongdoing. *Id.* This allegation, the court held, was a "conclusory allegation . . . unsupported by particularized facts." *Id.* Even if the allegation were supported by particularized facts, the court continued, Delaware law requires gross negligence before liability can be imposed, and gross negligence "in the corporate context, means 'reckless indifference to or a deliberate disregard of the whole body of stockholders' or actions which are 'without the bounds of reason.'" *Id.* (citation omitted). Even if accepted as true, the court stated, plaintiffs' allegations of negligence did not rise to this level of gross negligence. *Id.*

The court next addressed allegations that Merrill Lynch's directors knew or should have known that during the early 1980s Merrill Lynch and other brokerage firms had sold the City of San Jose "virtually identical highly-leveraged securities, which, as the result of a sharp increase in interest rates in 1984, resulted in a $60 million loss" by San Jose, that San Jose had sued Merrill Lynch and other brokerage firms, and that Merrill Lynch had contributed $750,000 to a $26 million settlement fund in that litigation. *Id.* at 231, 676 N.Y.S.2d at 534. The court also addressed allegations that "in 1993, Merrill Lynch made the 'extraordinary' decision to offer to buy Orange County's entire derivative portfolio for $3.5 billion, which offer was refused in a letter from Orange County's Treasurer in which he stated that 'it was only after extensive consultation with highly placed Merrill Lynch officials by conference call, in person, and in writing well over a year ago that we felt secure in investing an even larger percentage of our portfolio in derivatives securities.'" *Id.*

With respect to each of these allegations – "Merrill Lynch's decision to settle the San Jose litigation for $750,000, and its offer to buy back Orange County's derivatives portfolio" – the court held that "there are no particularized facts alleged that would create a reasonable doubt that they were anything but sound 'business decisions' made with the best interests of Merrill Lynch in mind." *Id.* at 235, 676 N.Y.S.2d at 536. The court reasoned as follows with respect to Merrill Lynch's offer to buy back Orange County's derivatives portfolio:

> There is no allegation that the buy-back offer was unreasonably high or low or did not reflect the actual market value of the portfolio. Instead, plaintiffs claim that "the major concern of Merrill Lynch's senior managers was not what losses the Orange County investment fund might suffer as a result of transactions entered into with Merrill Lynch, rather, the Company's concerns centered around the potential financial exposure Merrill Lynch itself might face. . . .
>
> Thus, it is just as reasonable to conclude that, if in fact the defendant directors were asked to approve the buyback offer, they determined that such offer was in the best interests of Merrill Lynch. As stated in an April 5, 1995 Wall Street Journal article quoted by plaintiffs, "[t]he risk managers' primary concern was a simple one: losing money. Merrill was lending against illiquid, volatile securities as collateral, and could have been on the hook for millions."

Id. at 235-36, 676 N.Y.S.2d at 536-37. This decision, the court stated, "[c]ertainly . . . does not appear 'so extreme or curious as to itself raise a legitimate ground to justify further inquiry and judicial review." 243 A.D.2d at 236, 676 N.Y.S.2d at 537 (quoting *Kahn v. Tremont Corp.*, 1994 Del. Ch. LEXIS 41, at *20, 1994 WL 162613, at *6 (Del. Ch. Apr. 21, 1994)).

The court also pointed to the following allegations in plaintiffs' complaint that "support the business judgment rule presumption as much as they seek to overcome it":

- "Merrill Lynch earned $35 to 40 million in commission revenues in 1992 and well in excess of $100 million in fees and commissions in 1993 and 1994 as a result of its aggressive sales to Orange County,"
- "[B]y 1993, profits from Merrill Lynch's municipal financing activities had risen dramatically to constitute between 5% and 10% of the Company's entire annual revenues,"
- "[D]espite internal memoranda urging caution, some Merrill Lynch executives continued to aggressively seek profits from the 'fast-growing business,'" and

- "Merrill Lynch undertook these sales despite unanimous agreement at the highest levels of the Company that they constituted a substantial risk to both the Company and Orange County."

Id. at 237, 676 N.Y.S.2d at 537-38. The court stated that "risk is at the heart of Merrill Lynch's business, or for that matter any business, and it seems as if the risk entailed resulted, for a substantial period of time, in what plaintiffs describe as 'huge fees and commissions to the company' and, presumably, financial benefit to Orange County." *Id.* at 238, 676 N.Y.S.2d at 538. The allegation that the "huge fees" Merrill Lynch obtained "were at the expense of Orange County and the result of breaches of fiduciary duties owed by the Company to Orange County," the court stated, was conclusory and therefore "insufficient to overcome the business judgment presumption that any action or inaction on the part of the defendant directors with regard to Merrill Lynch's dealings with Orange County was taken in good faith in what they thought was the best interests of the Company at that time." *Id.*

In sum, the court concluded, "despite all of plaintiffs' conclusory allegations, there is no well grounded evidentiary showing that a reasonable doubt exists as to whether any of the defendant directors' alleged actions or inaction with regard to the so-called 'red flags' cited by plaintiffs were other than valid exercises of the directors' business judgment and fiduciary responsibility to Merrill Lynch." *Id.* at 237, 676 N.Y.S.2d at 537.

Add the following at the end of the paragraph beginning and concluding on page 1543 (immediately after footnote 981):

A federal court construing Illinois law in *Silver v. Allard*, 16 F. Supp. 2d 966 (N.D. Ill. 1998), held that Illinois courts follow Delaware law with respect to the need for a demand and held that demand was required in a case where the plaintiff alleged that the directors of Unicom Corporation and its

Commonwealth Edison Company subsidiary, who were the same individuals, breached their fiduciary duties by

> (1) permitting ComEd and its employees to operate its nuclear power plants in violation of applicable government regulations; (2) failing to provide the financial and human resources necessary to insure that ComEd's nuclear power plants were operated in compliance with applicable government regulations; and (3) failing to implement remedial programs or establish procedures to monitor the effectiveness of such programs.

Id. at 968. The court stated that plaintiffs challenged "the absence of board action": "[r]ather than specifically allege the transactions Plaintiffs challenge, Plaintiffs merely allege, in a conclusory fashion, that the Directors failed to act." *Id.* at 970. The court pointed in particular to plaintiffs' allegations that "each Director Defendant knew or should have known of repeated transgressions by ComEd's senior managers, and did little, if anything, to rectify this conduct, which has jeopardized ComEd's and Unicom's continued financial integrity." *Id.*

The court stated that where the subject of a derivative action is the absence of board action, *Rales v. Blasband*, 634 A.2d 927 (Del. 1993), requires that plaintiffs must allege facts demonstrating "a reasonable doubt that the directors are disinterested and independent." 16 F. Supp. 2d at 970. The court held that plaintiffs had failed to do so because "[t]he only self-interest Plaintiffs allege is that the Directors are subject to personal liability" but "the mere fact that the directors are asked to sue themselves and risk personal liability is not enough to show lack of disinterest and independence." *Id.* at 970-71. The court added that even assuming that plaintiffs challenged conscious decisions by the directors to act or refrain from acting, demand only would be excused if plaintiffs alleged facts demonstrating "a reasonable doubt that the challenged transactions were the product of a valid exercise of the Directors' business judgment" and that plaintiffs had failed to do so. *Id.* at 970. The court explained as follows:

> Plaintiffs do not show that the challenged transactions "were 'devoid of a legitimate corporate purpose.'" In fact, Plaintiffs allege that the Directors were motivated by 'short-term sav-

> ings' and 'short-term profits' for Unicom and ComEd. Hence, the court cannot conclude that the transactions are '"so egregious on its face that [it] cannot meet the test of business judgment.'"

Id. (citations omitted).

Another federal court construing Illinois law reached the same result in *In re Abbott Laboratories Derivative Shareholder Litigation*, 126 F. Supp. 2d 535 (N.D. Ill. 2000). This case involved allegations that the directors of Abbott Laboratories failed to require Abbott's management to comply with federal requirements established by the Food and Drug Administration. The result, plaintiffs alleged, was a consent decree entered into by Abbott and the FDA on November 2, 1999 that required Abbot "to pay a $100 million penalty, withdraw 125 types of medical diagnostic test kits from the United States market, destroy certain inventory, and make various corrective changes in its manufacturing procedures." *Id.* at 536.

Plaintiffs alleged that Abbott's directors "were in knowing breach of their fiduciary duties by failing to correct and by failing to disclose the deficiencies that led to the consent decree." *Id.* at 537. In support of this allegation, plaintiffs pleaded that Abbott received warning letters from the FDA on October 20, 1993, March 28, 1994 and March 17, 1999, that Abbott representatives met with the FDA at least ten times during that period, that Abbott operated under an FDA-monitored compliance plan from July 19, 1995 through February 26, 1998 pursuant to which Abbott committed to make specific corrections and to submit progress reports to the FDA, and that the FDA conducted extensive inspections of Abbott's operations from May to July 1999 and detailed 45 deviations from FDA standards and Abbott submitted written responses that the FDA deemed insufficient. *Id.* at 537-38.

The court rejected these allegations as insufficient to excuse demand. The court pointed to the absence of any "allegation that the directors were even aware of the 1993 and 1994 warning letters, although apparently copies were sent to the chairman of the board, or that they had any reason to believe that appropriate corrective action was not being taken." *Id.* The court rejected an allegation that the directors knew about the March 1999 warning letter because it was publicly disclosed in two publications in June 1999. According to the court, "[w]e are left, then, to speculate as to whether plaintiffs claim that the directors knew of the representations in the March 18, 1999, warning letter at that time, or shortly thereafter," "whether they knew the results of the later inspection," and "whether they knew that corrective action was not being taken." *Id.* at 538. The court added that "[c]onceivably they were parties to a decision not to comply with federal requirements until the FDA threatened to file suits, or were advised that deficiencies were not being corrected and did nothing, but particularized factual allegations of what board members knew and when they knew it are lacking." *Id.*

The court added that plaintiffs' allegations that Abbott's directors "should have known" that appropriate corrective action was not being taken were insufficient to excuse demand because Abbott's directors were protected by a certificate of incorporation provision precluding "any liability that may arise from their negligence" and that "directors are entitled to rely upon the honesty and integrity of their subordinates until something occurs to alert suspicion." *Id.* at 536-37, 538. The court rejected plaintiffs' use of "a variety of pejorative words and phrases" – including "'sanctioning violations of federal laws and regulations,' 'caused,' 'knowing and culpable violation of their duties,' 'aware of . . . a risk of serious damage,' 'ratified and/or endorsed the ongoing violations of law,' 'an absence of good faith,' 'participated,' 'approved the wrongful acts complained of,' 'concealed' and 'misused'" – because these pejorative words and phrases were not supported by "particularized factual allegations." *Id.* at 537.

Section B 5 e

Add the following at the end of the paragraph beginning and concluding on page 1549 (immediately after footnote 1014):

Bansbach v. Zinn, 258 A.D.2d 710, 685 N.Y.S.2d 332 (N.Y. App. Div. 3d Dep't 1999), is illustrative. The plaintiffs in this action alleged that the directors of Besicorp Group Inc. breached their fiduciary duties to the corporation and wasted corporate assets by not taking action with respect to a scheme pursuant to which Michael Zinn, the president and chairman of the board of Besicorp, and Michael J. Daley, Besicorp's vice-president, chief financial officer and corporate secretary, violated federal campaign finance laws by soliciting campaign contributions from employees and reimbursing the employees for the contributions by means of falsely labeled "raises" and "bonuses." Besicorp and Zinn each pleaded guilty to two felonies – filing a false tax return and causing a false statement to be filed with the Federal Elections Commission. According to plaintiff, no effort was made by the directors of Besicorp to recover damages from Zinn and Daley for the harm caused to the corporation by their conduct or to obtain repayment from Zinn and Daley for sums advanced by the corporation to them for legal fees. *Id.* at 711, 685 N.Y.S.2d at 333.

The court held that a demand upon Besicorp's board – which consisted of Zinn and George A. Habib, Harold Harris and Richard E. Rosen – was excused because Zinn "so dominated and controlled Habib, Harris and Rosen that a demand upon the board would have been futile." *Id.* at 712, 685 N.Y.S.2d at 334. The court acknowledged that "the mere allegation of personal friendships is insufficient to establish domination and control" and relied instead upon the following alleged business relationships between Zinn and Habib, Harris and Rosen:

> [P]laintiff alleges that [Zinn] and a third party had once formed a corporation with Harris and that such corporation, in turn, did business with Besicorp. When such corporation failed to meet its obligations with Besicorp, plaintiff alleges, Besicorp

> "wrote off" a note payable to it in the amount of $127,500 and [Zinn] reimbursed Harris for a $14,000 payment made to finance the failed project. As to Habib and Rosen, plaintiff alleges that each had sought to do business with Besicorp and that Habib had submitted a written marketing and business consulting services proposal to Besicorp.

Id. at 713, 685 N.Y.S.2d at 334. The court noted that "[t]o the extent that plaintiff's complaint may be read as alleging that the board of directors' conduct . . . was so flagrant and egregious that it could not have been the product of sound business judgment . . . we find plaintiff's conclusory assertions in this regard to be insufficient to excuse demand upon this basis." *Id.* at 713 n.1, 685 N.Y.S.2d at 334 n.1.

Replace the Teachers' Retirement citation in footnote 976 on page 1543 with the following:

Teachers' Retirement Sys. v. Welch, 244 A.D.2d 231, 232, 664 N.Y.S.2d 38, 40 (N.Y. App. Div. 1st Dep't 1997).

Replace the Teachers' Retirement citation in footnote 1019 on page 1550 with the following:

No. 113271/94 (N.Y. Sup. Ct. N.Y. Co. Apr. 16, 1996), *aff'd*, 244 A.D.2d 231, 664 N.Y.S.2d 38 (N.Y. App. Div. 1st Dep't 1997).

Replace the Teachers' Retirement citation in footnote 1031 on page 1552 with the following:

No. 113271/94 (N.Y. Sup. Ct. N.Y. Co. Apr. 16, 1996), *aff'd,* 244 A.D.2d 231, 664 N.Y.S.2d 38 (N.Y. App. Div. 1st Dep't 1997).

Replace the Teachers' Retirement citation in footnote 1037 on page 1553 with the following:

Teachers' Retirement Sys. v. Welch, 244 A.D.2d 231, 664 N.Y.S.2d 38 (N.Y. App. Div. 1st Dep't 1997).

Replace the Woolworth citation in footnote 1038 on page 1553 with the following:

No. 109465/94 (N.Y. Sup. Ct. N.Y. Co. May 3, 1995) and N.Y.L.J., Apr. 22, 1996, at 28 (N.Y. Sup. Ct. N.Y. Co.), *aff'd*, 240 A.D.2d 189, 658 N.Y.S.2d 869 (N.Y. App. Div. 1st Dep't 1997).

Replace the Woolworth citation in footnote 1045 on page 1554 with the following:

240 A.D.2d at 189, 658 N.Y.S.2d at 689.

Delete "at 1-2" in the Woolworth citation in footnote 1047 on page 1554.

Replace the first sentence of the paragraph beginning and concluding on page 1557 (including footnotes 1065 and 1066) with the following:

The opposite conclusion is illustrated by two intermediate appellate court decisions in *Miller v. Schreyer*, 200 A.D.2d 492, 606 N.Y.S.2d 642 (N.Y. App. Div. 1st Dep't 1994), *subsequent proceedings*, 257 A.D.2d 358, 683 N.Y.S.2d 51 (N.Y. App. Div. 1st Dep't 1999), *leave to appeal denied*, 1999 N.Y. App. Div. LEXIS 5167 (N.Y. App. Div. 1st Dep't Apr. 29, 1999).

Replace "The court held" with "The court's first decision, issued in 1994, held" in the first sentence of the first paragraph beginning and concluding on page 1558 (immediately after footnote 1070).

Replace the first sentence in the second paragraph beginning and concluding on page 1558 (immediately after footnote 1072) with the following:

The Court of Appeal's decision in 1996 in *Marx v. Akers*, 88 N.Y.2d 189, 666 N.E.2d 1034, 644 N.Y.S.2d 121 (1996), rejected the *Miller* decision as wrongly decided.

Replace the third sentence (immediately after footnote 1073) in the second paragraph beginning and concluding on page 1558 with the following:

On a renewed motion to dismiss in *Miller* based upon *Marx*, the court's second decision, issued in 1999, adhered to its prior ruling pursuant to the law of the case doctrine. The court acknowledged that "the law of the case doctrine is not so inflexible as to preclude correction of a ruling based on a change in the law" but held that "'the error sought to be corrected must be so 'plain * * * [that it] would require [the] court to grant a reargument of a cause.''" *Miller v. Schreyer*, 257 A.D.2d 358, 361, 683 N.Y.S.2d 51, 54 (N.Y. App. Div. 1st Dep't 1999) (citations omitted), *leave to appeal denied*, 1999 N.Y. App. Div. LEXIS 5167 (N.Y. App. Div. Apr. 29, 1999). According to the court, "no compelling reason" was presented "for this Court to depart from the law of the case doctrine in what represents a largely factual determination, as opposed to a decision on a narrow point of law that clearly requires reversal in view of subsequent developments in our case law." *Id.* at 361, 683 N.Y.S.2d at 55. In the court's view, "[t]o abandon our ruling would require this Court to speculate whether, on a review of our original decision, with the advantage of the full record before it, the Court of Appeals would agree that Delaware case law . . . was improperly applied to the facts of this case." *Id.*

The court stated that "[i]t does not appear" that Delaware law absolves a board of directors "of all responsibility to prevent the repeated misuse of corporate resources for illegal purposes" and, the court noted, the Delaware Court of Chancery had described "our decision in this case" as one "based on 'obvious danger signs of employee wrongdoing.'" *Id.* at 362, 683 N.Y.S.2d at 55 (quoting *In re Baxter Int'l S'holders Litig.*,

654 A.2d 1268, 1271 (Del. Ch. 1995)). Under New York law, the court continued, *Marx* "imposes accountability for wrong-doing about which corporate directors unreasonably fail to inform themselves, as appropriate to the circumstances." *Id.* at 362, 683 N.Y.S.2d at 55. The alleged misconduct in this case, the court stated, involved "not one but a series of transactions, each involving hundreds of thousands of dollars, each executed on or about the last business day of the year, with the same client, in which the identical portfolios of Treasury securities and junk bonds were exchanged, only to be unwound within a few business days." *Id.* The court stated that "[i]n view of the illegal purpose of the transactions, their magnitude and duration, their timing and the identity of their beneficiary, the matter should have come to the attention of senior management even on a rudimentary audit," and that "[i]t is hardly unreasonable to require directors to implement basic financial oversight procedures sufficient to disclose a patently improper scheme extending over a five-year period." *Id.* The court added its view that "[n]or is it naive to consider it futile to expect the directors to launch a vigorous investigation well after the facts have come to light as the result of the insurer's insolvency," as "duly empowered regulatory agencies, notably the Securities and Exchange Commission and the Florida Department of Insurance" had done. *Id.*

The court accordingly held that "its ruling on the futility of service of a prelitigation demand on the board of directors of Merrill Lynch" was "not so clearly wrong, in light of subsequent case law, as to require departure from the well-established doctrine of law of the case." *Id.* The court accordingly determined to "adhere our original order." *Id.*

The same result was reached in *In re Oxford Health Plans, Inc.*, 192 F.R.D. 111 (S.D.N.Y. 2000), a case decided by a federal court in New York construing Delaware law. The court focused upon "allegations of misconduct in connection with the knowing or reckless issuance of materially false statements concerning financial results and operations of the company." *Id.* at 117. These "numerous breaches of fiduciary duty, intentional or as a result of reckless disregard," included

> failing to have in place sufficient financial controls and procedures to monitor the planned conversion to a new computer system; failing to implement and enforce procedures to prevent the wholesale appropriation of the Company's information and assets by certain of the Director Defendants (the "Insider Traders") who sold thousands of shares of their personal holdings of Oxford stock during the period of November 6, 1996 through August 20, 1997; knowingly or recklessly disseminating, or permitting to be disseminated, misleading information to shareholders; and allowing the Company to engage in wholesale improper billing practices and to violate numerous insurance regulations, thereby subjecting the Company to fines, penalties and further investigations. The Complaint also alleges against all Directors a generalized failure or neglect to monitor the activities of management, said to amount to reckless conduct as well as corporate waste.

Id. at 114. The court stated that a lack of good faith can be established "by showing a sustained or systematic failure to exercise oversight and assure adequate record keeping" and, citing *Miller*, stated that demand futility has been found in "cases where liability is based upon a failure to supervise and monitor, and to keep adequate supervisory controls in place, . . . especially where the failure involves a scheme of significant magnitude and duration which went undiscovered by the directors." *Id.* at 117.

A federal court in New York construing New York law similarly excused demand in *In re Bank of New York Derivative Litigation*, 2000 U.S. Dist. LEXIS 16502, 2000 WL 1708173 (S.D.N.Y. Nov. 14, 2000). The case involved allegations that the directors of Bank of New York Company, Inc. and its wholly-owned subsidiary, the Bank of New York, breached their fiduciary duties to shareholders by wrongfully permitting the Bank of New York "to aggressively expand its correspondent banking business in Russia" and "directly participated in, or knowingly or recklessly permitted the Bank to participate in, money laundering or other illegal activity with customers, including members of organized crime." 2000 U.S.

Dist LEXIS 16502, at *1-2, 2000 WL 1708173, at 1. The court held that the directors "failed to fully inform themselves to the extent reasonably appropriate under the circumstances" by "'ignor[ing] the clear risks of doing substantial wire transfer and other similar business with Russian correspondent banks,' 'fail[ing] to adopt reasonable internal controls and independent monitoring systems over [the Bank's] wire transfer business,' and 'ignor[ing] repeated specific warnings that [the Bank's] system of internal controls over its wire transfer business was a sham and that [the Bank] was aiding or participating in its customers' illegal banking activity.'" 2000 U.S. Dist LEXIS 16502, at *4-5, 2000 WL 1708173, at *2. The court also pointed to "numerous specific examples" in the plaintiffs' complaint of "publicly available and other information that plaintiffs contend should have put the individual defendants on notice, had they been acting with the diligence required of officers and directors of a bank, that the Bank was being exposed to unacceptable risks." 2000 U.S. Dist. LEXIS 16502, at *5, 2000 WL 1708173, at *2. The court quoted the *Oxford* court's statement that demand has been excused in cases "where liability is based upon a failure to supervise and monitor, and to keep adequate supervisory controls in place, . . . especially where the failure involves a scheme of significant magnitude and duration which went undiscovered by the directors." 2000 U.S. Dist. LEXIS 16502, at *6, 2000 WL 1708173, at *2 (quoting *Oxford*, 192 F.R.D. at 117).

Add the following at the end of the paragraph beginning and concluding on page 1559 (immediately after footnote 1084):

Additional decisions construing New York law and requiring demand include *Ciullo v. Orange & Rockland Utilities, Inc.*, No. 601136/98, slip op. at 6-7 (N.Y. Sup. Ct. N.Y. Co. Jan. 8, 1999), *aff'd*, 271 A.D.2d 369, 369, 706 N.Y.S.2d 428, 429 (N.Y. App. Div. 1st Dep't), *leave to appeal denied*, 95 N.Y.2d 760, 737 N.E.2d 952, 714 N.Y.S.2d 710 (2000), *Rudolph v. Panish*, No. 115585/98, slip op. at 6-8 (N.Y. Sup. Ct. N.Y. Co. June 4, 1999), and *Ash v. Alexander*, 2000 U.S. Dist. LEXIS

171, at *3-6, 2000 WL 20704, at *1-2 (S.D.N.Y. Jan. 12, 2000).

Add the following at the end of the first sentence (immediately after footnote 1096) of the paragraph beginning on page 1559 and concluding on page 1560:

An additional decision construing New York law and excusing demand is *Minzer v. Keegan*, 1997 U.S. Dist. LEXIS 16445, at *30 (E.D.N.Y. Sept. 22, 1997).

Replace "decision" with "and Minzer decisions" in the second sentence (immediately after footnote 1096) of the paragraph beginning on page 1559 and concluding on page 1560.

Section B 5 g

Replace "1996" with "Supp. 1998/99" in the Model Act § 7.42 citation in footnote 1112 on page 1562.

Replace "199" with "7-335" in the Model Act § 7.42 citation in footnote 1113 on page 1563.

Add the following at the end of footnote 1120 on page 1564:

See also Pace v. Jordan, 999 S.W.2d 615, 619-20, 625 (Tex. App. 1999) (Texas statute does not apply retroactively).

Replace "A fifteenth state," in the second sentence of the paragraph beginning and concluding on page 1564 (immediately after footnote 1120) with the following:

Hawaii, Utah and Wyoming also have adopted statutes enacting universal demand requirements. *See* Haw. Bus. Corp. Act § 414-172; Utah Bus. Corp. Code § 16-10a-740(3)(a); Wyo. Bus. Corp. Act § 17-16-742.

An eighteenth state,

Add the following at the end of footnote 1121 on page 1564:

See also Drain v. Covenant Life Ins. Co., 712 A.2d 273, 278-79 (Pa. 1998) (stating that universal demand requirement adopted in *Cuker v. Mikalauskas*, 692 A.2d 1042 (Pa. 1997), applies only in derivative actions filed after *Cuker* was decided).

Replace "7-343" with "7-336" in the Model Act § 7.42 citation in footnote 1150 on page 1570.

Delete "at 7–343-44" in the Model Act § 7.42 citation in footnote 1151 on page 1570.

Add the following at the end of the paragraph beginning on page 1571 and concluding on page 1572 (immediately after footnote 1161):

A New Jersey court *In re PSE&G Shareholder Litigation*, 718 A.2d 254 (N.J. Super. Ct. Ch. Div. 1998), a case where a demand was made, stated its view that "[r]equiring universal demand would place the burden of responding upon the board of directors, where it belongs, and would remove from the courts the necessity of engaging in a tortured inquiry of whether demand is excused." *Id.* at 260. According to the court in *PSE&G*, "[c]ourts would then be in a position to properly apply the business judgment rule to the action of the board of directors or any special litigation committee appointed to review and act upon a shareholder's demand." *Id.*

Section B 5 h

Add the following at the end of the paragraph beginning and concluding on page 1575 (immediately after footnote 1182):

The court in *Corwin v. Silverman*, 1999 Del. Ch. LEXIS 147, 1999 WL 499456 (Del. Ch. June 30, 1999), likewise held that the need for a demand is not altered by the filing of an amended complaint after a change in board composition where the amended complaint "spells out" allegations in the original complaint with "greater clarity" but the claims in the amended complaint cannot "fairly . . . be characterized as 'entirely new' claims." 1999 Del. Ch. LEXIS 147, at *18, 1999 WL 499456, at *5. A Minnesota court construing Delaware law in *Professional Management Associates, Inc. v. Coss*, 598 N.W.2d 406 (Minn. Ct. App. 1999), *review denied*, 1999 Minn. LEXIS 780 (Minn. Nov. 23, 1999), similarly held that a demand was not required where a demand previously had been excused, the board was newly constituted, and each of the counts stated in the amended complaint was contained in earlier complaints. The court stated that "[a]lthough not every specific issue raised within these counts was previously raised, the new language is only an expansion of the claims already raised." *Id.* at 411.

Add the following at the end of the paragraph beginning and concluding on page 1576 (immediately after footnote 1195):

A federal court in New Jersey construing Delaware law in *In re Cendant Corp. Derivative Action Litigation*, 96 F. Supp. 2d 394 (D.N.J. 2000), held that demand was not excused with respect to a cause of action against directors seeking contribution for amounts paid by the corporation to settle a claim alleging a violation by the corporation of Section 11 of the Securities Act of 1933, which prohibits false or misleading statements in a registration statement, because a majority of the corporation's board consisted of disinterested and independent directors at the time this claim first was asserted. *Id.* at 401-02. The court rejected plaintiff's reliance upon a finding earlier in the case that demand was excused with respect to causes of action for breach of fiduciary duty and gross negligence in a complaint that referenced the corporation's potential liability under Section 11 because the complaint that referenced the corporation's potential liability under Section 11 did so "merely to illustrate the depth of the individual defendants' alleged breaches of fiduciary duty." *Id.* at 398. The court noted that the complaint alleging causes of action for breach of fiduciary duty and gross negligence focused "on events which occurred in April 1998" and that there was no reference in that complaint to the corporation's announcement two years later of the proposed settlement of Section 11 claims for which a cause of action for contribution later was asserted. *Id.*

Add the following at the end of the paragraph beginning on page 1577 and concluding on page 1578 (immediately after footnote 1206):

Another federal district court in New York, *Strougo v. BEA Associates*, 2000 U.S. Dist. LEXIS 346, 2000 WL 45714 (S.D.N.Y. Jan. 19, 2000), followed the Delaware Court of Chancery's decision in *Harris v. Carter*, 582 A.2d 222 (Del. Ch. 1990), in a case governed by Maryland law and held that the need for a demand should be assessed "as of the time of the filing of the original complaint with respect to claims the allegations of which are raised both in the original complaint and in an amended complaint." 2000 U.S. Dist. LEXIS 346, at *12, 2000 WL 45714, at *5. The court stated that the Second Circuit's conclusion in *Brody v. Chemical Bank*, 517 F.2d 932 (2d Cir. 1975), that the need for a demand should be assessed as of the date an amended complaint is filed "appears to have relied exclusively on federal law in reaching this conclusion," but the Supreme Court held in *Kamen v. Kemper Financial Services, Inc.*, 500 U.S. 90 (1991), that state law governs the need for demand and "[s]ince the *Kamen* decision, *Brody* has not been cited for the proposition stated above, and thus no longer appears to be controlling." *Id.* The court stated its view that "the reasoning of the *Harris* Court is persuasive" and pointed to the Court of Chancery's "well-recognized expertise in the field of state corporation law." 2000 U.S. Dist. LEXIS 346, at *11, 2000 WL 45714, at *5.

By contrast, another federal court in New York, *Ash v. Alexander*, 2000 U.S. Dist. LEXIS 171, 2000 WL 20704 (S.D.N.Y. Jan. 12, 2000), in this case construing New York law, followed *Brody* and held that when a board has been replaced by a new board following a merger, "it would make no sense to permit plaintiff to amend yet again unless he could allege, which he concededly cannot, that he has made a demand on this new board." 2000 U.S. Dist. LEXIS 171, at *5-6, 2000 WL 20704, at *2. The court stated that *Harris* "is not here relevant" because "it did not involve New York law" and "did not involve, as here, an attempt to second-amend a complaint after the deficiencies involving the original failure to demand had repeatedly been brought to plaintiff's attention while the old board was still in existence." 2000 U.S. Dist. LEXIS 171, at *6 n.1, 2000 WL 20704, at *2 n.1.

A New York state court construing Delaware law in *Lushbough v. Merchants Group, Inc.*, No. 115600/93 (N.Y. Sup. Ct. Apr. 7, 1997), *motion for reargument denied*, No. 115600/93 (N.Y. Sup. Ct. N.Y. Co. Sept. 4, 1998), considered the standard of judicial review that governs a decision by disinterested directors that pursuit of derivative litigation would not serve the best interest of the corporation where an interested board at the time the litigation is commenced is replaced by a disinterested board, the new board appoints a special litigation committee consisting solely of new directors elected by shareholders for the sole purpose of serving on this committee, and the committee concludes that the prior board acted reasonably with respect to the conduct challenged in the litigation. Apr. 7, 1997 slip op. at 4; Sept. 4, 1998 slip op. at 3. The court stated that a new demand was not required under *Harris v. Carter*, 582 A.2d 222 (Del. Ch. 1990), but held that the business judgment rule – the standard that ordinarily governs board decisions to refuse demand where demand is required (*see* Chapter IV, Section B 6) – governed judicial review of the committee's decision that pursuit of the litigation would not serve the best interest of the corporation even though demand was not required. Apr. 7, 1997 slip op. at 5-7; Sept. 4, 1998 slip op. at 3-4.

The court explained that "*Harris* recognized . . . that where a new disinterested board comes into existence 'the (new) board may cause the corporation to act in a number of ways with respect to that litigation.'" Sept. 4, 1998 slip op. at 4-5 (quoting 582 A.2d at 230). One possibility, the court stated, is that "the board may, after deliberation on the matter, move to dismiss the case as not, in the board's business judgment, . . . in the corporation's best interest.'" *Id.* at 5 (quoting 582 A.2d at 230).

The court rejected a contention that cases where demand is excused but a new disinterested board has replaced the previous interested board are governed by the same standard that ordinarily applies where demand is excused – i.e., the two pronged standard first stated in *Zapata Corp. v. Maldonado*, 430 A.2d 779 (Del. 1981), pursuant to which "the court first inquires into the independence and good faith of the committee and the bases supporting its conclusions, with the burden "on the corporation to prove the independence, reasonableness of investigation and good faith" of the committee, and "[i]f the Court determines that the committee was independent and showed a reasonable basis for good faith findings, the Court then determines, applying its own business judgment, whether the motion to dismiss should be granted." Apr. 7, 1997 slip op. at 5-7; Sept. 4, 1998 slip op. at 4-5; *see also* Chapter IV, Section C 2 b-c (discussing *Zapata* standard). Rather, the court stated, "[w]here a majority of the board are not subject to a disqualifying self-interest, the board can decide for itself whether a derivative action should be dismissed and then cause a motion to dismiss to be made," and "[u]nder these circumstances, the Court will respect the business judgment of the board of directors." Apr. 7, 1997 slip op. at 7.

Section B 5 i (i)

Add the following at the end of the first sentence (immediately after footnote 1249) of the paragraph beginning and concluding on page 1583:

An Illinois court in *Miller v. Thomas*, 656 N.E.2d 89 (Ill. App. Ct. 1995), and a District of Columbia court construing Illinois law in *Flocco v. State Farm Mutual Automobile Insurance Co.*, 752 A.2d 147 (D.C. 2000), also followed the Delaware rule that "a shareholder who makes demand may not later assert that demand was in fact excused as futile." *Miller*, 656 N.E.2d at 97, *quoted in Flocco*, 752 A.2d at 153. The courts in *Miller* and *Flocco* stated the following: "We see no reason to deviate from Delaware's standard, as this rule makes a great deal of sense from an efficiency standpoint. It would be a waste of time and resources to allow a shareholder to make a demand and have the claim investigated by the company, only to allow the shareholder to declare the investigation meaningless when unhappy with the results." *Miller*, 656 N.E.2d at 97, *quoted in Flocco*, 752 A.2d at 153.

Add the following at the end of the paragraph beginning on page 1585 and concluding on page 1586 (immediately after footnote 1277):

A Texas court in *Pace v. Jordan*, 999 S.W.2d 615 (Tex. App. 1999), also held that a demand by one shareholder binds other shareholders. The court stated that the claims asserted by two shareholders, one of whom made a demand and the other of whom did not make a demand, were identical, and in order to succeed either shareholder "had to prove that he or she fairly and adequately represented the remaining shareholders." *Id.* at 621. The court stated that "[w]e discern no logical reason why a board's decision should not bind similarly situated shareholders making identical claims." *Id.* The court added that "[j]udicial economy demands that identical claims, which in actuality belong to the corporation, be simultaneously disposed of by one demand." *Id.*

Section B 6 a

Add the following at the end of footnote 1325 on page 1594:

See also Harhen v. Brown, 730 N.E.2d 859, 865 (Mass. 2000) ("[i]f the plaintiff chooses to make demand, the board may institute suit, take action short of litigation to resolve the issues the demanding shareholder has identified, or determine that no action is appropriate at that time").

Add the following at the end of footnote 1331 on page 1595:

See also Sterling v. Mulholland, 1998 U.S. Dist. LEXIS 19550, at *5, 1998 WL 879714, at *2 (S.D.N.Y. Dec. 16, 1998) (rejecting claim that "the board's initial position that the board 'prefers not to be a party to the action [but] does not oppose the action' constitutes tacit board approval of this derivative suit" because "stating that the corporation does not wish to be a party to the suit but does not otherwise oppose it makes no sense, given that the corporation would inherently be a party to the derivative suit" and "[i]n light of such contradictions, it is impossible to tell what exactly the board meant," and holding that "the board, having previously 'not opposed' a suit, can subsequently clarify, or change, its position upon further reflection" and oppose the litigation).

Section B 6 b

Add the following at the end of the paragraph beginning and concluding on page 1601 (immediately after footnote 1369):

The court in *Miller v. Thomas*, 656 N.E.2d 89 (Ill. App. Ct. 1995), reached the same result in a case where plaintiffs sought a response to a demand within two weeks. The court stated that "plaintiffs have not presented what the board should have done other than address the issue at its next meeting, and we do not believe that this insignificant delay [from the September 15, 1992 date of the demand until the October 16, 1992 date of the board's next meeting] could have justified any belief by the plaintiffs that demand was futile." *Id.* at 91, 97.

Section B 6 c

Replace "1997" with "2000" in the Fletcher citation in footnote 1397 on page 1605.

Add the following at the end of footnote 1427 on page 1610:

See also Grimes v. Donald, 673 A.2d 1207, 1220 (Del. 1996); *Grimes v. Donald*, 2000 Del. Ch. LEXIS 162, at *10 & n.9, 2000 WL 1788784 at *3 & n.9 (Del. Ch. Nov. 30, 2000).

Add the following at the end of footnote 1428 on page 1610:

See also Sterling v. Mulholland, 1998 U.S. Dist. LEXIS 19550, at *4-8, 1998 WL 879714, at *2 (S.D.N.Y. Dec. 16, 1998).

Add the following at the end of footnote 1431 on page 1611:

See also McDermott, Will & Emery v. Superior Court, 83 Cal. App. 4th 378, 383, 99 Cal. Rptr. 2d 622, 625 (Cal. Ct. App. 2000).

Add the following at the end of footnote 1436 on page 1611:

See also Flocco v. State Farm Mut. Auto. Ins. Co., 752 A.2d 147, 153 n.8 (D.C. 2000); *Miller v. Thomas*, 656 N.E.2d 89, 94 (Ill. App. Ct. 1995).

Add the following at the end of footnote 1437 on page 1611:

See also Harhen v. Brown, 730 N.E.2d 859, 865-66 (Mass. 2000) (citing this text).

Add the following at the end of footnote 1442 on page 1612:

But see In re PSE&G S'holder Litig., 718 A.2d 254, 261 (N.J. Super. Ct. Ch. Div. 1998) (adopting "a modified business judgment rule, the key feature being that the corporation, not the shareholder, would have to meet an initial burden of proof": "Courts would have to dismiss a shareholder derivative suit in accordance with management's recommendation so long as the corporation could establish the decision maker acted reasonably, in good faith, and in a disinterested fashion. The suggested standard would not permit the court to substitute its own business judgment for that of management. In determining whether the corporation has met its burden, the court would be able to consider all relevant justifications for management's determination, including the seriousness and weight of the plaintiff's allegations. This rule would protect corporate management by disallowing judicial intrusion into the substantive allegations except to the minimal extent necessary for the corporation to meet its burden. . . . [T]he standards of good faith and reasonableness are quite low and should be readily met.").

Add the following at the end of footnote 1446 on page 1612:

See also Pace v. Jordan, 999 S.W.2d 615, 623, 624 (Tex. App. 1999).

Add the following at the end of the paragraph beginning on page 1611 and concluding on page 1612 (immediately after footnote 1447):

The business judgment rule also governs decisions by board committees consisting of disinterested directors where the board that appoints the committee includes a majority of disinterested directors. *Harhen*, 730 N.E.2d at 867.

Add the following at the end of the paragraph beginning on page 1611 and concluding on page 1612 (immediately after footnote 1447):

A court construing Louisiana law has reached the same conclusion. *See Atkins v. Hibernia Corp.*, 182 F.3d 320, 324-25 (5th Cir. 1999).

Section B 6 d

Add the following at the end of the paragraph beginning and concluding on page 1613 (immediately after footnote 1452):

"It would be a waste of time and resources to allow a shareholder to make a demand and have the claim investigated by the company, only to allow the shareholder to declare the investigation meaningless when unhappy with the results." *Flocco v. State Farm Mut. Auto. Ins. Co.*, 752 A.2d 147, 153 (D.C. 2000) (quoting *Miller v. Thomas*, 656 N.E.2d 89, 97 (Ill. Ct. App. 1995)).

Section B 6 e

Add the following at the end of footnote 1485 on page 1619:

See also Dean v. Dick, 1999 Del. Ch. LEXIS 121, at *10, 1999 WL 413400, at *3 (Del. Ch. June 10, 1999) (stating, in the context of a limited partnership not involving the demand requirement, that "nothing in our partnership law requires a general partner to meet with limited partners at their every request").

Section B 6 f

Add the following at the end of the second paragraph beginning and concluding on page 1635 (immediately after footnote 1582):

A state court in New York construing Delaware law in *Brinckerhoff v. JAC Holding Corp.*, No. 663438/97 (N.Y. Sup. Ct. N.Y. Co. Sept. 30, 1998), *aff'd*, 263 A.D.2d 352, 692 N.Y.S.2d 381 (N.Y. App. Div. 1st Dep't 1999), reached the opposite conclusion in a case where plaintiffs "raised issues regarding the *bona fides* and adequacy" of an investigation conducted by a board committee considering a shareholder demand asserting that the corporation had sold its 41 percent interest in JAC Products, Inc. for "grossly inadequate" consideration to an entity affiliated with the corporation's controlling shareholder. Plaintiffs alleged that the committee failed to retain independent counsel (and instead was advised by the attorney who represented the corporation in the challenged transaction), ignored critical documents, did not interview a central figure in the challenged transaction, did not engage an independent financial advisor, did not perform an appropriate valuation of the corporation's 41 percent interest in JAC Products, and improperly applied a 50 percent discount due to "purported unmarketability." Slip. op at 10-12; 263 A.D.2d at 353, 692 N.Y.S.2d at 382. The court accordingly concluded that "plaintiffs have met their burden of raising a reasonable doubt as to the adequacy of the Special Committee's investigation of the JAC Products transaction, which would preclude the application of the business judgment rule." Slip op at 12.

Section B 6 g

Replace the heading in the first paragraph beginning and concluding on page 1636 (between footnotes 1582 and 1583) with the following:

g. Decisions Construing Massachusetts, New York, Illinois, Michigan and Texas Law.

Add the following at the end of the first paragraph beginning and concluding on page 1636 (between footnotes 1585 and 1586):

State court decisions in *Harhen v. Brown*, 730 N.E.2d 859 (Mass. 2000), and *Pace v. Jordan*, 999 S.W.2d 615 (Tex. App. 1999), illustrate the law in Massachusetts and Texas, respectively.

Add the following at the end of the paragraph beginning on page 1648 and concluding on page 1649 (immediately after footnote 1657):

The Supreme Judicial Court of Massachusetts in *Harhen v. Brown*, 730 N.E.2d 859 (Mass. 2000), held that "the business judgment rule is applicable in the context of a refusal of a presuit demand made either by a board composed of a majority of disinterested directors or its committee, whose members, in turn, are also disinterested." *Id.* at 867. Applying this standard, the court held that the business judgment rule protected a decision by a disinterested committee appointed by a disinterested board to refuse a demand seeking corporate action against directors and employees of Hancock Mutual Life Insurance Company alleged to have participated or acquiesced in illegal lobbying by Hancock of members of the Massachusetts legislature. The court rejected a claim that "the plaintiff has alleged sufficient facts that either the board or its committee acted in bad faith, or failed to investigate the claims adequately." *Id.* at 867. The court pointed to the fact that "at the time the demand was made, Hancock had already performed an internal investigation, reassigned or retired Sawyer and Hathaway [Hancock's senior registered lobbyist and the head of Hancock's government relations department, respectively], and instituted a moratorium on entertaining government officials." *Id.*

The court also held that the committee's letter refusing the demand, "while brief, was adequate" because "[i]t referenced to the plaintiff's demands and stated that those demands had been 'carefully reviewed.'" *Id.* "[L]engthy explanations of a demand refusal are not required," the court stated, and the "brief nature" of a reply to a demand "does not impugn the reasonableness of the board's investigation." *Id.* The court rejected a claim that a refusal by two Hancock employees to answer questions asked by plaintiff's counsel concerning why the demand was refused demonstrated bad faith. *Id.* at 868.

Pace v. Jordan, 999 S.W.2d 615 (Tex. App. 1999), also involved a demand that litigation be commenced on behalf of a utility company, in this case Houston Industries, Inc. ("HII"), against directors and officers of the corporation. Letters sent in October 1992 and March 1993 demanded litigation in connection with "bad investment strategies, legal malpractice and misappropriated lumber," and a letter sent in July 1993 demanded litigation in connection with mismanagement that led to the shutdown of HII's South Texas Nuclear Project ("STP") facility in February 1993 and increasing regulatory activity. *Id.* at 618-19. The corporation's board referred the charges in the first two demands to the board's audit committee for investigation, and the audit committee, with the assistance of an outside accounting firm and outside counsel, investigated the charges and found that they were unsupported by facts. The board accordingly refused the demands. *Id.* at 618. After refusing the second demand and before receiving the third demand, the board studied the causes of the regulators' concerns about the STP facility's operation and met with regulators to discuss issues relating to STP. The third demand then was received, and the corporation's directors voted to refuse the demand "based on their familiarity of the events and their discussions with federal regulators." *Id.* at 618-19.

The court rejected plaintiffs' contention that the board's investigation before the vote on the demand was inadequate "because the board was not fully informed about all of the allegations." *Id.* at 624. The court reasoned as follows:

> Director Milton Carroll stated that he and other voting directors had at times served on the personnel committee and were familiar with the management abilities of corporate officers, including appellees Jordan and Sykora. The board had obtained outside assessments of Pace's earlier claims, heard management's responses, and was unable to substantiate the claims. Throughout the ongoing assessment of STP, the directors had received regular reports from the Vice President, Nuclear, and from the board's own Nuclear Committee. Before considering Pace's claims, the directors knew of the management initiatives that had been and were being implemented to address the problems at STP. The directors had met with regulatory authorities only weeks before voting on Pace's demands and were satisfied that the regulators' concerns were being addressed. Based on this information, it was the directors' judgment that Pace's claims did not justify litigation. There was no genuine issue of material fact regarding whether appellees Jordan and Sykora carried out the corporate objectives set by the board, or whether they wavered in their loyalty to HII, HL&P [a wholly owned subsidiary of HII], or the shareholders.

Id. at 624. The court pointed to plaintiffs' acknowledgment that "the board, before its meeting to discuss Pace's demands, had reviewed the executive summary of the diagnostic evaluation team report," which "outlined the regulatory authority's assessment of the causes of the outage at STP." *Id.* The court also pointed to the lack of authority for the proposition that "information is insufficient to support a board's decision merely because the information is obtained before a demand is received." *Id.* at 624-25. The court added that the regulatory agency's findings and fines imposed against the corporation "are not pertinent to the sufficiency of the board's investigation" because "[a] derivative suit on the corporation's behalf cannot be maintained by merely showing that the board's decision not to act was unwise, inexpedient, negligent, or imprudent." *Id.* at 625.

Section B 6 h

Add the following at the end of the paragraph beginning on page 1650 and concluding on page 1651 (immediately after footnote 1671):

The same conclusion was reached by the Supreme Judicial Court of Massachusetts in *Harhen v. Brown*, 730 N.E.2d 859 (Mass. 2000). The court stated that "where the failure to pursue a claim in itself is an illegal act, the business judgment rule does not apply." *Id.* at 866.

Add the following at the end of the second paragraph beginning and concluding on page 1654 (immediately after footnote 1699):

The court in *Finley v. Superior Court*, 80 Cal. App. 4th 1152, 96 Cal. Rptr. 2d 128 (2000), a case involving a special litigation committee defense – pursuant to which independent directors form a committee in a case where demand is excused to consider whether litigation of a shareholder claim will serve the best interests of the corporation (*see* Chapter IV, Section C) – likewise distinguished between the "two distinct exercises of business judgment" that potentially may be exercised in the context of ultra vires, illegal or unconstitutional acts. *Id.* at 1161, 96 Cal. Rptr. 2d at 135. First, the court stated, the defendants in the case invoked the business judgment rule to protect their decision to make contributions to a political action committee. The court "assume[d], without deciding," that "the business judgment rule would not apply to this decision if the contributions were ultra vires or illegal." *Id.* at 1161-62, 96 Cal. Rptr. 2d at 135. Second, defendants invoked the business judgment rule to protect the special litigation committee's decision that this derivative action is not in the best interest of the corporation. "Even assuming the underlying contributions were ultra vires or illegal," the court stated, "the decision not to pursue a derivative action regarding them was not ultra vires, illegal, or unconstitutional" and thus "this decision was entitled to the protection of the business judgment rule." *Id.* at 1162, 96 Cal. Rptr. 2d at 135.

Section B 6 i

Replace "7-351" with "7-347" and replace "1996" with "Supp. 1998/99" in the Model Act § 7.44 citation in footnote 1711 on page 1656.

Replace "7-356" with "7-347" in the Model Act § 7.44 citation in footnote 1715 on page 1657.

Replace "7-354" with "7–47-48" in the Model Act § 7.44 citation in footnote 1716 on page 1657.

Add "at 7-348" in the Model Act § 7.44 citation at the end of footnote 1717 on page 1657.

Add the following at the end of footnote 1718 on page 1657:

See also Einhorn v. Culea, 612 N.W.2d 78, 86 (Wis. 2000) (stating, in a case construing statute based upon the Model Act, that "the presence of one or more of these factors is not solely determinative of the issue whether a director is independent" but that a court may "give weight to these factors").

Replace "7-356" with "7–48-49" in the Model Act § 7.44 citation in footnote 1719 on page 1658.

Add the following at the end of the first sentence of the second paragraph beginning and concluding on page 1658 (between footnotes 1722 and 1723):

Hawaii, Utah and Wyoming also have adopted statutes containing universal demand requirements. *See* Haw. Bus. Corp. Act § 414-172; Utah Bus. Corp. Code § 16-10a-740(3)(a); Wyo. Bus. Corp. Act § 17-16-742.

Add the following at the end of the second sentence of the second paragraph beginning and concluding on page 1658 (immediately after footnote 1724):

Hawaii also has enacted a statute identical to Section 7.44 of the Model Act. *See* Haw. Bus. Corp. Act § 414-175. These statutes require courts "to defer to the business judgment of a properly composed and properly operating special litigation committee." *Einhorn*, 612 N.W.2d at 84.

Add the following at the end of the second paragraph beginning and concluding on page 1658 (between footnotes 1724 and 1725):

Utah and Wyoming also have enacted statutes similar to the Model Act but with the differences summarized below.

Replace "7-351" with "at 7-344" in the Model Act § 7.44 citation in footnote 1730 on page 1660.

Add the following at the end of the paragraph beginning and concluding on page 1664 (immediately after footnote 1752):

Utah's statute provides that "[i]f a corporation proposes to dismiss a derivative proceeding" pursuant to the statute, discovery "shall be limited" to facts relating to whether the directors who determine that maintenance of the derivative proceeding is not in the best interests of the corporation are "independent and disinterested" and "the good faith of the inquiry and review" by the directors. Utah Bus. Corp. Act § 16-10a-740(3)(e). The statute states that "the reasonableness of the procedures followed" by the directors in conducting their review "may not extend to any facts or substantive matters with respect to the act, omission, or other matter that is the subject matter of the derivative proceeding." *Id.*

Add the following at the end of the paragraph beginning on page 1664 and concluding on page 1665 (immediately after footnote 1756):

The Wyoming statute provides for dismissal only if a court-appointed panel of one or more independent persons determines that maintenance of the derivative proceeding is not in the best interests of the corporation. Wyo. Bus. Corp. Act § 17-16-744(a), (b). The plaintiff bears the burden of proving that the statute's requirements have not been met. *Id.* § 17-16-744(b).

Section B 7

Add the following at the end of footnote 1779 on page 1673:

See also Brehm v. Eisner, 746 A.2d 244, 266 (Del. 2000).

Add the following at the end of footnote 1780 on page 1674:

See also Miller v. Thomas, 656 N.E.2d 89, 96 (Ill. App. Ct. 1995).

Replace the Teachers' Retirement citation in footnote 1789 on page 1676 with the following:

Teachers' Retirement Sys. v. Welch, 244 A.D.2d 231, 232, 644 N.Y.S.2d 38, 39 (N.Y. App. Div. 1st Dep't 1997);

Add the following at the end of the first paragraph beginning and concluding on page 1676 (immediately after footnote 1789):

A trial court in New Jersey in *In re PSE&G Shareholder Litigation*, 718 A.2d 254 (N.J. Super. Ct. Ch. Div. 1998), after adopting "a modified business judgment rule" requiring the corporation to meet "an initial burden of proof" and "establish the decision maker acted reasonably, in good faith, and in a disinterested fashion," permitted discovery "limited to the narrow issue of what steps the directors took to inform themselves of the shareholder demand and the reasonableness of its decision." *Id.* at 261. The court stated that this discovery could include "depositions of all the directors and officers who were on the board when the demand was refused," "minutes of any meetings in which the decision to either proceed with the litigation or reject the demand was discussed," and "any documents which were generated to inform the directors upon which they based their decision to reject the demand." *Id.* at 261-62. The court added that "[p]laintiffs may not have discovery on the merits of their claim nor may they require defendants to produce documents which were utilized in making the decisions which resulted in alleged mismanagement." *Id.* at 261. The court stated that "discovery should be made available from the time the demand was made" and "[a]ny discovery which relates to actions that occurred prior to the demand would go to the merits of the litigation" and not the "narrow issue" of the board's response to the demand. *Id.*

Replace "7-356" with "7–48-49" and replace "1996" with "Supp. 1998/99" in the Model Act § 7.44 citation in footnote 1792 on page 1676.

Add the following at the end of the paragraph beginning on page 1676 and concluding on page 1677 (immediately after footnote 1796):

Defendants likewise cannot rely upon affidavits in support of a motion to dismiss for failure to comply with the demand requirement "since such a motion is directed to the face of the complaint." *Mizel v. Connelly*, 1999 Del. Ch. LEXIS 157, at

*15, 1999 WL 550369, at *5 (Del. Ch. July 22, 1999). The court added that allowing a defendant to introduce affidavits in support of a motion to dismiss for failure to comply with the demand requirement "would create a gross imbalance" because plaintiffs are not entitled to discovery to assist their compliance with the demand requirement's pleading with particularity requirement. 1999 Del. Ch. LEXIS 157, at *16, 1999 WL 550369, at *5.

Add the following at the end of the paragraph beginning and concluding on page 1679 (immediately after footnote 1816):

The Delaware Supreme Court in *Brehm v. Eisner*, 746 A.2d 244 (Del. 2000), summarized the law governing Section 220 actions and how Section 220 actions constitute one of the "'tools at hand' to develop the necessary facts for pleading purposes" as follows:

> [P]laintiffs may seek relevant books and records of the corporation under Section 220 of the Delaware General Corporation Law, if they can ultimately bear the burden of showing a proper purpose and make specific and discrete identification, with rifled precision, of the documents sought. Further, they must establish that each category of books and records is essential to the accomplishment of their articulated purpose for the inspection. We do not presume to direct the Court of Chancery how it should decide any proceeding under Section 220. From a timing perspective, however, we note that such a proceeding is a summary one that should be managed expeditiously.

Id. at 266-67 (footnotes omitted).

The Delaware Court of Chancery in *White v. Panic*, 2000 Del. Ch. LEXIS 14, 2000 WL 85046 (Del. Ch. Jan. 19, 2000), stated that a shareholder who fails to conduct the "pre-suit investigation recommended by the Supreme Court in *Rales v. Blasband*" is not entitled to "a broad reading" by the court of the facts alleged in his complaint or for the court to infer from the facts alleged in his complaint "the existence of other facts that would have been proven or disproven by a further pre-suit investigation." 2000 Del. Ch. LEXIS 14, at *20, 2000 WL

85046, at *6. The court stated that the plaintiff in a shareholder derivative action may "rely on the truthfulness of reports published by reputable media," but added that this principle "hardly relieves a plaintiff of the responsibility addressed in *Rales* of using the 'tools at hand' to engage in further investigation needed to flesh out the matters reported upon." 2000 Del. Ch. LEXIS 14, at *22, 2000 WL 85046, at *7.

The court noted that "more information could and should have been obtained" in the case before the court and that "[i]nformation gained by means of a request to inspect corporate books or records might have led to the facts justifying an inference that the Director Defendants reached their conclusions because of considerations other than stockholder interest" or "might also have led plaintiff and his counsel to abandon their claim or to acknowledge that demand was not excused." 2000 Del. Ch. LEXIS 14, at *22-23, 2000 WL 85046, at *7, *quoted in In re Delta & Pine Land Co. S'holders Litig.*, 2000 Del. Ch. LEXIS 91, at *21 n.17, 2000 WL 875421, at *7 n.17 (Del. Ch. June 21, 2000); *see also Ash v. McCall*, 2000 Del. Ch. LEXIS 144, at *55 & n.56, 2000 WL 1370341 at *15 & n.56 (Del. Ch. Sept. 15, 2000) (dismissing claim without prejudice and "leav[ing] it to plaintiffs" to adduce facts "sufficient to impute knowledge . . . to the company's board of directors" "through various pre-discovery fact-finding methods they have at their disposal," and noting that "the Delaware Supreme Court has repeatedly exhorted" that "shareholders plaintiffs should use the 'tools at hand,' most prominently § 220 books and records actions, to obtain information necessary to sue derivatively").

The Delaware Court of Chancery's decision in *Grimes v. DSC Communications Corp.*, 724 A.2d 561 (Del. Ch. 1998), addressed the scope of discovery permitted in a Section 220 proceeding seeking the inspection of corporate books and records in order to obtain facts to be used in an attempt to satisfy pleading requirements in a derivative action. The decision involved the shareholder, Charles L. Grimes, whose derivative claims had been dismissed due to his failure to make a demand in *Grimes v. Donald*, 673 A.2d 1207 (Del. 1996), one of the Supreme Court decisions pointing to the availability of the summary procedure provided for in Section 220 "as an information-gathering tool in the derivative context." *Id.* at 1216 n.11.

On June 5, 1996, Grimes made a demand. On May 20, 1997, DSC sent Grimes a one-page letter informing him that his demand had been refused by DSC's board following a special board committee investigation and recommendation to refuse the demand. DSC's letter read as follows:

> As you know, the Board of Directors of DSC Communications Corporation (the "Board") appointed a special committee of independent directors (the "Special Committee") to investigate the issues raised in your demand letter to the Board dated June 5, 1996 (the "Demand"). The Special Committee conducted an extensive investigation, including a review of relevant documents and interviews of numerous individuals with knowledge of the issues raised in the Demand.
>
> Based upon its investigation and consideration of applicable law, the Special Committee prepared a comprehensive report to the Board recommending that the Board reject the Demand. The report was presented to the Board at its meeting on April 30, 1997. After full discussion at that meeting and a meeting held on May 15, 1997, the Board decided to accept the recommendation of the special committee.
>
> Accordingly, the Board has rejected your demand and has declined to take any of the actions requested in the demand.

724 A.2d at 564 & n.2.

Grimes made a written request to inspect and copy the DSC books and records "relating to the formation, investigation and report of the Special Committee and the board's decision to accept the Special Committee's recommendation." *Id.* at 564. Grimes stated that the purpose for this request was "to determine the independence of the Special Committee and whether the Special Committee and the Board have complied with Delaware law in their analysis and rejection of the Demand." *Id.* at 564-65. DSC produced some documents, but refused to produce or produced redacted documents in the following categories:

> 1. Documents produced or prepared by the Special Committee including its report recommending refusal of the plaintiff's pre-suit demand.
> 2. Documents referring or relating to interviews conducted by the Special Committee.
> 3. Documents referring or relating to any legal authorities relied on or considered by the Special Committee.
> 4. Documents referring or relating to meetings held by the Special Committee or actions taken by the Committee in lieu of a meeting, including minutes of such meetings.
> 5. Documents reflecting disbursements made in connection with investigations conducted by the Special Committee.
> 6. Documents reviewed or provided to the board in connection with its acceptance of the Special Committee's recommendation.
> 7. Other documents referring or relating to the board's rejection of the plaintiff's pre-suit demand.

Id. at 565 & n.5.

The court stated that under Section 220, "a record stockholder of a Delaware corporation is entitled to inspect corporate books and records if . . . the inspection is for a proper purpose which is 'reasonably related to such person's interest as a stockholder.'" *Id.* at 565 (citations omitted). The court added that "[p]roper purpose has been construed to mean that a shareholder's *primary purpose* must be proper, irrespective of whether any secondary purpose is proper," that "the primary purpose may not be adverse to the corporation's best interest," and that "[i]t is the stockholder's burden to establish by a preponderance of the evidence that his purpose is proper." *Id.*

Applying these principles and citing the Supreme Court's decisions in *Grimes*, *Rales v. Blasband*, 634 A.2d 927 (Del. 1993), and *Scattered Corp. v. Chicago Stock Exchange, Inc.*, 701 A.2d 70 (Del. 1997), the court held that the stated purpose for Grimes' demand – to obtain access to DSC's books and records in order to determine whether there are grounds to assert a claim that his demand was wrongfully refused, and, if so, to assist him in meeting the particularized pleading requirements of Delaware law – was a proper purpose under Section 220. 724 A.2d at 566. The court reasoned as follows:

> [T]he plaintiff has taken to heart the Supreme Court's admonition. He made a demand and, nearly one year later, was told without explanation, or "peremptorily," that the board of directors, on the recommendation of the Special Committee, had refused his demand. Plaintiff is now attempting to "use the tools at hand," in order to determine whether his demand was wrongfully refused. *Grimes* and *Scattered Corp.* clearly indicate that a Section 220 request for documents under these circumstances is proper.

Id.

The court next held that "the right to obtain corporate records for the purpose of determining whether or not a demand was improperly refused focuses on the committee process itself and extends at least to 'reports or minutes, reflecting the corporate action.'" *Id.* at 567 (quoting *Grimes*, 673 A.2d at 1218). Stockholders thus are "entitled to receive copies of the Special Committee's report, minutes of the meetings of the Special Committee and minutes of any meeting of the board of directors relating to the creation or functioning of the Special Committee, including any meeting of the board of directors at which the recommendation of the Special Committee was considered or approved." *Id.* at 567. The court also required production of "documents reflecting payments made to or on behalf of the members of the Special Committee." *Id.* The court, however, held that plaintiff was "not entitled to receive or examine copies of other documents not directly related to the Special Committee's conclusions and recommendations." *Id.* As examples, the court pointed to "interview summaries prepared by counsel to the Special Committee" and "records of every disbursement made in connection with the investigation." *Id.*

The court explained the distinction it was drawing between these categories of documents by reasoning that "[o]rdinarily . . . basic documents" of the type the court was allowing Grimes to obtain in his Section 220 action "should suffice for the purposes of establishing or raising reasonable grounds for suspicions about a special committee's independence, good faith and due care." *Id.* The court left upon the possibility of broader discovery where a plaintiff "can articulate a reasonable need to inquire further after review of those basic documents." *Id.* The court described its conclusions as "broadly consistent with decisions of this Court in defining the scope of allowable discovery in the analogous context of a motion by a special litigation committee to dismiss or settle properly instituted derivative litigation." *Id.* (citing *Kaplan v. Wyatt*, 484 A.2d 501 (Del. Ch. 1984), *aff'd*, 499 A.2d 1184 (Del. 1985), and *Carlton Invs. v. TLC Beatrice Int'l Holdings, Inc.*, 1997 Del. Ch. LEXIS 4, 1997 WL 38130 (Del. Ch. Jan. 28, 1997)).

The court then turned to DSC's contention that the special committee report, which was prepared by the committee's counsel, and minutes of special committee and board meetings (and other documents that the court had ordered DSC to produce) were protected by the attorney-client privilege. The court relied upon the doctrine first articulated by the Fifth Circuit in *Garner v. Wolfinbarger*, 430 F.2d 1093 (5th Cir. 1970), *cert. denied*, 401 U.S. 974 (1971), and discussed in Chapter IV, Section E 1. Under the *Garner* doctrine, "where the corporation is in suit against its stockholders on charges of acting inimically to stockholder interests, protection of those interests as well as those of the corporation and of the public require that the availability of the privilege be subject to the right of the stockholders to show 'good cause' why the privilege should not apply." *Grimes*, 724 A.2d at 568 (quoting 430 F.2d at 1103-04). The court pointed to the following five factors enumerated in *Garner* "for determining whether good cause exists" that were "[o]f particular relevance" in this case: "(i) the number of shares owned by the shareholder and the percentage of stock they represent; (ii) the assertion of a colorable claim; (iii) the necessity of the information and its unavailability from other sources: (iv) whether the stockholder has identified the information sought and is not merely fishing for information; and (v) whether the communication is advice concerning the litigation itself." *Id.*

The court acknowledged that the *Garner* test usually is applied in the context of a pending lawsuit, while here "the plaintiff seeks access to DSC's books and records in order to determine whether the board wrongfully refused his demand, and if so to assist him in meeting the particularized pleading requirements of Rule 23.1." *Id.* at 568. The court concluded that "while as of yet no action has been filed, the current posture of the case contemplates the possible filing of a derivative suit sometime in the future" and as a result "it is appropriate to analyze whether the plaintiff has demonstrated 'good cause' under the factors set forth in *Garner*." *Id.* at 568-69.

"Giving due weight to the factors set forth in *Garner*, and in particular the ones listed above," the court held that "the plaintiff has demonstrated 'good cause' for production of the privileged documents." *Id.* at 569. The court explained that "[o]f particular import is the fact that the documents sought are unavailable from any other source while at the same time their production is integral to the plaintiff's ability to assess whether the board wrongfully refused his demand – the stated purpose of his Section 220 demand." *Id.* The court continued:

> In *Grimes*, the Supreme Court specifically stated that a stockholder who makes a demand and receives only a preemptory refusal has "the right" to use the "tools at hand" to obtain relevant corporate records for the purpose of determining whether the demand was wrongfully refused. The Supreme Court specifically identified, without limitation, reports, minutes and other related information reflecting the corporate action taken as documents which a shareholder was entitled to receive. Further, in making these statements, the Supreme Court contemplated that these documents would be available to a shareholder in the context of a Section 220 demand.

Id.

The court also rejected DSC's contention that the documents requested were protected by the work product doctrine, which the court explained is "intended to protect 'materials an attorney assembled and brought into being in anticipation of litigation.'" *Id.* at 569-70 (citation omitted). Under Delaware law, the court explained, "a party may obtain information otherwise protected by this doctrine upon a showing that it has substantial need for the materials and is unable, without undue hardship, to obtain the substantial equivalent of the materials by other means." *Id.* at 570. The court stated that "[f]or the same reasons that the plaintiff has shown 'good cause' to overcome the claim of attorney-client privilege, . . . he has also shown a substantial need for the information for purposes of the work product doctrine." *Id.* In the court's words:

> As discussed *supra*, in order for the plaintiff to be able to determine whether the committee and the board wrongfully refused his demand he needs to have access to documents which reveal the deliberative processes which the committee and the board underwent. The only place the plaintiff can obtain this information is in such documents as the report of the special committee and the minutes of the meetings of the board at which it discussed the committee's report and voted to accept its recommendation. Accordingly, under the circumstances, just as the defendant's attorney-client privilege claim fails, so too must its work product immunity claim

Id.

DSC also sought to prevent production of the requested documents based upon a contention that these documents were protected by the self-critical analysis privilege, a privilege that "where recognized . . . protects confidential, non-factual deliberative material, including recommendations or opinions resulting from internal investigations, reviews or audits." *Id.*

The court stated that "Delaware courts have thus far refused to recognize the privilege," and held that "even if Delaware were to adopt this privilege, it could not properly be asserted in the present situation." *Id.* at 570, 571. The court reasoned that "courts that recognize the self-critical analysis privilege apply a four factor test in determining whether the privilege applies." *Id.* at 570. These four factors consist of the following: "(i) the information in question results from a self-critical analysis; (ii) the information was intended to be and has been kept confidential; (iii) the public has a strong interest in preserving the free flow of the type of information sought; and (iv) the free flow of that information would be curtailed if the information were discoverable." *Id.*

The court focused primarily upon the fourth factor and DSC's claims that "rejection of the privilege will have a chilling effect on the special committee process of corporations residing in Delaware." *Id.* at 571. According to DSC, "if committee reports are not privileged, the integrity of the process itself is likely to be compromised because corporations will no longer be honest in their self-evaluations" and this "will have an adverse impact on shareholders." *Id.* DSC also contended that "in the shareholder demand context, absent assurances that its determinations and recommendations will be kept confidential, boards and special committees would no longer have any incentive to perform an objective and candid analysis of the issues raised by the demand." *Id.*

The court rejected these contentions. The court stated that "[i]n a shareholder demand situation, far from discouraging candor and objectivity, subjecting the report to disclosure should encourage the committee and the board to undergo a thorough investigation." *Id.* According to the court: "A thorough report may convince a shareholder not to file a derivative suit or, if one is filed, provide strong evidence that the committee and the board undertook a comprehensive investigation which fully supported its determination to refuse the demand." *Id.*

The Delaware Court of Chancery in *Harbor Finance Partners v. Huizenga*, 751 A.2d 879 (Del. Ch. 1999), after concluding that "[c]lose familial relationships between directors can create a reasonable doubt as to impartiality" and that "[t]he plaintiff bears no burden to plead facts demonstrating that directors who are closely related have no history of discord or enmity that renders the natural inference of mutual loyalty and affection unreasonable," added that "one wonders how a plaintiff could use tools such as 8 Del. C. § 220 or public filings to generate such facts." *Id.* at 889 & n.32.

Section B 10

Replace "1996" with "Supp. 1998/99" in the Model Act § 7.42 citation in footnote 1862 on page 1687.

Add the following at the end of footnote 1864 on page 1687:

See also Harhen v. Brown, 730 N.E.2d 859, 868 (Mass. 2000) ("Although California, Delaware, and New York have eliminated this requirement, a 'substantial minority' of jurisdictions, including Massachusetts, continue to require that demand be made on other shareholders") (citing this text).

Add the following at the end of footnote 1865 on page 1687:

See also Harhen, 730 N.E.2d at 868 ("[t]he rationale for demand on other shareholders is that such a requirement allows the majority of shareholders to determine whether legal action is in the corporation's best interest").

Add the following at the end of footnote 1868 on page 1688:

See also Harhen, 730 N.E.2d at 867 ("[A]n exception to the shareholder demand requirement, where a very large number of shareholders is involved, as in this case, is eminently reasonable, and we therefore adopt such an exception. To hold otherwise would place a tremendous financial and administrative burden on plaintiffs; in this case requiring the plaintiff to make demand on the seven million other policyholders.").

Section C

Add the following at the end of footnote 1879 on page 1690:

See also Atkins v. Hibernia Corp., 182 F.3d 320, 325 n.3 (5th Cir. 1999); *Sterling v. Mulholland*, 1998 U.S. Dist. LEXIS 19550, at *7 n.4, 1998 WL 879714, at *2 n.4 (S.D.N.Y. Dec. 16, 1998); *Miller v. Thomas*, 656 N.E.2d 89, 94 (Ill. App. Ct. 1995); *Harhen v. Brown*, 730 N.E.2d 859, 867 (Mass. 2000).

Add the following at the end of footnote 1883 on page 1690:

See also In re General Instrument Corp. Sec. Litig., 23 F. Supp. 2d 867, 873 n.6 (N.D. Ill. 1998) ("Of course, a finding of demand futility does not preclude the corporation from subsequently appointing a disinterested litigation committee to assess the merits of going forward with the litigation. But this prospective right has nothing to do with whether the plaintiff's demand on the Directors when the suit was filed would have been futile.") (citations omitted).

Section C 1 a

Add the following at the end of footnote 1919 on page 1695:

See also Drilling v. Berman, 589 N.W.2d 503, 506-07 (Minn. Ct. App. 1999), *review denied*, 1999 Minn. LEXIS 306 (Minn. May 18, 1999).

Add the following at the end of footnote 1922 on page 1695:

See also Finley v. Superior Court, 80 Cal. App. 4th 1152, 1158-61, 96 Cal. Rptr. 2d 128, 132-34 (2000).

Add the following at the end of footnote 1927 on page 1695:

See also Strougo v. Bassini, 112 F. Supp. 2d 355, 361 (S.D.N.Y. 2000); *Strougo v. Padegs*, 27 F. Supp. 2d 442, 447 (S.D.N.Y. 1998); *Strougo v. Padegs*, 1 F. Supp. 2d 276, 280 (S.D.N.Y. 1998).

Add the following at the end of the first sentence (between footnotes 1933 and 1934) in the paragraph beginning on page 1695 and concluding on page 1696:

A federal court construing Louisiana law has reached the same conclusion. *See Atkins v. Hibernia Corp.*, 182 F.3d 320, 325 (5th Cir. 1999).

Section C 1 b

Add the following at the end of the paragraph beginning on page 1698 and concluding on page 1699 (immediately after footnote 1948):

"In repealing the section, the legislature made it clear it was not commenting on the substance of the section and that its repeal 'must be interpreted in the same manner as if section 302A.243 had not been enacted. The legislature took that action in recognition that Minnesota was one of the few states with legislation governing judicial review of special litigation committees. The repeal represented 'a commitment to let our caselaw develop,' and a desire to give our courts flexibility." *Drilling v. Berman*, 589 N.W.2d 503, 506 (Minn. Ct. App. 1999), *review denied*, 1999 Minn. LEXIS 306 (Minn. May 18, 1999) (citations to legislature history omitted).

Section C 2 a

Replace the period at the end of footnote 1979 on page 1704 with the following:

See also Lichtenberg v. Zinn, 260 A.D.2d 741, 742, 687 N.Y.S.2d 817, 819 (N.Y. App. Div. 3d Dep't), *leave to appeal denied*, 94 N.Y.2d 754, 723 N.E.2d 89, 701 N.Y.S.2d 340 (1999) (quoting *Auerbach v. Bennett*, 47 N.Y.2d 619, 631, 393 N.E.2d 994, 1000-01, 419 N.Y.S.2d 920, 927 (1979)).

Add the following at the end of footnote 1981 on page 1704:

See also Lichtenberg, 260 A.D.2d at 742, 687 N.Y.S.2d at 819 (quoting *Auerbach*, 47 N.Y.S.2d at 623-24, 393 N.E.2d at 996, 419 N.Y.S.2d at 922).

Add the following at the end of footnote 1982 on page 1704:

See also Lichtenberg, 260 A.D.2d at 742, 687 N.Y.S.2d at 819 ("the business judgment doctrine shields the substance of a special litigation committee's decision from judicial inquiry").

Add the following at the end of the paragraph beginning on page 1706 and concluding on page 1707 (immediately after footnote 1999):

The same result was reached by an intermediate appellate court in *Lichtenberg v. Zinn*, 260 A.D.2d 741, 687 N.Y.S.2d 817 (N.Y. App. Div. 3d Dep't), *leave to appeal denied*, 94 N.Y.2d 754, 723 N.E.2d 89, 701 N.Y.S.2d 340 (1999). The court stated that there was not "sufficient admissible proof to raise a question of fact as to the disinterested independence of the SLC members" and that "we cannot say" that the investigative procedures and methodologies of the committee were "'so restricted in scope, so shallow in execution, or otherwise so pro forma or halfhearted as to constitute a pretext or sham.'" 260 A.D.2d at 743-44, 687 N.Y.S.2d at 820 (quoting *Auerbach*, 47 N.Y.2d at 634, 393 N.E.2d at 994, 419 N.Y.S.2d at 920). The court pointed to the board's grant to the committee of "unfettered and unlimited authority to conduct its investigation," the committee's retention of "experienced independent counsel and three unaffiliated experts to assist it in evaluating the specific allegations set forth in the complaint and, further, in reviewing the multitude of documents requested by the SLC," and the fact that the committee "extensively deliberated and considered the issues before it." 260 A.D.2d at 744, 687 N.Y.S.2d at 820. In short, the court concluded, "even a cursory review of the SLC's summary of findings and conclusions belies plaintiff's assertion that the SLC's investigation was perfunctory." The court accordingly affirmed a grant of summary judgment dismissing the complaint. 260 A.D.2d at 741, 744, 687 N.Y.S.2d at 818, 820.

Add the following at the end of the third sentence (immediately after footnote 2003) of the paragraph beginning and concluding on page 1707:

The same result also was reached by a trial court in New York in *Kahn v. Buttner*, No. 600456/97 (N.Y. Sup. Ct. N.Y. Co. Sept. 28, 1999), another case where a special litigation committee moved to terminate litigation. *Id.*, slip op. at 4-5.

Add the following at the end of footnote 2012 on page 1708:

See also Drilling v. Berman, 589 N.W.2d 503, 506-07 (Minn. Ct. App. 1999), *review denied*, 1999 Minn. LEXIS 306 (Minn. May 18, 1999).

Add the following at the end of the third sentence (immediately after footnote 2016) of the paragraph beginning on page 1707 and concluding on page 1709:

A third federal court construing Maryland law held in decisions in related cases that Maryland would follow the Delaware standard adopted in *Zapata Corp. v. Maldonado*, 430 A.2d 779 (Del. 1981), rather than the New York standard adopted in *Auerbach*. *See Strougo v. Bassini*, 112 F. Supp. 2d 355, 361 (S.D.N.Y. 2000); *Strougo v. Bassini,* 1999 U.S. Dist. LEXIS 5951, at *13-14, 1999 WL 249719, at *5 (S.D.N.Y. Apr. 28, 1999); *Strougo v. Padegs*, 27 F. Supp. 2d 442, 447

(S.D.N.Y. 1998); *Strougo v. Padegs*, 1 F. Supp. 2d 276, 280-81 (S.D.N.Y. 1998).

Add the following at the end of footnote 2026 on page 1711:

See also Cuker v. Mikalauskas, 1998 Phila. Cty. Rptr. LEXIS 2 (Pa. Common Pleas Ct. Phila. Cty. Feb. 26, 1998) (granting motion for summary judgment seeking termination following evidentiary hearing).

Section C 2 b

Add the following at the end of the second sentence (immediately after footnote 2064) of the paragraph beginning on page 1721 and concluding on page 1722:

A third federal court construing Maryland law held in decisions in related cases that Maryland would follow the Delaware standard adopted in *Zapata Corp. v. Maldonado*, 430 A.2d 779 (Del. 1981), rather than the New York standard adopted in *Auerbach v. Bennett*, 47 N.Y.2d 619, 393 N.E.2d 994, 419 N.Y.S.2d 920 (1979). *See Strougo v. Bassini*, 112 F. Supp. 2d 355, 361 (S.D.N.Y. 2000); *Strougo v. Bassini,* 1999 U.S. Dist. LEXIS 5951, at *13-14, 1999 WL 249719, at *5 (S.D.N.Y. Apr. 28, 1999); *Strougo v. Padegs*, 27 F. Supp. 2d 442, 447 (S.D.N.Y. 1998); *Strougo v. Padegs*, 1 F. Supp. 2d 276, 280-81 (S.D.N.Y. 1998).

Section C 2 c

Add the following at the end of the paragraph beginning on page 1730 and concluding on page 1731 (immediately after footnote 2123):

The opposite result was reached in *Electra Investment Trust PLC v. Crews*, 1999 Del. Ch. LEXIS 36, 1999 WL

135239 (Del. Ch. Feb. 24, 1999), another case where a special litigation committee formed to investigate the merits of a derivative action negotiated a settlement. This action involved allegations that Robert B. Crews, Jr., the president and chief executive officer of The Benjamin Company, Inc. ("TBC"), misappropriated TBC funds for his personal use and caused TBC to enter into agreements with persons or entities with whom Crews had a financial interest without disclosing those financial interests. 1999 Del. Ch. LEXIS 36, at *1, 5-6, 1999 WL 135239, at *1, 2-3. The proposed settlement required Crews "to pay back the misappropriated funds" and thus "solve[d] Crew's most egregious (alleged) abuses." 1999 Del. Ch. LEXIS 36, at *2, 1999 WL 135239, at *1. The court thus stated that "[i]n many respects" the SLC did "an admirable job of addressing the issues" raised by the litigation, including, in particular, obtaining "Crews' promise to repay allegedly misappropriated funds" – an agreement that provides "the remedy that my reading of the complaint indicates is most suitable." 1999 Del. Ch. LEXIS 36, at *16, 1999 WL 135239, at *6.

Nevertheless, the court concluded, the settlement agreement "downplay[ed] the significance of some of Electra's claims without engaging in a reasonably thorough investigation of the facts underlying those allegations." 1999 Del. Ch. LEXIS 36, at *2, 1999 WL 135239, at *1. The court focused upon three issues: (1) child support payments, (2) a refusal by TBC's outside auditor, Coopers & Lybrand, LLP, to issue an audit opinion, and (3) travel and entertainment expenses.

With respect to child support payments, plaintiff alleged that Crews used TBC funds to pay a total of $2,618 in child support payments that were accounted for on TBC's books as payments for cleaning supplies. Crews denied the allegation and the special litigation committee concluded that it was "not in the best interests of the Company, nor is it cost effective, to pursue litigation to seek payment of $2,600.00." 1999 Del. Ch. LEXIS 36, at *10, 1999 WL 135239, at *4. The court stated that "I do not quibble with the need to factor cost into the SLC's decision as to how far to pursue its investigation" but concluded that this argument was "unpersuasive" in this case because "a phone call or two" to the woman who was the mother of the child and to the person to whom the payments were made (the child's grandfather) "would not have drastically raised the cost of the SLC's investigation." 1999 Del. Ch. LEXIS 36, at *11-12, 1999 WL 135239, at *4. This course, the court continued, not only "might have provided the facts necessary for the SLC to reach the merits of this claim" but also "would have potential value for the SLC and the Court in examining Electra's remaining claims" because Crew's integrity was called into question in connection with other claims and "exoneration of Crews in this matter would have added to his credibility." 1999 Del. Ch. LEXIS 36, at *12, 1999 WL 135239, at *4. The court added that "[t]he mere recital of the SLC's conclusion that a particular claim is not worth pursuing effectively leaves this Court with no record to review" and "no tenable basis upon which to assess the SLC's recommendation." 1999 Del. Ch. LEXIS 36, at *12-13, 1999 WL 135239, at *4.

With respect to Coopers & Lybrand's refusal to issue an audit opinion, the court stated that the committee's investigation concerning this subject relied exclusively upon (1) an allegation that Coopers & Lybrand had questioned the same financial abuses that were challenged in the litigation, (2) Crews' claim that Coopers & Lybrand refused to issue an audit opinion because TBC's chief financial officer, who had been informed that his employment contract would not be renewed, refused to sign off on the financial statements, and (3) a summary written by Crews' personal attorney of a conversation in which Crews, his attorney and one member of the special committee had participated. 1999 Del. Ch. LEXIS 36, at *13-14, 1999 WL 135239, at *5. The court stated that the committee never contacted Coopers & Lybrand directly to learn why the accounting firm would not issue an opinion. 1999 Del. Ch. LEXIS 36, at *14, 1999 WL 135239, at *5. This failure by the committee "to conduct such a fundamental and simple inquiry," the court held, "constitutes a failure to pursue adequately and independently the facts necessary to its investigation." *Id.*

With respect to travel and entertainment expenses, the court stated that the committee's report documented claims and Crews' rebuttal to these claims and reported the committee's conclusion that "it would not be cost effective to further investigate this claim" and the fact that the committee therefore did not engage "in the effort and expense of retracing Crews's travels and auditing his entertainment activities." 1999 Del. Ch. LEXIS 36, at *15, 1999 WL 135239, at *5. The court stated that these conclusions were not "unreasonable on their face" but concluded that "the scope of the underlying investigation" was "most troubling" because "[n]o outside source of information was contacted to verify or contradict Crews's version of the facts." *Id.* This "factual vacuum" underlying the committee's conclusions, the court held, "prevents me from finding that the SLC's investigation was reasonably thorough." 1999 Del. Ch. LEXIS 36, at *15-16, 1999 WL 135239, at *5

In sum, the court concluded, "in the three areas described above" the committee "engaged in a pattern of glossing over . . . claims . . . without even attempting to investigate or resolve the dispute." *Id.* This "selective investigation" and "package of piecemeal reforms," the court held, was insufficient to permit a conclusion that the investigation was "reasonably thorough." 1999 Del. Ch. LEXIS 36, at *17, 1999 WL 135239, at *6. The court accordingly denied the committee's motion to approve the proposed settlement. *Id.*

Add the following at the end of the paragraph beginning and concluding on page 1731 (between footnotes 2123 and 2124):

Strougo v. Bassini, 112 F. Supp. 2d 355 (S.D.N.Y. 2000), a decision by a federal district court in New York construing Delaware law, held that a special litigation committee "pursued its investigation in a thorough and diligent manner" and in good faith. *Id.* at 366. The court pointed to a five month investigation that included 11 witness interviews and a "comprehensive review of approximately 36,000 pages of documents" and stated that committee members "personally reviewed all of the documents that 'counsel believed were particularly pertinent,' in addition to the documents used in the witness interviews and any other documents that the SLC members specifically requested to review." *Id.* at 365. The court also pointed to the fact that the committee invited "potentially 'unfriendly' witnesses" such as the shareholder who had commenced the litigation underlying the investigation and his counsel to be interviewed twice, but they refused to be interviewed. *Id.* The court also pointed to the committee's report and five volumes of exhibits, which the court stated "outline the SLC's reconstruction of the history of the events" surrounding the allegations investigated by the committee and the committee's findings and conclusions. *Id.* at 366-67. The court concluded that the committee had reasonable bases for its conclusions that the corporation's directors did not breach their fiduciary duties and that there was no basis for the allegations in the litigation underlying the committee's investigation. *Id.*

The court also examined the discretionary second step of *Zapata*, which permits the court to undertake "its own independent review of the merits of the derivative claim" before approving the committee's recommendation. *Id.* at 368. The court concluded that the "core liability theory" underlying the claims examined by the committee was "unlikely to prevail," that there was "no supportable theory of damages that could be recouped by continued litigation," and that "this stockholder grievance does not merit further consideration in the corporation's interest." *Id.; see also Strougo v. Padegs*, 27 F. Supp. 2d 442, 451-54 (S.D.N.Y. 1998) (same conclusion based upon similar reasoning in related action).

Section C 2 d

Add the following at the end of the paragraph beginning on page 1743 and concluding on page 1744 (immediately after footnote 2213):

A California court in *Finley v. Superior Court*, 80 Cal. App. 4th 1152, 96 Cal. Rptr. 2d 128 (2000), held that a court may bifurcate a litigation and try an affirmative defense based upon a special litigation committee determination before addressing other issues. *Id.* at 1162-63, 96 Cal. Rptr. 2d at 135-36.

Section C 2 e

Add the following at the end of footnote 2215 on page 1745:

See also Einhorn v. Culea, 612 N.W.2d 78, 86 (Wis. 2000) (it is not enough to name all directors as defendants because if it were "a shareholder could prevent the entire board from serving on the special litigation committee merely by naming all the directors as defendants").

Add the following at the end of footnote 2216 on page 1745:

See also Strougo v. Padegs, 27 F. Supp. 2d 442, 449 (S.D.N.Y. 1998) (interest not established where committee member was named as a defendant and joined a motion to dismiss the action and filed a brief in which, according to plaintiff, "he contended, gratuitously, that plaintiff's allegations had no merit").

Add the following at the end of footnote 2219 on page 1746:

See also Strougo v. Bassini, 112 F. Supp. 2d 355, 362 (S.D.N.Y. 2000); *Padegs*, 27 F. Supp. 2d at 448; *Einhorn*, 612 N.W.2d at 81, 89.

Add the following at the end of footnote 2220 on page 1746:

See also Bassini, 112 F. Supp. 2d at 363-64 (finding disinterestedness where committee members were not named as defendants); *Padegs*, 27 F. Supp. 2d at 445, 448-51 (finding disinterestedness where one of two committee members was a defendant); *Lichtenberg v. Zinn*, 260 A.D.2d 741, 742, 687 N.Y.S.2d 817, 819 (N.Y. App. Div. 3d Dep't), *leave to appeal denied*, 94 N.Y.2d 754, 723 N.E.2d 89, 701 N.Y.S.2d 340 (1999) (finding disinterestedness where committee members were not defendants); *Kahn v. Buttner*, No. 600456/97, slip op. at 5 (N.Y. Sup. Ct. N.Y. Co. Sept. 28, 1999) (finding disinterestedness where two of three committee members were defendants but "no specific allegations" were made against them); *Einhorn*, 612 N.W.2d at 89, 91 (noting this factor).

Add the following at the end of footnote 2221 on page 1747:

See also Einhorn, 612 N.W.2d at 89 (noting this factor).

Add the following at the end of footnote 2222 on page 1747:

See also Bassini, 112 F. Supp. 2d at 363-64 (finding disinterestedness where committee consisted of outside, non-management directors); *Padegs*, 27 F. Supp. 2d at 445, 448-51 (same); *Buttner*, slip op. at 5 (finding lack of disinterestedness where committee members were non-employee directors and thus "are presumably and apparently independent"); *Cuker v. Mikalauskas*, 1998 Phila. Cty. Rptr. LEXIS 2, at *5 (Pa. Common Pleas Ct. Phila. Cty. Feb. 26, 1998) (finding disinterestedness where committee consisted of outside directors who were "experienced, sophisticated business executives with impeccable backgrounds"); *Einhorn*, 612 N.W.2d at 91-92 (questioning disinterestedness of a special committee member where the committee member was a corporate employee, the case involved a bonus to the corporation's president and majority shareholder, James D. Culea, and the committee member "received a $25,000 bonus at the same meeting of the compensation committee at which Culea's challenged bonus was approved").

Add the following at the end of footnote 2223 on page 1748:

See also Bassini, 112 F. Supp. 2d at 363-64 (finding disinterestedness where committee members joined the board after the alleged wrongdoing occurred); *Padegs*, 27 F. Supp. 2d at 445, 448-51 (finding disinterestedness where one of two committee members joined the board after the alleged wrongdoing occurred); *Lichtenberg*, 260 A.D.2d at 742, 687 N.Y.S.2d at 819 (finding disinterestedness where committee members "were not members of Besicorp's board of directors at the time that the challenged transactions are alleged to have occurred"); *Buttner*, slip op. at 5 (finding disinterestedness where one of three members of committee joined the board after the alleged wrongdoing); *Cuker*, 1998 Phila. Cty. Rptr. LEXIS 2, at *8 (finding disinterestedness notwithstanding the fact that committee members "were participating members of the PECO board and two of the three served on the board's audit committee at the time of the allegedly wrongful actions," which involved credit and collections issues).

Add the following at the end of footnote 2224 on page 1749:

See also Lichtenberg, 260 A.D.2d at 742, 687 N.Y.S.2d at 819 (finding disinterestedness where committee members were not "implicated in the alleged corporate wrongdoing"); *Einhorn*, 612 N.W.2d at 89 (noting this factor).

Add the following at the end of footnote 2225 on page 1749:

See also Padegs, 27 F. Supp. 2d at 449 (finding disinterestedness where one of two committee members participated in the approval of the challenged conduct); *Einhorn*, 612 N.W.2d at 89 (noting this factor).

Add the following at the end of footnote 2228 on page 1750:

See also Lichtenberg, 260 A.D.2d at 742, 687 N.Y.S.2d at 819 (finding disinterestedness; discussed in text later in this Section).

Add the following at the end of footnote 2229 on page 1750:

See also Bassini, 112 F. Supp. 2d at 363 (finding disinterestedness where one member of a two member committee was "acquainted" with an outside director "due to the fact that both men served on the boards of directors" of the two other corporations and had "no social contact . . . outside of their board appointments" and the second member of the committee had met another outside director "through their appointments at Columbia University"; the court stated that "such associations and contacts arise in any business setting and are neither inappropriate nor do they suggest that McGuire and Vasarhelyi would not faithfully discharge their obligations to the Fund's shareholders"); *Padegs*, 27 F. Supp. 2d at 445, 450 (finding disinterestedness where one member of a two member committee was described by a director who was a defendant as a "good friend" but the committee member testified that his friends did not include any other director, and the committee member had asked the director who described him as a "good friend" if he "would mind talking to his son who recently graduated from Yale"; the court stated that "[i]n any business setting, associations and contacts of the type which Da Casta has had or may have had with some of the individual directors and the Fund are neither inappropriate nor do they suggest that Da Costa would not faithfully discharge his obligations to the Fund's shareholders"); *Lichtenberg*, 260 A.D.2d at 742, 687 N.Y.S.2d at 819 (finding disinterestedness; discussed in text later in this Section); *Cuker*, 1998 Phila. Cty. Rptr. LEXIS 2 at *7-8:

> Plaintiffs also pointed to the fact that many of the PECO directors named as defendants in the shareholder derivative suits, as well as the non-defendant board members and the SLC members, served on business and charitable boards to-

> gether. Although it is true that there may have been some interlocking directorships (the record is unclear what particular PECO board members served on what particular boards with the SLC members), there was no evidence that any relationships which might have developed as a result impinged upon the objectivity of the SLC members. For example, it appeared that numerous PECO board members were involved with the United Way charity, and that Mr. Harris and Mr. Hagen served on the board of the Philadelphia First Corporation with Mr. Paquette. It cannot be said that Messrs. Harris and Hagen were rendered incapable of disinterested or independent action as a result, however, as virtually all of the board members were associated either with United Way or with charities like the Philadelphia First Corporation. If SLC members were to be disqualified based on interlocking directorships, then it is likely no one would have been eligible to serve.

See also Einhorn, 612 N.W.2d at 89, 92 (noting this factor).

Add the following at the end of footnote 2231 on page 1752:

See also Bassini, 112 F. Supp. 2d at 363-64 (finding disinterestedness in case involving two member committee notwithstanding challenges to both committee members); *Padegs*, 27 F. Supp. 2d at 448-51 (same); *Lichtenberg*, 260 A.D.2d at 742-43, 687 N.Y.S.2d at 819-20 (finding disinterestedness in case involving three member committee notwithstanding challenges to all three members); *Buttner*, slip op. at 4-5 (finding disinterestedness in case involving three member committee); *Cuker*, 1998 Phila. Cty. Rptr. LEXIS 2, at *5-9 (finding disinterestedness in case involving three member committee notwithstanding challenges to all three committee members); *Einhorn*, 612 N.W.2d at 90 (noting this factor).

Add the following at the end of footnote 2234 on page 1753:

See also Bassini, 112 F. Supp. 2d at 359 (noting use of "separate counsel"); *Padegs*, 27 F. Supp. 2d at 446 (noting use of "independent counsel"); *Lichtenberg*, 260 A.D.2d at 744, 687 N.Y.S.2d at 820 ("the SLC retained experienced independent counsel and three unaffiliated experts"); *Buttner*, slip op. at 2 (committee's investigation included "retaining independent counsel" and "retaining independent compensation expert"); *Cuker*, 1998 Phila. Cty. Rptr. LEXIS 2, at *9 ("counsel appointed to represent the SLC . . . was fair, impartial, disinterested and independent"); *Einhorn*, 612 N.W.2d at 90 (noting this factor); *cf. Electra Inv. Trust PLC v. Crews*, 1999 Del. Ch. LEXIS 36, at *13-14 n.7, 1999 WL 135239, at *5 & n.7 (Del. Ch. Feb. 24, 1999) (not resolving issue but noting the "troubling fact" that the two members of a special litigation committee, Robert C. Hill and Patricia Ryan, "were first informed that they were likely candidates" for the committee by Jack Jackson, the personal attorney for the "main target" of the investigation, and that "Jackson may have assisted Hill and Ryan in obtaining Delaware counsel" to represent the committee).

Add the following at the end of footnote 2242 on page 1755:

See also Einhorn, 612 N.W.2d at 90-91 & n.39 (noting this factor).

Add the following at the end of the paragraph beginning and concluding on page 1761 (immediately after footnote 2283):

The same result was reached in *Lichtenberg v. Zinn*, 260 A.D.2d 741, 687 N.Y.S.2d 817 (N.Y. App. Div. 3d Dep't), *leave to appeal denied*, 94 N.Y.2d 754, 723 N.E.2d 89, 701 N.Y.S.2d 340 (1999), a case involving allegations that Michael F. Zinn and two other corporate officials "caused the corporation to grant them substantial stock options and warrants for little or no consideration, thereby wasting corporation assets and increasing their control of the company while diluting the power of the public shareholders." 260 A.D.2d at 741, 687 N.Y.S.2d at 819. A special litigation committee was formed consisting of three directors who were not named as defendants, were not members of the board at the time of the challenged transactions, and who were not implicated in the alleged corporate wrongdoing. *Id.* On a motion for summary judgment, the court held that "plaintiff simply failed to tender sufficient admissible proof to raise a question of fact as to the disinterested independence of the SLC members." 260 A.D.2d at 743, 687 N.Y.S.2d at 820.

The court rejected plaintiff's reliance upon allegations that one committee member and Zinn had children who attended the same dance class, that a second committee member occasionally played tennis with Zinn, and that a third committee member held a "rather casual" social relationship with Zinn. 260 A.D.2d at 742-43, 687 N.Y.S.2d at 819-20. The court also rejected plaintiff's reliance upon allegations that one committee member was one of the corporation's original investors and had served on the corporation's board of directors and had done business with the corporation during the early 1980s (the alleged wrongdoing occurred during the early 1990s) and that the other two committee members had submitted consulting proposals to the corporation that had not been accepted. 260 A.D.2d at 743, 687 N.Y.S.2d at 820. The court also held that the record did not substantiate plaintiff's assertions that Zinn "hand-picked" each member of the committee, that Zinn "controlled and dominated the investigative process," and that the committee members each were "mere puppets" and "cronies" of Zinn. *Id.* The court stated that the committee members "each had substantial, relevant business experience" and "there is nothing in the record" suggesting that any of the committee members formed an opinion concerning the litigation before joining the corporation's board "or, more to the point, to substantiate plaintiff's assertion that each was chosen in an effort to preordain the outcome of the SLC's investigation." *Id.*

Section C 2 f

Add the following at the end of the first sentence (immediately after footnote 2341) of the paragraph beginning on page 1771 and concluding on page 1772:

"The majority view" thus "recognizes that independent directors are capable of rendering an unbiased opinion despite being appointed by defendant directors and sharing a common experience with the defendants," and "only a minority of courts have found that structural bias taints the independence of litigation committee members." *Strougo v. Bassini*, 112 F. Supp. 2d 355, 362 (S.D.N.Y. 2000); *Strougo v. Padegs*, 27 F. Supp. 2d 442, 448-49 (S.D.N.Y. 1998).

Add the following at the end of footnote 2342 on page 1772:

See also Bassini, 112 F. Supp. 2d at 362; *Padegs*, 27 F. Supp. 2d at 449.

Replace the period at the end of the paragraph beginning on page 1771 and concluding on page 1772 with a comma and add the following immediately after footnote 2344:

and the result would be "the rejection of special litigation committees in their entity." *Bassini*, 112 F. Supp. 2d at 363; *Padegs*, 27 F. Supp. 2d at 449.

Replace "94,850" with "98,590-91" in the Illinois Power citation in footnote 2345 on page 1773.

Add the following at the end of footnote 2345 on page 1773:

See also Bassini, 112 F. Supp. 2d at 362 *and Padegs*, 27 F. Supp. at 448 ("courts have 'almost universally determined that the standards of review developed for derivative suits are designed to overcome the effects, if any, of structural bias'") (both quoting *Weiland v. Illinois Power Co.*, [1990-1991 Transfer Binder] Fed. Sec. L. Rep. (CCH) ¶ 95,747, at 98,590 (C.D. Ill. Sept. 17, 1990)).

Section C 2 h

Add the following at the end of the second paragraph beginning and concluding on page 1778 (immediately after footnote 2390):

The court in *Strougo v. Bassini*, 112 F. Supp. 2d 355 (S.D.N.Y. 2000), rejected a challenge to a special litigation committee report where one member of a two member committee attended three of ten committee meetings in person and six meetings by telephone, both members of the committee participated (in person or by telephone) in seven witness interviews, one member of the committee participated in three additional witness interviews, neither member participated in the interview or follow up telephone interview of one witness, and "[a]fter every interview, the SLC's counsel drafted an in-depth summary, which was received and approved by the members of the SLC." *Id.* at 360, 364. The court stated "scheduling conflicts" have "no bearing" upon whether a committee member carries out his duties in an independent manner. *Id.* at 364. The court also relied upon the review by the committee members of "all of the documents that 'counsel believed were particularly pertinent,'" in addition to the documents used in the witness interviews and any other documents that the SLC members specifically requested to review." *Id.* at 365.

The court in *Drilling v. Berman*, 589 N.W.2d 503 (Minn. Ct. App. 1999), *review denied*, 1999 Minn. LEXIS 306 (Minn. May 18, 1999), also concluded that a contention that a special litigation committee "relied too heavily on its counsel" in the questioning of witnesses "does not weigh adversely on the good faith of the committee." *Id.* at 510. The court stated that "[t]he committee members independently determined when they had heard enough testimony from each witness," that plaintiffs "do not assert the information gained during the interviews was insufficient," and that "the use of capable counsel is generally seen as demonstrative of good faith." *Id.*

Add the following at the end of the second paragraph beginning and concluding on page 1780 (immediately after footnote 2402):

The court in *Weiser v. Grace*, 179 Misc. 2d 116, 683 N.Y.S.2d 781 (N.Y. Sup. Ct. N.Y. Co. 1998), also relied upon *Peller v. Southern Co.*, 707 F. Supp. 525 (N.D. Ga. 1988), *aff'd*, 911 F.2d 1532 (11th Cir. 1990). As in *Peller*, the court in *Weiser* stated, the special litigation committee in *Weiser* "relied heavily on counsel who conducted 10 of the 14 interviews which formed the factual basis" for the committee's report. 179 Misc. 2d at 121, 683 N.Y.S.2d at 786. As in *Peller*, the court continued, "the witness interviews were not transcribed" and the "only written record of the interviews are counsel's notes, outlines and summaries." *Id.* The court stated that "[l]ike the *Peller* court, this court is troubled by the issue of whether the SLC acted in good faith when it preserved the interview testimony in such a way that it could then protect it from examination by asserting privilege." *Id.* at 122, 683 N.Y.S.2d at 786.

The court in *Strougo v. Bassini*, 1999 U.S. Dist. LEXIS 5951, 1999 WL 249719 (S.D.N.Y. Apr. 28, 1999), distinguished the *Weiser* case on the ground that in *Weiser* "counsel conducted ten out of fourteen witness interviews without any participation from the SLC members," while in *Strougo* "only one witness interview and two follow up interviews were conducted without the participation of at least one SLC member." 1999 U.S. Dist. LEXIS 5951, at *21 n.5, 1999 WL 249719, at *7 n.5.

Section C 2 i

Replace footnotes 2410 through 2412 with the following:

2410. 2 Model Bus. Corp. Act Annotated § 7.44 Official Comment at 7-351 (3d ed. Supp. 1998/99).

2411. *Id.* §§ 7.44(a), (d), (e) & Official Comment at 7-351.

2412. *Id.* Official Comment at 7-351.

Section C 3 a

Replace "1996" with "Supp. 1998/99" in the Model Act § 7.43 citation in footnote 2433 on page 1785.

Add the following at the end of the first sentence (immediately after footnote 2430) of the first paragraph beginning and concluding on page 1785:

An intermediate appellate court in New York in *Lichtenberg v. Zinn*, 243 A.D.2d 1045, 663 N.Y.S.2d 452 (N.Y. App. Div. 3d Dep't 1997), noted a trial court decision not to stay proceedings pending a determination by a special litigation committee. *Id.* at 1046, 663 N.Y.S.2d at 453.

Add the following at the beginning of the first paragraph beginning and concluding on page 1785 (immediately after footnote 2432):

A federal court construing New York law in *In re Bank of New York Derivative Litigation*, 2000 U.S. Dist. LEXIS 16502, 2000 WL 1708173 (S.D.N.Y. Nov. 14, 2000), stated that "[c]ourts have discretion to stay discovery of a derivative suit pending a special litigation committee's decision on whether the corporation should pursue the claims against the officers and directors." 2000 U.S. Dist. LEXIS 16502, at *8, 2000 WL 1708173, at *3. The court, however, declined to stay this particular litigation before the for three reasons: (1) the case "has already been pending for more than a year," the committee could have been created a year earlier, and "a stay of the case at this juncture will only delay matters"; (2) discovery was proceeding in a parallel state court action; and (3) there were "substantial questions" concerning the disinterestedness and independence of the members of the committee, one of whom already had resigned due to a potential conflict of interest and the remaining two of whom were defendants in the action and had joined a motion to dismiss "in which they and the other defendants have strenuously denied any wrongdoing" and thus it was "difficult to imagine" that the committee "will reach any conclusion other than that the complaint lacks merit." 2000 U.S. Dist. LEXIS 16502, at *9-10, 2000 WL 1708173, at *3; *see also Katz v. Zucker*, No. 604465/99, slip op. at 1-3 (N.Y. Sup. Ct. N.Y. Co. Dec. 6, 2000) (parallel state court proceeding following federal court decision to deny stay discovery pending the completion of the committee's investigation).

Section C 3 b (i)

Add the following at the end of the paragraph beginning on page 1792 and concluding on page 1795 (immediately after footnote 2482):

- *Strougo v. Padegs*, 1 F. Supp. 2d 276, 282 (S.D.N.Y. 1998), and *Strougo v. Bassini*, 1999 U.S. Dist. LEXIS 5951, at *17-22, 1999 WL 249719, at *6-7 (S.D.N.Y. Apr. 28, 1999) (both permitting discovery, including inspection of all documents made available to the committee, inspection of notes of interviews by the committee and drafts of the committee's report, and depositions of the members of the committee, and both not permitting depositions of the committee's counsel).

The court in *Weiser v. Grace*, 179 Misc. 2d 116, 683 N.Y.S.2d 781 (N.Y. Sup. Ct. N.Y. Co. 1998), a decision by a trial court in New York construing Delaware law, ordered the production of notes, summaries, and witness outlines or lists of questions prepared in advance of 14 interviews conducted by a special litigation committee or its counsel. The plaintiffs sought these documents due to the absence of transcripts of the interviews. Plaintiffs contended that these materials were needed (1) to enable them to challenge whether the committee "discharged its duties with diligence and zeal or whether it 'played softball with critical players.'" *Id.* at 119, 683 N.Y.S.2d at 784 (quoting *Peller v. Southern Co.*, 707 F. Supp. 525, 529 (N.D. Ga. 1988), *aff'd*, 911 F.2d 1532 (11th Cir. 1990)), (2) to shed light on the committee's resolution of factual disputes between alleged statements by two directors, one of whom was interviewed and one of whom was not interviewed, concerning the extent to which the corporation's board was informed with respect to alleged overpayments being investigated by the committee, and (3) to contest the committee's reliance upon its counsel and to support plaintiffs' contention that the participation of committee members in the interview process was "perfunctory, or otherwise deficient." 179 Misc. 2d at 119, 683 N.Y.S.2d at 784.

The court held that production of the notes, summaries and outlines of the committee's interviews of witnesses did "not constitute all-encompassing merits discovery" and "is necessary and will facilitate determination of the reasonableness and good faith of the SLC's investigation" because "[i]n order for plaintiffs to reasonably challenge the thoroughness of the SLC's factual investigation, they must be able to examine the questions posed and the subjects explored in the witness interviews." *Id.* at 121, 683 N.Y.S.2d at 785. The court also stated that "it is impossible for the court to assess whether the SLC pursued its charge with diligence and zeal, if the court is unable to review the development of the factual record" that underlies the committee's report. *Id.*

The court also held that the committee "relied heavily on counsel who conducted 10 of the 14 interviews which formed the factual basis" for the committee's report and, because the interviews were not transcribed, "[t]he only written record of these interviews are counsel's notes, outlines and summaries." *Id.* According to the court, "[t]o deny plaintiffs the opportunity to discover the questions asked of the key witnesses, and whether the responses thereto were used or ignored by the SLC in forming its conclusions and preparing its report, would impermissibly allow the SLC to insulate its investigation from scrutiny by simply using counsel to conduct the interviews." *Id.* at 122, 683 N.Y.S.2d at 786. The court stated that it was "troubled by the issue of whether the SLC acted in good faith when it preserved the witness testimony in such a way that it could protect it from examination by asserting privilege." *Id.* The court added that "[t]o successfully challenge the committee's good faith reliance on counsel, plaintiff must show overreaching by counsel or neglect by the SLC," and "the SLC's notes, outlines and summaries of witness interviews provide the only means by which to make an assessment of the reasonableness and good faith of the SLC's investigation, to the extent that the information is otherwise unavailable." *Id.* at 122, 124, 683 N.Y.S.2d at 786, 787.

Section C 3 b (ii)

Add the following at the end of the paragraph beginning and concluding on page 1796 (immediately after footnote 2496):

An intermediate appellate court in New York in *Lichtenberg v. Zinn*, 243 A.D.2d 1045, 663 N.Y.S.2d 452 (N.Y. App. Div. 3d Dep't 1997), has read *Auerbach v. Bennett*, 47 N.Y.2d 619, 393 N.E.2d 994, 419 N.Y.S.2d 920 (1979), and *Parkoff v. General Telephone & Electronics Corp.*, 53 N.Y.2d 412, 425 N.E.2d 820, 442 N.Y.S.2d 432 (1981), to permit discovery concerning a special litigation committee investigation where the discovery is not limited in scope "to the issues of the SLC's disinterested independence and its methods and procedures." 243 A.D.2d at 1046, 663 N.Y.S.2d at 453.

The court stated that *Auerbach* "clearly held that the business judgment rule barred judicial probing into the substantive aspects of a special litigation committee's decision not to pursue claims advanced in a derivative action" but "nothing therein specifically limits a party's ability to engage in discovery." *Id.* at 1047, 663 N.Y.S.2d at 453. The court pointed to language in *Auerbach* "[r]ecognizing that 'those responsible for the procedures by which [this] business judgment is reached may reasonably be required to show that they have pursued their chosen investigative methods in good faith'" and stating that "the proof necessary to achieve this end 'depend[s] on the nature of the particular investigation, and the proper reach of disclosure at the instance of the shareholders will in turn relate inversely to the showing made by the corporate representatives.'" *Id.* at 1047, 663 N.Y.S.2d at 454 (quoting *Auerbach*, 47 N.Y.2d at 634, 393 N.E.2d at 1002-03, 419 N.Y.S.2d at 929). The court also pointed to language in *Parkoff* stating that "a plaintiff in this type of action 'must necessarily be given more latitude to discover' and 'the legitimate interests of shareholder plaintiffs' should not be frustrated, especially when all relevant information pertaining to disinterestedness and independence, as well as the propriety and completeness of the SLC's investigation, is necessarily in defendants' possession." 243 A.D.2d at 1047, 663 N.Y.S.2d at 454 (quoting *Parkoff*, 53 N.Y.2d at 417-18 n.2, 425 N.E.2d at 822 n.2, 442 N.Y.S.2d at 435 n.2). Significantly, the court added, the depositions already had been completed and there was no showing in the record that "information with regard to the substantive deliberations was sought and actually received." 243 A.D.2d at 1047, 663 N.Y.S.2d at 454.

Add the following at the end of the paragraph beginning and concluding on page 1798 (immediately after footnote 2507):

The court in *Kahn v. Buttner*, No. 600456/97 (N.Y. Sup. Ct. N.Y. Co. Sept. 28, 1999), rejected a request for depositions of three special litigation committee members by a plaintiff challenging the committee's recommendation that a derivative action be dismissed in a case where each of the committee members had submitted affidavits in support of the committee's recommendation that the action be dismissed. *Id.*, slip op. at 5. The court stated that depositions of the three committee members "would serve no purpose other than encourage a fishing expedition based on wishful thinking." *Id.*

Section C 3 b (iii)

Replace "7-95" with "7–348-49" and replace "1996" with "Supp. 1998/99" in the Model Act § 7.44 citation in footnote 2513 on page 1799.

Add the following at the end of footnote 2516 on page 1800:

See also Cuker v. Mikalauskas, 1998 Phila. Cty. Rptr. LEXIS 2 (Pa. Common Pleas Ct. Phila. Cty. Feb. 26, 1998) (granting motion for summary judgment seeking termination following evidentiary hearing).

Section D

Add the following at the end of footnote 2523 on page 1804:

See also Dean v. Dick, 1999 Del. Ch. LEXIS 121, at *6-7, 1999 WL 413400, at *2 (Del. Ch. June 10, 1999) ("[d]erivative suits involving limited partnerships have been few and far between").

Replace the third sentence (immediately after footnote 2523) in the paragraph beginning and concluding on page 1804 (including footnotes 2524 through 2526) with the following:

Decisions since the early 1990s have expanded the law in this area considerably.

Additionally, least two decisions, *Elf Atochem North America, Inc. v. Jaffari*, 727 A.2d 286 (Del. 1999) and *Weber v. King*, 110 F. Supp. 2d 124 (E.D.N.Y. 2000), have considered derivative litigation issues (although not the demand requirement or termination of derivative litigation by special litigation committee) in the context of limited liability companies. *See* 727 A.2d at 294 ("Delaware law allows for derivative suits against management of an LLC"); *Weber*, 110 F. Supp. at 130-

32 (a member of a New York LLC "may sue derivatively on behalf of the LLC").

In the general partnership context, "barring express agreement to the contrary, no correlative derivative litigation exists because in a general partnership everyone has a right to manage the affairs of the business, including the right to sue in court." *Gotham Partners v. Hallwood Realty Partners, L.P.*, 1998 Del. Ch. LEXIS 226, at *16 n.14, 1998 WL 832631, at *5 n.14 (Del. Ch. Nov. 10, 1998).

Section D 1

Add the following at the end of the second paragraph beginning and concluding on page 1806 (immediately after footnote 2539):

The Court of Chancery again re-affirmed these principles in *Dean v. Dick*, 1999 Del. Ch. LEXIS 121, 1999 WL 413400 (Del. Ch. June 10, 1999), stating that "the rule regarding demand futility in the corporate context is nearly the same as that in the limited partnership context." 1999 Del. Ch. LEXIS 121, at *7, 1999 WL 413400, at *2. The court, however, focused upon an important distinction: "[i]t is not sufficient to excuse demand (in a corporate context) to simply allege a director would be required to bring suit against himself," but "there is at least some doubt as to the disinterest" of a general partner that is 100 percent owned by one person and the demand seeks the commencement of litigation by the general partner against the person who owns the general partner. 1999 Del. Ch. LEXIS 121, at *8, 1999 WL 413400, at *3. The court explained that "[w]hen demand is made in a corporate setting, the board of directors has some pressure to at least consider the suit, as some directors may feel they are not as liable as others, or at least some directors may take their responsibilities seriously, or all directors may be protected by directors and officers insurance, or several of the defendants may be non-director officers of the company and so the potential liability may fall more squarely on those defendants." 1999 Del. Ch. LEXIS 121, at *8-9, 1999 WL 413400, at *3. "[W]hen a majority of the board of directors is beholden to the person from whom the damages (or return of funds) will be sought," the court continued, "demand is excused." 1999 Del. Ch. LEXIS 121, at *9, 1999 WL 413400, at *3. In the context of a limited partnership having a general partner owned by one person and "where the only party against whom relief is sought is the 100% owner of the party that would be requested to prosecute the lawsuit – what could be closer to beholdenness?" *Id.* Thus, the court held, "MDD [the general partner] is beholden to Dean [the person from whom damages were sought] because MDD is 100% owned by Dean. And so, demand is excused." *Id.*

The court nevertheless dismissed the case. The court explained that "[m]erely because demand was excused . . . does not mean that Becker's underlying claims are valid." 1999 Del. Ch. LEXIS 121, at *10, 1999 WL 413400, at *3. The court examined each of the claims and held that "they (a) receive business judgment rule protection, and (b) survive scrutiny under that standard." *Id.* The court reasoned that the claims were improperly vague, did not involve amounts that were material to Dean, did not involve gross negligence, involved injury suffered by Dean in the same proportion as his partners, and/or failed to state claims upon which relief could be granted for other reasons (for example, a claim for failing to respond to demands for information from a limited partner was rejected because "nothing in our partnership law requires a general partner to meet with limited partners at their every request" and there was no showing that the limited partner was entitled to see the information demanded either pursuant to "the partnership agreement or, in the absence of anything in that agreement, by the fiduciary duty owed by the general partner to the limited partner"). 1999 Del. Ch. LEXIS 121, at *10-17, 1999 WL 413400, at *3-5. None of the underlying wrongs, the court held, were "so egregious as to warrant second-guessing . . . in contravention of the business judgment rule." 1999 Del. Ch. LEXIS 121, at *12, 1999 WL 413400, at *4.

A intermediate appellate court in New York in *Broome v. ML Media Opportunity Partners, L.P.*, 273 A.D.2d 63, 709 N.Y.S.2d 59 (N.Y. App. Div. 1st Dep't 2000), similarly held that limited partners lack standing to assert derivative claims on behalf of a limited partnership without complying with the demand requirement. 273 A.D.2d at 64, 709 N.Y.S.2d at 60.

The Court of Chancery in *Gotham Partners, L.P. v. Hallwood Realty Partners, L.P.*, 1998 Del. Ch. LEXIS 226, 1998 WL 832631 (Del. Ch. Nov. 10, 1998), rejected a contention that where a general partner is a corporate entity, the need for a demand is measured with respect to the board of directors of the general partner rather than the general partner itself. The court explained that "the presence of a majority of interested directors within a corporate general partner might be one way of demonstrating demand futility as to the corporate general partner," but that fact does not make the corporate general partner's board of directors the "organizational subcomponent" to whom a demand should be made. 1998 Del. Ch. LEXIS 226, at *17, 1998 WL 832631, at *5. Rather, the law requires that courts look "to the person owing the fiduciary duty" and not the "individuals who make decisions in that entity's best interest." 1998 Del. Ch. LEXIS 226, at *18, 1998 WL 832631, at *5. The court added its view that any other rule "would require the Court to look into the form of entity of each general partner in order to determine whether the entity's internal decision-making individuals (or aggregate of individuals if that decisionmaker was also a business entity) were independent." *Id.*

The court stated that any other rule also would be "counter to the contractual freedom granted parties to a limited partnership" because "it forces them to treat a corporate general partner's board of directors as the de facto general partner" and "would ignore the reality that it is the general partner who owes the limited partners fiduciary duties, not the management of the general partner, even though they make the decisions for that business entity." 1998 Del. Ch. LEXIS 226, *18-19, 1998 WL 832631, at *5. The court added that "[t]he fact that the general partner is a corporation is a fortuity; many general partners are not," and therefore "it should be sufficient to make the demand upon the general partner, whatever its form," with the "manner in which the response to the demand is made" depending "upon whatever form of internal governance the general partner utilizes" – an issue that "is purely internal" and that "should be of no concern to a court." 1998 Del. Ch. LEXIS 226, at *19, 1998 WL 832631, at *5. The court acknowledged that under this rule "even where the limited partnership agreement permits self-dealing, limited partnerships with only one general partner may be exposed to derivative challenges in which the plaintiff limited partner will plead demand futility." 1998 Del. Ch. LEXIS 226, at *20 n.18, 1998 WL 832631, at *6 n.18. The court concluded, however, that "it is, after all, that one general partner who owes the limited partners the duty to act consistently with established fiduciary duty law." *Id.*

The court in *In re Cencom Cable Income Partners, L.P. Litigation*, 2000 Del. Ch. LEXIS 10, 2000 WL 130629 (Del. Ch. Jan. 27, 2000), held that "[i]n the partnership context, the relationships among the parties may be so simple and the circumstances so clear-cut that the distinction between direct and directive claims becomes irrelevant," such as "where a partnership is in liquidation and *all* non-defendant partners in the resulting litigation constitute a uniform class of limited partners." 2000 Del. Ch. LEXIS 10, at *8, 2000 WL 130629, at *3. Thus, the court held, "[i]f: (1) a business association consists of only two parties in interest, one a putative class of injured plaintiffs and the other the defendant party that controls the business association; and (2) the business association is effectively ended, but for the winding up of its affairs; and (3) the two sides oppose each other in the final dispute over the liquidation of that association; then a claim brought in that context is direct." 2000 Del. Ch. LEXIS 10, at *2, 2000 WL 130629, at *1. The court stated that under these circumstances, "classifying claims of collective injury as derivative ignores the reality that the dispute is really between the *only* two entities that make up the business association – the limited partner class and the general partner. It is not an action brought on behalf of the partnership itself." *Id.* Put another way: "With the partnership in dissolution the 'partnership' entity is simply an artifice representing the relationship between two legally juxtaposed parties and is no longer relevant as a distinct legal creature for the purpose of resolving the final claims between these parties." 2000 Del. Ch. LEXIS 10, at *19, 2000 WL 130629, at *6. Under these circumstances, the court concluded, "superimposing derivative pleading requirements upon claims needlessly delays ultimate substantive resolution and serves no useful or meaningful public policy purpose." 2000 Del. Ch. LEXIS 10, at *9, 2000 WL 130629, at *3.

Section E 1

Add the following at the end of the paragraph beginning on page 1820 and concluding on page 1821 (immediately after footnote 2628):

Additional cases finding good cause and piercing the attorney client privilege include *Sealy Mattress Co. v. Sealy, Inc.*, 1987 Del. Ch. LEXIS 451, at *8-9, 1987 WL 12500, at *3 (Del. Ch. June 19, 1987), and *In re Halter*, 1999 Tex. App. LEXIS 6478, at *9-10, 12-15, 1999 WL 667288, at *3, 4-5 (Tex. Ct. App. Aug. 27, 1999). Another case finding an absence of good cause and refusing to pierce the attorney client privilege is *In re Fuqua Industries, Inc. Shareholder Litigation*, 1999 Del. Ch. LEXIS 190, at *5-8, 1999 WL 959182, at *2-3 (Del. Ch. Sept. 17, 1999). Accordingly, "[d]iscovery of lawyer-client communications is not automatic in shareholder suits." *Id.*, 1999 Del. Ch. LEXIS 190, at *8, 1999 WL 959182, at *3 (quoting *Deutsch v. Cogan*, 580 A.2d 100, 106 (Del. Ch. 1990)).

The *Garner* doctrine also was applied in *Grimes v. DSC Communications Corp.*, 724 A.2d 561 (Del. Ch. 1998), a Section 220 proceeding seeking the inspection of corporate books and records in order to obtain facts to be used in an attempt to satisfy pleading requirements in a derivative action. The *Grimes* decision is discussed in Chapter IV, Section B 7.

Add the following at the end of the paragraph beginning on page 1822 and concluding on page 1823 (immediately after footnote 2636):

A trial court in New York construing Delaware law in *Weiser v. Grace*, 179 Misc. 2d 116, 683 N.Y.S.2d 781 (N.Y. Sup. Ct. N.Y. Co. 1998), however, held that special litigation committee notes, summaries and outlines of witness interviews that were not transcribed could be discoverable for "good cause" under *Garner v. Wolfinbarger*, 430 F.2d 1093 (5th Cir. 1970), *cert. denied*, 401 U.S. 974 (1971), even if these materials constituted work product. 179 Misc. 2d at 123, 683 N.Y.S.2d at 787. The court stated that the plaintiffs in the case included one of the corporation's largest shareholders, that the plaintiffs had demonstrated that the documents they sought were not available from other sources because the interviews had not been recorded, and that the documents they sought "do not necessarily disclose counsel's advice." *Id.* The court accordingly ordered an in camera review of the documents to "protect against disclosure of the mental impressions, conclusions, opinions or legal theories" of counsel. *Id.* With respect to the attorney-client privilege, the court stated that the committee's counsel represented both the committee and the corporation as a whole, including the plaintiff shareholders, and "[u]nder such circumstances, the attorney-client privilege would not bar discovery of all communications between counsel and the SLC." *Id.* at 122, 683 N.Y.S.2d at 786.

Replace the words "Section 7.13(e) of Principles of Corporate Governance does address the issue and" in the second sentence (between footnotes 2636 and 2637) of the paragraph

beginning on page 1823 and concluding on page 1824 with the following:

The court in *Drilling v. Berman*, 589 N.W.2d 503 (Minn. Ct. App. 1999), *review denied*, 1999 Minn. LEXIS 306 (Minn. May 18, 1999), held that shareholders are not entitled to legal memoranda prepared by a special litigation committee's counsel because the law in Minnesota, a jurisdiction following the approach adopted in *Auerbach v. Bennett*, 47 N.Y.2d 619, 393 N.E.2d 994, 419 N.Y.S.2d 920 (1979), "precludes courts from performing a substantive review," and thus "any information regarding the committee's reasoning is not relevant to our review." 589 N.W.2d at 510-11; *see also* Chapter IV, Section C 2 a (discussing *Auerbach* approach). Section 7.13(e) of Principles of Corporate Governance

Add the following at the end of the paragraph beginning on page 1825 and concluding on page 1826 (immediately after footnote 2646):

A New Jersey court in *In re PSE&G Shareholder Litigation*, 726 A.2d 994 (N.J. Super. Ct. Ch. Div. 1998), reached the same conclusion as the court in *Joy v. North,* 692 F.2d 880 (2d Cir. 1982), *cert. denied,* 460 U.S. 1051 (1983). The court in *PSE&G* stated that "when the opinion of counsel or advice of counsel is injected into the case, the attorney-client and work product privilege have been deemed waived." *Id.* at 996. Applying this rule, the court concluded that "the defendants rely in part on the opinion of their special counsel in rejecting plaintiffs' demand," and accordingly "[t]he court will grant plaintiffs' motion to compel the directors to respond to the questions concerning their conversations with special counsel in connection with the preparation and the submission of counsel's report." *Id.*

An intermediate appellate court in New York in *Lichtenberg v. Zinn*, 243 A.D.2d 1045, 663 N.Y.S.2d 452 (N.Y. App. Div. 3d Dep't 1997), declined to follow *Joy.*

Add the following at the end of the first paragraph beginning and concluding on page 1826 (immediately after footnote 2648):

An intermediate appellate court in California in *McDermott, Will & Emery v. Superior Court*, 83 Cal. App. 4th 378, 99 Cal. Rptr. 2d 622 (Cal. Ct. App. 2000), held that a shareholder derivative action on behalf of a corporation cannot be asserted against the corporation's outside counsel because an action of this type would raise attorney-client privilege issues that foreclose the attorney from mounting a meaningful defense. The court explained that shareholders in a shareholder derivative action "stand in the shoes of the corporation for most purposes" but not for the purpose of waiving the attorney-client privilege. *Id.* at 383, 99 Cal. Rptr. 2d at 625-26. Allowing a suit of this kind therefore "would place the defendant's attorney in the untenable position of having to 'preserve the attorney client privilege (the client having done nothing to waive the privilege) while trying to show that his representation of the client was not negligent.'" *Id.* at 384, 99 Cal. Rptr. 2d at 626.

The court rejected the view adopted by federal courts in cases such as *Garner*, which permits a case-by-case finding of "good cause" for allowing the shareholders access to privileged information in a derivative action. The court stated that "[w]e simply cannot conceive how an attorney is to mount a defense in a shareholder derivative action alleging a breach of duty to the corporate client, where, by the very nature of such an action, the attorney is foreclosed, in the absence of a waiver by the corporation, from disclosing the very communications which are alleged to constitute a breach of that duty." 83 Cal. App. 4th at 385, 99 Cal. Rptr. 2d at 626-27. The court stated that "long standing California case authority has rejected" the federal *Garner* doctrine because "it contravenes the strict principles set forth in the Evidence Code of California which precludes any judicially created exception to the attorney-client privilege." *Id.* at 385, 99 Cal. Rptr. 2d at 627. Accordingly, the court concluded, "the creation of any shareholder right to waive the privilege in a derivative action should be left to the California legislature. And, in the absence of such a right, this derivative action, necessarily brought in equity, cannot go forward." *Id.*

CHAPTER V

Introduction

Add the following new footnote 0.1 at the end of the first sentence of the first paragraph beginning and concluding on page 1851:

See generally Chamison v. HealthTrust, Inc. – The Hosp. Co., 735 A.2d 912, 917 n.12 (Del. Ch. 1999) (noting two uses of the term "indemnification": (1) "the term of art defining a corporation's reimbursement of a director, officer or employee for the costs incurred by that individual in defense of an action brought against that individual in his capacity as a director, officer or employee of the corporation," and (2) "the more general concept of liability-shifting from the party who paid a claim to the party who should have paid it"), *aff'd*, 748 A.2d 407 (unpublished opinion, text available at 2000 Del. LEXIS 95, 2000 WL 275649) (Del. Mar. 6, 2000).

Section A 1

Replace "1997" with "2000" in the Bishop citation in footnote 3 on page 1852.

Replace the Olson citation in footnote 3 on page 1852 with the following:

John F. Olson, Josiah O. Hatch III & Ty R. Sagalow, *Director and Officer Liability: Indemnification and Insurance* §§ 4.05 - 4.11 (2000) (same).

Add the following at the end of footnote 3 on page 1852:

See also VonFeldt v. Stifel Fin. Corp., 714 A.2d 79, 84 (Del. 1998) (citation omitted):

> Delaware's first general corporation law, enacted in 1899, contained no provision for the indemnification of corporate officers and directors. Indeed, in the pre-World War II era, indemnification statutes did not exist anywhere, as the topic was exclusively one of judge-made law. In the 1940s, however, a codification movement began to gather momentum, as state legislatures sought to clarify what had become "an intolerable common-law muddle."

Add the following at the end of footnote 5 on page 1853:

As stated by the Delaware Supreme Court in *VonFeldt*:

> We have long recognized that Section 145 serves the dual policies of: (a) allowing corporate officials to resist unjustified lawsuits, secure in the knowledge that, if vindicated, the corporation will bear the expense of litigation; and (b) encouraging capable women and men to serve as corporate directors and officers, secure in the knowledge that the corporation will absorb the costs of defending their honesty and integrity.

714 A.2d at 85 (citing *Hibbert v. Hollywood Park, Inc.*, 457 A.2d 339, 343-44 (Del. 1983)); *see also Owens Corning Fiberglass Corp. v. National Union Fire Ins. Co.*, No. 3:95 CV 7700, slip op. at 6 n.3 (N.D. Ohio Mar. 31, 1999); *Cochran v. Stifel Fin. Corp.*, 2000 Del. Ch. LEXIS 179, at *24, 2000 WL 1847676, at *7 (Del. Ch. Dec. 13, 2000); *Chamison v. HealthTrust, Inc. – The Hosp. Co.*, 735 A.2d 912, 925 n.45 (Del. Ch. 1999) (quoting *Hibbert*, 457 A.2d at 343-44), *aff'd*, 748 A.2d 407 (unpublished opinion, text available at 2000 Del. LEXIS 95, 2000 WL 275649) (Del. Mar. 6, 2000).

Replace the period at the end of footnote 7 on page 1854 with the following:

, *quoted in part in Cochran v. Stifel Fin. Corp.*, 2000 Del. Ch. LEXIS 58, at *30, 2000 WL 286722, at *9 (Del. Ch. Mar. 8, 2000).

Add the following at the end of the paragraph beginning on page 1853 and concluding on page 1854 (immediately after footnote 7)

The Delaware Supreme Court has stated that "[w]e eschew narrow construction of the statute where an overliteral reading would disserve these policies." *VonFeldt*, 714 A.2d at 84.

Replace "8-290" with "8-281" and replace "1996" with "Supp. 1998/99" in the Model Act § 8.50-8.59 citation in footnote 8 on page 1854.

Section A 2

Add the following at the end of footnote 13 on page 1856:

See also Channel Lumber Co. v. Simon, 78 Cal. App. 4th 1222, 1232, 93 Cal. Rptr. 2d 482, 490 (Cal. Ct. App. 2000) ("an outside attorney retained by a corporation to represent it at trial, who then is sued by the corporation for alleged legal malpractice while representing the corporation, is not a party to the malpractice suit 'by reason of the fact [the attorney] is or was an agent of the corporation,' within the meaning and purposes of section 317"); *Cochran v. Stifel Fin. Corp.*, 2000 Del. Ch. LEXIS 58, at *48-49, 58, 2000 WL 286722, at *14, 16 (Del. Ch. Mar. 8, 2000) ("a director or officer of a wholly-owned subsidiary is only an agent of the parent . . . if the common law agency test is satisfied"; "a showing that the director merely 'served at the request of' the parent is insufficient under § 145 to prove 'agency' status; the director must go farther and demonstrate that he was the parent's agent under the traditional agency definition"; "the hardly uncommon term 'agent' must be given its usual meaning").

Replace "1996" with "Supp. 1998/99" in the Model Act § 8.56 citation in footnote 15 on page 1856.

Replace "8-369" with "8–368-69" in the Model Act § 8.56 citation in footnote 16 on page 1856.

Section A 3

Add the following at the end of the second paragraph beginning and concluding on page 1857 (between footnotes 18 and 19):

Even where indemnification (or advancement – a subject discussed in Chapter V, Section A 5) is mandatory, only reasonable expenses are required to be indemnified (or advanced). In Delaware, "[t]his element of reasonability is derived solely from the overall requirement of reasonableness found in the Delaware General Corporation Law," but a charter, bylaw or contract provision may address this issue in a more specific manner. *Dunlap v. Sunbeam Corp.*, 1999 Del. Ch. LEXIS 126, at *18 n.9, 1999 WL 1261339, at *6 n.9 (Del. Ch. June 23, 1999); *see also Dunlap v. Sunbeam Corp.*, 1999 Del. Ch. LEXIS 132, at *1-5, 1999 WL 413299, at *1-2 (Del. Ch. June 7, 1999) (in dispute concerning the reasonableness of defense costs incurred by former corporate officers for which advancement was sought, court permitted discovery by the former officers of the amounts spent by corporation's counsel relating to the matters concerning which the corporation contested the reasonableness of the defense costs incurred by the former officers).

Section A 3 a

Add the following between "where" and "the person to be indemnified" in the first sentence (between footnotes 18 and 19) of the paragraph beginning on page 1857 and concluding on page 1858:

"the matter at issue [is] covered" by the indemnification statute (*Cochran v. Stifel Fin. Corp.*, 2000 Del. Ch. LEXIS 179, at *33, 2000 WL 1847676, at *9 (Del. Ch. Dec. 13, 2000), and

Add the following at the end of footnote 20 page 1857:

See also Dunlap v. Sunbeam Corp., 1999 Del. Ch. LEXIS 126, at *15, 1999 WL 1261339, at *5 (Del. Ch. June 23, 1999) ("it does not matter whether Sunbeam's board votes to disapprove of indemnification of these expenses – if Dunlap and Kersh prevail 'on the merits,' indemnification is automatic"); *Chamison v. HealthTrust, Inc. – The Hosp. Co.*, 735 A.2d 912, 917 919 (Del. Ch. 1999) ("[I]t is beyond dispute that Chamison's dismissal with prejudice from the *Anderson* suit constitutes a 'success[ ] on the merits or otherwise in defense of [the] action.' Thus, it falls squarely within the mandatory indemnification provision of § 145(c).") (footnote omitted), *aff'd*, 748 A.2d 407 (unpublished opinion, text available at 2000 Del. LEXIS 95 and 2000 WL 275649) (Del. Mar. 6, 2000).

Replace "1996" with "Supp. 1998/99" in the Model Act § 8.52 citation in footnote 23 on page 1858.

Add the following at the of the first sentence (immediately after footnote 24) of the paragraph beginning and concluding on page 1858:

Delaware law thus "permits – nay, mandates – indemnification of directors and officers who satisfy the success criteria . . . regardless of their good faith." *Cochran v. Stifel Fin. Corp.*,

2000 Del. Ch. LEXIS 58, at *63, 2000 WL 286722, at *18 (Del. Ch. Mar. 8, 2000).

Replace "8-343" with "8–330-31" in the Model Act § 8.52 citation in footnote 28 on page 1859.

Add the following at the end of footnote 28 on page 1859:

See also Cochran, 2000 Del. Ch. LEXIS 58, at *64 n.73, 2000 WL 286722, at *18 n.73 ("the phrase . . . 'on the merits or otherwise,' permits the indemnitee to be indemnified as a matter of right in the event that he wins a judgment on the merits in his favor or if he successfully asserts a 'technical' defense, such as a defense based on the statute of limitations'") (quoting Veasey, Finkelstein & Bigler, *Delaware Supports Directors with a Three-Legged Stool of Limited Liability, Indemnification and Insurance*, 42 Bus. Law. 399, 406 (1987)).

Replace the Folk citation in footnote 31 on page 1859 with the following:

I Rodman Ward, Jr., Edward P. Welch & Andrew J. Turezyn, *Folk on the Delaware General Corporation Law* § 145.4, at GCL-IV-231 (4th ed. & Supp. 2001-2).

Replace the Mayer citation in footnote 40 on page 1861 with the following:

Mayer v. Executive Telecard, Ltd., 1997 WL 811691 (S.D.N.Y. Apr. 30, 1997) (determining amount owed).

Add the following at the end of footnote 40 on page 1860:

See also Owens Corning Fiberglass Corp. v. Nat'l Union Fire Ins. Co., No. 3:95 CV 7700, slip op. at 1, 5-6 (N.D. Ohio Mar. 31, 1999) (also following *Waltuch v. Conticommodity Servs.,*

Inc., 88 F.3d 87 (2d Cir. 1996), in a case involving a settlement).

Add the following at the end of the fourth sentence (immediately after footnote 40) of the paragraph beginning on page 1860 and concluding on page 1861:

As stated by the Delaware Court of Chancery in *Cochran v. Stifel Financial Corp.*, 2000 Del. Ch. LEXIS 179, 2000 WL 1847676 (Del. Ch. Dec. 13, 2000), "[a]lthough Cochran may not have emerged from the Criminal Proceeding with his reputation intact, he did emerge from that proceeding with an acquittal on all counts against him," and "[t]hat outcome is sufficient to satisfy the success standard . . . , which simply requires 'success[ ] on the merits or otherwise.'" 2000 Del. Ch. LEXIS 179, at *33-34, 2000 WL 1847676, at *9.

Add the following at the end of the paragraph beginning on page 1861 and concluding on page 1862 (immediately after footnote 53):

The Delaware Court of Chancery in *VonFeldt v. Stifel Financial Corp.*, 1999 Del. Ch. LEXIS 131, 1999 WL 413393 (Del. Ch. June 11, 1999), noted – but did not decide – a claim that a $6,000 settlement payment represented no more that the "nuisance value" of a suit and thus constituted "success on the merits or otherwise." 1999 Del. Ch. LEXIS 131, at *4-5, 1999 WL 413393, at *1-2. The court described the opposing views of the parties as "equally inadequate":

> On the one hand, the principle might be that a party seeking indemnification has been successful on the merits or otherwise *only* where he has obtained a final judgment in his favor or a dismissal with prejudice without the payment of any consideration. On the other hand, room might exist for recognizing that dismissal with prejudice with the payment of nominal consideration, amounting perhaps to the nuisance value of the suit, is an appropriate understanding of the phrase "success on the merits or otherwise." Of course, the latter approach could be

> problematic, requiring a potentially burdensome inquiry into the underlying action in order to determine its nuisance value.

1999 Del. Ch. LEXIS 131, at *15-16, 1999 WL 413393, at *4. "Fortunately," the court concluded, "resolution of this question at this time is unnecessary." 1999 Del. Ch. LEXIS 131, at *16, 1999 WL 413393, at *4.

Add the following at the end of the paragraph beginning on page 1862 and concluding on page 1863 (immediately after footnote 58):

The court in *First American Corp. v. Al-Nahnyan*, 17 F. Supp. 2d 10 (D.D.C. 1998), construing Virginia law, which mandates indemnification where a director "entirely prevails in the defense of any proceeding," stated that it would be "very difficult" for the persons seeking indemnification in that case to contend that they had "entirely prevailed" in Senate Subcommittee and Federal Reserve Board proceedings because the Senate Subcommittee issued a report finding that they participated in wrongdoing and a settlement agreement in the Federal Reserve Board proceeding required them to relinquish stock. *Id.* at 31. The court, however, held that a jury should decide whether expenses incurred in preparing testimony in the Senate Subcommittee and Federal Reserve Board proceedings also were incurred in connection with state and federal court criminal cases in which the persons seeking indemnification indisputably had "entirely prevailed" (one of the individuals seeking indemnification was acquitted in the state court proceeding, the charges against the other individual seeking indemnification were dropped in the state court proceeding due to the individual's failing health, and the federal charges against both individuals were dropped). According to the directors seeking indemnification, "anything they said under oath" in the Senate Subcommittee and Federal Reserve Board proceedings "could and would be used against them in the criminal cases." *Id.* at 31.

Where indemnification is mandatory because the person seeking indemnification has been successful in the defense of an action, indemnification is not required for expenses incurred following dismissal of the claims against the person seeking indemnification, such as monitoring the litigation due to a concern that the person seeking indemnification may be called as a fact witness or named as a defendant in another suit arising from the same underlying conduct. *Chamison v. HealthTrust, Inc. – The Hosp. Co.*, 735 A.2d 912, 928 (Del. Ch. 1999), *aff'd*, 748 A.2d 407 (unpublished opinion, text available at 2000 Del. LEXIS 95, 2000 WL 275649) (Del. Mar. 6, 2000). These types of defense costs, the court held, "go far beyond reasonable 'winding up' activities." *Id.* If another action is filed and later dismissed, the court stated, "such preparatory efforts" would be considered in determining the indemnification owed in the later action, but are not relevant to the defense and dismissal of the first action. *Id.*

Replace "8-343" with "8-331" in the Model Act § 8.52 citation in footnote 75 on page 1865.

Replace "applies" with "was amended in 1997 to apply" in the first sentence (between footnotes 81 and 82) of the paragraph beginning on page 1866 and concluding on page 1867.

Add "thus" between "This provision" and "does not apply" in the second sentence (immediately after footnote 82) of the paragraph beginning on page 1866 and concluding on page 1867.

Add the following at the end of footnote 83 on page 1867:

See also Cochran v. Stifel Fin. Corp., 2000 Del. Ch. LEXIS 58, at *6, 54, 2000 WL 286722, at *2, 15 (Del. Ch. Mar. 8, 2000) (the 1997 amendment to § 145(c) eliminated any reference to the term 'agent', thus ending the right of a corporate agent to demand mandatory indemnification from his corporate principal if the agent otherwise satisfied the terms of the subsection").

Add the following at the end of the second sentence (immediately after footnote 83) of the paragraph beginning on page 1866 and concluding on page 1867:

"[T]he rationale for this change had nothing to do with restructuring the ability of corporations to provide indemnification to employees and agents and everything to do with permitting corporations greater freedom to decide what indemnification coverage to provide to them." *Cochran*, 2000 Del. Ch. LEXIS 58, at *67, 2000 WL 286722, at *19.

Section A 3 b

Replace "1996" with "Supp. 1998/99" in the Model Act § 8.58 citation in footnote 86 on page 1867.

Add the following at the end of the second sentence (immediately after footnote 86) of the paragraph beginning on page 1867 and concluding on page 1868:

Charter, bylaw or contract provisions that require indemnification "to the full extent authorized by law" require indemnification whenever indemnification "would be permissible" under the law; "[t]hat is, if the [law] does not forbid such indemnification, such indemnity is authorized, or in other words, permissible." *Cochran v. Stifel Fin. Corp.*, 2000 Del. Ch. LEXIS 179, at *29-30, 2000 WL 1847676, at *8 (Del. Ch. Dec. 13, 2000).

Add the following at the end of the paragraph beginning on page 1867 and concluding on page 1868 (immediately after footnote 92):

Charter, bylaw or contract provisions mandating advancement also have been enforced in *VonFeldt v. Stifel Financial Corp.*, 714 A.2d 79, 81, 83-86 (Del. 1998), and *Cochran v. Stifel Financial Corp.*, 2000 Del. Ch. LEXIS 179, at *29-42, 2000 WL 1847676, at *8-11 (Del. Ch. Dec. 13, 2000). A corporation also may contractually commit itself to indemnify directors of a corporation that it is acquiring, as the Delaware Court of Chancery found to have occurred in *Chamison v. HealthTrust, Inc. – The Hospital Co.*, 735 A.2d 912, 919-20 (Del. Ch. 1999), *aff'd*, 748 A.2d 407 (unpublished opinion, text available at 2000 Del. LEXIS 95, 2000 WL 275649) (Del. Mar. 6, 2000).

Where a charter, bylaw or contract provision provides that a corporation "shall indemnify to the full extent permitted by Delaware law," the use of "the phrase 'shall indemnify' . . . not only mandates indemnification; it also effectively places the burden on [the corporation] to demonstrate that the indemnification mandated is not required." *VonFeldt v. Stifel Fin. Corp.*, 1999 Del. Ch. LEXIS 131, at *10, 1999 WL 413393, at *3 (Del. Ch. June 11, 1999).

Add the following at the end of footnote 92 on page 1868:

See also Frater v. Tigerpack Capital, Ltd., 1998 U.S. Dist. LEXIS 19128, at *4-14, 1998 WL 851591, at *1-4 (S.D.N.Y. Dec. 9, 1998), *subsequent proceedings*, 1999 U.S. Dist. LEXIS 6, at *4-16, 1999 WL 4892, at *2-6 (S.D.N.Y. Jan. 5, 1999) (denying claim for mandatory indemnification because the bylaw and contract provisions relied upon in support of that claim did not reflect an "unmistakably clear" intent to indemnify under the circumstances in this case); *Harhen v. Brown*, 710 N.E.2d 224, 237, 239-40 (Mass. App. Ct. 1999), *rev'd on other grounds*, 730 N.E.2d 859 (Mass. 2000) (denying motion to dismiss claim challenging indemnification by a corporation – a life insurance company owned by policyholders – of an officer for expenses incurred defending federal criminal charges that were dismissed as part of a plea agreement pursuant to which the officer pleaded guilty to mail fraud and the sentencing judge stated that the guilty plea did not represent a finding by the court that the officer acted in good faith or bad faith; the corporation contended that the indemnification was authorized by a bylaw that required indemnification for expenses incurred in defending any civil or criminal action, but the court held that the copy of the bylaw requiring indemnification submitted by the corporation to the court was inadequate because it lacked a "secretary's certificate attesting to a meeting of the members held following a legally sufficient notice of meeting and to the outcome of the vote that was taken" and plaintiffs alleged that the corporation had not sent notice of the meeting at which the bylaw was adopted to policyholders).

Add the following at the end of the first sentence (immediately after footnote 94) in the paragraph beginning on page 1868 and concluding on page 1869:

The Delaware Supreme Court likewise observed in 1998 that "'[v]irtually all' public corporations have extended indemnification guarantees via bylaw to cases where indemnification is typically only permissive." *VonFeldt v. Stifel Fin. Corp.*, 714 A.2d 79, 81 n.5 (Del. 1998) (quoting *Advanced Mining Sys., Inc. v. Fricke*, 623 A.2d 82, 83 (Del. Ch. 1992)).

Add the following new footnote 96.1 at the end of the third sentence of the paragraph beginning and concluding on page 1869:

See VonFeldt, 714 A.2d at 81, 83-86; *Cochran*, 2000 Del. Ch. LEXIS 179, at *29-42, 2000 WL 1847676, at *8-11 (both requiring indemnification by a parent corporation of a person sued by a wholly-owned subsidiary of the corporation, and both discussed in Chapter V, Section A 9).

Replace the Olson citation in footnote 98 on page 1870 with the following:

John F. Olson, Josiah O. Hatch III & Ty R. Sagalow, *Director and Officer Liability: Indemnification and Insurance* § 7.10, at 7–15-16 (2000).

Add the following at the end of footnote 102 on page 1871:

See also VonFeldt, 1999 Del. Ch. LEXIS 131, at *10, 1999 WL 413393, at *3 ("[b]y using the mandatory word 'shall' in the indemnification bylaw, Stifel has contractually agreed to indemnify the persons covered by the bylaw").

Add the following text and new Section A 3 c at the end of the paragraph beginning on page 1870 and concluding on page 1872 (immediately after footnote 105):

A mandatory indemnification provision in a charter, bylaw or contract may include a restriction requiring the payment of attorneys' fees and expenses incurred by a counsel "*selected by* [*the corporation*]." *Chamison*, 735 A.2d at 916, 920. In a decision involving a provision drafted in this manner, the court held that the corporation had broad discretion in selecting counsel, but in light of the "implied covenant of good faith and fair dealing" that "inheres in every contract" the provision "cannot be construed so broadly as to permit it to force clearly inferior representation" upon a director in the absence of evidence that the parties' agreement "contemplate[d] sacrificing a director's defensive options to [the corporation's] counsel selection prerogative." *Id.* at 920, 923. The court found that the corporation's interpretation of the counsel selection provision was unreasonable because the law firm selected by the corporation contemplated a group defense strategy that ignored unique defenses available to a director who sought separate counsel for himself. *Id.* at 921-22. These unique defenses included the fact that this director was the only one of the corporation's directors who did not have a financial interest in stock appreciation rights ("SARs") underlying the litigation and a claim by this director that he had been misled by the corporation's chief executive officer concerning the value at which the SARs were repurchased by the corporation in the transaction challenged in the litigation. *Id.* at 915-16, 921-22.

The court stated that nothing in Delaware's indemnification statute "indicates that a counsel selection clause trumps a director's right to utilize his best legal defenses," and added that the statute's "purpose – to enable Delaware companies to attract competent directors by offering them indemnification for suits arising from their service to the company – runs counter to the notion that an indemnitor could, through a counsel selection clause, foist a less-than-the-best defense upon an indemnitee." *Id.* at 922. Thus, the court concluded, the corporation "unreasonably restrict[ed]" the director's defense "through manipulation of the counsel selection provision" and "violated its implied covenant of good faith and fair dealing." *Id.*

Section A 3 c

c. *Contribution.* The indemnification statutes in Delaware and most other jurisdictions "clearly contemplate the possibility that more than one corporation may be the indemnitor of a director, officer, employee or agent who is a party to an action from which an indemnification obligation arises." *Chamison v. HealthTrust, Inc.– The Hosp. Corp.*, 735 A.2d 912, 925 n.44 (Del. Ch. 1999), *aff'd*, 748 A.2d 407 (unpublished opinion, text available at 2000 Del. LEXIS 95 and 2000 WL 275649) (Del. Mar. 6, 2000). This is because "[a] corporation has the power to indemnify a director, for example, who is serving, at its request, on the board of another corporation," and in that circumstance, the requesting corporation and the corporation that the requesting corporation's designee is serving "are potentially liable as joint indemnitors." *Id.*

The Delaware Court of Chancery has held that where more than one corporation is liable under mandatory indemnification provisions as joint indemnitors, each is liable for the full amount and the joint indemnitors have contribution rights against each other. *Id.* at 924-26. The court based this determination upon (1) the court's fear that a rule not permitting contribution "would undermine the very purpose of indemnification" because "[i]f a corporation thought it could escape the responsibility of indemnifying a director on the chance that the entire obligation could be shifted to another contractually obligated indemnitor, the director would suffer the same lack of protection that indemnification . . . is intended to permit," and (2) "conventional insurance law . . . under which co-insurers insuring the same risk share ratably and have rights of contribution against one another." *Id.* at 925.

Thus, where two entities (Tenet Healthcare Corporation and HealthTrust, Inc. – The Hospital Company) were equally obligated to indemnify a director (Alan Chamison) for his successful defense of an action, the court determined that Tenet and HealthTrust should "share the indemnity ratably, i.e., by each paying half." *Id.* at 926. The court accordingly found that Tenet, which indemnified Chamison after HealthTrust improperly refused to do so, was entitled to contribution from HealthTrust in an amount equal to one-half the amount Tenet had paid to Chamison. *Id.*

The court rejected HealthTrust's contention that it had a right to set off from its contribution toward Tenet's expenses on behalf of Chamison the defense expenses that HealthTrust claimed it incurred on behalf of Chamison. The court explained that the defense provided by HealthTrust for Chamison was not a good faith defense because Carrington Coleman Sloman & Blumenthal, the law firm selected by HealthTrust to represent Chamison, contemplated a group defense strategy that ignored unique defenses available to Chamison. *Id.* at 921-22, 929; *see also* Chapter V, Section A 3 b (discussing this aspect of decision). The court stated that there was no evidence that the Carrington Coleman firm shared work product with the counsel Chamison selected to represent him and that there was no evidence linking Carrington Coleman's efforts to Chamison's successful defense. *Id.* at 929. The court added that HealthTrust had arrived at its $208,113.76 set-off "by claiming that Chamison, as one of five directors, was responsible for twenty percent of Carrington Coleman's total bill, arising from its common defense of all five directors." *Id.* at 930. The court stated that "[b]y this means, HealthTrust effectively tries to impose on Chamison, a disinterested director, part of the cost of defending" four directors who were not disinterested directors because they had a financial interest in stock appreciation rights ("SARs") underlying the litigation for which indemnification of defense costs was sought. *Id.* This result, the court concluded, would be "inequitable and unfair" because "Carrington Coleman's efforts, so far as I can tell on this record, had no connection with Chamison's dismissal" from the litigation. *Id.*

The Delaware Supreme Court affirmed, stating that "[t]o the extent that (a) the issues raised on appeal are factual, the record evidence supports the trial judge's factual findings; (b) the errors alleged on appeal are attributed to an abuse of discretion, the record does not support those assertions; (c) the issues raised on appeal are legal, they are controlled by settled Delaware law, which was properly applied." *HealthTrust, Inc. – The Hosp. Corp. v. Chamison*, 748 A.2d 407 (unpublished opinion, text available at 2000 Del. LEXIS 95, at *1 and 2000 WL 275649, at *1) (Del. Mar. 6, 2000).

Section A 4

Replace "1996" with "Supp. 1998/99" in the Model Act § 8.51 citation in footnote 107 on page 1872.

Add the following at the end of footnote 109 on page 1873:

See also Frater v. Tigerpack Capital, Ltd., 1998 U.S. Dist. LEXIS 19128, at *13, 1998 WL 851591, at *4 (S.D.N.Y. Dec. 9, 1998) (N.Y. Bus. Corp. Law § 723(c) "is permissive, stating that a company 'may' reimburse a director" and thus "codifies the right of corporations to indemnify their officers and directors if they so desire"); *Iberti v. Walker & Zanger (W. Coast)*

Ltd., No. 602113/99, slip op. at 7 (N.Y. Sup. Ct. N.Y. Co. Sept. 22, 1999) ("BCL § 722(c) authorizes, but does not require, a corporation to indemnify its directors and officers"; "[i]n contrast to BCL § 722, which merely permits indemnification, BCL § 724 specifies the standards and procedures by which a court may order such indemnification").

Section A 4 a

Replace "1996" with "Supp. 1998/99" in the Model Act §§ 8.50 and 8.51 citation in footnote 121 on page 1876.

Add the following at the end of the first sentence (immediately after footnote 123) of the paragraph beginning on page 1876 and concluding on page 1877:

The text of Delaware's statute "makes plain the legislative intent that the good faith requirement is central to the policy underlying the statutory language," and "as a matter of public policy it simply would not make sense for a corporation to have the power to indemnify agents who do not act in its best interests." *VonFeldt v. Stifel Fin. Corp.*, 1999 Del. Ch. LEXIS 131, at *5-6, 1999 WL 413993, at *2 (Del. Ch. June 11, 1999). Unlike the case in an action brought by or in the right of the corporation such as a derivative action (discussed in Chapter V, Section A 4 b), "a director found liable for a breach of fiduciary duty in a direct action brought by the company's stockholders can be indemnified" because "the legislature appears to believe that the good faith safeguard . . . is sufficient even though the underlying breach may be no different in nature than that involved in a derivative action." *Cochran v. Stifel Fin. Corp.*, 2000 Del. Ch. LEXIS 58, at *50, 2000 WL 286722, at *14 (Del. Ch. Mar. 8, 2000).

Add the following at the end of footnote 124 on page 1877:

See also Biondi v. Beekman Hill House Apartment Corp., 257 A.D.2d 76, 83, 692 N.Y.S.2d 304, 310 (N.Y. App. Div. 1st Dep't 1999) (rejecting claim that the prohibition against indemnifying directors for bad faith acts is restricted "to instances where the corporation was the target of bad faith," and stating that it would "stand reason on its head" to accept a contention that a director "may have acted in good faith for a purpose he reasonably believed" was in the corporation's best interest while "willfully violating the civil rights" of third parties: "[a] director cannot willfully violate the Civil Rights Law and act in bad faith, thus exposing the corporation to potential liability, and, at the same time, reasonably believe that in so doing he is acting in good faith and in the corporation's best interests"), *aff'd*, 94 N.Y.2d 659, 666-67, 731 N.E.2d 577, 580-81, 709 N.Y.S.2d 861, 865-65 (2000) ("the key to indemnification is a director's good faith toward the corporation" and "a judgment against the director, standing alone, may not be dispositive of whether the director acted in good faith," but a judgment for "willful racial discrimination cannot be considered an act in the corporation's best interest" and thus is dispositive and precludes indemnification).

Replace "8-339" with "8-322" in the Model Act § 8.51 citation in footnote 132 on page 1878.

Section A 4 b

Replace "1996" with "Supp. 1998/99" in the Model Act § 8.51 citation in footnote 141 on page 1880.

Add the following at the end of footnote 141 on page 1880:

See also Cochran v. Stifel Fin. Corp., 2000 Del. Ch. LEXIS 58, at *38, 2000 WL 286722, at *11 (Del. Ch. Mar. 8, 2000) ("Section 145(b) has much tighter restrictions on the scope and availability of indemnification than does § 145(a)").

Add the following at the end of footnote 142 on page 1881:

See also Cochran, 2000 Del. Ch. LEXIS 58, at *38, 40, 43, 2000 WL 286722, at *11, 12 (the statute treats direct actions brought by the corporation itself and derivative actions brought by shareholders on behalf of the corporation identically).

Add the following at the end of the paragraph beginning on page 1880 and concluding on page 1881 (immediately after footnote 142):

Actions by or in the right of a wholly-owned subsidiary of a corporation are not actions by or in the right of the corporation. *Cochran*, 2000 Del. Ch. LEXIS 58, at *37-54, 2000 WL 286722, at *10-15 (discussed in Chapter V, Section A 9).

Add the following at the end of footnote 152 on page 1883:

See also Cochran, 2000 Del. Ch. LEXIS 58, at *41 & n.48, 2000 WL 286722, at *12 n.48.

Add the following at the end of the paragraph beginning and concluding on page 1883 (immediately after footnote 150):

"Reading those two subsections together, it is plain that the omission of a power to indemnify in derivative suits was intentional. . . . '[T]he express inclusion of the broader indemnification power in (a) and its exclusion in (b) demonstrates the legislative intent to prohibit indemnification of judgments or amounts paid in settlement in derivative suits.'" *TLC Beatrice Int'l Holdings, Inc. v. Cigna Ins. Co.*, 1999 U.S. Dist. LEXIS 605, at *14-15, 1999 WL 33454 at *5 (S.D.N.Y. Jan. 27, 1999) (quoting earlier edition of what now appears at 1 R. Franklin Balotti & Jesse A. Finkelstein, *The Delaware Law of Corporations and Business Organizations* § 4.22, at 4-84 (3d ed. 2001)).

Replace "8–337-38" with "8-321" in the Model Act § 8.51 citation in footnote 153 on page 1884.

Add the following at the end of footnote 153 on page 1884:

See also TLC Beatrice, 1999 U.S. Dist. LEXIS 605, at *15-16, 1999 WL 33454, at *5 ("The reason for the distinction between § 145(a) and (b) apparently is that the ultimate plaintiff in a derivative action is the corporation on whose behalf the suit is brought. To permit a corporation to indemnify an officer or director for amounts paid in settlement or satisfaction of a judgment in a derivative action would permit the management of the corporation to deprive the corporation, as ultimate plaintiff, of the very benefit it is meant to receive.").

Replace "1998" with "2001" in the Balotti citation in footnote 154 on page 1884.

Add the following at the end of footnote 154 on page 1884:

See also TLC Beatrice, 1999 U.S. Dist. LEXIS 605, at *15, 1999 WL 33454, at *5.

Replace "8-358" with "8-350" in the Model Act § 8.54 citation in footnote 162 on page 1885.

Section A 4 c

Replace "8-363" with "8-359" and replace "1996" with "Supp. 1998/99" in the Model Act § 8.55 citation in footnote 176 on page 1888.

Replace "8–295-96" with "8-286" in the Model Act § 8.50 citation in footnote 191 on page 1890.

Replace "8-364" with "8-360" in the Model Act § 8.55 citation in footnote 201 on page 1892.

Add the following at the end of footnote 201 on page 1892:

See also Nakahara v. NS 1991 Am. Trust, 739 A.2d 770, 787-89 (Del. Ch. 1998) (in a case where the term "independent" was not defined in the governing instrument of NS 1991 American Trust, a business trust, the court relied on "basic 'independence' concepts" and stated that "Delaware law only requires that there be no disqualifying conflict of interest" and "does not require that otherwise 'independent' counsel be brand new to the scene, with no prior contact to any party or to any relevant facts"; applying this standard, the court concluded that "[i]t is my belief that the term 'independent' in § 4.2(d)(ii) means independent of the managing trustees seeking the advancements and independent of any other interested parties who oppose such advancement" and that "[b]ecause the advancement decision is to be made by the American Trust itself and a decision that has direct consequences to the American Trust – because it decides whether to disperse money from the American Trust accounts – it would be unreasonable for the term 'independent' to mean free of allegiance to the American Trust itself").

Replace "8-364" with "8-359" in the Model Act § 8.55 citation in footnote 210 on page 1893.

Add the following at the end of the first paragraph beginning and concluding on page 1894 (immediately after footnote 215):

Payments of defense costs to directors sued as individuals must be made in "the only legally proper way" – indemnification (or advancement) in accordance with the applicable statutory requirements. *Technicorp Int'l II, Inc. v. Johnston*, 2000 Del. Ch. LEXIS 81, at *158, 2000 WL 713750, at *43

(Del. Ch. May 31, 2000). Fees paid by the corporation to fund a director's defense of an action are improper where directors "never invoke[ ] the machinery, or satisf[y] the legal requirements, for indemnification." *Id.*

Section A 5

Replace "8–348-49" with "8-337" and replace "1996" with "Supp. 1998/99" in the Model Act § 8.53 citation in footnote 216 on page 1894.

Replace the Watson Wyatt citation and the parenthetical following that citation in footnote 216 on page 1895 with the following:

Tillinghast-Towers Perrin, *2000 Directors and Officers Liability Survey* 69 (2001) (of the 1,102 claims reported as closed, the average cost where an insurance payment was made was approximately $3.23 million, and "[c]laims from shareholders – historically the most costly – averaged $9.62 million per claim award, an all-time high"; these calculations do "not reflect the possibility that the open claims may eventually close for greater amounts, on average" and "[t]hus the ultimate cost in today's dollars could be substantially higher").

Replace "8-348" with "8-337" in the Model Act § 8.53 citation in footnote 217 on page 1895.

Section A 5 a

Replace "to the contrary," in the first sentence (between footnotes 218 and 219) of the paragraph beginning on page 1895 and concluding on page 1896 with the following:

requiring advancement (*see* Chapter V, Section 5 b) or limiting advancement (*see In re Cencom Cable Income Partners, L.P. Litig.*, 2000 Del. Ch. LEXIS 10, at *20-28, 2000 WL 130629, at *6-9 (Del. Ch. Jan. 27, 2000),

Delete ", not mandatory" in the first sentence (immediately before footnote 219) of the paragraph beginning on page 1895 and concluding on page 1896.

Replace "1996" with "Supp. 1998/99" in the Model Act § 8.53 citation in footnote 219 on page 1895.

Add the following at the end of footnote 252 on page 1902:

; *see also Active Asset Recovery, Inc. v. Real Estate Asset Recovery Servs., Inc.*, 1999 Del. Ch. LEXIS 179, at *57-61, 1999 WL 743479, at *18-19 (Del. Ch. Sept. 10, 1999) (stating that general partner of a limited partnership "cannot advance fees to or indemnify itself or its affiliates unless it demonstrates that it is fair for it to do so" because "[t]he business judgment rule does not apply to such a self-interested decision, nor does it apply if the general partner did not act in an informed manner," and concluding that the advancement decision in this case was not fair).

Replace footnotes 273 through 276 on page 1905 with the following:

273. 2 Model Bus. Corp. Act Annotated § 8.53 Official Comment at 8-338; *see also* Chapter I Introduction and Chapter II, Section A 2 (discussing Model Act § 8.30).
274. *Id.* § 8.53 Official Comment at 8-338.
275. *Id.* at 8-339.
276. *Id.* at 8-340.

Replace "8-349" with "8–337-38" in the Model Act § 8.53 citation in footnote 283 on page 1907.

Add "at 8-338" at the end of the Model Act § 8.53 citation in footnote 284 on page 1907.

Replace "1998" with "2001" in the Balotti citation in footnote 287 on page 1907.

Section A 5 b

Replace "1996" with "Supp. 1998/99" in the Model Act § 8.58 citation in footnote 296 on page 1909.

Replace the VonFeldt citation and the parenthetical following that citation in footnote 306 on page 1910 with the following:

VonFeldt v. Stifel Fin. Corp., 714 A.2d 79, 86-87 (Del. 1998) (advancement not required where director was unable to produce a signed indemnification agreement and the evidence offered in support of the director's claim that an indemnification agreement had been entered into "either lacked credibility or was susceptible of an explanation consistent with Stifel Financial's claim that no agreement existed");

Add the following at the end of the third sentence of the paragraph (immediately after footnote 306) beginning on page 1909 and concluding on page 1911:

Charter, bylaw or contract provisions mandating advancement also have been enforced in *Truck Components Inc. v. Beatrice Co.*, 143 F.3d 1057, 1061 (7th Cir. 1998) (Delaware law), *Greco v. Columbia/HCA Healthcare Corp.*, 1999 Del. Ch. LEXIS 24, at *16-22, 1999 WL 1261446, at *6-8 (Del. Ch.

Feb. 11, 1999), and *Dunlap v. Sunbeam Corp.*, 1999 Del. Ch. LEXIS 126, at *3-18, 1999 WL 1261339, at *1-6 (Del. Ch. June 23, 1999).

Add the following at the end of footnote 309 on page 1911:

See also Truck Components, 143 F.3d at 1062 ("Section 145(k) allocates jurisdiction among Delaware courts. Delaware maintains separate systems of courts in law and equity. Claims based on corporate arrangements go to the Court of Chancery rather than to the law courts, where other contracts are litigated. Such an intra-state allocation has no effect on federal litigation, which merged law and equity long ago."); *Johnston v. Caremark Rx, Inc.*, 2000 Del. Ch. LEXIS 46 at *10, 2000 WL 354381, at *3 (Del. Ch. Mar. 28, 2000) (Del. Gen. Corp. Law § 141(k) provides the Court of Chancery jurisdiction "exclusive of any other *Delaware* court" but "Delaware clearly does not have *exclusive* jurisdiction"); *Rudebeck v. Paulson*, 612 N.W.2d 450, 455 (Minn. Ct. App. 2000), *review denied*, 2000 Minn. LEXIS 563 (Minn. Sept. 13, 2000) (Delaware statute granting Delaware Court of Chancery exclusive jurisdiction over indemnification claims does not preclude a Minnesota court from hearing an indemnification claim under Delaware law because "a state legislature cannot create a transitory cause of action and confine its enforcement to its own courts" and an indemnification claim "is in the nature of a transitory cause of action").

Replace "8-380" with "8-369P" in the Model Act § 8.58 citation in footnote 312 on page 1911.

Add the following at the end of the paragraph beginning and concluding on page 1913 (immediately after footnote 323):

Greco involved claims that a former corporate officer committed breaches of fiduciary duty, fraud and racketeering. 1999 Del. Ch. LEXIS 24, at *13, 32-33, 1999 WL 1261446, at *5,

11. *Sunbeam* involved claims against two former corporate officers terminated by the corporation in connection with restatements of financial statements. 1999 Del. Ch. LEXIS 126, at *2-3, 1999 WL 1261339, at *1. The court in *Truck Components* rejected a claim that a provision mandating advancement was not enforceable because a corporate officer "engaged in misconduct" on the ground that this reason "has nothing to do with the agreement" to advance expenses. 143 F.3d at 1061. The court in *Greco*, however, noted that "I do not and need not decide" whether "the unclean hands doctrine may in certain circumstances bar recovery in an action under § 145(k)." 1999 Del. Ch. LEXIS 24, at *35 & n.7, 1999 WL 1261446, at *12 & n.7.

Replace the Christman citation in footnote 341 on page 1915 with the following:

Christman v. Brauvin Realty Advisors, Inc., 1997 U.S. Dist. LEXIS 19563, at *5, 1997 WL 797685, at *1 (N.D. Ill. Dec. 3, 1997) ("indemnification of legal expenses is a separate issue from advancement of these expenses"), *appeal dismissed*, 134 F.3d 374 (unpublished opinion, text available at 1998 U.S. App. LEXIS 1123 and 1998 WL 31755) (7th Cir. Jan. 21, 1998).

Add the following at the end of the paragraph beginning on page 1925 and concluding on page 1926 (immediately after footnote 400):

In sum, hardship – on the part of either a corporation that has committed itself to pay advancement or a former corporate director, officer or employee who cannot fund a defense without advancement – "is not a factor . . . typically considered in determining whether to provide for the advancement of fees, although that does not foreclose the future possibility of a party making that argument successfully." *Dunlap v. Sunbeam Corp.*, 1999 Del. Ch. LEXIS 126, at *17 n.8, 1999 WL 1261339, at *6 n.8 (Del. Ch. June 23, 1999).

The court in *Nakahara v. NS 1991 American Trust*, 739 A.2d 770 (Del. Ch. 1998), held that trustees of a business trust were entitled to advancement pursuant to the governing trust instrument but that this right was defeated by the doctrine of unclean hands in the case before the court. The court explained that the trustees seeking advancement, in violation of a standstill agreement and in "utter disregard of ongoing judicial proceedings" and "under the guise of 'self-help,'" had "wrongfully, without permission, and surreptitiously" taken the funds they sought for advancement rather than await the court's judicial determination of their rights. *Id.* at 791-96. The court subsequently held that the trustees who sought advancement could not "avoid the impact of their inequitable conduct by attempting to undo that conduct after an adverse verdict." *Nakahara v. NS 1991 Am. Trust*, 718 A.2d 518, 519 (Del. Ch. 1998). The court reasoned that "[i]n effect, Plaintiffs would return the money with one hand and then reach out to take it right back with the other. Effectively, Plaintiffs now seek to avoid all consequences of their inequitable actions." *Id.* at 521.

Replace "8-349" with "8-337" in the Model Act § 8.53 citation in footnote 419 on page 1928.

Add the following at the end of the paragraph beginning and concluding on page 1928 (immediately after footnote 419):

Where advancement is mandatory and the required undertaking is provided, "the possibility of prevailing on the merits" – which would mandate indemnification – leads to the conclusion that "a board vote not to indemnify . . . is not sufficient to 'call back' the advances. Therefore, repayment of the advance would not be required until after the completion of the lawsuits – and then only if (a) [the persons to whom advances have been paid] do not prevail on the merits, and (b) the [corporation's] board votes not to authorize indemnification." *Sunbeam*, 1999 Del. Ch. LEXIS 126, at *17, 1999 WL 1261339, at *5.

Section A 5 c

Replace the first sentence (including footnote 421) of the paragraph beginning and concluding on page 1929 with the following:

The Delaware Supreme Court in *VonFeldt v. Stifel Financial Corp.*, 714 A.2d 79 (Del. 1998), cited the Delaware Court of Chancery's decision in *Advanced Mining Systems, Inc. v. Fricke*, 623 A.2d 82 (Del. Ch. 1992), for the proposition that a "mandate to indemnify does not include [a] duty to advance litigation expenses." 714 A.2d at 86 n.28. Rather, "advancement and indemnification are entirely distinct types of legal rights, and entitlement to one does not necessarily entail entitlement to the other." *Nakahara v. NS 1991 Am. Trust*, 739 A.2d 770, 795 (Del. Ch. 1998). "The converse is also true. Lack of entitlement to advancement does not necessarily entail lack of entitlement to ultimate indemnification." *Id.*

The *Advanced Mining* case involved charter and bylaw provisions stating that the corporation "shall indemnify" its directors and officers "to the extent permitted" by Delaware law. These provisions, the court held, mandated indemnification but not advancement. 623 A.2d at 84.

Add the following at the end of footnote 427 on page 1929:

See also Dunlap v. Sunbeam Corp., 1999 Del. Ch. LEXIS 126, at *10 n.3, 1999 WL 1261339, at *4 n.3 (Del Ch. June 23, 1999) (requiring advancement where provision requiring advancement was unambiguous but stating that where there is ambiguity concerning whether advancement is required the "ambiguity must be interpreted in favor of the statutory discretion that is accorded directors under 8 Del. C. § 145(e)").

Add the following at the end of the paragraph beginning and concluding on page 1929 (immediately after footnote 427):

As stated in *Cochran v. Stifel Financial Corp.*, 2000 Del. Ch. LEXIS 179, 2000 WL 1847676 (Del. Ch. Dec. 13, 2000), advancement is a form of relief that "to a large degree" is "different in kind, rather than degree, from traditional indemnity." 2000 Del. Ch. LEXIS 179, at *41 n.41, 2000 WL 1847676, at *10 n.41; *see also Active Asset Recovery, Inc. v. Real Estate Asset Recovery Servs., Inc.*, 1999 Del. Ch. LEXIS 179, at *22 n.15, 1999 WL 743479, at *17 n.15 (Del. Ch. Sept. 10, 1999) ("case law . . . distinguishes between the right to advancement and the right to indemnification").

The court in *Nakahara v. The NS 1991 American Trust*, 739 A.2d 770 (Del. Ch. 1998), again held that "surely the holding of *Advanced Mining* is still good Delaware law." *Id.* at 783. The court in *Nakahara*, however, distinguished *Advanced Mining* in a case involving the Delaware Business Trust Act (the "BTA"), which refers to indemnification but not to advancement. The court stated that the BTA and the Delaware General Corporation law (the "GCL") contain "many differences" and are "simply too different to draw *any* conclusions from a comparison of their various provisions," including the explicit mention of indemnification and advancement in the corporation statute and the explicit mention of indemnification but the absence of any explicit mention of advancement in the business trust statute. *Id.* at 782. The court explained:

> [T]he BTA was not modeled after the GCL. Moreover, the BTA and the GCL are different in scope, purpose and approach. The BTA simply was intended to be more flexible than the GCL. Section 3821(b) of the Act says as much: "It is the policy of this chapter to give maximum effect to the principle of freedom of contract and to the enforceability of governing instruments." This highly permissible language reveals a clear intent on the part of the General Assembly to grant business trusts broad freedom in establishing their internal governance mechanisms. In marked contrast, the corporate code contains no such broad directive. Though flexible in many respects, the GCL places many restrictions on how a corporation may be organized.
>
> The permissible language of § 3817(a) itself suggests that the General Assembly intended the BTA's indemnification provi-

> sion to be interpreted broadly. Unlike § 145 of the GCL, which lays out express limitations on who, and then under what specific circumstances, may be indemnified by the corporation, the language of the BTA's indemnification provision is broad and flexible. Such a general authorization of indemnification compels a permissive interpretation, with the language intended to authorize as much as possible and exclude only that which is expressly prohibited.

Id. at 782-83 (footnotes omitted). For these reasons, the court held that "absent an express prohibition in the BTA, there is an implicit authorization for business trusts to organize themselves in any way that is consistent with general contracting principles" and that "[t]his includes authorizing the advancement of litigation expenses to trustees if those establishing a Delaware business trust so choose." *Id.* at 784.

Replace the Christman citation in footnote 430 on page 1930 with the following:

1997 U.S. Dist. LEXIS 19563, 1997 WL 797685 (N.D. Ill. Dec. 3, 1997), *appeal dismissed*, 134 F.3d 374 (unpublished opinion, text available at 1998 U.S. App. LEXIS 1123 and 1998 WL 31755) (7th Cir. Jan. 21, 1998).

Replace "8-381" with "8-369P" and replace "1996" with "Supp. 1998/99" in the Model Act § 8.58 citation in footnote 437 on page 1931.

Section A 6 a

Add the following at the end of the second sentence (immediately after footnote 447) of the paragraph beginning and concluding on page 1933:

By contrast, the Court of Chancery also has stated that "it makes little sense . . . to decide claims for indemnification – as opposed to claims for advancement of litigation expenses – in advance of a non-appealable final judgment" because "[t]here is simply too great a risk that the appellate courts will take a different view than the trial court for it to make much sense to grapple with indemnification claims until the underlying litigation is concluded with finality." *Simon v. Navellier Series Fund*, 2000 Del. Ch. LEXIS 150, at *33-34, 2000 WL 1597890, at *9 (Del. Ch. Oct. 19, 2000). Thus, "[i]n the absence of a showing of undue hardship," adjudication of an indemnification claim should "wait until the outcome of the underlying matter is certain" in order to "reduce the chance that the court will engage in a wasteful exercise in predictive justice, only to see its work undone by a reversal of the trial court's judgment in the underlying matter." 2000 Del. Ch. LEXIS 150, at *35-36, 2000 WL 1597890, at *9; *cf. Witco Corp. v. Beekhuis*, 1993 U.S. Dist. LEXIS 17289, at *10, 1993 WL 749596, at *4 (D. Del. Oct. 22, 1993), *aff'd*, 38 F.3d 682 (3d Cir. 1994) (a claim that "is final enough to be appealed is final enough" to warrant mandatory indemnification if the statutory requirements for mandatory indemnification have been met).

Add the following at the end of the paragraph beginning and concluding on page 1933 (immediately after footnote 448):

There is no requirement that a director or officer make a demand for indemnification to the corporation's board before commencing a litigation seeking indemnification, but a corporation that wishes to make a demand a predicate to indemnification "can do so by requiring such a demand in its bylaws." *Cochran v. Stifel Fin. Corp.*, 2000 Del. Ch. LEXIS 58, at *33-36, 2000 WL 286722, at *10 (Del. Ch. Mar. 8, 2000).

Add the following at the end of footnote 449 on page 1933:

See also Greco v. Columbia/HCA Healthcare Corp., 1999 Del. Ch. LEXIS 24, at *37-41, 1999 WL 1261446, at *12-13 (Del. Ch. Feb. 11, 1999) (enforcing contract and charter provision stating that "[s]hould any dispute arise concerning this agreement or its interpretation, then the courts shall award legal fees to the prevailing party"); *Chamison v. HealthTrust, Inc. – The Hosp. Co.*, 735 A.2d 912, 927 (Del. Ch. 1999) (enforcing charter and contract provisions requiring payment of fees), *aff'd*, 748 A.2d 407 (unpublished opinion, text available at 2000 Del. LEXIS 95, 2000 WL 275649) (Del. Mar. 6, 2000).

Replace the second Mayer citation in footnote 451 on page 1934 with the following:

1997 WL 811691 (S.D.N.Y. Apr. 30, 1997).

Replace the Model Act § 8.54 citation in footnote 459 on page 1935 with the following:

what now appears at Model Bus. Corp. Act Annotated § 8.54(b) (3d ed. Supp. 1998/99)

Add the following at the end of the paragraph beginning on page 1935 and concluding on page 1936 (immediately after footnote 467):

The Court of Chancery in *VonFeldt v. Stifel Financial Corp.*, 1997 Del. Ch. LEXIS 108, 1997 WL 525878 (Del. Ch. Aug. 18, 1997), *aff'd in part and rev'd in part*, 714 A.2d 79 (Del. 1998), thus stated that "[t]his Court has clearly held that the right to advancement of and indemnification against fees and expenses incurred in a successful action to obtain indemnification is not found in section 145 and must be based on express provisions found either in corporate by-laws or separate agreements." 1997 Del. Ch. LEXIS 108, at *5, 1997 WL 525878, at *2. The Delaware Supreme Court in *VonFeldt v. Stifel Financial Corp.*, 714 A.2d 79 (Del. 1998), noted the result reached in this line of decisions but stated that "we do not reach this issue and we express no opinion" on the issue. *Id.* at 86 n.29. The Court of Chancery re-affirmed its prior decisions in *Dunlap v. Sunbeam Corp.*, 1999 Del. Ch. LEXIS 126, 1999 WL 1261339 (Del. Ch. June 23, 1999), another case where nothing in the governing charter, bylaw or contract provisions required the corporation to pay "fees in connection with any action to enforce the right to advancement or indemnification." 1999 Del. Ch. LEXIS 126, at *20, 1999 WL 1261339, at *6. The same result was reached in *Cochran v. Stifel Financial Corp.*, 2000 Del. Ch. LEXIS 58, at *75-76, 2000 WL 286722, at *21 (Del. Ch. Mar. 8, 2000).

In *Chamison v. HealthTrust, Inc. – The Hospital Co.*, 735 A.2d 912 (Del. Ch. 1999), *aff'd*, 748 A.2d 407 (unpublished opinion, text available at 2000 Del. LEXIS 95, 2000 WL 275649) (Del. Mar. 6, 2000), the court distinguished the rule that "[o]rdinarily, under Delaware law, a successful suit for indemnification does not entitle the successful director or officer to recover 'fees for fees'" in a case that was "not like the typical case where a director seeks fees incurred in prosecuting an indemnification action to a successful conclusion." *Id.* at 926. Instead, the court explained, the case involved two equally obligated co-indemnitors – each of whom had agreed to indemnify the individual seeking indemnification, but one of whom "refused, unreasonably . . . , to acknowledge its obligation from the beginning" and thus required its "equally obligated co-indemnitor . . . to pay the full amount of . . . bills when and as presented." *Id.* at 926-27.

The court pointed to the two distinct uses of the word indemnification: (1) "the term of art defining a corporation's reimbursement of a director, officer or employee for the costs incurred by that individual in defense of an action brought against that individual in his capacity as a director, officer or employee of the corporation," and (2) "the more general concept of liability-shifting from the party who paid a claim to the party who should have paid it." *Id.* at 917 n.12. This case, the court continued, involved a situation that was "more analogous to the concept of indemnification that involves shifting liability from the party who paid a claim to the party who should have paid it." *Id.* at 926. According to the court, the purpose of indemnification would be "undermined seriously" if the law required an equally obligated co-indemnitor who paid the full amounts owed by two co-indemnitors also to pay the attorneys' fees and the costs of a lawsuit to enforce its co-indemnitor's obligation to indemnify, and, if that were the law, then similarly situated co-indemnitors "would have an economic incentive to refuse payment of what it should pay in the first place." *Id.* at 927; *cf. Sunbeam*, 1999 Del. Ch. LEXIS 126, at *20 & n.11, 1999 WL 1261339, at *6 & n.11 (stating that "[w]hile this Court has on occasion awarded 'fees for fees' [citing *Chamison*], I do not find Sunbeam's actions in disputing this matter to be so egregious or in such bad faith as to require that special form of discipline).

Replace "Two courts" in the first sentence (between footnotes 467 and 468) of the paragraph beginning on page 1936 and concluding on page 1937 with the following:

A federal court construing New York law in *In re Health Management Systems, Inc. Securities Litigation*, 82 F. Supp. 2d 227 (S.D.N.Y. 2000), reached the same result. The court stated that "[i]nasmuch as a promise by one party to a contract to indemnify the other for attorney's fees incurred in litigation between them is contrary to the well-understood rule that parties are responsible for their own attorney's fees, the court should not infer a party's intention to waive the benefit of the rule unless the intention to do so is unmistakably clear from the language of the promise." *Id.* at 230 (quoting *Hopper Assocs., Ltd. v. AGS Computers, Inc.*, 74 N.Y.2d 487, 492, 548 N.E.2d 903, 905, 549 N.Y.S.2d 365, 367 (1989)). The court acknowledged that "there may be an element of illogic in denying fees on fees" because "the purpose of indemnity is to make someone whole," but concluded that "the appropriate resolution of this problem is to amend the applicable instrument, be it a contract or a corporate by-law, explicitly to authorize fees on fees, rather than to conclude that language which is ambiguous is, actually, 'unmistakably clear.'" *Id.* at 231 (footnote omitted).

By contrast, two courts

Add the following at the end of footnote 478 on page 1937:

See also Fleischer v. Fed. Deposit Ins. Corp., 70 F. Supp. 2d 1238, 1242 (D. Kan. 1999) (construing Kansas statute and bylaw to require indemnification of fees incurred in action seeking enforcement of indemnity agreement).

Replace "1996" with "Supp. 1998/99" in the Model Act § 8.54 citation in footnote 479 on page 1937.

Section A 6 b

Replace "1996" with "Supp. 1998/99" in the Model Act § 8.54 citation in footnote 481 on page 1938.

Section A 6 c

Replace the Bear Stearns citations in footnotes 499 through 505 on page 1941 and 1942 with the following:

499. 243 A.D.2d 252, 663 N.Y.S.2d 12 (N.Y. App. Div. 1st Dep't 1997).
500. *Id.* at 252-53, 663 N.Y.S.2d at 13.
501. *Id.* (quoting N.Y. Bus. Corp. Law § 725(b)(1)).
503. 243 A.D.2d at 253, 663 N.Y.S.2d at 13 (citations omitted).
504. 243 A.D.2d at 253, 663 N.Y.S.2d at 13.
504. *Id.*
505. *Id.* at 253-54, 663 N.Y.S.2d at 13.

Add the following at the end of the first paragraph beginning and concluding on page 1942 (between footnotes 508 and 509):

Additional decisions – *136 East 56th Street Owners, Inc. v. Darnet Realty Associates*, 248 A.D.2d 327, 670 N.Y.S.2d 97 (N.Y. App. Div. 1st Dep't 1998), *Iberti v. Walker & Zanger (West Coast) Ltd.*, No. 602113/99 (N.Y. Sup. Ct. N.Y. Co.

Sept. 22, 1999), and *Brittania 54 Hotel Corp. v. Freid*, 251 A.D.2d 49, 673 N.Y.S.2d 668 (N.Y. App. Div. 1st Dep't 1998) – also illustrate the operation of Section 724(c) of the New York Business Corporation Law.

Add the following at the end of the paragraph beginning on page 1945 and concluding on page 1946 (immediately after footnote 533):

The court in *136 East 56th Street Owners, Inc. v. Darnet Realty Associates*, 248 A.D.2d 327, 670 N.Y.S.2d 97 (N.Y. App. Div. 1st Dep't 1998), reached the same result in a case where directors and officers succeeded in dismissing some of the breach of contract claims asserted against them and all of the fraud and Racketeer Influenced Corrupt Organization Act ("RICO") claims asserted against them. *Id.* at 327-28, 670 N.Y.S.2d at 97-98. The court accordingly held that "genuine issues of fact and law" were raised warranting advancement of reasonable attorneys' fees and expenses pursuant to Section 724(c) "subject to repayment should defendants ultimately be found guilty of the wrongdoing alleged in the complaint." *Id.* at 328, 670 N.Y.S.2d at 97-98.

The court in *Iberti v. Walker & Zanger (West Coast) Ltd.*, No. 602113/99 (N.Y. Sup. Ct. N.Y. Co. Sept. 22, 1999), held that former directors of a corporation had raised "genuine issues of fact or law" warranting payment by the corporation of attorneys' fees and other expenses the former directors had incurred during the pendency of a litigation brought by the corporation against the former directors. *Id.*, slip op. at 7-9. The court rejected a contention that Section 724(c) is inapplicable where the corporation's bylaws do not provide for indemnification because "the cited provisions of the BCL do not provide that a corporation's by-laws must provide for indemnification as a prerequisite to an indemnification application to the Court" and thus an indemnification award under Section 724(c) "can be made independently of any charter, bylaws or resolution of the corporation." *Id.* at 9 (quoting *Marco v. Sachs*, 201 Misc. 928, 932, 106 N.Y.S.2d 522, 527 (N.Y. Sup. Ct. Kings

Co. 1951)). The court also rejected contentions that "genuine issues of fact or law" must be raised with respect to the right to indemnification and that Section 724(c) is inapplicable where the person seeking indemnification has been sued by the corporation for wrongdoing against the corporation. *Id.* at 10. The court stated that "where, as here, 'the director or officer satisfies the BCL's requirements, the Court may order their corporation to advance litigation expenses, notwithstanding the corporation's allegations that the director or officer engaged in wrongdoing against the corporation.'" *Id.* (quoting *Sierra Rutile Ltd. v. Katz*, 1997 U.S. Dist. LEXIS 11018, at *8, 1997 WL 431119, at *1 (S.D.N.Y. July 31, 1997)).

The opposite result was reached in *Brittania 54 Hotel Corp. v. Freid*, 251 A.D.2d 49, 673 N.Y.S.2d 668 (N.Y. App. Div. 1st Dep't 1998). The court held that "[d]efendant's submissions were insufficient to raise a genuine issue of fact regarding his assertion that he held the office of president or chief executive officer in plaintiffs' corporation, in light of compelling documentary evidence submitted by plaintiff establishing that defendant never was a corporate officer." *Id.* at 50, 673 N.Y.S.2d at 669.

Replace the Model Act § 8.54 citation in footnote 534 on page 1946 with the following:

2 Model Bus. Corp. Act Annotated § 8.54(a)(3) & Official Comment at 8-350 (3d ed. Supp. 1998/99).

Section A 7

Replace the Olson citation in footnote 536 on page 1947 with the following:

John F. Olson, Josiah O. Hatch III & Ty R. Sagalow, *Director and Officer Liability: Indemnification and Insurance* § 5.03[1][b], at 5-15 (2000).

Replace "1996" with "Supp. 1998/99" in the Model Act § 8.50 citation in footnote 537 on page 1947.

Section A 8

Replace "1996" with "Supp. 1998/99" in the Model Act § 8.51 citation in footnote 539 on page 1947.

Section A 9

Add the following at the end of the first sentence (immediately after footnote 573) of the paragraph beginning on page 1952 and concluding on page 1953:

"'By reason of' claims are essentially claims that challenge conduct by the party seeking indemnity in his official corporate capacities." *Cochran v. Stifel Fin. Corp.*, 2000 Del. Ch. LEXIS 179, at *3, 2000 WL 1847676, at *1 (Del. Ch. Dec. 13, 2000).

Replace "(1994)" with "(3d ed. Supp. 1998/99)" in the Model Act §§ 8.51 and 8.56 citation in footnote 574 on page 1953.

Add the following at the end of footnote 604 on page 1957:

See also Nakahara v. NS 1991 Am. Trust, 739 A.2d 770, 773 n.2, 785-87 (Del. Ch. 1998) (finding that trustees of a business trust were sued "by virtue of [their] being or having been [ ] Trustee[s]").

Add the following at the end of the paragraph beginning on page 1956 and concluding on page 1957 (immediately after footnote 604):

The court in *Rudebeck v. Paulson*, 612 N.W.2d 450 (Minn. Ct. App. 2000), *reviewed denied*, 2000 Minn. LEXIS

563 (Minn. Sept. 13, 2000), construing Delaware law, held that employees who successfully defend sexual harassment suits brought by co-workers are sued "by reason of the fact" they are employees because "'social interactions among employees * * * are broadly incidental to the enterprise of an employer,'" "expressions of human nature are incidents inseparable from working together" and "involve risks of injury . . . inherent in the working environment," and "'the risk that one worker may accuse another of sexual harassment to deflect an adverse performance review is a risk inherent in employment.'" *Id.* at 455-56 (quoting *Jacobus v. Krambo Corp.*, 78 Cal. App. 4th 1096, 1103-04, 93 Cal. Rptr. 2d 425, 431 (Cal. Ct. App. 2000), a case construing California Labor Code § 2802, which requires an employer to indemnify an employee for all expenses and losses incurred "in direct consequence of the discharge of his duties").

Add the following at the end of the paragraph beginning and concluding on page 1958 (immediately after footnote 615):

The Ninth Circuit in *Brush Creek Mining & Development v. Lawson*, 205 F.3d 1350 (unpublished opinion, text available at 1999 U.S. App. LEXIS 33675 and 1999 WL 1253370) (9th Cir. Dec. 20, 1999), construing Nevada law, held that officers of Brush Creek Mining & Development Company were not entitled to indemnification of attorneys' fees incurred in an action by the corporation against them that alleged that they "improperly, if not fraudulently, caused shares of the corporate stock to be issued in violation of federal and state statutes." 1999 U.S. App. LEXIS 33675, at *2-3, 1999 WL 1253370, at *1. The court stated that to be entitled to indemnification "[t]he conduct of the agent which gives rise to the claim against him must have been performed in connection with his corporate functions and not with respect to purely personal matters," "[w]here personal motives, not the corporate good, are predominant in a transaction giving rise to an action, indemnification is not warranted," and that the reasoning of the courts in *Plate v. Sun-Diamond Growers*, 225 Cal. App. 3d 1115, 275

Cal. Rptr. 667 (1990), and *Petty v. Bank of New Mexico Holding Co.*, 787 P.2d 443 (N.M. 1990), "apply with equal force here." 1999 U.S. App. LEXIS 33675, at *5, 1999 WL 1253370, at *1-2. A state court construing New York law in *Brittania 54 Hotel Corp. v. Freid*, 251 A.D.2d 49, 673 N.Y.S.2d 668 (N.Y. App. Div. 1st Dep't 1998), similarly held that an action had not been commenced against the defendant in that case "'by reason of' the fact that he was an officer, or for any action allegedly taken by him as an officer." *Id.* at 50, 673 N.Y.S.2d at 669.

The court in *First American Corp. v. Al-Nahnyan*, 17 F. Supp. 2d 10 (D.D.C. 1998), stated that "under Virginia law, the fact that a person was an officer or director of the corporation must have been a substantial factor in causing that person to be made a party to a proceeding" in order for the person to be entitled to indemnification. *Id.* at 30. The court denied a motion for summary judgment and held that a jury should decide whether each of two individuals was made a party to a criminal proceeding "because he is or was a director of the corporation," and, if he was made a party for multiple reasons, whether and how expenses should be apportioned. *Id.* at 30-32.

The Delaware Court of Chancery in *Scharf v. Edgcomb Corp.*, 2000 Del. Ch. LEXIS 130, 2000 WL 1234650 (Del. Ch. Aug. 21, 2000), denied a motion for summary judgment by Michael J. Scharf, a former chairman, chief executive officer and director of Edgcomb Corporation seeking indemnification for legal expenses incurred in connection with a Securities and Exchange Commission securities fraud investigation following which the SEC determined to take no action against Scharf. 2000 Del. Ch. LEXIS 130, at *1-2, 2000 WL 1234650, at *1. The court held that "a dispute regarding the actual scope of the SEC investigation exists": according to Scharf "*all* the SEC investigated was Scharf's handling of inside information regarding Edgcomb that he obtained within the scope of his Edgcomb duties" and thus the investigation was "by reason of his being a director, officer, employee or agent of the corporation," and according to Edgcomb "the SEC investigation centered on Scharf's *personal* trading" and thus was not "by reason of his being a director, officer, employee or agent of the corporation." 2000 Del. Ch. LEXIS 130, at *7-8, 2000 WL 1234650, at *2-3. The court permitted discovery on this issue. 2000 Del. Ch. LEXIS 130, at *8-9, 2000 WL 1234650, at *3.

Add the following at the end of the paragraph beginning on page 1958 and concluding on page 1959 (immediately after footnote 618):

The Delaware Supreme Court's decision in *VonFeldt v. Stifel Financial Corp.*, 714 A.2d 79 (Del. 1998), addresses the rules governing indemnification of directors or officers who serve entities other than the corporation (in this case a wholly-owned subsidiary of the corporation) at the request of the corporation. The case also addresses "good" – but not required corporate practice – with respect to requests by one corporation that its directors or officers perform services for another entity and the fact that "in today's corporate world, directors will commonly extend their official activities beyond the four walls of the boardroom" and assume "multiple roles in the corporation." *Id.* at 85 & n.26.

The case involved Stifel Financial Corporation and a wholly-owned subsidiary of Stifel Financial, Stifel Nicolaus Corporation ("SNC"). From 1971 through 1994, Dewayne R. VonFeldt served as an SNC director, officer and employee. From 1983 through 1987 and 1992 through 1994, VonFeldt also served as a Stifel Financial director. VonFeldt sought indemnification from Stifel Financial for expenses incurred in defending and amounts paid to settle an action by Mid-America Healthcare, Inc. (the "MAH action") and a National Association of Securities Dealers, Inc. proceeding (the "NASD action"). These actions arose out of events in the late 1980s involving VonFeldt's conduct as a director, officer and employee of SNC. Stifel Financial was not a party in any of the actions, the actions did not involve VonFeldt's service as a Stifel Financial director, and VonFeldt was not a director of

Stifel Financial at the time of the events underlying these lawsuits. *Id.* at 80.

VonFeldt sought indemnification pursuant to a Stifel Financial bylaw that was "maximally broad, mandating indemnification to the full extent permitted" by Delaware law. *Id.* at 81. The bylaw thus protected not only Stifel Financial directors, officers and employees, but also persons serving other enterprises "at the request of" Stifel Financial. *Id.* at 81 & nn. 4-6. VonFeldt contended that he served SNC at the request of Stifel Financial and, indeed, that "his work for SNC had, in effect, Stifel Financial's 'fingerprints' all over it." *Id.* at 83. Stifel Financial sought to rebut VonFeldt's claims "with evidence that it was not a party to VonFeldt's employment contract" and contended that it "bore no direct responsibility for VonFeldt's conduct as an officer and employee of SNC." *Id.*

The Supreme Court stated that because "the record is ambiguous, it falls on the trier of fact to evaluate the relative credibility of the parties' evidence." *Id.* In this case, the Supreme Court continued, "the Court of Chancery resolved these factual disputes in favor of Stifel Financial" and held that "aside from evidence that Stifel Financial elected him to the SNC board, 'VonFeldt provides no other persuasive evidence suggesting that he was serving SNC at the request of [Stifel Financial].'" *Id.* at 83 & n.15. The Supreme Court stated that "we defer to the trial court's findings of fact, and accept, for purposes of this appeal, Stifel Financial's contentions that it is not responsible for VonFeldt's employment contract, and that it was never active in setting the terms or conditions of VonFeldt's employment with SNC." *Id.* at 83.

As a result, the Supreme Court stated, "VonFeldt has but one arrow left in his quiver: SNC's status as a wholly-owned subsidiary of Stifel Financial." *Id.* The court stated that "[t]his appeal, then, reduces to a narrow legal question" and an "issue of first impression": "whether the election of a director to the board of a wholly-owned subsidiary by the 100% stockholder parent constitutes a 'request' that the director serve the subsidiary" for the purpose of indemnification under Section 145(a) of Delaware's General Corporation Law. *Id.* at 83-84.

The court stated that "[w]hen faced with an interpretive problem of this sort, it is proper to search for guidance in legislative history." *Id.* at 84. Here, however, a search for guidance in legislative history was "unavailing" because "[t]he origins of the language in question – specifically, the portion of Section 145(a) that includes within the class of permissible indemnities those who serve one corporation 'at the request of' another – are irretrievably obscured by the fogs of time." *Id.* The court summarized the history of the "at the request of" statutory language as follows:

> The very first corporate indemnification statutes, Delaware's included, spoke of directors who serve one enterprise "at the request of" another, but so few legislative documents remain from the relevant time periods that reliance on legislative history is nearly impossible.
>
> Delaware's first general corporation law, enacted in 1899, contained no provision for the indemnification of corporate officers and directors. Indeed, in the pre-World War II era, indemnification statutes did not exist anywhere, as the topic was exclusively one of judge-made law. In the 1940s, however, a codification movement began to gather momentum, as state legislatures sought to clarify what had become "an intolerable common-law muddle." New York was first out of the box with an indemnification statute in 1941, but Delaware quickly followed with its own in 1943.
>
> Since its original incarnation, Delaware's indemnification statute has included the language at issue in this case. Sadly, there is nothing in the way of legislative history to tell us what motivated its inclusion. Any official documents that could have shed light on the textual meaning are evidently lost or destroyed. All we know is that the "at the request of" language . . . was not an original invention of the drafters, for it was apparently commonplace for corporations to include such language in their indemnification bylaws in the pre-codification era.

Id. (footnotes omitted).

In the absence of historical guidance, the court turned to "legislative intent and policy." *Id.* The court stated the "dual policies" of Section 145 as follows:

> (a) allowing corporate officials to resist unjustified lawsuits, secure in the knowledge that, if vindicated, the corporation will bear the expense of litigation; and (b) encouraging capable women and men to serve as corporate directors and officers, secure in the knowledge that the corporation will absorb the costs of defending their honesty and integrity.

Id. In accordance with these dual policies, the court held that the election of a director to the board of a wholly-owned subsidiary constitutes "a 'request' on the part of the parent." *Id.* at 85. The court reasoned that "[t]he vote of a 100% stockholder is a public expression of support for the elected candidate." *Id.* This "public expression" of support in "unmistakable fashion . . . broadcasts the stockholder's preference to have the candidate serve on the subsidiary's board." *Id.* The court stated that "[t]his must amount to a 'request' in the eyes of the law" and that "[t]o require a director to prove additional facts – such as a direct communication from the parent, explicitly invoking the term *request* – would lend undue importance to the incantation of magic words." *Id.* The court stated that "[w]e do not believe the General Assembly intended such a formalistic reading of the statute." *Id.* Accordingly, the court concluded, "where a 100% stockholder elects a director to the board of a subsidiary, that director thereafter serves the subsidiary 'at the request of' the stockholder, within the meaning of 8 Del. C. § 145(a)." *Id.* Thus, "[b]y virtue of the fact that Stifel Financial elected VonFeldt to the board of its wholly-owned subsidiary, VonFeldt is deemed to be serving the subsidiary at the request of the parent." *Id.*

The court also relied upon the Official Comment to Section 8.50 of the Model Business Corporation Act. Section 8.50 "contains 'at the request of' language similar to what appears in" Section 145(a) of Delaware's statute. *Id.* at 85 n.26. The Official Comment to the Model Act states the following:

> A special definition of "director" and "officer" is included in subchapter E to cover individuals who are made parties to proceedings because they are or were directors or officers or, while serving as directors or officers, also serve or served at the corporation's request in another capacity for another entity. The purpose of the latter part of this definition is to give directors and officers the benefits of the protection of this subchapter while serving at the corporation's request in a responsible position for employee benefit plans, trade associations, nonprofit or charitable entities, domestic or foreign entities, or other kinds of profit or nonprofit ventures. *To avoid misunderstanding, it is good practice from both the corporation's and director's or officer's viewpoint for this type of request to be evidenced by resolution, memorandum or other writing.*

Id. (quoting what now appears at 2 Model Bus. Corp. Act Annotated § 8.50 Official Comment at 8-50, at 852 (3d ed. Supp. 1998/99)). The court stated that "[t]he final sentence of the comment – and, in particular, its use of the phrase 'good corporate practice' – strikes us as telling." *Id.* at 85 n.26. According to the court, the drafters of the Model Act commentary "suggest by negative implication that the statute does not require proof of an explicit communication between the parties, even though the failure to memorialize the request may not be good corporate practice." *Id.*

The court acknowledged that "the pleadings in the MAH action named VonFeldt as a defendant in his capacity as an officer and employee of SNC, rather than as an SNC director." *Id.* at 85. The court, however, rejected this distinction as "immaterial." *Id.* The court explained that it would not "engage in the hyper-technical exercise of trying to measure the 'scope' of Stifel Financial's request against the various roles VonFeldt filled at SNC." *Id.* Stifel Financial, the court stated, "was surely aware that, in today's corporate world, directors will commonly extend their official activities beyond the four walls of the boardroom." *Id.* Sometimes, the court continued, "directors will involve themselves in the day-to-day management of the firm's operations, thereby assuming multiple roles in the corporation." *Id.*

"Where such is the case," according to the court, "the director seeking indemnification is not required to prove the existence of a request relating specifically to his work as an officer and employee of the subsidiary." *Id.* To the contrary, the court held that "as a matter of law, the request to serve as an officer and employee of a wholly-owned subsidiary is inferred from the director's election to the subsidiary's board." *Id.* The court thus held that "[i]n accordance with the terms of Section 145(a) and Stifel Financial's bylaws" VonFeldt was entitled to indemnification for expenses incurred in the MAH and NASD actions even though those actions "implicated his conduct only as an officer and employee of SNC." *Id.*

The court was careful to point to the narrowness of its holding.

First, the court expressed no view with respect to "whether a parent's consideration and approval of an employment contract" between an officer or employee of a subsidiary and the subsidiary "amounts to a 'request'" triggering an obligation to indemnify pursuant to a bylaw requiring indemnification of persons who serve an entity other than the parent corporation "at the request of" the parent corporation. *Id.* at 83 n.17. The court also expressed no view with respect to whether an officer or employee of a subsidiary "could establish the existence of a 'request'" by a parent corporation to serve a subsidiary "by proving that defendant corporation set the plaintiff's compensation, entered into a termination fee agreement with plaintiff, or was ultimately responsible for firing plaintiff from the entity at which he was serving." *Id.* The court noted that "[w]e decide only the case before us," and "[t]his decision speaks only to the facts of this case and similar cases where a parent corporation has elected the putative indemnitee to the board of a wholly-owned subsidiary." *Id.* at 85. Other cases, the court continued, "will have to be decided on their own facts concerning what constitutes one corporation's request to serve another corporation." *Id.*

Second, the court stated that its decision "does not perforate the limitations on inter-firm liability that are a *raison d'etre* of wholly-owned subsidiaries." *Id.* The court stated that "Stifel Financial is liable in this case only because it voluntarily extended its indemnification duties to cover circumstances where indemnification is permissive." *Id.* The court stated that "Section 145(a) does not oblige Delaware corporations to indemnify those who serve other enterprises at their request." *Id.* at 85-86. Accordingly, "[i]f a corporation wishes not to extend indemnification rights to those who serve elsewhere at its request, it can say so in its bylaws, or it can say nothing at all, thereby achieving the same result." *Id.* at 86; *see also Chamison v. HealthTrust, Inc. – The Hosp. Corp.*, 735 A.2d 912, 925 n.44 (Del. Ch. 1999) ("[a] corporation has the power to indemnify a director, for example, who is serving, at its request, on the board of another corporation"), *aff'd*, 748 A.2d 407 (unpublished opinion, text available at 2000 Del. LEXIS 95 and 2000 WL 275649) (Del. Mar. 6, 2000).

In *Cochran v. Stifel Financial Corp.*, 2000 Del. Ch. LEXIS 58, 2000 WL 286722 (Del. Ch. Mar. 8, 2000), *subsequent proceedings*, 2000 Del. Ch. LEXIS 179, 2000 WL 1847676 (Del. Ch. Dec. 13, 2000), another case involving Stifel Financial and its wholly-owned Stifel Nicolaus subsidiary, Robert M. Cochran sought indemnification from Stifel Financial predicated on Cochran's service as a director, officer and employee of Stifel Nicolaus. Cochran alleged that he served Stifel Nicolaus as a director, officer and employee at the request of Stifel Financial and therefore was Stifel Financial's agent. 2000 Del. Ch. LEXIS 58, at *1-2, 2000 WL 286722, at *1. Cochran based his claim upon (1) (i) Section 145(a) of the Delaware General Corporation Law, which permits indemnification in actions other than actions by or in the right of the corporation where the person to be indemnified has acted in good faith and in a manner the person reasonably believed to be in or not opposed to the best interests of the corporation, and (ii) Stifel Financial's "maximally broad" bylaw "mandating indemnification to the full extent permitted" by Delaware law

(*VonFeldt*, 714 A.2d at 81), and (2) Section 145(c) of the Delaware General Corporation Law as it existed until July 1, 1997, which mandated indemnification "[t]o the extent that a director, officer, employee, or *agent* of a corporation has been successful on the merits or otherwise in defense of any action" (as discussed in Chapter V, Section A 3 a, Section 145(c) was amended in 1997 to change the words "director, officer, employee or *agent*" to "director or officer"). 2000 Del. Ch. LEXIS 58, at *5-6, 2000 WL 286722, at *2.

Cochran sought indemnification for two matters: (1) an SEC investigation into Stifel Nicolaus's Oklahoma City Municipal Bond Underwriting Department, which led to an indictment of Cochran for criminal fraud and a conviction that was reversed on appeal, and (2) an arbitration brought by Stifel Nicolaus against Cochran before the National Association of Securities Dealers, Inc. involving an unearned compensation claim, a promissory note claim, a breach of fiduciary duty claim and a non-competition claim arising out of a non-competition provision in Cochran's employment contract with Stifel Nicolaus. The arbitration resulted in a $1.2 million judgment against Cochran on the unearned compensation and promissory note claims but no liability on the breach of fiduciary duty and non-competition claims. 2000 Del. Ch. LEXIS 58, at *7-11, 2000 WL 286722, at *2-4. According to Cochran, he was entitled to (1) indemnification under Section 145(a) and Stifel Financial's bylaw with respect to all claims, and (2) indemnification under Section 145(c) with respect to the SEC, criminal, breach of fiduciary duty, and non-competition claims. 2000 Del. Ch. LEXIS 58, at *9, 11, 2000 WL 286722, at *3, 4.

Section 145(a) Indemnification. With respect to permissive indemnification under Section 145(a) and Stifel Financial's bylaw, the court rejected Stifel Financial's contention that indemnification of the judgment assessed against Cochran in favor of Stifel Nicolaus on the unearned compensation and promissory note claims was barred because the arbitration commenced by Stifel Nicolaus against Cochran was an action "by or in the right of the corporation" and thus was governed by Section 145(b), which bars indemnification of judgments in actions by or in the right of the corporation. *See* Chapter V, Section A 4 b. The court acknowledged the "substantial logic from a policy perspective" and "great first-blush appeal" of Stifel Financial's contention that the words "by or in the right of the corporation" should be read "as implicitly including the concept that any action brought by or in the right of a wholly-owned subsidiary must also be deemed one 'by or in the right of' the parent corporation." 2000 Del. Ch. LEXIS 58, at *45, 2000 WL 286722, at *13. The court likewise acknowledged that "to require Stifel Financial to indemnify Cochran for judgments he owes to Stifel Financial's wholly-owned subsidiary . . . would let Cochran off scot-free, to the detriment of both Stifel Financial and Stifel Nicolaus." 2000 Del. Ch. LEXIS 58, at *41, 2000 WL 286722, at *12.

The court concluded, however, that the arbitration commenced by Stifel Nicolaus was not an action "by or in the right of the corporation" and thus that Section 145(a) – which governs actions other than actions by or in the right of the corporation and does not bar indemnification of judgments – governed and permitted indemnification by Stifel Financial of the judgment against Cochran. "[T]he language of the statute cannot bear the construction Stifel Financial advances," the court reasoned, because "[b]y its plain language, the 'corporation' that is referred to in the phrase 'by or in the right of the corporation' is the corporation from which indemnity is sought" – i.e., Stifel Financial, not Stifel Nicolaus. 2000 Del. Ch. LEXIS 58, at *42, 2000 WL 286722, at *12. "Had the General Assembly wished § 145(b) to apply to suits 'by or in the right of the corporation or the wholly-owned subsidiary of the corporation,'" the court stated, "it could have easily written § 145(b) in that manner." *Id.*

The court also observed that "Section 145(b) may be written the way it is" – i.e., barring indemnification of judgments only in actions brought by or in the right of the corporation and not in actions brought by or in the right of the corporation *or* a controlled corporation – "for rational reasons" arising out of the fact that "many corporations have controlled subsidiaries that are not wholly-owned." 2000 Del. Ch. LEXIS 58, at *45, 2000 WL 286722, at *13. The court offered the following example:

> Posit, for example, a parent corporation that owns 80% of the stock of a subsidiary. Assume that the parent purchases a division of the subsidiary. The directors of the subsidiary, who serve at the request of the parent, approve the sale. The public stockholders of the subsidiary then file a derivative action alleging that the directors of the subsidiary breached their fiduciary duties because the sale was unfair to the subsidiary and overly advantageous to the parent. Under a plain reading of § 145(b), that situation would implicate § 145(a), not § 145(b). And under § 145(a), the parent corporation could indemnify the subsidiary directors for an adverse judgment against them so long as the directors "acted in good faith and in a manner [they] reasonably believed to be in or not opposed to the best interests of the [parent] corporation."
>
> Although this scenario is obviously different from one involving a wholly-owned subsidiary, it does illustrate one reason why the General Assembly may have chosen to craft § 145(b) the way it did and to give flexibility to a parent corporation under § 145(a) to indemnify a director it asks to serve on a subsidiary's board.

2000 Del. Ch. LEXIS 58, at *45-46, 2000 WL 286722, at *13.

The court noted that its ruling was limited to corporations that have adopted bylaws mandating indemnification to the full extent permitted by law. Section 145(a), the court stated, "does not impose the obligation on a parent corporation to indemnify a director it asks to serve on a subsidiary board; rather, it simply gives the parent corporation that option if the conditions set forth in § 145(a) exist." 2000 Del. Ch. LEXIS 58, at *46, 2000 WL 286722, at *13. According to the court, "[p]arent corporations can avoid the absurd result Stifel Financial believes Cochran's claim presents through careful drafting of their own bylaws." *Id.*

The court also noted that "[i]n rejecting Stifel Financial's argument, I, of course, in no way imply that Cochran will ultimately be entitled to indemnity" for the judgments against him under Section 145(a). 2000 Del. Ch. LEXIS 58, at *50, 2000 WL 286722, at *14. "[I]f Cochran knowingly took excessive or unearned compensation or failed to repay sums he clearly owed on a promissory note," the court stated, "then his conduct would not have been in good faith or in the best interests of Stifel Financial" because "Cochran could not simultaneously act in bad faith toward Stifel Nicolaus while acting in good faith towards Stifel Financial when he bases his claim to indemnification on Stifel Financial's alleged request that he serve Stifel Nicolaus as a director, employee, and officer." 2000 Del. Ch. LEXIS 58, at *50-51, 2000 WL 286722, at *14.

The court nevertheless concluded that Cochran was not entitled to permissive indemnification pursuant to Section 145(a) because Cochran was not seeking indemnification for conduct that occurred "by reason of the fact" that Cochran was serving SNC "at the request" of Stifel Financial.

First, in a decision denying a motion to dismiss, the court stated that it had "grave doubt that a person can sign a binding agreement with a wholly-owned subsidiary, commit himself to abide by the contract, and then refuse as a matter of economic reality (by seeking indemnity from the subsidiary's parent) to repay sums that the relevant decisionmaker under the contract had ruled were owed to the subsidiary." 2000 Del. Ch. LEXIS 58, at *51, 2000 WL 286722, at *15. The court reasoned as follows:

> [I]t appears that Cochran bound himself to an employment contract and a promissory note with Stifel Nicolaus that contained arbitration clauses. Although § 145(a) contains expansive language governing actions against a person "by reason of the fact that the person" was serving another corporation "at the request of the parent," the obvious intent of the statute is to govern actions against such a person as a result of his actions in his official capacity. When a person signs an employment agreement or promissory note with the corporation he serves, he is, one would think, acting as an individual. To the extent that a dispute about his compliance with such an agreement later arises, it would appear to be "by reason of the fact that the person" allegedly breached his individual obligation to the corporation, and not "by reason of the fact that the person" inci-

> dentally was serving the corporation in a position "at the request of" another corporation.

2000 Del. Ch. LEXIS 58, at *52, 2000 WL 286722, at *15. The court concluded, however, that "I cannot dismiss the complaint on this basis" because this "precise argument" had not been made by Stifel Financial and as a result the court had "not had the benefit of briefing on this question" and "its resolution may turn on the substance of the underlying contracts." 2000 Del. Ch. LEXIS 58, at *52-53, 2000 WL 286722, at *15.

Subsequently, on cross-motions for summary judgment, the court held that Cochran was not entitled to indemnification under Section 145(a) or Stifel Financial's indemnification bylaw on the excessive compensation, promissory note and non-competition claims (Stifel Financial did not seek summary judgment on the breach of fiduciary duty claim because it acknowledged that the breach of fiduciary duty claim against Stifel Financial was brought against Cochran "by reason of his" service in his official capacities as Stifel Nicolaus). The court found that these claims "were not brought against Cochran 'by reason of the fact' that he was serving in indemnification eligible positions at Stifel Nicolaus, but 'by reason of the fact' that he had allegedly breached a personal contractual obligation he owed to Stifel Nicolaus." *Cochran v. Stifel Fin. Corp.*, 2000 Del. Ch. LEXIS 179, at *13, 24, 2000 1847676, at *4, 7 (Del. Ch. Dec. 13, 2000). The court reasoned as follows:

> When a corporate officer signs an employment contract committing to fill an office, he is acting in a personal capacity in an adversarial, arms-length transaction. To the extent that he binds himself to certain obligations under that contract, he owes a personal obligation to the corporation. When the corporation brings a claim and proves its entitlement to relief because the officer has breached his individual obligations, it is problematic to conclude that the suit has been rendered an "official capacity" suit subject to indemnification under § 145 and implementing bylaws. Such a conclusion would render the officer's duty to perform his side of the contract in many respects illusory.
>
> In contracting with Stifel Nicolaus, Cochran bound himself to important personal obligations. Those obligations included a

> commitment to: (1) repay any excessive compensation he received within ten days after he was provided proper notice by Stifel Nicolaus; (2) repay the balance of the Promissory Note in the event that he was terminated for cause in accordance with the Agreement; (3) not to compete with Stifel Nicolaus for one year after his contract was terminated; and (4) arbitrate any disputes arising out of the Agreement.
>
> As a matter of law, Stifel Financial's decision to elect Cochran as a member of the Stifel Nicolaus board of directors is deemed a "request" by Stifel Financial to have Cochran serve Stifel Nicolaus in all his capacities – as a director, officer, and employee. But it is inconceivable that Stifel Financial "requested" Cochran to serve Stifel Financial under employment contracts that, by operation of the Indemnification Bylaw, implicitly required Stifel Financial to indemnify Cochran for any "good faith" breaches of those contracts that he *committed.* Rather, the only plausible conclusion is that Stifel Financial expected that the terms of Cochran's employment contracts with Stifel Nicolaus would be paramount and exclusive as to any claims for breach of those contracts, absent a provision in those contracts to the contrary. That is, if Stifel Financial is deemed by law to have "requested" Cochran's service at Stifel Nicolaus in all of his capacities, so too should it be deemed to be an implied beneficiary of his employment contract – a beneficiary entitled to have Cochran live up to his bargain with Stifel Nicolaus without assistance from Stifel Financial itself.

2000 Del. Ch. LEXIS 179, at *20-22, 2000 WL 1847676, at *6 (footnote omitted). Any other result, the court stated, "rewrites [Cochran's] employment contracts," "subverts the contractual arrangement between Cochran and Stifel Nicolaus," and "leaves Stifel Nicolaus without a genuine remedy against Cochran." 2000 Del. Ch. LEXIS 179, at *23, 2000 WL 286722, at *7. Cochran, the court added, "is a sophisticated businessman and cannot have rationally believed that Stifel Financial would indemnify him if he breached his own contractual obligations to Stifel Financial's corporate child, Stifel Nicolaus." 2000 Del. Ch. LEXIS 179, at *24, 2000 WL 1847676, at *7.

The court summarized its holding as follows:

> I grant summary judgment for Stifel Financial as to . . . Cochran's claims [that] seek to have Stifel Financial indemnify Cochran for a judgment and other costs he suffered in litigation with Stifel Nicolaus based on his breach of his employment contract and a related promissory note. As to these claims, this court concludes that Cochran's contractual claims against Stifel Nicolaus were not brought "by reason of" his service in indemnification-eligible positions at Stifel Nicolaus "at the request of" Stifel Financial. "By reason of" claims are essentially claims that challenge conduct by the party seeking indemnity in his official corporate capacities. By contrast, Stifel Nicolaus's claims alleged that Cochran breached his personal contractual obligations to Stifel Nicolaus. Holding that Stifel Financial must indemnify Cochran for the costs he incurred in living up to his end of his employment agreement with Stifel Nicolaus would rewrite those agreements and render many of Cochran's purported duties thereunder illusory. Rational contracting parties could not have believed that Stifel Financial would "request" Cochran's service at its wholly-owned Stifel Nicolaus subsidiary and yet agree to pick up any liability Cochran incurred as a result of his breach of his employment contracts.

2000 Del. Ch. LEXIS 179, at *3-4, 2000 WL 1847676, at *1.

Section 145(c) Indemnification. With respect to mandatory indemnification under Section 145(c) from Stifel Financial with respect to the SEC, criminal, breach of fiduciary duty and non-competition claims on which Cochran had not been held liable to Stifel Nicolaus and thus was "successful on the merits or otherwise," the court rejected Cochran's claim that he was eligible for mandatory indemnification as Stifel Financial's agent "because he was asked to serve as a director, officer and employee of Stifel Nicolaus by Stifel Financial." 2000 Del. Ch. LEXIS 58, at *53-55, 2000 WL 286722, at *15-16.

The court pointed to *VonFeldt*, which held that "the request to serve as an officer and employee of a wholly-owned subsidiary is inferred from the director's election to the subsidiary's board." 2000 Del. Ch. LEXIS 58, at *55-56, 2000 WL 286722, at *16. *Von Feldt*, the court explained, involved indemnification under Section 145(a), which, like Section 145(b), provides for indemnification for persons who serve one corporation "at the request of" another corporation. Cochran, by contrast, sought indemnification under the pre-1997 version of Section 145(c) as an "agent" of the corporation. 2000 Del. Ch. LEXIS 58, at *56, 2000 WL 286722, at *16. According to the court, "[t]his choice" – the words "at the request of" in the permissive indemnification provisions in Section 145(a) and 145(b) versus the word "agent" in the pre-1997 version of the mandatory indemnification provision in Section 145(c) – "would appear to reflect a considered decision to apply stricter criteria" in cases involving mandatory indemnification under Section 145(c) than in cases involving indemnification under Sections 145(a) and 145(b) and to limit mandatory indemnification under Section 145(c) "to those persons who can demonstrate that, pursuant to Delaware's law of agency, the corporation from which they seek indemnity acted as their principal." 2000 Del. Ch. LEXIS 58, at *56-57, 2000 WL 286722, at *16.

Moreover, the court continued, "the term 'agent of the corporation' is included in § 145(a) and (b) alongside language covering persons who serve another corporation in certain capacities (including as an agent) 'at the request of' the parent." 2000 Del. Ch. LEXIS 58, at *57, 2000 WL 286722, at *16. "Therefore, the mere fact that one serves another corporation 'at the request of' the parent does not automatically make that person an 'agent of the corporation.'" 2000 Del. Ch. LEXIS 58, at *57-58, 2000 WL 286722, at *16. As a result, the drafters of the statute "cannot have intended that the use of the word 'agent' in § 145(c) encompassed any person serving another corporation as an officer, director, employee, or agent 'at the request' of a parent corporation." 2000 Del. Ch. LEXIS 58, at *58, 2000 WL 286722, at *16.

Rather, the court stated, "the hardly uncommon term 'agent' must be given its usual meaning." *Id.* Under Delaware law, "[a]n agency relationship is created when one party consents to have another act on its behalf, with the principal controlling and directing the acts of the agent." 2000 Del. Ch. LEXIS 58, at *59, 2000 WL 286722, at *17 (citation omitted). Here, the court concluded, Cochran alleged facts that, if true, would support the first part of the agency definition ("one party consents to have another act on its behalf") but failed to allege facts that, if true, would support the second part of the definition ("the principal control[s] and direct[s] the acts of the agent").

With respect to the first part of the agency definition (whether Stifel Financial consented to have Cochran act on its behalf), the court stated that "[u]nder the *VonFeldt* decision, the fact that Stifel Financial elected Cochran as a director of Stifel Financial is deemed to constitute a decision by Stifel Financial to have Cochran act at its request as a director, officer, and employee of Stifel Nicolaus." 2000 Del. Ch. LEXIS 58, at *60, 2000 WL 286722, at *17. According to the court, "[t]his would appear to go a long way toward establishing that Stifel Financial had 'consented to have [Cochran] act [in those capacities] on its behalf.'" *Id.*

With respect to the second part of the agency definition ("whether Stifel Financial retained the power to 'control' and 'direct' Cochran's actions in those capacities"), the court stated that "[w]ithout more, the mere fact that Cochran was a director of Stifel Nicolaus and elected by Stifel Financial would not make him subject to Stifel Financial's control and direction in that capacity." *Id.* To the contrary, "[t]he traditional approach of our law is to respect the separate identities" of parent and subsidiary corporations and "to assume that the subsidiary's board governs it, until there is some showing to the contrary." 2000 Del. Ch. LEXIS 58, at *61 n.70, 2000 WL 286772, at *17 n.70. Similarly, the court added, "there is no basis to believe that Stifel Financial had the legal authority to direct Cochran in his managerial role at Stifel Nicolaus." 2000 Del. Ch. LEXIS 58, at *62, 2000 WL 286722, at *17. The court acknowledged that "[u]ndoubtedly, a person in Cochran's situation would not last very long if he did not perform in accord with the expectations of the corporate parent" but held that "as a matter of law, one would think that an employee of Stifel Nicolaus would be directed and controlled by the Chief

Executive Officer of that subsidiary, not the CEO or directors of the parent." *Id.*

Additionally, Section 145(c) has the same "by reason of the fact" requirement as Section 145(a), so to the extent that Cochran was not entitled to indemnification pursuant to Section 145(a) for the excessive compensation, promissory note and non-competition claims on this ground, he also was not entitled to indemnification pursuant to Section 145(c). *See* Del. Gen. Corp. Law §§ 145(a), (c); 2000 Del. Ch. LEXIS 179, at *19, 2000 WL 1847676, at *5.

Section 145(f) Indemnification. The court nevertheless ruled in favor of Cochran on his claim that indemnification was required by Stifel Financial's bylaw mandating indemnification "to the full extent authorized by law" with respect to the criminal, SEC and breach of fiduciary duty claims upon which Cochran had been "successful on the merits or otherwise" pursuant to the non-exclusivity provision in Section 145(f) of Delaware's statute. This aspect of the *Cochran* decision is discussed in Chapter V, Section V A 10.

Section A 10

Add the following at the end of footnote 623 on page 1960:

See also Biondi v. Beekman Hill House Apartment Corp., 94 N.Y.2d 659, 665, 731 N.E.2d 577, 580, 709 N.Y.S.2d 861, 864 (2000):

> Business Corporation Law former § 721 previously made [the] statutory indemnification provisions exclusive. However, in 1986, in an attempt to "attract" capable officers and directors, the Legislature amended Section 721 to expand indemnification to include any additional rights conferred by a corporation in its certificate of incorporation or by-laws, provided that "no indemnification may be made to or on behalf of any director or officer *if a judgment or other final adjudication adverse to the director or officer establishes that his acts were committed in bad faith* or were the result of active and deliberate dishonesty and were material to the cause of action so adjudicated" (Busi-

ness Corporation Law § 721 [emphasis added]; Governer's Approval Mem. Bill Jacket, L 1986, ch 513, § 1, at 9, reprinted in 1986 McKinney's Session Laws of NY, at 3171-3172).

Replace "1996" with "Supp. 1998/99" in the Model Act § 8.59 citation in footnote 626 on page 1961.

Replace "8-384.1" with "8-369U" in the Model Act § 8.59 citation in footnote 627 on page 1961.

Add "at 8-369U-V" at the end of the Model Act § 8.59 citation in footnote 628 on page 1961.

Replace "8-384.1" with "8-369U-V" in the Model Act § 8.59 citation in footnote 654 on page 1967.

Add the following at the end of the first sentence (immediately after footnote 656) in the paragraph beginning and concluding on page 1967, and begin a new paragraph after the following:

The Delaware Court of Chancery in *VonFeldt v. Stifel Financial Corp.*, 1999 Del. Ch. LEXIS 131, 1999 WL 413393 (Del. Ch. June 11, 1999), restated these principles as follows: "While § 145(f) permits indemnification on terms other than as set forth in the rest of § 145, such other indemnification must be consistent with the policies expressed in the other parts of § 145," and thus "Delaware corporations lack the power to indemnify a party who did not act in good faith or in the best interests of the corporation" (unless, as discussed below, indemnification is mandatory because the person seeking indemnification has been successful on the merits or otherwise). 1999 Del. Ch. LEXIS 131, at *8, 1999 WL 413393, at *2. The court pointed to the fact that the text of Delaware's statute "makes plain the legislative intent that the good faith requirement is central to the policy underlying the statutory language," and "as a matter of public policy it simply would not make sense for a corporation to have the power to indemnify agents who do not act in its best interests." 1999 Del. Ch. LEXIS 131, at *5-6, 1999 WL 413393, at *2. The court also pointed to the Delaware Supreme Court's statement of the policies underlying Section 145 – "(a) allowing corporate officials to resist unjustified lawsuits, secure in the knowledge that, if vindicated, the corporation will bear the expense of litigation; and (b) encouraging capable women and men to serve as corporate directors and officers, secure in the knowledge that the corporation will absorb the costs of defending their honesty and integrity" – and stated that "[t]he Supreme Court's analysis takes as given the good faith of the officers, directors, or employees who seek protection from expense under § 145. It follows that when a corporation . . . undertakes to adopt a bylaw that expands the permissive nature of indemnification to mandatory indemnification the good faith requirement survives." 1999 Del. Ch. LEXIS 131, at *7, 1999 WL 413393, at *2 (quoting *VonFeldt v. Stifel Fin. Corp.*, 714 A.2d 79, 85 (Del. 1998)).

The same result was reached in *TLC Beatrice International Holdings, Inc. v. Cigna Insurance Co.*, 1999 U.S. Dist. LEXIS 605, 1999 WL 33454 (S.D.N.Y. Jan. 27, 1999), a federal court decision construing Delaware law. The court stated that "a corporation's indemnification powers cannot be inconsistent with the substantive statutory provisions of § 145, notwithstanding the broader grant of powers under § 145(f)," and that pursuant to this "consistency" rule "the indemnification rights provided by contract may not exceed the 'scope' of a corporation's indemnification powers as set out by the statute." 1999 U.S. Dist. LEXIS 605, at *14, 1999 WL 33454, at *4. Applying this rule, the court held that Delaware's statute intentionally bars indemnification of amounts paid to settle actions by or on behalf of the corporation and thus indemnification of amount paid to settle actions by or on behalf of the corporation is not permitted by the statute's non-exclusivity provision. 1999 U.S. Dist. LEXIS 605, at *14-16, 1999 WL

33454 at *4-5; *see also Biondi*, 94 N.Y.2d at 655, 731 N.E.2d at 580, 709 N.Y.S.2d at 864 ("[w]hile section 721's non-exclusivity language *broadens* the scope of indemnification, its 'bad faith' standard manifests a public policy limitation on indemnification" that "is reflected in the statutory indemnification provisions . . . which restrict indemnification to acts of 'good faith' that are 'reasonably believed to be in * * * the best interests of the corporation") (quoting N.Y. Bus. Corp. Law §§ 722(a), (c)).

The court in *Cochran v. Stifel Financial Corp.*, 2000 Del. Ch. LEXIS 58, 2000 WL 286722 (Del. Ch. Mar. 8, 2000), *subsequent proceedings*, 2000 Del. Ch. LEXIS 179, 2000 WL 1847676 (Del. Ch. Dec. 13, 2000), described the non-exclusivity provision in Section 145(f) as "obviously a difficult provision to implement in actual practice because it appears to collide with other provisions of § 145." 2000 Del. Ch. LEXIS 58, at *65, 2000 WL 286722, at *18. Nevertheless, the court concluded, "§ 145(f) suggests that a corporation's decision to provide broader indemnification rights should not be disturbed unless those broader rights are 'contrary to the limitations or prohibitions set forth in the other section 145 subsections, other statutes, court decisions, or public policy.'" *Id.* (quoting Veasey, Finkelstein & Bigler, *Delaware Supports Directors with a Three-Legged Stool of Limited Liability*, 42 Bus. Law. 399, 415 (1987)).

Applying this standard in a decision denying a motion to dismiss, the court held that Delaware law does not preclude indemnification of a person serving a wholly-owned subsidiary of a parent corporation at the request of the parent corporation who has been "successful on the merits or otherwise" simply because the person is not entitled to mandatory indemnification under the mandatory indemnification provision in Section 145(c) of the Delaware General Corporation Law because Section 145(c) reaches only directors and officers and the person is not a director or officer. The court explained that "[i]t is difficult to see why it would offend public policy or conflict with the other subsections of § 145 to permit corporations voluntarily to indemnify persons who are not within the class of persons entitled to mandatory statutory indemnification" – i.e., directors or officers – "but who otherwise satisfy the requirements of § 145(c)" – i.e., they are "successful on the merits or otherwise in defense of an action or proceeding." 2000 Del. Ch. LEXIS 58, at *66, 2000 WL 286722, at *18. Indeed, the court continued, "our law typically applies the most rigorous indemnification procedures to directors and officers, who are entitled to mandatory indemnification under § 145(c) and more flexible procedures in the case of mere employees or corporate agents" due to "the greater responsibility of directors and officers and the greater likelihood that indemnification decisions as to them might be tainted by possible conflicts of interest." *Id.*

Accordingly, the court concluded, "[t]o the extent our public policy permits such high-ranking corporate officials to receive indemnification on a showing of success (regardless of whether it was because of a merely technical defense), it is difficult to conceive why it would offend public policy for a corporation to accord equal treatment to employees and agents who can demonstrate success." *Id.* In short, "because Delaware permits – nay, mandates – indemnification of directors and officers who satisfy the success criteria in § 145(c) regardless of their good faith, . . . Delaware should surely permit a corporation to provide contractual indemnification rights to a person who serves another corporation at its request and who shows, per § 145(c), that he was 'successful on the merits or otherwise in defending any action . . . .'" 2000 Del. Ch. LEXIS 58, at *63, 2000 WL 286722, at *18 (quoting Del. Gen. Corp. Law § 145(c)).

The case before the court involved a person, Robert M. Cochran, who served Stifel Financial Corporation as a director, officer and employee of Stifel Nicolaus & Company, Inc., a wholly-owned subsidiary of Stifel Financial, and who sought indemnification pursuant to a Stifel Financial bylaw mandating indemnification "to the full extent authorized by law." 2000 Del. Ch. LEXIS 58, at *71, 2000 WL 286722, at *20. If Cochran "was the former Chairman of the Board and CEO of Stifel Financial," the court stated, "Stifel Financial would be statutorily required to indemnify him" because Section 145(c) protects directors and officers and Cochran had been "successful on the merits or otherwise." *Id.* The court therefore concluded that no "Delaware public policy would be offended if Stifel Financial afforded indemnification to Cochran where he has been successful in defending actions brought against him in his capacity as a director or officer of Stifel Nicolaus, which he served at Stifel Financial's request." 2000 Del. Ch. LEXIS 58, at *71-72, 2000 WL 286722, at *20. "To conclude otherwise," the court stated, "would require a determination that the General Assembly intended to accord corporations greater flexibility to indemnify their most important corporate officials – i.e., their directors and officers – than to indemnify mere employees, agents, or persons serving other corporations on an 'at request of' basis." 2000 Del. Ch. LEXIS 58, at *72, 2000 WL 286722, at *20. The court stated that "I see no basis for so concluding." *Id.*

The court rejected a claim that good faith is required for indemnification pursuant to a non-exclusivity provision adopted pursuant to Section 145(f) where the person seeking indemnification has been "successful on the merits or otherwise" but is not entitled to mandatory indemnification under Section 145(c) because the person is not a director or officer and thus is not covered by Section 145(c). The court stated that "I do not believe that one can read" Delaware law "as embracing the notion that it is mandatory as a matter of Delaware public policy to indemnify a director or officer solely upon a showing of success but impermissible as a matter of Delaware public policy for a corporation contractually to indemnify an employee, agent, or person in an 'at the request of' status in the identical circumstances." 2000 Del. Ch. LEXIS 58, at *74, 2000 WL 286722, at *20.

In a subsequent decision on motions for summary judgment, the court re-affirmed its prior conclusions "that a corporation's decision to provide broader indemnification rights should not be disturbed unless those broader rights are 'contrary to the limitations or prohibitions set forth in the other section 145 subsections, other statutes, court decisions, or public policy. . .'" and that "because Delaware law would require Stifel Financial to indemnify its CEO if he were to have achieved the same result as Cochran did . . . without an examination of the CEO's good faith, § 145(f) of the Delaware General Corporation Law permits Stifel Financial to indemnify Cochran in the identical circumstances." *Cochran v. Stifel Fin. Corp.*, 2000 Del. Ch. LEXIS 179, at *31-36, 2000 WL 1847676, at *8-9 (Del. Ch. Dec. 13, 2000) (citing earlier decision and Veasey, Finkelstin & Bigler, 42 Bus. Law. at 415). "Because Delaware permits such indemnification," the court stated, "Stifel Financial is contractually bound to provide it." 2000 Del. Ch. LEXIS 179, at *36, 2000 WL 1847676, at *9.

The court elaborated upon its reasoning with the following illustration:

> Imagine the following scenario. Suppose Cochran had told Stifel Financial that he would not continue at Stifel Nicolaus unless he was given the same right to indemnity that he would have as a director and officer of Stifel Financial itself. Why, Cochran reasoned, should he continue to be afforded second-class indemnification rights simply because he worked at Stifel Financial's wholly-owned subsidiary, which was very important to Stifel Financial's overall success? Hence, assume Cochran demanded and received a contract with the following key provisions: (1) Cochran would serve as a director, officer, and employee of Stifel Nicolaus, a wholly-owned subsidiary whose performance is important to Stifel Financial; and (2) in partial exchange for his service at Stifel Nicolaus, Stifel Financial would indemnify Cochran if he met the success standard of § 145(c) in an action brought against him by "reason of his" service at Stifel Nicolaus. That is, assume the contract would give Cochran the same indemnification rights as if he were a director and officer of Stifel Financial itself.
>
> Given the existence of § 145(c) and (f), the court fails to see how such a contract would violate Delaware public policy. If such an explicit contract would be valid because the indemnification it provided was not inconsistent with Delaware public policy, and thus authorized by § 145(f), the provision of the

> identical indemnification pursuant to a maximally expansive bylaw is not contrary to Delaware law, either.

2000 Del. Ch. LEXIS 179, at *36-37, 2000 WL 1847676, at *10 (footnote omitted).

In sum, the court held, a parent corporation that "has promised to provide indemnification to the fullest extent permitted by Delaware law" must provide indemnification when "(i) a party serving another corporation at the parent corporation's request (ii) who is covered by the parent corporation's indemnification provision, (iii) shows that the corporation would have been required under § 145(c) to indemnify its own CEO in the identical circumstances for the claims at issue." 2000 Del. Ch. LEXIS 179, at *40, 2000 WL 1847676, at *10.

The court rejected Stifel Financial's contention that the court's ruling was "inconsistent with the legitimate expectations of 'hundreds' of corporations like it, which all had assumed (it confidentially asserts) that a good faith requirement was implicit in their maximally broad indemnification bylaws" and that "only the permissive indemnification provided for in § 145 (a) and (b) would fall within the ambit of a bylaw providing indemnity to . . . 'the full extent authorized by law.'" 2000 Del. Ch. LEXIS 179, at *39, 2000 WL 1847676, at *10. The court stated that "[t]he answer to any problem . . . posed by this court's plain meaning interpretation of its maximally broad Bylaw is simple: the affected corporations can redraft their indemnification bylaws to be more precise." 2000 Del. Ch. LEXIS 179, at *39-40, 2000 WL 1847676, at *10.

Add the following at the end of footnote 658 on page 1967:

See also Owens Corning Fiberglass Corp. v. Nat'l Union Fire Ins. Co., No. 3:95 CV 7700, slip op. at 4 (N.D. Ohio Mar. 31, 1999) (permitting indemnification pursuant to Delaware's non-exclusivity provision where there was no evidence of bad faith).

Replace "1998" with "2001" in the Balotti citation in footnote 659 on page 1967.

Replace the Olson citation in footnote 659 on page 1967 with the following:

John F. Olson, Josiah O. Hatch III & Ty R. Sagalow, *Director and Officer Liability: Indemnification and Insurance* § 5.04[5], at 5–40-42 (2000);

Section A 11

Replace "8-289" with "8-280" and replace "1996" with "Supp. 1998/99" in the Model Act §§ 8.50-8.59 citation in footnote 668 on page 1969.

Replace "8–289-90" with "8–280-81" in the Model Act §§ 8.50-8.59 citation in footnote 670 on page 1969.

Replace "8-290" with "8-281" in the Model Act §§ 8.50-8.59 citation in footnote 671 on page 1969.

Replace "1998" with "2001" in the American Jurisprudence citation in footnote 672 on page 1969.

Add the following at the end of the second paragraph beginning and concluding on page 1969 (immediately after footnote 672):

Thus in *Biondi v. Beekman Hill House Apartment Corp.*, 94 N.Y.2d 659, 731 N.E.2d 577, 709 N.Y.S.2d 861 (2000), the court held that a director is not entitled to indemnification for an award of punitive damages imposed for acts of bad faith such as racial discrimination. *Id.* at 663-64, 731 N.E.2d at 579, 709 N.Y.S.2d at 863. The court stated that racial discrimination "is precisely the type of conduct for which public policy should preclude indemnification," and to allow a director "to shift that penalty" to the corporation "would eviscerate the deterrent effect of punitive damages, and 'violate the 'fundamental principle that no one shall be permitted to take advantage of his own wrong.''" *Id.* at 664, 731 N.E.2d at 579, 709 N.Y.S.2d at 863 (quoting *Messersmith v. Am. Fid. Co.*, 232 N.Y. 161, 165, 133 N.E. 432, 433 (1921) and *Public Serv. Mut. Ins. Co. v. Goldfarb*, 53 N.Y.2d 392, 400, 425 N.E.2d 810, 814-15, 442 N.Y.S.2d 422, 427 (1981)).

Replace "1997" with "2000" in the Corpus Juris Secundum citation in footnote 672 on page 1970.

Add the following at the end of footnote 676 on page 1970:

See also Fromer v. Yogel, 50 F. Supp. 2d 227, 238 (S.D.N.Y. 1999) (indemnification "is not available in a case where the party seeking indemnification has knowingly and willfully violated the federal securities laws").

Add the following at the end of the paragraph beginning on page 1970 and concluding on page 1971 (immediately after footnote 686):

The Seventh Circuit in *King v. Gibbs*, 876 F.2d 1275 (7th Cir. 1989), extended its ruling in *Heizer Corp. v. Ross*, 601 F.2d 330 (7th Cir. 1979), to reach "an innocent defendant, rather than a wrongdoer" in a case involving Section 10(b) of the Securities Exchange Act of 1934. 876 F.2d at 1276. Unlike most other courts that have considered the issue, the court in *King* reasoned that "[t]here is simply no congressional intent to create a right to indemnification under Section 10(b)" and stated that "policy analysis has no role to play in the question of whether there is a federal right to indemnification." *Id.* at 1283. The court noted, however, that "[i]t is difficult to see how a right to indemnification for even innocent persons would serve the deterrent function which underlies the statute" because "innocent parties who would qualify for indemnification, because they lack the scienter required by the rule, cannot be found liable for damages" and thus "a right to indemnification would have no effect on their conduct and would not serve the deterrent function of the statute." *Id.* at 1282 n.10 (citation omitted).

The Tenth Circuit in *First Golden Bancorporation v. Weiszmann*, 942 F.2d 726 (10th Cir. 1991), held that indemnification was not permitted in a case seeking to recover short-swing profits by corporate insiders under Section 16(b) of the Securities Exchange Act of 1934, "a prophylactic anti-fraud statute" written to impose strict liability in order "to deter transactions which have a high potential for fraud." *Id.* at 729. The court stated that "the public policy behind section 16(b) renders invalid any attempt by an insider to seek indemnification for his liability under section 16(b)." *Id.*

Replace "9-16" with "9-17" and "1997" with "2000" in the Bishop citation in footnote 709 on page 1975.

Section A 12

Replace the Olson citation in footnote 711 on page 1976 with the following:

John F. Olson, Josiah O. Hatch III & Ty R. Sagalow, *Director and Officer Liability: Indemnification and Insurance* §§ 7.16, 9.02, 9.05-9.07 (2000);

Section A 13

Replace the Olson citation in footnote 726 on page 1979 with the following:

John F. Olson, Josiah O. Hatch III & Ty R. Sagalow, *Director and Officer Liability: Indemnification and Insurance* § 5.04[5], at 5-42 (2000).

Replace "1996" with "Supp. 1998/99" in the Model Act § 16.21 citation in footnote 728 on page 1979.

Replace "16-86" with "16-82" in the Model Act § 16.21 citation in footnote 729 on page 1979.

Section B 1

Replace "1996" with "Supp. 1998/99" in the Model Act § 8.57 citation in footnote 732 on page 1980.

Replace "8-376" with "8-369H" in the Model Act § 8.57 citation in footnote 734 on page 1981.

Section B 2

Add the following at the end of the second paragraph beginning and concluding on page 1983 (immediately after footnote 744):

The court in *TLC Beatrice International Holdings, Inc. v. Cigna Insurance Co.*, 1999 U.S. Dist. LEXIS 605, 1999 WL 33454 (S.D.N.Y. Jan. 27, 1999), explained that rules limiting indemnification create "a monetary risk to officers and directors who, in order to avoid lengthy and unpredictable litigation, are forced to make settlement payments," and that "[w]ithout the authority to indemnify or insure their directors and officers, one might argue, Delaware corporations would be at a distinct disadvantage in attracting qualified candidates for those positions." 1999 U.S. Dist. LEXIS 605, at *17-18, 1999 WL

33454, at *6. The court stated that "Delaware's solution to these problems was not to authorize indemnification of directors and officers" for amounts paid to settle claims by or on behalf of the corporation but "rather to authorize the purchase of insurance for these persons." 1999 U.S. Dist. LEXIS 605, at *18, 1999 WL 33454 at *6. The court described the "rationale for choosing insurance over indemnification" under these circumstances as a balance between "the employment concerns of corporations and the Delaware legislature's wish for a 'non-circular' solution in a derivative action." *Id.* This is accomplished, the court explained, "because the corporation is paying only a premium and not the full settlement amount" and thus "only slightly diminishes the potential benefits to the corporation." 1999 U.S. Dist. LEXIS 605, at *18-19, 1999 WL 33454 at *6.

Replace the Olson citation in footnote 747 on page 1984 with the following:

John F. Olson, Josiah O. Hatch III & Ty R. Sagalow, *Director and Officer Liability: Indemnification and Insurance* § 6B.01, at 6B-3 (2000).

Add the following at the end of footnote 748 on page 1984:

See also In re Pintlar Corp., 124 F.3d 1310, 1313-14 (9th Cir. 1997) (holding that a directors and officers insurance policy was not "property of the estate" and that "litigation concerning its scope" brought by the insurer against directors and officers was not required to be stayed during bankruptcy proceedings because the prospect for recovery by a creditors' litigation trust in claims brought in the name of creditors against directors and officers, the directors' and officers' claims for coverage, and the insurer's right to litigate coverage "all implicate interests independent of the debtor's," and because the action brought by the insurer did not name the debtor as a party and thus a judgment involving the insurer and the directors and officers would have a persuasive but not controlling effect in any subsequent action involving the debtor's coverage and "the persuasive effect of a judgment involving third parties does not have a sufficient potential impact on the value of the estate to fall under the Bankruptcy Code's stay provision"); Paar, Silverschotz & Stern, *D & Os May Be Exposed in Corporate Bankruptcy*, Nat'l L.J., Jan. 25, 1999, at C6.

Section B 3

Replace "1997" with "1997 & Supp. 2000" in the Couch citation in footnote 750 on page 1985.

Replace the Lunceford citation in footnote 757 on page 1986 with the following:

Lunceford v. Peachtree Cas. Ins. Co., 495 S.E.2d 88 (Ga. Ct. App. 1997), *cert. denied*, 1998 Ga. LEXIS 558 (Ga. Ct. App. 1998),

Section B 4

Replace the Olson citation in footnote 763 on page 1988 with the following:

John F. Olson, Josiah O. Hatch III & Ty R. Sagalow, *Director and Officer Liability: Indemnification and Insurance* § 10.05, at 10-13 (2000);

Add the following at the end of footnote 764 on page 1988:

See also TLC Beatrice Int'l Holdings, Inc. v. Cigna Ins. Co., 1999 U.S. Dist. LEXIS 605, at *9-10, 1999 WL 33454 at *3 (S.D.N.Y. Jan. 27, 1999) ("pursuant to the plain meaning of Exclusion (G) of the insurance policy, a director or officer may not make a direct claim under Part One unless the Company is prohibited from indemnifying the director or officer under the Company's charter or bylaws, or under applicable state law").

Add the following at the end of footnote 765 on page 1988:

See also Rosenberg, *Insurance Coverage and Securities Litigation*, 31 Rev. Sec. & Comm. Reg. 213, 214-15 (Nov. 4, 1998); Tillinghast-Towers Perrin, *2000 Directors and Officers Liability Survey* 3 (2001) (noting that in 2000 "[m]ore than 90% of U.S. insureds purchased entity coverage, up dramatically from less than 30 percent four years ago").

Replace "10-27" with "10-28" in the Olson citation in footnote 770 on page 1990.

Add the following at the end of footnote 772 on page 1990:

See also Citizens First Nat'l Bank v. Cincinnati Ins. Co., 200 F.3d 1102, 1108-09 (7th Cir. 2000); *Stauth v. Nat'l Union Fire Ins. Co.*, 185 F.3d 875 (unpublished opinion, text available at 1999 U.S. App. LEXIS 14006, at *22, 30 and 1999 WL 420401, at *8, 10) (10th Cir. June 24, 1999).

Add the following at the end of footnote 775 on page 1991:

See also Rosenberg, 31 Rev. Sec. & Comm. Reg. at 219-20.

Add the following new footnote 793.1 at the end of the first sentence of the paragraph beginning on page 1994 and concluding on page 1995:

See Rosenberg, 31 Rev. Sec. & Comm. Reg. at 220-21.

Add the following at the end of footnote 800 on page 1995:

See also Federal Ins. Co. v. Hawaiian Elec. Indus., Inc., No. 94-00125 HG, slip op. at 17-23, 26-34 (D. Haw. Dec. 15, 1995) (holding that insurer's "reservation of rights and its statements and conduct surrounding it reservation of rights," including acting in "an equivocal manner" over "a long period of time," constituted "the functional equivalent of a denial of coverage," that the insurer unreasonably withheld its consent to a proposed settlement, and that the lack of an agreement on allocation of a settlement payment between the insurer and the insured does not provide a reasonable basis for withholding consent to a settlement because the insurer can consent to the settlement while reserving its rights to subsequently argue allocation and coverage issues).

Add the following new footnote 800.1 at the end of the first sentence of the paragraph beginning and concluding on page 1995:

See, e.g., TLC Beatrice Int'l Holdings, Inc. v. Cigna Ins. Co., 2000 U.S. Dist. LEXIS 2917, 2000 WL 282967 (S.D.N.Y. Mar. 16, 2000).

Add the following at the end of the second sentence (immediately after footnote 801) of the paragraph beginning and concluding on page 1995:

Once an insurer has denied coverage (or acted in a manner that is the equivalent of a denial of coverage), however, the insured no longer is bound by the insurance policy's provisions governing settlements. *Hawaiian Elec.*, slip op. at 25.

Add the following at the end of footnote 805 on page 1996:

See also Rosenberg, 31 Rev. Sec. & Comm. Reg. at 221.

Section B 5

Replace the Olson citation in footnote 812 on page 1997 with the following:

John F. Olson, Josiah O. Hatch III & Ty R. Sagalow, *Director and Officer Liability: Indemnification and Insurance* § 10.06[1], at 10-17 (2000);

Replace the Klein citation in footnote 813 on page 1998 with the following:

Klein v. Fidelity & Deposit Co. of Am., 700 A.2d 262 (Md. Ct. Spec. App. 1997), *cert. denied*, 703 A.2d 1265 (Md. 1998).

Add the following at the end of footnote 813 on page 1998:

See also Zunenshine v. Executive Risk Indem., Inc., 1998 U.S. Dist. LEXIS 12699, at *2 n.1, 1998 WL 483475, at *1 n.1 (S.D.N.Y. Aug. 17, 1998), *aff'd*, 182 F.3d 902 (unpublished opinion, text available at 1999 U.S. App. LEXIS 14629 and 1999 WL 464988) (2d Cir. June 29, 1999).

Add the following new footnote 814.1 at the end of the first sentence of the paragraph beginning on page 1998 and concluding on page 1999:

See Sapp v. Greif, 141 F.3d 1185 (unpublished opinion, text available at 1998 U.S. App. LEXIS 6668, at *9 and 1998 WL 165116, at *3) (10th Cir. Apr. 3, 1998) ("[g]enerally, under a claims made policy, coverage is triggered only when an insured notifies the insurer during the policy period of claims against the insured," but "[t]he specific language of the policy in question, of course, circumscribes any general rules").

Add the following at the end of footnote 821 on page 2000:

See also Foster v. Summit Med. Sys., 610 N.W.2d 350, 354-55 (Minn. Ct. App. 2000), *review denied*, 2000 Minn. LEXIS 432 (Minn. July 25, 2000) (holding that a subpoena duces tecum issued by the Securities and Exchange Commission seeking to compel the production of documents did not seek "relief" and thus policies that defined a "Securities Action Claim" as "any judicial or administrative proceeding initiated against any of the Directors and Officers or the Company based upon, arising out of, or in any way involving the Securities Act of 1933, the Securities Exchange Act of 1934, rules or regulations of the Securities Exchange Commission under either or both Acts, similar securities laws or regulations of any state, or any common law relating to any transaction arising out of, involving, or relating to the sale of securities *in which they may be subjected to a binding adjudication of liability for damages or other relief, including any appeal therefrom*," did not require coverage because "[t]he SEC's ability to compel production of documents does not fit any reasonable reading of the term 'relief'"); Rosenberg, *Insurance Coverage and Securities Litigation*, 31 Rev. Sec. & Comm. Reg. 213, 216 (Nov. 4, 1998) (stating that the definition of the term claim "typically encompasses lawsuits and may also include written or verbal demands for monetary or non-monetary relief," that "[a]dministrative or arbitration proceedings may be covered as well as criminal proceedings commenced by return of an indictment or similar charging document," and that "[m]any policies provide coverage for administrative proceedings commenced by a 'filing of a notice of charges, formal investigative order or similar document against Directors or Officers,'" and reporting that some insurers that exclude coverage for costs incurred in the investigation or evaluation of shareholder demands offer an endorsement providing up to $250,000 in insurance for these costs).

Replace the Klein citation in footnote 844 on page 2002 with the following:

700 A.2d 262 (Md. Ct. Spec. App. 1997), *cert. denied*, 703 A.2d 1265 (Md. 1998).

Add the following at the end of the paragraph beginning on page 2001 and concluding on page 2003 (immediately after footnote 847):

- *Hyde v. Fidelity & Deposit Co.*, 23 F. Supp. 2d 630, 632-33 (D. Md. 1998) (holding that an investigation by the Resolution Trust Corporation involving a potential claim was not a claim because "[a] claim is something demanded as of right in a court" and the RTC "merely gave the Directors notice that they intended to hold the Directors liable" but "did not subsequently file a claim in court").

Section B 6

Replace the Olson citation in footnote 878 on page 2008 with the following:

John F. Olson, Josiah O. Hatch III & Ty R. Sagalow, *Director and Officer Liability: Indemnification and Insurance* § 10.06[6], at 10-44 (2000).

Add the following at the end of footnote 878 on page 2008:

See also Rosenberg, *Insurance Coverage and Securities Litigation*, 31 Rev. Sec. & Comm. Reg. 213, 217-18 (Nov. 4, 1998) ("policies differ as to whether the claim must be reported within a set amount of time or simply 'as soon as practicable'" and may provide that the reporting obligation is not triggered "until as soon as practicable after the company's risk manager or general counsel first becomes aware of the claim").

Add the following at the end of paragraph beginning on page 2020 and concluding on page 2021 (immediately after footnote 956):

The court in *Sapp v. Greif*, 141 F.3d 1185 (unpublished opinion, text available at 1998 U.S. App. LEXIS 6668 and 1998 WL 165116) (10th Cir. Apr. 3, 1998), held that notice was inadequate in a case where the governing policy language required "written notice to the Insurer of the circumstances and the reasons for anticipating such a claim, with full particulars as to dates and persons involved." 1998 U.S. App. LEXIS 6668, at *10-11, 1998 WL 165116, at *3. The wrongful acts for which coverage was sought involved claims by three borrowers – Fletcher, Janet and Ronald Sapp – who contended that Leopold Grief misapplied funds while he was a bank officer and director. 1998 U.S. App. LEXIS 6668, at *14, 1998 WL 16516, at *4. The Sapps obtained a judgment for over $900,000 in a state court action against Grief and then brought an action against the corporation's directors and officers liability policy insurer. 1998 U.S. App. LEXIS 6668, at *2, 1998 WL 16516, at *1.

First, the court held that a March 30, 1993 letter by the corporation's president informing the insurer "generally of potential claims for 'mismanagement of lending by the institution and for other activities which may constitute 'wrongful acts' as defined in the . . . policy'" was "clearly too general and vague to provide notice." 1998 U.S. App. LEXIS 6668, at *12-13, 1998 WL 165116, at *3.

Second, the court held that a June 30, 1993 letter by the FDIC, after it had become the corporation's receiver, informing the insurer concerning "claims the FDIC may have against former bank directors and officers with respect to loan transactions involving eleven entities or groups of borrowers" was "more specific" but still not sufficient to constitute notice. 1998 U.S. App. LEXIS 6668, at *12-13, 1998 WL 165116, at *4. The FDIC's letter listed the following wrongful acts:

1. Failure by the directors to exercise adequate supervision over the bank's officers and employees.
2. Failure to establish and enforce adequate debtor repayment programs.
3. Extending credit with an over-reliance on collateral, rather than cash flow.
4. Extending credit to borrowers who were not creditworthy or were known to be in financial difficulty.
5. Failure to employ sound internal controls.

6. Failure to supervise, manage, conduct and direct the Banks' business and affairs to ensure compliance with law, the banks' by-laws, and prudent banking principles.

1998 U.S. App. LEXIS 6668, at *15 n.6, 1998 WL 165116, at *5 n.6. The court stated that the "general description of the 'wrongful acts' that might give rise to a claim" in the FDIC's letter "did not include anything like misapplication of funds." 1998 U.S. App. LEXIS 6668, at *15, 1998 WL 165116, at *5. The court also stated that the letter identified "a bank loan officer, Bruce Rhoades, as being involved in the relevant loan transactions, but does not mention Grief, and it identifies claims that the FDIC might have, not the Sapps." *Id.* The court added that "the circumstances described that might give rise to a claim occurred sometime after July 15, 1992, well after the date of Greif's alleged actions." 1998 U.S. App. LEXIS 6668, at *14-15, 1998 WL 165116, at *4.

The court thus found that "plaintiffs have not produced any evidence linking the conduct mentioned in the FDIC letter to the conduct on which their [state court] lawsuit and judgment are based." 1998 U.S. App. LEXIS 6668, at *16, 1998 WL 165116, at *5.

Section B 7

Replace the Olson citation in footnote 957 on page 2021 with the following:

John F. Olson, Josiah O. Hatch III & Ty R. Sagalow, *Director and Officer Liability: Indemnification and Insurance* § 10.06[3], at 10-22 (2000);

Replace "1998" with "2001" in the Securities Law Techniques citation in footnote 957 on page 2021.

Add the following at the end of the paragraph beginning on page 2024 and concluding on page 2025 (immediately after footnote 981):

Coverage also was denied in *Cincinnati Insurance Co. v. Irwin Co.*, 2000 Ohio App. LEXIS 6045, 2000 WL 1867297 (Ohio Ct. App. Dec. 22, 2000). The case involved an informal buy back policy by The Irwin Company, a closely held corporation pursuant to which "[w]hen feasible, an employee's stock would be purchased by the company at or below book value." 2000 Ohio App. LEXIS 6045, at *3, 2000 WL 1867297, at *1. Two groups of shareholders sold shares to the company treasury for $28 per share, and the corporation's chief executive officer and largest shareholder then offered these treasury shares to certain directors and officers at $28 per share at a time when these directors and officers knew that a strategic alliance was being negotiated and anticipated a purchase of all corporate shares at a price in the range of $83 to $107 per share. 2000 Ohio App. LEXIS 6045, at *3-4, 2000 WL 1867297, at *1. Following a merger a short time later in which the corporation's shares were acquired for $131.54 per share, the selling shareholders sued and the case ultimately was settled. 2000 Ohio App. LEXIS 6045, at *4, 2000 WL 1867297, at *1.

The court held that the amounts paid by the directors and officers to settle the litigation were for acts performed in their personal capacities rather than acts performed in their corporate capacities. The court reasoned that there was no prior corporate approval for the purchase of the treasury stock, that the settlement amount was allocated based upon the number of shares owned by the directors and officers rather than their relative liabilities for actions taken as directors and officers, and that the settlement amount "represented a return of the personal profit that was realized on the purchase of treasury shares from Irwin and the subsequent sale of the appreciated shares" in the merger. 2000 Ohio App. LEXIS 604, at *8-9, 2000 WL 1867297, at *3.

Section B 8

Replace the Olson citation in footnote 982 on page 2025 with the following:

John F. Olson, Josiah O. Hatch III & Ty R. Sagalow, *Director and Officer Liability: Indemnification and Insurance* § 10.06[3], at 10-22 (2000);

Replace "1998" with "2001" in the Securities Law Techniques citation in footnote 982 on page 2025.

Add the following at the end of footnote 982 on page 2025:

See also Rosenberg, *Insurance Coverage and Securities Litigation*, 31 Rev. Sec. & Comm. Reg. 213, 216 (Nov. 4, 1998).

Replace "10-24" with "10-25" in the Olson citation in footnote 984 on page 2025.

Add the following at the end of footnote 992 on page 2027:

See also Rosenberg, *Insurance Coverage and Securities Litigation*, 31 Rev. Sec. & Comm. Reg. 213, 221 (Nov. 4, 1998) (noting policy provision providing for the governing law to be the law of the jurisdiction most favorable to coverage for punitive damages).

Add the following at the end of the paragraph beginning on page 2028 and concluding on page 2029 (immediately after footnote 999):

By contrast, the court in *Level 3 Communications, Inc. v. Federal Insurance Co.*, 1999 U.S. Dist. LEXIS 13338, 1999 WL 675295 (N.D. Ill. Aug. 18, 1999), rejected a claim that an amount paid to settle a litigation was "uninsurable under the law" because, the insurer claimed, the settlement payment was "a disgorgement by the company of wrongfully acquired funds" allegedly obtained "by wrongfully concealing information when purchasing the plaintiffs' stock." 1999 U.S. Dist. LEXIS 13338, at *3-4, 11, 1999 WL 675295, at * 1, 3.

The court, construing Nebraska law, stated that the definition of loss in the governing policy "does not distinguish among types of loss in terms of compensatory or rescissionary damages" and pointed to the insurer's failure to cite any "Nebraska case or statute indicating that the Nebraska Supreme Court would find the settlement at issue here 'uninsurable' under the law." 1999 U.S. Dist. LEXIS 13338, at *11-12, 1999 WL 675295, at *3-4. The court declined to follow *Reliance Group Holdings, Inc. v. National Union Fire Insurance Co.*, 188 A.D.2d 47, 594 N.Y.S.2d 20 (N.Y. App. Div. 1st Dep't), *motion for leave to appeal dismissed in part and denied in part*, 82 N.Y.2d 704, 619 N.E.2d 656, 601 N.Y.S.2d 578 (1993), because "[t]he court in *Reliance*, rather than relying on the policy's plain language, instead made a policy-based decision based on a hypothetical that it constructed," and "[a]s such, the case is inapplicable to the court's determination here." 1999 U.S. Dist. LEXIS 13338, at *11-12, 1999 WL 675295, at *3-4.

Section B 9 a

Replace the Olson citation in footnote 1004 on page 2030 with the following:

John F. Olson, Josiah O. Hatch III & Ty R. Sagalow, *Director and Officer Liability: Indemnification and Insurance* § 10.06[5][d], at 10-41 (2000).

Add new footnote 1005.1 between "legally entitled," and "illegal remuneration" in the second sentence of the paragraph beginning on page 2030 and concluding on page 2031:

See Jarvis Christian College v. Nat'l Union Fire Ins. Co., 197 F.3d 742, 748-49 (5th Cir. 1999) (the term "personal profit or advantage" "is broader than the term 'profit'"; "it does not mean a balance-sheet profit; rather, it encompasses any gain or benefit").

Replace "10–27-32, 10–39-40" with "10–29-33, 10–41-42" in the Olson citation in footnote 1008 on page 2031.

Replace "1998" with "2001" in the Securities Law Techniques citation in footnote 1008 on page 2031.

Add the following at the end of footnote 1008 on page 2031:

See also Owens Corning v. Nat'l Union Fire Ins. Co., 1998 U.S. App. LEXIS 26233, at *3-5, 10-17, 1998 WL 774109, at *1-2, 4-6 (6th Cir. Oct. 13, 1998) (exclusion barring coverage for acts, errors or omissions with regard to "any asbestos related injury or damage" does not bar coverage for a securities class action claim alleging that filings by Owens Corning with the Securities and Exchange Commission "misrepresented the company's future financial exposure to asbestos claims, that the defendants had 'failed to disclose the danger' that Owens Corning's product liability insurance coverage would eventually be exhausted, and that the defendants had 'misled investors concerning the impact that asbestos claims would have on [Owens Corning's] future financial condition and prospects'"; the court stated that the alleged wrongdoing was "misleading investors" and "was not based upon the use of asbestos" and that if the insurer "intended to exclude coverage of shareholder derivative suits and securities class-action suits entirely, it could have done so specifically").

Replace the Donald Sheldon citation in footnote 1011 on page 2031 with the following:

In re Donald Sheldon & Co., 186 B.R. 364, 370 (S.D.N.Y. 1995), *aff'd*, 182 F.3d 899 (unpublished opinion, text available at 1999 U.S. App. LEXIS 13954 and 1999 WL 459778) (2d Cir. June 22, 1999);

Replace footnote 1013 on page 2032 with the following:

186 B.R. 364 (S.D.N.Y. 1995), *aff'd*, 182 F.3d 899 (unpublished opinion, text available at 1999 U.S. App. LEXIS 13954 and 1999 WL 459778) (2d Cir. June 22, 1999);

Add the following at the end of the paragraph beginning on page 2032 and concluding on page 2033 (immediately after footnote 1016):

The Second Circuit affirmed "substantially for the reasons stated" in the district court's "well-reasoned opinion." *In re Donald Sheldon & Co.*, 182 F.3d 899 (unpublished opinion, text available at 1999 U.S. App. LEXIS 13954, at *2 and 1999 WL 459778, at *1) (2d Cir. June 22, 1999).

Add the following at the end of footnote 1020 on page 2033:

See also Citizens First Nat'l Bank v. Cincinnati Ins. Co., 200 F.3d 1102, 1107-09 (7th Cir. 2000) (finding that provisions excluding coverage for "actions taken in bad faith" and "dishonest" acts require "some sort of intentional wrongdoing" and do not reach reckless breaches of fiduciary duty committed by a corporate officer who acted with a "pure heart, but empty head").

Replace "10-30" with "10-31" in the Olson citation in footnote 1021 on page 2033.

Add the following at the end of the paragraph beginning on page 2033 and concluding on page 2034 (immediately after footnote 1025):

Summary judgment also was granted in favor of an insurer in *Zunenshine v. Executive Risk Indemnity, Inc.*, 1998 U.S. Dist. LEXIS 12699, 1998 WL 483475 (S.D.N.Y. Aug. 17, 1998), *aff'd*, 182 F.3d 902 (unpublished opinion, text available at 1999 U.S. App. LEXIS 14629 and 1999 WL 464988) (2d Cir. June 29, 1999). The court held that claims by a group of institutional investors who purchased $71 million in notes from SLM International, Inc. in March 1994 and who alleged that SLM directors and officers negligently misrepresented SLM's financial condition in the months before the notes were sold (the "Noteholders' Lawsuit") were excluded from coverage by "pending litigation" and "prior notice" exclusions that read as follows:

> The Underwriter will not pay Loss, including Defense Expenses, for Claims based upon, arising out of, directly or indirectly resulting from, in consequence of, or in any way involving:
>
> (1) any fact, circumstance, situation, transaction, event or Wrongful Act underlying or alleged in any prior and/or pending litigation or administrative or regulatory proceeding as of May 24, 1996 [the "pending litigation exclusion"];
>
> (2) any fact, circumstance, situation, transaction, event or Wrongful Act which, before May 24, 1996, was the subject of any notice given under any policy of directors and officers liability or other similar insurance [the "prior notice exclusion"].

1998 U.S. Dist. LEXIS 12699, at *3-4, 1999 WL 483475, at *1.

These exclusions, the court held, were triggered by federal securities law claims by a class of former SLM shareholders alleging that SLM directors and officers had issued false and misleading statements concerning SLM's financial condition between July 12, 1993 and November 21, 1994 (the "Shareholders' Lawsuit"). The court reasoned as follows:

> The Policy's "pending litigation" and "prior notice" exclusions are clear and unambiguous. By their terms, they exclude coverage for claims "arising out of, directly or indirectly resulting from, in consequence of, or in any way involving any fact, cir-

> cumstance, situation, transaction, event or Wrongful Act" alleged in a pending lawsuit or made the subject of a prior notice given to another insurer. "Wrongful Act" includes "any actual or alleged act, error, omission, misstatement, misleading statement or breach of duty" by a director or officer in his official capacity. Nothing in the plain language of either exclusion is ambiguous.
>
> * * *
>
> Comparing the Noteholders' and Shareholders' Lawsuits reveals that there is a strong factual nexus between the two. The Noteholders' Lawsuit alleged that plaintiffs misrepresented SLM's financial condition both in December 1993 and in March 1994 by issuing false statements concerning: SLM's net income for the first three quarters of 1993, the percentage of its sales spent on television advertising, and the effect of the trademark infringement action. Similarly, the Shareholders' Lawsuit alleged that four of the same six plaintiffs made virtually identical false statements in reports, press releases, and other public statements issued between July 12, 1993, and November 21, 1994. That lawsuit alleged also that plaintiffs made these statements to prevent SLM's investment rating from being downgraded before the notes could be sold. Because the same "fact[s], circumstance[s], situation[s], transaction[s], [and] event[s]" underlie both the Noteholders' and Shareholders' Lawsuits, plaintiffs' claims are excluded from coverage by the Policy's "pending litigation" and "prior notice" provisions.

1998 U.S. Dist. LEXIS 12699, at *11-13, 1998 WL 483475, at *4-5 (citations omitted).

The court rejected the insured's contention that "the two lawsuits involved different parties, legal theories, 'Wrongful Act[s],' and requests for relief" because, the insureds argued, "the Noteholders' Lawsuit was based on false statements plaintiffs allegedly made to the noteholders in the offering memorandum and at the closing, whereas the Shareholders' Lawsuit arose from false statements plaintiffs allegedly made to the general public." 1998 U.S. Dist. LEXIS 12699, at *13-14, 1998 WL 483475, at *5. The court reasoned that "these small differences are not material given the explicit language of the Policy at issue here":

> Nothing in the Policy requires that a claim involve precisely the same parties, legal theories, "Wrongful Act[s]," or requests for relief for the "pending lawsuit" or "prior notice" exclusions to apply. Indeed, both exclusions are phrased in the disjunctive, that is, a claim is excluded if it arises out of "any fact, circumstance, situation, transaction, event or Wrongful Act," alleged in a pending lawsuit or made the subject of a prior notice. To read the additional terms suggested by plaintiffs into these exclusions would be at the same time to render them virtually meaningless: a claim would be excluded only it if were based on an identical lawsuit or were the subject of an identical prior notice given to another insurer.

1998 U.S. Dist. LEXIS 12699, at *14-15, 1998 WL 483475 at *5 (citations omitted).

On appeal, the Second Circuit defined the "dispositive issue" to be whether the Noteholders' lawsuit filed during the policy period was "sufficiently similar" to the Shareholders' Lawsuit filed prior to the coverage period. 1999 U.S. App. LEXIS 14629, at *3, 1999 WL 464988, at *1. The Second Circuit agreed with the district court that "the language of the policy is unambiguous" and "clearly applies to exclude coverage for losses in connection with the Noteholders' lawsuit." 1999 U.S. App. LEXIS 14629, at *3-4, 1999 WL 464988, at *1. The court continued:

> The Noteholders' claim are based upon the defendants' alleged underestimation of (1) SLM's earnings, especially for the first three quarters of 1993, (2) SLM's advertising expenditures, and (3) the potential impact of a pending trademark infringement action against SLM. The same series of underestimations (whether it be considered a "fact, circumstance, situation, transaction, event or Wrongful Act") underlay the Shareholders' lawsuit and, therefore, was the subject of prior notice. These commonalties clearly trigger the coverage exclusions.
>
> As the district court concluded, it is immaterial that the two lawsuits involved different parties and somewhat different legal harms (negligent misrepresentation vs. securities fraud), because the above-quoted policy terms clearly focus on the existence of common facts. It is also immaterial that the underestimations were conveyed to the Noteholders and Shareholders in somewhat different forms (private communications vs. public disclosures), because the underestimations themselves

> clearly underlay both suits. Finally, it is immaterial that the Shareholders' claims also involved a series of additional misrepresentations beyond those connected with the Noteholders' lawsuit, because the exclusions apply if the Noteholders' claims were based on any fact underlying the Shareholder litigation.

1999 U.S. App. LEXIS 14629, at *4-5, 1999 WL 464988, at *1-2. The court added that "[c]learly, the common facts were sufficiently prominent in both lawsuits that it is in no way unfair to enforce the result that the unambiguous language of the policy requires." 1999 U.S. App. LEXIS 14629, at *6, 1999 WL 464988, at *2.

Add the following at the end of footnote 1035 on page 2036:

See also Foster v. Summit Med. Sys., 610 N.W.2d 350, 353-54 (Minn. Ct. App. 2000), *review denied*, 2000 Minn. LEXIS 432 (Minn. July 25, 2000) (holding in favor of insurer on motion for summary judgment based upon retroactive date exclusion where improper revenue recognition was made before the policy's retroactive date and the improper revenue recognition later became the basis for a claim when false and misleading statements were made to the public; the court stated that the policy excluded coverage for a claim that "even 'indirectly results from or [is] in consequence of, or in any way involve[s]'" a wrongful act that occurred before the retroactive date).

Add the following at the end of the paragraph beginning and concluding on page 2036 (immediately after footnote 1035):

Stauth v. National Union Fire Insurance Co., 185 F.3d 875 (unpublished opinion, text available at 1999 U.S. App. LEXIS 14006 and 1999 WL 420401) (10th Cir. June 24, 1999), involved (1) a 1993 pricing action brought by a customer of Fleming Companies, Inc. against Fleming and one of its officers that resulted in a $207 million verdict against Fleming and, after a judgment in the case was vacated, a $19.9 million settlement, and (2) 1996 class actions by Fleming shareholders and noteholders against Fleming and Fleming officers and directors alleging that Fleming violated the federal securities laws by not disclosing the existence of the pricing action. 1999 U.S. App. LEXIS 14006, at *5-11, 1999 WL 420401, at *2-3. The governing policy aggregated all loss arising out of "interrelated wrongful acts," which the policy defined as acts that are "causally connected." 1999 U.S. App. LEXIS 14006, at *18, 1999 WL 420401, at *6.

The court stated that "there are two general lines of authority dealing with the term 'interrelated acts' in insurance policies." 1999 U.S. App. LEXIS 14006, at *21, 1999 WL 420401, at *7. The first line of authority involves policies that do not define the term and "[m]ost courts faced with such policy language have generally taken a pro-insured approach to defining 'interrelated'" based upon "the maxim that ambiguities in insurance policies 'must be interpreted in favor of the insured'" and "have held that 'legally distinct claims that allege different wrongs to different people' are not 'interrelated' claims." 1999 U.S. App. LEXIS 14006, at *21-22, 1999 WL 420401, at *7-8 (citations omitted). The second line of authority involves policies that

- define "interrelated wrongful acts" as acts "'which have as a common nexus any fact, circumstance, situation, event, transaction or series of facts, circumstances, situations, events or transactions,'"
- define "interrelated wrongful acts" as acts "which are the same, related, or continuous" or "which arise from the same, related, or common nexus of facts," with the policy specifying that "[c]laims can allege Interrelated Wrongful Acts regardless of whether such claims involve the same or different claimants, Insureds, or legal causes of action," or
- exclude coverage whenever "all or part of [any] claim is, directly or indirectly, based on, attributable

> to, arising out of, resulting from or in any manner related to the Insured's Wrongful Act(s)."

1999 U.S. App. LEXIS 14006, at *23-24, 1999 WL 420401, at *8 (citations omitted). "Courts interpreting these specific definitions have been much more willing to find acts to be 'interrelated'" and "[s]ome of these courts have even concluded that 'but for' causation is enough, under such policy language, to render two acts 'interrelated.'" 1999 U.S. App. LEXIS 14006, at *24, 1999 WL 420401, at *9.

Here, the court held, "the policy language does not fit neatly into either of these two general lines of authorities" because the policy "does contain a definition of 'interrelated,' but this definition is not as specific as the definitions in the second group of cases discussed above." 1999 U.S. App. LEXIS 14006, at *25, 1999 WL 420401, at *9. Instead, the policy "merely defines 'Interrelated Wrongful Acts' as 'causally connected' wrongful acts" – a definition that "does not greatly advance our inquiry because . . . it merely poses a further question: What is the meaning of 'causally connected'?" *Id.*

The court defined the governing rule as one of "proximate causation" – rather than "mere causal relation" – and held that "[c]ertainly the 1996 and 1993 actions relate to each other at some level" but "whether they interrelate in the sense of being proximately causally connected" is "more speculative and argumentative than not" because the court could not "say with any confidence that the pleadings portray a continuous unbroken sequence of events." 1999 U.S. App. LEXIS 14006, at *27-29, 1999 WL 420401, at *9. The court determined to "construe any ambiguity surrounding the term 'causally connected' against the insurance company and in favor of coverage," and on this basis concluded that the actions were "not 'causally connected.'" 1999 U.S. App. LEXIS 14006, at 30, 1999 WL 420401, at *10.

In *ML Direct, Inc. v. TIG Specialty Insurance Co.*, 79 Cal. App. 4th 137, 93 Cal. Rptr. 2d 846 (Cal. Ct. App. 2000), the court held that a prior litigation exclusion that read as follows and identified the "Pending Litigation Date" as March 11, 1997 was clear and unambiguous:

> This insurance does not apply to any Claim made against any Insured arising out of any of the following:
>
> A. Any litigation, proceeding, or administrative act or hearing brought prior to or pending as of the Prior or Pending Litigation Date as shown in Item 8 of the Declarations, as well as any future litigation, proceeding, administrative act or hearing based upon any such pending or prior litigation, proceeding, administrative act or hearing or derived from the essential facts or circumstances underlying or alleged in any such pending or prior litigation, proceeding, administrative act or hearing. . . ."

Id. at 142, 93 Cal. Rptr. 2d at 850-51. The court rejected a contention by a corporation and one of its directors that the provision was not clear and unambiguous. The court reasoned as follows:

> Pointing to its 40-word length, appellants characterize the policy's prior litigation exclusion as convoluted and incomprehensible. We disagree. Of those 40 words, more than half are devoted to a six-word phrase which is repeated four times – ". . . litigation, proceeding, administrative act or hearing . . . ." The obvious purpose of this grouping of terms is to identify the kinds of prior or pending actions which bring the exclusion into play. Nine words are devoted to the phrase "Prior or Pending Litigation Date as shown in Item 8 of the Declarations." Since this date is readily ascertainable from the face of the policy, the phrase is easily collapsed into meaning the date of March 11, 1997.
>
> We agree that his phrasing is inelegant, but we are reviewing an insurance policy, not literature. If these phrases are viewed in context, the clause can easily be understood as referring simply to a specified class of proceedings pending as of March 11, 1997, and is thus read as follows: "This insurance does not apply to any Claim made against any Insured arising out of any of the following: A. Any proceeding [from the specified group] brought prior to or pending as of March 11, 1997, as well as any future proceeding based on such pending or prior proceedings or derived from the essential facts or circumstances underlying or alleged in any such prior proceeding." The meaning of this clause seems clear enough. If a claim is

> made during the policy period, but the claim arises from a proceeding pending as of March 11, 1997, the claim is not covered. If a claim is made during the policy period, but arises from proceedings instituted after March 11, 1997, which are based on or properly connected to other proceedings pending before that date, then the claim is not covered. We therefore hold that the exclusion is not ambiguous.

Id. at 145, 93 Cal. Rptr. at 852-53.

The court also rejected a contention by the corporation and one of its directors that the exclusion was inapplicable because the director sought coverage for a class action lawsuit filed in a New York federal district court – the Petit action – and the prior proceedings were SEC and NASD proceedings in which the corporation and the director were "not parties" and were "mentioned briefly, it at all." *Id.* at 145, 93 Cal. Rptr. 2d at 853. "As a result," the corporation and its director contended, the allegations which related to them were not essential to the SEC and NASD pleadings." *Id.* The court stated that this argument "overlooks the other portion of the exclusion, which applies if the claim is based on the prior proceedings," and here the class action lawsuit "expressly alleged that it was based on the SEC and NASD complaints and the factual relationship between all three pleadings is not disputed." *Id.* at 145-56, 93 Cal. Rptr. 2d at 853.

The court also rejected a claim that the prior litigation exclusion was "at odds with the policy's retroactivity provisions" and thus "enforcing the exclusion would rob" the insureds of their "bargained-for coverage." The court explained:

> Reading the provisions together, the policy provides coverage for claims made during the policy period for acts occurring after June 22, 1995, unless those acts were the subject of prior litigation or proceedings under the prior litigation exclusion. If the SEC and NASD complaints had been filed after March 11, 1997, the Petit action would have been a covered claim. We cannot rewrite the policy to provide greater coverage than that which was agreed to.

Id. at 146, 93 Cal. Rptr. 2d at 853.

Add the following at the end of the second paragraph beginning and concluding on page 2037 (between footnotes 1040 and 1041):

Other examples include claims related to initial or secondary public offerings and claims alleging that the corporation paid an inadequate or excessive purchase price for the stock or assets of another entity. Rosenberg, *Insurance Coverage and Securities Litigation*, 31 Rev. Sec. & Comm. Reg. 213, 221 (Nov. 4, 1998).

Add the following at the end of footnote 1056 on page 2040:

See also Nat'l Bank of Ariz. v. St. Paul Fire & Marine Ins. Co., 975 P.2d 711, 715-16 (Ariz. Ct. App. 1999) (following *Olympic Club v. Those Interested Underwriters at Lloyd's London*, 991 F.2d 497 (9th Cir. 1993): "In both of the underlying lawsuits against NBA, none of NBA's directors and officers were named as defendants, nor were they subject to any demands for relief, payment, or something as a right or as due. . . . NBA's directors and officers did not face any liability, thus NBA is not entitled to any coverage or reimbursement under its D & O Policy. To find coverage under NBA's D & O Policy under these circumstances would be to transform it into a corporate liability policy.").

Section B 9 b

Replace the Olson citation in footnote 1058 on page 2040 with the following:

John F. Olson, Josiah O. Hatch III & Ty R. Sagalow, *Director and Officer Liability: Indemnification and Insurance* § 10.06[5][c][iii] (2000);

Replace "1998" with "2001" in the Securities Law Techniques citation in footnote 1058 on page 2040.

Section B 9 c

Replace the Olson citation in footnote 1086 on page 2044 with the following:

John F. Olson, Josiah O. Hatch III & Ty R. Sagalow, *Director and Officer Liability: Indemnification and Insurance* § 10.06[5][c][i], at 10–34-37 (2000);

Replace "1998" with "2001" in the Securities Law Techniques citation in footnote 1086 on page 2044.

Replace "10-33" with "10-35" in the Olson citation in footnote 1088 on page 2045.

Add the following at the end of the third sentence (immediately after footnote 1089) of the paragraph beginning on page 2044 and concluding on page 2046:

As explained by two commentators:

> The purpose of the exclusion, now standard on almost all D & O policies, is easy to understand. The underwriting philosophy behind a D & O insurance policy is to provide coverage for claims brought by third parties against an insured corporation's management.
>
> There are two reasons classically given for the insured v. insured exclusion. First, providing coverage for a claim brought by an insured against another insured or brought by the company against an insured would support potential collusive arrangements between insiders. Second, even in the absence of collusion, the insured v. insured exclusion is needed to prevent coverage for "boardroom infighting."

John F. Olson, Josiah O. Hatch III & Ty R. Sagalow, *Director and Officer Liability: Indemnification and Insurance* § 10.06[5][c][i], at 10-35 (2000).

Replace the paragraph beginning and concluding on page 2046 (including footnotes 1091 through 1093) with the following:

Early forms of this exclusion were read by some to exclude coverage in shareholder derivative actions, but most insured versus insured exclusions used in policies today create broad exceptions for shareholder claims that have not been asserted in collusion with an insured party. Some insured versus insured exclusions also add an exception for wrongful discharge or termination claims, employment practices claims, or claims by a bankruptcy trustee. An example of a typical provision is the following:

> The insurer shall not be liable to make any payment for Loss in connection with a Claim made against an Insured:
>
> * * *
>
> (i) which is brought by or on behalf of any Insured or the Company; or which is brought by a securities holder or member of the Company, whether directly or derivatively, unless such securities holder's or member's Claim is instigated and continued totally independent of, and totally without the solicitation of, or assistance of, or active participation of, or intervention of, any Director or Officer or the Company; provided, however, this exclusion shall not apply to:
>
>> (1) any Claim brought by a Natural Person Insured in the form of a cross-claim or third-party claim for contribution or indemnity which is part of and results directly from a Claim which is not otherwise excluded by the terms of this policy;
>>
>> (2) any Claim alleging an Employment Practices Violation brought by any past or present Natural Person Insured other than a past or present Natural Person Insured who is or was a member of the Company's Board of Directors or, in the case of an LLC, the Board of Managers;
>>
>> (3) any Claim brought by or against an Employee; or
>>
>> (4) in any bankruptcy proceeding by or against the Named Corporation or any Subsidiary thereof, any Claim brought by the Examiner or Trustee of

> the Company, if any, or any assignee of such Examiner or Trustee.

John F. Olson & J. Hatch § 10.06[5][c][i], at 10–36-37. This type of exclusion is intended "to screen out the possibility of suits by the company or by individuals acting as proxies for the company, while at the same time permitting most noncollusive shareholder class or derivative actions to be covered." *Id.* at 10-37; *see also* Weiss, *Filling the Gaps in D & O Insurance*, 6 Bus. Law Today No. 3, Jan./Feb. 1997, at 44, 47; Weiss, *Doing D & O Insurance Right*, 4 Bus. Law Today No. 2, Nov./Dec. 1994, at 50, 53; *Int'l Ins. Co. v. Morrow, Inc.*, No. 86-1247-JU, slip op. at 8-12 (D. Or. Oct. 23, 1987) (policy provided that if notice is given to insurer of an occurrence that may subsequently give rise to a claim against the insureds for a wrongful act, then any claim that subsequently is made arising out of that wrongful act shall be treated as a claim made during the policy year when notice of the occurrence was provided to the insurer; court held that an amendment of the policy to include an insured versus insured exclusion did not exclude coverage of a later filed action for conduct arising out of a previously reported insured versus insured occurrence).

Add a comma between "Co." and footnote 1096, delete the second "and" (immediately after footnote 1096) and add the following immediately after footnote 1097 in the first paragraph beginning and concluding on page 2047:

and the Seventh Circuit in *Level 3 Communications, Inc. v. Federal Insurance Co.*, 168 F.3d 956 (7th Cir. 1999).

Add the following at the end of the paragraph beginning on page 2048 and concluding on page 2049 (immediately after footnote 1109):

The Seventh Circuit in *Level 3 Communications, Inc. v. Federal Insurance Co.*, 168 F.3d 956 (7th Cir. 1999), held that the presence of one "Insured" in a group of plaintiffs is sufficient to trigger an "Insured versus Insured" exclusion in a directors' and officers' liability insurance policy, but only with respect to the insured plaintiff.

The policy in the case excluded liability for "any 'Claim made against an Insured Person' if the Claim is 'brought or maintained by or on behalf of any Insured.'" *Id.* at 957. The insured, Anthony J. Pompliano, Sr., a former director of a subsidiary of Peter Kiewit Sons, Inc., had joined a securities fraud action as a plaintiff against Kiewit six months after the action had been filed. The insurance policy defined the term "Insured Person" to include a "person who *has been*, now is, or shall become a duly elected director or a duly elected or appointed officer of the Insured Organization" and defined the term "Insured Organization" as the corporation and its subsidiaries. *Id.* The court held that the Insured versus Insured exclusion thus was applicable and therefore "the contract clearly excludes coverage" for expenses "allocable to Pompliano." *Id.* at 958.

The court then explained that the policy defined "claim" as "a civil proceeding commenced by the service of a complaint or similar pleading" and stated that this definition could be construed to mean that if any of the plaintiffs were Insureds there would be no coverage, particularly if – unlike this case – the insured were a current officer or director and the principal plaintiff. *Id.* at 960. Here, the court concluded, however, "the contract deals with this problem in another way, by requiring allocation of covered and uncovered losses." *Id.* Accordingly, the claim "was against Insured Persons, but it included uncovered matters because one of the plaintiffs was an Insured, with the result that his part of the Claim was not covered by the insurance contract." *Id.*

The court rejected a claim by the insured corporation that the insured versus insured exception should be read not literally but "in light of its purpose, which is to exclude coverage both of collusive suits – such as suits in which a corporation sues its officers or directors in an effort to recoup the consequences of their business mistakes, . . . thus turning liability insurance into business-loss insurance – and of suits arising out of those particularly bitter disputes that erupt when members of a corporate, as of a personal, family have a falling out and fall to quarreling." *Id.* at 958. According to the insured, this case was "of neither sort." *Id.* The court explained its rejection of this claim as follows:

> The fallacy in the argument is in confusing a rule with its rationale, or in turning a rule into a standard by reference to its rationale. There is a tradeoff between clarity and ease of application, on the one hand, and a tight fit between a legal or contractual norm and its purpose, on the other. A simple, flat rule is deliciously clear and easy to apply, but it may be both underinclusive and overinclusive in relation to the purpose that animates it. A standard, like "no coverage for collusive suits or lovers' quarrels," is contoured exactly to its purpose, but it cannot be applied without a potentially costly, time-consuming, and uncertain inquiry into the nature of the underlying dispute sought to be covered. It is apparent from the wording they chose that the parties opted for the rule, not the standard in agreeing to the "Insured versus Insured" exclusion.
>
> But when the application of a rule leads to a truly whacky result, a more than suspicion arises that the parties can't have set so high a value on clarity that they would have thought such an application a proper interpretation of the rule . . . . Kiewit argues along these lines that the "Insured versus Insured" exemption can't mean what it says, because if it did then even if Pompliano were merely an unnamed class member in a securities class action, with a stake of $10 in the outcome of the suit, and even if he had resigned his directorship in a subsidiary of Kiewit 20 years ago, Kiewit would lose its insurance coverage. To this, Federal weakly replies that a suit by a class of which an Insured is an unnamed member is not a suit "brought or maintained by or on behalf of any Insured." Of course it is; a class action is brought by the named plaintiff or plaintiffs on his (their) own behalf and on behalf of the unnamed class members. Federal further argues that the "on behalf" language of the contract was not intended to apply to an unnamed or "passive" litigant. But in so arguing Federal is abandoning its primary argument, that the contract means what it says.
>
> Maybe applying the contract's "or on behalf of any Insured" language to the case of the unnamed class member is so absurd that the language must bend. Or maybe not, because . . . the

> insurance contract requires allocation of covered and uncovered losses rather than barring all recovery because of the presence of an insured on the plaintiff's side of the case . . . . But even if the application of the "Insured versus Insured" exclusion to the unnamed class member would be too nutty to be tolerable as a contractual interpretation despite its literal accuracy, we do not think it follows that the rule barring coverage when an insured is suing another insured collapses into a standard that would require the district court to inquire into the collusive potential of the securities suit or the bitterness of the feelings between Pompliano and the defendants in that suit. It is one thing to carve a hard-edged exception, necessary to avoid absurdity, say for the case in which an "Insured" is an unnamed class member; it is another thing to replace the hard-edged rule of "Insured versus Insured" with a mushy, messy standard that would be hell for an insurance company to apply when asked to indemnify its insured. A rule plus exceptions is not the equivalent of a standard.

Id. at 958-59 (citations omitted).

Replace "The same result has been reached" with "Insured versus insured exclusions also have been enforced" in the first sentence (between footnotes 1109 and 1110) of the paragraph beginning and concluding on page 2049.

Replace "10-34" with "10-36" in the Olson citation in footnote 1123 on page 2051.

Section B 9 d

Add the following at the end of the paragraph beginning on page 2064 and concluding on page 2065 (immediately after footnote 1200):

The court in *Hyde v. Fidelity & Deposit Co.*, 23 F. Supp. 2d 630 (D. Md. 1998), also granted summary judgment in favor of the insurer. The court reasoned that the insured versus insured provision in the governing insurance policy "specifically excluded coverage for cases 'on behalf of' the Bank, and not just 'by' the Bank." *Id.* at 634. The court stated that the bank's receiver, the Resolution Trust Corporation, asserted claims "solely on behalf of" the bank and that the receiver was "'to all intents and purposes the bank – at least he stands in place of the bank.'" *Id.* (quoting *Landy v. Fed. Deposit Ins. Corp.*, 486 F.2d 139, 147 (3d Cir. 1973), *cert. denied*, 416 U.S. 960 (1974), and *O'Connor v. Rhodes*, 79 F.2d 146, 148 (D.C. Cir. 1935), *aff'd sub nom. U.S. Shipping Bd. Merchant Fleet Corp. v. Rhodes*, 297 U.S. 383 (1936)).

The court added that D & O insurance "does not protect the insureds from claims by the corporation itself." 23 F. Supp. 2d at 634. Quoting *Mt. Hawley Insurance Co. v. Federal Savings & Loan Insurance Corp.*, 695 F. Supp. 469 (C.D. Cal. 1987), the court stated the following:

> "It is difficult to argue that it is within the reasonable expectations of the parties to such an insurance contract that the corporation was paying D & O insurance premiums to protect the directors and officers from the consequences of breaching their duty to the corporation. If coverage for claims made by the corporation against the officers and directors does not fall within the scope of the 'insured's reasonable expectation of coverage,' there is no reason for the insureds to suppose that these same claims would be covered if brought by the receiver for the corporation." *Mt. Hawley*, 695 F. Supp. at 484. Because "[t]hese claims would not be covered under the policy if asserted by [the bank]; it is difficult to argue that they should be covered when asserted on behalf of [the bank] by its receiver." *Id.* at 481.

23 F. Supp. 2d at 634. "To find otherwise," the court concluded, "would be an affront to the purpose of the insured-versus-insured exclusion." *Id.*

Section B 9 e

Add the following at the end of the paragraph beginning on page 2073 and concluding on page 2074 (immediately after footnote 1261):

The court in *In re Buckeye Countrymark, Inc.*, 251 B.R. 835 (Bankr. S.D. Ohio 2000), similarly held that a policy provision excluding claims "brought by or on behalf of the Insured" (*id.* at 838) does not exclude claims brought by a bankruptcy trustee. The court explained that the insurers' contention that the trustee "stands in the shoes" of the debtor "ignores the very real differences between the Trustee and the Debtor":

> [A] bankruptcy trustee is a separate legal entity that neither represents the Debtor nor owes the Debtor a fiduciary obligation. Instead, the Trustee's responsibility is to the bankruptcy estate that he or she represents. As such, the Trustee and the Debtor often take adversarial positions. In these respects, the Trustee and the Debtor are neither the same entity nor alter egos of each other.

Id. at 840 (citations omitted); *see also id.* ("[a]s representative of the estate, the Trustee brings his claims on behalf of the Debtor's creditors rather than on behalf of the Debtor"). The court added that "the very purpose of an 'insured vs. insured' exclusion" is "to protect insurance companies against collusive suits between the insured corporation and its insured officers and directors" and "does not apply to adversarial claims brought by the Trustee against the Debtor's directors, officers and managers" because "[w]hen the plaintiff is not the corporation but a bankruptcy trustee acting as a genuinely adverse party to the defendant officers and directors, there is no threat of collusion." *Id.* at 840-41. The court also relied upon "the rule of construction requiring the court to construe ambiguous language in an exclusionary provision liberally in favor of coverage." *Id.* at 841.

As discussed in Chapter V, Section B 9 c, some policies include an express exception to insured versus insured exclusions for claims by bankruptcy trustees against directors and officers.

Section B 9 f

Replace the Olson citation in footnote 1262 on page 2074 with the following:

John F. Olson, Josiah O. Hatch III & Ty R. Sagalow, *Director and Officer Liability: Indemnification and Insurance* § 10.06[5][c][ii] (2000);

Replace "1998" with "2000" in the Securities Law Techniques citation in footnote 1262 on page 2074.

Section B 10

Replace the Olson citation in footnote 1367 on page 2093 with the following:

John F. Olson, Josiah O. Hatch III & Ty R. Sagalow, *Director and Officer Liability: Indemnification and Insurance* § 10.07[3], at 10-54 (2000).

Replace "10–54-55" with "10-57" in the Olson citation in footnote 1371 on page 2093.

Replace "1998" with "2001" in the Securities Law Techniques citation in footnote 1371 on page 2093.

Section B 11 a

Replace the fifth, sixth and seventh sentences in the paragraph beginning on page 2109 and concluding on page 2110 (including footnotes 1480 through 1482) with the following:

A recent survey concluded that the corporation is a defendant in approximately 87 percent of the cases in which D & O claims are made. Of those cases where there was a non-zero allocation, the average allocation percentage of judgments or settlement payments was 63 percent to the D & O insurer in 1998, 60 percent to the D & O insurer in 1999, and 60 percent to the D & O insurer in 2000. The average allocation percentage of defense costs was 62 percent to the D & O insurer in 1998, 67 percent to the D & O insurer in 1999, and 66 percent to the D & O insurer in 2000. Tillinghast-Towers Perrin, *2000 Directors and Officers Liability Survey* 6, 69 (2001); Tillinghast-Towers Perrin, *1999 Directors and Officers Liability Survey* 6, 68 (2000).

Add the following at the end of footnote 1485 on page 2110:

See also Owens Corning Fiberglass Corp. v. Nat'l Union Fire Ins. Co., No. 3:95 CV 7700, slip op. at 8 (N.D. Ohio Mar. 31, 1999); *Piper Jaffray Cos. v. Nat'l Union Fire Ins. Co.*, 38 F. Supp. 2d 771, 775 (D. Minn. 1999).

Add the following at the end of footnote 1488 on page 2111:

See also Owens Corning, slip op. at 8; *Piper Jaffray*, 38 F. Supp. 2d at 775.

Add the following at the end of footnote 1490 on page 2111:

See also Owens Corning, slip op. at 8; *Piper Jaffray*, 38 F. Supp. 2d at 775.

Section B 11 b

Change "six" to "seven" in the first sentence (between footnotes 1494 and 1495) of the paragraph beginning and concluding on page 2113.

Delete "and," between footnote 1499 and "in 1997" and add the following at the end of the first sentence (immediately after footnote 1500) of the paragraph beginning and concluding on page 2113:

and, in 1999, *Stauth v. National Union Fire Insurance Co.*, 185 F.3d 875 (unpublished decision, text available at 1999 U.S. App. LEXIS 14006 and 1999 WL 420401) (10th Cir. June 24, 1999).

Add the following at the end of the paragraph beginning and concluding on page 2113 (between footnotes 1500 and 1501):

The 1999 decision in *Stauth* declined to make an allocation decision prior to an actual settlement or judgment in the underlying litigation. *See also Nat'l Union Fire Ins. Co. v. Liberty Nat'l Bancorp, Inc.*, 1998 U.S. App. LEXIS 26942, at *7-8, 1998 WL 773673, at *3 (6th Cir. Oct. 16, 1998) (holding that insurer was not required to contribute to a $6.21 million "global settlement" of a series of claims because all claims involving directors or officers were dismissed prior to the settlement or involved only injunctive relief; the insurer was liable, however, for the cost of defending the directors and officers before the claims against the directors and officers were dismissed).

Add the following at the end of the paragraph beginning and concluding on page 2113 (following new footnote 1500.1):

As a result of these decisions, insurers have sought to incorporate the relative exposure test into policy language. *See*

Rosenberg, *Insurance Coverage and Securities Litigation*, 31 Rev. Sec. & Comm. Reg. 213, 221-22 (Nov. 4, 1998).

Add the following at the end of the first paragraph beginning and concluding on page 2127 (immediately after footnote 1584):

The Tenth Circuit's decision in *Stauth v. National Union Fire Insurance Co.*, 185 F.3d 875 (unpublished decision, text available at 1999 U.S. App. LEXIS 14006 and 1999 WL 420401) (10th Cir. June 24, 1999), noted the larger settlement and relative exposure rules and that stated "the allocation landscape was altered in December 1995, when Congress passed the Private Securities Litigation Reform Act of 1995" (the "PSLRA"). 1999 U.S. App. LEXIS 14006, at *34-35, 1999 WL 420401, at *12. The PSLRA, the court explained, "abolished joint and several liability in private securities lawsuits, except in cases where the defendants committed knowing violations of the securities laws" and requires determinations of "the discrete percentages of responsibility attributable to the various liable defendants in the lawsuit." 1999 U.S. App. LEXIS 14006, at *34-35, 1999 WL 420401, at *12. "Thus, in securities suits covered by the PSLRA that actually go to trial, the entire question regarding the proper allocation rule is rendered moot" and as a result unless the action is settled before trial the court "need not determine whether the larger settlement rule or the relative exposure rule is the better one." 1999 U.S. App. LEXIS 14006, at *36, 1999 WL 420401, at *12.

The court accordingly declined to decide the allocation issue because the underlying securities class action had not yet been tried or settled. "For our opinion on the allocation issue to have any relevance," the court stated, "parties other than the insured," such as the corporation, underwriters or uninsured individuals "must be found liable in the underlying litigation," and the case must be settled rather than tried because if the case is tried allocation will be determined "by the procedures set forth in the PSLRA." 1999 U.S. App. LEXIS 14006, at *40,

1999 WL 420401, at *14. As a result, the court concluded, "an opinion on the allocation issue in this case, at least before any settlement or judgment has been rendered, would be premature and, because of the many contingencies involved, would be advisory in nature." 1999 U.S. App. LEXIS 14006, at *41, 1999 WL 420401, at *14. The court therefore remanded the case to the district court "with orders to hold the case in abeyance until the Class Actions have either been settled or dismissed or have proceeded to judgment." 1999 U.S. App. LEXIS 14006, at *44, 1999 WL 420401, at *15. The court noted that "neither side has cited to us, nor can we find, any case in which allocation questions were decided prior to an actual settlement or judgment in the underlying litigation" and stated that "[w]e decline the invitation to become the first court to do so." 1999 U.S. App. LEXIS 14006, at *43, 1999 WL 420401, at *15.

Replace "California, Colorado and Maryland" with "California, Colorado, Illinois, Maryland, Minnesota and Ohio" in the first sentence (between footnotes 1598 and 1599) of the second paragraph beginning and concluding on page 2129.

Add the following at the end of the third sentence of the paragraph beginning on page 2129 and concluding on page 2130 (immediately after footnote 1603):

Level 3 Communications, Inc. v. Federal Insurance Co., 1999 U.S. Dist. LEXIS 13338, 1999 WL 675295 (N.D. Ill. Aug. 18, 1999), the federal district court decision in Illinois, applied the larger settlement rule because the policy in this case obligated the insurer to provide coverage for "the total amount which any insured person becomes legally obligated to pay" and "the settlement amount was not increased by any uninsured employee." 1999 U.S. Dist. LEXIS 13338, at *15-16, 19, 1999 WL 675295, at *5, 6. The court acknowledged that the insureds were named as defendants only in one (a federal securities law claim) of the four counts (the other claims were breach of fiduciary duty, breach of contract and breach of the duty of good faith and fair dealing) in the plaintiffs' complaint, but stated that all of the counts were based on the same alleged wrongdoing and all involved the same allegations concerning damages. As a result, when the corporation – which was uninsured – settled the claim against its insured officer, "the simultaneous settling of the claims against the corporation did not increase the settlement amount." 1999 U.S. Dist. LEXIS 13338, at *16-18, 1999 WL 675295, at *5.

Add the following at the end of the paragraph beginning on page 2129 and concluding on page 2130 (immediately after footnote 1605):

Piper Jaffray Cos. v. National Union Fire Ins. Co., 38 F. Supp. 2d 771 (D. Minn. 1999), the district court decision in Minnesota, also adopted the larger settlement rule. Applying this rule, the court denied a motion for summary judgment by an insured corporation, Piper Jaffray Companies, Inc., after finding that "there exists a genuine issue of material fact as to whether Piper as a corporate entity experienced joint but independent liability due to the actions of uninsured employees that increased the McDaid settlement costs." *Id.* at 780. The court pointed to disputes with respect to "the level of involvement of the officer and directors in the employee activities alleged by Defendants [the insurers] as giving rise to independent corporate liability" and the absence of evidence demonstrating "the extent to which insured officers and directors directly or indirectly controlled" alleged wrongful actions by uninsured Piper employees. *Id.* at 778. The court rejected the insurers' contention that "Piper as a corporate entity faced direct, independent corporate liability" pursuant to Section 10(b) of the Securities and Exchange Act and Rule 10b-5 promulgated thereunder "under a theory of 'collective scienter,'" pursuant to which plaintiffs could show scienter on the part of "members of top management" but not any particular officer. *Id.* at 778-79. The court stated that "[t]heoretically, collective scienter could be a basis for liability," but "there is no case law supporting an independent 'collective scienter' theory." *Id.* at 779 (quoting *Nordstrom, Inc. v. Chubb & Son, Inc.*, 54 F.3d 1424, 1435 (9th Cir. 1995)).

Owens Corning Fiberglass Corp. v. National Union Fire Insurance Co., No. 3:95 CV 7700 (N.D. Ohio Mar. 31, 1999), the district court decision in Ohio, also adopted the larger settlement rule. The court held that the corporation's liability did not exceed the liability of directors and officers on a claim for which the corporation was "independently but jointly liable" in a securities class action litigation. *Id.*, slip op. at 10. The court rejected an insurer's contention that several factors "unrelated to the liability of the insured directors and officers contributed in the determination of the settlement amount," including the following "corporate considerations": "(1) avoidance of the expense and negative publicity associated with the lawsuit; (2) the potential negative effect on employee morale; (3) the possibility of disclosure of sensitive corporate information, and (4) the general distraction of the corporation's employees." *Id.* at 11-12. The court stated that "[t]his 'evidence' can be said to be present in any corporate litigation which contemplates settlement; in an of itself that is not sufficient to raise a factual issue on allocation." *Id.* at 12.

Section B 11 c

Add the following at the end of the paragraph beginning on page 2133 and concluding on page 2134 (immediately after footnote 1624):

Additional cases placing the burden of proof upon the insurer include *Piper Jaffray Cos. v. National Union Fire Insurance Co.*, 38 F. Supp. 2d 771, 775 (D. Minn. 1999), and *Owens Corning Fiberglass v. National Union Fire Insurance Co.*, No. 3:95 CV 7700, slip op. at 10 (N.D. Ohio Mar. 31, 1999).

Section B 11 d

Replace "one court" with "two courts" in the parenthetical (immediately before footnote 1633) in the second sentence of the paragraph beginning and concluding on page 2135.

Add the following at the end of footnote 1633 on page 2135:

See also Caterpillar Inc. v. Great Am. Ins. Co., 864 F. Supp. 849, 852 (C. D. Ill. 1994), *aff'd*, 62 F.3d 955 (7th Cir. 1995). Other courts have rejected this view. *See Safeway Stores, Inc. v. Nat'l Union Fire Ins. Co.*, 64 F.3d 1282, 1289 (9th Cir. 1995) (a policy requiring that parties "'use their best efforts to determine a fair and proper allocation of the settlement amount' . . . 'requires an allocation analysis,' but not necessarily an allocation"), *quoted in Stauth v. National Union Fire Ins. Co.*, 185 F.3d 875 (unpublished decision, text available at 1999 U.S. App. LEXIS 14006, at *33 and 1999 WL 420401, at *11) (10th Cir. June 24, 1999); *Owens Corning Fiberglass v. Nat'l Union Fire Ins. Co.*, No. 3:95 CV 7700, slip op. at 7 (N.D. Ohio Mar. 31, 1999).

Add the following at the end of footnote 1633 on page 2135:

See also Level 3 Communications, Inc. v. Fed. Ins. Co., 1999 U.S. Dist. LEXIS 13338, at *15-16, 19, 1999 WL 675295, at *5, 6 (N.D. Ill. Aug. 18, 1999) (stating that policy provision requiring the insureds and the insurer to "use the best efforts to agree upon a fair and proper allocation . . . between covered loss and uncovered loss" "provides rather limited guidance as to how allocation should be determined," and allocating the full settlement amount to the insured where the policy provided coverage for "the total amount which any insured person becomes legally obligated to pay" and "the settlement amount was not increased by any uninsured employee").

Add the following at the end of footnote 1634 on page 2135:

See also Rosenberg, *Insurance Coverage and Securities Litigation*, 31 Rev. Sec. & Comm. Reg. 213, 221 (Nov. 4, 1998).

Delete the Watson Wyatt citation in footnote 1636 on page 2136.

Add the following at the end of footnote 1636 on page 2136:

See also Rosenberg, 31 Rev. Sec. & Comm. Reg. at 221.

Add the following at the end of footnote 1637 on page 2136:

See also Rosenberg, 31 Rev. Sec. & Comm. Reg. at 221; Tillinghast-Towers Perrin, *2000 Directors and Officers Liability Survey* 3 (2001) (noting that in 2000 "[m]ore than 90% of U.S. insureds purchased entity coverage, up dramatically from less than 30 percent four years ago").

Add the following at the end of the first paragraph beginning and concluding on page 2136 (immediately following footnote 1638):

Some policies extend coverage to non-insured corporate employees if a claim also is made against an insured director or officer. These policies eliminate the allocation issue where directors and officers and a non-officer employee are sued. Rosenberg, 31 Rev. Sec. & Comm. Reg. at 221.

Section B 12

Replace "1998" with "2000" in the Appleman citation in footnote 1660 on page 2139.

Replace "1997" with "1997 & Supp. 2000" in the Couch citation in footnote 1660 on page 2139.

Replace the Olson citation in footnote 1660 on page 2139 with the following:

John F. Olson, Josiah O. Hatch III & Ty R. Sagalow, *Director and Officer Liability: Indemnification and Insurance* § 10.08[3][d], at 10-81 (2000).

Replace "10-77" with "10-81" in the Olson citation in footnote 1661 on page 2140.

Section B 12 a

Add the following at the end of the paragraph beginning on page 2140 and concluding on page 2144 (immediately following footnote 1684):

- *2575 Owners Corp. v. Federal Insurance Co.*, 1998 U.S. Dist. LEXIS 18822, at *1-8, 1998 WL 846123, at *1-2 (S.D.N.Y. Dec. 3, 1998) (granting insurer's motion for summary judgment and holding that coverage for a claim under a directors and officers liability insurance policy was excluded where the insureds had answered "no" to the following policy application question: "Is the undersigned, or any individual proposed for this insurance, aware of any fact, circumstance or situation involving the organization, its affiliates or its subsidiaries which he/she has reason to believe might result in any future claim which would fall within the scope of the proposed insurance?"; the court stated that "[t]he application, in simple and straightforward terms, required plaintiffs (who were not unsophisticated) to disclose any facts that gave them reason to believe a future claim might be made within the coverage of a standard 'D & O' policy protecting against litigation risk," but the insureds did not disclose receipt of a letter that challenged a board decision, alleged specific injuries and threatened "'unpleasant actions,' including resort to legal channels such as the Attorney General").

Replace the Mt. Airy citation in footnote 1697 on page 2148 with the following:

Mt. Airy Ins. Co. v. Thomas, 954 F. Supp. 1073, 1079 (W.D. Pa. 1997), *aff'd mem.*, 149 F.3d 1165 (3d Cir. 1998);

Add the following at the end of footnote 1697 on page 2148:

See also 2575 Owners, 1998 U.S. Dist. LEXIS 18822, at *6, 1998 WL 846123, at *2.

Replace the Fabric citation in footnote 1699 on page 2148 with the following:

Fabric v. Provident Life & Accident Ins. Co., 115 F.3d 908, 913 (11th Cir. 1997), *cert denied*, 523 U.S. 1095 (1998);

Section C

Replace the Olson citation in footnote 1736 on page 2153 with the following:

John F. Olson, Josiah O. Hatch III & Ty R. Sagalow, *Director and Officer Liability: Indemnification and Insurance* §§ 9.02, 9.03 (2000);

Add the following at the end of footnote 1740 on page 2154:

See also Bermuda Takes the Risk: From Tourist Paradise to Haven for Insurance Businesses, N.Y. Times, Apr. 28, 1999, at C1 (discussing regulatory and tax advantages possessed by Bermuda insurers and noting efforts by United States regulators to ease regulatory restrictions in an effort to assist United States insurers to compete against Bermuda insurers).

Replace "1998" with "2001" in the Balotti citation in footnote 1744 on page 2155.

Section D 1

Replace the Olson citation in footnote 1786 on page 2163 with the following:

John F. Olson, Josiah O. Hatch III & Ty R. Sagalow, *Director and Officer Liability: Indemnification and Insurance* §§ 4.11, 10.02 (2000);

Section D 2 a

Replace "1996" with "Supp. 1998/99" in the Model Act § 2.02 citation in footnote 1812 on page 2168.

Section D 3

Replace the paragraph beginning on page 2172 and concluding on page 2173 (including footnotes 1830 through 1834) with the following:

D & O insurance has been somewhat more available since the late 1980s. Weiss, *Filling the Gaps in D & O Insurance*, 6 Bus. Law Today No. 3, Jan./Feb. 1997, at 44; Weiss, *Doing D & O Insurance Right*, 4 Bus. Law Today No.

2, Nov./Dec. 1994, at 50. One consulting firm has offered the following thoughts concerning market conditions, first, at the end of 1999, and then at the end of 2000:

> *1999:* The D & O insurance market continued to be very competitive for most market segments, according to our 1999 survey respondents, with a majority of purchasers paying less on renewal (on a price per $million of coverage basis). Most purchasers also obtained a better D & O insurance product this year, as both buyers and insurers continued to pay special attention to coverage wording. Competition today involves much more than just pricing, it also involves the quality of the D & O insurance product, as reflected in the breadth of the coverage wording. We have seen the quality of the D & O coverage form improve consistently since 1990, following a steady stream of new restrictions and exclusions between 1984 and 1990.
>
> * * *
>
> *2000*: The D & O insurance market continued to be very competitive for many market segments, according to our 2000 survey respondents, but several key segments in the U.S. saw sharp increases in premiums as well as more stringent underwriting. In short, it appears that after a lengthy period of significant annual price decreases the D & O market has firmed overall – and for some segments, it has turned sharply.

Tillinghast-Towers Perrin, *1999 Directors and Officers Liability Survey* 2 (2000); Tillinghast-Towers Perrin, *2000 Directors and Officers Liability Survey* 2 (2001). This consulting firm has created a standardized premium index (established at a value of 100 for the average D & O policy, measured in terms of policy limits, corporate reimbursement deductibles and other coverage features) that indicates the following leveling off and decline of premiums during the 1990s, but also a more than 11 percent increase in the index average in the year 2000:

Historical D & O Premium Index

Year	Index Median	Index Average
1974	90	100
1976	69	81
1978	77	103

1980	76	99
1982	55	71
1984	38	54
1986	415	682
1988	513	746
1990	481	704
1991	513	720
1992	515	720
1993	526	771
1994	548	806
1995	550	793
1996	498	726
1997	459	619
1998	402	539
1999	356	503
2000	349	560

Id. at 4. During 2000, approximately 36 percent of surveyed firms reported premium increases, 16 percent reported decreases, and 48 percent reported no change in premium. *Id.* Many of the surveyed firms reporting premium increases obtained higher policy limits and improved coverage at a favorable price. *Id.*

Replace the Wyatt citations in footnote 1835 on page 2173 with the following:

2000 Tillinghast-Towers Perrin Survey at 2.

Replace "or a weak economic region or industry" with "or those operating in a weak economic region or industry" in the fourth sentence (immediately before footnote 1836) of the paragraph beginning and concluding on page 2173.

Replace the Wyatt citation in footnote 1836 with the following:

1999 Tillinghast-Towers Perrin Survey at 2-3.

Add the following at the end of the paragraph beginning and concluding on page 2173 (immediately after footnote 1836):

The increased stock volatility caused by new technologies such as the Internet (which adds a technology component to many businesses that previously were not technology businesses), changes in investment activity, and recent market trends all have added to the challenges facing D & O carriers and pressures to the D & O insurance market. Meiners, *New Challenges for the D & O Market*, Directors & Boards, Summer 2000, at 42.

Replace "2-17" with "2-16" and replace "1996" with "Supp. 1998/99" in the Model Act § 2.02 citation footnote 1837 on page 2174.

TABLE OF AUTHORITIES

Cases: **Page(s):**

Federal Statutes and Rules:

State Statutes:

Model Statutes, Restatements and Recommendations:

Books:

Articles, Reports and Book Chapters: